THE COVE DIARY 2

The Last Cove Diary Book, Ever (Honest!)

By Andrew Carne

Cover design Alison Taylor
Map drawing Neil Willis

Shield Crest

ISBN: 978-1-910176-70-2

MMXV

Published by
ShieldCrest
Aylesbury, Buckinghamshire, HP22 5RR
England

www.shieldcrest.co.uk

Acknowledgements

Thanks are due to various people, dumb animals and, particularly the weather that has permitted me to carve this obelisk out of pure nothingness.

I ran into all sorts of problems last time by leaving the Missus until last. She promised faithfully to leave if I ever produced another book but has nonetheless encouraged me to continue, unflinching through thick and thin. Is she trying to tell me something?

I must once again thank my sister for her editing skills and for supporting me through the trauma of actually deleting substantial sections of boring script; each word gone was like losing a treasured limb and it is a wonder that there is anything left. I must also thank Neil W for producing some incredible art – he did the map - after I was told last time that people wanted pictures and in the final furlong, Rose G, who ran with the proof read and ensuing amendments.

Finally I must thank you, the general public, for providing some memorable moments, some positive, others not quite so and of course, last but not least, the bleddy hound for making my life intolerable.

INTRODUCTION

It has been four years since The Cove Diary was published, well almost. Since the enclosed pages herein describe two years this rather means it has taken an entire two years to bring this monument of literature into being. Believe me, that is not a long time.

On the face of it this time, the book looks like an edifice, a mighty volume, an insurmountable peak, unclimbable by normal common folk. Ordinarily I would agree with you but let us face it, we are talking about The Cove Diary here, not some intellectual, academic or historical masterpiece - you know, proper books. This is a book so vacuous that I am sure it is but a featherweight in your hands and anyway it is also available through the miracle of modern electronics as an e-book which weighs nothing at all.

It would be unfair of me to suggest that this is a great work of note or that it is a work of note or even a work. Therefore I will not. It is however full of words, bigger than the last book, thus enabling higher shelves to be reached if you stand on it, and heavier, lending itself to greater impact if thrown.

You may well ask, why so big? Why indeed when so many of the world's great works are slim volumes: Wuthering Heights, 260 pages; To the Lighthouse, 320 pages (Barrett, hard of hearing edition); Noddy goes to Toyland, 32 pages. What they lack in volume they make up with talent in spades; I had to compensate. Additionally many of the copies of the first book ended up in holiday lets in The Cove. Holiday makers told me that they read the book during their two week stays – for free. A book twice the size, then, should deter even the most avid reader from completing it inside an average holiday stay and therefore they would have to buy a copy to finish it. Up top for dancing, I say.

So, having established why size matters (in this case, at least) we should proceed to why you should buy it; why your life would be incomplete without a copy in your possession.

If you have never heard of The Cove Diary before nor have you been drawn to witness the grievous stain on the Internet that is the daily witterings-on of a dangerously unstable (fear not, I mean in literary terms only) shopkeeper plying his trade in the Far West of Cornwall, I heartily commend this volume to you as a toe in the water of light – very light - entertainment. After all you know no better, do you? If on the other hand you are a seasoned reader of the online issues and, perhaps, the previous book there is no more wool to be pulled over your eyes. Should you purchase a copy of this lump and are thereafter disappointed, you should surely have know better.

—

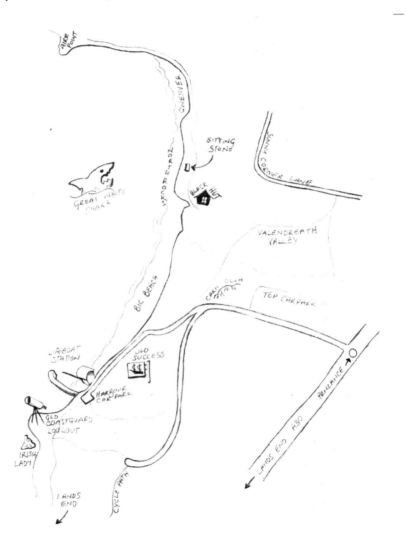

April 1st – Friday

The thick fog from last night had cleared up a little but still hung around all day in one form or another.

In fact, this morning I should have missed it completely. The Missus had offered to get up early and do my normal chores, bless her. As it happened my cardboard man dropped in unexpectedly and I had to get up anyway.

Our cardboard man is a very useful chap indeed so it is best not to upset him. You see we generate an extraordinary amount of cardboard each year and need to get rid of it on a regular basis. We are not allowed to put this into the corporation recycling facilities, being a business, nor can we take it to the tip for recycling. Our normal business waste collectors will not touch it either, unless it is bailed into precisely weighed packages and bound by their own special cord. Oh, and they charge an exorbitant fee for the privilege too.

Cardboard man does this service for free, currently, and does not care how it is presented either. He also provides me with the all important transfer note that, should the thought police ask, proves that I have disposed of my cardboard through an official route. Nothing quite like an infrastructure that is designed to make it as easy as possible for business to thrive, is there?

Yup, thought all that would keep you on the edge of your seat, no doubt poised to throw yourselves off.

You might have expected a little jolly jape in today's page given the date. I would have been pleased to oblige too had this page actually appeared on the date stated at the top. I have also avoided relaying any news stories from today's papers just in case I find myself duped and an unwitting party to propagating an April 1st joke. That would be just a little too embarrassing.

April 2nd – Saturday

Well it cleared up into a pretty little day with bags of blue sky and sunshine. No wind to speak of and in the sunshine perfectly warm.

Not exactly the busiest day we have had but there were a fair few around and it rather looks like some schools up country may already have gone on hols. Awkward then that the two orders I put together last night never materialised this morning. It might possibly have something to do with the fact that I completely forgot to send them off. Whoops!

All a bit of a fairy tale really and why should it not be, especially as Hans Christian Anderson was born today in 1805. He was a great fan of Dickens, apparently, and spent five weeks at his house. I cannot see Dickens being the most attentive host during that period as shortly after Anderson left, Dickens published David Copperfield.

"'Ere Cath, look after 'ans will you, I'm off to do a bit of writing."

"Oh, not again, Charlie!"

"You'll be alright, luvver. I can't understand a blessed word 'ee says either. Just show 'un our collection of tin soldiers or maybe that thumb puppet of yours and take 'un down to Regent's Park and feed they darned ugly cygnets down there. If that dunt do it just say 'es in the right places and show 'ee a bit of ankle."

You'll be most familiar with the Saturday night routine by now, down to the starry sky walk home. The lighter evenings, though, give the bleddy hound a better chance of chasing rabbits up in the field behind the F&L so we tarried there for a while first.

The walk home was a little more precarious than usual as someone's left a bleddy big hole at the bottom of Stonechair. Good job I remembered my torch.

April 4ᵗʰ – Monday

What an absolutely blinding sunrise. Very much like a sunset in reverse.

The shock, horror news of the day is a Kookaburra has gone missing from Paradise Park in Hayle. Perhaps the sunrise made it homesick.

We know from the rhyme that Kookaburras are merry creatures and have a gay life. We also know that they sit in gum trees and chase monkeys. This gives our peripatetic bird something of a problem: West Cornwall, as far as I know, is devoid of gum trees, in fact has few trees at all. As for monkeys, well, I have not seen too many of them either. It is not looking at all good for our escapee.

We had more gulls than we had visitors today, which could be something to do with mating season, the gulls that is, not the visitors although that is just a supposition on my part. Who knows what the visitors are up to but they are not down here. Shame really; it is a cracking little day out there.

I actually remembered to send off our fresh fruit and veg order last night. Well when I say remembered, I remembered after I had shutdown the computer for the night and had, in fact, retired. It will be all right, come October I will have got the hang of this shop keeping lark.

Is that the sound of hysterical laughter I hear, deriding my best efforts to keep a lid on management operations? No, just a lost Kookaburra. He should laugh; I am not the one up a gum tree – yet.

April 5ᵗʰ - Tuesday

What a grey and miserable day. Rain at first turned to mizzle then the low cloud hung around all day. It appears that everyone else wrote the day off as well as we can count the customers we had on one hand. All right both hands and a foot, maybe.

At least it gave us some time to clear the two big orders that came in today. Time to prepare for what we hope is a busy Easter time. Our shop hours extend from Saturday so someone better turn up else we will cut very lonely figures gazing out on deserted streets.

I trust you will not be fooled by the report in today's paper that put St Ives as the number one beach in the UK and sixth in Europe. This is the outcome of a survey by Trip Advisor, the criteria for which is a bit unclear. They seem to have included the Hepworth Museum and the Tate Gallery, one of which is nowhere near a beach. However when it comes to taking your own medicine Trip Advisor must be in the bottom quartile: one look at their own website's top ten European beaches and the UK, let alone St Ives, is nowhere to be seen.

We had an invitation from LT to attend a tasting at his new fish & chip place up in Sennen this evening. An invitation I tell you! Makes a change from having to gate crash all these events.

Unfortunately I had a prior arrangement with a pack of cards at the OS so the Missus went by herself.

We have been well aware of the hype and the hope that we would be blessed with a top quality purveyor of the deep fried piscatorial delight. Fresh fish from Newlyn and proper local potatoes traditionally chipped. The Missus returned with a big beaming grin. Looks like we no longer have to trek to PZ for a decent fish & chip meal from Thursday on.

Talking of salt, the weather rubbed some into our open sores by turning out a cracking clear and dry evening. Thanks for that.

April 6ᵗʰ – Wednesday

That is a bit better: an absolutely cracking day out there today, blues skies with a few mares tails, even the sea has calmed down a bit.

The beach looked stunning too although there is a fairly large patch of oar weed dumped in the middle after the big seas of the last few days. And with the blue skies a few less blue people and a few more happy ones, despite it being 'worse-off Wednesday'. Quite a few dipping in the sea and even saw a couple in swimming costumes, the brave souls.

Each day now more 'stuff' arrives at our door. It would be quite exciting but for the certain knowledge that we are going to have to cough up for it before too long.

One of the 'stuff' that arrived today was our Cornish tea. You might remember not so long ago that the Missus supped on some at Claridges when she went up for her girly day out in the big city. You may assume that it is not what you would call cheap but I can offer that it will be a sight less expensive than taking it at Claridges. And if you are of the mind that tea is just tea this brew may just change your mind.

Talking of expense, let us have a 'here we go again' moment. Why in the world would anyone come into a shop with the express purpose of purchasing something and then not have any money to buy it? Somehow this very often translates into my fault and worse still that we do not accept payment cards on purchases where to do so would cost us more than the profit made on the item. Then the unkindest cut of all is the retort that Tesburys do it.

I must cast my mind forward now to the forthcoming week when, with a fair wind, things will get busier. I must also cast my mind back because I cannot for the life of me remember all those things we have to do to be prepared for it. Ah yes, I remember now, polish the seat of my pants.

April 7ᵗʰ - Thursday

Strike a light! Today's weather is no match for yesterday's sunny skies. I was not sure that fog was on the agenda a couple of days ago when they said it was going to be fine for a few days. One might consider it to be the work of Lucifer. I am just glad I did not invest a bit in sun screen lotion. Anyway who cares if today is no match? Stick to what we have and be grateful, I say.

Despite it being a good bit chillier today it seems we were a little busier than yesterday. Indeed, we actually had a veritable crowd in the shop at one point and the first queue at the till – albeit three customers. It helped that the fog backed off from mid morning and hung around on the horizon. It is scheduled to revisit beyond evening.

I was toying with the idea of making a few daffodil references and perhaps throwing in a few floating clouds on account of it being Wordsworth's birthday today in 1770. However, having already taunted you with some match gags I thought you might be a little worn out. As indeed, I am sure, Mr Wordsworth was waiting to be made poet laureate, a title he eventually achieved when he was 73.

Yes, the match references stem from Mr John Walker who invented them in 1827. The chemicals were sufficiently toxic to see off many match makers, he clearly not being one of them. He lived to be 78.

So back in The Cove a little light Lifeboat launching to while away the hours. Between launch and recovery we had a few chums around for tea. Missus despatched herself off to the new chippy at the top. She took a while, as it was very busy on its first day of opening.

Worth the wait? I'd say, fresh fish from Newlyn, proper chips and not a drop of grease in the box. TL looked pretty much done in when I bumped into him just locking up when I returned from the last pound a pint session at the F&L. He did have a mighty grin on his face though.

April 8ᵗʰ – Friday

What a curious day. Certainly not in a bad way, the weather is delicious with a bit of an easterly breezing in. Now, usually easterly would be preceded by a nagging, knicker-tugging or similar derisory prelude. However this particular easterly has me flummoxed and lost for a suitable adjective. It is, you see, an unusually mild blow, from the deserts of far off Africcy and laced with the promise of exotic spices, dusky maidens and depleted uranium.

Curious it may be but it just kept getting better and better. The Cove was definitely looking very much alive by mid afternoon with visitors beginning to trickle in. We even had the first yacht arrive, a catamaran no less, moored out in the bay. Just hope that this continues as we have three weeks of extended opening to look forward to from tomorrow.

Missus upped sticks and took the bleddy hound down to the big beach. The poor, hard done by, dog has not had a decent run for a few days since our neighbours up the back went home. She will be even more hampered in a few weeks when dogs are banned from the beaches. I still cannot find a definitive notice regarding dog restrictions as the Council website seems to point to an outside source of information. This still says that the dog walking will be restricted to morning and evenings, let us hope its right.

A nice, quiet evening in, I think, tonight. We might actually have to do some work tomorrow.

April 9ᵗʰ – Saturday

An encouraging start to the Easter break under a somewhat hazy sun with that easterly, while still mild, has increased in velocity taking the edge off what is otherwise a lovely warm day.

It is on days such as this that the bleddy hound likes to sun bathe on the flat roof of our store room. In fact 'likes' may not quite cut the mustard in terms of an adequate description; the mere mention of r-o-o-f has her up the stairs like a robber's dog (some customers may unkindly suggest that this is exactly what she is) bumping her nose against the window should it be closed.

It is an ordinary felt roof with those loose stones scattered over it. The Missus has adorned it with a garden of plant pots containing lifeless twigs and solar lights hang from bits of trellis. We have no idea if the solar lights work as the blinds are closed at night. Over the years the roof has collected an additional covering of dirt and moss that the bleddy hound routinely paints onto the sofa and the carpets with her paws.

The Missus has long been searching for a solution to the mucky problem despite my suggestion that closing the window would probably work. This year she has hit upon the idea that synthetic grass is the very thing. Naturally it has to be bedded on two types of underlay so that the bleddy hound may find some comfort while lying on it.

I shall keep you posted on the efficacy of this approach. Since both the moss and the dirt arrive from the adjacent rooftops I suggest the only benefit that will be derived is that we shall have a comfortable hound spreading moss and dirt over the sofa and carpet.

I think, despite our late closing, that I shall repair to the F&L tonight to consider these matters of greatness. I shall, no doubt, avail myself of one or two ales and I shall do my best not to slip from the kerb on my way home and break a couple of fingers. That would be such a bizarre and freakish accident I could not imagine it happening to anyone, other then EA, of course.

April 10ᵗʰ – Sunday

By Jove! We were warned to expect an overcast day with rain clearing from the morning so we anticipated a pretty much sedate day. What we got was big blue skies from the off, temperatures increasing during the day and an influx you'd expect to see during a good August day.

We had a bit of a Head Launcher's convention over a fine breakfast next door, sitting out in the warming sunshine ahead of today's Lifeboat exercise. Nothing like a few rashers of back bacon, something that our International Correspondent is deprived of, I understand. Rather oddly back bacon is not available in the most advanced country in the world MM tells me. Makes you glad to be here, doesn't it?

There is an outside chance that, in the event that insufficient numbers of Boat Crew turn out for a shout, then the Coxswain of the day may call upon the ranks of the redoubtable Shore Crew. So there I was waiting to launch the Lifeboat when skipper, OG, called me onto the boat for a bit of experience. And what an experience it was too, a cracking day to be out on the water and a trip round to Porthcurno.

The coast looked magnificent from the water. PK beach was busy and a few were scattered over Pednevounder too, some even with clothes on. There appears to be some building work going on at Minack, a new dressing room, I understand. Being on the edge of a cliff this clearly requires some innovative thinking to get materials down to the lower levels, hence the steeply sloping chutes and proliferation of scaffolding. Rather them than me, thank you.

When we returned the Missus made it clear that I had been allowed quite enough fun for one day and nailed my feet down behind the counter. We probably were not quite as busy as a summer day but not far off it. How very lovely it was and how very encouraging for an embattled shopkeeper in the middle of a recession – oops, recovering economy, sorry. Gives you goose bumps all over.

And if that had not given me goose bumps then the mist that rolled in at six fifteen certainly did. An instant chill hit the air and for a while we could not see the sea at all. That just about finished off the day.

Ah well into every life a little fog must creep, I suppose.

April 11ᵗʰ – Monday

We seem to have a foggy hangover this morning with occasional heavy mizzle; did not stop everyone coming in though.

As you know we have odd requests from time to time. Today's came from a very charming young lady who was after a copy of Yoga magazine. Now, we do try and stock a fairly wide range of magazines attempting to encompass both local foible and visitor whim. Titles such as "Oblivion: drinking for love and success" and "Rolly: smoking hints for the under sixteens" seem to go down well as does "Gurgle: surviving the surf on eight pints and a reefer".

I did try and explain that down here Yoga would be confused with a character from Star Wars and Pilates usually had Pontius in front of it. I think she left with a packet of something from our pet food selection - muesli I think.

The fog cleared out by mid morning letting go to some serious blue skies again. The westerly that is slowly increasing in volume and veering up to the north west had started chopping up the sea by mid afternoon. This seems to have put off most of the surfers and less serious players. The gannets, on the other hand, are loving it. And I do not need to imagine it is a cracking afternoon for kite flying, as there are people down on the beach proving it. Most other people saw the fog this morning and made other plans, I suspect.

Ah well, gives me a few minutes to delve into this month's "Mask: the Dick Turpin guide to shop keeping".

April 12ᵗʰ - Tuesday

It did not look much to start with but turned into a surprising good day; surprising for a number of reasons.

First there was the blue sky and a lightening wind veering round to the west again. Sun hats, shorts and good moods were out in abundance.

Sorry to interrupt but why do people find it necessary to screech to a halt, half way up the pavement outside the shop. Surely it is not that far to walk from the kerb. If the bleddy hound had been tied up there she would have lost her nose, for heaven's sake.

Secondly, some chap turned up and started painting the front of the shop. He looked strangely familiar. It took a few minutes but I recognised in those roughly hewn features, the one leg a tad shorter than the other and the slight hump on the left shoulder, the devilishly 'ansum visage of Picasso, our local painter. I was going to mention that I was sure the hump was on the other shoulder last time I saw him but thought better of it.

Perhaps I should have been embarrassed by my inability to remember him but, in my defence, it has been more than twelve months since he started and last worked on this project; dreckly is just too soon for this man.

After working for ten minutes he offered me down to the OS to celebrate his birthday. I could hardly refuse; he would have cut a sad and lonely figure else. We did not stay long but in the little time we had he regaled me with tales and how he lost his leg in the Crimean wars. I did not believe him, of course; his leg is as good as mine – just a little shorter.

Earlier in the day we had a little Lifeboat shout. The Inshore Lifeboat was launched into some bouncy water to investigate a life jacket adrift out by Brisons. Fortunately the jacket had some identification that allowed it to be attributed to the institution to which it belonged, ahem.

Just another day at the sharp end in Sennen Cove.

April 13th – Wednesday

The promised rain took its time getting here today and when it did it was not half so bad as we were warned of, or what it looked like on the MO website. Apparently big lumps did fall on Penzance where, I was told, a large number of visitors went today. Perhaps they would have been better going up Camborne Hill.

It was also quite fresh as well, (spelt c-o-l-d), and not the sort of day for white stockings, though I did remind everyone, including myself, that this is actually normal weather for April and the good stuff we have been getting has been somewhat exceptional. There is no point in getting steamed up about it; good stuff is on the way for the weekend apparently.

Good then that at last the artificial grass for the roofing project has arrived. The Missus will be out there as soon as the rain abates planting it so that the bleddy hound may enjoy its comfort come the sunshine. Trouble is she gets so hot in the sun that she pants away excessively, the dog, that is, not the Missus. Like a little puffing devil, she is.

I know that you, dear reader, are not one to have wool pulled over your eyes, no matter how pleasant it makes the day look. You will, by now, have discerned that I have alluded to Mr Trevithick's birthday in 1771 with my references to white stockings and steam. A very clever man, by all accounts, though he would have done well to employ a business manager. He died penniless in Dartford, of all places.

There are two gulls that have been plaguing the environs of the waste bin across the road from the shop. They had some of the contents out on Sunday when the bin became full. Since then they have had their beady little eyes on the shop and have become increasingly brave as the week has progressed. Today they have been standing on the newspaper box surveying what I assumed to be our postcards. I was still puzzling over this when one started pecking at the window. At the place it was pecking is a poster for an art exhibition and the painting displayed depicts some berries on a leaf.

Margaret Collins, if you are reading this, not only has your work made it to an exhibition, so realistic is it you have even fooled the birds of the air. If you call round next week we can discuss some commission work; I was thinking ten pound notes to start with.

April 14th – Thursday

A bit of a mixed up day with cloud, some mizzle and bright spells. We even had a bit of blue sky at one point – something for everyone, perhaps.

Regardless of the weather it was a day that lightened my spirit and put a geet smile on my face.

I can promise you that it was not because our favourite brewer has launched its own smart phone 'app'. Apparently you can order beer from your mobile telephone and provide feedback on the public houses you might have had the misfortune to pay large amounts of your hard earned in. There is one advantage that might make the whole thing worthwhile - you can find out where its ale houses are and drive to somewhere else instead.

If you are driving, of course, you should be aware that the Highway Code was first published today in 1931. I might venture that this could be the most popular driving book and probably the least read. In fact observing some of the driving antics I am sure we have all seen, the book may as well have been written in Esperanto.

If it had been, Dr Lazurus Ludwig Zamenhof would have been delighted if he was still around in 1931 for he invented Esperanto and died today in 1917.

Even a well attended Lifeboat launch this evening, as delightful as it was, was not the chief reason for my elation. Both boats were sent thither with a decent sized audience to see them off and returned quite late for a near perfect recovery. Not that our audience cared a jot – they had all gone home.

But none of these little nuggets, handily dropped into my metaphorical, Diary writing, lap compare to the news, that The Sennen Cove Diary has cracked the southern hemisphere.

Surprisingly H did not look the least embarrassed admitting her guilty secret. I suppose it helped that the shop was empty at the time. I hope she drops us the occasional mail; it would be nice to have the odd snippet from down under. Heaven knows how much help this page needs. She originally hails from Carnyorth, which is odd as I did not know they spoke Australian up there.

For a change, we repaired to the OS for an evening of quiet contemplation interrupted only by a revival of the quiz night. Our small team of shy and retiring launchers (and Fred) beat the considerable opposition into a cocked hat. Oh what joy, what rapture for such a modest band.

Things just keep getting better and better. Shame there was not a lottery result tonight.

April 15ᵗʰ – Friday

It is quite curious how some things conspire together to bring about a circumstance so much greater than the sum of its parts.

I am sure I should have mentioned this sooner but I shall tell you now and trust that your lives have not been too much diminished by the ignorance of it. The Missus has recently caught a bug. Perhaps it is more of a hobby or even a fetish so bizarre is it. You see she had become a Twitterer (one who Twitters has not yet attained OED approval. Sorry, I just checked; it has and it is. An acquaintance suggested a much less complimentary but probably more accurate term). She has several minor celebrity notches on her smart phone cover already.

I have to admit that I have not quite grasped the attraction of such activity but there have been some amusing moments. She seems to have formed something of a virtual relationship with one chap in particular whose name I clearly must withhold for the sake of the children. All I can say is that his television appearances have been prolific of late.

You will remember that I mentioned the arrival of the plastic grass, set to make spoiling the bleddy hound complete in every way. Well the laying of the artificial turf is now finished. As TS noted, we could run bowling competitions up there throughout the summer. In fact there may be endless uses, having seen the light, but I fear it may just be a false lawn.

Irritating though the admission is, I have to say it does look rather smart. Just do not tell the Missus I told you that. I will never hear the end of it. Leonardo da Vinci himself would have been proud of such innovation and artistic flair and should be mentioned on account of it being his birthday today in 1452.

"What do you think to this 'ere plastic grass, Leo?"

"Bleddy 'ansum. That maid of yours certainly knows a good thing when she sees it. Just think what I could have done with some of that in my day."

With such a glowing endorsement, simply letting the moment of completion pass unmarked is out of the question. Now that the Missus is chummy with so many of the glitterati we shall set about inviting one or two of them down to do a grand opening. How could they refuse?

So if you find that your favourite episode of East Emmer Street is not being aired next week it is because they are all down here, sipping rough cider and chomping on award winning pasties on our new grass, darling!

April 16ᵗʰ – Saturday

One look at the MO website, well two looks actually, showed PZ as a place of sun and delight while St Mary's on Scilly would be fog bound all day. There were we in the middle without a clue how this would turn out. As it happened geet black clouds hung over PZ all day and we were blessed with blue skies for the main part; very nice too.

If the gods are smiling on us this should be a very busy week. The weather will be all important and it would have been nice to see a falling tide in the afternoon. As it stands, for the busy part of the day, most of the beach will be covered up, especially on a burgeoning spring tide. Fussy ain't we.

We are quite used to being asked questions and our advice sought on a wide range of topics. Today's question quite floored me. "What do you drink?"

Well, I am ashamed to say that reflex kicked in and my immediate response was, "That's very kind. I'll have a pint please."

Having realised my mistake I think I recovered quite well. It appears that the young lady wanted to establish what might be a similar drink to the type she drank in her native land. Now, she was speaking with an accent that could either have been German or Dutch. It is certainly not done to confuse the two, so rather than risk a faux pas I asked her what she drank at home which only confirmed my ignorance by not having a clue what she just said but it did confirm she was German.

Still clueless as to what might suit I packed her off with a couple of Doom Bars and a four pack of Fosters. It might not taste the same as her brew from home but it would certainly have her on her back in no time, so the effect would be the same. It just goes to show that we still have much to learn when it comes to the purveying of beers to our cosmopolitan customer base.

Now, it strikes me that the F&L may have some experience in this area, being a popular public house on the visitor circuit. Naturally, being a busy time, I would ordinarily eschew my regular trip to the F&L on a Saturday night. However I have a duty to my customers to resolve the issues at hand. I shall repair to the F&L forthwith to make my enquiries.

You may consider this a selfless act of some note; I can only tell you these sacrifices are but commonplace activities, undertaken to satisfy our customers.

April 19ᵗʰ – Tuesday

Crikey! We would be lucky to get weather like this in August, never mind April. The easterly has dropped out too and that has made all the difference. It has also pinned a lot of people down on the beach soaking up the rays, which is no good I tell you. They need to be up and about buying things in the shop. See you just cannot make a shopkeeper happy.

I had a bit of a moment when a vintage tractor pulled up outside today. I thought we might have been a victim of a late April fool and that the new tractor delivered for the Inshore Lifeboat was a cruel joke. It was not, of course, and we had a nice new shiny trailer delivered today to go with it.

And when my witterings take on fabrication of this enormity it is very definitely time to stop and take a cold bath.

April 20ᵗʰ - Wednesday

That medium level cloud that rolled in just before sunset gave rise to a rather pretty little sunrise this morning. Now, come on, let us stay positive, it was not exactly a *red* sky.

A nasty little surprise down at Land's End last night was reported on the radio this morning. An oil slick, about a kilometre square in size last night, appeared off the point, possibly spillage from a passing ship. By this morning it had broken down considerably and was reported as covering around 100 square metres. It was not thought likely that it would affect any of the local beaches. Phew!

And at last some good news, at least for H in Australia who probably would not be there if it was not for Captain James Cook, the first European to discover it in 1770. The chap left a trail of places named after him, his ships and his pet cat, probably. By the time he reached the north west of America he started on the climate (Cape Foulweather) and other vagaries (Isle of Sailorwithoddwartonnose). It is believed he knew he had gone too far when the inhabitants of Hawaii took ultimate umbrage at having their islands called after a sliced bread snack.

I will not dwell on this too long, as Radio Pasty devoted an entire day to it. It is the twentieth anniversary of the county final between Cornwall and Yorkshire at Twickenham. I also know as I was living there at the time. The place was a sea of black and gold; Cornwall was empty.

Returning to matters nautical, our new lifeboat tractor was used in anger today. Twice in an hour! The sea has looked deceptively inviting all day but there was a nasty swell underlying it and several rips that were not all that obvious. The first shout might have been a little over cautious but the second got a surfer in close and going nowhere. The ILB stayed on the beach for the rest of the afternoon. Lifeguards on duty from Friday, I believe.

Now it is off to dip my feet in a nice secluded little bay I know. I named it myself: Bay of WaterIhadapeein.

April 21ˢᵗ - Thursday

As I looked over the beach this afternoon I had the uncanny feeling I had just missed three months. There really is little difference between today and an August day, except that it is not raining - yet.

It was also our busiest day so far. We were pinned down behind the counter all morning apart from a restocking trip to our store. Wish I could have done that with milk. We ran out mid afternoon, which is unheard of, and by the looks of disbelief and incredulity on people's faces they had not heard of it either.

I was about to slip on my hair shirt and cilice and commence beating myself with daffodil stalks (I have told you before we have very few trees here and certainly no birches) when a customer came in and told me Julia Bradbury, her on Countryfile, was down at the OS filming. There was no possible way I could get there so I concluded that that was punishment enough.

There was no Lifeboat exercise this evening so I left the others nosing around the new tractor and returned to the shop to let the Missus do her bit of restocking. Honestly this is more like summer behaviour than Easter time.

April 22ⁿᵈ - Friday

A bit off patch this but I could not resist. It seems that at least some thieves in Devon are blessed with a sense of irony. They broke into the car of the Chief Constable of Devon & Cornwall Police and helped themselves to his police radio and other gadgets. Mr Otter swore blind he had locked it but could not see how they could have broken in, as there was no damage caused.

Sensing some irony of their own, the force sent a couple of Bobbies around to give the chief a leaflet on crime prevention and drop him a few tips. I imagine they suggested not leaving valuables in the car and perhaps buying a motor less attractive to the criminals, like the old bangers the rest of us can afford.

Further afield still, some enterprising Cornishman has opened a pasty shop in Copenhagen. He ships them in from a bakery in Crantock and if it is the one I am thinking of they are not bad for a mass produced, frozen jobby. He better do a good job; we do not want to scare the Danish off before they even get here.

We tied off the day nicely with the first of the summer type Lifeboat shouts - a yacht with engine failure off Logan Rock. Fair enough there was very little wind and the poor chaps must have been getting wet out there. Penzance harbour was closed due to some technical error so she was berthed up for the night in Newlyn.

Lifeboat in and tidied up by 8:45 pm; me in and tidied up with a small beer in front of the tele' by nine. Shame then that the television people had failed to schedule in any programmes worth watching.

April 23ʳᵈ - Saturday

Well, at least the rain has gone. The forecasters tell us that the chance of it moving off Scilly and heading towards us is slim. Let us hope they are right for a change.

Nevertheless it was cloudy for most of the day, the sun only deigning to break through after about four o'clock. The wind, punching in from a northerly direction is really giving us the cold shoulder and the cold everything else too.

With the weather set against us it is nice to see that the Exeter based airline, Flybe, is doing its bit to promote Cornish tourism. I have mentioned on these pages before how Rosamunde Pilcher has captured the hearts (and wallets) of our German friends. Flybe, bless 'em, have introduced a new weekly Dusseldorf to Exeter schedule to cart all those Pilcher enthusiasts over here.

They could, of course, have stopped there but it seems the little airline is keen to go the extra mile for its literarily bent passengers. There will be opportunity at the check in to have your picture taken with a cardboard cut-out of the lady herself and if that was not enough another cardboard cut-out will be taking the flight with you. No, wait, there is more. Every passenger will be given a Rosamunde Pilcher face mask to wear and when you take your seat you will hear Rosamunde Pilcher's dulcet tones welcoming you on board.

The Samaritans are so concerned about the psychological effect all this will have on passengers they have set up a desk at the arrivals gate at Exeter airport. You will be able to recognise them immediately; they will all be wearing Winston Graham masks.

If some of these avid readers do manage to arrive in a stable condition they will be able to take advantage of the tour bus that started again yesterday. This is the open top bus that does a circular route in both directions from Penzance through St Ives, taking in Land's End and St Just on the way. What I did not realise is that the road between Penzance and Land's End has got a little longer since last year, at least on one side.

I was checking the times for the printed summary timetable I put in the shop window when I noticed it. The journey from Penzance to Land's End takes three minutes longer than it did last year. Having changed all the entries on the clockwise route I set about changing the anti-clock table. Oddly it is exactly the same as last year.

On reflection I suppose it makes sense. On the clockwise journey the bus is on the outside of the circle, a slightly longer journey – but only on the first leg. The bends on the road from St Just to St Ives must cancel out the effect on the rest of the route.

I am so glad we sorted that out.

At last knockings we had a bus pull up outside. It had "Positive Attitude College" written down the side, which I had not heard of. They were very nice people and I wished them good evening. They said they were not so sure it would be, as they were certain they would not find anywhere to stay. Still, I told them that tomorrow would be fine weather so they bought couple of umbrellas just in case.

visit, so she told us, the outcome of which was that we were now served by this very fine little chap.

"Ah, Mr Holmes I presume," said the taller of the two gentlemen. "We are representatives of the ... ."

"United Kingdom Border Agency." Cut in Holmes.

"Good Lord! How the deuce ... .?"

"From the cut of your suit it is evident that you are comfortably off. The slight sheen on the seat of your trousers suggests much time in a sedentary pose and the noticeable dent in the crook of your index finger tells me that much time is devoted to holding a tea cup, Staffordshire stoneware if I'm not mistaken. The distinct lack of furrows on your forehead is the mark of a man who is certain of an early retirement on a final salary pension, a luxury that very few private firms could indulge their staff in. Our national borders are bounded by the sea; your boots show a small white salt residue around the welt suggesting much time spent by the coast. All quite elementary, I can assure you, sir. Quite apart from that the name badge that you neglected to take off when leaving the office has "UK Border Agency" written upon it."

"Well, well Mr Holmes. Allow me to introduce myself. I am Mr Stoppham and this is my colleague, Mr Grabham," said the tall gentleman, sounding suitably impressed.

"So, gentlemen, how may I be of service to you?" said Holmes settling back onto a nearby packing case and watching Gagan shuffle noiselessly out of the door.

"It's a rum do," said Mr Stoppham, gravely. "Each year Cornwall hosts a male voice choir festival with choirs attending from all the corners of the Empire and beyond. This year one of the choirs has gone missing."

"Missing, Mr Stoppham?" I asked.

"Yes, sir, the contingent from Nepal has completely vanished," continued Mr Stoppham. "They disembarked at Falmouth docks and that's the last anyone saw of them. We believe that they may have done a runner, sir, lured by the promise of cheap houses and medical benefits this fine country of ours offers. In less than a century we'll be offering state benefits too, I've no wonder."

"Nepal, eh, Holmes. Isn't that where Mrs Hudson ... .?" I exclaimed.

"Yes, Watson. Quite right," interrupted Holmes. "Pack your overnight things, Watson. If we hurry we'll make the Paddington to Penzance night train."

Without delay we hastened to Paddington and were soon on our way to Penzance. As we sat in the dining carriage a young lady approached us and introduced herself as Elaine.

"A platter of sandwiches, sirs?" she asked in a thick London accent.

"A platter?" I queried.

"Ellie meant tray, my dear Watson," Holmes returned.

We ate the half filled morsels and retired to our berth. I attempted to sleep while Holmes practised his violin. Even the clatter of the wheels on the track could not drown out the awful caterwauling.

After a less than restful night we arrived at Penzance early the next morning. The sun was breaking over the bay as we stepped down from the carriage. I looked out towards the sea to a strange line of exotic trees. Holmes followed my line of vision.

"A lemon tree, my dear Watson," he said answering my unasked question. "It is a fact, Watson, that the far west of our country enjoys a climate conducive to the early production of fruit and vegetables and allows the cultivation of sub tropical flora."

It was odd because from where I was standing they did look ever so like palm trees but there again that would have entirely ruined the joke.

A porter trotted up behind us pushing a barrow containing our bags and singing quietly to himself. He was a short, dark man with oddly oriental type features. I tipped him a couple of pennies to load our baggage onto the nearby cart. The driver was coincidentally of similar stamp.

We made the short journey into town to visit the organiser of the male voice choir festival while the driver hummed a rather tuneful melody. The streets were strangely quiet so I was about to enquire of the driver where all the people were when Holmes spoke.

"Driver, I expect that the streets hereabouts are quiet due to the occasion of Trevithick Day in Camborne where everyone celebrates the wonderful inventions of the late inventor."

"I dunno, sir," replied the driver in a curious accent, "I'm from Tibet, honest."

"Tibet, eh?" I ventured. "The porter at the railway station bore a striking resemblance to your good self. Is he from Tibet too?"

"Yes sir, he's my brother."

Our enquiries with the festival organiser brought us no closer to a solution to the mystery and neither did interviews with members of some of the choirs, so we retired for the evening to a busy inn in the town. Here we were served by a waiter who bore more than a casual resemblance to the cart driver and the porter. As he took away our order he broke into a delightful little song that amused us greatly.

We returned to London after a day's investigation at Falmouth still no closer to finding the missing choir. I had never seen Holmes in such a dark mood. By the time we reached Paddington he had snapped the stem on his pipe and broken a string on his violin he had played it so fervently. At least I had a decent night's sleep.

In our absence Mrs Hudson had returned and led us up to our newly refurbished lodgings. The door frame had been painted a light shade of yellow which was most unusual, as Holmes noted.

"A lemon entry, my dear Watson."

This time I ignored Holmes as he retreated to his room with a bag of opium, his broken pipe and a pot of horse glue and welcomed home Mrs Hudson. I must confess that I thought Mrs Hudson looked a little sheepish as I related the tale of the missing Nepalese choir. I was minded to ask her where she found our decorators at such short notice especially as I dimly recalled hearing them singing whilst they worked.

She reasoned that having just returned from Nepal she would know if the workers were Nepalese. She assured me that she was certain that they were from...

"Tibet?" I queried.

The End

Well not quite. The Nepalese choir really did do a disappearing act from this year's Male Voice Choir festival throwing proceedings into turmoil. The immigration authorities were alerted over fears that they may have absconded. Last night these fears seemed to be unfounded when the choir turned up in London as if nothing had happened. The last word was that they were heading for Cornwall to pick up their bookings.

I also have to thank the late, great Mr Barker for a couple of the 'elementary' gags, bless him; the highly contrived one is my own but I imagine you guessed that.

May 1ˢᵗ – Sunday

May Day. All that dancing around maypoles, young ladies in white frocks and men with bells on their legs thumping each other with big clubs; the idyllic spring scene with the sun beating down on happy, laughing faces.

Yeah, right. It's pelting down here today and by the looks of the rain radar it will be all day in varying degrees of wetness. Still, we have had three important weeks of sunshine that has made all the difference to our little business concern here in The Cove.

I have lost count of the times I have told you that we get all sorts of random and bizarre questions thrown at us from time to time. Today brought another from a chap who looked like he had a sense of humour. Well I have not got a black eye so I could have been right. He asked what he should do with a brood of young children who were causing mayhem on account of the weather. I am quite ashamed to say that I actually verbalised the first thought that came into my head, which was to tie a brick to their ankles and toss them off the end of the harbour wall.

I did make a hasty recovery and told him not to be such a wuss and to get them out on the beach. Most kids do not give a monkey's about the weather when they are knee deep in sand castles. Of course what I should have said was that our middle aisle has all sorts of activity books, pens and coloured pencils, which may not have made any difference to his predicament but at least would have put a few shillings in my till. Ah, the benefits of hindsight.

Of course the rain today makes for a splendid link to the birth of Arthur Wellesley in 1769 especially if you are wandering around in a pair of wellies. The good old 1ˢᵗ Duke of Wellinington gave his name to the footwear as well as knocking Boney off his perch with the help of some Prussians as well as being noted for having a huge conk (that is nose if you are reading this in the colonies and have now got a fit of the giggles, you naughty things). He was awarded the nomenclature of Iron Duke after he had iron shutters fitted to his London home when his parliamentary reforms led a few disaffected voters to throw rocks at them. And in a stunning example of sociological progress, nearly 200 years later some disaffected voters still think throwing rocks will change things; not overly encouraging, is it?

May 3ʳᵈ - Tuesday

We have had rather an alarming time of late. Not due to the weather for a change, though it has been very windy again today. Yesterday it stopped the Scillonian reaching its berth for three hours, which after a rocky trip, I am sure, gave some alarm of its own.

I imagine there was no small amount of alarm within the authorities shortly after 3ʳᵈ May when it is largely believed the first Cornish rebellion commenced in 1497. Being a while ago now it certainly was not the root of our current discomfiture although the modern day authorities do have much to do with it.

It was the Building Regulations (Approved Document B, specifically Part B of Schedule1 – er, possibly) that almost had me start a small rebellion of my own. It was at the tail end of some building work in our flat a while back that the electrician informed me that I must have a fire alarm installed. Despite showing him one that I already had one tastefully installed upon the ceiling he was adamant that another needed to be installed, in fact another two.

Both of the new devices are connected to the main electricity supply but have a battery installed to act should the mains supply fail, as it does here quite frequently. Further, one of the new, clever little flying sauceresque devices measures heat alone and the other smoke. Curiously the Regulations demand that the one that measures heat must be situated in the kitchen where heat is routinely generated and as a consequence our alarm is routinely tested.

The machines are smart enough to detect when the backup battery is nearly expired, (but not that you're only cooking bacon), and emits an annoying little bleep even if, as I discovered, you remove the unit from its base, which is confusingly above it. It had started to do this at 5:30am one morning last week but by 6:00am had given up bleeping and I forgot about it.

Forgot, that is until 10:00pm last night when it started to bleep again but this time without respite. I was fortunate enough that I had one battery left of the type required to silence the cursed disc and set about working out how to remove the unit from its base. The instructions suggested the dextrous use of a screwdriver inserted in slot 'A' but surely they really meant a big hammer, as the recommended tool appeared to have no effect however dextrously the user employed it.

I had quite forgotten that operations of such delicacy require utterances of keen rhetoric and blasphemy such that would bring colour to the cheeks of a stoker. Once recalled, of course, the device came apart with ease.

Replacing the battery was thankfully a simple affair as was replacing the unit back on its base in the ceiling. Pressing the test button set it and its sister unit in the kitchen singing away merrily; job done and a peaceful night in store.

Bleep! Followed several moments later by another, then another. What manner of foul deed is this that smells above my head I had to ask myself? If the deployment of a £4 battery could not silence this technical demon, what other recourse could I contemplate? The battery was obviously one of the best money could buy; it came from our shop, for heaven's sake.

Perhaps I should be brief when I describe that I exhausted my not inconsiderable fault management skills in identifying the root cause of the bleep and my increasing frustration. I should tell you that I replaced the kitchen heat sensor battery with the one taken from the smoke unit, (I did not have another spare new one), and that even when I had turned off the mains power, removed both units from their bases and taken out the batteries the blasted unit still cocked a snook at me and bleeped in defiance.

We slept all night with the invention of Beelzebub bleeping every forty seconds. I had resolved to go to another shop and get second battery and replace them in both units. The next stage of the plan, had that failed, was to seek out the hammer I should have employed in the first place, determining that a death in some raging inferno preferable to a slow demise by interminable bleep.

It was in the morning, standing under our original smoke detector, glaring angrily at the gleaming technical wizardry of the new one that I realised where the bleep was coming from.

Never mind, I won the poker game at the OS in the evening.

Our nice weather seems to have brought out the stars too, or at least one star. Leonardo Di Caprio is down at The Beach doing a spot of cooking in their kitchen. Actually it might be Gino D'Acampo, I could not be sure but he sent off a runner to Breakers next door for bacon sandwiches this morning. You would think he could cook his own so perhaps it is Leonardo, who probably could not or would not.

It is rather odd that the lifeguards are still on the beach. For the last few days they were about the only people on the beach. I would have thought that they would have been better value the week before Easter and the week after when it was busier. I'm pretty sure that they will go again at the end of this week and be back at the Whitsun half term.

With the brighter weather came a few more, brighter faces; we have been pretty much down on numbers since bank holiday Monday. Though we know it's coming, and hence our hours reduce, it still never fails to amaze how quickly The Cove empties out.

Neither Leonardo or Gino deigned to come down to the 'downstairs' end of The Cove to see their adoring public. That is the last of his spaghetti westerns I will eat, I can tell you.

May 6ᵗʰ - Friday

I regularly berate customers, in a jovial sort of way, when they ask for some sauce with their pasties. The latest, an Australia was most bemused at my look of horror when he popped the question. Apparently in Australia they always have red or brown sauce when they have a meat pie. Worse still an English customer asked if I had ever had my pasty fried! I mean for the love of St Piran, who would want to do that to a perfectly good pasty.

Quite clearly the moral of this story is if you ever go to Australia or certain parts of England take a good supply of sauce with you – the food's clearly not palatable without it.

We had quite a few Australians in this week and today especially. You can generally tell even before they start speaking; they are the ones with big heavy coats on and fingerless mittens. I did mention to one that this was a particularly warm day today due to our 'Spanish plume' to which she retorted that warm was the forty degrees she left behind and a feather, wherever it came from, would not convince her otherwise.

Still none of this weather compares to that which our American friends have had to endure recently. Our international correspondent reports that though she's had some tornado warnings South Carolina had been very lucky. In fact I saw a newspaper report that showed that major damage had been sustained in all the surrounding states but had somehow spared SC.

So thanking our lucky stars for a quiet little day, I think a quiet little night is in order with a bit of fish and chips from our most excellent new chippy. Pass the ketchup – only kidding.

May 7ᵗʰ – Saturday

I have a little tune running around in my head this morning: Pom, pom, di, pom, pom, pom. I cannot imagine where it came from.

It was raining first thing but that very quickly blew through and left a rather jolly little day from mid-morning. There is a fair old breeze stomping in from the southeast today but find a sheltered spot and I reckon it would be rather warm. Nevertheless it rather looks like everyone has danced off somewhere, so perhaps they will be on the floor all day, didi, pom, pom, didi, didi, pom, pom, pom.

I looked rather hopefully at the open top bus coming down the hill at lunchtime but they all stayed on board. I am rather glad that the council has not wielded its axe in that direction; it is a cracking little service. It was preceded by a little coach full of French-Canadians who jumped off, thought it a bit breezy and jumped back on again. Apparently they are off a big cruise liner moored up at Falmouth. There are 31 big coaches down there at their disposal, according to the coach driver, and we get the 29 seater, and not one wanting a shop. Pom, pom, pom, didi, pom, pom, pom.

Five minutes later a big German coach pulled up outside the shop, turning out half the occupants onto the path. To a man they beggered off in the direction of Land's End without so much as a vigates liebchen. I considered letting down the tyres but then I'd have a bleddy geet coach outside the shop all day.

It was busier upstairs than it was in the shop. The bleddy hound had her mutt mate from next door 'round to play; there was carnage in the living room. Just how they are going to do a five kilometre walk together for charity at the start of next month I have no idea. Sorry, did I not tell you that they are doing a sponsored walk and that you can sponsor them by following the link on the home page of the website? How remiss of me. Pom, pom, pom, didi, didi, didi, pom.

I rather hope that you have the name of the tune by now as I am running out of words to wrap around it, pom, pom, pom, didi, pom, pom, pom. I also got confused and had to write the whole thing down in 'poms' and 'didis' to find out where I had got to. There is, of course, the rather obvious clue in the second paragraph and if that didn't tell you then here comes the last line, pom, pom, didi, didi, pom, pom, pommmmmm.

There, I knew that would give it away. Written, apparently by Kate Moss in 1911, (must have been the thin one's gran), based on the traditional music of the Furry Dance. She managed to get the name wrong and called it the Floral Dance. The people of Helston must have forgiven her years ago because they play it every year at their Flora Day celebrations. I have to say I still prefer butter, myself.

The rain came back in force in the evening but I am a lucky chap. There was a break between showers that just so happened to coincide with my walking home from the F&L. Perhaps it wasn't such a bad day after all.

May 8ᵗʰ - Sunday

"What's the weather going to be like today?"

"Let me have a look at the Met Office website, madam. Ah, yes. Wall to wall sunshine until tomorrow afternoon."

"Is that the wall to wall sunshine with big black clouds and heavy showers like the one just coming?"

"Yes, that's the one, madam. Have a nice day."

To be fair the majority of the day was dry and sunny but the most incompetent weather watcher could see that there was a good chance of a shower in the morning. Well, perhaps not in this case.

Talking of incompetence, the people who produce 'Hello' magazine quite rightly anticipated some additional demand for their glossy prints following William and Kate's wedding last week. They trotted out the magazine a few days early and had them sent to newsagents on the Sunday. They were reckoning without the spoiling tactics of the Laurel and Hardy Newspaper Company who rallied to the cause and sent us three copies. In an ordinary week we would normally expect six copies at least. They lasted about five minutes.

Not to be confounded, the 'Hello' magazine people had another crack at it this week with royal wedding part two. The highly refined computer system at the Laurel and Hardy Newspaper Company kicked into action and, yes, sent us another three copies. This is the same finely tuned system responsible for sending us such relevant titles as 'London Street Map', 'Highland Cattle Weekly' and 'Crofting Times'. You may take as read that we do not rely on magazine sales to make our fortune.

The bleddy hound played an absolute blinder today. We rather foolishly left a bowl of fishy pasta on the side next to the cooker and the window to the new roof 'lawn' open, which is doing very well in all this rain, thanks for asking. Well, no prizes for guessing the outcome but she ought to get some respect for determination; it is quite a reach from windowsill to where the bowl was. She did look a little sheepish when caught and did not move much for the rest of the day.

I took both her and her mate around the block later in the day. It was positively balmy in the shelter from the southerly wind. The hillside up towards Sennen Heights is aglow with crocosmia x crocosmiiflora, (all right, we can all look up montbretia on the Internet and sound smart), which looks very pretty with the sun lighting up the leaves until you realise that there is probably twice as much as there was five years ago. In another five years there probably will not be anything but montbretia up there.

My turn to cook tonight; a nice little stir fry with plenty of chillies; I made sure to leave a bowl on the side and left the window open.

May 9ᵗʰ - Monday

Whitesands Bay seems so much bigger on days like this. From where we stand we can look around from Cowloes, taking in the far off Brisons, Cape, Nanjulian Cliffs, Aire Point and the expanse of the beach before that long pan peters out. I am quite surprised that the hang gliders are not out today as I am sure they would never land.

It might have been a little busier today, or perhaps we have honed our ability to hook more customers or maybe it is me. Anyway I have not been plagued by the ticking of the clock today like it has been following me around. And talking of clocks my alarm did not go off this morning. I think I shall have to tinker with the bell before we go to bed.

There are many walking types at this time of year. Today was no exception with a group of young chaps hanging around outside the café earlier today. I heard the fellow next door ask, "Are you lost, boys?" but I think they were just checking their maps. Either way they seemed properly kitted out.

With so much time on our hands we are able to spend a bit more time experimenting in the kitchen. We are doing some barbeque chicken type thing tonight with a little chilli and lemongrass. It has a very Southeast Asian flavour, chiefly Indian in a Thai grilly sort of way.

It is, of course, on account of Sir J M Barrie's birth in 1860, that I have once again strained against all reasonableness to try and get as many Peter Pan references into today's wibblings. I really am sorry for that last one, by the way, but you try and get Tiger Lily into a sentence.

May 10ᵗʰ - Tuesday

I find it somewhat irksome when things or people do not perform to expectations. It is even worst when the person or thing performing has provided that expectation in the first place.

For example we have a very nice, friendly fish supplier who did exactly what he said he would. He said he could not deliver any wild bass and he did not. I do like our nice, friendly fish supplier but it did mean I had to go to another supplier who is not so nice and friendly and has previous for not doing what they said. When I asked for 500 grams of sea bass I did rather expect roughly 500 grams of sea bass to turn up. In fact I said to the young lady on the telephone that I expected roughly 500 grams of sea bass to turn up and not nearly two kilograms like the last time I ordered 500 grams sea bass. She told me that this was extremely unlikely as the largest fish they had was two kilograms and you cannot get two kilograms of fillet off a two kilogram fish.

It was fortunate indeed that the Missus was working when nearly a kilogram of sea bass fillet turned up in the afternoon.

I suppose it is much the same when you go to the big supermarket, (if you really must), to buy some beef. It is probably reasonable to expect it to come from a British cow. After all one of the big chains makes a big song and dance about its buying British credentials. Mr T is not claiming their Black Angus beef from the USA to be anything else but there again I imagine there is not a big label on its beef that says 'cheap, inferior quality beef shipped half way round the world and we are probably only buying it to squeeze the price on British producers' either.

Then we can add into the mix the fact that the batteries we had delivered to expressly work in digital cameras do not work in digital cameras and you almost have the perfect day for things not happening as they say on the tin.

And so it came as no surprise that we learnt today that Sennen Cove has lost its Blue Flag status, the only beach in Cornwall to do so. To be fair the accreditation can easily be affected by such vagaries as when water samples were taken, the state of facilities and beach management. Now it also includes whether or not you have a 'real time' warning system that alerts you if there has been a sewage overflow in your area, an extremely unlikely event in this neck of the woods during the season, at least. As yet we do not quite know what tipped us off our pedestal but we do not expect bodies of poisoned surfers to be washed up any time soon.

And if you are looking for the joie de vivre that this page normally fosters, all I can tell you is that our sunny day has turned all cloudy and I got wet coming home from cards at the OS. I lost too.

May 11ᵗʰ - Wednesday

Ah, a little ray of shine both literal and metaphorical today.

We have a definitive answer to our lack of Blue Flag hanging over Sennen beach: we will not pay for it. Yup, it is just as simple as that. No dire change in the quality of the water, no threats from angry little pressure groups and no dump of toxic waste littering the beach, despite The much maligned council withdrawing its beach cleaning service this year.

The information is from the horse's mouth so I shall brook no argument. The much maligned council has in the past paid for the application process, the first step in trying to obtain Blue Flag status. This year they demurred and asked if Sennen would pay for it instead. The rest, as they say, is history. So we have not 'lost' our Blue Flag status as the national media quite irresponsibly put it, we simply did not relish coughing up for it.

May 12ᵗʰ - Thursday

Another cracking good day in the offing but the wind has moved round to the northwest so it's our turn for a bit of a blast. It certainly took the edge off the balmy temperatures we've been having.

Still, things will be looking up in the forecasting stakes if the latest recommendation is followed up. Some bright spark MP reckons that with another £10 million of our hard earned bunts the Met Office will be able to accurately forecast conditions well in advance, such as the big snow last year. I would think some money being diverted to accurately forecast tomorrow's weather might be more appropriate. Mind you if that sort of spare cash is floating about, a few million aimed at grafting wings onto pigs or, perhaps, breeding MPs with half an ounce of common sense would not go amiss either.

I am sure all you readers of a certain age remember when the children's television programme, Blue Peter, would have a spot where they would show you how to make Saturn V rockets out of old loo rolls and sticky backed tape, which you eventually worked out was Sellotape. When you tried it at home you ended up with something that looked like a bunch of loo rolls stuck together with Sellotape. Good, keep that in mind.

The plastic stand that sits outside the shop and displays our footballs gave up the ghost recently; it falls apart when you attempt to move it. Finding a replacement has been impossible.

Enter the modern Blue Peter equivalent: the Internet. I found a site that showed how all sorts of things could be made using PVC piping, similar to that which plumbers use to transport water. One of the creations pictured on the website looked remarkably like a ball display stand.

I can see your minds racing ahead of me here, so I shall cut to the chase. Armed with my rolled up blueprints I repaired to my friendly PVC pipe retailer who furnished me with the requisite lengths of pipe, elbow and T joints to bring my vision into the realms of reality. I had already anticipated a little issue with robustness and built into the design some plywood to strengthen the structure.

It took all afternoon. There was the addition of cable ties and, yes, some sticky backed tape that was not in the original plan. Despite my best efforts the structure does have a little movement reminiscent of a tall, badly set, jelly. It drew some comment, mostly unkind, from the small crowd of sceptical onlookers that had gathered.

I am not disheartened, however. You know, in a certain light and from a kind angle it does rather look like a Saturn V rocket.

May 13ᵗʰ - Friday

You will be pleased to note that my construction project survived being put away last night and rolled out again today. I have enjoyed biting my thumb all day in the general direction of my detractors and shouting 'yah boo sucks' at inappropriate intervals too. I have, though, resolved to remodel the design slightly. This should not be seen as any sort of admission that there is anything wrong with the existing structure; it was, of course meant to wobble as a defence against earthquakes. I simply mean to improve its aesthetic qualities, you understand.

It is interesting to note that today is the anniversary of Alison Hargreaves, a mother, becoming the first woman to conquer Mount Everest, in 1995, without oxygen or Sherpas. Interviewed afterwards she seemed quite nonplussed by all the attention. She said she was sure her husband had said to take the second left at the third roundabout.

Moving very swiftly on I meant to tell you yesterday that I detoured on my return home yesterday from PZ. I needed to go to St Buryan as I prefer to use my local petrol station to fill up the van. It is a much more private place to burst into tears when they give you the bill. However the point of telling you this is to explain how I found myself on the back road returning to Sennen.

It has been a while since I last used this route and I had quite forgotten the abundance of flora that can persist along the hedgerows. It must have been some time since it was trimmed back, as the road was very much over hung with flowers of every hue. With the sun as bright as a button the hedgerows were alive with colour: the whites of alexander; tri-cornered garlic and blackthorn flower; bluebells, campion, pinks and purples of other blooms. I couldn't begin to tell you all the names as I am no expert and as the road is single track in many places watching the hedgerows in detail can be detrimental to your well-being. It was nevertheless a right good feast for the eyes and a pleasure to witness.

Perhaps I should have headed out there again this afternoon. It would have beaten standing behind the shop counter and scratching my behind; it was quiet as the grave after lunchtime.

Having been bored witless behind the counter, I decided to slip up to the F&L in the evening for a little excitement as they had a band playing. I was in good company as there was a good representation of the Lifeboat crew up there including our esteemed, (off duty), coxswain. A little after nine o'clock and our pagers went off sending us all looking for kindly teetotal drivers to take us down to The Cove. Do not be concerned; there was no proposal that we should send off wobbly lifeboat men into the blue. It is more a natural reaction for each of us to respond.

The shout concerned a broken yacht out towards Wolf Rock and a long tow ensued. Our trusty Shore Crew held the vigil for the return and recovery of the Lifeboat.

A very sleepy shopkeeper returned to his nice comfy bed at two in the morning.

May 14th – Saturday

Well that is it then. A guarantee for sporadic downpours, damaging storms and a washout summer is heralded in the Daily Express today with the front page title "Super Summer to Last Months". You will, of course, recall that this is the newspaper that headlined the 'barbeque summer' two years ago and "scorching temperatures' last year.

May 17th – Tuesday

You may be pleased to know that I am in the rude of health, as right as nine pence, as fit as a fiddle - oh, let us not be modest - as finely tuned as a Stradivarius and I have the blessing of the National Health Service to underwrite that opinion. In fact it was them that told me.

This may not hold sway with the erstwhile opinion you may have held of your Diarist. It has been reported back to me on a couple of occasions that 'all he seems to do is go to the pub a lot'. So while you may express some surprise, or possibly disappointment, if you were keen to see the end of this daily bilge, I can tell you that my regular intake of pasties, cider by the vat full and geet heaps of rough shag stuffed into my clay pipe while a woodbine smoulders 'twix index and middle finger has not, at least so far, done me any harm whatsoever.

I perhaps would not go so far as to recommend this lifestyle to young people today; they are not made of the same grit any more. It may even be that there has been a fair amount of luck attached to my current state of survival. For example I have not yet come across a box of potentially live ammunition lying on the beach, ready to explode into my face while I passed by, unlike a couple of ladies from Cape National Coastwatch Institute today. I must hurriedly add that they were lucky too and survived the experience.

Quite why they waited until they got to the shop before revealing their lucky escape perhaps we shall never know. It was to the Missus that they poured out their woeful tale and she called me and I called Falmouth Coastguard. The Land's End team were on site pretty sharpish and threw a cordon around the offending box, at the north end of Gwenver. After a little investigation and reporting back to Falmouth it was decided to call out the Navy, unfortunately meaning ES and company had to run shifts looking after the little explosive box for around three hours. It also took a little longer than I imagined before some clever soul worked out they would be getting their feet wet before the senior service arrived.

At least the team were not sitting in an icy northwest blast and although it has been overcast all day it is not that cold. It is probably just as well since when the bomb squad arrived they discovered that the box contained nothing more dangerous than the clips to which the rounds were secured.

Well after such excitement it is off to treat my perfect cholesterol score and my scarcely-worth-mentioning triglyceride count to some fabulous fish and chips from LT's most excellent chippery. Later I shall, no doubt, exercise my exemplary liver function by imbibing some unwholesome, (and over priced), beverage at the OS and, later still, wonder at the youthful efficiency of my kidneys.

Enough, I am sure, to make you clean living, health conscious readers as sick as a parrot.

May 19ᵗʰ - Thursday

Well, what a wholly different morning we had today. What more could a poor boy want?

How about weekly bin collections? Our jolly councillors have been talking rubbish. Perhaps I should be a little more specific, as that probably is not news to a lot of us. They have been talking rubbish and what to do with it and in doing so have held a consultation. This is a process whereby a lot of random people are given the opportunity to feel that they have been able to influence outcomes that, in reality, have long since been cast in stone.

It must have been a little upsetting for the council when they realised that the decision to maintain weekly bin collections actually coincided with what the majority of consultees wanted. I cannot help feeling that there will be blood on the carpet in some oak panelled suite up at County Hall over this.

And talking of consultations I think I must have missed the one about cutting our bus services. When you have a Cove full of German visitors all wanting to take the bus to Land's End then onto Penzance, even if the timetable was written in German I think they would struggle. It therefore came as no surprise that we were deluged with bus time questions.

What was most embarrassing was their utter disbelief that they had to wait for an hour and a half for an appropriate bus. All I could do was agree with them that while we want them here to spend their schillings we are not prepared to spend our shillings in making it easy for them to spend them. Somewhere along the line someone is not concentrating; there seems to be a lot of focus on saving money and none on what is making it.

You cannot possibly have missed the little nugget that the Olympic flame will start its UK journey at Land's End for the 2012 Olympics on May 19th. I mentioned yesterday that the press were up there yesterday in numbers. They upset our man that looks after the famous sign post up there - they brought their own! What I did not realise is that the bleddy torch, sorry, flaming torch is due in London on 27th July. I can only suppose they intend to take it by bus.

Still, at least the Lifeboat seems to be a constant in these crazy times. We treated some of the Lizard crew to some Tamar slipway experience tonight. Their slipway is due for completion this summer and they really needed to see why a Head Launcher needs a cowboy hat to recover a boat. I think they understood.

May 20th - Friday

So, yesterday was a bit of a flash in a pan, then. The weather was not a whole lot different today, perhaps a little more cloud, but we are back to tumbleweed rolling down the street. Even the beach was pretty much deserted by mid-afternoon save for a few lonely lifeguards busy moving their flags around. Perhaps someone told our visitors that the in-laws are coming to stay today and they have gone off to greet them as they arrive in the county. You did not for a moment think I was going to say that they heard the in-laws were coming and left town, did you? Tish, tish, if you did.

It could be quiet in PZ too by next year as the Isles of Scilly helicopter people have found a potential new home in St Erth. Cue formation of the Friends of St Erth Industrial Estate dusting off Friends of PZ Harbour's banners and placards to oppose the move. It is not the worst place it could be, close to the A30 and easily accessible by train and, dare I say, bus.

(Oh no, that's it; he's mentioned the bus word. Here he goes again.)

Look it is not my fault that someone asked me to plan a route for a day trip to Falmouth, is it? As it happened to be the in-laws what could I do? It only took an hour to work out that the return journey could be done in a day, if you leave early enough, do not want to spend more than an hour and a half in Falmouth and do not mind getting back late.

Dear visitor to Cornwall, I sincerely recommend you hire a vehicle, the biggest, gas guzzling, carbon generating, environmentally unfriendly monster you can find. The authorities here have not the remotest genuine desire to encourage you to use public transport and saving planet Earth is a great idea as long as it does not cost anything or involve any work.

Just to underline this view the council has just decided to build the biggest bonfire in the country to burn all our rubbish. The residents of St Dennis were so overjoyed with the news they burst out onto the street in celebration. I am afraid that any protest will have to wait until St Erth has finished with the banners and placards.

I think the bleddy hound is next in line to use them after that to complain about spring high tide that coincides with her ball chasing time down in the harbour. She is most put out that she now has to wait. What an outrage.

May 23rd - Monday

It is, a day I have been looking forward to for some time, over six weeks in fact. Up until my permit arrived this morning I have been prevented from visiting our local dump, excuse me, Household Waste Recycling Centre. You see I run a vehicle that is on the council's list of vehicles most likely to be used for dumping, sorry, recycling commercial waste. In response they introduced a snappily named Household Waste Recycling Centre Vehicle Permitting Scheme. When I applied I was led to believe that I would have my nice shiny permit within two weeks. My application clearly took far longer to scrutinise and prepare than even the council anticipated and I am not surprised.

My permit was delivered with a letter setting out the 'Rules' that I must adhere to while throwing away rubbish, I mean submitting my waste for recycling. There are no less than 14 terms and conditions to be mindful of, including having to fill out a trade waste disclaimer, having my waste examined to ensure it complies with the 'Rules' and visiting no more than once per month. These stringent and restrictive conditions, they assure me, are accidental:

"These regulations are not designed to discourage householders from recycling, or make it more difficult."

At least they are not charging yet, although, to be honest, I subscribe to that idea for non-recyclable waste. I know that this is not a popular view and I probably agree that it will lead to an increase in fly tipping. However I use the facility rarely where others use it on a regular basis and yet we are all being charged the same. That does not strike me as very fair.

How do you send a postcard to China? It is a conundrum that I would warrant has teased the greatest minds of our time. Indeed one I have pondered long and hard for many years. If the postcard is written in Chinese then how do our postal workers know what address to send it to and if it is written in English the Chinese postal workers will have the same problem?

I have to thank the young Chinese maid who came in today and proceeded to borrow a pen to write a rather long postcard to her mother in China – in Chinese. We shall waive any comment that she positioned herself at the counter with her rear hung out such that it blocked the doorway, a mere trifle in this weighty matter. I watched with breath bated as she drew the Chinese characters in the address portion of the card and then with deft flicks of the biro, one word in English – 'China'.

And with that momentous revelation reverberating across the planet I shall leave you to your own contemplations.

May 25ᵗʰ - Wednesday

A stuttering start to today with it not knowing whether it wanted to be sunny and warm or cloudy and chill; we had a few longer spells of nice through the afternoon before it went to cloud again for the evening. A few spots of rain around too.

The in-laws decided that today they would do their big bus adventure to Falmouth. I am sure Newquay was very pleased to see them. We do not expect to see them much before the end of next week. As it happened they arrived back in time for tea up the F&L. I think they must have threatened the bus driver that they'd follow him home had he not dropped them back.

And finally today it gives me great pleasure to announce May's winning entry for 'Question of the Month'. For this month we have, "where can we go rock pooling?" which you would think was a perfectly reasonable question to ask, now would you not?

"Well it's not bad the other side of the harbour wall. The tide's dropping off so you'll have plenty of time."

"Ah, but I have a pushchair with me. This 'getting over the wall' business seems like it might be a bit difficult."

"Mmm, in that case you might find it a bit difficult in the next place I was going to point out too. You see, as the name suggests, rock pools tend to be where it is rocky and not at all conducive to the smooth transport of a push chair."

As it was, he was too busy answering his mobile telephone to listen to what I was saying anyway.

Batten down your loose bits; it has started blowing a hooley out there.

May 26ᵗʰ - Thursday

Lummie! That is some wind blowing around and worse still it looks like it will veer round to the northwest, straight in our door.

Time to take a little trip out to do some small stocking up before, what we hope, is a busy weekend. Given that I would be passing by the door of our Household Waste Recycling Centre I took the opportunity to try out my new Household Waste Recycling Centre Vehicle Permitting Scheme permit. It has twelve little white circles on the back just begging to be stamped with a date marker saying that I have visited. If I collect all twelve perhaps I get a prize.

You have no idea how disappointing it is to arrive at your Household Waste Recycling Centre expecting to be challenged, directed to a separate, razor-wire surrounded enclosure and strip searched for contraband commercial waste, only to breeze in unnoticed. I even parked outside the site office to excite some reaction. When this failed to awaken the jack-booted agents of oppression I boldly asked an attendant where I should put the contents of my commercial-looking van. I was directed to the appropriate bin without so much of a flicker of suspicion.

You, dear reader, probably cannot divine the utter emptiness and desolation that my spirit endures at this moment; the complete futility of owning a Household Waste Recycling Centre Vehicle Permitting Scheme permit; the wasted weeks of my life in waiting anxiously for its arrival in the post.

The only crumb of solace that I might garner from this sorry affair is that there is a team of people up at County Hall who spent hours, possibly, dreaming up this hair-brained scheme, drinking gallons of tea and coffee in conference rooms discussing it and spending many precious pounds on printing the little tickets, who will feel twice as bad as me when they find out it failed miserably at the point of delivery. I hope so anyway, although deep in my heart I know that they will not give two hoots and, thinking about it further, it was my money they squandered in the first place.

It is at times like this that a chap has to know it is time to make a last stand. It was part of the reason for venturing out in the direction of Hayle, alongside restocking the shop for the long weekend. The last stand in this case is the revision to my previous last stand, made out of water pipes. Today's weather highlighted a hitherto unexpected flaw in the original design that while it might be adequately resilient against violent earthquakes it is a little on the light side and has a tendency to migrate in a high wind.

You will be delighted to know that the second iteration of the design is without peer. The planning process would equal that of a Vehicle Permitting Scheme but with an outcome that will be heralded throughout the realm of innovators and creators.

It did very nearly come to grief today, though, when I discovered that you can buy dowel of most any size but you cannot necessarily buy a drill bit that will make a hole the same size for the dowel to be inserted into.

The problem was duly resolved with the application of some deep thought and a Philps pasty. (Don't tell the Missus – about the pasty, that is; she would never believe you if you told her I had been caught thinking.)

The production and delivery of this Brunelian creation will have to wait, as there is Lifeboat training to consider and a quiz night to disrupt. Unfortunately we only managed a dismal third in the quiz. Much of our time was spent restraining an incensed Head Launcher who felt that a team of twelve was unfair cheating – as opposed to our, much more subtle, fair cheating.

May 27ᵗʰ - Friday

A distinctly better day than yesterday with that gusty wind dying off just ever so slightly and some serious blue skies breaking through in the afternoon. And coming down the hill later in the morning, after a trip to Shrew House, the sea was looking some serious blue, and very clean too.

I mention our clean blue water, and sorry to harp on about this, but the Marine Conservation Society (MCS) has just published its Good Beach Guide for this year, based on water quality.

It comes as no surprise to most of us that the Sennen Cove waters have been issued with a MCS Recommended categorisation. While critics will say that the award is based on samples taken throughout the previous year it is still pretty much a seal of approval similar to that of the Blue Flag status and, what is more, it cost us nothing!

And blow me if it does not just keep getting better and better. Condé Nast Traveller, the luxury travel magazine, (I am sure you are a subscriber, dear reader), has included Sennen Cove as one of its top spots to holiday in this country. Unfortunately the inference is that you also need to be seriously loaded to come here. It is not true; I can tell you I know several people who come here and have less than a couple of million to their name.

And talking of a millionaire lifestyle, the Missus went shopping again this afternoon. She is after a wedding dress, or rather a dress to go to a wedding in. I am rather glad it was the latter as the last time she did the former I ended up married. A couple of friends of ours are getting married tomorrow, which is as good a reason as any for buying a dress for a wedding. I shall be wearing a suit, one that I have had for some time, of course.

Given that we have a shop to run we shall be attending the wedding in relays. The Missus is going to the church bit and I shall be attending the serious celebrations afterwards. That seems fair as it plays to each of our particular strengths.

Anyway, I wish I was getting married tomorrow – I'd cancel it.

With the Missus out shopping that just left me, the bleddy hound and a ball stand to make. I gave the dog a run down on the Harbour Beach first; it is littered with oar weed, the beach, not the bleddy hound, well not to start with anyway. That wore her out sufficiently to give me a bit of peace while I sawed, sanded and drilled.

Now I hinted yesterday that the solution to the drilling part required some careful consideration. The only drill bit I found of the correct size is about eight inches in length and will drill through high tensile steel. It is a begger to get it straight in the chuck and all this for a fifteen millimetre deep hole in a piece of soft wood.

I was benighted before I managed to get to the painting stage and I cut the first dowel to the wrong size. Completion of my magnificent edifice will now have to wait until after the half-term break. I realise that this will be a huge disappointment to many of you who are down this week. I can only apologise.

If you ask nicely, as a sop, I shall invite you upstairs and show you the prodigious size of my bit.

May 28ᵗʰ – Saturday

This is the Sennen Cove Diary Home Service page of the day and here is a picture of me reading it.

Flatten me crackers and nosh my flappers! What a day. Well, that is not very nice, a complete covering of cloud with bits of mizzly rain blowing through from time to time. Do they not know there's a wedding on?

Despite the less than clement weather it was pleasingly busy and got increasingly so during the day. If it was not for the bottle-neck up at Temple I think we would have had them all at once. It beats all that standing around doing nothing. People were beginning to think we were workmen.

Talking of which the road works signs have been removed from along the road. It must be part of the cut backs; the council can afford to put up signs but cannot stretch to doing the work.

It was rather jolly seeing so many smiling, familiar faces again. Many treat us like old friends now. They reach out and give you their hand. I give them a foot; it is a fair swap.

By mid afternoon I should have been ensconced with the wedding party for the after event do, but late yesterday I bowed out. I had imagined it would be busy this afternoon in the shop, which it was, and going to the evening affair made much more sense. I suppose I should have felt a little left out, like a Scillonian who does not get to play with the Olympic torch even though the people of Jersey will. Mind you I can appreciate their chagrin, and that would have been something, to start the torch on Scilly, bring it into The Cove by Olympic swimmer and then up to Land's End. I can see the report now, 'he swam for 28 miles, the last two were agony – they were over land'.

For the first time in many years the Missus and I will spend an evening out together. It probably would not be the first time that a wedding ends in divorce. Actually it was fine. The weather was a little damp and it was cold too, in that breeze, but a finer bunch of folk you could not have contemplated.

Quite often things do not go according to plan. I had started out thinking I could do today's page in the style of someone else. I have seen it done on occasion and it looked so easy. I can tell you it is not. It accounts, now, for the smattering of comic references throughout, borrowed from a famous radio show that started life sixty years ago today as Those Crazy People and ended nine years later as The Goon Show.

Well it is time now to damp down the steam powered wireless and head to bed. It is very likely to be busy from the off tomorrow. And you will be pleased to know that the Missus and

I are still talking, well, we are together anyway, for the sake of the bleddy hound. You know.

May 30ᵗʰ – Monday

Looks like we are at war again with the weather. Not to worry, it will all be over by Christmas. Actually we are rather hoping it will all be over by lunchtime with some very welcome blue skies on the menu. It really does not help with Radio Pasty playing 'Mr Blue Sky' again first thing.

Quite how we missed it I do not know but there was a delicate rescue performed round the other side of Land's End last night. A climber had fallen off the cliff and, with LE Coastguard team in attendance, they took four hours to take him off. According to our inside man the helo had to come in three times in thick mist to drop the diver off and get them out again. Each time the rotor blades were no more than twenty feet off the cliff face and the team at the top were looking down directly on top of it.

Meanwhile another of the Culdrose helos was out on Scilly for a badly broken foot; they have no idea who left it there. The conditions were so bad last night that both helicopters were grounded at Treliske until later this morning.

Just before lunch the sun broke through and we had instant crowds. Ran out of bleddy pasties again but at least it was not our fault this time. Our rather good baker had a bit of a hiccup and short supplied us this morning. I guess you cannot win them all.

And just when we thought it was all over and the Met Office forecast of sunshine and warmth was true a few sharp showers blustered in. It is frightfully cold too; the bleddy hound's tail has turned pink.

May 31ˢᵗ – Tuesday

Well, that is a nice surprise, a nice big fat sunshiny day albeit with a chill wind blowing through it. It took a little while for that to get through to our visitors but once it had there was no stopping them.

Now we all know how hard it is to get people down here and when they are here the trick is to keep them without making it look too obvious. Today we pulled a bit of a blinder, although it did take two attempts to get it right. First we got a Western Greyhound bus to break down on the hill, which was great for a while but it was a little too early and stopped people coming down. Next we got the tour bus to break down at the turn around point in The Cove completely blocking the road. What a jolly wheeze that was.

It must have worked to some degree as we did not stop being busy all day. Still, not a patch on what we are used to at this time of the year. I watched it all play out from behind the counter as the Missus laboured away clearing our grocery delivery. The bleddy hound sulked under her shop bed trying to hide her pink tail.

All right, I will tell you the tale of the pink tail. She and her mate from next door are doing the Race for Life in PZ on Wednesday night. Both hounds already have pink leads and collars with rosettes for the event. The Missus felt that it would be the icing on the cake to paint their tails pink too.

Pink dog tails is not the half of it. It must be a day for momentously bad things going on: the Titanic was launched today in 1911; the last battle on English soil was fought after a slightly mad Cornishman led a bunch of somewhat impressionable Englishmen on a bit of a rampage in 1838; the top brass at The much maligned council could not quite make up their mind how many of its staff they had given corporate charge cards to.

I cannot see me getting to bed very early tonight; we still have daylight until almost ten o'clock. It is not that I do not like going to bed when it is still light but you do not think for a minute I am taking the bleddy pink tailed hound for her last walk while I can still be seen, do you?

June 1ˢᵗ – Wednesday

I knew it would happen eventually, early mornings and late nights, exacting customers and small children all taking their toll. I am pretty sure it is the stress as I am sure I only put tobacco in my hookah this morning; I have started seeing things.

Permit me to hallucidate. Just before I placed my bread and pasty order yesterday I looked at the Met Office website to see whether it would be sunny or not today; it gives me a small clue as to how busy it might be. There on the screen were several little sunshine symbols running from early morning to late into the evening - a busy day.

When I looked out of the window this morning there were dark grey clouds all over the sky. You might divine how perturbed the already fragile state of my mind became; how I must have imagined the little sunshine symbols on the Met Office web site yesterday and where they sat little grey cloud symbols now were. These chaps have multi-million pound computers and experts, paid a fortune with our hard earned pennies so, let us face it, they cannot possibly have been wrong. No, that is it for me; I am giving up the wine gums and remonstrating with small children for good.

As it happened the skies brightened in the afternoon and, gosh, did it start to get ever so warm. The sea has calmed down to a rippling pond and there was a small flotilla of little rubber boats out there whizzing around on it.

Our road works signs are back and at last I have deduced what is going on. The builders carrying out the controversial building works at the bottom end of Stonechair Lane have to load their building supplies in Cove Road as the lane up beside them is too small and the locals a tad close. Their risk assessment must demand that they inform the council that loading will be carried out on the main road. They no doubt pay dearly for three chaps in a van to come down and set out the road works sign to mitigate any risk to the public.

To say that the building work is universally detested might be slightly understating things. However it is evident that the builders feel a bit more comfortable in their somewhat hostile environment up there; they have stopped wearing their stab vests.

As you know the Missus is out tonight doing her bit for the Race for Life by escorting the bleddy hound and her mate around the sponsored walk course. The poor beast, the bleddy hound that is, not the Missus – she had a choice - had to undergo a re-pinking of her tail as it was thought not to be quite pink enough.

I do not know how long this walk is but it is ten o'clock now and they are still not returned. With the Missus in possession of a bottle of shocking pink dye I am darned if I am going to sleep before her.

Oh to blazes with it! Pass the wine gums and the hookah pipe.

June 2nd - Thursday

My equilibrium was already off balance from yesterday; there is a family here this week whose mere presence in the vicinity of the shop sets my nerves jangling. The parents, such as they are, seem constantly remote, lost in some immediacy that demands their undivided attention while letting their numerous offspring run riot in the shop. I waited patiently for the parents to snap out of their reverie and demand some restraint from their little horrors but they seemed unaware that they were there. After my patience expired I acted and gave each a clip around the ear 'ole, verbally, of course, (although I doubt that a literal one would have so much as raised an eyebrow), which did nothing to assuage my ire.

Fortunately we have more than sufficient happy, polite and well behaved youngsters to make up for it. One of which enlightened me to an occurrence in The Cove that amazes me how I missed it. In fact, had I seen it yesterday, I really would have thought I was hallucinating. Apparently, earlier in the week, there was a little steam engine chugging up and down the road. I have no further detail than that. I have no reason to doubt her; she did not look at all mad.

It is nice to see a good turnover of our perishable stock. We have been able to experiment with some of our new baker's cakes and whatnot as well as some more exotic vegetables such as peppers (yes, peppers are classed as exotic this far down, unlike our International Correspondent who is boasting some cantaloupes this year – I hope there is a cure).

A little Lifeboat jollity in the evening followed by our usual quizzing down the, very busy, OS. There must have been a dozen teams and how did our Head Launcher do this week? Two points off beating the winning team, darn it; not bad for three dodgy characters from the back woods.

June 3ʳᵈ - Friday

Well, I think that is the weather we have been wishing we had all week. Big, big sunshine from first thing and more people than you could shake a bucket and spade at.

We have had a very special visitor down here today, someone we have not seen for quite a while. Yes, BG has not been down here with a fish order for at least a month; we do miss him so.

Of course, I josh with you. Her Maj. chuffed into PZ station this morning on her way to the Isles of Scilly. Her train was not in the least bit late but I bet you everyone else's was. It was also the root cause of a thirty minute delay in the delivery of my bread and pasties today. Still, she had a lovely day for it and I understand that the islanders let her off again.

Good moods all around and what would you expect from the first just perfect day of the year. We had a happy chap in who asked if we did not feel a little aggrieved that we had to stay in the shop on a day like today. I told him no, as we did not have to go home after a week.

Our shelves have been pretty much cleared out and it seemed right and proper to spend our evening restocking and making sure everything was tickety boo for everyone first thing. So we gathered our good neighbours and beggered off to Trewellard for an evening of fun and frolic instead. It is away from the mainstream holiday bustle and we made merry all evening. I am certain we will regret this at six o'clock tomorrow morning, but what the heck. For a spontaneous repost to the vagaries of life it was just the tonic.

Even at midnight o'clock, which was the time we eventually bailed out, it was still quite temperate. No doubt I shall have a panting bleddy hound in my ear 'ole all night.

June 4ᵗʰ - Saturday

Looks exactly the same as yesterday but if you step out there is quite a stiff northeasterly blowing. We did not expect it to be quite so busy today as yesterday but we were wrong and have now run out of pasties, darnn it. With the sun and the wind mix I think we'll be selling a bit of sunburn lotion tomorrow; it is rather deceptive out there.

We were not the only ones caught out either. A chap in a little Laser sailboat took a tumble three miles nor' west of Cape and precipitated a rather rapid Lifeboat launch right in the middle of the Missus's bacon sandwich. Our good doctor who turned up a bit late for the shout was called back a few minutes later when it transpired the Lifeboat was bringing the casualty back to the station. The chap was a tad cold and shaken but otherwise unharmed. The Lifeboat then went back out to look for his boat.

In circumstances such as these both the boat crew and Falmouth Coastguard have some clever sums to work with that calculate the expected position of adrift items based on last position, (other than desperate), tide and wind speeds. The Lifeboat will then execute a search pattern of the area indicated. While other facts can play a part such as local currents the formula is tested regularly during exercises.

The boat was nowhere to be seen and therefore presumed sunk. Falmouth Coastguard has recorded a description of the craft just in case it turns up in the Azores in a month or two.

And I can confirm that it is rather deceptive out there, having spent the best part of an hour in the sun on the long slip, as my pate is sizzling a bit. I also believe that there is a broad white stripe from ear to ear across the top of my head where my headphones were. Seen from the top I probably resemble a 'no entry' sign.

June 5th – Sunday

Noticeably quieter today with all our lovely visitors gone home until next time; shame too as that geet blue sky is back with lots of lovely sunshine and the wind has dropped off too. So if you are reading this after you got home, you should have stayed, shouldn't you?

We narrowly missed another Lifeboat shout today with reports of a kayaker gone missing from yesterday. He is on his was to Hayle, apparently, and there was quite a lot of chatter on the radio with Land's End Coastguard out looking for him. Rescue 193 spotted him in the end and it was reported by

Falmouth CG that he was at the Land's End complex. No wonder he is taking so long; it must be murder paddling across the moor but certainly a lot safer than going by sea.

It is a shame that it clouded over in the evening as we could have had a little look for a planet. Although a Cornishman did not actually find it, he did prove that it was there. He did not even use a telescope. No, our lad used a pencil. From a humble farm background our man had a bit of a gift for mathematics and used it to prove theoretically that Neptune existed because of 'peturbment' in the orbit of Uranus. When Verrier and Galle spotted it the traditional way they showed that the Cornish lad had it right to within one degree. We are talking about John Couch Adams who would not have found it at all if he had not been born today in 1819.

We made a little discovery today as well. We found that our little Chinese take-away in St Just has closed down and we had to trek all the way into PZ for some nosh tonight. I do not think I have ever been to PZ on a Sunday evening before and I think that must be much the same for everyone else; it was like a ghost town. I was very pleased to get out of there; it was very eerie.

I suppose we could have had a barbeque down on the beach if we had thought about it. Someone else did and I would not have known anything about it had the bleddy hound not sniffed her way down there tonight on her last run around. She says thank you very much, by the way, for leaving her a bit.

June 6ᵗʰ – Monday

Still sunny today but a wind from the north that really rattled me bloomers and sent me scurrying for a jacket. It was quite chilly that is for sure.

Not exactly ideal weather for the bleddy hound to have a haircut; she looks a completely different hound altogether, and a lot smaller. The tail is still pink though and she has her curly top intact. I shudder to imagine how much a cut and blow dry for a female dog is. If it were down to me it would have been a quick short back and sides at Luigis, if I could find one. When was it that all barbers stopped being Italians with rude pictures of women on the wall and copies of *Penthouse* littered about the place?

No rain again today but some may be on the way. Good old South West Water is doing its best to save us all from drought, though. They again met their leakage targets for last year and that is for the twelfth year running. The regulator Ofwat set a target of no more than 84 mega litres, including on private land, should be dripped from pipes across the region. In an amazing show of precision SWW capped their leakage at, wait for it, yes, 84 mega litres. Oh, that is per day, by the way. Anyone else find that incredible?

To give them credit SWW is one of the better ones, reducing leakage by 60 percent since 1989. Across the country we are losing more than we did ten years ago, that's 3.3 billion litres of treated water not down the tubes per day or if you prefer twenty percent of the nations supply.

I still do not think that gives SWW the right to cream an increase of 8.7 percent profit off us though.

A few pigeons obviously thought that was good enough news to keep them here instead of flying off home to Northern Ireland. Veteran readers of the Diary will recall we have an annual visit of pigeon fanciers to test the navigational abilities of their birds. Unfortunately the dropouts are far too domesticated to last long in the rugged and unforgiving environment hereabouts, especially when they favour walking around in the middle of the road.

And talking of the road, our roadwork signs are back. I spoke to our beleaguered builder today and he denies any knowledge of the signage; back to the drawing board on that one then.

And talking too of off course lost souls we had a couple of foreign visitors in today asking directions. At first I thought they were asking the location of Lamorna Cove until they wrote down the name. It was Lulworth Cove they were after, 190 miles to the east; a mere stone's throw for these globe trotting adventurers, I am sure.

Time to close the shop and retire to our tea. My culinary skills are to be tested to the limit tonight with a dish that requires a bag of coriander. It will be interesting since our grocery supplier sent us flat leaf parsley instead. Bon appetit!

June 7th - Tuesday

Must be the day of a thousand coach trips today; we have been inundated. Of course we have had the usual drop off and walk past by the more sprightly ones but we have also had others come into the shop, for fridge magnets, thimbles and postcards mainly; we are not complaining, that is why we stock them. It is a bit of a worry as some of them look like they're on their last legs. If this was a SAGA bus holiday it took a long time to get here. Good job none of them was in a hurry as they all want to find you the 'right coppers' to save our change, bless 'em.

Shame the tour companies did not have a few more to send us as it went dead quiet in the afternoon, or perhaps that was a bad choice of metaphor. It has still been a bit windy but at least it was coming in from the west. Most of the customers we did get were refugees from the odd shower that breezed through from time to time today.

The expected worsening of the sea state has scuppered all our fish orders for tomorrow and cancelled our expected Lifeboat launch. So all in all not the most perfect day we have ever had. This must be why they call it flaming June; flaming winter, more like. Still we can only hope that bad weather now means an absolute cracker during August – what do you reckon our chances of that then?

I would say about the same amount of chance I have of winning at cards tonight, which is back on thanks to the cancelled exercise. I will probably get wet on the way back as well.

I did, by the way, get absolutely soaked as I took the bleddy hound around for her last run and after losing at cards too. I am seeing my accountant tomorrow; I hope he has good news or I shall start to feel victimised.

June 8th - Wednesday

Well what a day I had. Well, what a morning anyway. High adventure is not the word for it, definitely not the word for it but what else would you do on a day of strong sunshine marred by passing showers in the morning and high winds all day. Even the fishing fleet was confined to harbour.

First stop, as I suggested yesterday, was my accountant. He is a jolly nice chap and at this time of the year entertains me with lots of pretty pictures with lines in all sorts of colours. He looks at my confused expression and tells me that these graphs are much easier to understand than the horrible looking jumble of numbers on the other pages. I told him I liked the colours that he used and the fact that the lines on the graph marked 'sales' went in a different direction to the one on the graph marked 'expenses'. He agreed that they were very pretty but he suggested that they would look better if the lines were going in the opposite direction on each of the graphs.

Next, after stopping the other side of PZ for some lightbulbs, was a little foray into St Ives. Yes, you read that correctly, I voluntarily went to St Ives for the second time in a year. This, however, was not a pleasure trip, well, neither was the first visit. Let me re-phrase: this was a business trip, of sorts. The company that is printing the forthcoming blockbuster, The Cove Diary, is situated in St Ives. They will, of course, require offices in London, Paris and New York after the book goes on sale, but until then they are down a little back alley off High Street.

Now for those of you unfamiliar with St Ives, how lucky you must consider yourselves, but let me also explain that it is a warren of tightly connected streets and lanes. From the street map that I perused before I left, the route was quite clear. The streets, however, when you get there do not, as cruelly hinted at on the map, have their names written in the middle of the road. Neither in fact are they signed upon the buildings as you might expect.

Having walked into the main shopping street so that I had a known starting point I decided to seek assistance in the nearest likely shop; surely they would know where High Street was.

"High Street? You're in it mate."

"No, no, the street actually named High Street, not the one that shows all the normal hallmarks of a typical high street, that is to say being lined with shops. This, I think you will find is Fore Street, for example, … mate."

I left the shop assistant looking dumb, which was not far from accurate and headed for the nearest hostelry, which is where I should have gone in the first place and where I probably would have ended up if I got any more daft answers. As I imagined I got a pleasant and precise response and was at my printers in a jiffy.

Of course it was right and proper to be in St Ives today. Without a birth today in 1724 one of its most painted icons would never have come into existence. Mr John Smeaton built the lighthouse and the pier it sits on, well he probably drew a picture of it and had several dozen navvies actually do the building, but you know what I mean. He also invented concrete that goes off underwater, which is rather handy when you are building piers and lighthouses.

On the way back from St Ives I went in search of 14 millimetre dowel to finish off ball stand mark II. I could only find 15 millimetre dowel which will present something of an issue when it is faced with the 14 millimetre hole I have drilled to insert it into. I wager Mr Smeaton never had to put up with that.

The rest of the day was dull by comparison being filled with fridge magnets and 20p postcards but I guess you cannot have it all. It fell into line with discovering that the Harbour Beach was filled with oar weed after twenty four hours of big sea, when I took the bleddy hound down for her run.

And as I drilled my 14 millimetre holes for my 15 millimetre dowel I pondered the sad news that Zippy and Bungle have slipped off to the big Rainbow in the sky and have taken Mr Roy Skelton with them.

June 9th - Thursday

I was at something of a loose end today. The Missus is off to the Royal Cornwall Show tomorrow and to assuage her guilt about deserting me for a whole day has given me a bit of a day off.

I have to say I am not very good with day offs during the season; I never know what to do. So I still got up and did the early shift and gave her a couple of breaks during the day, (there is just no beginning to my generosity). However, at the back of my mind was the burgeoning urge to complete ball stand mark II, having purchased the wherewithal yesterday.

I was mindful that the top shelf of the existing stand, and one that will be recycled for the new one was looking a little tired after a year in the elements. Eager to avoid the same fate for the new shelves I had acquired some yacht varnish. This is the last job before final construction and borrowing the shelter of the Lifeboat mechanic's garage I set about the task with some fervour. If I get time tomorrow, when all the paint is dry, I shall complete the final build. Look upon my wonders and despair. Although I rather imagine the despair may well be all mine.

The wonder is how some people in power stay there. The Corporate Director of The much maligned council, for example thought perhaps he was being quite smart in telling a select group of MPs that Cornwall had up its sleeve some money making schemes so no need to worry. As it happened some sharp reporter noted that one of these money making schemes was to charge visitors £1 per head per night to stay here - a bed tax.

This has been mooted before and as before sent a shiver of terror, not to mention the sound of combined palms slapping foreheads, through the county's businesses that rely on tourism to make a living. In fact it is very much the whole county that relies on tourism to make a living. Perhaps someone should show the chap around some Georgian buildings and point out what happened when some smarty-pants introduced a window tax.

Still, with boards, dowels and uprights duly varnished it was time to attend a Lifeboat practice. No sooner had we arrived than DS announced a surprise Lifeboat launch. It seems the weather at the weekend, when the next one was due, is looking decidedly grim and adverse to Lifeboat exercises.

While we waited for the boat to return the very excellent Shore Crew entertained a foreign visitor. He arrived by motorbike all the way from the USA, west coast, I think, although I surmise he must have taken an alternative mode of transport some of the way as he was not at all wet. He stood out from the crowd by dint of the fact he had a camera on his helmet. A very affable chap in his fifties, at a guess, he was keen to trade lifeboat talk and surfing both sides of the Atlantic and beyond. I got the impression that we could have waxed lyrical over a pint or five and had a most enjoyable evening. Shame we both had other things to do.

June 10th - Friday

I met up with the ancient mariner today. This is the chap who, if you recall, sparked off a search when he failed to check in at the appointed time as he kayaked around Land's End. According to him he was having trouble paddling against the tide so stopped by for some shelter until it abated. He was unable to use his mobile telephone as there was no signal.

He asked about the weather conditions for the next few days as he wanted to get around to Zennor and was fed up with getting bum steers off the Met Office website. I sympathised with him entirely. He was going to paddle over to Cape this afternoon but had left some equipment with our neighbours who, of course, were up at Royal Cornwall all day. I expect he will be off in the morning instead. I will call Cape National Coastwatch Institute first thing!

I know you will all be disappointed but I did not get a chance to finish off the ball stand mark II today, although I did make some headway. A few customers asked what I was building. I did not wish to be too precise but said it was a work of art and if it did not work out I was thinking of calling it 'firewood' and sending it to the Tate as this year's Turner entry.

Firewood would probably be more useful than a ball stand at the moment; it is bleddy freezing out there.

June 11th - Saturday

It is a case of making the most of today; we have dire warnings of heavy weather heading in and the mare's tails this afternoon are a bit of a portent of doom. And what a day to make the best of with lots of sunshine and blue skies and, if you could find some shelter from the cool breeze, it was perfect.

We had a lovely couple in this morning, stocking up on supplies and their little eyes lit up when they saw we took orders for local fish. So what local fish did madam desire, our locally caught pollock, mackerel, megrim sole or perhaps some locally landed cod or haddock? No? Madam would like some of that famous Newlyn salmon; how discerning madam is.

And no, ball stand mark II is still not complete, thank you for asking. I will spare you the technical detail but because it is designed to come apart at the end of the season it wants to come apart now. Some well placed ratchet straps are required to hold it together, which will not be here until Tuesday at the earliest. In the meanwhile I have to find a way to stop people breathing near it.

Stop Press: as I consign these scribblings to the interweb the following morning, the morning that is my turn for a lie in, that is, I must tell you I have just returned from the Lifeboat station. I was rudely awakened at 4:15am, on the morning that is my lie in morning, by my pager requesting me to launch the Lifeboat ...

To be continued in tomorrow's exciting episode of The Sennen Cove Diary, same channel, same time.

June 12th – Sunday

I do apologise. There was me leading you to believe I had to get up half way through the night to attend a Lifeboat shout. Indeed, I was mislead and only found out my error when I looked at my pager later and realised that it is still set in Greenwich Mean Time. So I actually got up at 5:15am, not an hour before my normal waking time, except this was my morning to have a little lie in, if you recall.

Now where was I? Ah, yes, I do believe I left you on a bit of a cliff-hanger yesterday. Batman was tied to a lifeboat slipway with the boat about to launch, the tide was coming in and hungry sharks were circling below. Then the Shore Crew arrived, rescued Batman, Pow, Zap, and launched the Lifeboat for a chap on a yacht just the other side of Cowloes with a nasty injury to his arm.

Once again we called on the services of SuperDoc by shining the boat's search light up into the fog. Our hero arrived in a muddy Land Rover Defender, which was a bit unimpressive but I imagine it is part of his cover. Not only did he attend to the injured party's wounds and pile him off in the ambulance but he almost single-handedly skippered the yacht back to Newlyn for shelter.

I could also tell you that at the helm of the Lifeboat was The Blue Hornet, (green's unlucky on a boat), with Dan Dare alongside him and the boat recovery was masterminded by

Captain Marvel aided and abetted by the Fantastic Four but you probably would not believe me.

That big lump of rain we were threatened with all day seems to have blown through early. It was still rather misty but otherwise fine and dandy. I am sure the German coach party that landed here were grateful and some of them even came in the shop rather than shooting off to Land's End. The tour guide stopped by too and bought a gallon jug of Buryan cider for her party to try; they must have been on some kind of beano.

And talking of the Beano, DC Comics have revamped Superman for new millennium children. He now does not wear pants! At least not on the outside - he wears jeans instead. Outrageous!

Mind you the Germans were not the only ones to be making the best of it. Three ladies in bikinis could barely be seen through the mist running into the rather cool waters at the near end of the beach. I would have missed them completely had their shrieks, which could be heard half way to PZ, I imagine, not alerted me to their frolic.

So, after all that excitement, it was a weary shopkeeper that took the bleddy hound out in the thick mist for her last run tonight. I tell you it is hard work keeping up with all these super heroes around here but, no doubt, you will be relieved to know my underpants will be staying on in very much the traditional manner.

June 13ᵗʰ - Monday

All right, I will take the blame; shoulder the responsibility; put myself in the frame; take one for the team. Ok, ok, it was my fault. I mentioned sharks yesterday.

You mention sharks around here and all of a sudden there are pictures of basking shark fins in the tabloids with big headlines saying the great whites are here and everyone runs screaming out of the water. The *Western Morning News* latched on a bit sharpish, running a story today of a sighting of an oceanic white tip shark off St Ives. These little beauties have a bit of a reputation and are responsible for more bites out of humans than any other shark and this one was cold and very, very grumpy.

What is slightly worrying about this report is that it was called in by a St Ives fisherman, a man who has been fishing these waters all his life. He got a pretty good look at it too by his account, as it bumped his boat. The paper went on to say that a second, independent report also confirmed this story. This is not exactly true. The first fishermen, on doing a runner from the scene, met two more fishermen on another boat and told them what had happened. Now if an old fisherman told me to look out for an oceanic white tip and then ten minutes later I saw a shark I would be inclined to believe that it was an oceanic white tip when in fact it could have been a porbeagle with mould.

Be that as it may the weather took a turn for the better this afternoon and turned a little warm too; people in shorts and t-shirts instead of big thick jumpers and waterproofs. The big seas we were told to expect never materialised making it just right for kayakers, surfers and swimmers or, as we call them around here, dinner.

Seems like a nice evening. Wonder if the bleddy hound fancies a swim?

June 14ᵗʰ - Tuesday

What a blistering day. Well, as close to blistering as we have had so far this year and only up to mid afternoon when the clouds started to gather. It was very busy today though, which was encouraging; could have had something to do with our shark sighting that has now turned into a shark attack since it reached the nationals. It is becoming something of an annual tradition so we really ought to tart it up a bit, you know, a brass band and a few flags and some chaps dressed up as a big fish to celebrate the annual sharking day.

We may soon be able to guarantee good weather for the event too, though I would not hold your breath. The Met Office has teamed up with the US National Weather Service and what a formidable pairing that will be. Between them they clearly believe that they have the forecasting of terrestrial weather sewn up because this union is to predict the weather in space. The focus of their attention will be solar storms that can knock out large areas of the national electricity grid. The most notable event, apparently, was over twenty years ago where half of Canada and the USA were plunged into darkness for a while, so it is obviously a bit of a priority.

Call me cynical if you will but I can only see our power disruptions becoming increasingly more common. Not only will the electricity companies have their supplies interrupted by solar storms that the Met Office fail to predict but they will also shut down their circuits for the solar storms that the Met Office predict but never happen. It is just nice to see that our hard earned shillings are being thoughtfully invested and not being frittered away on some pie in the sky, er space, idea.

But things are looking up, not only did I come third at cards tonight, having suffered ignominy and derision for the last few weeks, but the ratchet straps for the ball stand have turned up. With any luck my balls will be out on display again from tomorrow.

June 15th – Wednesday

I think our taxi driver is going to be busy for the next few days. We have had nothing but enquiries for his services today. So concerned was one customer that the taxi service he commissioned was up to scratch he asked if it was a reputable service. I had to think about that one. I know he has a bit of a reputation. I do not know if that amounts to the same thing.

The Lifeboat launched this afternoon to carry out some equipment tests. With the Missus away deep I could but watch from the shop. I do not miss too many launches but there were more than enough of the excellent Shore Crew to carry out the necessary. They did not say, because they are shy and retiring to a man, but I am sure they missed me terribly.

All right, I know I have kept you on tenterhooks for far too long. I am sure you are all deeply concerned about the outcome of the completion of the ball stand. Well, what can I say? Did you hold any doubt in your bosom that it would be a run away success? Yes, I know you have already written down your orders for firewood but contrary to all expectation the thing worked a treat.

And talking of firewood, MM, our International Correspondent in case you have forgotten, tells me that they are having a bit of a drought in her neck of the woods and that the weather is so good they had a barbeque – around the Olympic sized swimming pool, of course.

We do not have an Olympic sized swimming pool, (neither does she, really), but we do like a good barbeque. It was when MM mentioned it that I realised that we would have had at least a couple of barbeques ourselves by now. Although our weather has been dry and largely fair it is not what you would call 'sitting out' weather yet, just a bit mediocre, really.

It was warm and dry enough today, though, to take the bleddy hound down the beach again this evening. She will normally chase a ball to the exclusion of all other distractions until it is lost or, as in this case, the beach is littered with bits of crab and fish the gulls had been having a go at.

She is definitely sleeping at the other end of the bed tonight.

June 16ᵗʰ – Thursday

What a helter skelter, roller coaster sort of day it has been. Well, this morning was anyway.

I had several errands to perform this morning. If I was lucky and I could get bean sprouts in St Just then all I needed to do was go and count some wetsuits in our store, collect some change from the post office and come home. I am not very lucky; you should know that by now, which meant a trip into the metropolis.

Actually I have been meaning to go into town for a week or so. Some while ago I discovered the joys of LED lighting, particularly as a replacement for those little 50 watt spot lights that we have in abundance and cost a fortune to run. We had already replaced the ones in the shop for those energy saving ones and for all the good they did I may as well have glued a dead glow worm to the ceiling. Last year I had intended to experiment with some LED bulbs I had upstairs to see if they were any better in the shop, but as usual I never got around to it until a couple of weeks ago when I replaced three of the nine. Let there be light! So by going into town I now have the full set and you can actually find your way around the shop without the aid of tactile signage.

However illuminating the last paragraph was for you, I digress just ever so slightly. Bean sprouts. One of our too many supermarkets, (potentially soon to become three too many), has just installed those self service terminals and unlike the other supermarket outside town these ones talk to you.

The people who manufacture these systems generally spend millions of pounds on Interactive Design, (IxD), ensuring that the human interactive elements sit comfortably with the types of people likely to use the machines. The company that installed these particular units probably spent three shillings and sixpence on a bloke who had read a bit about it in a magazine once.

"Have you got your own bag?"

Well, no, but then again I don't actually need one; I only have a bag of bean sprouts. Press NO, then.

"Take a bag from the dispenser and place your bag in the bag holding area."

Um, I don't need a bag. Press BACK and chose YES, I have a bag.

"Place your bag in the bag holding area."

Oh 'eck, let's see if it will scan anyway. Bleep. Fantastic.

"Place your bag in the bag holding area."

Maybe I can do without bean sprouts.

Here is a light hearted story to ease the tensions of automated shopping. On this very day in 1961 Rudolf Nureyev defected at Paris airport. Two years later to the day and inspired by his success, a somewhat short-sighted housewife from Moscow, Valentina Tereshkova boarded what she thought was the 6:15 to Paris and inadvertently became the first woman in space in Vostock 6.

Back on Earth, with a Lifeboat launch yesterday, training was cancelled for tonight. At a loose end I sat myself down in front of the television only to discover that our satellite television recording box has gone belly upwards.

You know what this means, don't you? Facing the labyrinthine automated voice response systems of the television company.

"Place your receiver box in the receiver box holding area."

June 18th – Saturday

I loathe the feel of rain drops in the morning; it feels like misery, to parody a well know film quotation and boy did it lash down. Of course it worked out all right for Mr Duval with his 19th century cavalry hat, Huey helicopters and soldiers with surf boards – how on Earth did they win that war? Oh yes, they did not.

We have surf boards too, well, body boards anyway, and it seems to be going the same way for us at the moment. Perhaps we ought to choose a different war to analogise; a different weather forecast would help too.

The weather has made today a date that will live in infamy as one of the most boring and slow at this time of year than we can remember. I suspect the lights are going out all over Sennen and we will be lucky if we see them lit again before tomorrow night. All that bleddy sweat and tears we put into opening today – wasted, and people wandering around in thick jumpers and cagoules, for heaven's sake. What is going on?

Never mind, a trip up to the F&L will sort out all my worries, I am sure. And sure it did with the Navigators, who managed to find their way here again. What a joyous and entertaining bunch they are.

And why was it such a battle against the odds today? I almost feel we met our Waterloo and probably not a surprise since it is the anniversary of that famous confrontation today. But even then we needed the Germans to give us a helping hand and today, as ever, they just walked on by.

June 20th – Monday

It was never going to be that easy, was it?

You remember a few days ago I reported that we were having some difficulty with our satellite television box; the sort of trouble that makes the Missus miss East Emmer Street, and that is trouble, I can tell you. I also laid bare my fear and trepidation at having to battle my way through the endless lines of defence that is the big corporate's Interactive Voice Response telephone system.

Well, had I been wearing it, I would have eaten my leopard skin liberty bodice. I only had to press two numbers and I was through to a human voice, albeit one that had difficultly grasping my regional brogue and me his. Never mind, with the clever use of semaphore to fill the gaps we established that an engineer

would be despatched yesterday to sort the problem and all for a
£65 fee including parts and labour.

Now I am sure you can guess, by virtue of the fact that you
are reading this today and not yesterday that the chap with the
spanner never showed up. The lady that I asked this morning
told me that my booking had been 'unfulfilled' and I told her I
knew how it felt. She also told me that the next available booking
was 7th July to which I replied that I felt even more unfulfilled. I
only lightly toasted her, which resulted in not having to pay for
the engineer when he eventually turned up and a rebate on my
subscription for the intervening period. I still do not feel in the
least fulfilled but perhaps slightly mollified. In the meanwhile it is
cold turkey, Coronenders Farm style, for the Missus.

Ironically a van bearing the television company's logo pulled
up outside this afternoon. A young lady passenger got out to buy
a towel and I buttonholed her at the till. She had obviously had
lessons in dealing with cheeky shopkeepers and ably gave me a
snappy reply:

"You're the second person to ask me this morning. We're on
honeymoon and you're not 'aving him."

"Congratulations," I said, unable to think of an equally
snappy reposte, "but you wouldn't be able to tell me what
happened in Emmeration Enders last night, would you?"

Oh, the innocence of youth. Ah, the hiding someone is
going to get when she gets home. On the diminishing beach with
the bleddy hound tonight, two young first schoolers, boy and
girl, making sandcastles. Nothing wrong with that I hear you cry.
Of course, sandcastles are best made with damp sand and where
shall we find some? Oh yes, what a clever girl, at the water's edge
between waves is an excellent place. And oh, how hard it is
gathering that wet sand when it slips between your small fingers.
So what shall she use to gather that wet, clingy sand in a much
more sensible way? Oh yes, my smart school shoes are just the
things.

And lastly, as Wimbledon fortnight begins, I will cast caution
to the wind and advise you gentlemen to loosen your collar studs
as I entice you to think of 'Gorgeous' Gussie Moran. She raised
more than an eyebrow or two, I would wager, when she was the
first to sport frilly knickers at the tournament in 1949. The All
England Lawn Tennis and Croquet Club committee were

scandalised and accused her of bringing 'vulgarity and sin into tennis'.

What a girl! I would not be at all surprised to find that she once used her shoes to build sandcastles.

June 21ˢᵗ – Tuesday

You might have noticed that yesterday I deliberately avoided mentioning anything at all to do with the weather. If you did not notice I can only conclude that I am wasting my time looking after your sensibilities or you are not paying attention. Either way you are not getting away with it today.

We actually have some sunshine and lots of happy people wandering around. There was a large crowd of pensioners, while joyful at the good weather, would have preferred some yesterday when they visited the Scilly Isles. Apparently their trip back was a little bouncy too.

I am not keen to advertise our closest competitors and even more so since this particular snippet has already reached Radio Pasty today. A major supermarket has brought out a new sandwich in its range especially for Wimbledon. I am sure you have already guessed that its filling is strawberries and cream. What you may not have discerned is that the cream is Rodda's clotted, though how they could have lowered themselves to such depths I have no idea; clearly if they start stocking a certain author's forthcoming book it will be because my publisher authorised the deal without my consent, honest.

I am beginning to think I have a lot in common with Luis Freg the way my luck has being going, what with the weather, oh, and with cards tonight, before you ask. Oh, come on, you must have heard of Luis Freg, he was born today in 1890 – all right, I had not either. Luis was a bull fighter, a Mexican of such monumental bad luck that he suffered 57 life threatening injuries, five of which required the application of the last rites. Another 58 were mere flesh wounds. Nevertheless he managed to retire in 1932 and two years later, maintaining his run of bad luck took a boat trip party out on the worst day of the year and was drowned. As if that was not bad enough sharks had his head and legs before the body was recovered.

If we get much more bad weather I am off to Mexico with my red cape. Olé.

June 24ᵗʰ - Friday

It is remarkably warm, and humid too, especially by comparison to what we have been used to recently. It must be summer. Indeed it is and midsummer's day today to boot, which seems a little obtuse of it given that summer started on June 21ˢᵗ. But the good folk of PZ will not let a little incongruity spoil their Golowan festival, culminating in Mazey Day tomorrow.

As it happens I trekked into the big metropolis today on a couple of errands, (one of which was spelt s-h-o-p-p-i-n-g, as the Missus sent me). There are colourful flags adorning Causeway Head and other parts visited by the festival organisers. I have to say they do a wonderful job, (both the banners and the organisers), of setting off against the graffiti on the boards shoring up the empty shops, the cracked and dilapidated cobbles and general signs of abandonment that the town has presented for many years. I understand that the town council is going to give permission to let the flags and bunting remain for the rest of the season. Given a few weeks the elements will have them ripped and stained so that by September they should fit in quite nicely.

Never mind, behind that tired façade the heart still beats strong in many areas. There are numerous little shops where the customer is still king and the bright lights of customer service excellence shine through the faded and peeling paintwork. The flower shop, Fur and Feathers, I think, is one, an independent shoe shop another and a haberdashery, in fact two haberdasheries come to think, are just the first four that sprang to mind. Other good retailers are available, as they might say on the BBC.

It was to the flower and pet shop, (they do both), that my errand took me; flowers for a friend's birthday. They could not do my order right away but if I came back in ten minutes it would be ready. Crikey, you can spend ten minutes in the queue at Tesburys waiting for some sullen, spotty teenager to throw your goods down a chute for you to pack yourself.

I spent my ten minutes in the shoe shop buying some more robust and luxurious flip-flops since I spend all day in them. I was served by a lady who wanted to talk to me rather than her mate behind the counter and knew all about the shoes she was selling. When I got back to the flower shop ten minutes later my flowers were ready. Things happen like that in proper shops. I heartily recommend you try them.

If we are talking about proper customer service I would bet my new, luxurious flip-flops that William Henry Smith spins horrified in his grave. He was born today in 1825 and ran newsagent shops in an era when the sort of service to which I refer was commonplace. Unfortunately the wholesaler which is part of his legacy, the one I affectionately call the Laurel and Hardy Newspaper Company, is bent on making my life a living hell through the administration of the most appalling service I have ever witnessed. I wish the flower shop was delivering my newspapers in the morning.

And talking of which, if I do not get my head down in a minute I will be a grumpy shopkeeper in the morning and we cannot be having that, now can we?

June 25th – Saturday

The Missus has some of her family staying here in the form of her sister and husband for a few days from today. Interestingly my family are a little more discerning who they spend time with. I cannot blame them; if I had the choice I would not spend time with me either.

The visitors brought their dog, Bessie, with them. This one is bigger and noisier than ours, if that is possible, and the bleddy hound definitely has her nose put out of joint. I believe she thinks that the etiquette that guest dogs are permitted some privileges is a little outmoded and, that after Orwell, all dogs being created equal, just some more equal than others actually applies in her case.

She has some smarts, our dog, thinking of that Orwell reference especially, as it was his birthday today in 1903. Of course the bleddy hound knew that. She probably also knows better than to make her distaste for our new visitor too overt.

She is clearly aware it is the anniversary of The Battle of Little Bighorn and she knows all too well what happened there.

And just to make my 'overt' statement a nonsense, when we got home from our evening at the F&L the two dogs had a catfight (?). This should make the rest of the weekend interesting.

June 26ᵗʰ – Sunday

The bleddy hound was strutting around this morning proudly showing off her battle scar. I have got to take her into town tomorrow, not for the vet; she wants a skull and cross bones tattoo with "Mum" written underneath on her front right leg. What a bruiser.

But I digress. A lady came into the shop with a very reasonable complaint about our crayons. She was an amateur artist and been down in the Harbour sketching various scenes into her sketchbook. When she came to colouring in, if that is an appropriate term, she found that there was no blue crayon. As I said, it was a very reasonable complaint. If you are colouring in a harbour scene you will almost certainly come to a point where you have to find some blue for the water and very possibly some blue for the sky, especially today.

Thinking that the box of crayons must have been put together in error I reached for another box off the shelf, then very quickly another. Do you know, not one box had a blue crayon within it. I would have sent them back to where I got them but for the fact that I have sold most of them. I am now seriously concerned that children all over the country have been chastised on returning their 'what I did on my holidays' illustrated compositions with purple seas and brown skies. To all you disadvantaged children I apologise profusely.

On the off chance that the weather may not be that good tomorrow we headed down the Harbour beach to watch the dogs have a show down. Fortunately they were far too busy chasing their respective ball and flying ring to worry about each other. Still it was pleasant enough and the first day this year I've been down without a coat on.

If it is foggy tomorrow I shall try and get rid of the rest of my crayons. I shall check if there's a grey in the box.

72

June 27th - Monday

Phew, what a scorcher! At least in London, Kent and parts of East Anglia I understand.

I am not going to say a word about the Met Office's £1.3m of performance bonuses; after all they got today's weather spot on – eventually. As I looked out of the window this morning I saw my groggy face reflected against the backdrop of the thick fog filling the bay. And we have no sour grapes at all about those areas suffering thirty-degree temperatures and full on sunshine today. And, no, that is not a smug little grin I have on my face at hearing they will suffer torrents of rain and lightning tonight. There should be fire and brimstone too if there is any justice in the world.

There was a palpable easing of tensions upstairs today as our visitors have gone home, or perhaps I should specify particularly because their dog has, much to the relief of our rough-house bleddy hound. Actually I am not so sure she was not secretly looking forward to another dusting up.

June 28th - Tuesday

The sun is out now but it took a while,
At first this morning it was rather vile.
Our happy shopkeeper did wear a frown,
At the thought he might need to trip to town

For groceries our wholesaler is known to deliver
But in error we forgot to order them hither.
Instead we resolved to carry on with next to nowt,
And to blow the customers if we run out.

Our neighbours, two, took the bleddy hound away
To walk to Land's End, it being bright and gay.
We know from old that it is her intent
To come back smelling of excrement.

You may be confused and ask why it be
A frail poem is in place of today's Diary.
Don't be alarmed and don't be terse
Cos I'll explain why it's writ in verse.

Rupert Bear is the boy we must blame,
That's the one of dodgy trouser fame.
When Mary Toutel dropped down dead,
At the easel, Alfred Bestall went in her stead.

From on this very day in 'thirty five
The Bestall boy would with Rupert thrive.
He went on drawing 'til he was ninety plus
If I were 'ee I would have cussed.

To write for that long in rhyming couplets
Would for sure have driven me nutlets.
As you can well see it's not been easy
To come up to scratch with Alf's legacy.

And in your home, no doubt tomorrow,
Your lives, I know, will be dogged with sorrow.
Because in your head you will be thinking
In bleddy couplets that'll drive you drinking.

June 29ᵗʰ - Wednesday

It never fails to astound me what people will do to get noticed or to get their names in the record books or both. On Saturday we had over nine thousand people in PZ dressed as pirates to wrest the record from another seaside resort for which pirates were frankly an incongruous affectation.

Then there is Lisa Clayton from Birmingham who, on this day in 1995 became the first woman to sail solo around the world from the northern hemisphere. It took her 285 days. Of course, it would have been a lot less had Birmingham been on the coast.

The latest was a young chap who has made his presence felt for a long time by buzzing up and down Cove Road from time to time on a noisy motorbike. He made a record today by being unable to demonstrate to the police officers that stopped him that he had insurance cover. To compound his woes and salve ours, his loud machine was put on the back of a flatbed truck and taken away to be squashed.

Something much more appealing, although not a record really, more an achievement: Cornwall Food and Drink celebrated a year of promoting the Cornish food scene. It is what is known as a hub; a group of facilitators that identify market opportunities then find Cornish food suppliers to meet the need. They have had some marked success, for example helping develop a special Cornish menu for First Great Western trains. All said they are making a real difference for Cornish producers who would otherwise have struggled for recognition.

There, stick that in your pipe if you thought this was nothing but a frivolous and fatuous set of scribblings by a wittering shopkeeper.

Oh, all right, it is nothing but a frivolous and fatuous set of scribblings by a wittering shopkeeper but it now has one serious paragraph, the first in eighteen months.

June 30ᵗʰ – Thursday

Another rip-snorkelling, blinder of a day. It was also a helter skelter, scramble of a sort of day. Mid morning I had to trip into the big city to keep an appointment with my bone cruncher. For a little girl she is quite adept at making various parts of me crack like the snapping of a dry twig. It is a preventative measure in the main and permits me to continue to perform heroic feats in the manner of a teenager such as hefting litres of milk into carrier bags without grunting like a champion tennis player.

On the way back I stopped off at Shrew House, our store, to rearrange things for a large delivery coming in tomorrow. This sufficiently tested my newly straightened bones to know that they were working in perfect harmony once more.

There was no let up in the frenetic pace once I returned to the shop either. Another delivery arrived just as I was putting the van away and the Missus was finishing off putting out one that arrived the previous day. This is Sennen Cove on the cusp of a busy summer, I can feel it in my bones, or perhaps that is just them still rattling from my bone cruncher's ministrations.

Now here is a spooky goings on. We have a clock in the shop just above the ice cream freezer. It has been there for a few years; I think we have replaced the batteries once. It keeps reasonable shop time, you know, a little slow before opening and a little fast before closing, but otherwise quite an unremarkable clock.

Just a couple of weeks ago we noticed that a crack had appeared in the face just around the '8'. Neither of us admitted to dropping the clock or even finding it off its perch and having to replace it. When I returned home from town I noticed that another crack had appeared, close to the '4'. Again we were pretty sure that it had not fallen and it is in such a remote position that it is highly unlikely that a customer managed to reach it let alone knock it down. Perhaps it is a malevolent spirit whose time on Earth was cut short and now is anti clock, so to speak. I read somewhere the best way to rid yourself of malevolent spirits is to drink them. I shall try later.

Quite a jolly event in The Cove this evening: a gig race. The first I knew of it was when one of the organisers asked us to put a poster up in the window, an hour before the start. A small group of gigs, (a giggle, perhaps), set off for a little row around Longships and back with the Lifeboat and Inshore Lifeboat in escort. Unfortunately when they got to Land's End the tide was a little severe so they turned tail and headed back. Do not ask me who won; they all look the same from a distance.

To round off a spanking evening we repaired to the OS for the usual; 'twas rather busy but the Head Launcher's team acquitted itself with some aplomb, (debatable), and reached a respectable, (arguable), joint second place.

Had we not, I suspect, we would have deserved to be pilloried but for the fact there is very little in the way of rotten fruit, since the introduction of sell by dates, and the dashed Parliament of 1837 abolished the practice.

I shall retire now and contemplate ascending to Eden.

July 1st – Friday

Well it just keeps getting better and better, although there were some distinctly dodgy looking clouds around mid morning. It is much warmer today as that cooling breeze dies away.

We had the usual Friday morning rush to buy going home nick knacks that kept us pinned down in the shop for a while. When it settled down I disappeared upstairs for a bit of croust and I was just into my first mouthful when the pagers went off. Falmouth had called for the Inshore Lifeboat to help out a Penberth fishing punt that had run into a little difficulty round by Gwennap Head. Coxswain considered the big Lifeboat a better option, which allowed me to do my charade of Chariots of Fire, (I mimic the guy at the back of the field who collapses before the finishing line), as I was up in the Inshore's boathouse at the time. The Lifeboat did a fast launch from inside the boathouse.

When I got back to the shop we had three delivery lorries and vans queued up just dying to fill our little shop to the gunwales, if it had any. This made life a tad interesting when I had to shoot off to recover the Lifeboat, leaving the Missus, bless her, to salt away the frozen goods all by herself. She told me later how delighted she was.

But there was only one thing today was made for. As I tantalisingly told you yesterday my every intention was to ascend up to Eden, and this I very much did. Not wishing to depart alone I took my very good friend Picasso, or Picasso Titmarsh to give him his full name, (he paints gardens or grows brushes or some such in case you were wondering). It did not take us long to get there and a very nice man on the gate that showed us where to go and before very long we achieved rapture.

I am, of course, talking about the Eden Sessions, musical performances held each year at the Eden Project. Tonight we were blessed with performances from, no less than four excellent bands. The theme was pretty much folky throughout and we enjoyed sounds from the Bees, Kola, Villagers and lastly Fleet Foxes. Good though they all were, and memorable, like the crystal voice of Villagers front man, Dubliner, Conor O'Brien the best was definitely last. The Fleet Foxes were absolutely astounding with heavy acoustic guitar, vocal harmonies and a multitude of instruments, likened in the press to Crosby, Stills, Nash and Young. Though we could see what they meant this six piece ensemble are accomplished musicians to a man and generate their own melodies from thumping rhythmic enterprise to haunting vocal triumph. At one point lead guitar was being played with a bow, bass guitar was replaced with double bass and the keyboard player played just about everything you can imagine. Simply brilliant.

Worn out and late though I was, when I returned home the bleddy hound was sitting by the window looking out for me to take her blasting around the usual circuit.

Quite fit to drop now, thank you.

July 2ⁿᵈ – Saturday

I am quickly running out of superlatives for the weather. I shall just note that we are basking in the best weather this year so far, we hope, but unfortunately for the surfers the sea is flat as a dish.

This is particularly not helpful for the annual Ashley Moffat memorial Surf Rodeo. Even worse the fragile Picasso will be down there on the beach trying to organise the event. That will teach him to go out and enjoy himself last night.

Never mind perhaps we will have another Lithosphere-Atmosphere-Ionosphere Coupling mechanism event like we had last week and, believe me, that will make the hairs on the back of your neck prick up. That is what they reckon happened alongside our tide-going-the-wrong-way business earlier in the week and had the Mount's ferryman report that the ladies' hair was standing on end from increased static in the air.

Here is the science bit. Most boffins, the majority of whom believe that a sub-ocean mudslide caused the mini tsunami we experienced, say that the static was caused by quartz crystals in the rock, prevalent in this area, being squeezed in what is termed the piezoelectric effect. They cite the recording of high temperatures in the upper atmosphere directly above the epicentre of both the Japanese and Haitian earthquakes. This, they say, is caused by the large amount of radon gas released by the squeezing of the rocks that ionises in the atmosphere and the associated radioactivity heats up the air.

Enter Dr Simon Boxall, an oceanographer who disagrees with this hypothesis of our event. He notes that there was no seismic activity ahead of the tidal anomaly and puts forward the theory that what we got was a seiche, a freak wave caused by areas of intense high or low pressure over water. If the speed of the weather system is right this can cause the water to resonate.

In these conditions the air would be charged with static and evidences the large number of electrical storms that followed across the country.

It is also hypothesised that today in 1961, after a remarkable moment of prescience that anticipated this entry in The Sennen Cove Diary, Ernest Hemingway shot himself.

Still there is hope. The World Harmony Run that has been going for thirty years and has covered 140 nations has finally recognised that there is a bit of this country that they have not yet covered. Yesterday they visited the Eden Project, thankfully before we got there, and handed out prizes for promoting peace, love and harmony. Today they reach Land's End. I do not think they will be handing out many prizes in this neck of the woods and will probably give up all together if they find their way back to the F&L tonight and witness the seismic upheaval that is the Surf Rodeo party.

All I can say is where is a Lithosphere-Atmosphere-Ionosphere Coupling mechanism event when you need one?

July 3ʳᵈ - Sunday

Dag nammit, I miss all the fun when I have a lie in. The Missus got the pleasure this morning of serving a transvestite itinerant and a pushy chap who could not wait until we opened to get his newspaper. Let us face it there is nothing remotely time critical about the contents of the Sunday newspapers; they are mostly rehashed stories from the previous week. The Missus had not even had time to put all the inserts together and found him helpfully carrying in the bundles for her so he could get at them.

The wanderer was a bit more patient; although keen not to miss our opening time he pulled a carriage clock from his belongings and placed it in front of him on one of our benches while he read a book. The cross dressing aspect may have been temporary as he was overheard asking about the Surf Rodeo that he had apparently travelled miles to attend. Whoops, sorry, a day too late.

We were busy throughout the day, which was gratifying, and the sun shone all the day long. All bread and all pasties went with no one left wanting and it is not often we get that. All in all pretty much a spot on day with an Augustesque emptying of shelves that was a pleasure to watch – if I had time to watch it.

There was not much in the way of a beach for the bleddy hound to run around on when we got down there. The tide was up just about on the slip and throwing the ball required some timing skills so it was not sucked out by the retreating waves. And just to make it a little more awkward a kayak arrived from around the corner and parked across the running zone. Of course the bleddy hound was not in the least put out – ah, a steeple chase.

After such an exciting weekend it is an early bath tonight. Just enough time to watch a lone cyclist tuck his skirt into his draws and cycle up the hill.

July 4ᵗʰ – Monday

A bit of a different day today and a subject not usually broached in the pages of the Sennen Cove Diary. Your somewhat unserious Diarist attended a shuffling off ceremony this morning, that of an aged Aunt who regularly attended Phillack Parish Church and where the service was held. For me, at least, it did not appear to be an overly sad occasion and there was no reason why it should have been. She was 93 and a jolly little woman, by all accounts, and that is certainly my recollection and she popped off peacefully in her armchair. My strongest memory of her is in that very room, a dark back parlour of her cottage in Hayle, having a two bob piece being conspiratorially pressed into my youthful hand and being told to go buy an ice cream with it.

As Cornish family gatherings go it was a small circle. I imagine that when you reach 93 your circle of contemporary family has shrunk a fair bit. The Aged Parent was there and an 'aunt' who was just as jolly and fun as I remember her, again, a long time ago. But some things do not change and at our Cornish family gatherings someone will always mention the one thing I have been made to regret my entire life.

Look, I was only six for heaven's sake. How was I supposed to know that the water pump had rusted through and the wooden supports become rotten after years of neglect? If I was twenty six I would have pointed out that it did not have a big sign on it saying 'VERY OLD RUSTY PUMP WITH ROTTEN WOOD SUPPORTS – CAUTION, MAY FALL ON ANNOYING SIX YEAR OLDS THAT INSIST ON PLAYING WITH IT' and reported Aunt Janey to the Health and Safety Executive. As it was I was six and have suffered years of jibes and embarrassment ever since. Is it any wonder I wound up running a shop in West Cornwall and writing esoteric platitudes on the Internet.

Apparently the Missus was overrun while I was away, which is a lot better than the other way around. It was a little quieter when I got back as people enjoyed the last of the present run of gorgeous weather down on the beach. The Met Office has painted a pretty bleak picture for the next few days but take heart; they have been known to be wrong on the odd occasion.

Time, then, to break into a bit of a barbeque, the first this year, with our good neighbours and friends of which we have some. Everyone brought a little something along and I cooked it on the gas-powered cooking machine. It is an amazing device that runs on what appears to be napalm and is adept at creating its own charcoal. The salad was very nice, though, and the garlic bread too.

As I attempt to prise the last of the blackened lamb from between my molars I should wish MM, our International Correspondent, hearty congratulations on her Independence today.

I should also point out that, having shared a deeply personal experience with you, it would be highly inappropriate of any of you to take advantage. It will not be a jolly jape and looked upon with the least amusement to overhear in the shop the slightest mention of Aunt Janey's water pump.

July 5ᵗʰ - Tuesday

Bad weather, what bad weather? After a bit of a wetting first thing the sun broke through around mid morning and just got brighter and warmer. I of course took no delight in the reports from PZ and Camborne that it was grey and showery.

It was quiet, though. That dire forecast had chased all our good people up to Eden, Flambards, Land's End and, no doubt, the pub. At least it gave us the opportunity to clear the rather large grocery order that arrived today. If you are arriving next week at least you will have something to eat while you are here.

Our satellite television repair man eventually arrived today. You wait for three weeks for a satellite television repair man to turn up and two come at once – and his dog. They have obviously heard about the dangers of travelling in West Cornwall alone and sent two vans. They were here for less than half an hour and we have a nice shiny new dish and recording box. At least the Missus will be able to settle down with Emmeration End tonight.

I, on the other hand, ensconced myself across the road with a little bit of on demand Lifeboat practice. The wandering waif, OG, has returned on a spot of leave from his new occupation oiling windmills and took the helm.

I returned to help close the shop and had just finished up when Head Launcher Hawkeye, and his Native American Indian mate spotted a kayak in trouble out in the bay. The Inshore Lifeboat launched in a bit of a hurry to recover a local man who was more concerned that he had just lost an expensive new rod and reel and several sizable pollock than the fact he nearly met a soggy end. Apparently he was tugging on a bit of a monster when it let go and sent him toppling backwards, comic book style.

In the meanwhile the Missus took the bleddy hound to the vet. She has been stoical about a sore paw for a few days now. It came to a bit of a head while chasing her chicken down the hall when she suddenly stopped and, roughly translated from bleddy houndish said, "look, my bleddy paw is a brea bit sore, how about you take me to the vet and get it sorted out."

Well, you cannot pass up a request like that, now can you? The vet removed a slice of something sharp from under her pad and all is well in the world of chasing balls and chickens again.

July 6th – Wednesday

Less a red letter day and more a yellow book day, really.

I was off first thing for a trip to St Ives. Joy, Anticipation and Excitement were my companions but I turfed them out at PZ as they would not stop singing. Radio pasty told me that the road into St Ives was blocked by an accident so I had to come in over the moors, which is probably a quieter route at this time of year anyway.

My destination, as if you had not guessed by now, was the printers situated in the heart of the Penbeagle Industrial Estate. There, gleaming on the table was the first pile of "The Cove Diary", your Sennen Cove Diary in printed form. It may well be an egotistical delusion to think that anyone might want to buy a copy but it was still a bit of a heart brimming moment to actually see it there.

I have to confess that it looks the part; a very attractive cover design that looks ever so professional and will no doubt make an excellent talking point on your coffee table and at, oh, such a reasonable price, compared to a Faberge egg, for example. I can say this without a shred of one iota of a scintilla of hubris as I contracted out its design to a world famous designer, or at least she will be when or if I manage to sell a few copies.

Anyway, I digress. Having loaded the boxes carefully into the back of the van and packed them with cotton wool, love and care for the long journey home I started to head back the way I came. On a sudden whim and because I had no reason to venture again into PZ I took the coast road back via St Just. This is a route of some beauty and has been noted as such by winning, at least twice, the best drive in the country.

It is a long while since I travelled this road and it was not long before I remembered why - it is bleddy windy and takes forever. You would need to have taken leave of your senses to want to tow a caravan along this route. I passed three bags of senses, carelessly tossed into the hedgerow before being trapped behind three caravans. It is some pretty, though, which allows you to plough effortlessly into the caravan in front because you are not paying attention and following far too closely because your van does not do five miles per hour very well.

Having posted off a handful of books to deserving homes, (I am sorry, that was a bit heartless. I am sure your home is equally deserving but, alas you will have to purchase your copy), I returned to my post behind the counter with expectations of countless people queuing to acquire a copy of my magnum opus, whatever one of those is.

So there I was on my own in the shop, with the bleddy hound minding her own business from her lofty bed, when along came a chap with a scabby looking bruiser of a dog. Sorry, but it was.

"My dog attacks other dogs. Okay if I bring it in?"

Now, I cannot possibly have heard that correctly.

"Did you just say your dog attacks other dogs and you'd like to bring it into the shop, past my bleddy hound?"

"Yes."

"No."

"Well can I tie it up outside, [next to the bleddy hound]?"

"No."

"Well, I won't fing come in then."

"Correct, you won't."

I have had some surreal moments and had discussions at length that afterwards I could not recall a word of but, please someone, tell me that conversation never happened.

And talking of surreal conversations I was entertained by my insurance broker while I waited for the Missus to return from the hair and foot dressers. Not that I am for one moment suggesting the good Missus has hairy feet, you understand, just that the hairdresser does things with feet as well.

Anyway, I digress. Where was I? Ah, yes, my insurance broker, bless him, has been instructed this year to find an insurer who is willing to only charge a leg rather than two limbs. Rather than find an aggressive competitor my man has elected to reduce my cover in order to mitigate the payment. It seems another two limbs will still be required but this year, maybe, I get to keep the stumps.

With the Missus still missing I took the bleddy hound down to the Harbour Beach where we both enjoyed being sand-blasted in the gale force winds. When I took her down again for her last wander out later in the evening the sea, near high water, was huge and very angry.

Still, we sold four books today. I think I got the timing just right; Booker Prize nominations go in before April next year.

July 7ᵗʰ – Thursday

As news of the book release spreads, congratulations have been pouring in from the around the globe. I thank both of you very much for your kind words. There, I promise I will not mention the book again, honest guv. Well, not for a couple of paragraphs anyway.

We were threatened with a bit of rain today but it never materialised. Instead we had some gorgeous sunshine and warm too with that wind easing back. And, of course, with the weather the visitors came pouring down to The Cove in their fives.

Not so warm, though, that it means you can take off your old, stiff greatcoat if you were an old tramp. I am probably not supposed to use that term anymore but I suspect it is, perhaps, marginally better than calling him a cantankerous and smelly old goat, which he was.

He asked directions to the church so I pointed down the road and told him it was up the hill and that is where it started to go wrong. He told me rather brusquely I should make my mind up as I was pointing down the road and telling him to go up the hill. It then got very silly as he kept asking if it was straight down the road at which point, my patience sorely tested, I said that it was not as the road has a curve and if he went straight he would walk into a house, which would hurt.

That was this morning and it rather appears he got as far a two doors down where he has been all afternoon nursing a large bottle of Lambrusco and a small bottle of spirit that, I hasten to add, he did not get from us. He did try and buy some more later in the day from us and was politely turned down, which elicited a less than polite response.

Once again we have got to closing time without a clue what we shall do for tea. The shop, when we are in full swing is all consuming, apart from trips to the hairdressers, Eden Sessions, vet, pub, Lifeboat... ahem ... the shop was all consuming today and we completely forgot about our tea. Lifeboat training was cancelled tonight since we had a launch on Tuesday so we were not pressed for time although enthusiasm was in rather short supply. I feel a something-out-of-the-freezer coming on.

The weather is closing in again so I best take the bleddy hound around for her last run. The Cotswold Courier has reminded me that the International Correspondent had her Independence Day barbeque a few days ago. I suspect the subsequent warming of the atmosphere and the pall of smoke hanging over the Eastern Seaboard has grievously affected our weather system.

July 8th - Friday

I think I must have slept in this morning ... 'til November. What a grey and miserable day, well most of it anyway; then at half past four lovely sunshine for about five minutes. I imagine that new solar farm up at Wheal Jane is just about kicking out enough electricity to power the forty watt bulb in the on-site portaloo.

In fact it was a rather odd day altogether, from waving off our foul-mouthed itinerant this morning to the lack of five-minutes-to-closing rush. Even the bleddy hound got bored and demanded to be taken upstairs and that was only half way through the morning.

To add at least some sparkle to the day I tripped up to the post office, yes to post off some more books, (that promise not to mention the book only lasts a day, you know). Oddly they weigh slightly more in Sennen than they do in St Just, must be the distance from the pole or something. Anyway, on my return I bore witness to the latest member of the excellent Shore Crew helping an old lady across the road. You see what a fine and upstanding bunch we are; he was not even wearing his woggle, or shorts for that matter. I hope she checked her handbag.

Since I did not go to the OS last night I was issued forth with instructions tonight not to return home before bedtime. As the good souls of the F&L have agreed to conspire with me to sell the book, (oh darn, I mentioned it again), I took a copy or two with me. Boy, was that a mistake. How I suffered! Derision and torment the night long – 'my friends are strange, more stranger than the rest'.

I shall leave you with a bit of Shelley, mainly because he met his demise today in 1822 just before his 30th birthday but also because I have a soft spot for him. You have to admire a man who carried the middle name Bysshe with such aplomb. The choice of poem is quite apt since he drowned.

Unfathomable Sea! Whose waves are years,
Ocean of Time, whose waters of deep woe
Are brackish with the salt of human tears!
Thou shoreless flood, which in thy ebb and flow
Claspest the limits of mortality,

And sick of prey, yet howling on for more,
Vomitest thy wrecks on its inhospitable shore;
Treacherous in calm, and terrible in storm,
Who shall put forth on thee,
Unfathomable Sea?

July 9ᵗʰ – Saturday

Ah, that is better. Some little drops of sunshine dripping down on us today and does it not just make everything so much better and all those good folk much, much happier. Even grumpy old shopkeepers can crack a bit of a grin on days like these.

That is until you get little text reminders, (I cheated and looked at the Missus's mobile telephone), from the Teenager that time is ticking away for her arrival here at the shop. She stayed with us last year for her summer holiday and it seems she is planning a reprise for this year. I will tell her she is on early shift for the six weeks and hopefully that will sort things out in my favour.

And, of course, you could not have a perfectly good day without there being a Lifeboat shout. A yacht had been spotted north of Levant acting suspiciously, and possibly lurking with intent, by some good natured soul. Land's End Coastguard was already up there keeping an eye on it and directed the Lifeboat in. Other than having a bicycle strapped to the aft rail, as you do, the craft and crew were found to be in good condition.

And then up to the F&L, you must know the drill by now. Actually it was a little different as we went up with the neighbours for a first class tea first. And we could not get away without letting the bleddy hound chase rabbits in the back field before that. Although I did not say, we let her chase rabbits last night too and so chill it was I had to wear a jacket. No such thing tonight; much warmer.

I stayed, of course, after the grownups had gone home and what an event it turned out to be. Jonestown were playing their stuff and the joint was jumping; it was packed to the gunwales. If you come down here visiting and you happen upon an F&L spontaneous happening, take it home with you and enjoy it forever.

July 10th - Sunday

For once all the weather agencies agreed that it was going to be a super, sunny day today, which is probably why it was cloudy and rained this morning.

TG delivered us some fine pollack this morning as the younger model is off at Silverstone today watching the motor racing. This is the same as watching tennis but you get a crick in your neck much faster. I did speak to young BG but he said the fishing at Silverstone was not up to much. Still, what I had not appreciated is that the Missus had taken orders for fillets of pollack.

Now, I can fillet a fish but I am not the fastest in the world so it was a happy coincidence that our esteemed Head Launcher happened by just as I was taking the fish upstairs. He has, in a varied career, at one time worked in a fish market and can, so he says fillet a mean fish. All I can say is that it must have been a right good while ago; I finished the rest myself.

It is sad to think that plans are afoot to make it even harder for these fishermen in small punts to scrape a living out of, possibly, the most sustainable method of fishing. Individual Transferable Quotas (ITQs) are being proposed for under ten metre boats. While of some benefit to the bigger boats it is feared the small punts will be put out of business. Part of the problem is that the quotas will be based on a period of poor fishing weather and when the small boats had to rely on non quota species to survive; flexibility is a key factor for the smaller boats and the ITQs are rigid instruments.

What we need is a paragon, a man of steel and vigour who can wield his influence in the corridors of power and overturn this grossly unfair ruling. What we got is our local MP, so if you fancy any locally caught fresh fish I would get your order in sharpish.

There I was minding my own business when a 'fat bloke on a moped' turned up, or rather his support van did. This was another well-meaning lunatic doing an end-to-end for charity. I do not take too much umbrage at being asked for rock or novelties with "Land's End" written on them as this chap did. I simply say that I have never heard of the place and tell them how lucky they are to have found Sennen Cove instead.

He wanted sticks of rock for his children and had already got the ones from the top end. He cited the fact that he was not paying what he called exorbitant fees to park up at Land's End to get them. It seems odd to come all this way and not finish the trip for the sake of a few quid.

Unlike our fisherman from yesterday who was doing a sponsored fish from Dover to Land's End in support of the RNLI whose grand finale was spoilt through no fault of his own. His plan was to hold a barbeque on the Harbour Beach to celebrate the end of the line. It was at the last minute it all came to grief when the well known tool hire company that had promised him the loan of three large barbeques changed their mind. With a bit of lateral thinking, of course, he could have had a word with the Roundhouse and set up a sushi bar on the old capstan. Instead he spent the day sitting across the road selling raffle tickets and trying to be philosophical. He must have enjoyed himself anyway as he now plans to carry on up the north coast, I suppose until he can find some more barbeques or runs out of fish. The wife and daughter with him looked utterly delighted at the prospect.

The Missus was a bit tardy cooking my tea tonight so I took the bleddy hound down the beach for a change. There was a local family already there and from their perch on the harbour wall spotted a sizeable turbot in the water at the bottom of the ladder. I can tell you that trying to catch a turbot with the aid of a teenage boy and a child's spade, with or without ITQs, is unlikely to become vogue.

Well, that is us at the end of another gruelling day at the beach face. It's a constant wonder to me how we manage to carry on sometimes.

July 11ᵗʰ - Monday

The Scottish are coming! In fact they have arrived, along with quite a few Germans, French and a couple of Canadians who have been keeping us busy since Saturday with daily fish orders. It seems they have resolved to eat nothing but fish for the week. They must come from a part of Canada that does not have fish. I must remind myself not to go there, although the Missus would love it; the Missus hates fish.

I had quite forgotten the Scottish schools went on holiday this weekend; we were mobbed first thing and the till is full of funny looking bank notes. One family had travelled through the night to be here, after breaking their journey in North Wales; they had started from Aberdeen and still looked pretty chipper to me.

The bleddy hound has been getting a fair amount of attention of late. She is getting the idea that she is famous for some reason or other; although I am not sure she is all that keen on the attention. After getting a prolonged bout of petting she tends to look pleadingly in our direction then looks hopefully at the way out.

Sad news: Stanley fell apart in my hands this morning. It was my favourite, in fact my only, craft knife that I use very regularly to open packaging and to stab myself in the leg when I forget to put the blade away as I stuff it back in my pocket. I am quite upset; I have had this knife since we first opened and it was in the shop when we arrived so I suppose it has served very well. My leg and I will miss it awfully.

And talking of knives I made comment yesterday about filleting fish and the expert help who said my filleting knife was not sharp enough. I thought I would look about to see what knives are recommended as I suspect I shall be doing some more slicing before long. I found buried on the Internet a likely candidate with more than one purpose, it seems. "Best for filleting salmon or large trout and the more experience angler" sounds ideal.

And in honour of a particular children's programme that first aired today in 1950 I shall clamber into my toy box with Looby Loo while the chap in the striped romper suit waves you all goodbye.

July 12ᵗʰ – Tuesday

Earlier in the year I reported that Sennen Cove had spurned the chance of applying for Blue Flag status again this year mainly due to the council not wanting to fork out for what they regarded as a privately owned beach. Contributory to the decision was that the council had also decided not to send their beach cleaners down this year either. Subsequently I heard that the council had reversed their decision and were going to clean the beach regardless and it is only now we know why.

Sennen School found itself in the *Western Morning News* today with a picture of a bunch of smiling youngsters on the beach down under the OS. Now here is the clever bit: they were taking part in the Safer, Cleaner, Greener project organised by The much maligned council. This sumptuous plan is so Machiavellian and so deliciously dastardly I wish I had thought of it myself. The project involves getting young children to sweep their local beaches for rubbish on the pretext of identifying it and understanding the lifecycle of waste. How absolutely delightful is that. Substantial costs are saved, heath and safety issues are wrapped up with the school's liability and all that nonsense covered in the child employment laws, all just swept away. Simply genius!

The Old Boathouse Stores will shortly be running a project aimed at teaching young children about small independent businesses during a downturn in the economy. They will be able to watch a shopkeeper put his feet up and read the newspaper, uninterrupted, while they sweep floors, fill shelves and serve alcohol and cigarettes to grown ups. They will of course benefit enormously from the process, mainly learning how not to run a business during a downturn in the economy. They will also appreciate the real world of working their little fingers to the bone for scant reward and mean conditions offered by their boss.

In true form this fat cat boss gave himself a record bonus this evening by making a second visit this year to the Eden Sessions, with his good mate, Picasso Titmarsh. Tonight's headline act was Brandon Flowers of Killers fame. What an energetic chap he was with his songs that make the pulse race and the feet tap uncontrollably. So much so I am rather afraid I must retire at once.

July 13th – Wednesday

I was having another lie in this morning after my late exertions of last night; that is two in the same week. Well almost. I was awoken by the sudden recall that I had to go to St Ives again today to pick up another batch of books from the printer.

If you would like to scroll down, (or turn back the pages, if I ever am sorry enough to print another book), to July 6th and read that day's entry you will save me an awful lot of typing. Just re-read paragraphs six to eight and replace the word 'caravan' with 'open top bus'. There, perfect. Thank you. You might just like to add that there was a little incident with a hedge trimmer in the chicane just after the airport straight, just when I thought I was on the home run.

There, who says I do not recycle.

Yes, I know I said I was not going to go that way again but it was such a beautiful day I just could not resist. Did I say it was a beautiful day? Oh, yes it was a gribbling snorkeler of a day to be utterly honest and you do not get many of those, I can tell you.

My new mate, Stanley, arrived today. This knife is made of metal so should go on forever and I will be able to pass it onto the next Old Boathouse shopkeeper should I ever decide to hang up my metaphorical brown housecoat.

As I said, it is metal and therefore much heavier than its plastic predecessor. The disadvantage of this is that I am very aware of it, as it sits in my right hand trouser pocket and I am sure that given no time at all it will wear its way through the cloth. The advantage of this, is that I am very aware of it as it sits in my right hand trouser pocket and I am sure I am less likely to find myself, inadvertently, in the middle of Penzance with a very offensive weapon squirreled away, which of course is something I have never, ever done, officer.

I would not have you believe that I am simply a knife toting brute of an alpha male dragging the Missus around by her curly locks; gosh if you only knew. No, not at all, I shall have you know that I am well versed in the domestic activities of the household.

As if to demonstrate this fact I cooked this evening's repast. Of course I first had to hunt it down and tear open the packet with my steely knife. I do like to dabble in the culinary arts provided that it requires just one pot to cook it in and the dish has a masculine aura to it, such as chilli, curry and, in this case, sweet and sour pork. In fact I excelled myself and used two pots as I made my signature special fried rice to go with it.

Naturally, being a complicated recipe it did take a while and I might have heard the Missus grumble that I was a bit tardy with her tea. Nevertheless it was a dish worthy of the table of a better than average restaurant, even though I do say so myself.

So there, I do hope that I have convinced you that I am not the slovenly, archetypal husband and that the balance of the relationship is one of shared responsibility across all aspects of domesticity. I reflected on this pleasing rumination in front of the television with my feet up while the Missus scrubbed the pots and mopped down the kitchen floor.

I shall go now and dust off my stab vest that I will, no doubt, require tomorrow while serving any incensed lady readers that might venture into the shop tomorrow.

July 14ᵗʰ – Thursday

Another grip nobbling corker of a day; we must have been, oh, so good to be having weather like this. All those happy, smiley faces and all those colourful shorts, swimsuits and summer dresses brightening up The Cove. Throw into this mix a pod of playful dolphins messing about among the delighted surfers then you have just about the perfect sunny day.

Sad too, that we wave goodbye to some of our visitors. Especially, for example, the happy and ever so polite young couple we have had this week coming in every morning for their family's daily shopping. The little blondie looks after the money, though she can barely see over the counter, and elder brother takes care of picking and carrying; what a team.

Anyway this was far too good a day not to take full advantage of. The Missus loves to take advantage and organised a little picnic down on Harbour beach this evening. We had little hot sausage rolls, slices of pizza and lots of various sandwiches with the crusts cut off, cucumber I would not be surprised. And naturally we had absolutely lashings and lashings of homemade, well, lemonade actually. Clearly it should have been ginger beer as it scans so much better than lemonade, but we had run out of ginger and the Missus does not like it.

And, because I had the call from our esteemed Head Launcher, I retired to the OS for what normally would have been an after Lifeboat training beer or five. However training was cancelled due to the launch on Tuesday, which I missed because of Mr Flowers at the Eden Sessions.

July 16th - Saturday

One of the big supermarkets in town has finally admitted that it cannot do without us. They very clearly instruct their drivers now to stop at the Old Boathouse to seek final directions to their destinations. This also serves as very useful intelligence, as I now know who is spurning our good services for produce of generally questionable quality with long, long food miles and covert pricing structures.

For these people I will do all I can to ensure that my levels of service match those of our closest competitor: no newspapers will be saved for you; our fresh local fish will come in a little plastic container all the way from the furthest port we can find and labelled as fresh; I shall ask Mr Olds, our butcher, to cut the bacon wafer thin and inject it with as much water as he can; if the shop is empty I shall endeavour to gather as many people as possible to form a queue, each paying for their £1.50 worth of goods with a credit card and when you get to the counter I shall close it and ask you to join another queue. Oh, and I will close at 4pm on Sunday. For everyone else our normal highly personalised, if quirky, service will continue as will the provision of high quality, locally produced foods alongside our choice of more generally produced and branded products.

If you think that sounds incensed then you need to have seen our German visitor who, very calmly, asked where our fishermen were as he needed to borrow some tools for his car. I asked what the problem was and he assured me that with the light application of an angle grinder there would be no problem at all. It transpires that he had been clamped and that there was no way on Earth that he was going to part with eighty pounds of his hard earned. Unfortunately I have insufficient information whether the clamping might have been justified or not but it does rather seem extraordinary that we can treat our bread and butter in such a way.

But at least we do not have odd visitors of the slithery kind such as frequented a Camborne estate agency. One young lady turned up to witness a five foot long snake of the constrictor kind lying on the office carpet. She thought her friends had played a joke on her with a plastic snake, unfortunately her friends thought it was she playing the joke. It all got a bit surreal when the thing started moving. It was then one of them remembered that the tenant living above had lost his snake six months previously. At least it explains the disappearance of several small children in the vicinity.

The afternoon stayed quite bright and busy and brought forth our new contingent of happy visitors. It also brought forth our first request for a multi-buy discount. Even writing the word brings on a near apoplexic condition. Our prices are honest and so keen you could almost cut yourself on them and if one is insistent on paying by credit card it is not easy to explain that any leeway has already been soaked up by the credit card company. If you'll excuse me I shall just go and lie down in a darkened room for a while.

Alternatively, of course, I could always repair to the F&L for the usual beering and music session with Dolphins Fly entertaining us, which I duly did. The band played their own tunes, which is refreshing, and to be honest they were quite brilliant; I even paid real money for their compact disc, (it was only a fiver).

I wasn't wholly prepared for the walk home. The wind in my face was more than a stiff breeze and for July quite outrageous. The sea is a boiling mess that will very likely put the mockers on sending the Lifeboat round to Penberth for their Lifeboat Day.

Here comes summer.

July 17th – Sunday

Crikey, we do not often see weather like today's outside winter time, which is where it belongs, frankly. How is a hard pressed shopkeeper supposed to cut a meagre living out of a day lashed with showers and gale force winds? Even if I had a business selling waterproofs and wellies I still would not get very far as there was no one here to buy them.

Ok, weather grumble over.

As expected the Lifeboat launch was cancelled, but Penberth Lifeboat Day still went ahead as planned. At least the boys and girls of the supporter's guild, (except it is not called guild any more), have a tent to sit in. Surprisingly the Lifeguards had the beach open for swimming first thing but closed it at around low water when the sea was a little too far away from their nice warm hut. Only kidding chaps, honest.

Amazing what you can get done on a Sunday around here. Take, for example, the RNLI car park entrance that used to have a nice red and white striped barrier across it. The alterations were so swift we did not even know it was scheduled, and certainly did not see the operative from BA Construction and Demolition turn up. I am led to understand that the method employed was somewhat unorthodox, although very effective. It is called not making sure that the handbrake on your car is properly on and placing the vehicle into a gear opposite from the direction of the slope, to stop it rolling forward and taking out the mechanics of the barrier. I cannot, of course, reveal the contractor's name, but I can tell you that he will have to win a few more quizzes to pay for his handiwork.

I have to confess that I am somewhat shop fatigued today. The parents-in-law are turning up tomorrow for a few days and the Missus has been running around in the flat like a little Tasmanian devil vacuuming and dusting while yours truly takes care of the store. It has its rewards though. The very nice lady from Boscawen Community Farm, the beneficiaries of this year's counter top collection, dropped off some very nice looking potatoes from the farm. I am rather hoping they will expand to developing beef cattle, pork production and, perhaps, cider from their apples in the near future; just a thought.

And finally I thought you would be pleased to note that the sun did put in an appearance today. It was at ten past nine just as I took the bleddy hound across the car park in the freezing cold. Briefly before it set the little blighter poked a nose through a tiny break in the cloud. Thirty seconds of setting summer sun, what more could a poor boy ask for?

July 18th – Monday

First off let us wish our glorious Head Launcher a very happy birthday. It is time for him to put the brakes on and put a barrier up to the world and enjoy a nice quiet day for a change. He is sure to be running into a bar later, perhaps he will roll down into the one at the bottom of the hill.

Well it certainly could not have got any quieter in The Cove this afternoon as we were treated to another deluge of the wet stuff. Apparently it had dogged the parents-in-law all the way during their journey and did not start here until just after they arrived. Far be it from me to draw any conclusions from this untimely coincidence, especially as they are demanding a copy of the book. I am holding back on their request until such time as I have been able to go through it and sanitise any passages that might disadvantage my continued health and well being.

We had a very pleasant young lady in the shop this afternoon, in fact the Missus dealt with her. She is apparently finishing her final year at some prestigious educational establishment reading psychology. Given that I can barely spell psychology I imagine she is a very intelligent young lady; not only intelligent, but clever with it. This comes from the poster she left us, asking for people to contact her to assist her with her dissertation.

"Surfing is of great importance to psychology researchers as what we refer to as 'serious leisure'. ... an activity of great importance and psychological benefit to those who take part."

Ok, luvver, I got you. While her mates are doing psychological effects of drug abuse in deprived inner city areas or gang mentality in city ghettoes she is down here doing psychological benefits of surfing in Cornwall. Oh, yes, I love it. Come start of autumn term she will not be the one with the haunted, staring eyes of those who have seen the edge and beyond, she will be the one with a deep coastal tan, sea-bleached hair and bare feet, if she went back at all. She is going to go far, that one.

I am sure the boys will be more than willing to help her out too but not for the cup of coffee and a bun she is offering in her poster. Now, now, I meant that she would have more luck suggesting a pint or five at the OS though it will make a serious dent in her student loan that is for sure.

If that is on offer I will call her up and give her chapter and verse on the psychological benefits of shopkeeping in a wind and rain battered Cornish cove.

Talking of which there was a sizeable yacht passing close to Cowloe this evening, battling against the elements. You could just about make out the sails against the last light in the sky. I am not sure about the psychological benefits of hanging, white knuckled, onto a handrail as geet buckets of sea water land on your head but it is definitely what you call 'serious leisure'.

July 19ᵗʰ - Tuesday

Another birthday today, this time the father-in-law's and no doubt we shall be having jelly and ice cream later. As you can witness I am still in fine fettle, or at least my fingers are, as I am able to type. It was touch and go there for a minute when the mother-in-law came down to the shop with a copy of the book in her hand and I thought, here we go. As it turned out she was very proud at having spotted a typo, another typo that is; I have dropped an 'o' out of Mrs Woolf's surname too.

My thanks to R&G who dropped me an email with some kind comments and a dire warning; they suggest that the Murdoch Empire may be eyeing up The Diary as a suitable replacement for that gap in the Sunday newspaper market. It should be said that I narrowly evaded arrest myself until I pointed out that the bleddy hound did not actually have a mobile telephone that I could hack.

They have sent me an anagram that I might like to share with you. Of course having read The Diary you will have determined already that I have barely learnt to string two words together and that words jumbled about to make other words will clearly be a bewilderment to me. Nevertheless, I will share with you their offering of 'old hen buddy'. It would give you an unfair lead if I gave you a clue, but keep chasing the chicken and I am assured you will get there. I am not entirely sure I did that justice. There will be a million pound prize for the first correct entry; the address to write to will be encoded into next year's book and I dearly wish I had thought of that ruse for this year's.

The arrival of a Welsh coach this afternoon reminded me of cheese. It was just at the end of last week that our long term supplier, Rodda's, turned up as they do three times a week to deliver fresh supplies of their very excellent clotted cream. They also furnish us with yoghurt, milk and, until now, Wyke Farm cheese. Now, Wyke Champflower is very close to the birthplace and family home of my mother and so I always felt some affinity to the place and, consequently, to some degree the product. It is a little on the expensive side but there again it is a product of superior quality.

Having supplied Wyke Farm cheese for the last eight years I was mildly surprised when we were presented with another cheddar upon placing our order. It took less than a few seconds to determine that the inferior, (my subjective opinion, naturally), replacement was Welsh in origin. I have nothing against the Welsh, I am sure they have very nice hills, sheep and food products, all rather pleasingly several hundred miles away.

What possessed Mr Rodda to select such a remote alternative is beyond me. There must, surely, be adequate suppliers closer to home. In fact there is because our milkman provides a very reasonably priced Cornish cheddar, which I have sampled and found very toothsome. When the last of our Wyke Farm cheddar is sold you will be able to judge for yourselves.

One glimmer of light in this otherwise glower day came from an elderly group that bussed in at lunchtime. A very elderly gent and his wife reached the till with their postcards and newspaper and a cheery greeting. It was then the old chap's mobile telephone rang and I have to say I laughed out loud; it fitted so well. The tune? The theme from Steptoe and Son.

What more appropriate point in the drivel to tell you about our birthday dinner at the F&L to celebrate the father-in-law's birthday, he is 88, you know. And what a fine repast it was with steaks and pies and ribs for mother-in-law and the Missus. I note particularly that they did not provide a finger bowl; the mother-in-law will drink anything with a lemon in it. The good staff at the F&L even went to the lengths of creating a makeshift cottage pie for the birthday boy. Now that is what you call service.

Back home and the Missus had prepared a Delia of a strawberry Pavlova. She does it so well she could almost open a Deliaship!

And on that note I should retire, permanently. I am sure you agree.

July 20ᵗʰ - Wednesday

Culdrose Air Day: a traditional event where many people from the locality go to listen to aeroplanes perform various manoeuvres in a mix of low cloud and heavy rain. No aeroplanes have yet been seen at one of these events and the conspiracy theorists are postulating that, especially now with cut backs, that the Navy is using recordings and large loud speakers to convince the public that real aeroplanes are being deployed.

No less exciting than the shout we had first thing for one of our local fisherman with an engine failure. He was fortunate in that he was still attached to a buoy when the engine failed and the Inshore Lifeboat was sent out to give him a tow back in.

It was not so fortunate that I had a crab order to place with this very fisherman. I was torn, it had to be said; no one would be so crass and objectionable to call a man for a crab in his hour of distress. So I gave it a minute and called him when he was on top of the store pots. Oh, come on, he was not driving at the time. Still he very kindly dropped in the crab and a bonus too, a crab with only one claw, worthless at market, unless, of course, the giving of a one clawed crab has some significant meaning of which I am, as yet, unaware; a bit like being given the 'black spot'.

If it is I really do not need any further misfortune. Customers are staying away in droves; the weather has been utterly pants for the last few days. Did I say days? Try months. We even had one young lady asking where she could get firewood, in July for heaven's sake! Perhaps that is where the new, post climate change, economy is. I shall have to buy a forest. I could also sell people buckets of water. When they get home they can dowse themselves and remember with fondness their time here. I understand that some people have even cut short their stay because of the weather. Well there is no need for that sort of thing.

We even laid on a Lifeboat exercise to stimulate a little interest. It seemed to work as the harbour wall was lined with spectators and the viewing gallery was packed. Where were they all when the shop was open is what I want to know?

July 21st – Thursday

A cross party group of MPs are to scrutinise the performance of the Met Office, the *Western Morning News* tells us this morning. They are concerned about the accuracy of forecasts after a string of failures. Something would appear to be awry here. Either the MPs are as woefully inaccurate in their assessment, as the Met Office apparently is in its forecasts or the performance criteria on which the Met Office won their bonuses are based on the wrong criteria.

Still, they appear to have got today's right, the Met Office that is, not the MPs (although they probably had as much chance as anyone), with blue skies this morning but there were still a fair few threatening clouds out there to make us feel a little uncomfortable. As it happened it turned out rather well and all that nasty cloud seemed to be hanging around over PZ direction.

Some more news broke this afternoon regarding our bus services here in Cornwall. The council has written to the bus companies apparently telling them that their subsidies will be reduced. As if that was not bad enough the reduction would be backdated to April, which seems a little unfair since the services have already been provided. One of the bus companies has threatened to withdraw completely from the county and the council has subsequently explained that the letter was merely a proposal.

Only a cynical commentator, after a cheap laugh, might suggest that in these parts no one would notice a bus company withdrawing its services. As you would quite rightly point out this commentator is not one of those commentators ... well, not all the time. I, indeed, would note the sad loss of their regular visits to The Cove, both of them, and would sorely miss not getting stuck behind one when it breaks down on the hill or having to take holiday makers back to their campsite because the last one never turned up.

Apparently there are 13 million people that use the Cornish bus services, which would explain why it has been so quiet down here all week. They will, no doubt, arrive all at once tomorrow.

July 22ⁿᵈ - Friday

Well here we go again. The dummer holiday sash is on its way. A small hong of thrappy clampers arrived in The Cove first thing this morning having started in the niddle of the might from the far reaches of the known Universe. Some even came from Lincolnshire. We weren't exactly overrun today but it was enough of a tease to speak of better things to come, provided the weather holds out. There were notable moments of busyness and an actual queue once or twice.

We started out under a blanket of cloud, which was a bit worrying, but the sun broke through at around dinnertime accompanied by a chively and lilly wind from the north, though frankly it could have been coming from anywhere.

It is at this moment that I realised that I might just have made a small error with our hop showers. Usually we close a little later a week before the main holidays then, when the brools shake up, we go to sate light nopping. It seems I whipped up by a sleek. It was probably just as well given the weather we had in the last few days so hopefully no harm done and we can always stay open a little longer if required anyway, as was the case tonight

The Missus took a fate lorry into town this evening to exchange a DVD; the shop had mistakenly put the wrong disc into the box. She had already changed it once, a couple of days ago, and the shop gave her a copy of Little Ted Goes to Town, which she hadn't noticed was the wrong disc *and* the wrong box. I suspect she just likes going to town really. Anyway she said she really fancied a kebab. You know the sort, the ones you see trodden into the pavement on a Saturday night or more often shown your dirt front on Sunday morning. Unfortunately the mere mention of it had me fancying one too and I was intrigued as to how it would taste *before* I drent out winking. I also realised too late that it is one of those things that is much better in the anticipation than in the consumption.

The OS had a bit of a blues band in attendance and I thought it churlish not to go and sneak a peak. And I can honestly state that if it were not for the attendance of some chewed gums I might have posed off at the dumps.

And I have to thank the stars that this entry has come to an end. I mean 'brools' and 'drent', for heaven's sake. I'm sure it was closer to Lewis Carroll than the Reverend Spooner who was clearly such a smart Alec that he only confused his words to confound latter day writers, such as myself. He was born today in 1844.

Darn it, I almost published without mentioning the heddy blonde!

July 23rd – Saturday

For one day only, the bright, the incredible, the rare as hens teeth, Mr Sunshine.

But hold. What is this, great tidings from the Palace at Westminster? A noble knight, (or probably Lord after he's finished skinning the country), has mounted his mighty steed and sallied forth, his breast plate gleaming in the sun, (they have some where he's from), and the banner of seaside resorts fluttering from the point of his lance. He has promised gold in great store for us who have long been shackled to the lumbering lame giant that is the UK tourist industry. Well, great store translates directly into today's currency of £23 million and that is for the whole of the UK.

Sticking with our medieval theme you can imagine the cart carrying our portion of wonga, wobbling down the rutted road in our direction. It passes Torbay and Brixham where thieves and blackhearts fall upon it and ravage most of the prize. When it gets to Penzance there are slim pickings indeed. By the time it reaches Sennen we will be lucky if we can use the cart for firewood, especially if it came via St Just.

I did not hear the statement our knight in shining armour made but you can bet it included, 'except in the far west'.

Still our own council is trying its best to look after us. They voted, by the narrowest of margins, to make St Piran's day a public holiday in Cornwall. I am sure it will make all the difference to the tourism dependent Cornish workers who will most likely be out of work anyway that early in the season.

With a name like *The Harry Peanut Show* for the band at the F&L there was only one of two ways it could go. Luckily it was the right way and they were pretty much full on and brilliant. Let me see, the play list included Dexy's, Dusty, Withers and just about anybody decent you would care to name across a spectrum of musical genres. With drums, bass and lead guitar, sax, trombone and trumpet with two lead singers, male and female they had the joint jumping from the first. They also did a little tribute Winehouse number who, I understand, left the planet this afternoon, the poor troubled lass.

And what more from a Saturday night could you possibly want?

Well, I will tell you what, a walk home in the dry when the forecast tells you that the only wet stuff is likely to fall on the moors. Please, then, tell me why my jacket is soaked from the heavy, all pervading, mizzle that seemed to surround me. To be honest, though unexpected, it was balmy and refreshing at the same time. Sadly it has been spoiled rather by a damp, bleddy hound nicely drying on my pillow. I promise you this, it could only happen in the far west.

July 24th - Sunday

We started off today with total cloud cover and the sea as flat as a dish, ruling out sunbathing and surfing in one fell swoop. At least it was looking good for Cape Swim, rescheduled from June due to poor weather and we were paged to expect a quarter past one launch of the Lifeboat to support the swimmers.

Half an hour later we were paged again saying that the swim had been cancelled; no surprise really as you probably could not see the Brisons from Cape and you certainly could not see it from here due to the fog bank that rolled into the bay. The fog stayed with us all day and we had no end of jolly visitors popping in to tell us how bleddy glorious it was in PZ.

Half way through the morning, just as I was tucking into some croust, I caught some action in the water out of the corner of my eye. A couple of pods of dolphins had slipped into the bay at one of the less foggy moments and were quite close in, playing around. In all the years we have been here I have never managed to capture a photograph of these beasts. Today was no different. By the time I grabbed my camera and fitted the long lens the dolphins had moved back out into the bay. Still they were good to watch. They do seem to have a sense of the theatrical about them as if they know there's a big crowd watching.

Despite the fog it was quite warm and the lack of vision certainly did not deter people from spreading out on the beach. It was busier than yesterday in the shop too and all our body boards went, precipitating a trip up to Shrew House.

It was the Missus who suggested since we were going that way we may as well have tea up at the F&L. I have to say I could not fault her judgement and the neighbours came too, which was all very pleasant.

104

When it came time to exit we found that the fog had really closed in; it was as thick as two bags. As we had stopped to restock on the way up we had not had time to let the bleddy hound chase rabbits in the back field prior to eating, so we hung back and took her out there afterwards. I have to say there is something quite surreal about throwing the ball into the fog and watching the bleddy hound disappear after it. You can hear the ball thump to earth then a second or two silence, then the patter of paws before she re-emerges running at you like a very small hound of the Baskervilles.

So as the cargo ship of Eternity passes slowly through the mists of Time until the skipper realises that the fog horn of Fate is the knock off siren at Castle Bromwich car plant it's time to say goodnight.

July 25th – Monday

Woke up with my head in a cloud again. I was not sure whether it was as a result of being at the F&L for two nights running or the fog had not gone away. Unfortunately it was the latter and thicker than yesterday and once again hung around all day.

And once again it seems that everywhere else was basking in brilliant sunshine while we just batted off the same question again and again, 'when's the fog going to lift?' Well if I knew that I certainly would not be a member of the Met Office who said it was going to lift in the afternoon. This is actually when it got thicker.

Still it was warm and dry, but it still does not take the edge off the late afternoon visitors returning to The Cove with tales of how wonderful it was, not a couple of miles distant on the south coast. I told them it was a shame they left as they missed the dolphins in the bay, along with several basking sharks, a killer whale and a white tipped oceanic. Well, there might have been, we will never know. I tell you if I could have found an albatross coming through the fog I would have shot the begger with perhaps some chance of being becalmed under a blazing hot sun.

At least we could have had albatross burgers. Instead I tripped off to St Just to fetch back some Chinese culinary delights. It is difficult to find the motivation to cook at the end of twelve hours in the shop, and the Missus has been labouring in the flat getting everything ready for the arrival and lengthy stay of the Teenager in a couple of days. The fog on the St Just road was wafting in and out and I spent much time trying to avoid the many cars without headlights on and a dozen suicidal cyclists in dark clothes. Just how foggy does it have to be … ?

After tea I took the bleddy hound down the Harbour Beach to chase a ball around. It was quite spooky down there with the Lifeboat station looming above us and the boats on the slip barely visible from the bottom end of the beach. The ball chasing aspect of this enterprise lasted as long as it took for her to find a bit of fish bone. I felt a bit surplus to requirements after that, standing around with a ball thrower while she demolished the length of backbone.

Oh, the albatross reference, I am sure you guessed, is for Samuel Taylor Coleridge who popped off today in 1834 and despite an addiction to opium, (two quarts of laudanum a week), managed a respectable 62 years.

July 26th - Tuesday

I would be a frightful bore to mention it again. I am not going to mention it, I won't, I won't. I am not going to use the 'f' word. I will make no reference at all to there being none first thing but by the time I turned round it was back with a vengeance. Having suffered for two days and resigned ourselves to a third it was with some joy that the sun broke through just after dinner and got the 'f' out of here.

I have never really 'got' the attraction of celebrity. I steer clear of those reality shows on the television especially the ones that televise endless footage of grim wannabes sleeping. The glamorous magazines that show currently in vogue celebrities in all their fragile glory seem a little strained to me. OK they sell very well but I mean, Hello!

With this in mind you will appreciate my consternation when I discovered the gentlemen of the press camped outside my door. I thought what, in the 'f'? Well, when I say camped, I mean they arrived, and gentlemen was one man and his camera crew. Well, when I say camera crew, I mean a man with a camera. Celebrity may be a little strong a word as the chap from the press was from

The Cornishman and his editor will decide when, or even if, my image will appear in the newspaper.

One person who will certainly make it into the newspaper is the lady who drove her car off the cliff at St Agnes. For those of you unfamiliar with the cliffs at St Agnes they are no small fry. Nearly all the motoring organisations will tell you that driving your motorcar over the edge of cliffs at St Agnes can seriously damage the paintwork and, regardless of the efficiency of your air bag system, their effectiveness is thought to be negligible in such an event; the cliffs are 200 feet high.

The lady in question was exceedingly lucky, not for driving over the cliff in the first place, but for finding a fortuitously placed ledge upon which her motorcar came to rest. It is likely that she would have been blissfully unaware of the remaining 180 feet drop, for which she should thank the 'f'. It is understood she spent the night there until discovered by a passer by whom, as well as raising the alarm, very bravely descended to provide what aid he could until the emergency services arrived.

The Bleddy Hound

You will also, no doubt, cast me as tedious if I should tell you that I took the bleddy hound down to the Harbour beach again and I expect that you would be right, so I will not, save but to mention this. The Missus told me that she had developed a new trick, the bleddy hound, that is, not the Missus, that she employs when she does not want to leave the beach. Well, it is more a behaviour, really, that is worthy of any child's naughty step or, as we used to call it, a clip 'round the ear 'ole, which enjoyed the advantage of not having to carry a step around with you.

Anyway, I digress. Where was I? Oh, yes, the bleddy hound was being troublesome again by bothering some nice people with a barbeque and anyway she had had a good run and swim, so I started up the slipway. She followed in that stamp-my-paw-I'm-not-going sort of way, carrying her ball. Half way up the slip she drops the ball. Whoops, I have to run back after it. This process is repeated at several points up the slipway until you manage to wrest the ball from her. It is like having an unruly and petulant child and I have had quite enough of those, thank you.

I must go and gird my loins now as the Teenager arrives tomorrow, who is wholly less unruly and petulant.

July 27ᵗʰ – Wednesday

Well this is more like it, wall to wall sunshine and the shop mobbed from the very start. If every day were like that I would be a little worn out heap on the floor but a happy little worn out heap on the floor. I might yet be a little worn out heap on the floor but less because I think that we'll have sunny days for the rest of the summer and more because the Teenager arrived with her mum this morning.

It started as it will probably continue. I had to go to the Post Office to post some more books away and stopped at Shrew House to restock with some essential supplies. When I got back our visitor had parked, not right outside the shop, that would have been far too easy, but half way across next door as well, effectively using up all the available space where I could have parked to unload the van, bless her. You have to appreciate the skill, not everyone could have done that in a car no bigger than a shoe box.

Before I knew it the morning had disappeared and it was time to go launch both Lifeboats for the Lands End Lifeboat Day. Torn as I was about leaving the shop on a busy day there were precious few of us shore side. Our glorious Head Launcher was invited aboard to teach the boat crew a thing or two about swagger and style; he was sorely missed, at least for a second or two. The three of us remaining on shore executed a text book recovery, as I'm sure you'd expect from three highly trained and dedicated individuals. Unfortunately those three weren't available so we had to do it. I returned to the shop with renewed vigour, if that's what you call a state of near collapse.

For the first time in a long while we were unable to fulfil a fish order today. I called our St Ives contact for mackerel first thing, only to be told that there was no mackerel. This is most unusual for the current sea state and our man blamed the tides. I heard later that there was rumour of a super-pod of dolphins thought to be in the area and, if true, the superior number of predators would certainly explain the mackerel making themselves scarce. I know the feeling, the Teenager and her Mum are here and I intend making myself very scarce indeed.

As a bit of practice I disappeared to Shrew House for the second time today, early in the evening. I followed on to the first class chip shop at the top to bring back some excellent fish and chips for the assembled masses and an extra bit of cod for the bleddy hound, (yes, she is spoilt beyond reason). The place was heaving and so was the cod but very much worth the wait.

After tea we repaired again to the shop to restock the shelves and unload the van. This activity is usually reserved for mid high season, not the start of it. Long may it continue; just look for the worn out little heap behind the counter.

July 30th – Saturday

And what a rip-kiddling sparker of a day to welcome our new intake; big, big blue sky, sun splitting the hedges, crystal, (but flat), sea and hardly a hint of a breeze to take the edge off. By the middle of the day the top end of the beach was packed with sizzling candidates for tomorrow's sunburn cream sales.

It was the sort of day that you could imagine wandering over the hills and breaking into song. It was so much that sort of day that I almost went and put on some leather shorts and a pork pie hat with a feather sticking out of it. Then to underline the point and crown it with an umlaut, seven girls walked into the shop in height order. Well, it was almost there; except they were all girls and they were not singing Doe a Deer. They were all related - I asked -sisters and cousins who probably will not come back in again to 'that shop with the slightly unbalanced shopkeeper'.

Perhaps not as unbalanced as some it seems; a couple of young gentlemen with short cropped hair and gothic tattoos came in late in the afternoon and I thought that, being not entirely English, they might ask me to leave their country, which might have initiated a slightly strained conversation. But no, instead they asked the somewhat surreal question, did I have somewhere they might boil a kettle.

Almost as interesting as a German gentleman who asked where he might "renew" his mobile telephone, proffering a two pin European type electrical plug. I had to sell him a UK visitor's adapter, naturally, but was more than happy to fulfil his renewable request. I bet you do not get that sort of service in Tesco, whoops, I meant some nameless supermarket chain.

One of our neighbours asked if their ward could take the bleddy hound for walks. We had assumed a fee was required for such a useful service but having paid the young lady for the first of such outings we were told to desist, that the young girl in question would do it free, gratis and for nothing and purely for her own enjoyment. How much input she had in this decision I would imagine is minimal but we would never stand in the way of family matters, and let her take the dog as requested. I have no idea what she does with her, but the bleddy hound returns absolutely knackered.

July 31st - Sunday

We're dreaming of a damp summer, overcast, grey and mizzly, just like the ones we used to know. I trust you made the most of yesterday, as it will be an enjoyable but distant memory to cling onto in the howling wind and persistent rain that is August in this neck of the woods. Cheerful soul ain't I?

At least we managed to get some mackerel today. I cornered BG at the F&L last night and told him of the countless numbers of mackerel hungry people waiting on his fishing skills. I made sure of getting some too by going to the Harbour and getting them off his boat. The down side to this over enthusiasm was that they had, as yet, not been gutted. If you ever want to liven yourself up after an evening of excess at your local drinking establishment find yourself a good few bags of ungutted mackerel and get to work with a sharp knife. It is the stuff of life, I promise you; even better if you manage to stab yourself a few times with the needle-like spine that protrudes from the fish's bottom. If anyone knows why any living beast would want a spike there, (with the possible exception of boyish looking incarcerated criminals), please let me know.

And while on the subject of beasts, despite dire warnings that the adder population in this country is in decline no one seems to have informed the adders around here; there are hundreds of the beggers. It is for this reason, and also that we do not have the time, that we do not let the bleddy hound up the hill off her lead at this time of year.

It appears that it is not just the coast path that is their domain. I heard today that one of the residents half way up the hill came home during the week to an adder in his bathroom. He got his son-in-law around to oust the beast but it had other ideas and slipped behind the bath panels. The son-in-law, not to be outdone, removed the panels but the snake, also not to be outdone crawled into a gap in the wall and disappeared. The poor chap now lives in trepidation that the adder might put in a reappearance at a less than convenient time. He has dusted the floor with flour so that at least he will know if the snake has shipped out in the night as well as being ready for frying when he eventually catches it.

But for it being Lifeboat Flag Day here in The Cove I think we would have cut very lonely figures down this end. As it was the bright flags and general commotion attracted the majority of people down to us and, I suspect, we had a better day than we would have else. The Lifeboat launched in front of a crowd of people lining the harbour wall to rousing cheers of hoorah and hats being thrown into the air, well, not quite, but you get the picture. The boat then performed a little rescuing of our Head Launcher who very helpfully rowed out in his little boat for this very purpose. The Lifeboat then beggered off around the corner where no one could see it, so everyone beggered off too.

After such a flat out day I shall retire to my bed. Before I do I shall check carefully under it and in the folds of the covers with a long stick, just in case. I shall also check my flip flops in the morning. I trust you too sleep well tonight, especially if you have ophidiophobia.

August 1ˢᵗ – Monday

I think that the fact that it is 10pm and I am just sitting down to write today's entry is indicative of the sort of day it has been. Oddly it did not seem that busy but looking at the empty shelves and spaces where body boards once were either we have been set upon by thieves or we have had quite a few sales today.

It was a slow start on an overcast day but the build up was gradual, which is probably why we did not notice. We also had a fair amount of quiet moments interrupted by long periods of shopping madness and I had to dash off on errands twice, no, thrice today so I was not in the thick of it all the time.

Our International Correspondent had placed a shipping order on our website before the weekend and because of the distance the goods would have to travel we took some extra care in packing them up. I have long since worked out that a 'Fragile' sticker placed on a package is an open invitation to those gentlemen of the Post Office to use it as a football; I have three rolls of 'Fragile' printed tape going for a good price if anyone is interested.

Having pointed my single stream concentration in the direction of securing the packets properly I completely forgot to weigh them. For those of you unfamiliar with the complexities of international postage I should enlighten you. Any packet weighing over two kilograms is considered by the Royal Mail as too heavy to send by air, regardless of the fact that people weighing considerably more than two kilograms travel by air on a regular basis. The restriction, I imagine, is rooted in the distant past when the only air travel across the Atlantic was by airship and the doyens at Royal Mail have not quite caught up yet.

So back at the post office having reached the front of the queue I was roundly denied an airmail stamp for one of my packets. I could however send it by surface mail, for just slightly less than the airmail price, which would secure its arrival at the destination address in the region of 56 days later. Needless to say I elected to return home and split the package into two and trek back up to the post office to try again.

It was only after this complex postal arrangement that I discovered, courtesy of an Internet search, that I could have used a courier service that would have delivered my goods in one package. They also would have picked it up from my door and delivered it for less than the price I paid for three packages with Royal Mail. Darn it!

The Missus has been shopping again but this time for stock for the shop. One of the lines that arrived today is a series of bird boxes. Do not ask, I could not see them selling either, but the Missus is adamant that they will fly out, so to speak. They are artfully crafted into a coffee shop, a surf shack and some sort of caravan and given some of the spellings I believe that they originate from the United States of America. I bet our supplier never had to pack them into discrete, less than two kilogram packets either.

I was asked to hang some on the wall to entice customers who know people who like birds and whom they utterly detest. For such circumstances they are the ideal gift and I shall be watching you all very closely to see who buys one.

Such was my disgust I duly hung these monstrous articles on the wall using screws that were vaguely in the correct place already, to avoid the expenditure of any unnecessary energy on them. While the positioning seemed fairly satisfactory to my untrained eye the Missus took me to task and demanded that one be moved half an inch to the left.

And this is where the story really starts. You will, of course, remember that I am intimately familiar with the properties of wood and the art of woodcraft; it is not just any shopkeeper who can fashion an aesthetically designed stand for his balls out of pieces of random timber I will have you know. I am also intimately familiar with the wooden façade from which the newly purchased bird boxes now hang. The screws that hold them in place are in their current position for a reason. That reason being that the screws are cheap and blunt and not the entire wooden surface readily accepts cheap blunt screws being forced into its fibres. Whichever side of the fence you are sitting at this juncture, dear reader, you will, of course, appreciate that such a reasonable excuse is entirely unreasonable.

Nevertheless, being a man of principle and stout hearted to boot I stood my ground and thought, "If you want that moved half a bleddy inch you can do it yourself." So I said to her, "I'll just get my screwdriver, my love".

I will spare you the graphic detail of how the cheap and blunt screw met insurmountable resistance from the wooden surface and how the screw slipped, followed by the sharp point of the screwdriver. Suffice it to say that I now find it excruciating to roll a cigarette or perform any activity that requires the use of my left thumb pad. I am sure the claret tint on the wall and the roof of one of the bird boxes will fade with time. I just hope that the article is never found at the scene of a particularly heinous criminal act else my DNA will be well and truly in the frame.

August 2ⁿᵈ - Tuesday

We had an inkling that today would be busy and we were not wrong. We would normally expect to have a few lulls during the main part of the day but there were none.

It was so busy, in fact, that I hardly noticed the departure of the Teenager's mum other than the fact the ringing in my ears stopped. I forgot to mention it yesterday, with everything else going on, but she deterred a couple of young boys trying to wreck our benches across the road. They had decided it a great plan for one of them to film the other performing skateboard tricks atop one of the benches. I was on the telephone at the time and could only tap impotently on the window as their antics became more destructive. It was then I heard a loud bellow telling the little oiks to get off. They stopped and ran off, I imagine to change their underwear; I certainly had to.

We now have the Teenager to help around the shop and the flat for a further five weeks. Clearly, without a guardian in tow we are free to exploit her in the most gratuitous way. We will set her to work straight away, just to keep her from becoming bored, you understand. A little break around midday, perhaps, we are not slave drivers after all, and a meal thrown in.

She will, no doubt, leave here a well-rounded individual and altogether fit to join society. If all goes well we will be offering this as a service next year, for an appropriate fee, of course.

August 3ʳᵈ - Wednesday

I was up before any self-respecting lark or the most flatulent of sparrows this morning and you all probably know why by now as it was on the national news broadcasts. Our pagers went off at around half past four this morning for the Lifeboat to assist the *Karin Schepers* that went aground, well ashore really, just about at Pendeen Lighthouse. I am sure the Sennen Cove Lifeboat web site has the exact spot.

I will spare you the detail of the grounding as that is more than adequately documented elsewhere. What I can tell you is that after the excellent end of the Shore Crew watched the Lifeboat disappear out towards Brisons and, as a man, we wiped our fevered brows, Head Launcher turned up fag in one hand and brew in the other. He had made the assessment that it was far too early for the rest of his dedicated team to want a cup of tea, so he just made himself one; just as long as he remembers that precept in the OS tomorrow night.

August 5ᵗʰ - Friday

I may have mentioned before that we get an array of small children coming to the shop without parental supervision. Sometimes this goes horribly awry, for us anyway, but in the main they are a joyful and polite bunch and a pleasure to welcome. I can imagine that to send the children down to the shop in some of their home environments is fraught with difficulties such as heavier traffic and a greater potential to meet unsavoury characters. Down here it is excellent territory to give the little ones a modicum of responsibility in a very safe environment. One such lad arrived this week asked, "Please can you direct me to the white sliced bread", in a very clear and precise voice. No doubt we shall be hearing him on the BBC news in twenty years time or, after a graduating from our state school system, Waterloo Station announcements.

Strangely enough we do have the occasional adult frequent the shop and every now and again one will have a story to tell. We have had one such lady in and out a couple of times today. She has been following her family around. Apparently there is not enough room for her in the family car so, having a bus pass, she has followed them around on the bus. I think this is an excellent idea. I shall suggest it to the mother-in-law next time she is down.

Only a week into our busy run and any pretence of cooking proper meals has already melted away. We resort to running to a take-away restaurant sometimes but after fourteen or fifteen hours in the shop even that seems too much effort. It would seem that even ready-meals have their limitations. Tonight, for example, I was pointed at a platter of some anonymous pasta promising comestible delight after just eight minutes in the microwave.

Now, our microwave is rarely used and as such is pushed into a corner in such a position that the door will not open fully. It is also quite a small machine. With this in mind imagine a plastic ready-meal dish some twelve inches across. By tipping it at an angle I could just fit it into the cabinet, unfortunately the dish was so wide it would not rotate on the turntable. Being an innovative sort of chap, (did I mention my ball stand?), I resorted to scraping the contents onto a smaller plate and covering the resulting, somewhat less aesthetically pleasing, goo with cling film.

Despite the plate being smaller and more than capable of turning in the microwave I still had to tip the plate to get it in through the door. Having squeezed it into the machine I set the dial for the requisite eight minutes. It had not occurred to me that the heated meal would be somewhat less viscous when hot. Not only this, but the heated meal was still sizzling on the plate requiring the use of bulky oven gloves to remove the completed meal. It was on tipping the plate to remove it through the narrow gap that it became apparent that the super-heated contents were by now quite fluid and only by the good grace of the properties of warm cling film did the sludge not slip from the plate.

Salad tomorrow night, I think.

Last thing, while penning this very page, I was tormented by the bleddy hound wishing to play chicken. I turned round to ask if her owner might rid me of this turbulent beast only to find that the Missus and the Teenager were sitting about their recreation with their feet in mop buckets of sudsy water. I did not ask.

August 6th - Saturday

I could tell you all sorts of mundane drivel about how the usual leavers and joiners bought things and complained that we had not ordered sufficient pasties and that we should not be charging for 'cash back' even though we get charged and the machine in the pub charges three times as much, but I will not. I will not because all you want to know is what happened at the F&L tonight don't you?

Alright, you asked for it but first I must tell you that the bleddy hound has had her nose put seriously out of joint. There are campers in her rabbit field. She winds herself up as the van climbs the hill, by the time she sees the church tower she is shaking like a leaf. When we turn into the F&L car park she is just about ready to jump through the window and she did once. Tonight as we turned in it was obvious there was no way she was going to get her run.

If you are a camper and feel a visit to the shop necessary, for the next few weeks please tread carefully. The bleddy hound is very upset and she has no way of telling if you are from the field at the back of the F&L or not.

I had to slip out of the van while she was distracted and restrained. The evening was special, as it most usually is, due to the nature of the participants and, musically, a first class band. Crickey, you waited two paragraphs for that!

I thought I might have been in for a slow traverse of Esther's Field on my way home as I gazed at the canopy of stars, the first for a long time, at least on my Saturday night wend home. As it happened Head Launcher spotted my obvious frame bouncing off the hedges and offered me a lift that I have to say was very welcome. I must also explain that my lack of navigational direction was a result of my upward glances rather than the effects of over imbibing. Honest.

August 7th - Sunday

I would just like to say happy birthday to Libby. She is a little Asian girl who popped her head around the door to ask the way to Land's End. She was delightfully happy, effervescent in fact, and her joy was quite infectious. I told her the way and she thanked me and left. Two seconds later her head popped round the door again and said that it was her birthday today, so, as you do, I wished her happy birthday and on a whim offered her a lollipop. She became even jollier, if one can attain a higher state of happiness from the one she was already in, and asked if she could take a small video of me wishing her happy birthday and giving her a lollipop.

You, like me, dear reader, probably saw in that last paragraph a selfless act; a sharing of a moment of beauty; a celebration of all that is good in people; a touch of joie de vivre. You, like me, dear reader, would probably need it pointed out to you that I should make it clear that I am not in the habit of proffering lollipops to young girls that I meet and that the young girl in question was probably in her twenties and armed with a hefty metal tripod. I trust that has averted any misunderstanding especially when the video goes viral on *MeCylinder* under the title 'Object Lessons in Personal Safety for Young Ladies Travelling Alone'.

An Act of Parliament passed today in 1840 really did for us struggling employers; boys were no longer allowed to go up chimneys to clean them. Fortunately we have a girl staying with us so I guess the rules do not apply and it is all right to set her to work for little pay, (well, no pay actually), and grim working conditions. Of course even this is not quite like the good old days. She does not emerge until long after we open and will not do anything that might ruin her nails. Nevertheless she helped stock the shelves between texts, swept the shop floor only stopping twice to fix her makeup and ran the bleddy hound down the beach in her Jimmy Chung's (me, top man in fashion or what?).

Well, it could be worse, but for the Chimneys Sweepers and Chimneys Regulations Act we might have ended up with a small blackened boy dropping soot everywhere.

August 8ᵗʰ – Monday

It started out looking decidedly dodgy despite a good forecast with some ominous clouds floating about over The Cove. There was a stiff breeze that made me very grateful that I decided to restock the windbreak stand; I should have been a boy scout. I would have been if it had not been for that somewhat misunderstood incident with Brown Owl at the Jamboree. It was all perfectly innocent, I tell you. She was just helping me with my woggle.

Anyway, I digress. Where was I? Ah, yes, stiff breeze, bit of cloud. Well the cloud soon cleared away and we had a half decent day despite the breeze. In fact it was the sort of day where people are quite happy to wander about buying things. It is also quite obviously a day for doing things a little out of the ordinary.

I was fiddling with some newspapers and cooking some bread, which is what I do before we open in case you were wondering, when a little article on the radio caught my attention. It was only on our radio because there is a Cornishman involved in the enterprise and, frankly, I thought he would have known better.

It appears he is part of a team that intends to row a boat to the Magnetic North Pole. Now, I do not want to pour cold water on their efforts, although I suspect that may help considerably, but I always imagined that the North Pole, magnetic or otherwise, had rather an abundance of ice about it. I have seen pictures, you know. I also know a thing or two about rowing, not a great deal, I grant you, but enough to understand that some water is usually required.

I have no doubt that this bunch of dedicated and enthusiastic chaps have all the best intentions in the world; their stated aim is to highlight the effects of climate change. Darned right too. It was cold down on the beach this evening when I took the bleddy hound down for a run. But however dedicated or enthusiastic you are please do not call an expedition a 'row to the pole', when for much of it you are dragging your boat over lumps of ice. If I were one of their extensive sponsors I might feel just a little hoodwinked.

In all seriousness I had to do some actual research for today's entry, yes, real looking up facts. If you look at the pictures of ice coverage today compared to 2005 there is quite a lot of blue where there was once white. The main shrinkage appears to be on the south side, er, the south side opposite from our south side, that is, so I think it's fair to say it was all the down to them not us, which will probably explain why The much maligned council has taken all the recycling bins away from The Cove. Sorry I did say I was going to be serious.

119

No doubt all this climate change malarkey will be at the root of a major feeding frenzy just off Gwennap Head at the end of last month too. In just a few hours 10,000 Manx shearwaters, (come on, how do you count that many? One, two ... fifteen ... twenty-five "Coffee?" "Yes please". Begger! One, two ...); hundreds of gannets; one percent of the world's population of Balearic shearwaters and common dolphins; along with bottle nose and Risso's dolphins; Minke whales and harbour porpoise; all after a large shoal of mackerel and other baitfish, astounded the team of volunteer watchers stationed there.

August 9th – Tuesday

The Aged Parent has been in contact with some advice on counting large numbers of Manx shearwaters. Being that he is a Cornishman and of such years of experience that he is known locally as Yoda of the West, I can only wonder in amazement at his sage advice. Apparently the trick is to count the legs then divide by two. I can only hope that one day I shall attain such wisdom.

August 10th – Wednesday

You will have to forgive me; I have been somewhat overawed today.

First we were absolutely mobbed in the morning. Actually it was second but I am employing some dramatic effect here so you have to be patient. It was by far the busiest morning we have had all year and we were pinned down behind the counter for quite some time. As it turned out it was a bit of a false dawn as the afternoon went as flat as a dish.

But no matter, I was floating on a cloud of elation. It is not often you find your name in the same journal as Brad Pitt and in fact I got a bigger picture and a more column space than he did. Eat your heart out Brad. Yes, I opened up the *Western Morning News* first thing to find my smiling and finely chiselled features looking back at me. An editor, clearly blessed with excellent taste and a sense of fair play and decency (or came back from a particularly fine lunch and in a forgiving mood), allowed the review of my book to be published. Not only was the review

120

published, it nigh on took over two thirds of the page and, not only that, it was a good review, with nice words and a cheering slant. That shilling pressed into the reporter's hand clearly paid dividends.

Here is an interesting fact and apropos of nothing at all, something of a small aside. On this day in 1842 the government of the day passed the Mines Act, forbidding women and children to work down mines, (shame on them, I hear you cry). Obtuse though it may appear, after 133 years of protest, campaigning and burning their brassieres women won the right, through the sex discrimination laws, to work back down them again.

In the last few days we have had any amount of requests for mackerel. I reported last week that we were having some difficulty in obtaining any. The fishermen are up against some stiff competition, namely 10,000 Manx shearwaters, gannets, dolphins and Minke whales.

I managed to get half a dozen yesterday, much to the chagrin of another customer who wanted some but had not ordered any. I tried again today to get some but our man was out for pollack. However, hidden amongst the bigger fish was a single mackerel. It will be in the shop tomorrow and will go to the highest bidder. I have asked the police to attend in case there are any ugly scenes.

I was just vacuum packing the last of the pollack fillets and the precious mackerel near closing time when the Lifeboat pagers went off. The big boat launched at around 8pm in search of a yacht whose skipper was reported as being tired and disorientated, out of fuel, (it's a yacht, it was windy!) and not a blind clue where he was. With some sort of electrical failure he only had a mobile telephone and had called in the Coastguard using that.

St Ives Lifeboat was also launched and both boats sent up parachute flares in their respective search areas to establish whether the yacht could see them but with no result. Just as our boat was being stood down, on the basis that searching an indeterminate area of sea for a boat that may not be there is a somewhat hopeless exercise, another boat reported in that they had found the yacht. It was some five miles south of Porthcurno. Sennen Cove Lifeboat proceeded to recover the boat and tow it back to Penzance. We recovered the Lifeboat up the long slip at about 1am.

Now that we are practically best buddies I might give Brad a call to ask what he thought of my review; these A-listers are always up all night at some party or other. Do not worry I will not offer him our mackerel. Do you think I am shallow or something?

August 11ᵗʰ – Thursday

A grey and miserably start to an August day scaring off all but the most hardy customer. It is surprising just how many hardy customers we have. They were even queuing outside the shop door first thing, which was a surprise as well until I remembered our lonely mackerel.

I thought I would be a bit more bleary-eyed this morning after being late to bed last night. It helped that the Missus gave me an extra hour in bed while she did the necessary downstairs. Unfortunately while the Missus was happy for me to have an extra hour in bed the bleddy hound was not and it is so difficult to zizz with a warm canine tongue in your ear.

For those of you taking advantage of the poorer weather and tripping into PZ keep an eye out for the facelift the empty shops are getting. I mentioned a while ago that the town is not as aesthetically pleasing as it could be. One chap on the town council, the deputy mayor, has taken it upon himself to brighten the place up and bully for him too. He has come up with the idea of putting wallpaper covered with iconic PZ landmarks in the empty shop windows. Although I suspect he will run out of landmarks before he runs out of shops at least someone is taking some positive action instead of just sitting in a chair at a keyboard and moaning about it (ahem!).

I have been warned that we will be outgunned again at the OS quiz tonight. As every good cowboy knows when you are out gunned you keep your mouth shut and your pistol in your pants – it is difficult to circle your wagons when there are only two of you. The problem is that there are some things some of us are not good at and keeping your mouth shut is one of them. I am not going to name names but it is one of the two-man Head Launcher's team and it is not me. Best, then, I start practising some of the in'jun talk so we merge in seamlessly … "eee bah gum", "well, ah'll goo to the foot of ower stairs", "'appen a've lost me whippet in t' pigeon loft". There, they will not rumble us now.

As it turned out it was to little avail. The mizzly night drove the majority inside and we were left to lose miserably, (actually we came forth in a crowded field), with only a few keen supporters.

Time now to get my wagons rolling in the direction of my bed, I think.

August 12ᵗʰ - Friday

As if to answer a shopkeeper's prayer a little body called Community First has entered the scene. The merry chaps there have created a project called Store is the Core and have already run a, presumably successful, pilot in Wiltshire. They aim to help 150 rural community shops in eighteen months by sending in advisors and mentors, well, to advise and mentor I suppose. They reckon that shopkeepers do not go and visit other shops, (they obviously did not ask the Missus who is never out of other shops), and a fresh pair of eyes can very often provide useful feedback on product positioning and shop layout. The mentors will be able to provide advice on grants and facilities available through various channels. I cannot see them coming down here any time soon; they would be here for weeks. "I'd get rid of those bird houses if I were you, my 'ansum."

If you are here regularly, dear reader, or have not been but are a proud owner of The Cove Diary in book form that had an ace review in the *Western Morning News,* (sorry, have I mentioned my excellent *WMN* review before?), you will be aware that I have a little aversion to small children running amok and unsupervised, or even amok and supervised, through the shop.

It was early in the evening when a family came in including a couple of small children who, on the face of it, appeared well mannered and well supervised by their mother. They were in the middle aisle when I heard the crash of objects falling to the floor. It did not sound terminal so I decided to wait until the family came to the till. The mother explained that she had tutored the offspring to behave themselves in shops and not to touch anything. She then added that she had not expected to perform similar training for the grannies that, she said, were the perpetrators of the heinous deed of scatting items off our shelf.

Naturally I berated the offending pensioners when they arrived at the till and hoped that they would not burst into tears. I did advise that they should look with their eyes and not their hands in future and that if they wanted to visit the shop again they should make sure they were supervised by one of the very well behaved children.

Mind you by the time the rain and the mizzle hit us in the late afternoon I would have settled for a shop full of shelf-destroying grannies as long as they had a shilling or two in their pockets. I do not know how much Store to the Core could help with this dilemma; I think I would rather employ the services of Cecil B De Mille, born today in 1881. At least he could get a crowd together, although I think I might be slightly disconcerted if the cast and extras from *Ben Hur* walked through the door.

I shall close my eyes now and hope it is all better in the morning.

There I was closing my eyes and hoping that things would be better in the morning when I was wrested from my bed by the Missus. She had received a call from a concerned neighbour fearing a John Carpenteresque character issuing from the fog; in the bay, close to the shore was an eerie light. Although the Teenager suggested an octopus with a torch I concluded that some insomniac was spear fishing; an enterprise not without risk at this time of the night as, had he run into trouble, it is unlikely that anyone, apart from the Missus and the neighbour would have seen him.

Of course had they seen him in trouble they would have assumed that the unworldly creature from the deep, with a flashlight, had been rightly consigned back to the hellish deep and gone to bed - as indeed shall I, again.

August 13ᵗʰ - Saturday

Well, it was a little better this morning although there was a suspicion of rain in the air that lingered for most of the day. The wind has come around a bit and is north by northwest or thereabouts. These Augusts are becoming notorious for throwing bad weather at us and without a shadow of a doubt we'd be much better without it. You'd think sometimes it was the work of some vengeful saboteur.

As seems to be normal for the new arrivals there is a bit of a frenzy of wetsuit buying. Two little girls were fitted out first thing, Rebecca and Marnie I think their names were and they seemed spellbound by the whole process of trying them on. As also seems to be normal, if one or two get wetsuits the rest of the family eventually follow suit. We use the storeroom in the shop if people want to try the suits on, which is recommended. We have a curtain that we can draw across and it has been there as long as we have. It is getting a bit threadbare in places and the slightest wrong move I'm sure will result in a torn curtain.

It appears that the best way of breaking in a new wetsuit, especially if you are an older child, is to jump off the breakwater as soon as you've squeezed yourself into it. It was pretty crowded out there around midday with both jumpers and fishermen. Of course, you would not get me out there, what with my touch of vertigo but they seemed to be having fun and, at least, if they fall in you would not have to launch the Lifeboat to go and get them.

Most people come down here by car but every now and again you find people who have travelled down by train or by coach. Two families came in today and they were saying how they were strangers on a train together and just by chance got to talking when they overheard one of them say they were coming down to Sennen. What are the chances of that?

I would say the same as to catch a thief. We have various items go missing off our shelves from time to time, the odd figurine or a bit of topaz jewellery, perhaps. I caught one arch criminal today, a small boy making off with a bar of chocolate. I think that at his age it was more that the concept of having to pay for goods was still a bit alien and he had all the sweet innocent looks too, which left me a dilemma. For murder he could have got away scot-free, I am sure, but for theft, not a chance. His dad coughed up for the little Raffles.

We are used to being asked many questions every day and the questions seem to go in weekly cycles. The usual directions to Land's End, bus times to Porthcurno, time of high water and how long is a piece of rope are almost reflex now but I was floored when someone asked me how many litres are in our gallon cider flagons. Anyone accusing me of being the man who knew too much has definitely got the wrong man especially when it comes to metric measurements.

I watched two sparrows outside the shop door this afternoon. The birds were busy picking up crumbs and it was interesting to see that the female was feeding hers to her mate. That reminds me that I have to make my own tea tonight as the Missus was going into town to get some tea for her and the Teenager, MacDoughnuts or some such. It must be something to do with being born under Capricorn, the Teenager, not the Missus.

By sheer coincidence I decided to go to the F&L tonight for a spot of music and a few beers. The Missus dropped me up there on her way into town. I am sure she watched me out of the rear window as she sped away. What a wonderful night it was and the band were superb; no hint of stage fright with this lot unless you happen to be sharing a stage with them. You could not really call them psycho but they are pretty loud and aggressive.

I am sure you were hoping deep down that there was some reason behind the absolute drivel that constitutes today's Diary entry. Well, for once there was. Alfred Hitchcock was born today in 1899 and I have included most of his major, (and one minor), film titles. You have less than twenty-four hours to save the world and come up with a total and I will let you know tomorrow how many I knowingly wrote in and what they were, which gives me a good sized paragraph for free in tomorrow's Diary. So not only have you had to face consternation and bewilderment reading today's wibblings once, you are now going to have to read it all over again. Sorry.

And for those of you reading this in book form no sneaking a peak at tomorrow's entry.

August 14ᵗʰ - Sunday

"All right Form 3C, settle down. No Watkins, you can't leave the room, you've only just got here. You'll have to hold on to it. No, Watkins, I was talking figuratively, you disgusting boy".

"I have marked your mid-term examination papers and we shall shortly go through the answers. First, hands up who got 25 film titles? Very clever Simpkins, but 'The Odd Figurine' is not a film title that Alfred Hitchcock had anything to do with or for that matter any other film producer, you made it up out of your over active imagination. Yes, Digby-Smyth, it will hurt if you shut the lid of you desk on it, won't it. Stop whingeing lad, it's a muscle, you can't break it".

"Yes, Goode, it is a lovely day out there today and the beach is looking particularly attractive, I grant you, and with all those people going into the sea together it does rather look like the River Ganges on a holy day, but we will continue this class in the sweaty environs of the classroom. Perhaps if Wilkins actually let the soap come into contact with his body in the showers after games it would be a little more fragrant in your quarter of the room".

"Now, the answers to yesterday's examination. What was that you just flicked at Clark, Ridley? Really? That is utterly vile. Report to me after class".

"I shall read out the answers as they appeared in the text to give the simpletons among you a chance of following, eh Johnston. There is one answer I shall leave until last as, by the look of your answer sheets, it eluded most of you. Perkins, they *all* seem to have eluded you but I can't leave them all until last, can I?"

"First there was *Suspicion* and in the same paragraph, *North by Northwest*, *Notorious*, *Shadow of a Doubt* and *Saboteur*. Then we have *Frenzy*, *Rebecca* and *Marnie*, difficult to work into the text in any other way than as names, followed by *Spellbound* and *Torn Curtain*".

"Are those sweets Billinghurst? I hope you have enough for the whole class".

"In the third paragraph we have *Vertigo* and *Lifeboat*, starting to slow down now. Oh, for heaven's sake Pitt, squeeze the bridge of your nose until it stops. Stop crying girl. You can change your blouse at the next break".

"Can we continue, now? Good. No, not you Goode, good as in splendid. Stop tittering Clark and you too Watkins. Tittering is not funny because it has the syllable 'tit' in it. Syllable, lad. Look it up, you stupid boy".

In the fourth paragraph we have just the one, *Strangers on a Train*. Moving swiftly onto the fifth paragraph you will find *To*

Catch a Thief and *Topaz* and in the sixth, *Rope*, *The Man Who Knew Too Much* and *The Wrong Man* followed by *The Birds* and *Under Capricorn* which was a tough one until I discovered that the Teenager really does have her birthday under that sign.

Lastly in the penultimate paragraph we have the remaining *Rear Window*, *Stage Fright* and, of course, *Psycho*.

"How many is that so far, Perkins? Yes, use Watkins's fingers if you must but I think you will still struggle unless Watkins has grown some extra digits, as the answer is 23 so far".

"The last one will make you want to throw odd pieces of rotten fruit at me and I am speaking metaphorically, Withers, and if you do have rotten fruit in your desk I suggest you remove it before it ferments. Now look again at the fifth paragraph and open your minds, "... dilemma. For murder ..." Well you try and get *Dial M for Murder* into a sentence".

"Very well class I shall hand back your papers now. Perkins, come and collect yours I have no wish to risk my health by touching it again".

"In tomorrow's lesson we will discuss how we watched the Lifeboat launch in the afternoon and heard St Buryan Male Voice Choir sing on the quay. Yes, I am well aware that it is the first time in eight years that it hasn't rained for this event. It did look rather special with the Lifeboat moored in the Harbour while they sang. Well done, Goode, for noticing how brave those Shore Crew chaps were since there was quite a swell running when they recovered the Lifeboat".

"That's all for today, Form 3C. Class dismissed".

August 15ᵗʰ - Monday

It had to happen; I have been too lucky so far this season. Yes, it was the first wild child incident this year, I think. To be fair the children were far too young to be culpable; one was barely walking. I watched with what must have been a dumb look of suspended belief on my face as the mother attended to composing a lengthy text on her mobile telephone while the offspring laid waste to the shop. I intervened eventually, which is rare for me. I normally just burst into tears in the corner and clean up the mess later. I cannot be growing a backbone at this late stage in my life, surely.

Fortunately we have more than enough friendly, fun and pleasant characters frequenting the shop to make these instances insignificant. We even have DI who, despite her frosty demeanour in my direction, made me some scones the other day. I asked the Missus and the Teenager if they wanted to try some and both said no. I took that to mean that they did not want to taste some of the homemade scones with lashings of Sisleys strawberry preserve and Rodda's clotted cream (other brands are available but I doubt that they are a patch on these).

Did you see what I did there? I have learnt that putting derisory comments in The Diary about people or towns may bring me nothing but grief if ever we get to publish book two. By mentioning Sisleys and Rodda's as being the best, other makers of strawberry jam and clotted cream will read this entry and be encouraged to send lots of samples of their own brands such that I might be swayed to include theirs in future entries. I think they call it product placement. Smart, eh? Next week Ferrari, Cartier and John Deere – well, why not? Always fancied having a tractor.

Anyway, I digress. Where was I? Ah yes, I offered the Missus and the Teenager a bit of my cream tea and they said no. I am guessing that my gentlemen readers are already streaks ahead of me here, having, no doubt, been in the same pot of boiling ire and my lady readers are already tut tutting in the knowledge that I ate the cream tea, all of it, myself. It was, of course, only after the last morsel passed my lips that I was roundly castigated for not sharing my calorie-laden delight. No doubt I shall be reminded of my social and/or marital ineptitude for the rest of my born days. The Missus will probably ensure I live to 120 so that I receive full retribution for my inability to realise that when she said no she actually meant "of course I want a bit of your cream tea and if you don't save me a bit you'll suffer big time".

Well, if I am going to live that long I had better get some rest. I will probably be still wheeling out my ball stand in the mornings when the two wayward infants from today come and clock me with their walking sticks for being rude about them.

August 16ᵗʰ – Tuesday

The mist and low cloud pulled out fairly early this morning but the day did not amount to a hill of beans despite a slice of blue sky visible for about five minutes. How cruel was that? Even so it did not stop us from being mobbed for much of the day.

As you will know by now Tuesday is the day for the main delivery of our weekly groceries. Last week our good neighbour lent a hand and we had the van empty in double quick time. This week one of our customers offered to help, she of the troublesome scones. Normally I would have offered, and I am sure she expected, a "wouldn't dream of having one of our customers put themselves out in such a manner" but instead, and mindful of the punishment of the scones, I replied "you carry on", so she did. She got her own back later by returning the sieve that she had borrowed to make the scones minus the handle.

It seems that Rock has pushed the boat out with a new hotel. It has en-suite bathrooms, king sized beds and a cordon bleu restaurant. Nothing out of the ordinary there you would think, especially for an area such a Rock. Nothing at all until you find out that the whole thing is under canvas rather than bricks and mortar. I think the team to which the radio article referred was the Pop Up Hotel that sets up in various locations across the UK depending on events, basically chasing the money. With the en-suite option a weekend's bed and breakfast will set you back the best part of five hundred quid.

The concept is not new. They have been doing this at the back of the F&L for the last few years. The en-suite option, if you pitch next to the portable toilet, is fifteen quid for the weekend. If you book for August you are almost guaranteed an outside shower.

Even in this inclement weather we are still selling summer wear including any number of flip flops. A lady bought some today and as I was just about to throw away the labels she stopped me and explained she wanted to make sure there were no instructions she had to be aware of. Fearful that she may be missing some technical detail I offered to write 'left' and 'right' on them for her. Fortunately she laughed.

The Lifeboat was called out in the afternoon for a scheduled rendezvous with St Ives Lifeboat that was towing a Fastnet Race casualty. Sennen Cove Lifeboat took over the tow and handed on to Penlee and was due to return to station at around 7pm. They must have made better time than was expected and I nearly missed the recovery at shortly before six o'clock.

Best I get some sleep now. It looks like I will have a busy day tomorrow counting the raindrops.

August 17ᵗʰ - Wednesday

And count the raindrops we did, at least for the morning. Having been alerted by the Met Office to expect rain all day it was hardly a surprise that it brightened considerably in the afternoon with some patches of blue sky. In fact it went on to be quite a stonkingly fabulous afternoon. Well done, lads.

Nice to see that Cornwall has been awarded Enterprise Status by the Government; these zones will be "trailblazers for growth, jobs and prosperity" and are designed to encourage business growth outside London and the South East. We can expect to see tax breaks handed out to the resurgent mining industry, the fishing ports around the county benefiting from reduced red tape and the fostering of increased employment and farming attracting better export potential and higher yields through investment in new technologies.

Well, no, actually. So let me re-phrase that. Nice to see that a 55 hectare site in Newquay, most of which has aeroplanes landing on it, has been awarded Enterprise Status by the Government for the development of that bedrock of Cornish industry – aerospace.

All cynicism aside I am sure it is a very good thing and far in away better than not being awarded it. However I cannot see it making a ha'penth worth of difference to most hard-pressed Cornish workers, who will still be reliant on the struggling industries that may well suffer further as focus is diverted to a small site on the north coast.

The Missus and the Teenager did their bit to promote local business by tripping off to the Trewellard Meadery tonight. I, of course, did my bit to promote our local business by staying behind to run the shop and not a tax break or reduction in red tape to be seen. I just do not know how we do it.

One thing is for sure if this up and down weather keeps disrupting business I am moving the shop to the end of runway one at Newquay. Things are looking up there, apparently.

August 18ᵗʰ - Thursday

I have to tell you I am absolutely fed up with this rain we keep getting. It must be rain because the Met Office said it was. It was the sort of rain that made everyone strip down to their swim suits and head down to the beach. How awful is that? And what is worse is it lasted all day long and we ended up being flooded ... with customers.

It was a perfect day, then, for the BBC to come down and film the Lifeboat all day. Word has obviously got around regarding the elite Shore Crew at Sennen Cove. Naturally being modest and retiring chaps, in fact most of us should have been retired years ago, we spurned their advances and suggested they film the Boat Crew instead. Apparently there is a new series on rescue services and it was our turn to be filmed. Rescue 193 went over mid morning and I think they even took the camera out on Big J's boat to capture some footage.

The Teenager spent the day down on the beach. We keep ribbing her that she is only down there to look at the lifeguards. She is a brave little soul though, as she is quite happy to go and enjoy some rays down there all by her lonesome. She came back glowing, although it could have been the sun, it could equally have been from looking at lifeguards.

I could give you chapter and verse regarding the quiz at the OS but it would be much more interesting to tell you that we sold one of the bird boxes today. You must remember the bird boxes. This one was in the form of a surf shack and the chap that bought it must have been as mad as a big bag of marbles.

August 19ᵗʰ - Friday

Here in Sennen there are very few legal and free parking spots; driveways are jealously guarded. Come the end of September cars will be parked all along Cove Road, unlike August when only half the road is full. They cannot all have blue badges, surely. Until then, like today, the car parks were jammed with happy beach goers.

Not a problem when you have a spanking new 4x4 and a really expensive jet ski whereupon the signs that say no vehicles on the beach and no jet skis to be launched do not apply to you.

So you drive down onto the beach and launch your big expensive jet ski and park your 4x4 mid way down the beach. Then, when its time to leave, you find that a whole host of people have pitched their beach tents and windbreaks in your way and you have to ask them to move. It is then that you find that your spanking new 4x4 is not quite as 'all terrain' as the brochures suggest and you need the harbour tractor to pull you out. Not only that but you have been given some good advice to drive your jet ski around to the Harbour beach following the eastern channel markers. But, of course, a direct route is much better until you find your propeller lagged in weed.

And then we, or rather I, repaired to the OS where the rather wonderful *Dirty Living Rhythm Band* was playing. I have raved about them before on these pages so I shall not rave about them again … oh, go on then. She with a voice clear as cut glass and him with a seven shilling acoustic guitar that sounds like a telecaster-Stratocaster-Stradivarius, whatever-he-wants-it-to-sound-like. I spoke to a fellow guitarist about him and I was told that he plays chords that should be impossible to play.

Whatever it was it brought the OS back to life again, back to what it was and what it should still be. See, it doesn't take that much. Anyway, those are my principles. If you don't like them, I have others.

August 21st – Sunday

The first evictions have happened in the Big Sennen Cove House. In fact there were three evictions at the same time. The votes were all counted and verified and three teenage boys were top of our list of mindless oiks. They were physically aged around fourteen or fifteen, acting out a mental age closer to their shoe size.

Judging from their accents they were from a more privileged background and if this is the product that our better educational establishments are churning out, heaven help the rest of us. They were twice warned to behave themselves, which was inadvertent, as The Missus did not know I had done it once already. On the third infringement, dispensing expensive hand cream for their pathetic amusement, the Missus turned them out.

What really got my goat was they appeared to be proud of this achievement. As they exited the shop they announced, to what appeared to be a parent, that they had been thrown out. The parent seemed unconcerned. Our future world is in their hands, burgeoning politicians I would not wonder.

Other than that little hiccup it was a rather pleasant day ... what am I talking about? It was a rip shocking crimbler of a day with wall to wall sunshine from early in the morning to last knockings at night. The beach was crammed full of happy holidaymakers and so was the shop for most of the day, which makes for jolly little shopkeepers too.

And what also makes a jolly little shopkeeper giggle is ladies coming in and asking what is in our cheese and vegetable pasty. She was keen to ensure that it contained no vegetables other than onion, as her daughter, who is a vegetarian, does not like them. We also enjoy meeting with librarians whose access to The Diary pages from her place of work is so strictly controlled I have to be careful not to use the words 'bottom' or 'catapult' less I be censored for pornography or promoting weaponry, (I will let you decide which word represented what offence). Oh, and I must say hello to her mother, M, who is an avid reader. Never mind; I am sure that with the right medical attention you will come to your senses in no time.

The Missus and the Teenager shipped off to Truro again before we closed. They wanted to go to our nearest Pizza Hut, though what it has to offer that induces people to drive an 80 mile round trip to visit it is beyond me. Nevertheless I suspect it was slightly better than what the bleddy hound found for her supper.

I left it half an hour after we closed before I took her down on the Harbour beach for a bit of chase the ball. I was pretty sure that there were people down there barbequing so I gave them some time to finish off else the dog would have been all over them. It was coming on dusk when we eventually got down there and it all started pretty well. Pretty well, that is, until she found her first scabby fish. The Missus had her down there a couple of nights ago and she ate so much of it she was sick when she got back. Anxious to avoid a repeat performance I threw the fish into the sea remembering only too late that she can swim. Fortunately the fish sank so she soon gave up and came back ashore. It was then she found her second fish. I managed to get her off that too and used the ball as a decoy while I threw it into the water. She was coming off the decoy ball looking rather disgusted that she had fallen for that old trick when she came across her third fish.

It was at this point I admitted defeat, hooked her up to her lead, dragged her home and re-evaluated the benefits of eating a Pizza Hut pizza forty miles away.

August 23rd - Tuesday

The Diary received a very pleasant email from a reader in Winnipeg this morning. It is childish, I know, but I always get rather excited when emails come in from readers and even more so when they are from as far away as Australia.

Childish indeed; after reading some of the texts herein some readers may say that The Diary could have been written by someone short of a developed mind. Regular readers of The Diary will have long suspected that I have a portrait of a small child chained to a computer in the attic. As any keen amateur cryptologist will tell you if you read The Diary entries backwards, hidden in the text, is a message that reads "I am a small child, chained to a computer in the attic writing inane diary entries everyday, please help me."

He would have been as perplexed as I that it was not raining this morning despite Radio Pasty's best efforts to foretell the weather in great detail. This rather means that the Met Office was actually spot on with its forecast displayed on the Internet. You would think that an organisation as prestigious as the Met Office would, at least, have the decency to get it consistently wrong; it plays havoc with my pasty orders.

And talking of wet stuff we had some in the shop this morning. Yes, I know we have gallons on the shelf in bottles, but this was on the floor and not in bottles. We suspected the freezer to start with but a casual check of the temperature gauges said otherwise, unless ice has started to melt at −22 degrees Celsius. The positioning of it was similar to that when the drain at the back overflows, but given we have had no rain this was an unlikely source and also there was no water in the store room that lies between our puddle and the drain. I checked round the back anyway, just in case it had rained there and we had not noticed. I had also checked the ceiling and the walls lest our flood had come from above but there was not even the suggestion of dampness.

It remains a mystery, but we have either sprung a very short-lived artesian spring or we have an incontinent ghost with a capacious bladder. We had all better hope it is the former when we start bottling it.

I have berated the portrait of a small child in the attic and given him a clip around the ear 'ole, (you can do that to portraits of small, tethered children hidden in attics that no one knows about), for saying that Winnipeg is in Australia. Everyone knows, of course, that it is in America.

Ouch!

August 24th - Wednesday

Having managed to upset around 650,000 people yesterday, twice, I felt I should make amends. What I did not realise yesterday is that a city whose name derives from a muddy lake has much in common with Sennen Cove. Other than the fact that it is in Canada, of course it is, and the last time I looked, Sennen Cove was not, it suffers from short summers and long cold winters. After this short summer our winter will be very long and bleak indeed; we are practically twins.

You Winnipegians will be pleased to note that I got my comeuppance this morning when I came down to the shop. Our artesian spring had sprung back to life overnight. Artful, possibly, but artesian it was not. We had set our dishwasher to run last thing and its murky, watery contents were liberally set about the shop floor. I had hoped for an easy morning with few magazines to put out and a falling order of bread to bake. Not a chance. Mop, bucket and lashings of soapy, disinfected water were time consumingly deployed. What joy! Feeling better already, Winnipeg?

Having established we had a drainage problem the next question was how bad was it? We had already discovered from our previous flood that we do not have a manhole cover to enable us to rod the main drain. Through a logical process of elimination we worked out that it was the foul water from shower and sinks, as opposed to the septic water from the toilet, which feeds into the main drain from a spur. I am sure I do not need to be explicit about how we worked that out, especially as at least two of you read this over breakfast.

It also did not take much working out that I could not go plumbing the depths of our drainage system myself; it is August after all. So, who you gonna call? Picasso Titmarsh, of course. A man for all seasons if ever there was one, particularly when there is a dirty hole that needs some attention. No sooner had he arrived he was shoulder deep in our drain, pulling out bits of rock, earth, pottery; a copy of a 1976 Playboy Magazine (minus centrefold); sufficient hair to put Rapunzel to shame; Lord Lucan, a cuddly toy and, right at the bottom, a Cornish miner. Wherever you go you will always find …

The Picasso man is a genius and should be applauded. Well, why not? He is unlikely to get paid. I might even withdraw the lawsuit against him for that unnecessary little piece on TG's forum on the main Sennen Cove website. I turned to thank him but there he was gone. All in a day's work, I guess.

Keeping with tradition we sent out for tea again; fish and chips from up the top. You just cannot beat them even if you do have to serve customers between mouthfuls. It will be quite a shock to the system to have to step into the kitchen and actually cook something.

It is the Teenager's last night after some four weeks. After some four weeks she decided that she better get her toes into the water since she has been living no more than 100 yards from it. Her actual words were, "going for a dip" which we assumed meant swimsuit and diving hat. Not exactly. She arrived on the beach in shorts and t-shirt and went in as far as her knees, and bearing in mind she is four feet three that is not very far. Ah, well, wet is wet I suppose.

Tomorrow we must face a tearful farewell to Teenager and mother. It will be a while since I laughed that hard.

August 25th – Thursday

So I said to this chap, "Dry as a bone today. See those little sunshine marks on the weather map – guaranteed."

He decided to stay in the shop for a minute or two longer to give the passing heavy shower a chance to blow through.

After that little interlude I ought to tell you about a short Inshore Lifeboat shout we had this morning. One of the local fishermen suffered engine failure in quite a precarious position out towards Nanquidno. By the time the ILB arrived the boat was making her own way back. Then later we had an impromptu exercise for the big boat.

We have a relief mechanic here for a week, who also happens to be a 2nd Coxswain. He has experience at both pontoon and slip based stations but, as yet, not with a Tamar on a slip. The exercise gave him a shot at putting the City of London III onto the short slip in some interesting conditions. He managed extremely well on three or four approaches. It goes without saying that the expert guidance of one of our excellent Shore Crew was available throughout the trials.

I did not quite make Lifeboat training tonight. While it was not what you would call busy, I had a constant line of customers from about 6:30pm including a couple of girls who were in and out for the best part of and hour. When questioned they told us that their parents were having dinner and they were told to amuse themselves. If their little pockets were full of shillings we would quite happily have amused them for hours, (you must have realised by now that we are not proud), but as it was we were expected to perform this child sitting service for next to nothing. If this year returns any profit at all we shall be investing in chimneys or a small tin mine for such eventualities in future.

And finally, as you know, the Teenager returned to her fold today.

Rarely, rarely, comest thou,
Spirit of Delight!
Wherefore hast thou left me now
Many a day and night?
Many a weary night and day
'Tis since thou are fled away.

August 26th - Friday

As if we needed further proof that we are blessed in this little corner of the Universe. While the drain covers in the city of sin were lifted by the force of flood water we, in Sennen Cove, remained dry and untouched. If you had seen the rain radar at around 10am this morning you would have seen what a miracle this was; there was rain everywhere.

We must have caught the edge of a squall at one point as our bodyboards nearly took a trip down the street. At least they could get down the street. In Truro cars were backed up to the A30 at Carland Cross and didn't clear until early evening.

I suspect Cornwall's woes are small beer compared to the threat that our International Correspondent is under at the moment. As I clatter my stubby fingers across the keyboard Hurricane Irene is heading in her direction. Her allotment may be at risk but at least her hot peppers are safe. She previously picked a pot of pickling peppers prior to the potential pandemonium precipitated by persistent precipitation and pressing, er, wind. It is possible, of course, that we may get the tail end of Irene ourselves 'ere long.

In the mean time it looks like we might be in for a fair weekend, fingers crossed and all that. I thought I'd get ahead of the posse and call into to Shrew House to fill our shelves to overflowing. The cunning plan is that I won't need to go up again until after the ball is over. Probably as cunning a plan as Philip VI of France had until the Brits turned up with longbows, today in 1346.

Of course we would prefer it if the next swathe of visitors turned up with purses and wallets filled to the brim with currency of the realm rather than longbows but at this stage of the game we'll take it as it comes, thank you. I hear you can get a good price for a decent longbow these days.

August 27th - Saturday

Mockery and derision I could probably live with, as it does not cost money. I did read, however, that there was a fifty percent increase in libel cases last year resulting from online defamation. I noted with a small chill that this is the period over which The Diary had its first outing. I do hope there are no nasty surprises in Tuesday's mail.

Talking of defamation, I notice that much has been said against all this Olympic torch business and how the council are advertising for a chap to project manage the event and coordinate various festivals and parties. Not only that, but they have decided to invest around £135,000 of our money in promoting the torch bearing and associated happenings.

Well, hang on just a minute all you dissenters. This is going to be absolutely massive for Cornwall and the Isles of Scilly, just like the eclipse in 1999. Well, when I say Cornwall and the Isles of Scilly I mean just Cornwall actually, as the Isles of Scilly have been excluded as being just a bit too far off the beaten track. Well, when I say Cornwall I mean the twenty communities that the torch will pass through.

Anyway, just think of all those opportunities that come with the bearing of the torch. The council reckons there will be up to seven million of them, although I cannot think of one at the moment, but that is why we are employing someone. Just bear in mind that £20k is just a pro rata amount and before tax. The contract is for eight months, and must attract someone educated to degree level, with project management, marketing and publicity experience who is able to organise meetings. No doubt they will also need to be able to cope with mockery and derision. The post runs until 31st May giving him or her two weeks to clear their desk after it happens.

Remember the torch will be in Cornwall for a whole day, well not exactly a whole day, some of a whole day, as it arrives in Plymouth later on. Whoever does this job is going to have one busy time on 19th May, for sure. Hang on a second, there, I have just had a look at my diary (my appointments diary, not this one) for that date and, you know, I do not have a single appointment. I live locally and have plenty of ideas how I could spend £135,000. In terms of publicity, through The Diary, (this one, not the appointments diary), we could have global exposure, well, Manitoba, South Carolina and New South Wales, oh, and Los Angeles, at least. I would say the job is pretty much in the bag.

While penning that load of drivel, I have been munching into a bag of chocolates. On the side of the pack it says that it is 'reclosable'; it is a fairly big bag after all. On first glance the design of the bag did not look that reclosable so I took a closer look and it has some instructions on the side. It suggests I pull out the sides to flatten the opening, fold down the top, and here is the really clever bit, I use some tape, (not supplied), to hold it down. Genius! It is a shame that all big bags of sweets do not have this reclosable feature; obesity would be a thing of the past. If the chap, (all right it could have been a girly), who came up with that idea is available I might have some competition for the torch coordinator post.

Talking of obesity, there is a beer festival on at the F&L over the weekend. It started last night, so I imagine most of the barrels are empty by now and half of Sennen is dozing fitfully. I know that many of you will be wanting to know the gritty goings on so I feel that it is my duty to attend and report back in graphic detail.

At your behest I dragged my sorry, weary and bent old frame up the hill after the shop shut. I would not do it for just anyone, you know. (Okay, the Missus drove me up there. And we had to stop at Shrew House for more stock – another cunning plan lying in tatters on the ground.)

The F&L has a marquee set up at the back to contain the additional beer stock. I have never known beer drinking to be so intense. Oh, come on you would not begrudge me the odd, heaven sent pun would you? Anyway the format works exceedingly well. The heavy duty, be-sandaled and bearded real ale drinkers stay outside in the marquee leaving the rest of us have some proper elbow room inside.

I could not pass by without trying a real ale or two. I had several options and asked the goodly bartend to recommend one. He suggested a Black Hole, but I really could not be drawn into that one. I opted for an Orkell's Red that was very hoppy. The first half was amusing but I had to quaff the second and returned to my usual brew thereafter.

The *Dirty Living Rhythm Band* was playing tonight and, as you know, I have waxed lyrical about them before, so I shall not again. All I can say that it was pretty much a full on night and anyone who is anyone in the village was there.

I hardly felt a breeze on the way home. But the skies were clear. Did I ever tell you about a walk home with clear skies, a still night and the stars sparkling? Man, you just got to be there.

August 29ᵗʰ - Monday

I think I told you a little while ago that South West Water has volunteered to put its hand up when some of its combined storm overflows, (cso), are activated. These safety valves let raw sewage spill into the sea when the water treatment plants have been inundated with heavy rain. Each cso event has to be agreed by the Environment Agency and when it happens little electronic gizmos fire off messages to the Surfers Against Sewage website and registered users' mobile telephones.

South West Water has spent some £2 billion of our money on its 'Clean Sweep' project to ensure bathing water meets rigorous EU standards. The expectation was that, possibly, two or three cso events may occur during a bathing season at each site. It was something of a surprise, therefore, when Surfers Against Sewage recorded 42 events, with nine occurring at one location alone, Salcombe, since you ask.

So let me summarise. We pay the highest water rates in the country, exacerbated by a project that South West Water had to carry out to comply with EU directives. The project was 100% successful – except when it rains. One thing is for sure, I am not going swimming in Salcombe.

The bleddy hound does not seem to mind swimming here though and she is quite good at it. Perhaps her partiality to swimming comes from her love of fish. When we go up the top to the fish and chip shop she always gets a bit of fish to herself, yes she is spoilt rotten and does like her fish fresh. Very fresh it seems.

The Missus took her down to the harbour tonight for a run around just as a chap on a kayak came in with his catch on the other side of the beach. She was in there like a robber's dog and had one of his mackerel away, quick as you like. The embarrassed Missus chased her around the beach for half an hour to get it off her. Apparently the fisherman was not that keen to have it back. Cannot imagine why.

Fresh mackerel in the shop tomorrow, if you are interested.

August 30ᵗʰ - Tuesday

The Marine Management Organisation has just released its 2010 figures for UK fisheries. I thought I would share some of the facts and figures with you, because it is a lot easier than making something up and takes up an awful lot of Diary space. There, how is that for honest deceit? Additionally you might actually, for once, learn something – I was going to say useful – from these pages and you might find it interesting. I didn't.

There were 606,000 tonnes of fish landed into the UK during the year, which includes shellfish. Prices went up, which I hardly imagine is a surprise. The value of the catch was £719 million, a seven percent rise in value against a four percent rise in quantity. Of the total UK fleet catch, 68 percent was landed into the UK, while 21 percent of total landings into the UK was by foreign boats.

More than a quarter of all the fish landed was mackerel, part of 286,000 tonnes of pelagic fish, (mackerel, herring, sprats, pilchards and anchovy), in total, an area where the value dropped by six percent, and 152,000 tonnes of shellfish.

The most telling statistic, however, is that ninety nine percent of all the pelagic fish and ninety six percent of demersal fish landed was by the class of vessel consisting mainly of boats over ten metres in length.

It begs the question, therefore, why there is such a high level of legislation, administration and, ultimately, constraint on the under tens including the small punts that operate here out of The Cove. Clearly mine is not a particularly informed opinion, but on the face of it the word disproportionate springs to mind. Where handline fishing and potting are such distinctly sustainable fishing methods why on Earth would anyone want to discourage it?

Our diminutive dog walker went home today. She gave the bleddy hound about a week's worth of exercise in the hour before she left. I think the girl's grandparents will miss her attendance in their back yard too, the bleddy hound, not the grandchild or that may also be the case, as she was doing a fair job of keeping the cats off the garden. Who would have thought that the bleddy hound actually did something useful in its over-fed and over-cosseted lifestyle.

We should spare a thought today for Clement Ader and Ernest Rutherford who come together for pulling things apart. With Clement it was sound when he demonstrated a stereophonic two-channel system using two telephone lines connected to the Paris Opera in 1881. Lord Rutherford, born today in 1871, split the atom and eventually created an even bigger noise.

I shall pull myself together now and have an early night for a change.

August 31ˢᵗ - Wednesday

Something of a corking sunrise this morning with just enough cloud to reflect its glory all around. That was not the only thing coming out of the east this morning. The wind has moved around and is a tad chilly, a real knicker-ripper too. We have had to tie down the bleddy hound lest she gets whisked away.

Still, windbreak sales are up! However you will be alarmed to hear that a wheel has fallen off my Turner Prize worthy ball stand. If the Missus had one criticism about it, no, I have to be honest she had a bag full of criticisms about it, one of which was the wheels were too small. Well, it is not as if it has to do the Dakar rally or anything; it just has to get in and out of the shop every day. I will add the repair to my growing list of 'now-that-we're-less-busy-you-can' jobs.

On the opposite slant we have a darned laid back lot of visitors this week. Not one of them has mentioned the Turner Prize worthy ball stand either. There is me getting up before dawn to bake bread, untie newspapers, dust down my sprindles and polish my gwelps. Well, that is it. I am not working my finger to the skin if you lot cannot be bothered. I am having a lie in tomorrow and you can all put up with dirty gwelps.

Which reminds me, I see that Wadebridge is to get its out of town supermarket after the inaptly named, (or should that have been just inept), Strategic Planning Committee reversed its decision of some seven months ago not to allow it. I am sure that the £10 million that the council will earn from the deal had no bearing on the decision at all. Still, on the up side the council will be able to use the money to board up Wadebridge town centre shops and maintain the derelict buildings for a few years.

And talking of scary endings a number of you have been in touch to ask what happened to the snake. If you remember I reported that an adder had crawled, er, slithered perhaps, into a nearby house and under the bath. Some of you said you could not imagine a worse situation. Well your imagination and wickedness need some cultivation. You could take a lead from our International Correspondent who clearly has an abundance of both and suggested that the snake could have been pregnant.

Sweet dreams all.

September 1ˢᵗ – Thursday

We could have done with a few days like this in August and with so many people around it is very much like high summer. We have even had the true mark of the season, totally unconcerned parents letting their children run riot in the shop. "Oh, I didn't realise you had that expensive vase in your hand Samantha." Well no, you wouldn't because you were looking the other way and so was Daddy. Bet you don't do that on a busy road. "Oh Samantha, what a mess you've made of yourself; you look quite squashed. I know, it was a very naughty bus."

The sea has been just about as packed as the beach today and for a change the swimmers and splashers about have had full command; the water is flat as a dish, at least until Monday, that is, when it is likely to go off the scale when Irene gets here.

I tripped off to St Just today to drop into the Cape Surgery on a routine matter. I said it was a routine matter, nothing at all to be concerned about. The Aged Parents do worry so at the mere mention of 'me' and 'doctor' in the same sentence. I have had two letters at the beginning of the season begging me to turn up for my annual review. I think they just like to count my arms and legs and make sure my head's in the right place.

Anyway, the point being, they have been having some building work go on there during the summer. The front door has been shut off and patients have had to use the tradesmen's entrance. I, of course, have refused to attend on principle. It has now been finished and it looks very grand indeed. They even have automatic sliding doors at the entrance, what you might call swish. The most worrying development is that they have doubled the waiting room seating. Shall we see a shortage of available doctors or are many more of us expected to be ill? I think we need to be told.

Whatever the case our Lifeboat Coxswain must have the inside track as he organised a Lifeboat exercise ahead of us all succumbing to the impending dreaded lurgy. The boat did not have to travel too far down the slip before it hit the water as we are still having those big spring tides. It also means we did not have far to fish it out at recovery either and our little tractor did not get its tracks sandy at all recovering the ILB.

The timing of the exercise nearly put our usual quizzing in jeopardy but fortunately they held it at the OS instead, which is a lot closer. It did not matter anyway as we were dreadful. I think we must have peaked too early.

I think I am going to have to call in the doc' again tomorrow; I am still feeling quite chipper.

September 2ⁿᵈ - Friday

Golly. I might just hazard that today was just about the finest of the summer, a real rip zipping cribbler of a day. It was not warm, it was hot and I do not think I have used that word to describe the weather this year. There was plenty of blue sky and again the sea looked inviting if a little flat.

And what a lot of happy little souls we had. For most, it was their last day and it really could not be more memorable. For one lady it was extremely memorable, as she had a car run into her in the Beach car park. She did not look too upset but I suppose as it happened yesterday she has time to become philosophical about it. She has asked me to pass on a message as she had heard that this organ, well, when I say organ, more of a squeezebox with a leaky diaphragm really, has the ear of the populous, well, eye, I suppose, if you want to split possums. I do not know where she heard that, but perhaps both of you could pass on the message to someone you know.

Anyway, I digress. Where was I? Ah, yes, for those of you unfamiliar with the terrain, the Beach car park is on a slope with most of the car parking spaces pointing down hill, or up hill if you prefer. No, it is definitely down hill; cars do not run away up hill, do they? The rescue service that turned up to tow her out told her that the event, cars rolling away and into others, was a frequent occurrence. He explained that cars that had come down the hill tend to apply their brakes for most of the journey thus heating up the discs and making them expand. When the car parks and the hand brake is applied all seems well until the heated disc cools and contracts thus loosening the grip of the brake pad. Sorry if that was a little technical for some of you. To summarise; the hand brake stops working after a while.

It is at this point in the proceedings that I should give you an extreme example to demonstrate the tragedy that might occur. However, our Head Launcher has made me promise faithfully never to mention the time when his hand brake slipped off and his new car ran away and scat down the lifeboat station car park barrier. So I will not. All I can say is that an incident might occur when someone does not put their car in a gear opposite to the direction of the slope, that the hand brake may slip off for the reasons already stated and roll away, maybe knocking over, say, a lifeboat car park barrier, for example.

Another thing that has not been working for a while is the Levant steam engine. The old boiler stopped working and I am sure that will resonate with many of you. I have to say that I had no idea that there had been a problem but in the news today there was a picture of the new boiler being installed. The engine, the beam of which was made by Harvey's of Hayle, was installed in 1840 and decommissioned in 1930. They certainly do not make old boilers like they used to. The previous modern boiler was only twenty years old when it gave up the ghost.

And we were about to give up the ghost in the shop when I was summoned to a Lifeboat shout. Both boats were launched to an incident over at Porthcurno. A reliable source told me that a lady surfer had gone to the aid of a couple of boys seemingly stranded on some rocks. When she arrived to help they promptly beggered off leaving her stranded. A fellow surfer then went to help her out and both were back on the beach by the time the Lifeboats arrived.

This made me a little late for my tea. We have had some pollack in our fridge for a couple of days and it had reached its sell by date. Alas and alack this rather meant I had to eat it myself. It was a little too large for one person and the Missus was not interested in sharing; the Missus hates fish. That only left the bleddy hound and she loves fish. Mine went into a Spanish style omelette and hers I poached in milk. I have to say hers looked so attractive I had some of that too. It also tasted attractive and is now earmarked for my breakfast. If the bleddy hound behaves herself I will let her have the poaching liquor.

Oh, come on, it is not like she *knew* I cooked it for her.

September 3ʳᵈ – Saturday

The Met Office should recommence its long-range weather forecast. So says a chap who used to work for them and now works for a European weather centre. Well, I suppose he can say that now because if the Met Office gets it wrong again he is not in the firing line. He went further and said that the perception of the Met Office getting it wrong is that they do not get enough air time on television and radio to explain the probabilities. Presumably he means that they get enough time to say, "It's not going to rain tomorrow", but not enough time to say, "It's not going to rain tomorrow but there again it just might".

Well they did say it was going to rain today and it did, bang on time as well. Luckily it gave us just enough time in the morning to say goodbye to all the leavers and their bags full of biscuits, fudge and other pressies. I would certainly rather be leaving today than leaving yesterday, that is for sure.

Gloomy though it was we did not see much of the rain during the day. There are some grave expectations, though. The tractor was down on Harbour beach pulling the punts up the slip; the tides are still quite big and the swell is set to increase over the next day or so. Regardless of the weather we shall have plenty of sea watchers, no doubt. A big crashing sea is a wonder to behold.

I had a call from one of The Diary's roving reporters this morning. He was at the Cornish Gorsedh's open meeting at Helston trying not to be spotted; he is from Redruth, you know. He tells me that among the serious tomes for sale tracking the history of the Gorsedh and other weighty matters was a copy of The Cove Diary, (did I tell you it had a review in the *Western Morning News?*). I can only assume it was there to make the other books look a little more attractive. Do not be ridiculous, The Cove Diary was there to excite readership in the less than interesting historic documents, I am sure.

148

September 4ᵗʰ - Sunday

I do not get accused of being overly cool very often, all right never, and it certainly was not going to happen today. You see our refrigerator, the one in our kitchen, has broken down. The Missus noticed last night and I certainly noticed this morning as the contents have become very aromatic.

It is not as big a disaster as, say, my beer fridge breaking down, which it did incidentally, at the beginning of the summer of all times. Because my beer fridge has broken down the failure of the kitchen fridge has become a major incident; I have nowhere to cool my beer.

If you live in the suburbs of one of our big cities or, heaven forefend, Birmingham, you probably have the choice of a cornucopia of several big stores, even on a Sunday, from which to choose your replacement refrigerator.

(Can someone please explain why the shortened version of refrigerator has a 'd' in it? Or is it a shortened version of Frigidaire, but that did not have the extra 'd' in it either? I mean why would you shorten a word then extend it with an additional letter? It is very confusing especially as I am alternating between the two so as not to be overly repetitive with one or the other).

Anyway, I digress. Where was I? Ah, yes buying a new refrigerator on a Sunday in big cities must be a cinch. Here we have the chain store Curly's or some such and that is it. If they have not got it, you do not have it and as luck would have it, they did not, so we have not, at least not our first choice. We did not get second choice either as the Missus did not like it when she came face to face with it.

So the upshot is that we still do not have a working refrigerator in our kitchen, at least until Tuesday. We found the article that we required online, eventually, and it has been ordered. On the first attempt the selected supplier promised free delivery until they found out where we lived, so we elected to buy from another supplier who will also pick up the old one for a tenner. This, believe me, is a mere bagatelle given the hoops I would have to jump through at the local tip, sorry, household waste recycling centre.

I put off emptying the old fridge until after our tea for obvious reasons but the steaming contents of the refrigerator needed to be dealt with. Sir Humphrey Davy must have had this very moment in mind when he invented the miners' safety lamp today in 1815. Were it not for the electric light in the kitchen I believe I would have been at grave risk of combustion had I lit a match.

The contents are now safely in our wheelie bin and thankfully it will be collected tomorrow unless the starving cats of the neighbourhood latch onto the subtle scent and get there first.

Tomorrow we shall have an object lesson in the safe manual handling of loads, namely refrigerators down narrow concrete stairs, followed by a dissertation on the availability of chiropractors in rural communities.

September 5ᵗʰ - Monday

The Missus has been working hard on clearing up our aisles and there has been one item especially that has stood in the way more than any other. It is a tall wooden structure that displayed magnets; little posts you press into the earth; and door hangers that held various witticisms that, for us, have long since ceased to be witty. If you have been in the shop you will almost certainly have snagged your bag/coat/arm/whole body*, (*delete as appropriate), on it and probably thought it your fault. Well, sorry, but it probably was as I have studiously avoided doing so for two years, but I am willing to concede that as a shop we probably attract more than our fair share of clumsy customers. Sorry, there was no easy way of breaking it to you.

Now that you know what it was and have reluctantly accepted that you are not the fleet footed sylph you thought you were, I can relieve you, somewhat, of your burden by telling you it has been dismantled. This object of dismay, along with a surfboard shaped jewellery display, have now been shipped off to Shrew House. I can tell you it was no mean feat hefting it up a ladder to the safe confines of the mezzanine either. The lengths that we go to for the comfort of our customers will one day be chiselled on our grave-stones, if they can find one that big.

The procedure did remind me that I really must do something about the mountain of cardboard in there as I can hardly move inside. It will be the best part of half a day's work, bailing and sorting and will no doubt be relegated to a day when I am feeling really enthusiastic. Sometime in November, perhaps.

I managed to get out twice today. It is part of my rehabilitation and integration back into society after the incarceration that is the summer holidays. I found myself, again, venturing into the bright city lights of the metropolis, except it was daylight and the lights were off. It is my second trip inside a week to St Just and I must say I am adjusting well to the experience. Next time I might even get out of the van.

I have really given myself a battering today, as I also had to do lots of accounting type things that have really got my head spinning. I really do not know which I detest the most, the pile of cardboard in Shrew House or the pile of paper on my desk. At least I am not compelled to keep the cardboard in Shrew House for seven years.

Well, after an entry of completely mundane drivel and the achievement of alienating the other half of my customers, (you remember I managed to finish off customers from Birmingham yesterday who are blest with such a keen sense of humour they must have forgiven me already), it is best I give up and lie down for a while.

September 6th – Tuesday

"We are such stuff as dreams are made on, rounded with a little sleep."

It was a tempest indeed over night and into the morning. The wind reached over 50 miles per hour this morning and was throwing some rain around. Thankfully by the time I had to come downstairs most of the rain had blown through. The wind veered round to the northwest by the afternoon, which was worse for us, but had lightened considerably and the day brightened up a bit.

For the last two days we have been treated to the sight of a large gathering of gannets throwing themselves forcibly into the water not a hundred yards offshore. My guess is that the stormy waters stir up additional grub and attract more fish. This would explain the appearance of seals in this sort of sea state too. Of course I could be mistaken and the fish tend to gather in stormy waters because they know the fishermen are too girly to throw a line into the sea at times like this.

It might have stopped the fishermen but the surfers, fair starved of a bit of a wave for the best part of a week prior, ventured out but only in ones and twos. Fair play, too, to the lifeguards who stayed their red flags to let the experienced few get their boards wet.

I see in the news that the Dogs Trust has reported that there is a 47 percent rise in the number of stray dogs being picked up. I casually wondered if they would notice one more. The Trust is blaming the rise on the dire economic situation, saying that families can no longer afford to run a dog.

While I agree that a dog can be expensive, especially if it breaks down a lot or is owned by my Missus, I cannot subscribe to the Dogs Trust assessment. My opinion stems from the number of homeless people I have seen here and in London, when I worked there, who beg on the streets with dogs in tow. I make no judgemental or social comment; it is purely an observation. The dogs seemed healthy enough and well looked after.

I have never been there, and I am therefore a lame commentator, but I cannot imagine a family, even in the extremity of its need, banishing a loved pet to the wilderness. I know for a fact that if push came to shove I would be out of the door long before the bleddy hound or for that matter the iPad, iPhone, collection of Eternal Bow crockery and back copies of Australian Woman's Weekly cookbooks.

I suspect the 47 percent rise is product of people who are more willing to latch onto popular clichés than do sensible research for themselves. Perhaps with a little less of our television screens filled with emotive pictures of neglected dogs in need of a good home that only your £5 per month will secure, fewer people would be inclined to get a dog for the wrong reasons.

On a less controversial note our new refrigerator arrived today. We were very impressed with the company that delivered it. We had a call last night stating, in recorded tones, that it would be delivered between 10am and 2pm. Today the driver telephoned to repeat the claim. He was 30 minutes late but had called to say so and, apart from a small issue with his tailgate not working, the delivery went very smoothly. Should this excellent company care to contact us I am sure we can come to some agreement about publishing its name in time for the new book. Product placement is all the rage, you know.

Now that our shop hours have returned to normal I felt it time to repair to the OS for a game of cards again. It is a small gathering of perfectly pleasant people that makes for an all round enjoyable evening. I lost, of course, but I shall look to exact my revenge in the weeks to come.

And as I said to the Missus just the other day, "A pox o' your throat, you bawling, blasphemous, incharitable dog." I did not, clearly, else I would be writing this among the 47 percent increase in homeless curs but I thought we had best end with a little Tempest since we started with one.

September 7ᵗʰ - Wednesday

If you do not see us for a while do not be too alarmed, The bleddy hound and I have gone on the run; fugitives from the law and an unjust society. If the sheriffs ask, you have not seen us. I have just enough time to scribble a few words before we take to the hills. Darn, no hills. South of the border then. It is St Levan for us.

It started out ordinarily enough; another day full of bluster and bustle. The wind kept up its bluster from yesterday but because there was no rain the people came out in their droves and created a bit of a bustle. It was therefore not the ideal day for the Missus to go away deep on some mission or other, no doubt connected to the prestigious National Cup Cake Week next week and probably the root cause of how the dog and I got into so much hot water.

What on earth do you mean you have not heard of National Cup Cake week? And no it is not the spa for pregnant women and new mums that you find if you search for cup cakes on the Internet. No, not at all, these are the good old traditional fairy cakes, recipes for which MI6 are replacing bomb making instructions on terrorist organisation's websites by hacking into them, the websites, not the cup cakes, (yes, really). I hope they did a good job or else we will be finding big, round, black cupcakes with fuses on the top in cake shops across the country.

I have to say I already feel somewhat robbed of the excitement of the event. I wanted to see whom the runners were in this year's National Cupcake Championships only to find that it had already taken place. The lady that won made a vegan cupcake with no butter or eggs. You would have thought that impossible, would you not you, but apparently she is a very knowledgeable young lady, a veritable fondant on all things cupcake.

Actually the Missus made some before the summer, with butter and eggs. They were very toothsome indeed, although the beetroot and dandelion took a bit of getting used to. Apparently cupcakes are back in fashion big time so perhaps I can persuade the Missus to make some more for you all to share next week in the shop.

Well, by closing time I was flagging a bit and clearly all reason had deserted me. It fell to me to take the bleddy hound down the beach for a run since the Missus was still away. I was keen, too keen, perhaps, to get back for my tea and this is where the story really starts, we cast caution to the winds and took on a devil-may-care air about us.

We could have claimed, I suppose, that we did not realise the time but like Washington, I cannot tell a lie; we did it because we are bad to the core. Or, perhaps, we are just born freedom fighters, striking a blow for common sense and railing against the machine of government and our authoritarian masters. In years to come I expect there will be a statue at the head of Harbour Beach of the two of us, like Robin Hood at the gates of Sherwood Forest, hopefully with me wearing a bush hat and carrying a whip and her with a bandolier striking an heroic pose.

You may ask why all the dramatics and I must tell you in confidence that it was before the 7pm deadline when no dogs should be seen on beaches in these parts. We felt very naughty, the pair of us. She is a little tearaway, you know, and I suppose that makes me a rebel without paws.

September 8th – Thursday

I had the impression that we had thick low cloud and mizzle most of the morning. Of course, I cannot possibly have been right, as most of the cars I saw on my way into PZ did not have any lights on. Surely they cannot all be congenital eejits. Sorry, have I mentioned before that this is one of my bugbears?

Anyway, despite the mist and heavy drizzle it was warm and clammy; I was perspiring at the mere thought of work. Mind you I did not do very much of either today, working or thinking, (but at least I thought to put my headlights on – oops, that just slipped out), at least not in the shop. I spent most of the morning in PZ on one errand or another; in fact I went in to do one errand and ending up doing half a dozen.

The first was to replace the shower head holder that snapped off this morning. The Missus, being quite short, has the shower head bent down, as she fits neatly under it, I, on the other hand, am quite tall and require it to be angled out, as I do not. All this switching it up and down has obviously caused some terminal fatigue and ended with me holding the shower head above me with one hand and trying to wash with the other. It is not my intention to put you gentlemen off your breakfast or to have womenfolk across the globe swooning with the thought of my Adonis-like frame glistening with suds under the cascading water of our shower. It is not that sort of Diary, although if it were readership might improve. No, I merely mean to set in your minds the importance that hangs on the proper operation of the shower head holder, not to mention the shower head itself.

Despite its grave import even the shower head holder was not the initial reason for going to PZ today. I was going anyway to deliver the quarterly paperwork to our accountant. This normally results in me swooning at the end of the month when the regular bribe to Her Majesty's Revenue is due, to stop them hammering on my door in the dark of night.

With the knowledge that I was heading towards a shop that purveyed shower fittings, the Missus promptly issued me with a list of other things to acquire. Chief amongst these was a longer hose that runs from the shower unit to the shower head, as the current one is too short. (Do not even contemplate asking why, as I have already indicated, with the use of an angled shower head, the facility already works efficiently for both of us. I did and was given short shift; why should I need to know why; surely the edict was clear enough? All right, apparently it does not reach the bleddy hound who cowers in the corner of the shower cubicle while being washed.) Add to this a halogen bulb the thousand hours of life of which we have amazingly consumed in less than a month, (where on Earth was the receipt we had with it) and a happy bunch of flowers.

Ah yes, the flowers. A neighbour, wife to he that makes Methuselah look like a teenager, was taken ill during the week, bless her and him for that matter. The flower shop, I have told you about this one before, did a first class job; a brighter and cheerier bunch you could not have contemplated. We think it was well received, although the saffron cake that went with it was probably more welcome. We wish her well, anyway.

Apropos of absolutely nothing at all, a small note in today's newspaper reporting that it is the anniversary of the opening of the first Severn Bridge in 1966, stirred a long distant memory. I recall sitting in a car, in a queue, with my grandfather in the driving seat waiting for one of the last Severn ferries, with the new bridge looming out of the mist above us. (My memory might have added the mist for dramatic effect.) It also demonstrates that while your Diarist may be advancing in years his memory is as sharp as a new pin.

And last, a little Sassoon, born today in 1886, who would, no doubt, berate me for so callously carving out such a short phrase from his poem but something we should all be doing at this time of night.

Falling asleep ... the herons, and the hounds....
September in the darkness; and the world
I've known; all fading past me into peace.

September 9ᵗʰ – Friday

But soft, what light from yonder ministry breaks? It is the east and a cut in VAT the sun. Yes, the Treasury has hinted that a cut in VAT is possible for tourism related industries. As hopeful as I might be, it is likely that this will only extend as far as hotels and restaurants, a model that has been tried in France and Ireland. Quite how they distinguish between a tourist hotel or restaurant and a non-tourist one I cannot imagine but a boost of some sort would be more than welcome.

Certainly more welcome than a Marine Conservation Zone, (MCZ), in the heart of a fishing area, I imagine. This has raised its ugly head again because the Finding Sanctuary project has reached the stage where its recommendations have been sent up to government for comment. They are still clinging to the policy that the decisions on management of the zones will be made after the areas have been designated. I infer from this that they are asking the stakeholders to agree the areas before they know what rules will apply to them but wait, there is more.

It would also appear that an area of sea from, roughly, Zennor in the north to Land's End in the south has already been submitted to our EU masters as a candidate to be a Special Area of Conservation, (SAC), in respect of its reef formations. This is part of the EU Habitats Directive and means that the area has already been designated as a Site of Community Importance, (SCI), which was news to me, and, I would wager, an awful lot of other people. Following so far? Similar to the MCZ it seems that decisions on the management of the SAC will only be made once the EU has ratified it as a SAC but unlike the MCZ there was no stakeholder consultation.

Enter the Marine and Coastal Access Act (2009), which incidentally spawned the Marine Management Organisation (MMO). This little piece of legislation has also demanded that areas of sea are set aside as special areas of conservation that will be called MCZs. Some of these MCZs encompass parts of the pre-existing and proposed SACs while others are completely new. Finding Sanctuary, bless them, have adopted a different approach to the EU and have actually gone around and spoken to people about the creation of these MCZs. It seems they did not have to, so bully for them in that respect. Whether anyone they have spoken to has actually been listened to is another matter; fishermen in generally believe they have been largely ignored.

Finding Sanctuary state that "there is no presumption that any particular human activity will be restricted" in any of the areas but the only MCZ that currently exists, around Lundy, is a no take zone.

It is of no surprise that the fishermen around here are concerned. Large areas of their fishing grounds, areas where they make their living, are being carved up into designated areas either through the EC Habitats Directive or the UK's Marine and Coastal Access Act. Complete uncertainty surrounds the management of both sets of areas and, it seems, that once the areas have been designated, Defra (or someone), will have carte blanche to impose restrictions as they see fit. Imagine a farmer being told half his wheat fields have been designated and he cannot use them any more.

Heavens to Betsy! I hope you found some of that interesting because I waded knee deep through electronic ink to extract all that. It was so gratifying to at last understand how much red tape this government has got rid of. I also hope that I understood as much as I think I did. I am sure someone will put me right if I did not.

Okay, wake up you lot; it is almost time to draw a close to today's Diary page. Was that a collective sigh of relief I heard?

Time for bed, I think.

September 11th – Sunday

This tropical storm is turning out to be more Kittia than Katia despite there being a stiff breeze from which we, in the Cove, are mainly sheltered. It is certainly not the devastating scythe of doom portrayed by the weather forecasters or the newspapers. Still, there's always tomorrow.

Mind you the bay was a dramatic seascape all day. Even at low water this morning the waves were crashing over the footings of Pedn-men-du, with some hopeful looking climbers looking down on it. I think looking at the sea state I would have taken a leaf out of the Marines' book who had taken the day off. They have been here all week leaping off cliffs, running up and down Cove Road carrying old tyres and sand bags and leaving behind them a trail of breathless ladies.

Those crashing waves over Pedn-men-du were even more eye-catching towards evening after it had clouded over. The spray jetting into the air was stark white against the grey sky backdrop. I watched from Harbour Beach where I was trying the throw a ball for the bleddy hound; even three hours after high water there was precious little beach for us to play on. Although not the best vantage point it certainly left this shopkeeper breathless.

The Lifeguards very sensibly red flagged the beach today and not very sensibly two surfers and a canoeist took to the waves. I cannot imagine why surfers would want to go out in it as it did not look very useable and clearly was not as after an hour of bobbing around they came out. I lost sight of the canoeist so he might still be out there.

We had a bunch of cyclists turn up late in the afternoon. A very nice gentleman, (he must have been as he bought a copy of the book), told me that they had cycled in from Northampton, presumably not just today, raising money for their air ambulance and the RNLI. Unfortunately the message had not got through that they were coming and we did not have time to roll out the flags for them. Happily our trusty Press Officer turned up to shake a few hands. Still, they looked like a very pleasant bunch, (even if they all did not buy a book), if a little saddle sore and worn out from pedalling into the wind for the last day and a half.

Now I would give you a little bit of DH Lawrence as he would have been celebrating his birthday today had he lived to be 126. He had connections to hereabouts. Last year I managed to fill a whole day chuntering on about him and his German missus, and at least this year I managed to get the reference in on the right day. But, no, I shall not be offering any of his verses here as they are a bit dower and frankly, if I may be so bold, a little misogynistic. He was a rum old chap. He did have the occasional moment though and I leave you with this.

"Be still when you have nothing to say; when genuine passion moves you, say what you've got to say, and say it hot."

Do you think he is trying to tell me something?

September 12ᵗʰ – Monday

I hear that Torbay is hoping for some support for its plan to sink the Ark Royal in the bay to act as a nature reserve and diving reef. It should also improve surfing waves in selected parts of the area.

Well, what is good for the goose is sauce for the gander and it is high time that Sennen Cove took up the baton, grasped the nettle and picked up the ball and ran with it; *carpe diem* as lake fishermen say. We all know that there will be no shortage of Royal Navy ships available in the near future but I also understand that they might be a bit pricey. On the basis that Sennen probably has not got two ha'pennies to rub together I expect that we will have to be a bit innovative. I suppose we could wait for another ship to forget to hanger starboard at the top of the Traffic Separation Scheme but even that is a bit hit and miss with only two ships failing to make the turn in the last eight years.

No, we need a here and now solution that will not cost us the Earth and I think I may just have the very thing. It was only recently that we discovered that the Head Launcher's punt has a couple of holes in it. Ideal. All we need now is a local hero, a man of fearless spirit, a paragon of noble virtue and a compete idiot to boot to row it out in the bay and pull the plug out.

I am much heartened as to the state of our nation after a chance conversation today. We have a couple of German ladies who come every year at around this time and, although their English is possibly not as good as some, it is far in away better than my German. By necessity our conversations tend not to be too complex and perhaps centre around how busy it has been, local changes and events and, of course, the weather.

I was surprised to learn that the winter in Berlin was long and harsh and that the Rhinelands, an area known for its mild climate, also unusually suffered. What surprised me most was to discover that their transport infrastructure fell apart, just like ours. Buses did not run and, scrunge me gobblers, the Deutsche Bahn train system, that model of German efficiency, ground to a halt. Warms the cockles to think that Britain, for once in a long while, is leading the world.

And lastly I have sadly to report that after a thorough search we have discovered that we have run out of paragons of noble virtue, men of fearless spirit and local heroes. Fortunately we managed to find a complete idiot.

I have to dash now; I have a boat to launch.

September 14ᵗʰ - Wednesday

It is gratifying to note that we have done such a good job on the front of the shop in making it alluring to the most discerning customer that it even attracts shoppers when the blinds are down, the closed sign is up and the door is shut. However, experience has shown that the majority of customers find that they are able to secure their goods in the nine hours and thirty minutes that we are officially open during the slower parts of the season.

Such is our popularity these days that we are getting fan mail through the post. Well, we had a letter in the post but I cannot really claim that it is very fanatical, more cryptic really. If I had just watched one of the psychological thriller films where the victim is plagued by mysterious notes left on steamed up mirrors I might be a little concerned. As it is a folded photograph taken from the top of the western slip and a credit card size RNLI calendar pinned to a corner it is more conundrum than alarming psycho-killer message – I hope. There is not even much of a clue to be garnered from the envelope either, although the writing style is vaguely familiar, the postmark is illegible.

It will have to remain a mystery, for the time being, until I find a bunny boiling on my stove one day. At least then I would be able to narrow the search to about twenty-five possibles. I do not know why you are looking so shocked; I simply meant the number of people I know who dislike the furry creatures.

Twenty-five is also about the same number of people who asked me if the Lifeguards would be opening up the beach today. We are clearly expected to know the ins and outs of a hen's behind. I suggested that they probably would around low water but to expect it to be closed again as the flood tide gathered momentum. I suppose it does not help, that that is exactly what happened, thus 'proving' that we are indeed intimately familiar with that part of a chicken.

September 17ᵗʰ – Saturday

It is 9:15am and I am looking at the Met Office forecast on the Internet. It tells me to expect sunny spells the day long, some rain overnight and another day of sunny spells tomorrow. Radio Pasty has just told me heavy showers are on the way some joining together this afternoon to give us some lengthy periods of persistent rain that will continue into the evening, overnight and well into tomorrow. They have suggested I consider building an Ark. To lend weight to their forecast a blustery shower, somewhat heavy, has just passed through The Cove.

I am sure you are fed up to the back teeth of me harping on about the MO, as indeed am I, but I find it difficult to restrain myself in the face of such buffoonery. How on Earth do they get away with this? I based my weekend orders on their inept forecast. If I put a sign outside my shop saying 'Best Pasties in the Universe Sold by the Sexiest Shopkeeper in Cornwall' Trading Standards would be down on me like a ton of bricks for failing to be honest; let's be fair, there are better pasties than ours.

But who needs a slightly misleading sign outside the door when we have a fair number of visitors for the time of year, despite the showers. I am sure, though, that one of our visitors today is used to much larger numbers of people. I was speaking to his companion unawares of the illustrious company I was in until he turned to join the conversation. He recognised me immediately, of course, from my picture in the newspaper, (did I mention I was in the *Western Morning News*?), and I him from his countless interviews each year as founder of the Glastonbury Music Festival, Mr Michael Eavis, CBE. He assured me my place on the Pyramid Stage was vouched safe at the next festival or, I am sure, would have done if the conversation got round to it. As it was we spoke about Chinese visitors, which was a bit surreal but is clearly the mark of greatness in a man that has rubbed shoulders with the likes of Bono, Neil Young, David Bowie, Paul McCartney and Orinoco.

September 18ᵗʰ – Sunday

I do wonder what goes through people's minds when, on a windy day, they ask if it is always windy here. On a sunny day, if anyone can remember one of those, I really cannot recall anyone asking if it is always sunny down here or even on a rainy day if it is always raining. I mean if it were always windy down here you would think word might have got around. It would not be called Cornwall for a start; it would be called Windyshire or County Gale. Not many people would come here either.

"Shall we go to the Westcountry for a week camping, dear?"

"Yes, all right, but leave out that end bit. Windy as 'ell down there. Never lets up. We'd need three foot tent pegs."

"Oh, yes, I saw a programme about it on the Geography Channel. All the people down there walk around leaning forwards. Shops sell umbrellas already inside out and there's that Newquay they call kiter's capital of the west."

"Yes, and that's how all that tin mining started; couldn't build a mud hut without it blowing flat so they started to dig holes in the ground and found tin and that."

If you really must know the Cairngorms are likely to be the windiest place in Britain. In December 2008 they recorded a wind speed of 194 miles per hour, however the Met Office could not verify it because its equipment was not working properly on that day. If I had to guess I would have said it was a smoke screen, as they had forecast a light breeze. They did manage to record the UK's highest wind speed there in 1986 which was 173 mile per hour. All right, so that is on top of a mountain so you would expect it to be windy so let me assure you that the windiest low altitude place is Fraserburg in Aberdeenshire with 142 miles per hour in 1989. See, both nowhere near Cornwall.

And while we are on the subject, research has shown that Britain is becoming less windy generally. Last year was the least windy since 1824 when records began. The research also shows that it becomes less windy when it is cold too, just when you might expect to need lots of electricity - electricity that is increasingly being generated, (or not), by those large windmills that they insist on building all over the pretty countryside.

So, just let us recap that little soupçon just when we need most electricity, windmills do not work very well. No wonder we need a lot of them.

Anyway, I digress. Where was I? Ah, yes, is it always windy here? No.

Just come in from taking the bleddy hound round for her last run out. That wind nearly took my shirt off.

September 19ᵗʰ – Monday

I had a letter from my bank this morning that, rather worryingly, has got my address wrong. It came via a neighbour who lives at the house where my letter was addressed. It is a copy of a letter that I got from them a couple of weeks ago and that one arrived at my door directly. Whether it was addressed correctly or the postman dynamically adapted because he recognised my name I shall never know as the previous letter has been consigned to the rubbish bin.

Either way it is an irksome thing as it means I must try and contact them again; the first time because the content of the letter demanded some response and this time because they have my address wrong. I have a telephone number to call and I have been informed that it is a special number because I am a special customer. I really do not think they like talking to their special customers though. This special number allows me to enter a maze like telephone system that requires the wits of a Zen Buddhist to negotiate and the patience of Job. I think I would prefer to lose 500 yoke of oxen, have my donkeys carried off by Sabeans, whoever they are, have 7,000 sheep burnt up and 3,000 camels taken by Chaldeans, (from somewhere near St Buryan, I think), than face that telephone system again.

I have a letter drafted and secured in twenty-five nested envelopes that I will send tomorrow. Each envelope has a number on each corner and an instruction to select the appropriate edge to open. The final envelope says there are not any envelopes available at the moment and could they try again later. I hope I have the address right.

September 20ᵗʰ – Tuesday

Never let it be said that I am unresponsive to approaches from The Diary readership. All right, I am generally, but never let it be said. I must tell you that I have been roundly berated by a reader for not pointing out that St Just Cricket Club were playing in the Barbados Cockspur Club T20 semi-final at Chelmsford against Ealing yesterday. I would have thought it preferable that it was not mentioned, as the comedy was all Ealing's. Apparently Neil Curnow lofted to long-on in the third over, whereas Mark George was promoted but failed to get bat on ball, which is odd because he hit a six – with what if not his bat - only to find his 18 came off 32 balls. There was some upping of tempo and some running out at the non-strikers' end too that I am sure was very exciting but not sufficient to secure a win.

And with that description ringing in your ears I expect never to be asked to comment on cricket ever again.

September 21st – Wednesday

The Aged Parents took to their feet and headed off to Land's End. They even took the bleddy hound or, probably more accurately, vice versa. This was even more poignant since they have studiously avoided dogs their lives long, well at least mother has. She came back suitably worn out and so did my father and the dog.

Another weekend and another surf competition. This one is at Praa Sands organised by a bit of a wag, (old meaning, at least I do not think he is the partner of a footballer), seemingly, as this is the World Championship of Crap Surfing. The poet Murray Lachlan Young, a self confessed, ahem, bad surfer, and his equally unskilled compatriots longed for the thrill of a surfing competition that they could join in with so they organised their own. The winner, across several categories, some of which I could not possibly repeat in such in polite company, will go to the person who displays the most effort and is still awful. Additional prizes will go to most genuinely upset loser, best wipe-out and worst wetsuit among others. Sounds right up my street especially if I did not have to get into the water, I could win laziest surfer.

My turn to take the bleddy hound out for a run down on the Harbour Beach tonight. The oar weed is a major problem down there, piled up in geet heaps. Fortunately the sea, even in the sheltered confines of the Harbour, is no place for little dogs to be swimming tonight. There is enough of a strip of sand at the top end of the beach to throw her ball and have her chase up and down. All this careful planning and consideration, however, is for nought. The bleddy hound chases the ball twice then, contemplating her busy day, casts a look of utter contempt at the ball thrower, me, and ball in mouth trots up the slip in the direction of home. And you wonder why I call her the bleddy hound.

She will have less time from now on for 'tis the autumn, sorry southern hemisphere readers, September equinox and our days will be shortening henceforth. Look out all, here comes the long darkness.

September 22nd - Thursday

Top of the news today is the threatened closure of a tortoise sanctuary near Liskeard. It is an issue that has been in the national press so I will not spend too much time elaborating. The whole issue pivots on whether the tortoise is a wild animal or not – grrrr. Anyone in an organisation with tight resources and a mandate to save money and with half a glimmer of common sense would have found themselves an expert who would swear blind that the tortoise was a domestic pet and thus save any further action and expense. I shall say no more than The much maligned council has dived in with both feet, the full force of the law and its attendant costs having come down on the side of the wild animal decision. Enough said, perhaps.

It puts me in mind of an old school teacher of mine; she taught us.

While you digest that I shall tell you we had another half decent day again today and again there were many people floating about. Today they seemed a little more reticent to part with their hard earned shillings. It is also very rare for us to have a visit by people from the home of the socially ill-prepared and the land of those blessed with little brain and as welcome as a Truro wind farm. These young blackhearts thought it highly amusing to launch one of our lightweight balls down the street. They left it to their father to replace it and provide an apology, for which I was grateful and somewhat surprised. I was surprised again by their temerity when they returned to use the shop for its proper purpose. It was then that the words of a dear but sadly departed sage rang in my ears, "smile and take the money." So I did.

Talking of being grateful I am exactly that to one Diary reader whose information has permitted me to remove my hair shirt and my two sizes too small thong, (I could not find a cilice for love nor money). My perfect pasties fell short of the mark a couple of days ago as my taters went floury on me. My informant and saviour has reliably enlightened me that some purportedly waxy potatoes grown during a dry season will do exactly what happened to me. So there you go, not my fault, reputation still intact and I can hold up my head again at the next meeting of the brotherhood of champion pasty makers. I imagine my voice will return to its normal baritone after a few days.

And so to Lifeboat training where no lifeboats were launched but we did clean the fabled bell. It may not be fabled yet but if we ring it often enough when the Lifeboat comes into view it will be fabled one day, I am sure.

We shall make sure our doors are firmly bolted tonight lest any of those wild tortoises escape and ravish us in the night.

September 23rd – Friday

Being as it was so nice today I decided to have a look at it from other places too. We have been running on existing stock for some while and sorely needed a top up. This means a trip up to Hayle, a Philp's pasty, without doubt, and a run around the cash and carry warehouse.

Philp's was heaving when I got there with a queue stretching out of the door. As ever it is well worth the wait and I also managed to cadge a parking space overlooking South Quay. Several of the small fishing boats there were just heading out. It is the first time in nearly twenty years of going there that I have seen The Pioneer, PZ 277, leave her mooring.

The Pioneer is a fine fishing boat with 'Dandy' rig of fore, mizzen and jib sails. Built at St Ives in 1903 for line, trawl and net fishing she is around 30 feet long with a central box cabin. She was originally owned by Henry Hendy of Penzance and skippered by him for at least 40 years, changing ownership several times. She was converted to motor at some point which is probably as well as she is too long to turn in the moorings and has to exit to the channel aft first.

We are under caution that a geet satellite, the size of a double decker bus, is heading our way tonight in a downwards kind of direction. NASA's game plan is that whatever does not get burnt up by the atmosphere on re-entry will splash into the western Pacific. However they admit there is a small chance of it coming down over that part of the western Pacific called Cornwall instead and an even smaller chance it will land on someone's head; probably about the same chance of getting run over by a double decker bus in these parts. Nevertheless I cast caution to the winds and went off down the OS for a spot of music wearing my tin hat, just in case.

The band did not bother turning up and as I certainly did not go down there for the cheap beer and legendary customer care, I came home.

On reflection a bit of satellite falling on my (protected) head would have been a bit more entertaining.

September 24ᵗʰ - Saturday

It is not often I find myself in agreement with the Government, or for that matter many figures that believe they are in authority over us. It was therefore something of a surprise to find that a group of MPs have roundly criticised the pub industry for failing to regulate itself properly. We have seen, at peak, 52 pubs a week closing, a figure that has now dropped to 14, probably on the basis that there is not many left to close. Chief among their concerns are the large pub companies that demand 'sky high' rents and control which drinks the pub sells and the prices they charge. That sounds kind of familiar but I cannot imagine whom they might be talking about.

The MPs and other supporters are calling for a "Pub Tsar" to step in and crack the whip with these naughty brewers. As shy and retiring as I am, according to a couple of readers, I really ought to put my hand up for this one. I can wear a funny woolly hat as well as the next man and I am very familiar with the pub trade, having spend around two thirds of my life in a cross section of them. The only fly in this pint of beer is the sticky end a lot of tsars seem to come to. I have no wish to find myself looking down the wrong end of a barrel or even a firkin in some dingy cellar.

Talking of authorities, The much maligned council has put in a fresh bid for £16m to complete an east-west link road through Redruth, Pool and Camborne. The project is highly commendable and seeks to complement the regeneration of those areas. Having been told that their original bid was too high, the council managed to reduce their first estimate from £44.5m by removing all the exit slipways from the project; their consultation process showed no one wanted to get off the road there.

And we should not forget that it is F Scott Fitzgerald's birthday today. He was born in 1896 and his name conjures up images of spats, posh cars with white wall tyres, (or should that be tires), speakeasies and smoky blues bars. Oddly, after eulogising him so, you know, I do not think I have even one of his records.

And what a gift of a link that is to my next subject which, of course, is a night at the F&L where Big Scott is singing, fronting his band Blues Connection. Not only is he a gentleman of prodigious girth, hence his nomenclature, but he is also blessed with a voice particularly suited to belting out blues numbers. His main advantage on this occasion is that he turned up.

I had to trot up to the top myself tonight as the Missus has a touch of woman flu. It is like man flu but obviously not as bad. With this in mind it was down to me to run the bleddy hound down the beach this evening. I cast caution to the dog warden's wind and ran her down a little before curfew ended. There is still a proliferation of oar weed down there and a scattering of fish remains; it was the devil's own job to keep her mind on the ball. I found myself having to toss various crab bits over the short slip between ball throws. It is certain that I covered more beach than she did trying to anticipate her every move. I have to admire her sense of selection. She was down at the water's edge picking at something big. When I got there it was the squashed, football sized head of a monkfish. You wait until I find out which fisherman that was.

Anyway, where was I? Ah yes, up at the F&L, that's where I was. Mr Big Scott and not Fitzgerald at that; Blues, rock, funk and quite an all round superb musical evening. And then I made the big mistake of paying attention to the MO forecast that said it would not rain tonight and elected not to take a coat. Boy, did I get wet getting home.

It was lovely.

September 25th – Sunday

We had a visit today from M who, I can only guess for her own disillusionment, reads the Diary every day, poor girl. I suppose it is a more ladylike version of wearing a hair shirt. Anyway she had come on a pilgrimage to the home of the Diary and to throw a few coins in our wishing well, which we call a till. She asked if we did Miles tea that she was convinced was from

Cornwall and which is readily available in St Ives apparently. I introduced her to our Tregothnan tea, grown here in Cornwall. I would be interested to hear how it measures up to Miles'.

I did say that I would investigate the Miles tea, as I had never heard of it. I am sorry M, the stuff comes from Somerset and is blended there from teas across the globe, most of the globe that is except Cornwall. I realise that this may be a further disillusionment for which, as a regular reader, you are probably becoming inured. However, I am sure you are right in that it is a perfectly fine tasting tea.

Being as I was confined to barracks I missed attending the Lifeboat exercise this afternoon. From what I could see my compatriots in the very excellent Shore Crew struggled through without me - the dogs. They could at least have soothed my hurt feelings by making it look like they had a bit of trouble.

No sooner had the big boat come in from the exercise than the little boat went out on a shout. Running up to high water the sea had quite a swell and then, one hour before high water, the swell seemed to settle but no more than half an hour after that the swell was back with something of a vengeance. One of the two canoeists, apparently a novice and instructor, that went out during the quiet time was caught out when the swell came back. The Inshore recovered the party but the other refused any help and did not want to come back in with the ILB.

I slipped down to the beach with the bleddy hound again tonight, it would seem mainly for her to admire today's piscine selection. I got a small soaking for my trouble as the promised rain sent in an advance party of one quick, heavy shower.

Talking of soakings I think this groaning and bent old shopkeeper is in for an early bath tonight. He is fair puffed out.

September 27th - Tuesday

I have just heard the latest weather forecast on Radio Pasty explaining that the good people of this country should expect some rather nice weather. How lovely, oh, except the far west of Cornwall and the Isles of Scilly. It was not just the once either. That last refrain was repeated for each day of the forecast through to the weekend.

It seems a little unfair to be singled out in this way. Imagine if it was always like that.

In the beginning God created the heaven and the earth, except for the far west of Cornwall and the Isles of Scilly. The lights are going out all over Europe, except in the far west of Cornwall and the Isles of Scilly where it happens on a regular basis anyway. Veni, vidi, vici, except for the far west of Cornwall and the Isles of Scilly. We shall fight them on the beaches … we will never surrender, except the far west of Cornwall and the Isles of Scilly.

To make matters worse it was very quiet today. I imagine people just could not find us in the fog. Adding insult to injury the wind went round to the south east and freshened making things very chilly. Just when you think it could not get any worse the ex-neighbour dropped in and asked what it had been like here all day. I, of course, told him it had been sunny and hot and he, of course, did not believe me. He had been in Hayle all day under a blazing sun. He was on his way back to his new home in St Just where I hope rain and sleet fall in abundance tonight. No bad feelings, of course.

September 28th - Wednesday

A youth of the parish arrived at the shop this morning for a little tuck. I felt it my social duty to ask why he was not at school today to which he replied he was on a school trip. I was minded to suggest that a school trip that delivered him to his doorstep was not much of a trip, especially as he was going to meet the other trippers here and therefore not a trip at all. Instead I asked what he was likely to learn from such an excursion. He told me that it was a geography trip and that they were to go surfing. Casting aside the fact that the sea was as flat as a dish today, I wondered what geographical nuggets of an educational nature could be extracted from driving from Cape Cornwall to Sennen Cove and taking to the sea on a surf board.

"All right, Robbins and Clarke, paddle out there. Now, what can you see Clarke?"

"Cliffs, sir."

"Very good Clarke. What sort of cliffs, Clarke?"

"Granite cliffs, sir."

"Right, Robbins but I didn't ask you, did I boy? All right, Robbins – watch out for that right hand break – very good, now what sort of rock is granite?"

"Hard, sir."

"Thank you, Clarke. When I want your opinion, Clarke, I will write my invitation on a cricket bat and hit you with it."

"Sedimentary, sir."

"Nice try, Robbins, but wrong. Anyone else? Nice hang ten there Ellis. Yes Ellis, I just caught that as you rushed by. Igneous, quite right. Ooh, bad luck Ellis. Yes, I'm sure it hurts. Yes, Clarke, we all know where Ellis's board hit him. And yes if they were called rocks I expect it would have been quite an amusing quip, Clarke. As it is, it is more likely you have them between your ears, boy."

No, I just cannot see that working.

In fact I spoke to the little herbert as he returned from his edifying experience and asked what he had learned today. "Nuffink. We just done surfing." Well, zackly.

And lastly it looks like the weed in the Harbour has eventually gone. I am not sure, as it was dark down there when I took the bleddy hound down for her last run. It would be rather nice if it has; we are only a couple of days off her being allowed down there during daylight hours. I know how much you must have missed the repetitive Diary pages endlessly documenting walks along the beach. Ah, those halcyon days.

September 29th – Thursday

As they say, it is a small world. There was a very pleasant couple in this morning. I watched, trying not to look too interested, as they admired the shapely form of the book of The Cove Diary. It took some wiles to convince them that their lives were incomplete without a copy of the book, poor souls. It was at this point that I learnt that they live where, for the most part, I grew up, if fact in the same road. I also learnt that my old alma mater, (if you can call a reform school that), has been half demolished, the familiar features of the watchtowers and the barbed wire removed. It has been taken over by a Swedish company that intends to turn it into an academy. How very grand, I thought. Then I thought it probably will not remain grand for long, if the same sort of hooligans that went there when I did, still go there today.

The little bit of our small world that I found myself in this morning was another wonder to behold. There was some mist around, clinging to the cliffs and the valley but this slowly moved away giving us an even better day than yesterday. There was a bit more of a swell around too today, although it looked deceptively calm, waves were fair thumping up Aire Point even at low water.

Talking of bold visions we were treated to an unusual sight at low water today. Our highly respected and clearly versatile, if not flexible, Lifeboat coxswain made an appearance, dressed in a dry suit, at the end of the long slip this afternoon. Nothing unusual about that you might think. But wait, watching closely you could see him twisting and turning, was that a fine pirouette? The finely tuned routine certainly appeared to be a series of dance moves. We believed that it was only a rumour that he had been invited to join the BBC's new programme, Strictly Come Dancing Underwater but now we have seen this we are not so sure. I shall ask him directly tonight but I expect he'll try and front it out by saying he was moving boulders off the bottom of the slipway, or something equally unbelievable.

September 30th – Friday

The last day in September and how on Earth did we get here so quickly. From tomorrow the whole street will be lined with parked cars, the beaches awash with hounds and the weather will improve dramatically.

Quite by chance this morning I bumped into a fellow who was off to see a man about a moth. Not just any moth I should have you know. This beast is a Dark Mottled Willow, I think, a rarity in these parts, in fact a rarity in Britain. I knew exactly who he was going to see, of course. I might have mentioned before we have a resident naturalist in The Cove who is an authority on just about anything with legs and quite a few things without legs too. Among his areas of expertise are moths that he captures, and kindly, releases after studying them.

Well that was all very interesting, I am sure, if you are a lepidopterist. What I did not realise is that news of this rare find had been posted on notice boards across the country and hundreds of avid fans had jumped into their butterfly-mobiles to come and get a glimpse of this beauty. Allegedly.

Sorry, did I just say beauty? Due to the expected deluge into The Cove our naturalist had the stunning good plan that this holy grail of moths should be displayed in The Old Boathouse, for the delectation of the arriving hordes. Our man arrived with a Perspex box, a very small Perspex box, with a bit of egg carton in it. In fact at first glance it was just a bit of egg carton. It took the application of my glasses and an almost painful squint to establish that there was a living beast within. It was about the size of an average house fly and brown in colour.

I am sorry. I would defy the combined wit and wordsmithery of Boswell, Johnson and Wordsworth to come up with a more interesting description than that. It is possibly the most ordinary thing I have seen and lives in such abundance in its home territories, that it is regarded a pest for doing unspeakable things to golf courses.

By half past five we had precisely two visitors wishing to see the moth. We have been instructed to release it into the wild after dark lest the sparrows get it. I imagine it must be the equivalent of a white truffle in the British bird world. We might drive over to Cape to find somewhere comfortable for it's reintroduction to the wild; next to the golf course, perhaps.

October 1st – Saturday

A rather large mini bus pulled up outside the shop late in the afternoon. It was full of jolly chaps, or perhaps more accurately merry chaps, from the Round Table somewhere up country. Their exit from the van was preceded by a case or two of empty beer cans and a green cloud. Apparently they were doing a Lifeboat challenge in aid of the RNLI, visiting every Lifeboat station in the UK and Ireland. I looked up this challenge on the Round Table website and it says that the challenge is to visit all the stations in 112 days, ending in March 2011. Given that it is now October, I rather think they may have got lost or extended the challenge to include all the pubs between the stations. Good luck to them.

I am a bit concerned about the Missus. At this time of year television schedules are scrutinised, recordings set and my ability to talk at leisure severely curtailed. It was me tonight that noticed that the television recorder was not running and the Missus, oblivious in the kitchen. For 'tis the season for Strictly Come Dancing and the Missus has demonstrated the attention of a goldfish with dementia. I know she was unwell last week but this just will not do. Next week I can only hope I will be complaining bitterly how I have been rudely ignored, I cannot watch Panorama and sequined leotards are hanging where my shirts should be.

So that is it, goodnight.

What do you mean you want to hear about the weekly trip to the F&L for a serious band night? It was only last week you were complaining that it was so routine that it had become boring.

So, no, I will not tell you that the rather loud *Sinpusher* were playing a spot on set including numbers from Mr Hendrix and The Who. I will not reveal that the night was rocking so much that ordinary punters were getting up to sing extracts, albeit from the wrong song, into the momentarily unattended microphone.

And I certainly will not expound on the vision of spangled heavens shining forth with myriad gleaming diamonds on my walk home, the sight of which would turn a simple boy's soul to jelly.

October 2ⁿᵈ – Sunday

Well, bladder my ghastlies, dear reader, I think I may have run out of rip gripping superlatives for such a day as this; a day where the sun shone incessantly; where people came flocking to the seaside from the corners of the known universe and St Buryan; where all the girls wore things that their grannies would not approve of, especially on a Sunday; a day where certain things that have been put off for far too long needed to be done.

The first thing that needed to be done was to explain to a Spaniard where the Men-an-Tol was. We have an Ordinance Survey map onto which we have marked various places of interest such as Men-an-Tol and Lanyon Quoit for just this purpose. I showed our visitor just where it was on the moor and the footpath that leads to it. Unfortunately this was not enough for our man, he wanted me to write down on his postcard the name of the place where it was. For those of you unfamiliar with the location of these prehistoric lumps of granite, they are on a bit of desolate moor between the parishes of Morvah and Madron. I tried in vane to tell him there was not a 'place' that I could write down that would help him but he was having none of it. What really finished me off was when he asked for the Men-an-Tol postcode to put into his satellite navigation system.

It must have been a day for grand meetings down here. In the morning we had a group of vintage motorcycle enthusiasts. I was going to mention a few motorcycle names like the 1961 Bantam that chugged in but to be honest I am a little nervous of doing so. You see there is a reader who came out of the closet a little while ago who is known locally as BP. He lived here once but now lives up country. He visited today and bought a couple of books, clearly an extremely nice and discerning chap, but unfortunately I was not in the shop to meet him. What I did notice is that he departed on a rather big motorcycle and I would venture that he is a bit of an expert. So you see if I start reeling off motorcycle names and get one wrong I am very likely to be taken to task. Best I just say they were old bikes and have done.

I know that I told you last year about the three marathon challenge. I think they start from Padstow and run three marathons over three days and end up at Land's End. We were blessed with them again this year thundering through The Cove followed by those hobbling through The Cove. As invigorating as that might be it certainly does not appear on my need to be done list.

I have always lived by the adage never to do today what I could quite feasibly put off until tomorrow. Unfortunately this particular task could not wait that long, else I would have to wait a very long time to try again. The Missus and I have tried this before and nearly met with disaster or, at the very least, embarrassment. It is an adventure that requires the perfect alignment of natural forces. It is, of course, to walk from Sennen to Gwenver across the beach, a walk that can only be completed at spring tide low water and only the very big springs at that.

To be honest I thought I might have missed my opportunity as the spring tides are diminishing, so to give myself the best chance I left to coincide being at Escalls Vean beach at dead low water, which today was half past three.

The top end of Sennen Beach was packed when we, the bleddy hound and I, got there. It was as close as we will ever get to knowing what it is like down on the beach in August, I suspect. Fortunately with the tide out so far there was plenty of room to let her off the lead without facing the danger of her seeking out and tucking in to someone's picnic. After the first twenty yards or so it became clear that wearing flip flops was not going to work, as the sand under the strap was doing a passable job of sanding the skin off my feet. She and I went bare foot, (and paw), together and I have to say I felt a certain freedom unshod. I had the smallest inkling that I could, to some degree, understand the naturists' way of life, unfettered by the bonds of clothing. Fear not, dear reader, there is a chasm between understanding and meeting a strong desire to rip all my clothes off. The sight of my bare legs alone is enough to send small children screaming and mothers swooning.

Anyway I digress, slightly. The long and the short of it is that there was sufficient gap to make it through to Gwenver and return. Then there was time to sit, while the bleddy hound dug a geet hole in the sand to bury her ball in, and come home across the expanse of beach under a warming sun, and dally a while to paddle a bit. I think that's the first time my feet have been dipped in the wet stuff out there for some years. How shameful and how bleddy cold must it be at other times of the year.

I tripped off to St Just a little before closing to gather up a bit of Chinese grub for our tea. The sun was beginning to set in a gathering haze. What an 'ansum sight to behold, with everything turning golden and a long sheen of sun on the sea. We are definitely long in the season now, as the sun is setting well behind Pedn-men-du as you head down the hill.

All in all I cannot for a long time remember such a fine day in The Cove for getting things done.

October 3ʳᵈ – Monday

There's absolutely no need to be rummaging around in the dark corners of my mind for some superlatives to describe today's weather. There was a small hint last night when some particularly thick and wet fog crept in after dark. I had resigned myself to a foggy day anyway, but there was a cruel twist this morning. As I looked out at first light we had the makings of a fine day. The first half of the morning was rather pleasant and again I made the mistake of revelling in the news that Penzance was cloaked. Then the curtains came down.

At least today we will not have too many access issues in The Cove. I was going to mention this yesterday but then I thought of other things to witter on about. A chance meeting with our local rozzer brought back to mind the hellish trouble we had yesterday, with a line of cars parked from the OS down to the bus turning restrictions. With half an ounce of common sense a few gaps could have been left to let traffic pass in both directions. As it was cars were parked end to end including across access roads and people's driveways.

It does not happen very often, but with October half term holiday looming we shall probably see more of the same. It will, no doubt, be raised at this Friday's Parish Council meeting. A recourse open to them will be to mark out some additional keep clear zones along the road, to force some passing spaces. If that does not happen I can see some local lads out with their paint brushes one dark night, doing it for them.

If we thought we had some bad fog here during the day, you should have seen it over St Just. For the second time in two days I found myself venturing forth in that direction, to our trusty butcher, Mr Olds. It took the use of some cunning navigation skills just to find the place; the fog was thicker than granny's thermal knickers.

We have not had a bit of a poem for a while and just by chance poor old William Morris poddled off today in 1896, apparently he did a good line in wallpaper too.

Come, shoulder to shoulder ere Earth grows older!
The Cause spreads over land and sea;
Now the world shaketh, and fear awaketh,
And joy at last for thee and me.

I wish I had found some of his wallpaper now, I rather think it would have been a sight more interesting.

October 4th – Tuesday

Well that is all right then. I thought for a while there we might be in serious trouble, but I need not have worried. Never mind that the tourist industry might collapse in a heap without a little help, the Chancellor is ploughing £150m into mobile telephone masts. It is heartening to note that when I am evicted from my home and living in a field in the middle of nowhere, I will still be able to text my great auntie Gertie, to ask her how her lumbago is.

All has become clear, I think. We had some cameras here last week filming down on the quay and around the fishing sheds. There is a possible explanation in the paper today, that help for our threatened fishing fleet may well be coming from a very unexpected quarter. A lawyer from Greenpeace is doing a tour of small fishing villages across West Cornwall asking what they would say to the fisheries minister, Richard Benyon. As you might expect from our venerable fishermen there are some succinct quotes, surprisingly all of them publishable, or at least the published ones were. The most telling is, "Nature regulates us. Weather is our control and a harsh one." The unnamed spokesman went on to say that with a 15 feet boat and a fishing radius of three miles, the idea of quotas on these boats is crazy and unmanageable. Well said that man!

At least the lady from Greenpeace had some decent weather to undertake her research. Today we were teased with some early blue sky before some cloud came over and by afternoon the fog was back. No wonder the in-laws spirited away the Missus to go shopping.

Oh yes, I did not mention the in-laws were here, did I? And very nice it is to see them and their wagon train of baggage. I have not asked how long they are staying this time, why should I? They are, of course, welcome to stay as long as they like because it is such a joy to have them here. And did I also mention that the mother-in-law has started reading The Diary?

I had to leave for cards night down the OS a good half an hour earlier than usual. Obviously, I would have preferred to stay to watch EastCorrienders Farm with them all but they would have none of it. Naturally I could not give cards my full attention while I worried how they might be doing without me, so I lost miserably.

Taking the bleddy hound around tonight reminded me that the toilets in the Harbour car park have become an inconvenience. A customer alerted me to the fact that, despite a notice warning customers that the toilets will close at the end of October, they have already been barred and locked. It is as well he told me, as I have been sending nervous looking customers in that direction all week. The council must be saving a penny or two but, for some reason, they have seen fit to leave the lights on.

October 5ᵗʰ - Wednesday

It turned distinctly chillier today which was probably why my new beer fridge arrived today. I was getting increasingly frustrated by having to move my beer from the fridge downstairs to upstairs in ones and twos, to avoid using up all the space in the food fridge. Then, of course, I would forget and either have warm beer or have to traipse downstairs to get it. I could feel the empathy from you bubbling up through the Internet as I wrote that.

Now all I have is the problem of getting rid of the old beer fridge. This has a glass front and I can just see the scrutineers at the rubbish dump, sorry, household waste recycling centre, getting a bit uppity about it being a commercial fridge, which it is not. The very nice chaps who collected the last refrigerator said that they are worth a few bob now, if I wished to take it to a scrap merchant, because of the price of steel. I really do not know if that is allowed though, either legally or morally. Since the tip, sorry, household waste recycling centre is on the way to the scrap merchants they have one chance to convince me to leave it with them.

At least there I will be speaking to human beings, without being held interminably in a queue.

My home contents insurer wrote to me in the middle of last month, telling me that my payment method was no longer valid and could I contact them to change it. The policy expired last month sometime and it is only now that I have had the time and inclination, mostly inclination, to do something about it.

I was very much delighted when I telephoned them, selected the option for 'accounts' and got through to a human voice straight away. Three cheers for you, I thought, and might even have said something to the agent, they like to be called agents, you know, like three cheers for you for answering the telephone and not keeping me waiting interminably in a queue. It was when

I told him why I was calling, he told me I needed to talk to 'renewals' instead and that he would transfer me.

I am sure, dear reader, you are way ahead of me and can see that, yes, I joined a queue for 'renewals' and had to wait for an agent to become free to answer my call. Eventually I spoke to a very nice chap, who said he could not find my details on his computer, and perhaps if I gave him the vehicle registration number that might help. I said that I very much doubted it, as I did not think my van was covered by my contents insurance, mainly because I find it difficult to get it up the stairs. He said that it was not and that I should be talking to someone in contents insurance rather than motor insurance, to which I said that I thought I was. He promised faithfully to transfer me to the correct person.

I had much time to consider the value I held for this company as I inched my way forward on yet another queue that promised me that my custom was very much valued. You know, I was starting to doubt their sincerity.

When the third person to whom I spoke said that I needed to speak to 'accounts' and if you are still awake, dear reader, that was the first department that I spoke to, I became somewhat agitated. He tried in vain to placate me with wild promises of action and remedy and said that he would call ahead to make sure that the person I spoke to next, was indeed the correct person. He put me on hold for a minute or two then spoke to me again. He apologised profusely and said that he had not yet been able to speak to the next agent as he was held in a queue.

I put the telephone down on him.

After that I was minded to see what other companies on the insurance market could frustrate me more. I decided not to use one of the comparison websites, as I am still getting about thirty unsolicited emails a week from the last time I did. I went directly to the website of a company chosen at random and completed their online form. I did not imagine that the premium would be much less and it was not. I also was not prepared for the telephone to ring twenty seconds after I pressed the 'get a quote' button, with a chap asking me how my experience was filling out their web form and could he help. I might telephone them tomorrow and see how quick they are off the mark when I call them.

You would think that after all that trauma and stress I would have been deserving of a little rest and relaxation, would you not? It was at this point I was told that the Missus was taking the in-laws out.

I understand that they do a fair dinner at Trevaskis Farm, I would not know, of course, as I have never been. When they came back, the Missus and the in-laws told me they still do a fair dinner at Trevaskis Farm and the shopping in Truro was good fun too. Then they told me they were far too full up to want any tea and, by the way, what was I going to have? Even the bleddy hound had her tea organised for her and she had not run the shop all afternoon.

Oh, yes, that tea and sympathy is just oozing through the wires. I can feel it.

October 6ᵗʰ - Thursday

I am sitting in the van eating my very excellent Philp's pasty and looking out over South Quay in Hayle. I do not want to offend anyone but it is a tip and not a household waste recycling centre at that, although I can see some household waste over there. There is no doubt that it is historic; big ships used to come in here and dock and it was once a centre of industry and bustling with activity.

There is a proposal to build a supermarket on the site, houses and other facilities too. The plan includes reviving the sluice that will improve navigation of the Hayle River channel and help preserve the sand on Hayle beach. For once it is not supermarket led. All right it is a supermarket, but it is not exactly out of town and the whole project is part of a well-considered regeneration of Hayle, certainly at Foundry end. It is not a panacea and not everyone's cup of tea, but on balance the advantages are thought to outweigh the disadvantages. The other offers on the table are for supermarkets at either end of town and they do not include the additional benefits, unless you count the football team getting a new pitch.

Why then would English Heritage, who consider the supermarket to be too large, want to scupper the whole thing by sticking their size nine boot in, threatening to strip Cornwall of its World Heritage Site status? Perhaps a desolate waste tip is a thing of beauty in some eyes. If so they will not have long to wait until there is an even bigger wasteland from Foundry to Loggans Moor.

So let me step down from my soapbox and tell you that it was my turn to venture forth today, in case you had not already guessed. I had such joyous things to do such as dump the old beer fridge and go to the cash and carry. Once again the very good chaps at the tip, sorry, household waste recycling centre, did not bat an eye when I turned up in my obviously commercial vehicle. They did not even ask to see my little card with six spaces on the back for their official stamp and they even unloaded the fridge for me. At this rate I will never win the free prize for collecting all six tokens.

It was a very windy picture that greeted me coming back down the hill into The Cove. The bay was filled with white-capped waves and a fair floshing of white water over the footings of Pedn-men-du. It has rather scotched the hopes of the in-laws who wanted some crab and lobster this morning, but it is at least real, manly weather unlike that girly stuff we had over the weekend.

We shall skip briefly over Lifeboat training tonight as you would not launch a kite in this weather let alone a big expensive Lifeboat, except in an emergency obviously, but I cannot think of any emergencies that demand the launch of a kite.

So it is onto the quiz at the OS where the Head Launcher's team made a valiant effort to become first – along with two other teams. We then promptly lost on the tie break. One of our number was then lucky enough to draw the winning ticket in the 'chase the ace' raffle, then promptly screwed it up by choosing the wrong card!

Do not think I will bother doing the lottery this weekend.

And then to end, a bit of Tennyson who popped off today in 1892 and then only so I can squeeze in an extremely poor pun.

On either side the river lie
Long fields of barley and of rye,
That clothe the wold and meet the sky;
And thro' the field the road runs by
To many-tower'd Camelot;
And up and down the people go,

Gazing where the lilies blow
Round an island there below,
The island of Shalott.

No more today, I think. That is shalott.

October 7th - Friday

There was a howlin' and a grindin' of teeth overnight. Well, a howling anyway, the teeth might have been mine. That wind was not so much strong but definitely in the wrong quarter for us, straight in from the nor' west. I have not been able to put my flags out this morning and it has already taken the lid off my carefully crafted ball stand.

There is some good news, for some at least, that I feel I should update you with. The much maligned council voted thirteen to six to be 'minded to agree' the Hayle, South Quay development proposed by ING, the harbour owners. The real decision needs now to go to the Secretary of State who will have to take into account English Heritage objections. Anything could happen, but it would be deeply disappointing if South Quay is a desolate wasteland for another 40 years and I don't even live there.

Then there is £2m for Jubilee Pool, £500,000 for a water sports centre on Albert Pier in Penzance and £2.3m for a treatment centre at West Cornwall hospital. Recesssion? What recession?

And why, you might ask, dear reader, have I spent two days harping on about Hayle? Well, I went there for one, and secondly it is, near enough, the family seat. When I say family seat think three legged milking stool in a rusty shed. And last, doings in The Cove over the last few days have been about as exciting as watching a Last of The Summer Wine box set with the repeat button on. I really should not have written that. I went to put my feet up around midday and you will never guess what the father-in-law had on the television.

We passed the time in the afternoon counting the tumbleweed as it rumbled across the front of the shop. Even taking the bleddy hound down to the Harbour beach was a welcome break from thinking up names for the pasty crumbs in the bottom of the warmer.

An early night, I think. I have to face the trauma of the in-laws leaving tomorrow and one interesting and one crucial rugby match to consider.

October 9th - Sunday - 1897

There was a bit of a stir up at Land's End today. I heard about it off Constable Ellis who was there when it all 'appened, so 'ee should know.

'Ee said there was this chap from up country with this bleddy geet contraption with four wheels on it. Looked a bit queer for a carriage and was stuck right in the way up there. Anyway the superintendent up there got a bit upset with it, what with all the crowds gatherin' an' that, and summoned up Constable Ellis to sort the whole thing out.

So Constable Ellis comes along and asks the gentlemen where his 'osses was and the chap said didn't need any as he already had four under his bonnet. Well, you know how Constable Ellis gets when he thinks someone is trying to pull one over on him, so 'ee says *'ees* got a steam engine under *'is* helmet and if the good gentlemen didn't want to spend the night in Penzance nick he'd better get 'is 'osses out from under 'is hat and get them hitched up quick, like.

The gent gets a bit agitated then and tells Constable Ellis that what 'ees sitting in is one of they new autocar jobs, called a Daimler with a Mulliner body what he designed 'isself. It don't need no 'osses and has some sort of engine inside it, the same as four 'osses. I can't see that being right. It would have to carry some lump of coal with it.

Anyway the gent asks Constable Ellis, 'ow would 'ee get to John O'Groats from here. Constable Ellis is getting a bit hot under the collar by now and tells the gent 'ees never heard of this chap John, let alone where 'ee lives and 'ees lived 'ere 40 odd years, man and boy. 'Ee did say he knew that there was an O'Mally working on Bolitho's farm and it sounded like it might be something to do with 'ee.

Our gent tells Constable Ellis that it's a place in Scotland and how 'ee intends to drive there in 'is motor car to prove to the world how reliable and sturdy they are. Well, I'm sure I don't need to tell 'ee how Constable Ellis took that. 'Ee says if the gentlemen wanted to know about places in Scotland 'ee should ask a Scotsman and there weren't too many of they around 'ere, but seeing how there was only one road out of Land's End, perhaps it would be a good start to follow it and ask again when 'ee got the other side of Lanson.

Constable Ellis said to me 'ee looked ever so determined and 'ee thinks 'ee just might do it. Anyway I had a shilling with Constable Ellis that 'ee won't get no further than Redruth. It wasn't until after 'ee took the bet I reminded Constable Ellis there in't no petrol stations yet.

* * *

Henry Sturmey did complete the journey from Land's End to John O'Groats, the first to do so, even without petrol stations. The 929 mile journey took him ten days to complete and he started off today in 1897. Sales of his Daimler motor car reached 89 the following year on the back of his promotional run. However he is best remembered for his collaboration with James Archer, for inventing the Sturmey-Archer three-speed gear drum for bicycles. I had one on my bicycle when I was a young teenager.

What an education it is reading The Sennen Cove Diary.

October 10th - Monday

All quiet on the western seafront again today. Heavy dark clouds with patchy mizzle make for a very grey day indeed. We are just marking time now until the half term week and our last week of opening.

So with beggar all happening in the shop and a nice big empty beach to play with, it seemed only right to take the bleddy hound down for a long jog across the sand. Well, more of a fast stroll than a jog, really. So there I was with knapsack and ball thrower all stowed and ready to take off when our neighbours from up the back turned up. Whenever they are down they take her out from time to time. It is most useful when we are busy and very often they go for miles and miles. So that left me all revved up and nowhere to go, as Mr Meatloaf would have it.

Not quite so revved up is the circus that hit town with their flyers and money off vouchers ahead of the big top event this week, cash only, of course. They were due to entertain us all in Penzance but word on the street is that the show has been cancelled. Their website shows nothing about the Penzance venue and their ticket hotline has gone a bit cold.

From what I hear those naughty clowns are to blame for dipping their hands in the till and nicking all the dosh from the last event. Police apparently found size 23 footprints by the safe and officials have been left with red noses after hearing a loud bang, and finding the thieves' getaway car in pieces on the road. Identikit pictures have been distributed and people have been told to look out for several very white men of medium size, large red noses, bowler hats with a flower sticking out and big baggy trousers. The public have been urged not to tackle the men who are believed to be armed with custard pies and extremely funny.

I do realise that this probably was not very amusing for the circus, so I do apologise, but please try and understand that this suffering Diarist needs all the help he can get at the moment.

The circus was not the only thing all washed up. A lady came running up to the shop this afternoon to report a baby seal on the Harbour beach. I gave her the number of the seal sanctuary at Gweek and she went away quite happy. I went down to have a little peek but it seemed the animal was up in the corner by the steps leading up to the wall; that far up it was unlikely to get out on the impending high water. Giving them their due, a maid from the sanctuary was here within the hour to sort it out. Nice shiny pelt coat she was wearing.

I must away now perchance to dream. I am glad I do not have coulrophobia else my dreams might turn to nightmares – clowns in seal skins coats walking around on the beach.

Sleep tight, children.

October 12th – Wednesday

The bleddy hound has been looking a bit nervous over the last couple of days. She keeps looking over her shoulder and leaps up at the slightest sound. Unusually she is avoiding the kitchen, particularly when I find it necessary to sharpen my big carving knife. She has also started to behave irrationally, barking and snarling at the television. It only seems to be when certain cookery programmes are on that feature the celebrity chef, Huge Leafy Wherewithall. I cannot imagine that she has read the newspaper report that the chef, who was highly successful in his campaign to promote sustainable fish, has suggested that, in principle, he has no objection to a "high-welfare organic puppy farm".

I felt a bit silly taking the bleddy hound out last thing. She has taken to wearing a long macintosh, dark glasses and a trilby hat and is walking about on her hind legs.

October 13ᵗʰ – Thursday

I got Scotland and Devon mixed up this morning. I was very confused. This in itself is probably not unusual, some might claim, as my demeanour is oft akin to that of the gently bewildered; 'twas the fog that was at the root of it all.

A regular customer noted that we might well be lost; cut off from the world so thick was the mist. My immediate response was Brigadoon and in my mind I had some mist covered moor in Devon. That, of course, was Lorna Doone, a completely different kettle of kedgeree altogether; Brigadoon was some mist covered moor in Scotland.

Then, of course, came the argument of who was in it, Brigadoon at first, and it was suggested Ned Kelly, or was that Nelson Eddy, I cannot quite remember. We all know that it was Gene Kelly, Van Johnson and Cyd Charisse, whoever he was. Nelson was Rose Marie, not to be confused with Rosalie, the Mounties and all that. You must see that we were entirely lost.

Thankfully the mist rose, gathered, regrouped, parted, made another approach, thinned, thickened, lifted and fell. Eventually it hung off in the environs of St Just, as it will, before returning for a reprise later in the day. Gosh it was ever so exciting guessing what it would do next, and very pretty watching it swirl.

I will not bore you with what is fast becoming a daily occurrence with the bleddy hound. Suffice to say the beach was a bit of a damp facsimile of what it was the past couple of days but with loads more surfers.

Now, I would not pretend that I know much about surfing other than it is, apparently, very bad for the hips. But when you are sitting on the beach and surfers start coming out of the dunes behind you as if out of nowhere you have to believe that the surf is good and must be enjoyed, despite the danger to your hips.

And then there was the Lifeboat exercise launch. There were sufficient of us to launch both boats into the fog, probably never to be seen again. Launching the little boat was a trial in itself as the beach is once again piled high with oar weed. The trial was mostly coping with the flies that have made the rotting seaweed their home. Within a couple of minutes of being down there the tractor was covered and I had to move it up the slip after the launch so that I would not be eaten alive when I went back to it.

By an amazing stroke of luck both boats made it back to the station. We put this down to the very excellent Shore Crew holding vigil with lanterns strategically placed at the end of the slipway. This was only made possible by the same dedicated crew spending hours on hand and knees clearing the weed from the said slip.

With duty done we marshalled our strength enough to play a rough game of quiz at the OS. It is demoralising to believe that there are other teams out there capable of cheating better than we, but it must be true as we lost miserably. We should point out to any potential quiz participants that we consider this sort of behaviour ungentlemanly, to say the least, and should be left to professional ungentlemen, such as Head Launcher and me.

October 14th - Friday

I mentioned a little while ago that the toilets in the Harbour car park have been closed. The sign still says that they are open until the end of October, which would have been convenient to cater for the increased population during half-term week. With little else to do I telephoned the council to ask the reason for the closure.

I can accept that if they are trying to save money closing the toilets early is not the end of the world. However an explanatory note would not have gone amiss and, after all, someone had to come and lock the gate so they could have pinned one up. It is also irksome that if economy is at the root of it, why leave the lights burning all night?

I would have telephoned the correct department but their website was not at all forthcoming about which department looks after public loos. A very polite young lady answered my initial call at the general enquiries desk and, unable to find out immediately the cause, transferred me to the correct person. At least she would have done if the correct person was not in a meeting. I left my number with an assistant to the correct person and received a promise that I would get a call back.

It is gone half past three so the council will have gone home by now and no call back. I assume it is part of the cut backs; efficiency and customer service just has to go. Of course it could be that they are still sulking after having their plans for a waste incinerator at St Dennis overturned at the High Court this week.

The boys from Falmouth Divers were here for most of the day for the bi-annual polishing of the Lifeboat channel markers. They made a satisfactory dent in my pasty supply for which I was very grateful. I have to say they look very spruce and shiny after their efforts, the channel markers, not the pasties, although they look pretty good too. We will have to see how many channel markers are left after the winter storms, but for the foreseeable future the sea state looks rather calm. I think there is a plan to give them a test drive this weekend.

A bit off the beaten track this one and rather more off the beaten track than First Group, the bus and train people, would have liked too it seems. The company has come in for a bit of stick for their latest advertising campaign, visit Dartmouth by train; a highly commendable promotion you would think. Certainly until you appreciate that the nearest First Group serviced station is six miles away and even that is on a branch line.

Still, it could have been worse; take a bus to sunny Sennen Cove and use the free toilets.

October 17ᵗʰ – Monday

Phew! That was hard work; pushing against quite a chilly southwesterly coming back over the beach. Oh, darn it. I spoiled the surprise. I was going to have a competition in today's page,

"Guess what I and the bleddy hound did today?" The winner would get a free copy of the book. Yes, I know second place gets two copies of the book. Still, it is not going to happen now.

The doom mongers have said that we will be getting power cuts before too long, when demand outstrips supply. I have to tell you that it might not be the only reason why the nation will be plunged into frozen darkness.

A chance conversation with some pals at the F&L on Saturday night sort of suggested I was paying three times the amount that they were for electricity. Seeing as they both have much bigger properties than I do, someone is making a lot of extra money out of me for nothing. As my supplier is the, currently, cheapest according to market observers, I could only assume it is because I have that money pit of a system, Economy 7 electricity and old storage heaters. Either that or the Lifeboat station is running off a spur or I have leaky wires.

For those of you unfamiliar with Economy 7, it is an excuse for the power company to pretend to supply you with cheap electricity overnight to charge up the radiators, while hiking up the normal electricity rate to compensate.

This wake up call has sent me scurrying to the Internet to seek out a solution to my dire circumstance. I had previously heard of a type of storage radiator, manufactured in Germany, that operates on normal electricity and is super efficient. My in depth research has discovered one company in Cornwall that will provide a complete service, disposing of the old heavy lumps of iron and installing the new and another company up t'north that will supply the radiators and leave me to do the installation. Naturally there is a dichotomy in pricing and, naturally, the do it yourself option is the most attractive on the grounds that I might just be able to afford to do it.

So that will be me, a screwdriver, lots of electric type wires and a couple of trips to the tip, sorry, household waste recycling centre. I will let you know when I start work to give you some time to get some candles in. When your lights start to dim and flicker off it probably is not the forces of supply and demand at fault. There is probably a little blackened shopkeeper with a bunch of wires in hand and a surprised look on his face at the end of it.

It looks like it might be a very cold winter this year.

October 18ᵗʰ - Tuesday

My Brigadoon lady was in again today. She travels a bit and today the conversation turned to Whitstable. There must be something about her, or at least the subjects she chooses to discuss, as I had another blinding flash of recognition. We agreed that Whitstable has a connection with oysters, which was right on subject as the Falmouth Oyster Festival has just ended. However I was minded that there was also a connection to Dickens that I just could not quite put my finger on. To add to the dilemma she also said that a major pub chain, that has the habit of converting old cinemas and other public buildings, has a hostelry there, called the Peter Cushing.

I refuse to be drawn this time though. I shall have to start calling my shop lady Lorna after Lorna Doone given the amount of grief it gave last time. Our friend in Winnipeg reminded me that it was Exmoor where she caused all the strife and heartache and partly Somerset, rather than the completely Devonian Dartmoor that I probably had in mind.

I think I am become somewhat obsessed with the project to replace our electric heaters. I have spent an inordinate amount of time researching just what we should do for the best. I have discovered, however, that our German radiators might not be all they have been hyped up to be. On the basis that all electric heaters are 100 percent efficient, it is unlikely that these can be any better than cheaper models. Similar to the advice of not to go shopping when you are hungry, choosing heaters should not be done when it has started to get cold.

I think I shall repair to the OS for a game of cards where it will, no doubt, be sweltering and make the decision from there.

In the meanwhile the bleddy hound made her position perfectly clear. She is just as bored with her trips down to the beach as the rest of you are. We were half way across when she stopped and looked at me. I asked her what the problem was and her response was to walk in the opposite direction, towards home and with her ball in her mouth, I had no choice but to follow. Well it was a tad chilly down there, the wind whistling down from the west; it is likely to be whistling through our door tomorrow.

And while I hate to admit my mental failings, which I am sure are legion, Dickens had absolutely nothing to do with Whitstable, though, apparently they do hold Peter Cushing walks in the town; he retired there, don't you know. I will not elaborate lest I have Whitstabolians on my case and, let us face it, I would not want to be shucked by a Whitstable oysterman; those knives are terribly sharp.

October 19ᵗʰ – Wednesday

What an auspicious day it turned out to be. It is a day that will go down in, erm, famy?

It certainly was not because of the weather. That turned out to be a bit showery and the wind was biting cold too. It is getting a little more difficult to maintain a stiff upper lip in my shorts and flip flops, although if you could have found some shelter, it would have been quite warm in the sunshine.

Nor was it that my bank manager came to visit with a man from his insurance branch. Needless to say they were here to relieve me of some more of my hard earned shillings, but hopefully less than I am paying now for my insurance. It is part of an important cycle, as I am sure the bank will want to lend it out as soon as possible to budding industries across the land. Anyway his attendance was quite timely as it permitted me to bend his ear.

Yesterday, along with my credit card machine bill, I received a notice that the machine can be switched to using the broadband connection. I have been hankering after this for some while, as it will make the card transactions almost instantaneous and save queuing up at the till. I made some enquiries about how we might implement this system and discovered that the blighters want to charge me £25 for setting it up, and a further £50 per year for "maintaining" my pre-authorisation key. The £25 I might just about have swallowed as someone at their end needs to kick off the process. However, "maintaining" the pre-authorisation key requires absolutely no human intervention; it is worse than money for old rope, especially as the machine is only used for eight months of the year. At least if you have parted with money for old rope, you have some old rope to show for your trouble.

I got a call from the bank manager later in the day after his promised enquiries with the card machine supplier, which is part of the bank. As I imagined he was not able to sway them. So if you are in the queue in the shop, as a string of people wade through the credit card machine process, you can shake your fist in the general direction of my bank, or me I suppose if you think I am just being too tight.

Not even the appearance of two nuns of the Franciscan order, I think, since they were wearing brown, meets today's necessary criteria for being auspicious. These two are annual visitors at this time of year and, judging from their ancient appearance, they were founder members of the order. This, of course, gives me carte blanche to mention my entire repertoire of nun, habit and wimple jokes. Fortunately for you I cannot recall any at present and I am keen to reveal the big news of the day.

All right, I shall hold you in suspense only moments longer, while I explain that I received a telephone call this afternoon to tell me that a rather special little girl has given birth to a special little girl of her own. What makes this even more special, is that the caller was my sister and the new mother is my niece. That makes me a great uncle, which is the first time I have been a great anything, other than a great lummox and also, rather amusingly, makes my sister a granny. I should be somewhat gentle in explaining that the Aged Parents are now, of course, Aged Great Grandparents. Interestingly, for us anyway, my sister thought that the date held some family significance. She telephoned back some while later to tell me that today was my late grandfather's birthday too, a man that I have always held in high regard despite, or perhaps because of, me being only six when he popped off.

So Happy Birthday Ellie Mae, (which might be Mary Jane or Doris Gertrude by the christening); one day you will understand that only very special people have their birthday telegraphed around the globe and then in an eminent publication such as The Sennen Cove Diary at that.

(All right, it's not that eminent, but small children are easily impressed.)

October 20th - Thursday

A couple of Cornish MPs have been having a pop at the proposed Marine Conservation Zones, bless them. They say that many are inappropriate and fail to strike a balance between social, economic and sustainable protection factors. They exemplified their argument with Falmouth, that is trying to attract large liners into the port and Cape Bank, where sustainable fishing would have to stop. You can just see them now, can you not, trilling their hearts out to rows and rows of empty seats and a couple of old codgers snoring in the back, while all the main players are at lunch. The Environment Minister, Mr Benyon, responded that ministers themselves would examine all the evidence, (put forward by the conservationists, incidentally), before deciding which sites go forward for public consultation.

Well, thank heavens for that. For a moment there I thought we were in trouble.

With all this good sense prevailing it was of no surprise that The much maligned council agreed the building of a Sainsbury's supermarket on the Scilly's helicopter site. That will be three within walking distance of each other. Clearly the £1.9 million that Sainsbury's were offering in local benefits had no bearing on the decision. They promise to create 400 jobs too, probably employing the 400 lost in the town centre.

One of the benefits Mr Sainsbury is paying for is a subsidy for off season town centre parking, which will be interesting. You might remember that central government handed out bags of cash to councils to help fill in pot holes that had appeared in the big freeze last year. The much maligned council saw fit to divert this cash to ease its car park deficit, preferring to leave pot holes alone until first quarter next year. Well, if the forecast is right, there will only be more pot holes by then.

All right, let us see if you have been paying attention. Hands up all those that think car park charges will go down after Sainsbury's is built. Yup, me too. It will not matter anyway, as you will not be able to get to the car parks for the pot holes in the roads and there is unlikely to be anything left to park there for.

I tripped out to Hayle for a spot of corporate shopping, after all we will be deluged next week with happy holiday makers keen to enjoy the howling wind and lashing rain. If British International Helicopters think they will have a clear run at their new site at St Erth they might be wise to tread carefully. There are huge banners all along the A30 there, telling them otherwise. Unfortunately they do not seem to have the odd couple of million to bribe the council with ... gosh, I am sorry, I think there is a problem with my keyboard. That should have read ... the odd couple of million to provide some additional community benefits with their proposal.

Back on safer ground I can tell you that after a bit of a Lifeboat training session we repaired to the OS to maintain our losing streak at the Thursday quiz. By some amazing stroke of good fortune we managed to uphold our miserable reputations in that regard.

It is a bit of a shame as I was saving up to complete my master plan of building a supermarket on the Harbour car park. The main building would have sufficient roof space for a heliport and if we concrete over the Cowloes, (let us face it when it is an MCZ the fishermen will not be able to fish there anyway), there should be enough car parking spaces, at least at low water.

I have, of course, factored in some community benefits that will see my proposal go through on the nod. All planning committee members will have free shopping for life, and any household within ten metres of the development will be able to rent ear defenders at a preferential rate. Job done.

October 21ˢᵗ - *Friday*

I have been trying to get to the bottom of this since last week. The Harbour car park toilets remain closed, which is hardly a convenience. I had left a message with the council for someone to return my call, which they have not. I should have called back earlier in the week but it was a news item today that spurred me into action.

My enquiries today reveal that I have spent a week waiting on the wrong man to call me back. The right man, naturally, was not available today, so it is unlikely that we shall see any action in the toilet department before the end of the half term, by which time it will be too late.

Oh yes, the news item. The much maligned council has announced the closure of approximately half of their 247 public loos to save in the order of £1.1 million. They are rather hoping that the parish and town councils will feel duty bound to pick up the bowl and run with it.

When the unitary authority was formed it was always stated that the parish and town councils would take on more responsibilities. When the unitary authority was formed, the parish and town councils always thought that taking on more responsibility would mean being handed the dirty end of the stick.

We are all aware that council tax is frozen, but at parish and town level the precept can still be raised. If I were a cynic, which thank heavens I am not, I might suggest that services are being passed down to a level where tax can be raised to cover them. At county level they can all sit around looking smug at all the cut backs they have made without effecting services.

We had some rather unsavoury pictures of Mr Gaddafi's demise on the front covers of the newspapers today. Neither eight independent editors nor I considered the impact of this. During the school holidays many small children are sent to collect the morning goods, including the daily press for their parents. Fortunately there are not that many small children about at the minute, but some did turn up with their grandmother this morning. It was not until I heard the grandmother trying to explain that they should take no notice, that it sunk home.

There have been times throughout the year when I have had to refuse to sell newspapers to minors as there has been an age-restricted movie enclosed. We are also asked to place certain mainstream magazines, with scantily clad ladies on the front cover, behind more innocuous titles. I would warrant the images on the front pages today were far more severe than anything in a PG, or even 18 film, and carry more impact than a lady in a bikini.

Gosh, that was all a bit serious. I will try and lighten the mood tomorrow.

October 22nd - Saturday

Our young visiting dog walker is back in town and the bleddy hound has been dragged from her pit every two hours today. With any luck she'll forget to bring her back one day.

I did not see the Missus for most of the day either. She was indulging herself in a little deep cleaning of the flat ahead of our own visitors arriving tomorrow. I have not mentioned this previously, on the grounds that I might have imagined it, or perhaps in the hope that they all found better things to do. There is still time, of course, but it does look rather likely that they will, indeed, turn up.

Yes, tomorrow I shall be beset with five females, six if you include the bleddy hound. Teenager is returning along with Big Sis, Friend and, for a shorter stay God help me, Mother. The alehouse and my bed will be my only refuge and my only succour for a week, away from the relentless chatter and personal abuse I shall, no doubt, suffer. In fact the alehouse as a bolt hole will be short lived; Big Sis and Friend are fast approaching the age when they will be able to fray my nerves there too.

October 23rd - Sunday

At around lunchtime the visitors arrived. I picked the wrong weekend to give up drinking. Mother had driven a considerable distance and claimed she was tired after the journey. She said she was lost for words. She was not. Fortunately it was busy in the shop and I managed to cling on to working, as an excuse for being somewhere else. I even managed a trip up to Shrew House for replenishment stock that was running thin. Once again it was a nightmare trying to get from one end of The Cove to the other, with cars parked with gay abandon along the road.

I must say I had not realised just how peaceful, (only in terms of the weather), a haven The Cove was today. Up at Shrew House it was breezy, but nothing much to write home about. It was not until travellers, (people that travel as opposed to the cultural group that do not), started coming into The Cove with tales of woe from the south coast that the severity of the blast became apparent. Large waves were spilling over Penzance

Promenade, and at Praa Sands wind had brought down a power cable cutting off electricity to the café.

Hold on to your hats, the wind is veering round to the northwest before it dies off. It could be our turn tomorrow.

October 24ᵗʰ – Monday

A very Italian feel to this morning: it was unseasonably warm; walking the bleddy hound felt very much like standing in the Trevi Fountain and there were three teenagers in my bed first thing. I should point out that I was downstairs working at the time, in case there are accusations of impropriety.

There was plenty of warning for the rain we were having today. We did not get a particularly heavy downpour but it was persistent. They said we would get a month's worth of rain in a single day, but they did not specify which month. Nevertheless the Missus felt it worthwhile to get geared up in her waterproof togs and take the bleddy hound down to the beach. I would have gone myself, although I do not know how much fun it would have been in shorts and flip flops.

Certainly a lot more fun than it was in the shop in the afternoon, that is for sure. We had a little flurry of activity late in the morning where, thankfully, all the bread and pasties disappeared but after that nothing; zilch; nadda; begger all. It took boredom to a whole new level and I think I read all the newspapers cover to cover, then progressed to *The Beano*, *Sparkle* and *Barbie*; that Ken is a bit of a boy, is he not? Even the news that the Tamar Bridge, (the new one), is fifty years old today could not inspire me to any delight.

Did you know that there is widespread concern that Himalayan yak herders are deserting their traditional role and instead gathering wild Cordyceps sinesis, a caterpillar originating fungus that sells for £50,000 a kilo? It has aphrodisiacal and health properties, apparently. No one would have noticed, except the herders are all sporting new American made bows and arrows and the women started turning up at market with Gucci shopping bags.

A little closer to home, Aldeburgh in Suffolk is to start fining people for feeding gulls. They dismissed a cull as too extreme and might make a worse mess of the seafront than the feeders.

Peter Aldous, the area's MP is to lead a parliamentary debate on 'Seagulls in Coastal Towns' this coming Wednesday. I imagine it will be riveting and will doubtless result in gulls being handed ASBOs, or being told they have not got planning permission to roost at the seaside, and being evicted.

We had a little gull plague of our own when the rain eased this afternoon. Hundreds of them gathered along the sea wall and eventually settled on the sea, close in. Our resident naturalist said that there were little black maggot type creatures down there that they were feeding on. He did not know what they were either.

The Missus took the visitors, minus Mother who went home this morning, off to the big city to indulge in a little light evening shopping and a visit to Pizza Shed.

They were gone for ages, which gave me enough time to indulge in a little squid cleaning; one of our friendly fishermen dropped by a few on his way through this morning. Cleaning involves gripping the slack leggy bit behind the eyes, twisting and with a sharp tug pulling the entrails out, hopefully without piercing the ink sacks. Having stripped the skin and fins away from the mantle, a cunning manoeuvre with the thumb on the base turns it inside out so that the inside can be cleaned. The larger ones were sliced up for rings, while the baby will be presented whole. Enjoying our breakfast are we?

Of course this whole Diary entry could have been condensed into fewer words. Got wet walking the dog, got bored senseless and read all the newspapers, watched some gulls and dissected some cephalopods. What a life!

If you do not hear from me for a while do not be too alarmed. I shall be off doing a spot of yak herding in the Himalayas for the winter and I am not entirely sure they have broadband.

October 25ᵗʰ - Tuesday

An all together better day today. While big splashes of rain fell on Penzance, Sennen Cove basked in the sunshine with only a light smattering of the wet stuff. Boy, were we busy because of it. It was like everyone was held back by a big elastic band yesterday and the sunny weather let them go with a big ping.

They must be a big fishy bunch too. Our fish orders have taken off in the last few days with squid top of the menu. I expect by the end of the week I will be sick of the sight of them.

Bristol University claim that due to global warming and the seas warming up, (did they try a dip this year?), stocks of previously little seen species are increasing. They have reached their conclusions by looking at landing data from the last twenty years. Among the species they mention are hake, gurnard, john dory and lemon sole. One seasoned fisherman has lambasted their findings as poppycock. Hake has been plentiful for more than 100 years, with most of it going abroad until recently. Gurnard was predominantly used as crab bait and not listed on landing figures. Fishermen used to exchange it, barter style, at the harbour with the crabbers. Thanks to celebrity chefs, it is now back in favour for eating and is landed, (and recorded), in numbers. Lemon sole was avoided too, until the European market was exploited. Lies, damned lies and statistics spring to mind. Some of these boys and girls will be running the country in a few years; heaven help us. Education is a wonderful thing but no match for experience and wisdom.

We best end with this, lest they be forgotten, as it was today 157 years ago it happened. The architects of the calamity were probably from the same stock as the lot counting fish.

When can their glory fade?
O the wild charge they made!
All the world wonder'd.
Honour the charge they made!
Honour the Light Brigade,
Noble six hundred!

October 26ᵗʰ - Wednesday

I have such a short memory. I had quite forgotten that The Old Boathouse has child care responsibilities. One parent took this to a whole new level by actually leaving his small ward in the shop. I had expected this to be one of those, 'I'll teach you a lesson' jobs, but he was gone long enough to suggest he was not coming back. Eventually the toddler had the same idea too and went in search of his runaway guardian.

We were just sighing combined relief when the mother returned with yet more offspring. These were permitted to run around the shop unsupervised, while mother perused the shelves on her own mission. It is so nice to see the summer traditions maintained. There is hope though, on the news this evening it was reported that the average global childbirth rate has fallen from five to two and a half.

Talking of surplus offspring, Big Sis and Friend managed to extract themselves from our sofas in front of daytime television to drag the bleddy hound down to the beach. There was plenty of it too. A large spring tide has opened out a big beach looking resplendent in the sunshine and packed with other dog walkers, surf lovers and ordinary walking folk.

The Missus took all the abundant visiting offspring on, what I was led to believe, a PZ shopping trip. It was not until a neighbour came in and taunted me about ladies being let loose in St Michael's, and we are not talking of the Mount here, that I realised that I had been hoodwinked as there is not a store with that association in PZ. When they had not returned by tea time, I telephoned to enquire what resolution they had in mind to ease my grumbling tummy. I was told that Big Sis was to cook this evening. When I responded that by that time I would be a withered pile of rags on the floor, Teenager, who had answered my call, told me to have a biscuit to tide me over. My insistence that a single biscuit was hardly likely to head off my early demise she told me to have two. She is sharp, that one, I have to admit.

Tea, when I eventually had it, was eminently palatable but by the time it was delivered I would have eaten a scabby donkey. No offence, of course, to superintendents of scabby donkey sanctuaries, I am sure they are just as edible as the non scabby ones.

In the later evening the living room was turned into a beauty salon, with hair being curled left right and centre. I was excluded from this enterprise, most certainly because nature has already adorned me with stunning good looks and absolutely nothing to do with the fact I have no hair. When they started painting their nails I skulked off to bed. I do have nails and they are far better in nature's hue and I wished them to remain that way.

October 27ᵗʰ - Thursday

An ideal morning for going to St Ives. The rain was lashing down first thing and a chilly blow from the northwest straight in the shop door. Fortunately we were one of the first to see it clear but that wind hung in there for the rest of the day.

Going to St Ives was exactly what the Missus, Teenager, Big Sis and Friend did via a dinner at Trevaskis Farm, Connor Downs. When they left, mid morning, the rain seemed to have largely stopped here but it was very likely to be largely falling on St Ives. As it was it came back with a vengeance here but there is no need to tell them that, is there dear readers? I said, is there dear readers?

We have had a 'lost c-a-t' notice in our window for a few days, possibly a week now. Sorry I cannot say the word out loud else the bleddy hound will go mad; she hates c-a-t-s. The story on the radio did not immediately trigger any recognition, and it was not until the cat, (oops), owner's husband came into the shop that I made the connection. It was eventually found up the chimney of a nearby holiday let and I am assuming that it was not the smell of singed fur that led to the discovery. However it would not come out for the owners, the fire brigade or the RSPCA. Crickey, all that lot for a cat! The bleddy hound would have had it out in a trice, albeit through the chimney pot. I have it on good authority that it has now been recovered and has had its paws glued to the floor. For the benefit of cat lovers everywhere that last bit was a joke; everyone knows six inch nails are much more effective.

And talking of cruelty to small animals, the cull of grey squirrels in the area goes on unabated. If you want to know the background to the cull you are going to have to buy a copy of the book, available on the website and all good bookshops that have been duped into stocking a copy. Oh, come on, winter's coming and a poor shopkeeper has to keep himself in beer and, well, beer really.

Anyway, I digress. Where was I? Ah yes, squirrels. The cull has had no shortage of volunteers, apparently. This has led to a surfeit of dead squirrel, which I am sure the local tip, sorry household recycling centre, will not allow in their pristine bins. Enterprising butchers from the locality have not been slow in capitalising on the situation and are now offering squirrel meat. Apparently, due to their diet of nuts and berries the meat is strong and flavoursome. I think the meat needs a name to disguise its source, much like venison draws our minds to Bambie. Perhaps skarol might suit if, like me, you are familiar with its Greek epithet, (another Internet Smart Alec – did you know there was a 1951 pornographic film called that, ahem, so I read), and no, nutkin really would not be a good idea. Come March it's skarol for my prize winning St Piran's Day pasty competition entry.

I would rather not go into the detail arising from tonight's OS quiz. They changed the rules down there and far too many people seemed to have adopted the Head Launcher method of game play. We apply cunning; they all cheated.

October 28ᵗʰ – Friday

All right, hang onto your hats, here come the superlatives. What a rip-strippling stonker of slib gribbling sort of day. The sun rose into a clear blue sky. I know because I saw it climb up there and shine splendour all around and down onto a crystal sea, with just enough waves to make surfing and body boarding worthwhile.

The acreage of golden sands was too much for a poor boy to bear and Teenager, me and the bleddy hound grabbed a few essentials and headed down there, just in time for low water. I have never been that close to a tide that low before; there were a few hundred yards between North Rocks and the nearest waves. Had I been on my own I probably would not have ventured far beyond Escalls Vean beach, but Teenager spurred us on into Gwenver and further to two huge sand bars that stretched out deep into the bay. We were able to walk all the way up to Aire Point.

I telephoned Big Sis from there as I promised we would wave when we got there. Unfortunately my mobile telephone lacked sufficient signal for a quality connection. The first mobile telephone call was made from a car in Cheshire to London today in 1959. Fifty two years later and I am struggling to make a call over a mile from Gwenver to Sennen. That is progress.

Still on Gwenver, but closer in, there was a large rock pool the size of a small swimming pool and probably around four feet deep. Teenager threw the ball to the far side and it landed above rocks just covered by the water. The bleddy hound duly plunged in and hauled herself up on the shallow rocks to retrieve the ball, then promptly decided she could not dive back in with the ball in her mouth. It took some cajoling and not a small amount of bravery on her part to overcome her concern and slip back into the deeper water and back to us.

It was warm and exceedingly pleasant down there, and coming back home took as much mental cajoling as it took the bleddy hound earlier. It is hard to believe that only yesterday we were in the grip of a wintry blast.

I thought I would spend some time on the beach in today's page. After all the shop closes in another two days from now and you need to become accustomed to day after day of walking the bleddy hound on the beach. You will love it, you know you will.

With the house full of voracious and should I say selective teenagers, cooking for ourselves has now gone out of vogue. First up on the eating out stakes was Trewellard Meadery. As I said earlier in the month it is wholesome food and apparently teenager friendly. Twice in the month was a little much for me, but it was worthwhile to demonstrate my dexterity at being able to catch a pickled beetroot, tossed into my lap by Big Sis, before it besmirched my attire.

Later in the meal Teenager managed to covertly slip me her glacé cherry; I hate glacé cherries. I suspect a conspiracy. I only have to survive another three days before they are packed off home. I shall be watching my back, I can tell you.

October 30th – Sunday

Well here we are at the end of the line with pages and pages of walking the bleddy hound on the beach or hither and thither in prospect for you lucky readers. Even the weather will cease to be important.

It did turn out to be the longest last day in history, thanks to the clocks going back last night and my body clock still stuck in yesterday's time frame. We did not do too badly in reducing the stock that will be out of date by Christmas, our next opening time. I think our worst mis-order was the number of saffron cakes we had left. Still, with some cunning use of a fine black pen to change the label and a sharp knife to scrape off the green bits we might just get away with it; it has worked loads of times before. I am only joshing with you, of course. It is far too difficult to remove the packaging to scrape the green bits off, so we usually leave them on and say they are herbs.

Ouch, did I use the C word in that last paragraph? At least I did not use it in September, which was the first festive advertisement I saw selling bookings in West Country hotels. No doubt it will be upon us in the blink of an eye. Ho, ruddy, ho … humbug.

In the morning we had a nice big patch of blue above us, although there was a fair amount of mist around. The sea was huge and the spray hung over the bay making it look even more misty. As the afternoon drew on the weather fell apart with thick fog creeping in, then mizzle and by the end of the afternoon some heavy rain. It was dark too. The last few hours of opening were completely miserable and a pretty much fitting end to a distinctly average year.

The girls are going home tomorrow and Mother turned up around closing. It is Halloween tomorrow after all. She was just in time, as we had agreed earlier that we would feast on a Chinese meal tonight. I was going to trip over to St Just, but a chance conversation with one of our very few customers reminded me that it is St Just Feast today and the place would be a vision of Bedlam. Teenager came with me to Penzance through the lashing rain and patchy fog. The whistling in my ear 'ole is beginning to abate now, just in time for it to be chewed off by Mother.

I shall miss them all dearly, I am sure.

October 31ˢᵗ – Monday

I did not reckon with Mother standing behind me chattering away in my ear 'ole while I tried to complete the Diary this morning. She did say that she liked being woken up by the sea in the morning. I shall remember that next time and throw a bucket of it into her.

I thought some natural justice had been meted out to me this morning. The early bus broke down, completely blocking the road out of The Cove. It looked for a while like the girls might have to stay an extra day. Then just as I had given up hope, the driver managed to get it going and moved into position at the bus stop, where it promptly broke down again. All would have been well, except someone had parked on the keep clear sign opposite and the road was still blocked. Fortunately the support vehicle turned up and pushed the bus back out of the way and the girls were off.

Being a Monday and bin day the big bus event caused some upset. The domestic bin collection lorry was trapped at the harbour end while this excitement played out. The bin lorry that empties our commercial bin could not get through, so we are left with an uncollected shop bin. This normally would not be an issue as at this time of year we only half fill it; we could skip a week and not notice. This, however, was to be our last collection for a while and I had intended to suspend collections from today.

Cove in winter

It was with heavy heart that I telephoned the bin company to resolve our dilemma. You just know that it would not be as simple as not charging us this week, have a collection next week then suspend the service thereafter. It was even worse than I imagined. They said that it was going to be as simple as not charging me for this week, making the collection next week and suspending the service thereafter. You just know that when they say it is going to be as simple as not charging me for this week, making the collection next week and suspending the service thereafter, they are going to get it unbelievably wrong. I am really not looking forward to my next bill and the ensuing confusion, explaining how they charged for both weeks and forgot to suspend my collection.

And now for the bit you have all really been waiting for. Yes, I took the bleddy hound down to the big beach. On a huge expanse of sand there were perhaps half a dozen other people and it was pleasantly mild today too. We even managed to get down there, run around and back again before the rain set in. What joy!

In the afternoon we did absolutely nothing, other than cook the tea, just because we can. If it were not for the bus breaking down it would have been a very short entry indeed.

Gosh, I am going to have to find something even more exciting tomorrow now that I have raised your expectations.

November 1ˢᵗ – Tuesday

Oh what a beautiful morning, oh, what a beautiful day. Rogers and Hammersmith must have been thinking about Sennen Cove on a morning such as this when they wrote those lines – well one of them was anyway.

The sea still has some swell left in it and is putting on a darned good show in the morning sunlight, crashing over the wall, dancing on Cowloe and climbing up Aire Point and the cliffs at Nanjulian. I know this because I booked the van in for some work and had to get up at the crack of dawn to take it in.

The dial that controls the heating in the van has been stiff since we acquired the van some years ago. Both the Missus and I have struggled with the stiff knob, playing with it until it eventually works. It was a little before the summer season started that while I was pulling at it I heard a bit of a twang from the guts of the machine rendering the stiff knob limp and useless. The Missus was most put out but since we rarely use it during the summer it seemed sensible to wait until we closed to have it fixed. It is unlikely that it would get any use until winter set in anyway.

I was going to finish with this yesterday but I held it back in case nothing happened today to write about, good job I did as I am stuttering already. A dirty trick, I know, but needs must and all that. We were given a carved out pumpkin by our young dog walker, which we placed at the top of our stairs with a tea light in it. To make it even scarier we daringly lit the tea light too. It did not chase off any young ghouls last night, but it did scare the tail off the bleddy hound when she came back from her walk.

Talking of the bleddy hound, for the past two Hallowe'ens one of the older girls that accompanies her sister around takes the dog with her. The Missus went to the lengths of buying, no doubt at great expense, a pointy hat and cloak - for the dog, that is; the Missus has her own. True to form, and in line with all these sorts of cunningly devised and carefully laid plans the lass did not show this year. Anyone in need of a pointy hat and cloak for a very small witch should apply here.

Happy to say I picked up the van this evening and my knob is fully operational again. This is something of a relief as I shall be going on a long journey soon and may be in need of it; more on that score at the end of the week. I hope you can stand the suspense.

Then, at the last, scupper me lummocks, I won at cards tonight. I have got a wonderful feeling, everything's going my way.

November 2nd - Wednesday

The Missus trekked off early up to PZ and shopping, (hopefully window), up at Truro. That took her out all day and left me nursing the bleddy hound. I took her down to the Harbour beach for a change and she pretty much wore a groove across the beach chasing a ball. When she tired of that she tried chasing a couple of birds instead, who very cleverly moved to the opposite end of the beach when they were rousted. This had the bleddy hound running to and fro across the beach for at least fifteen minutes, ideal. Do not ask me what kind of birds they were; I have not a clue. They had black and white stripes and definitely were not zebras and I hope they are there again tomorrow.

Down in the shop I was reminded that some of the freezers need to be defrosted and mothballed for next season. When they start to defrost you have to be there to catch the melt water else it flows like a river across the shop. I am of the school of thought that they should be left to flow; it is clearly the natural order of things. If you leave it long enough the water will dry by itself, although there will be a nasty stain across the floor. The Missus on the other hand prefers to do these things properly and will be down there for hours catching each drip. This will probably account for why it has not yet been done.

But everything is all right, I tell you. I am not worried. Apart from the pain and the agony I am quite happy. And now I am speechless. It has taken my breath away. I am overcome with the sheer magnitude of it. This will set the whole world buzzing with complete disinterest.

Quite perceptive that Tony Hancock who's Half Hour was broadcast for the first time today in 1954 and whose lines I have nicked and paraphrased above. He obviously saw the onset of The Cove Diary.

November 3rd – Thursday

Maybe it is the price of progress or maybe it is a conspiracy by technologists that will see us incapable of normal life without machinery. One thing is for sure and that is the long-term future of the 20p postcard is at stake, the lynchpin of Cove business and the barometer by which we measure success.

It was there in the newspaper, as bold as brass and they were hailing it a milestone in world-class learning. It seems that every pupil at the new Mounts Bay Academy, the first secondary academy in Cornwall, will be issued with an Apple iPad computer.

Well, what is so bad about that, you might ask? The Missus has one and I have to say I am mightily impressed. There is all sorts you can do with it, including my favourite that lets you point it up at the night sky and it tells you the names of every single star and planet, visible or not. So far she has not been willing to let me take it up the F&L on a Saturday night so I can star gaze on the way home, which is a bit unreasonable of her but it is early days yet.

There is also a plethora of 'apps' available to do everything imaginable, but I doubt that there is one that will reveal to the next generation that 'apps' is an abbreviation of the word applications. I can see that it will be a boon to the young people who come into the shop who have to buy one item at a time, because they are unable to calculate how much change they have left to buy the next.

The school believes that it will save them money on textbooks and PCs. The pupils are delighted, (obviously), and one is quoted as saying it would be really useful if the teacher did not know an answer, because they could look it up on the Internet. Most worrying is that the school believes they will eventually replace pens and paper. Well that is it, then. Not only will we have generations of young people unable to count, they will not be able to write either.

(Before any of my old class mates write in (they have computers in Pentonville, you know), I know that we did not have pens and pencils at our school either but that was different. It was because we were not allowed anything sharp.)

I will not have postcards in the shop next year. There will be a big console where you can chose the postcard image and type in the text you want on the back. You will be able to email it to your aunt in Solihull or print it, pre stamped, for popping in the post box opposite. My time will not be consumed with topping up postcards on the frame, instead I will be teaching grannies how to type postcards to their grandchildren on the postcard machine – for 20p, of course.

I should let you know that a few more of us very excellent Shore Crew are passed out at driving the ToolTrak machine that launches the Inshore Lifeboat. We took it to the empty Harbour car park tonight to put it through its paces as it is an awkward vehicle to manoeuvre and requires much practise to ensure we do not run anyone over en route to save someone's life.

After matters of such import the evening's quiz should have paled into insignificance. Little did we know.

I cannot say we were very successful at the quiz. I can only put it down to the fact that I was forced into using one of those awkward old-fashioned pens and I could not look the answers up on the Internet.

As you will know by now there is a little side game called 'chase the ace' that requires the purchase of a raffle ticket. Yes the purchase of a raffle ticket. This is a key element to being eligible to select an envelope out of a choice of four, one of which contains an ace that will win you the 'pot', which in this case amounted to a considerable sum, having accumulated over a number of weeks. With me so far?

Let me summarise the proceedings. TS bought a ticket for Head Launcher and Head Launcher won the big prize with it.

Much as we were overjoyed at Head Launcher's good fortune we would have expected the gentlemanly response to be to recompense the buyer of the ticket, TS, with a reward greater than the sum of its face value. Need I tell you that this was not forthcoming? Perhaps also, dear reader, as undoubtedly you and I would have done, it would have been right and proper to spread our new found wealth amongst our compatriots whose solid support we had enjoyed for years through toil and suffering.

Heartbreaking as it is, dear reader, I must share with you that our erstwhile friend spurned any such act of compassion. We are, of course, without malice or jealousy. It is the farthest thing from our minds to find, for example, a horse's head to slip into his bed. Even come the revolution will we heroically resist piddling in his swimming pool.

One thing is for certain, though. He will have to buy his own raffle ticket next week.

November 4ᵗʰ - Friday

One of the advantages, or possibly disadvantages, of having nothing to do is that I have time to take up various lost/daft/fruitless, (delete as appropriate), causes. Today it was triggered by finding an envelope, onto which I had scribbled the various contacts at The much maligned council who may be involved in the closure of the Harbour car park toilets before half term. I think that the chap who was apparently responsible and for whom I had left several messages, had rather hoped that I would go away after the end of the holiday. He is in for a surprise.

I telephoned him again only to find that once again his telephone was redirected to voice mail. I then telephoned one of the contractors responsible for cleaning the toilets. Because they are not council employees as such they are less politically minded and are likely to let out background information or contact names and numbers that the council would rather you did not have. I came away with another name and direct telephone number.

This chap, although surprised that I had managed to collar him, was a little more helpful. He told me that the first chap I tried to contact had indeed received my messages and had told him that the toilets had been closed because the lifeguard service had ended. I had to ask him to repeat that last bit as I really did not believe he had said it. What possible link was there between lifeguards and the state of readiness of our local conveniences? Does the absence of six or seven lifeguards tip the balance between having sufficient population to keep two public toilets open or closed?

Intrigued, I have to dig a bit deeper and get a more detailed response, preferably in writing. The chap I spoke to was more that willing to give me the name of his boss's boss, the Assistant Manager for Waste Disposal Services in Cornwall. I hope he is not a reader as it will spoil the surprise. Anyway a letter is winging its way to his door as we speak. I shall apprise you of developments as they happen, I promise.

I have also had some success with the electric company too. It did take two letters to elicit a response but nevertheless they called me, instead of having to battle their impossible telephone system. If all goes well a man will turn up at my door towards the end of the month to change my electric meter to get rid of the Economy 7 supply. All I have to do now is get rid of the chunky storage heaters and find some suitable ordinary heaters and all my problems will be over.

To celebrate this bright new dawn I took the bleddy hound down to the Harbour beach, while the Missus laboured away with the defrosting lark in the shop. For once she did not find any skanky fish to nibble at, the dog that is, not the Missus; the Missus hates fish, skanky or otherwise.

Late in the day the Missus took the bleddy hound to the vets, (it is all right, I can say vets as she is not here at the moment). She came back later with a curry and I had better add and the dog too, although the content of the curry was questionable. It seems our favourite curry house has slipped a bit, as it was not up to their usual standard.

I was rather hoping for a lay in tomorrow morning but my plans have been dashed. The Missus reports that the work we had done on the van earlier in the week has not been successful. I will need to call the garage first thing to be assured that the problem is cosmetic. I am going on a long journey on Sunday and need to know that the van will get me there and, more importantly, back home again.

The suspense must have you on the edge of your seat, I am sure. You will have to wait for tomorrow's exciting episode to find out what your Diarist has in store – if the van is fixed, of course.

November 5th – Saturday

Remember, remember the 5th of November ... how could you possibly forget, with fireworks banging off for weeks either side of the event? When I was little we all had sparklers to play with and it was a good excuse to tie bangers to old Airfix models and blow them up. Hands up how many of you thought I was going to say cats' tails?

These days, of course, small children, if they are allowed anywhere near a sparkler, must have arms six feet long, hold a safety certificate in manual handling of sparklers and wear safety glasses. Under no circumstances must they light them or show any indication of having the slightest bit of fun. Go on, buck the trend, show them a bit of risk.

Talking of not having any fun I must drive for four hours tomorrow in a direction that is away from The Cove. I cannot say I can see any joy in that at all, apart from the fact that at the end of this particular journey I shall be with the Aged Parents. While it would be sufficient reason in itself to make such a lengthy journey, it is but a staging point on an even longer one.

In order that I may dazzle website visitors with alluring pages of wonderment I have decided to go on a course to teach me how this might be achieved. Unfortunately this requires that I travel many leagues to the environs of London town and almost within earshot of the sound of Bow bells, to a place called Byfleet. (All right it is nowhere close to Bow church and you would need the auditory capacity of a bat to hear the bells from Byfleet but it sounded good when I wrote it down.)

When I enquired of the company that runs the course which Travel Hotel Inn Lodge I should stay at, they recommended that I find a bed and breakfast as there are several in the town, which are closer and possibly cheaper.

It was by chance that the Missus asked me the name of the small hostelry I had booked into and I said that it might go by the jaunty name of The Blue Anchor. She immediately suggested that this sounded very much like the name of a public house, rather than a bed and breakfast run by a chaste and stern maiden aunt that would not permit singing, let alone alcohol or evening guests to one's room.

I said that the possibility had not occurred to me, and that the cheerful sounds of clinking glasses and bonhomie in the background when I made the booking I took to be the cheeky cockney kitchen porters, merrily going about their duties.

I forget the exact form of words the Missus used to describe my selection and the manner with which I went about choosing it, but there might have been a hint of disapproval in her tone.

Needless to say there is likely to be a small break in transmission of The Diary pages until next Friday when you will be flooded with fives days all at once, unless I can find a way of remotely updating them. For those of you who may well be reading these lines in a good old-fashioned book, and not wishing to be excluded from the experience of Diary deprivation, I have asked the publisher to insert a blank page or two to simulate the hiatus – which he has clearly ignored.

Given that I too will be deprived of my exercise along the beach with the bleddy hound for several days I took her to the big beach for a run. It was a fine looking day for our last jaunt, with a big blue sky dotted with fluffy white clouds. There was a bit of a breeze from the northeast spiked with a nasty chill but not so much to force me to run for my big boy's trousers and boots, not just yet anyway. The sea temperature is still not unpleasant and the feel of it lapping around my ankles will be a memory I must cling to in the midst of the smog and cramped streets of the suburbs.

Another memory that should not be far from mind is the F&L on a bonfire night with hundreds of little urchins running about screaming and spilling my beer. Fortunately the majority made a hasty retreat home with their guardians after the firework display.

That said, and in all seriousness, the bonfire evening at the F&L is exceedingly well organised, not to mention free, funded by the good people that run the joint. It brings together the community and others from farther afield and is a benefit that should be greatly appreciated.

When I arrived the bonfire was well alight and the bar packed to the point that it was difficult to move. Even when the fireworks kicked off there were sufficient people still in the bar to make waiting for a drink a tad tedious. I did see most of the display and it was suitably impressive.

Then came the more serious business of a rocking band well suited to the temperament of the evening and the consumption of a few beers, although I had to exercise some restraint given my journey tomorrow.

Then to the walk home, with the breeze in my face and the stars up above and, without the Missus's iPad, not a clue what each one was. Nevertheless you would not want to have missed it with a half moon lighting the way.

It did make me think why on God's green earth would I want to travel three hundred or more miles to make my website glow in the dark.

November 6ᵗʰ - Sunday

I was woken with a tongue up my nose; even the bleddy hound could not wait for me to go.

So my bags were packed and I was ready to go, as Chantal Kreviazuk might have said. I had to dig out my big boy's trousers to come away in, which was a bit of a shame as it will be really hard to slip back into shorts again when I get back.

With all my goodbyes said I turned the van to the east and set the controls for the heart of the sun. Actually by the time I got going it was away from the sun but that does not sound so good. The going was relatively easy and with my main thrusters on I could start to feel the GH force, (Go Home force), pulling me back. I shot past the stars of Camborne, Bodmin and Launceston and at 13:22 precisely I left the gravitational field of

Cornwall. It was also a cracking day, which made it even more difficult to depart.

There was very little in the way of major traffic around and I made it to the Aged Parents well ahead of schedule. Nevertheless it is a long and often boring journey so I resorted to turning on the radio for a bit of entertainment. I started off with Radio Pasty that has, on Sunday lunchtime, a programme that is vaguely reminiscent of Family Favourites. This in turn reminded me of Sunday lunches years ago, with the family all sat around the communal table, so I rapidly turned it off again. Radio 2 offered Don Black does sounds from the musicals, which was absolutely terrible. Then as I sat in the only traffic jam of the journey on the Illminster bypass, (well it could have been Chard, Bristol or Nottingham for all I knew), I kicked the automatic search button and ended up with something classical.

Now. I do not mind a bit of classical music particularly as I was stuck in traffic and the music that was on was quite listenable to. I thought it might have been Franck or Bruch, as the violins put me in mind of those old black and white movies where the heroine is just about to lose her beau, or had just found one, or someone has used one to put an arrow in her beau. Anyway, I digress. Fortunately I had listened at the right moment and when it drew to a close I discovered that it was Nicholas Moore's Concerto for violin and rather good it was too. I was rather relieved that it was not his Odyssey, which is some 200 bars long and lasts for one and a half hours, the longest ever single movement, unless you play it at 45 or 78 rpm but I am not so sure you can do that with CDs.

My early arrival caused mayhem and consternation and made me wish I had gone around the block a few times. Many people will say that I already have, of course. Still, things quickly settled down and we made arrangements to go and see my new great niece in the morning. Tea was a wonder, mainly a wonder it made it to the plate, but was perfectly palatable despite the Aged Mother's protestations that she only knew how to cook for the Aged Father these days.

Since I was early when I first arrived I took the opportunity to pen the Diary entry for the day. This gave me two hurdles to cross. First that the Aged Parents do not have a wireless broadband connection, just a wired one, which not only gave rise to the issue of how to send my entry home, but also with no access to the Internet, how to spell Nicholas Moore's surname. Secondly my laptop is not blessed with Microsoft Word, which means I have to use a standard text editor, which you will lern over the next fow days dus not have a sepll checker.

November 7ᵗʰ – Monday

Overcast and miserable from the very outset this morning and the weather was not much better. I must be missing the sounds of the sea.

Given that I had to trek to the outer reaches of London town I did not want to leave it too late to be on my way. Part of the journey encompasses the dreaded M25 motorway, words that strike fear into the heart of seasoned travellers, let alone a country boy whose regular travels extended only as far as St Just or at a push, Penzance.

Before I could proceed, it seemed appropriate to go and see the great niece since they live less than an hour away. I think you may have got the impression that I think small children are best seen at a distance, and preferably a great enough distance that they cannot be heard either. You would not be wrong, but it is not every day a chap becomes a great uncle so I felt pressed to go and reassess my values, which might be the best way of putting it.

When we arrived it, sorry, Ellie Mae, was asleep which was ideal as far as I was concerned. I have to say she did not look one bit like Winston Churchill and appeared quite angelic in her slumber. The little mite is two and a half weeks old and remarkably small for a human being. Everything was going exceedingly well until the mother decided we should all get a closer look and hooked her out of her cot.

Now, I would have kept this next detail to myself, on the grounds that it will besmirch a perfectly miserable reputation that has taken me years to cultivate. Unfortunately someone took a picture of the event, which will no doubt be launched onto Face Page with a suitably caustic comment. Yes, the still sleeping babe was pressed into my arms and I was forced to hold it, sorry Ellie Mae, for what seemed like forever. My reputation may well be preserved to some degree as it was not long after the saintly item had been resting in my arms that it, sorry, Ellie Mae, started to ball her lungs out.

It was clearly time to make a hasty retreat to somewhere quieter and also to continue my journey Londonwards. I was relatively comfortable with the route I was to take, however the Aged Father suggested that I take his satellite navigation box with me. Of course, being at the forefront of technology myself, I had heard of these devices and their unerring ability to block narrow roads with juggernauts and leave seemingly intelligent people in the middle of riverbeds. Despite being au fait with these stories of woe I have never used one, or for that matter had the need for one; there not too many ways you can get lost going to St Just. I was, however, intrigued and decided to take up the kind offer and try it out on my journey.

Aberdeen is quite a cheery place at this time of the year, I can assure you. No, I am joshing with you. The machine spoke to me only a few times on the journey as most of it was in a straight line on the same road. It did go on a bit as I neared the destination but mainly because there were a few more turns and roundabouts. At one point it bleeped very loudly that gave me quite a start as I had no idea what was going on. It was not until I passed the speed camera at slightly above the limit that I realised what it was warning me about. This feature became rather irritating on the M25 as there are speed cameras every hundred yards or so.

Given a little common sense it is a useful tool. I found that I was more able to concentrate on the road and not worry too much about looking for sign posts. The road on which the bed and breakfast, (yes, all right it is a pub), sat was much smaller than I anticipated and I think without the satellite navigation tool I might have been concerned I was on the wrong track.

Having read a less than complimentary review on the Trip Advisor website I was slightly concerned about the condition of the accommodation. Nevertheless the maid who attended to me when I first arrived was most welcoming and even gave me a choice of room. The first was more than adequate. Modern it was not, but it was clean enough and spacious. They even had venison on the menu, which was a surprise but I imagine that it will not be when I tell you that it was rather dear. (I should apologise for that but you should be more than used to me by now)

It was only subsequently, having fallen in with some chatty types at the bar, that I understood that the place is over 100 years old. It is also, apparently, haunted by the landlord whose unfaithful wife's lover poisoned the chap and became the front page news of the time. Well, I shall have a comfortable night's sleep then.

From a room somewhere near London and whose television remote does not work, it is good night from me.

November 8ᵗʰ - Tuesday

Hmm, this is going to be difficult. I rather think you will not want to know about me sitting in a classroom all day and on this occasion being bored ridged. My course was not all I thought it might be and I am beginning to think that I would have got away with attending just the second day, which is going to be more in depth and, essentially, more interesting.

I should tell you that I tapped into the local knowledge and established that the journey to the place where the course was to take place was eminently walkable. This was attractive on two levels. First I did not want to lose my advantageous parking space in the cramped bed and breakfast, (all right, it is a pub), car park and secondly the bonhomie in the bar last night may still have been clinging about me. The only downfall in this operation was that there was a fair amount of mizzle in the air.

There is a wealth of difference in walking just less than two miles in Cornwall and the same distance in west of London suburbs as I am sure you can imagine. There is, for a start, a distinct lack of romanticism about the roar of traffic, clouds of motor fumes and the constant risk of being run over. There was also the intimidating experience of walking on a bridge that crosses the M25 with a parapet that was lower than I might have considered to be safe.

West Byfleet, it would appear, is populated by ugly winos who do not mind a cake or two. My observation is based purely on the number of hair dressers and beauty parlours, wine bars and bakeries in the place. I must hasten to add that I am utterly sure that West Byfleetonians are fine upstanding people. Indeed I witnessed no ugly winos eating cakes at all.

Unsurprisingly lunch was in a wine bar just without the wine, thankfully; I would surely have fallen asleep in the afternoon.

The walk back to the hotel was grim. It was raining and I made a fateful decision to cross the main road early on. It was a very busy road and I took a chance when one direction was stopped at some lights. I had not noticed on my walk up that there was no footpath on the other side and there was also no chance of crossing back.

I am rather afraid there will be rather more of this sort of thing tomorrow except I shall not be walking to West Byfleet. I am sure you can hardly contain yourselves. All I can tell you is, that if it was tedious reading it, bear a thought for the person living it.

November 9ᵗʰ - Wednesday

The weather was perfectly fine this morning; walking weather. Typical, as today I was driving into the course so that I could leave straight afterwards.

I will not bore you with the ins and outs of a deeply technical course that had my head near exploding with facts and nuances of the computer software that I had purchased some six months earlier. It was certainly more interesting than yesterday but left me with the impression that the software was designed by committee. Do not expect, in the near, or distant future, a glowing website that will make the eyes pop out of your head.

I shall move immediately to the journey home and the application of the borrowed satellite navigation system that would have had me hack across the suburbs to join the M3 rather than retrace my steps down to the A3, onto the M25 and join the M3 from there. Since it was perfectly comfortable with me taking this journey on the way in I could not quite see why it thought that the return journey should be different.

I overrode its insistence that I should veer from my brain planned journey. I have to say that although it was persistent for a while it very quickly accepted my supremacy and joined in directing me the way that I wanted to go. Three cheers for Mr

Tom whose parents had inexplicably allotted him a Christian name of Tom also.

I stopped by at the Aged Parents again as I certainly had no wish to continue for another four hours in the dark on busy road and in the wet. I had also been promised a first class meal in a local hostelry with the added attraction that the Aged Parents were paying as well.

The Stags Head rests in a peaceful settlement of Yarlington, which is steeped in history. It was once the seat of Simon de Montague, obviously before he had collected all his motor cars and moved them to Beaulieu. The place looked like what you might imagine a typical country pub to look like. The original building has been extended in modern times but has still retained its character. Although the inside has been tastefully done and is clearly modern, the feel of it has been maintained as old world with big chunky wooden tables, beamed rooms and open fires.

For a pub that lies miles from the beaten track it was clear that they need an attractive reputation to make people from beyond walking distance trek here. Food is central and was certainly different with Bobotsie, a minced lamb dish, and chicken cooked in beer with junipers being two that I can remember. The meals provided came in more than adequate portions. Add to this the provision of Thatcher's Gold cider a chap might be convinced that he had landed in Valhalla.

Phew, that was a relief. I thought for a minute there I would have nothing to have to entertain you with today. It is hardly a silk purse but if you do not mind your purse looking like a sow's ear I suppose it will do.

November 10th - Thursday

There is a calling from the West which I cannot ignore and I should be pressing on my way.

The roads were less than busy and I made good time back to sunny Sennen Cove. It was a joy beyond all joys to come down over the hill to that view and the sea sparkling in the sunlight.

The bleddy hound was clearly overjoyed to see me too. After her initial little howl hello she hid under a pile a cushions for a couple of hours. The Missus did not even give a little howl, but at least she did not hide in the furniture.

Then, before long, everything was back to normal and almost as if I had not been away. I managed to wade through my 67 emails of which five were worth reading and open the pile of post most of which were bills. I made some headway in getting back on an even keel with the Diary thanking my lucky stars and the Missus that I was able to post the entries, such as they were, from afar.

It being Thursday we pottered off to Lifeboat training and hung the boat out on the slip to give it some fresh air and watch a belated firework display on the beach.

Some things never change including a mediocre performance at the OS quiz and a run round of the noisy hound after I returned. She went belting after something in the Harbour car park in the dark, which was rather disconcerting. If it were a cat she would normally squeal frightfully while chasing it and if it is something she did not know she would stand and bark. Something that requires chasing quietly is a bit of a worrying mystery. All I know is it was not there when I got to where she was heading.

Yes, everything is definitely back to its odd little normality.

November 11ᵗʰ - Friday

I may not have told you, as I think I was waiting for something more momentous to happen, but now seems as good a time as any. You might recall I wrote to Visit Cornwall on the subject of the closure of Tourist Information Centres. I suggested that a network of shops in areas abounding with visitors might, in some small way, assist in providing information if it were properly supported.

Well, they took me at my word and we are now officially the network of shops called a Tourist Information Contact Point. It all sounds rather grand and I rather think they might have missed the bit about being properly supported.

They have told the world that we are to be contacted for information and to provide help and this has started to happen. Foreign students have been sending their CVs asking if they might come and work with us and I spent some time with one enquirer on the subject of public houses in the locality, although I did not need much support with that one. Unfortunately there does not appear to be a set of information databases I can trawl, or a list of telephone numbers I can call for help. If there is, they have not told me about them yet.

We do get emails every day from Visit Cornwall containing press releases and statistics and I have been provided with a little pile of pamphlets: a Guide to Wind Farms in Cornwall, if you are interested.

It is not exactly what I had in mind, though we were one of first to know the route of the Olympic torch and that we are to expect a visit from the Secretary of State for Culture, Olympics, Media and Sport, (presumably we should not consider the Olympics either cultural or sporting), in the near future. All very interesting, I am sure, but if you are expecting an in depth service at the moment you might be a little disappointed. Hopefully by the time we open properly in March we may have a better idea.

All this talk of tourist information is, of course, no more than a preamble to the main event of the day. I am sure that you guessed that it was.

You might well know, had you looked at the weather forecast, that after some early rain we were blessed with some 'ansum day. I had to rush to change into my little boy's trousers in case I missed any of it.

I had slipped out to St Just on errands and as I drove back into The Cove under a broadening blue sky it was obvious that the tide was on it's way back in. There was still plenty of golden beach down there, which could mean only one thing. Yes, it was ideal for taking the bleddy hound down for a run. It is still remarkably warm for a third of the way into November; I was down there in short sleeves and shorts and perfectly comfortable. What a tough life.

There, I knew you had all missed the tales of walking the bleddy hound on the beach. The paragraphs on tourist information were nothing more that a big red herring - a little tease. How could you think I would disappoint you so?

November 12th - Saturday

Up with the lark this morning. That is the after October when the shop in closed lark, as opposed to the after March when the shop is open lark that gets up much earlier. And why, you may ask, should I wish to torture myself so, with not a care in the world and nothing much to do?

I think I must have a subconscious hankering to regress; to relive those lost days of childhood, strapping a satchel to my back and heading off to school. Then, to find myself alone at a desk, not because I had no schoolmates to sit with but because my Mum had forgotten, so she said, that it was the weekend.

No, there has to be another reason why I should want to return to education after all these years by booking myself on yet another training course. This one did not require a long drive to foreign parts, however, as it was at the Penwith College in Penzance.

The last time I was there it was with the Missus for our Food Hygiene course. There the good chaps at Environmental Health felt it requisite that we learn how to design a kitchen so that we could sell a few pasties without poisoning anyone. Since then the place has had a bit of a makeover. This might be a little understated as they flattened the whole site and rebuilt it with stark modern buildings that thankfully cannot be seen from anywhere.

I may have mentioned once or a dozen times over the summer how I have had to fillet fish for customers, or explain how to fillet fish to customers, and in some cases how to skin or cook a particular type of fish. My experience in this whole area is limited to what I have learnt from some of our fishermen, fish suppliers and what I have seen on the Internet.

It was on this pretext that I booked myself onto a fish filleting and cooking course. In fact I booked onto two but more of that another day. Today's course was aimed at the domestic fish filleter and was run by a very pleasant lady who has been a fishmonger for many years. She also knows a thing or two about cooking fish but if you are thinking Jamie Huge-Stein then think again. This was simple home cooking.

Compared to the previous course I went on recently this was unadulterated joy. The lady knew her fish inside and out and was very good at demonstrating and teaching. The course being just down the road added immensely to the experience.

I sit here now stuffed with lemon sole, squid, mackerel and haddock. Since we were able to take home the fish that we had skilfully prepared and not eaten I shall be dining on hake this evening. The bleddy hound is getting the remnants of the sole and haddock. The Missus will be having noodles and lamb chops; the Missus hates fish.

When I returned home the Missus had already taken the bleddy hound down to the beach so you will, unfortunately, have to miss that dearly awaited description. That left us only one thing to do and that was to watch a welcome rerun of Singin' in the Rain, boy, can that Gene Kelly dance or what!

I would love to tell you that the F&L was alive with a big band that had the place electrified and people hitting the dance floor like never before. I would love to tell you that, but sadly we had some bloke doing a 60's disco that included 'Sweet Child of Mine', so he was not even very good at doing a 60's disco. Still, never mind, there was still sufficient convivial company to make it worthwhile turning up.

Even more worthwhile was walking home under a silvery moon.

Now, on Thursday night I regaled my compatriots with tales of the billet that I stayed at while I was away and its ghostly occupants. This, of course, triggered a stream of like stories, ghosts seen in and around the environs of Sennen and The Cove. One of which was the old lady that is oft seen stalking the length of Stonechair Lane.

Unsurprisingly the majority of the conversation last Thursday has melted into oblivion. But oddly one part of that conversation sprung to mind as my first step fell on the path down Stonechair Lane. If someone tells you they saw the ghost of Gene Kelly in The Cove I am afraid it was I, tripping at speed down the lane. Never before have my feet not touched the ground on that particular part of my way home, and never before have the willies been so firmly placed up me.

I shall retire now and try to put the willies behind me.

November 13th - Sunday

We have, for some time, considered changing the ceiling lights in the living room. They are very pretty but are as functional as a glow worm in a coal mine. Off then to Buyit & Quake for two sets of lights that the Missus had seen on a previous visit. Once these banks of spotlights are installed we shall be serious competition for Longships lighthouse and it is likely we will be seen from space. When all the supplied halogen bulbs have expired, probably next week, they will be replaced with kinder on the eyes LED bulbs. This will also take the strain off the wheel in the electric meter that will have been rotating faster than a proton in the Hadron Collider.

The installation of the lights can wait until tomorrow when I shall have plenty of energy to throw my toys out of the pram when I cannot find anything solid to attach the fittings onto and I discover I have drilled through the electric cables. I can hardly wait. That reminds me, I have to find my rubber wellies.

November 14ᵗʰ - Monday

I actually got a lie in this morning. It was all going rather well, until the bleddy hound noticed I had opened one eye for a nanosecond to check the time. I was fair game after that. I assumed that she wanted to go out, so I went and took a shower and got dressed. By the time I got back in the bedroom to see where she had gone, she had curled up on my side of the bed and was fast asleep. I am not falling for that one again.

With nothing better to do I turned my attention to the new light fittings. The old ones came down easily enough, too easily. Although the retaining screws ran in the direction of the rafters, no one had attempted to locate one to screw them into.

The retaining screws on the new fittings run across the direction of the rafters that gave me an even bigger problem. The ceiling is paper thin so even with a wall plug the anchorage is tenuous to say the least. I managed to get one of the screws into a rafter on each fitting so they will come down but they certainly are not rock solid. Nevertheless they work and I did not, to my knowledge drill through any cable. Odd, though, that the bathroom taps seem to be glowing in the dark.

While I was occupied on the ceiling the Missus went about taking apart one of our storage heaters. She made light work of it too. I will have to think of a good excuse not to do the other two.

Having acquired newfound website skills I put them to good use by including PayPal as a payment method on the online shop. I lost a direct sale because it was not there previously, so I thought I better do something about it before I lose any more. My whole day in a classroom in West Byfleet was not completely wasted, although the PayPal button has ended up on the wrong page and in the wrong position. I have tried moving it but it ceases to work as a button when I do. They did not cover that bit on the course so I shall have to telephone them for help. I wonder what else they did not cover?

It was while I was sitting down eating my Chinese meal that I noticed just how squint the light fitting is over by the window. It looked pretty straight when I was putting it up. The Missus has not said anything yet but it is only a matter of time before it will irritate the pants off me; something to do Wednesday perhaps, while the Missus tackles the other two storage heaters. Anyone would have thought I did it on purpose.

November 15th - Tuesday

And it is back to an early morning again, but today for a very good purpose, for me, at least, and perhaps for you too.

I might have alluded to this event a couple of days ago, in fact I did. I said that I had booked onto two fish filleting courses, and this was the second. Actually this was the first but I was not entirely sure that it would happen, which is why I booked onto the other one – just in case this one did not happen. Are you with me so far?

This course was run by Seafish, the organisation that sits behind our sea fishing industry. It was set up by the government in 1981 and strangely seems to have been highly successful. It supports all sorts of aspects of the fishing industry including training, technical research and development and industry accreditation of which I am now bestowed. It is funded by a levy of the first sale of seafood in the UK. However, on this particular occasion, the course was funded by a Cornwall food organisation on the basis that the more fish that they can sell in county the better. It is ours for heaven's sake; you best eat it here.

It was a much more intense course than the previous one and run by the same lady. We were encouraged to fillet several fish of the same breed to hone our skills. The slant was much more commercial too. Watch out when you are next in the shop ordering fish, I am fully armed and ready to go.

228

It was not until later in the evening that I became aware of the legacy that being trained so vigorously in fish filleting leaves you with. You may be familiar with Tuesday night being poker night. Yes, the game of poker that requires discipline, cunning, and a steely hard stare. Not all that easy when you have the distinct aroma of gurnard, hake and whiting wafting up from your finger tips, palms and even the sleeves of your shirt. Needless to say the others on the table made a concerted effort to get me off the table as quickly as possible and succeeded.

At least the bleddy hound did not seem to mind. Shame she cannot play cards, really.

November 16ᵗʰ - Wednesday

Rain for the first time in a while; a completely miserable day, even the bleddy hound did not want to go out in it. I had to carry her down the steps first thing and later, having dragged her down to the beach for some chase the ball, she gave me a you-must-be-kidding look over her shoulder and headed back up the slip.

In a rare moment of excitement today I got a letter from The much maligned council. This was the reply I have been waiting some time for, following my enquiry about the Harbour car park toilets being closed ahead of schedule. It was from the chap I had tried on numerous occasions to contact by telephone. He apologised for not returning my calls; he was on holiday, though it appears no one else was aware of it because calls were still being put through to him. So that is one job where no one notices if you go on holiday. I will leave that with you, dear reader, to contemplate.

Anyway, I digress slightly. The meat of the letter confirmed that the toilets had been closed to save money. The criterion by which they selected those toilets to close was indeed whether an extended lifeguard service was in operation. If this has been applied across the county more than fifty percent of the popular beach resorts in Cornwall were bereft of toilet facilities during the half term holiday. I can hardly imagine they saved very much money by closing the toilets a month early, especially as they left the lights on in ours. This hardly speaks of a welcoming Cornwall; a Cornwall that relies on the tourist pound for survival.

I had toyed with the idea of making this little story more public but I will probably find my bin suddenly not being emptied. Still our man did say he would come by and turn the lights off so perhaps I should be satisfied with that.

It looks like I might have a busy day tomorrow so I might just turn off my own lights now and head for bed.

November 17th - Thursday

The delightful sound of the bleddy hound being ill on the bed was not the gentle wake up call I had in mind but it was quite effective. It was a late night last night, with the Missus being out for a rare late evening with her friends, so I needed a bit of a kick this morning.

As I said yesterday, today was likely to be a bit focused on getting things done. The storage heaters that we have long wanted to replace needed to go, to make room for the new normal electric heaters that we have not chosen yet – or specified, or checked to see if they will work in the room space. It could be a cold winter.

For those of you with little experience with storage heaters, let me explain that they are large metal framed beasts stuffed full of heavy heat absorbent bricks. To be permitted to dispose of them at the tip, sorry, household waste recycling centre, they need to be stripped down into their component parts of metal, brick and fibreglass insulation. The most troublesome element, as you might imagine, is the bricks. These weigh approximately seven and one half kilograms each and there were sufficient to accumulate 300 kilos in total. You will be at one with my joy at having to move these from the flat, down the stairs and into the back of the van. As if this procedure were not sublime enough, I also had to remove them into the skip at the other end of the journey.

Disposing of three storage heaters in one go might have raised the eyebrows of a few diligent workers at the tip, sorry, household waste recycling centre, you would have thought. After all there are stringent measures in place to ensure that chaps of a distinctly commercial appearance do not use the facility inappropriately. No, the diligent workers were quite happy to direct me to the designated skips and watch on while I unloaded my waste. My little card with six little spaces for an official tip users', sorry, household waste recycling centre users', stamp that cost me the price of a postage stamp remains bleakly empty.

I do not know whether I am disappointed that my hard earned pennies were wasted on a totally pointless, and failed, plan to stop commercial waste being dumped or whether I am, er, appointed that common sense has prevailed, and that the coal-face workers can exercise their discretion at deciding who can dump and who should be turned away. Judging from the small sample I saw today I would suggest that there is a complete free for all, but at least there is no reason why our quiet beauty spots should be besmirched by fly-tippers.

All this lumping around of heavy bricks was good exercise for a chap who spends much time behind a counter and on a sofa or today, it seems, in front of a keyboard. For those of you visiting The Cove, less exercised and with frail heart, fear not. At Lifeboat training tonight we were coached in the dark arts of bringing the unfortunate back from the dead with cunning skills of resuscitation. Our good doctor led us in descending upon a plastic dummy on which we could practise cardiopulmonary resuscitation or CPR as it may be better known.

Thus revitalised it was of little wonder that the mighty Head Launcher team triumphed in the three team quiz at the OS tonight. Nice to see we are on top of our game again and we know in our hearts that, faced with stiffer competition, we would have overcome just the same. And for those of our vanquished foe that swoon and flutter lifeless to the floor after the effects of such a trouncing we will be more than able, with our first aid training, to bring you back for another go another week.

Taking the bleddy hound around last thing this evening I found it unusually dark in the Harbour car park; I could not see a thing. It turns out that some unsocial begger has turned out the lights in the public toilets.

November 18ᵗʰ - Friday

Twenty percent discount! The man has to be absolutely barking not to mention rude, using language like that in front of sensitive shopkeepers.

You might have heard on the news that we had a grand visitation from Jeremy Hunt, Secretary of State for Culture, Media, Olympics and something else; Tom Penrose, Minister for Tourism and James Berresford, CEO of Visit England. It was the latter Mikado who dropped the twenty percent bombshell. Suggesting that the Olympics year would be great for the South West, he extolled that we should be saying to our visitors, "Holidays are great and you can get them at a great price." I am sure he would be delighted to offer twenty percent of *his* earnings as a starting point.

That was not the only thing that ruined my day. We had planned to go to Travaskis Farm for dinner, a first for me, and then on the Gwithian beach to run the bleddy hound around. I was very much looking forward to it but one of us did not get out of bed 'til nearly half way through the day. It would be impolite to name names, but it was not me or the dog.

A spot of shopping was also required so I suggested we go visit the Pirates of Penzance and try out the new café that sells homemade burgers that I read about in *The Cornishman*. I recalled that it was on the terrace side of Market Jew Street, although we could not find any listing of it on the Internet. I walked the length of the street on that side and could not find anywhere advertising healthy burgers. We also tried Causeway Head and most of Bread Street in case I had not remembered the location correctly.

As we sat in the van in the car park eating a very disappointing sandwich from one of the many bakeries, I contemplated what on Earth else could possibly go wrong.

I dropped the Missus off at the supermarket despite the fact she could have got most of what we needed in town and probably for less. Unamused I ventured off with the bleddy hound and a ball thrower back to Long Rock beach. The tide was further out than the last time we were there, although the wind was as strong and in the same direction. Out in the rough sea there are some incongruous markers that look like a couple of passing gondoliers left their poles behind. It seemed a bleak and grey place, with a very hazy sun not adding to the picture at all. Even the sand is a muddy shade of grey and as solid as rock. I suppose I walked a couple of miles and she ran a good few more than that. She came back to the van covered in ruddy gore.

However the walking did the trick and she conked out for the rest of the afternoon and evening.

Part of the shopping is sufficient ingredients for me to make my prototype Yule log. I remember them being my favourite from Christmases long ago but suffered from a dearth of chocolate buttercream. (I am sure they did not really, it was just it was the best bit and always disappeared far too quickly.) I wanted to make one from scratch, including the Swiss roll bit, then I can add as much buttercream as I like. I will, of course, have to wear my pinafore as I fancy I will be covered in flour else. With any luck I will scoff the lot myself and feel very poorly afterwards. I will repent come Easter time. I owe Lent the price of a chocolate sponge cake.

I had thought that I might retire to the F&L for the first Friday in quite some time. When it came to it I could not quite summon up the energy, and it might take the edge off my cake baking skills tomorrow.

Well, that is quite enough of that. I am sure you noticed something afoot which comes from shoe horning Gilbert and Sullivan operetta titles into the prose. W.S. Gilbert was born today in 1836, I will have you know. I do apologise for Iolanthe (I owe Lent the), by the way, if indeed you noticed it.

November 19ᵗʰ – Saturday

For a day that, on paper at least, looked like it might be as dull as dishwater it thankfully turned up a few little treasures.

It was a very pleasant day too with lots of blue sky and a warm sun. So warm in fact that when I took the bleddy hound down the beach later in the afternoon it would have been churlish not to reach for the shorts and flip flops, so I did. Unfortunately by the time I had got down there, a big lump of black cloud came up from the south east bringing dusk on early.

Still, it was pleasant enough to carry on walking with the sand between my toes and the bleddy hound with the bit between her teeth. Worryingly, though, the bit between her teeth was a whole mackerel someone had carelessly discarded half way along the beach. I was too far away to get to her in time and she ate the lot, head, tail and guts. I am afraid I was laughing too much to be angry with her and it would not have done much good anyway, although she did look a little guilty when she eventually caught up with me.

With a whole lot of chasing the ball and vigorously digging holes in the sand it was no more than half an hour later that the fish made a reappearance, then again, and again and whoops, again. Sorry if you are eating your breakfast while reading this, dear reader, I did try and be as gentle with you as possible.

With unsavoury foodstuffs still in your mind I am sure you are dying to know the results of my Yule log baking experiment. Since this was my first foray into cake baking I felt it important that I follow the instructions to the letter, which I did. Things were going exceedingly well until it got to the bit where the mixture is poured into two 28 centimetres by 35 centimetres baking trays. First I could only find one such tray and secondly I really did not want to make two. I compromised by using the one and tipping the rest into cup cake cups.

Additionally the recipe made no specification of how deep the mixture should be in the tray. To me it seemed ever so thin and I am sure I used more than half the mixture in getting it to that point. This was not the only area that I found the instructions somewhat light on detail. When making the white chocolate buttercream the instructions demanded that I melt the chocolate, which seemed very fair. Yes, yes I know *now* that you are not supposed to do it in the microwave. It would not have hurt, would it, to include "over a bain marie" in the method, and would have had me on the right track straight away. It is only four words, for heaven's sake. It still puzzles me how chocolate in a microwave can appear to be melting one moment then the next be going as hard as rock the next.

So, my buttercream turned out a little crunchy, not helped by the fact that we had run out of icing sugar and I had to use caster sugar instead. My Swiss roll rolled up nicely nonetheless, once I had cut off the cardboard-like thin end of the sponge, (all right, I could have assumed "spread evenly"). I think I can count this as a success, particularly as no on else will be willing to eat any. If we had any milk chocolate I would do the outside as well. Maybe I will scoff the lot as is and just not feel as sick.

All right, we were terribly lazy and dined at the F&L tonight. It was every bit as good as it has always been; my Cajun chicken was spot on and the Missus's steak succulent and well presented. But of course that is not really why I was there.

Even Nine were playing tonight and they were probably the best band up there for a long while. Not that there has been anything wrong with the others, it was just that these guys are so good. They write their own tunes and play a few covers and unless you knew the covers it was difficult to distinguish between the two, the quality of their own songs being top notch.

Now, I mentioned last week, I think, that the spectre of the lady of Stonechair Lane was forethought in my mind. When I reached the end of the lane tonight I saw a vision that could well have been her, with long flowing blonde locks blowing in the wind that was not blowing. Spooky indeed until she asked me where the coastguard cottages were. She was not sure it was Coastguard Row so I suggested Smuggler's Rest in Robert's Row and she still was not sure. Crikey she managed to get this far with red, very pointy heel shoes, so I left her to it. She was not there when I returned with the dog so I guess she found her own way home or perhaps just evaporated into the ether.

If I find some pointy heel shoes tomorrow morning on my way round I will start to worry. There's no place like home, there's no place like home.

November 20ᵗʰ - Sunday

Definitely a lazy Sunday afternoon and we were not that active in the morning either.

The Missus has a little surprise in mind for a few weeks hence and required photographs of the church. You will be on the edge of your seat now, wondering what it might be, but I could not possibly divulge what it is. This will be on the basis that I do not really know either; I just do what I am bid – sometimes.

While I went about my duties with the camera, the Missus ran the bleddy hound around the back field. I took my time as it was not particularly warm up there, with a bit of a southeasterly breeze coming across the fields and I did not fancy standing watching the hound for too long. It is not an easy church to photograph, as the walls are quite close in and there are large

Cornish palms about it. Still I managed to get some suitable shots from the churchyard and went back to join the Missus.

I only mention this visit to demonstrate my heroic self-restraint at being that close to the F&L and not actually going inside. I am sure you are quite in awe. I also mentioned it because otherwise there would be begger all else to write about today.

We also had a nose around the community graveyard while we were there. We have been meaning to go for quite some time just out of interest. It was of no great surprise to see the familiar family names of Angove, Nicholas, Williams, Pender and etcetera, all recognisable from their relatives still living in the area. There are also two war graves standing out starkly against all the granite headstones. I did go home and look one up but could only establish that the chap was from Lancashire. I wonder what he was doing there?

We slipped back home with a soggy and aromatic hound for some more rest and relaxation. I took the risk of using another recipe, garnered from the Internet, to cook tea tonight. I must be cursed on the recipe front as this one came abruptly to a halt just before the last important phase of cooking, so I had to guess the last bit. I must have done all right, as there were no bits left over and we managed to eat it.

Then, just when the excitement was becoming unbearable the Lifeboat pagers went off. A fishing boat at the top end of the traffic separation scheme had broken down and required a tow back to Newlyn. As the pagers went off at around 7 pm we expected to be seeing the boat back at around 2 am. The Missus and I have an early start tomorrow morning too, of course.

As it turned out the boat elected to return for the morning low water at 6 am so I have a very early morning to look forward to.

November 21st - Monday

I leapt enlivened and sprightly from bed this morning at 5 am to face the day that had not yet dawned, and to recover the Lifeboat due at six.

I am sorry, there appears to be something slightly adrift with reality or is it my keyboard, or both? That previous sentence should, of course, have read, "I woke to the deafening trill of my alarm that some bleddy idiot had set for 5 am. It was still dark, for heaven's sake. Dragging myself from my inviting pit was a Herculean task and best left to Greek demi-gods. The whole exercise led to me having my underpants on inside out and my socks on the wrong feet. Of course the wrong feet, they should have been on someone else's, while mine remained sockless in bed."

There, that is much better.

There was a fair army of us gathered to welcome home the Lifeboat. Head Launcher and my good self managed to negotiate the skating rink that was the bottom end of the slipway, still upright. Even more miraculously we managed to reverse the performance upright as well, while being roundly abused for the cautious manner in which we did so. Still, the Lifeboat was recovered without incident and back in the boathouse washed and ready for service by 7 am, and still in darkness.

Even without the Lifeboat doings we would have had to be up early anyway, just not as early as 5 am. Our electric company had told us that today would be the day that an engineer would turn up to remove our Economy 7 electricity. They had given us a narrow window of expectation for the technician's arrival, somewhere between eight in the morning and eight in the evening. It was therefore of no surprise that he turned up half way through the construction of a bacon, cheese and onion toasted sandwich. He was good enough, though, to keep the electricity on for long enough to make him a cup of tea before he started.

Half an hour later he was all done and our Economy 7 money pit is a thing of the past. It is at this point that I discover that the root cause of my high bills was that my electricity is being used to light the street and the toilet block, whose lights are still on incidentally, and I need not have had the work done at all. It will ever be thus, I am sure.

With my cares, troubles and appointments over for the morning and the bacon toasty resurrected and consumed, it was fair and rightful that I be allowed to doze fitfully on the sofa. Fair and rightful it might well have been, but this holds little sway with a bleddy hound that wants to go for a walk. So insistent was she, that I roused myself from my recumbent posture and in doing so noted that there was no beach available for a run. This could only mean one thing, so I went and dug out my walking boots that have reposed in a cupboard all summer long.

I do not recall exactly, but I believe that there was snow on the ground the last time I took her up to Land's End. Despite the fact that it rained quite heavily last night the ground was still quite hard and there was not a great deal of surface water to contend with. It was also surprising how little flow there was down the few streams that cross the path, about half way up. I had just finished noting that very fact when I heard a splash behind me. I turned to see that the bleddy hound had dived in to the small pool I had just been looking at. She has never done that before. She clearly missed having her swim down on the beach.

Naturally no trip to Land's End would be complete without the bleddy hound adorning herself in her favourite perfume, courtesy of some passing fox or badger. It gave me great pleasure in handing the smelly beast over to the Missus, who had spent her time in my absence having a fair and rightful kip on the sofa.

There was a poker playoff at the OS tonight. This is to decide the third person who will be lucky enough to attend the regional heats at Bristol, and there to win a place at the national finals somewhere else. Frankly I have no wish to play poker beyond the confines of my own comfortable environment so, although there is a cash prize on the night, I had no other incentive to win, in fact completely the opposite. This is presumably why I won. The chap I beat into second place, by skill and cunning, (spelt playing with gay abandon), will go to Bristol in my stead. Quite right too; he is generally a much better player than I and with the other two attending, it is quite possibly the strongest team we have sent up there.

Fortunately we all retired early. I have a long drive tomorrow, and where once this would have threatened the continuity of these pages I have some new technology up my sleeve. If all goes well we will not miss a beat, if not there will be a short hiatus, unless you are reading a book in which case you will care not a jot.

November 22nd – Tuesday

I have a cold. It came on shortly after we crossed the border into Devon. I cannot possibly believe there is a connection, surely not?

Yes, we are here again visiting the in-laws in not so sunny Barnstaple and what a journey it was. For a start we left an hour later than planned, not a particularly major issue, as there was no definitive time that we had to be there, er, here. But we dallied and we dillied and although we did not loose our way, we did stop off on the way.

First there was Philp's, of course. It is a tradition that if the Missus and I are passing out that way we just have to stop and have a Philp's pasty. What we do not normally do is take a detour out to Travaskis Farm for a bit of breast of lamb for mother-in-law that they did not have. That is the breast of lamb, not the mother-in-law. If they start selling mother-in-laws I will start taking the Helston road when I drive out of Cornwall.

It was at the farm that the bleddy hound made a bid for freedom; well a bid for the butcher's counter anyway. The Missus caught up with her as she moved onto the restaurant. I would not necessarily take this as an endorsement of the quality of the food; you must remember the mackerel on the beach incident.

Apparently the coffee at the national chain outlet back down the road is better than the farm shop coffee, as that is where we headed next. Unbelievably we were on the road and heading in the right direction after that. Despite a road closure at Camelford we still went that way, it added a little interest to a very familiar journey. And then we were there, or rather here and to mark the occasion I promptly fell asleep on the sofa.

And now for the science bit. The reason you are able to read this today, all supposing you *are* reading this today, is that I have gone to some expense on your behalf to acquire a mobile broadband dongle, (whoever came up with the word 'dongle'?), that has allowed me to connect to the Internet. Of course, if you are not reading this today and you are reading four days in a row, the whole experiment has been a dismal failure. If this is the case, there will almost certainly be a mobile broadband dongle on the street somewhere in east Barnstaple, having been tossed forcibly out of the in-law's window in a fit of pique.

Now all I need is a dongle that makes a cold go away.

November 23ʳᵈ - Wednesday

The Missus took her mother and sister off to Exeter for a spot of shopping, (spelt full on, recession busting spend-a-thon), today. This in itself took a little bit of research, as the last time we were there we had a bit of trouble parking the van. Having followed the directions to a city centre multi-storey car park, it was only when we had driven up to the entrance that we were informed that the height restriction would not allow the van to pass, at least with its roof intact. By this time there was a queue of cars up behind us and the only option available to us was to get them all to reverse, so that we could get the van out of the way. Very embarrassing and never to be repeated.

So that was the girlies taken care of leaving me, the bleddy hound and father-in-law to hold the fort. The father-in-law is none too mobile these days and without the van we were pretty much housebound. In fact for most of the day I did not have a single interaction with another human being, other than the father-in-law. I did try taking the dog down the lane behind the house, but she was having none of it. I cannot say I blame her too much; it is not exactly a run down the beach or a trek to Land's End.

And neither is staying in all day and watching daytime television. At least *Last of the Summer Wine* was not being aired today, although I found out later the father-in-law has a whole list of them recorded on his magic box, which would have just about finished me off. There were, or course, the occasional conversations, which, with a loud television and me somewhat deaf from my head cold, were rather fraught and necessarily short.

After all this mind numbing, I found it very hard to be incensed by the news that car parking charges in Weymouth during the Olympics will be hiked by 300 percent. I know this is a little bit far off Cove life but, there again, so am I at the moment, so bear with me. Now wait a minute. Was it not just a few days ago the same Olympic chaps were advocating that we, in the Westcountry, should be dropping our prices by 20.12 percent to attract Olympic visitors. So the dastardly plan has been revealed. The Olympics lot will have milked the visitors so thoroughly, that in order to get any crumbs from the table at all, we will have to drop our prices as the poor beggers will have next to nothing left.

I still have my cold, by the way. Thanks for asking. It is worse now as I have a dose of cabin fever to go with it.

November 24ᵗʰ – Thursday

Still hanging on here in North Devon but it is my last day. I am heading back for Feast weekend in Sennen leaving the Missus behind.

It was my turn for a spot of shopping this morning, as I need a memory stick to be able to safely transport The Diary back to its rightful place in the world. I also needed a couple of other items, and the whole excursion would not take longer than an hour.

No more than an hour, that is, if, as I had expected, I journeyed into town by myself and not with the Missus and the mother-in-law, which is what actually happened. You would have thought that after a full day's shopping yesterday they would have had enough of it by now. Not a bit of it, it seems; we were there for hours.

The bleddy hound had been stuck indoors all yesterday, and the day before that she was in the van getting here. I suggested that she would benefit from a little run on the beach and, after yesterday, I certainly knew I did. I had checked the tide times for the area and knew that time was running out for both of us. Of course, my plea made absolutely no difference, this was shopping, after all.

I had selected, for no particular reason, Croyde beach to go and have a run around. Well, actually, I had selected Woolacombe beach to go and have a run around, but father-in-law said that parking might be a little fraught there and there might even be dog restrictions too. On previous visits we had been to Instow, as it is just down the road, but it is more river bank than beach and the sand on most of it is slightly reminiscent of mud. Yes, I am bound to upset someone by making derogatory comments about the place, but with my ears still ringing from my stinging indictment of Byfleet, what the heck. Er, the village is very pretty though, honest.

When we eventually got there we found that Croyde has a very attractive beach, with fingers of rocky strata running out to the sea at either end. The make up of the rock is shale, mudstone and, most importantly, red sandstone. There is also some rock called baggy beds, that sounds more like a bed spread made out of old trousers than a rock formation. I mention the red sandstone particularly, as the sand is much darker than at Sennen and has a deep red hue. Apparently it is also rich in lime and will explain the large kilns at the far end of the beach. That did surprise me, as there appeared to be no particular method of transport in and out. You certainly would not want to bring a boat in there.

Above all this, the bleddy hound had a whale of a time, variously chasing the ball and gulls and dipping into the many rock pools. I had a whale of a time, because I got to go outside on a pleasantly temperate day, parking was free and the seasonal toilets were not only open, but also sparkling clean. I am glad we got there when we did. The beach is funnel shaped and as such the tide seems to whip in there much more quickly than I had anticipated. Any later and we might have found ourselves in a spot of trouble.

On the way back from the beach we stopped off at a garden centre. Why, you might ask, would we want to go to a garden centre when we do not have a garden? I certainly did, (non verbally, naturally).

This aside, I noticed immediately the place had clearly stolen a march on its competitors by starting Christmas early. It was difficult not to notice. There were Santas, reindeers, fairies, trees covered in fake snow and all manner of seasonal decorations. I was led to the very epicentre of this cornucopia of Christmasness. It was like all my Christmases had come at once; I suddenly felt quite nauseous.

Clearly sensitive to my condition the Missus bought nothing more Christmassy than a pair of welly boots, green ones thankfully, and without any fur on the top. It is worrying to know that she will be here for another few days without my restraint.

Yes, all right that last sentence was completely meaningless, but you must be used to that by now, I certainly am.

November 25ᵗʰ - Friday

Well, that is me on my way home but first a stop off in Exeter, that will get me banned from education networks across the North West and will render JW's screen blank for a day or two. They will probably ban the book from the library for the same reason.

I harped on last year about getting a shotgun, (there you go JW, censored). It took me three months to get a licence and by then I had spent the money on less important things, such as stock. With the Feast shoot tomorrow, I was rather determined to fulfil my pledge to have one, while I can still mount it as opposed to using it as a walking aid.

Last year second hand guns were in plentiful supply. This year, what with a recession and the exchange rate with the Euro not exactly in our favour, old guns are as rare as rocking horse teeth. Our local gun shop in Helston has nothing at all, and the Exeter shop was not exactly bursting at the seams with them. Nevertheless they had some, and they had a very knowledgeable and worthy chap to help me make the selection. I even ended up with a gun that was less than I was willing to pay. All I need to prove now is that it, and I, can shoot without ending up with a comedy blackened face and the barrels peeling away like a banana skin.

With my booty in the back of the van, carefully covered in a blanket, I hacked home along the A30 in the direction of home. Having left too early for breakfast I was starting to feel a little peckish. I avoided going into Exeter services and if you have ever been to Exeter services you will understand why. Unfortunately, as it transpired, I might well have been better off there and if you have ever been to Exeter services you will know that is saying something.

Just after crossing the border, (what do you mean 'what border'?), there is a sign advertising services, parking and other facilities in three miles. It lies at the bottom of a dip and is reasonably wholesome, or so I have heard. I would not know because I never got there. The problem is, that at 2.9 miles, there is another services that is not anywhere close to being wholesome. It was into these services that I was duped to turn off.

Have you ever seen the film *Deliverance*, or perhaps *Southern Comfort?* If you have you will get some appreciation of the welcome waiting for me. If you have not seen those films, ask someone that has or skip to the next paragraph. It was all I could do to order a ham sandwich, smiling and hoping my gritted teeth were not too obvious. For two pounds, I wondered if they could spare the ham that they placed between two slices of limp plastic bread. A better, or more stupid, man would have complained I am sure. I was just grateful to get out of there without being poked with a pitch fork by a large chap, whose family tree had been recycled, asking me to squeal like a pig. I noted, for future reference, the other more mainstream rest area one tenth of a mile further on and was thankful that *my* ham was still firmly attached.

Home was a very quiet and lonely place when I arrived and so was my humble repast, (feeling sorry for me yet?), but I managed, just. It was right and proper that I find some solace and fine company at the F&L, so I resolved to travel up there.

All of a sudden it felt like a Saturday night; I have not been to the F&L on a Friday for quite some time. I had to ask where the band was just to ground myself and find some assurance that it was not actually a Saturday night. There were some wry comments, it has to be said, but overall we had a small gathering of good fellows, who were most convivial company.

I did not tell you that the walk up there was star studded and beautiful, which it was. You would expect that on my slightly squiffy way home, now, would you not? And, may I tell you, that I was just as uncertain of step on the way up as I was on the way down tonight, which just goes to show that my tripping really is not drink related – honest. You must conclude, therefore, that it is almost certainly due to not looking where I am going related – really you must.

And I suppose the most telling point, the one thing that epitomises my solitude, my utter isolation, was that when I slipped my key into the lock tonight I was not immediately bowled over by an overly exuberant bleddy hound, waiting for her last run around the block.

Utter bliss.

November 26th – Saturday

Odd is it not? I have free rein to stay as long as I like in bed, to do what I like and I am still up at eight o'clock, even without a wet (canine) tongue in my ear. And, despite my early rising, I am still late in completing all I want to do before it is time to go up the top, to help out with the Feast shoot.

Of course, this is the first outing of my new gun and it needs to prove itself. Strange, then, that I was improving all the while until the competition Parish and Open cups, when I suddenly could not hit the proverbial barn door. Nevertheless the gun felt good in my hands, I could feel the violence flow through it, death, maiming, blood, destruction, kill, kill … ahem, I mean it was well balanced, just like me.

It was one of those days that I should have stayed put and rode out the entire evening, but for some reason I decided to return home. Yesterday I felt like I was walking on air, running up the hill, tonight it felt like I was walking through glue. How does that happen? Further evidence that I would have been better off staying where I was.

Then there was the band that countered all that. I will withhold their name for fear of retribution or lawsuit. They were truly dreadful. They put up one poor chap to do some acoustic guitar work in the first hour, that really would not satisfy the hungry crowd that was slowly gathering. The second half was even more grim. Imagine Morrissey with a sore throat singing with his fingers in his ears, or perhaps the worst karaoke singer you ever saw, who would just not get off the stage. Bizarrely their instrumentals were fabulous and I could have listened to those all night.

Home, then through the mizzly wind and black as pitch night. Corking!

November 27th – Sunday

I took the traditional role of Sunday being a day of rest almost literally today. I got up late and lazed away the rest of the morning.

In celebration of this, and just to be perverse, I wore working overalls for the whole day. All right, it was not completely without purpose. We have two bare patches on the living room wall, where our old storage heaters used to reside. I quite rashly promised that I would make good the patches, before the Missus gets back. Since I was, ahem, busy yesterday that only left today to do the painting.

As luck would have it, I reserved some of the paint from the last painting of the hallway, which just happens to be the same colour as the living room, because the bleddy hound has chipped some paint off by the door with her exuberance, well her claws to be precise. That was about two years ago and the job has been outstanding since then. Well, you cannot rush these jobs, you know.

So armed with my reserved paint, a handy paint brush and a large screwdriver to prise open the paint tin, all that remained was to sand down the wall. In my tool drawer I had previously noticed a pack of fine sandpaper, such careful and detailed planning are the hallmarks of success, I find. I also found that the pack of fine sandpaper in the tool drawer was empty. It was an hour later when I found the other pack I had in the shop because I could not remember where I had left it.

With careful precision, I ensured that my brush strokes matched that of the surrounding wall and that the edges blended perfectly with the existing paintwork. I took time to allow the first coat to dry and a second was lovingly applied, with the same attention to detail as the first. I am glad I did it properly. Now, even with a bright light on the wall, it looks exactly like someone has painted over a patch.

Later in the evening, after making sure I properly cleaned the brush and tidied up the newspaper I had used to protect the carpet, I went downstairs to put the bin out. It was only then that I noticed it. I had completely forgotten about the paint chips by the front door.

Come to think, I have always liked those chips by the door; it makes the place look rustic and lived in.

November 28ᵗʰ – Monday

Up early today as I have a cross-border incursion to carry out, a commando raid, (and no, that does not mean I will not be wearing any underwear), to rescue the Missus from North Devon.

When I got there her bags were waiting in the back yard, ready for loading onto the van. Judging from the amount of shopping bags, I would say that Devon will be the only county in Britain not suffering a double dip recession in the new year. I can already tell you, that is more than can be said for the Old Boathouse household, which will be dining on bread and gruel for the foreseeable.

At least the bleddy hound was pleased to see me, with her trademark little howl of welcome. It is the most affectionate that I have seen her since we got her. I can only conclude that she is fed up with reruns of *Last of the Summer Wine* too. It did not last long though, the affection that is; *Last of the Summer Wine* will go on forever.

I had enough time for ten minutes kip, that was sufficient to reinvigorate me for the return journey. Two minutes into the trip back the Missus announced that she was hungry, which made me wonder what she had been doing since she got up. We had to get some of that gruel and dried bread for tea anyway, so we stopped off at the first watering hole, which was about ten minutes down the road.

Mind you, I did much the same on the journey up, but at least I had the excuse that I left before breakfast time. I stopped at Smokey Joe's just beyond Redruth. I have made mention of this place before. It is the closest approximation of an old style transport café and does a cracking good breakfast and mug of tea for a fiver, if you are not too greedy. The other good thing about it is that it is five minutes away from the post office in Blackwater, which was requisite, as I had some book orders to post.

Yes, people are still buying books and some people, like our International Correspondent, are buying more than one. This is essential if you want to read the new 3D version of the book, by the way. In the pack you will find an upmarket pair of hand crafted 3D spectacles; I cut them out of a cornflakes packet and glued in the red and green lenses myself. It is very realistic; you would almost think that the book is in the room with you.

Anyway I digress. Talking of spectacles, the post office at Blackwater is a building to behold. You could quite possibly believe you had stepped over the threshold and back in time, were it not for the modern chiller that is somewhat incongruous against the wall. The post office counter is tucked away at the back of a shop that, quite possibly, has not changed since Queen Victoria sat on the throne. There is even a door to a back room, that still has its original stained glass and a spiral staircase to an upper floor, that is currently being used as a store.

The queue up to the post office counter also looked like it had been there since Victorian times. The lady at the front of the queue apparently had saved up all her post office visits for the year, and was doing them all at once, this morning. At one point I wondered if we were in danger of being there for another monarchy she took so long. Fortunately, after she eventually left, the queue moved at a smarter pace, which was probably not a moment too soon for the little old grey-haired lady next in line.

I had a weather front chasing me on the way up and we found ourselves going through it on the way back. The weather forecast has it that we should expect some more of this and worse over the coming days, including a gale of wind tonight. I do not think the bleddy hound is going to be quite so overjoyed about coming home, when she finds out the weather she is going to be dragged out into in the coming week.

I am not going to be overjoyed either as the Missus did not get to see her favourite show, *I'm an Underexposed Has-been, Get Me Humiliated on Prime-time Television* and we have about six days worth to get through before nine o'clock when the next one starts.

I think I should sleep quite well tonight.

November 29ᵗʰ - Tuesday

It is odd how quickly things get back to normal when you return from a trip away. And now that the weather has caught up with what we should be having at the end of November, it definitely feels like normal.

What also felt like normal was waking up to a power cut after a stormy night. Western Power Distribution very kindly sent a text message to my home telephone telling me that they had a problem. My problem, apart from not being able to make a cup of tea, was that my home telephone does not work when there is no power to it. I must remember to let them know my mobile telephone number, but I suspect doing so will be a trial beyond its worth.

Nevertheless, shortly after I had retrieved some boiling water from the Lifeboat station for my tea, (it has a water boiler that was still hot), my power came back on again. It lasted long enough for me to be able to edit the Diary and post it, and failed again seconds after I had uploaded it to the Internet.

We, the bleddy hound and I, descended on the Harbour beach for a little run around once we were sure that the stormy rain had passed. It was not all that bad and I felt rather silly in full waterproof gear standing down there, throwing a ball around.

The weather behaved further while I gathered myself for a trip down to the OS for a game of cards. Things were going very badly for me in the first half, in a game populated with more players than normal. In the second half, and after a long time of hanging on, I found myself in the last three. Darn it and curses, I never checked how few chips the other player had and made my move too soon. A power cut just then would have been quite handy.

Maybe I was just too keen to get home and take that bleddy hound round the block, or it might have been that I am just a bad poker player. It is a close run thing, but I suspect the latter.

November 30ᵗʰ - Wednesday

The Missus spent most of the day in the kitchen cooking up things for Christmas. It seemed to involve an awful lot of chocolate of all types and descriptions and left the place looking like an explosion in a cake tin factory. I need not have worried overly about my waistline, though. Apparently none of the spectacular looking treats are destined for my tummy.

This did seem a little mean, especially as I was up dead early to take the van into the garage to get the heater fixed – again. The Missus will be taking the van on an extended journey next

week and will be less than pleased if she is chilly on the way. The
heater seemed to be working fine when I picked the van up later,
though it would have been a sight more economical for Missus
to buy a thicker coat and a pair of woolly socks.

Still, she redeemed herself by making me a chocolate log,
that she surprised me with at tea time. I could have made a
comment about the white chocolate being on the outside,
although I suppose it could have been a silver birch log, but it is
difficult to talk with your mouth full.

If you think this was the most boring entry in the year so far,
a) at least you did not have to live it and, b) wait for tomorrow's!

December 1ˢᵗ - Thursday

Well, stew me walnuts, it is December already. Only twenty
days to opening time and, she reminded me only yesterday,
twenty two days until the Teenager's birthday. You can send gifts
and greetings here and I will make sure she gets them, honest.

We had stopped off at Prussia Cove before with Teenager
and Big Sis but no one had wanted to get out of the van. I had
been determined since then to return for a proper look-see. I was
almost certain that it would have been a waste of time at anything
other than low water, so I made sure of my timings before I left.

I took the bleddy hound with me, naturally, and a ball
thrower, although I was not sure how much sandy beach we
would come upon. It is a little walk from the car park, down the
lane that winds between two semi-circular parts of Acton Castle,
which form a sort of courtyard. Try as I might, I have been
unable to discover any history of the building at all other than it
was the home of the Carters, famed for their smuggling prowess
and, after one of the brothers, Prussia Cove is named. The story
goes that in boyish games he called himself the King of Prussia
and one of the coves below the house was named King's Cove
after him.

The first cove that comes into view is called Bessie's Cove,
after a brewess who plied her trade on the headland above. The
way down looked steep and rocky and the cove was full of water,
so I walked on and down into King's Cove, originally Porth
Leah. Looking back west there is a small bunch of rocks off the
headland called the Enys, one of which looks like a miniature St

Michael's Mount. In the other direction, beyond a rocky outcrop, is a strip of sand called Kenneggy Beach, ideal for throwing a ball around on and the main reason for getting there at low water. Across the rocks was the only way onto it, so we picked our way slowly across; on dark shale it is not easy to discern safe or slippery rock. Once across we enjoyed the virgin sand all across to the far end.

As I turned back I could have sworn that the apparently dropping tide had swept in closer to shore. When I got closer to our outward footprints, I noticed that some had been swallowed up by the waves. I know I had taken my timing from Praa Sands, a little further down the coast, but it was very unlikely that the tide was coming in here before it had fully gone out a mile or two to the east. Was it a trick of the eye, the big swell, or had I got the time wrong?

We were not in any immediate danger of being cut off, but we had achieved what we had set out to do, a four paragraph filler for The Diary or five, if you want to include this one. I do hope you appreciate, dear reader, the sort of lengths I am willing to put the bleddy hound to for your entertainment. She is not overly keen on the longer journeys and she came back lagged in wet sand and mud. I will have the Missus give her a hose down later.

Lifeboat training was a perfunctory affair and we broke away early for an evening's quizzing, as you do. If I use the phrase, 'it's only a game', you will immediately realise that we lost. Not only did we lose, we came last for the first time ever. I blame it on the facts: that I was not there last week and my continuity was broken; we had, perhaps, lulled ourselves into some sort of complacency; I am playing in a team of dunces; our idiosyncratic method of play, that some unkindly call cheating, was not employed to its best advantage this week.

Whatever the cause you may expect a very short Diary entry tomorrow. I shall not be stepping out of the flat for fear of the public ridicule that will be awaiting me.

December 2nd – Friday

I woke up late this morning and dared to take the bleddy hound around the block. Something is afoot on the wharf, I see, with a twenty-five feet high aerial mast erected. I should not really let on, but as long as you promise not to tell anyone, I think I can let you know. This is a test to ensure that radio communications meet European regulations for when the Isles of Scilly helicopter link comes to Sennen Cove next year. Sure enough it will cause some problems with the parking, but I understand the project is likely to bring a million pounds worth of business into The Cove, so I am sure we can put up with a little inconvenience.

I had a couple of death threats this morning. Well, not exactly threatening death, but scratch your eyes out sort of comments. It seems I wrote the word 'dunces' yesterday where, of course, I really meant to write 'geniuses' relating to the other members of our quiz team. I cannot imagine how that little slip happened but I hope that all is right now, and fancy them thinking I could have meant that in the first place, the thickos.

I had intended to run out to get some provisions for next week; the Missus is off on some sojourn or other and will be leaving me on my own. Well, when I say on my own I think you can probably guess who will be here with me - leggy, curly and a propensity to use her tongue in my ear as a wake up alarm. No, not Pippa Middleton, the bleddy hound. That was what I intended to do, but the new heaters were delivered before I could get away and I was given instructions for their immediate installation.

Now all that remains is to convince the Missus not to have them blasting out morning noon and night and that wearing an extra pullover indoors is a perfectly acceptable alternative method of keeping warm. They did get a test run this evening and after four hours the room was roasting or, as the Missus put it, slightly warm.

So it is off to gather provisions tomorrow now. I cannot have another distraction else I will not eat next week, although I might make an exception for Pippa if she turns up.

December 3rd - Saturday

I managed to escape this morning to gather the supplies for my enforced isolation. I decided the best place to achieve my goal was the west's famous shopping centre at St Just. Free parking, no queues and everything you need under one sky.

All in all we had a very lazy day. I certainly did; I did not even have to take the bleddy hound around this morning. I did take her round a little later and just before our sparkling weather closed in with heavy mizzle. Apparently we have been singled out in the far west for some especially murky stuff into the evening. Even the tide was not conducive to taking her down to the beach today, so we ending up watching the television for some mind numbing afternoon entertainment.

This, of course, was only a small precursor to the evening up at the F&L for which I had finely attuned myself. That was until my pager went off, half way through my fish and chip dinner at ten to seven. As it happened there was no particular hurry as it was a crabber, the Intuition, which is a bit of a regular, with a fouled propeller, just North West of Pendeen Watch.

The big money was on the boat being held at Newlyn until the morning, as it would not arrive there until between one and two in the morning. It is a shame I had no big money, as the boat ended up being held at Newlyn, as it did not arrive until between one and two in the morning.

By the time we found this out TS had already arrived from Redruth. He is our stalwart, our main man who will stay the night, as required, waiting on information received, to command the rest of us to action. He is also the twonk that got the most important question of the quiz night wrong, so he deserved all he got, not that we in any way hold a grudge. He was also good enough to drop me up the F&L when we discovered that we would not be required until the morning, so I take it all back. He was also pulled by the sheriffs no sooner than he had driven out of the pub car park, but thankfully TS is as abstemious as a Wesleyan preacher in a Welsh mosque on a Sunday.

Ah well, all was forgotten when Big Scott started belting out good old blues numbers, like Stormy Monday, Bullfrog Blues and Pretty Vacant, yeah, go figure as they say in the colonies. Don't you just love the blues? And while I write this I have my headphones on listening to some Emmylou Harris, wondering what it was all about. Blues, rock, country, punk.

Never, ever think there are boundaries to your life.

December 4ᵗʰ - Sunday

Head Launcher, TS and I had agreed we would meet down at the Lifeboat station at ten o'clock this morning, as the boat was due at around eleven and there was a heap of weed on the short slip to dig away. The pagers went off at eight-thirty, inviting the crew to muster at nine-thirty to drive to Newlyn to pick up the boat. Following so far? When I turned up at nine forty-five the rest of the shore crew were already there, presumably heeding the nine-thirty boat crew muster, and most of the weed had been removed. Unfortunately I cannot see the short slip from the flat, else I would have turned up after they had finished.

The Lifeboat duly arrived at around eleven o'clock, in a very bouncy sea with strong breeze building from the west. There were some precautions taken, but the swell in the Harbour was not too bad and although it was not the easiest of recoveries, the boat was safely hauled up the slip in a textbook operation by the very excellent Shore Crew.

All this mucking about with Lifeboats rather put the boot in to my plans for today. Up until the shout last night I was all geared up for another trip down Geevor mine, with our tame mining guide. This time we were to traverse the crawling section out under Levant. With lessons learnt from the last trip I had invested in a helmet lamp and a waterproof grab bag to sling around my waist, now all destined to be unused. Although the trip did go ahead, a couple of hours later than planned, it would have interfered with the hastily arranged plans to ship the Missus off on her long journey a day earlier than originally scheduled.

As I sit penning this page I cut a lonely figure in our front room with just a ragged bleddy hound for company. It will be thus for the next few days while the Missus visits her mate up in a northern tundra, somewhere the other side of Launceston. It could have been worse; I could have been going too. There is a disadvantage to not being there, though. I cannot be the voice of restraint and there is a designer outlet village nearby and, I understand, an Ikea store. It is entirely possible that Northamptonshire will benefit from the Missus's largesse and avoid a double-dip recession along with Devon and, all before Christmas too.

I consoled myself by donning my waterproofs and heading down to the big beach with the bleddy hound. She did not get much exercise yesterday, or the day before that for that matter. She was her usual buoyant and enthusiastic self, charging down the road, but when we got there her mood suddenly changed. Whether it was the strong wind blowing up her bum, or the fact it was threatening rain I shall never know, but having given the ball a couple of half-hearted chases she turned around and headed for the slipway, taking the ball with her. Game over, as they say.

Ah well, it is not all bad. I have a couple of shooty bangy movies stashed away that I can watch at the proper volume – loud. I would never get away with that else.

December 5th – Monday

Golly, it was a wild and windy night, followed by a wild and windy morning and a wild and windy rest of the day. If it were not for the bleddy hound I would not have stepped outside the door at all. As I look out on the bay just now there is a deep grey mist descending and moving swiftly towards us, except it is not mist, it is a guts full of dark, hacking rain. Bleddy 'ansum.

There were enough breaks in the showers to manage to drag the dog around a few times today without getting wet. After yesterday's performance there was no way I was taking her down to the beach, so an alternative was required.

With this in mind the Missus rather fortuitously left me some presents, well, they are actually presents for other people that require putting in the post at the post office. As she had taken the van, this would require toting them up by hand and she very helpfully suggested I use one of the large re-usable carry bags, the type you get from supermarkets, to assist me in this task. I am guessing at this juncture that they do not have post offices in Northamptonshire, else I am certain she would have done the sensible thing and taken them with her.

There was no point in double guessing the weather, so I geared up in waterproofs and went in search of said large carry bag. Large though it certainly was, it would only accommodate two of the parcels and with a bleddy hound in one hand and the bag in the other, I had no choice other than select one to leave behind. Again I had to scratch my head somewhat, as one of the parcels is destined for the parents-in-law; the Missus is dropping in on them on the way home. There is bound to be some perverse logic that is eluding me as to why she could not have taken it with her.

Anyway, with bag and bleddy hound I set forth up Stonechair Lane. It is a stiff enough climb on its own, without having a small dog tugging you back down it because there was a blade of grass she forgot to sniff as she passed it the first time. One such omission I might have been persuaded to forgive, but by the time we had crested the incline she had missed more than a dozen such blades of grass. It did not help that the two parcels I was toting appeared to have gained weight the further I walked. The proof of this particular pudding was that they cost nearly fifteen quid to send, which is probably the main reason why I was the poor sod posting them.

It was less sheltered crossing Esther's Field, which is a bit of an understatement. It was here, of course, that the bleddy hound found it necessary to do something that required me to stop and wrestle a gossamer thin plastic bag from my pocket, unravel it inside out with one hand, while holding onto the dog and the carry bag with the other. It would have been easier to make a scale model of the houses of parliament out of matchsticks, while standing on your head and wearing boxing gloves.

We had a slightly better time of it on the way back and we detoured over Mayon Cliff to give her a bit of a run. By some miracle we managed to avoid being covered in fox or badger perfume too although she was a bit on the muddy side by the time we got home.

For the rest of the afternoon I did what I should have done in the first place and stayed indoors. This would have given me the ideal opportunity to test my theory with the matchstick houses of parliament, but would you guess it? No boxing gloves.

December 6th - Tuesday

By the miracle of modern mobile telecommunications I spoke with the Missus this morning. I told her that I had only been able to post two of the parcels she had entrusted me with, and that her Mum and Dad would have to wait for their parcel until I got the van back. She was a little put out, but I told her that under no circumstances, not even at the point that the Underworld suffered such a catastrophic climate change that it became ice-bound, would I even consider making another trip up to the post office with parcel and bleddy hound.

Once again I found that my waterproofs were superfluous on my way up the hill with the parcel and the bleddy hound. So far I seem to have managed to avoid the heavy showers that have plagued us. Since we were earlier than yesterday, and to avoid the onset of Groundhog Day, I took the high road and headed out towards Land's End.

We hacked across the moors and joined the coastal path back to The Cove. Despite the recent rain there was very little lying water, and the streams still had not swelled to their normal babbling brook-like selves. It was muddy in places, however, and the short legs on my companion soon meant her belly caked in black mire. I thought I might be able to get away with just rubbing her down with a towel, but by the time we got home she was lagged.

She has much improved her bath-time manners since I last hosed her down. She was happily led to the bathroom and jumped, without coercion, into the shower. She was a little less keen when I turned on the water, but it was still less than the battle of wills it was previously.

It was only when I got back into the living room that I noticed a note stuffed through the door. It told me that I had missed a delivery, one that I had been looking forward to. When I followed this up it seems it will be delivered tomorrow at some unspecified time, which means waiting in until it gets here. It rather means that the sparkling clean bleddy hound will have to forego her usual lengthy walk tomorrow and even the short ones will have to be carefully timed.

Because it is Tuesday and cards night at the OS I had arranged with our good neighbour, we have only one now, that she look after the dog for the evening. She never has been one to spend any time alone, that is the bleddy hound, not the neighbour, as far as I know the neighbour is quite happy spending time alone, anyway we have not bothered to train her to become accustomed to it.

I felt it polite to ensure she was empty before I dropped her around, so I ran her down to the slip. As we stepped out a hefty shower emerged from a sky that had been dry all evening. The battle of wills that I had evaded earlier, now ensued with full vigour. She wanted to go back indoors and I wanted her to have a wee. The end result was that, while I eventually won the day, we were both soaked through and you wonder why I call her the bleddy hound. The person that came up with the phrase, 'a dog is a man's best friend', clearly never had one, or at least not this one.

Poker at the OS was a cosy affair, with just eight of us vying for the spoils of war. I dropped out roughly in the middle of the field this week and returned to our neighbour to find my ward pressed up against the front door, waiting for me.

I am sure she takes some sort of perverse pleasure out of hounding me day and night. I am so looking forward to being stuck in the house all day with her tomorrow!

December 7ᵗʰ - Wednesday

Today was earmarked to be the laziest that I have spent in recent days and, believe me, that is saying something.

As you know I had to stay in, waiting on the delivery of our new toy, a technical gizmo that will connect all the Missus's Bramley computer products and allow their content to be presented on the television. As she has all her Bramley products with her, I imagined that setting it up and testing it would be rather limited, so I left it until quite late in the evening and now I wish I had not.

The box itself is tiny; it will fit in the palm of my hand. Wow. The set up was easy peasy and I have spent far too long looking at all the wonderful things it can do, even without the Missus's Bramley products. If I had set it up earlier, I would have spent many more hours playing with it.

As it was it sat in its box, while I discovered that I must now make another run up to the post office in the morning. The Aged Parent greased my palm with gold and asked that I send some packages to the far corners of the known world, when I visited some four weeks ago. The Aged Parent has waited until two days before the last posting day to the far corner of the known world, to let me have the addresses. Thanks for that Aged Parent. Fortunately for the Aged Parent, it transpires that I would have had to trek up there anyway, as someone has discovered that the website has a shop and has actually purchased something.

We have, sorry, we had, a sign attached to the railings at the far end of The Cove alerting anyone who might care that there is a shop at the other end of The Cove, namely The Old Boathouse. This sign has remained in place for two years or more, attached by no less than six man sized cable ties. When I last checked its security, a couple of weeks ago, all six ties were sound. Imagine my surprise then when Big A stopped by this morning to tell me that it was hanging precariously off one corner and in this wind about to blow away. As if to prove his report, another neighbourly character came along ten minutes later carrying my sign. Fancy that, two neighbourly characters passing by within a few minutes of each other. That is almost as coincidental as five sound cable ties all failing at the same moment.

And that was it. That was the full and unexpurgated story of the day. If you can stand the excitement, tune in tomorrow for some more dynamic and cutting edge literary gymnastics. Bet you cannot wait.

December 8th - Thursday

With my chores lined up for the day and the weather due to close in this afternoon in a very big way, it was only sensible to get moving early this morning. So with back pack full of packages and bleddy hound in tow, it was up the hill again to the post office. If I carry on like this I might actually get to enjoy these little scampers up Stonechair Lane, in the personal groove that I have worn. I do not think that the bleddy hound will ever get to enjoy being tied up outside the post office though.

I rewarded her with a walk down to the big beach afterwards. I have not been down the footpath alongside Cove Hill since at least the beginning of the year. I remember remarking then that the steps down were getting deeper and this time I am convinced they are deeper still. One step down was at least eighteen inches and with loose stones on the approach, I ended up taking it in a single bound, nearly landing on the dog.

Even last year, I cannot imagine it was a very attractive proposition with pushchairs and beach paraphernalia. Being the main safe route down from the top car park, perhaps it is about time it received some attention.

The beach was not as idyllic as it looked from the top. The wind was piling in from the west, with between forty and fifty miles per hour gusts. I threw the ball with the ball thrower a couple of times down wind, and the bleddy hound was gone for ten minutes trying to catch it up. I had taken her down Coastguard Row this morning and a single gust nearly scat her across the lane. On the beach it was much worse. I could not throw the ball at all in the windward direction, so we gave up and hacked back to the slip. I tried to keep on the wet sand so she was not too badly sand-blasted. It is the first time that I have seen the ripples in the sand running up the beach instead of across it. I think we were both grateful we did not hang around.

The Missus returned to the fold in the early evening, just in time for me to disappear across the road for a spot of Lifeboat training. Tonight we learned how to make the station floor sparkling clean, before trotting off to the OS for the obligatory quiz night. Modesty forbids me to tell you how miserably we did again, but it has to be said that most of the team deserted us midway, leaving us to suffer ignominy alone.

The wet deluge that we were promised had blown through, almost unnoticed, by the time I came home and the skies were clearing. It was almost pleasant running the bleddy hound round the block under the silvery moonlight. Not a bad consolation prize.

December 9ᵗʰ - Friday

Well, there is a turn up for the books; I got a lie in this morning for free. What happened was, the bleddy hound had a barking fit at around half past six. We know that around this time her arch enemy and her nemesis, is paraded past our shop. It is another hound that lives just down the road and the mere suggestion of her, sends the bleddy hound into apoplexy. The owner and his close associates, get a toned down version of the barking frenzy, even when the dog is nowhere to be seen.

I have been spared this reaction while the Missus was away and normally it is I, that am roused from my slumber. This morning, however, I turned my good ear to the pillow and let my deaf ear take the battering. The Missus, with two good ears, lost this war of attrition and, hey presto, I got to lie, fitfully snoozing, till long after what was good for me. I will, no doubt, be fitted up with a cold pudding of revenge when I least expect it and at a time that will wreak the most damage, which is very probably tomorrow morning.

December 10th – Saturday

Surprisingly I was up and at 'em before my alarm went off this morning. Although the bleddy hound got up to see what was going on, she did not take much convincing that she should return to bed, when the reveille did not include eating something or chasing a ball. So, with little formality, our Lifeboat was launched into a silvery sea, under a setting moon. The boathouse was battened down and I returned to my bed to finish off a fitful and necessary repose, only to find that the bleddy hound had taken my place.

We spent some time yesterday ferreting about in the loft, well the Missus did. This is where the Christmas decorations are stored for eleven and a half months of the year. It is a wonder of modern, or maybe quite old, engineering that the ceiling has, over the years, withstood the enormous weight; it is the stuff of legend. There must be some twenty or so boxes, bags and suitcases full of the sparkling and glittery objects, and each year this number increases.

Today I was entreated to ferry many of these boxes down to the shop, so that the Missus could make a start on the decoration of the window. I also had to remove the windbreak stand, the famous ball stand and the net bin up to Shrew House, as there is insufficient space to accommodate them all in the shop, with the grand display. I know already that all we will be asked for this Christmas is windbreaks, balls and nets.

While the Missus laboured away making a spectacle of the shop, I was rather alarmed to see a Lifeboat appear in the bay, nearly an hour ahead of schedule. Any hope of a swift response to prepare the scene for recovery was dashed, when I saw the amount of oar weed that had piled up on the short slip. It took us a good half an hour to clear it away. Just think Buster Keaton, and a plethora of banana skins, and you will have some idea of the problem we faced.

After such an arduous recovery, it was only fair that I should recoup and repair to the F&L for the evening. Since we still had no provisions worth a button, there was only one thing to do – take to the F&L for tea. You will understand that this requires an early attendance, to ensure that we are clear before the band kicks off and, therefore, an extended session of making merry. One has to make sacrifices, you know.

December 12ᵗʰ – Monday

The shop window looks very pretty even for those with SCAS, (severe Christmas aversion syndrome). Come on, it cannot possibly be my fault I do not like Christmas. Everything else has a syndrome, from obsessive cleaning to being an errant child, so I do not see why I should not have an excuse. There will be a drug out soon that will have me grinning from ear to ear all season long. After one Christmas of that, I imagine everyone will be more than happy to have the old miserable sod back.

December 13ᵗʰ – Tuesday

I noticed a while ago that the council has swapped those parking tickets that have a patch of sticky paper on the back, for ones that do not, roughly at the time they put up the prices, I think. It intrigued me how you would manage to rest these on top of the dashboard on a windy day. I found out today.

What happens is, you rest it on top of the dashboard and just as you are about to close the door, it blows off the dashboard and floats off into the van somewhere. You then spend ten minutes searching for it among the other, old car park tickets that you forgot to throw away. When you have found it, you then repeat the process of selecting a more sheltered part of the top of the dashboard. You then find that, although it has not been blown away by the wind, the mere act of closing the door creates enough draft for it to waft off the dashboard and onto the floor. By this time, you have fifteen minutes less parking than you did when you put the money into the machine. I did manage, in the end, to slip one edge of the ticket under the heating vent, which worked after a fashion but left the ticket in not the most visible location. I hoped for the best and left it there, before my time ran out completely.

I bumped into a chap in town who, from time to time, does some work for the Shark Trust. Rather him than me you might think as that is probably the last thing you would want to do to a shark. However, through him, I had some basking shark pictures published on the Internet a few years ago. He was delighted to inform me that the same pictures had now found their way into a brochure the Shark Trust had produced. They have had some success in using some photographs to identify individual sharks by their dorsal fin, so that they can be tracked. The idea being that by noting markings or scars on the fin, watchers from different locations may identify a particular shark that, one day, was seen in Cornwall and another off Scotland or Ireland, perhaps. It is unlikely that they will use my photographs for such a project, as the shark I photographed is unlikely to be spotted anywhere, as it was a tad dead at the time.

I know by saying this I will open the doors to the weather's raging fury, but I cannot help noticing how lucky I have been with my trips out with the bleddy hound. We seem to have found the optimum times for our walks where the rain has been slight or just ending. Today was no different, as no longer than thirty minutes after we got back home a series of squalls ran through The Cove.

Tune in tomorrow for a graphic description of me being soaked to the skin and the ensuing pneumonia, trench foot and distemper I suffered as a result. (Sorry about the distemper, but I needed a third gruesome illness to make it scan right and that was the first thing that popped into my head.)

I know, I know, there is usually a game of cards on a Tuesday night that I normally end up with. Did you really have to ask? Perhaps we can just skip to me feeling so confidant about missing the bad weather, that I decided not to be fully equipped with my waterproof over-trousers and how on the way home my nether regions, (below the thigh, ladies, you naughty things), were soaked through to the skin. Not exactly Mr Darcy, I am afraid.

December 14ᵗʰ – Wednesday

The bleddy hound had a visitor for most of the afternoon, the neighbour's dog, and she does not do the beach. So that was it. Very much a looking out of the window sort of day and spotting the two people that passed the shop and I think there were three cars. That is a busy day for mid December, but I have no idea what the commotion was all about.

One commotion that I am rather excited about is the news that the Eden Project is to host the first World Pasty Championships. Modesty prevents me from mentioning that a certain Cove shopkeeper is current holder of the best pasty in the parish title. Darn it, I mentioned it. Anyway it is knowledge already in the public domain, (it would be unnecessarily vulgar to suggest that it was I that put it there), so there probably was no need to mention it anyway. Clearly it is a little too early to expect my invitation to have dropped through the door, but being the aforementioned title holder it is surely just a matter of time.

There is only one fly in the proverbial shortcrust pastry; the championship is to be held on 3ʳᵈ March. Only two days later another such competition will take place at the F&L where I shall be expected to defend my title. You will, of course, appreciate the preparation, both physical and mental, that must be undertaken in such battles for supremacy. Even top athletes are given sufficient time to recoup between events to be able to compete at their best. I feel a sacrifice will have to be made and one of the competitions will have to manage without me.

Far be it from me to disappoint a world that is hungry for pasty perfection. Eden would be the pinnacle of a pasty making career stretching back, what, nearly ten months. So I will hold my head aloft, carry forth the flag of Cornish pasty making, cry God for cousin Jack, Cornwall and St Piran and make my stand at the F&L on March 5ᵗʰ.

Blow me, will I ever be hacked off if it gets cancelled because Manchester United are playing Real Madrid in some cup match.

AR has asked me to point out that the Southern Counties Ambulance Service, or SCAS for short, is not in any way connected with my use of the same initials which I suggested meant severe Christmas aversion syndrome. I should make it clear that, by using those initials that I willingly admit they have prior and exclusive use of, I made no implication either expressly or otherwise that the Southern Counties Ambulance Service is in any way averse to the season of joy, happiness and good will to all men.

I trust that puts that one to bed but come on, there must be a few miserable old goats among them; and anyway reading The Diary while driving an ambulance must be illegal, if not a tad dangerous.

I have written myself a mental note, (I find that increasingly I have to commit my mental notes to paper), never to succumb to illness or accident in the southern counties. I imagine the ambulance may inexplicably become lost on its way to my aid.

December 15ᵗʰ – Thursday

It looks like I have put my size nine in it again. Despite my best heartfelt regrets, (without prejudice, of course,) in using the initials SCAS it seems that I regretted to the wrong ambulance team. It was to the brave fellows and (feminine plural of fellow anyone? Fellas?), anyway, of the *South Central* Ambulance Service to which my disclaimer, sorry, regrets were meant. What makes it worse is that there *is* a Southern Counties Ambulance Service that has now been pulled into the fray. Oh bother, I will steer clear of making up acronyms in future.

I have not been to Porthcurno for so long that I almost missed the turn off. It would be ingenuous of me to recommend it, particularly in the pouring rain, but at least it was sheltered from the prevailing wind. There was even a rock pool, well, more a rock pond really for the bleddy hound to swim in. On closer inspection it seems that the tide had not refreshed the minor lake for some time, as it contained brackish and rather foul looking water. We avoided it.

As you might imagine the bleddy hound was fair covered in sand and dripping from the rain by the time we returned to the van. I invited her to climb into her own seat for the journey home, but first she preferred to jump over to the driver's seat and shake off the accumulated mire there, before settling on her throne. To ensure that I fully appreciated the gesture she did it again before I turned her out when we got home.

In our absence the Missus had gone about decorating the flat with Christmas lights and baubles of every sort. Even the lights have lights. It is very modern in appearance, with LEDs and fibre optics and 'SAMTSIRHC YRREM' written across our large picture window in lit perspex characters, the detail of which cannot, unfortunately, be seen from the road outside.

While I took the precaution of carrying waterproof trousers to ward against another soaking on my way home after Lifeboat training and the quiz night, of which I shall say very little, the promised deluge seemed to have avoided us. The clearing skies did afford me an excellent view of our humble abode from the other end of The Cove.

You can imagine my excitement when I returned home to find an email from NASA in my inbox. It informed me that the Voyager spacecraft has identified The Old Boathouse Stores from just the other side of Mars. They have asked that we dim our Christmas lights, just a little, as the reflection is inhibiting the Hubble telescope's view of distant galaxies.

December 16ᵗʰ - Friday

It must have been reasonably bad through the night as one of the power lines in Coastguard Row was down. We also noticed that the power pole across the road at the Lifeboat station was sparking last night in the rain. I reported both these events this morning and was rather impressed to see the electric company vehicles arriving no more that an hour later.

I do not quite know how it happened, but in the midst of doing stuff it was suddenly half past midday and I had not even missed my breakfast. I know I had invented quite a list of things to do, including switching allegiance to the incoming refuse collection company for this area who start in April next year. The trigger for this particular task was that I received a letter from the current commercial waste collectors telling me that my annual Waste Transfer Note renewal was due, er, at the end of February. It is a legal requirement to complete this form each year, but a reminder to complete it almost three months early was a black bag too far.

I note that Penzance is considering a design for a new logo. I have to confess that I did not know they had an old one. I am sure that we all know that designs for new branding can cost a fortune simply for the design, let alone the ensuing costs of new stationery and signage. It is clearly a priority, as I can think of nothing the town needs more. For what it is worth, I suggest a modern scene with a representation of Market Jew Street in the background complete with tumbleweed, being drawn to three black holes in the foreground named, for example, Tesco, Sainsburys and Morrisons. Should be spot on, that.

Now, with such a beautiful day set out before me, it was only fair that the bleddy hound should benefit from a little run down to the beach. Yes, I know that no particular thought or planning went into this adventure but, hey, sometimes you just need to take the world by the scruff of the neck, and the bleddy hound, obviously.

So off we went, directly to the beach this time. I must admit that it was a tad colder than I anticipated, with the wind coming in from the northwest. Still, it was not exactly howling and we had set up a good warming pace. It was not until I found a rock to perch on and throw the ball in this direction and that, that I noticed my fingers going blue. I will not pull my punches here, so children, close your ears, it was blinking cold.

We were down there for the best part of three quarters of an hour when I noticed a shower piling in across the bay. It did look like a big one and sported dark orangey colours in the low sun. As a precaution I started up the dune behind us towards Carn Keys, which was when the first wave of hail hit us. It was a good move, as we made it to the pillbox below the black huts just as the worst of it came through. It was probably the first, and only, time anyone has thought that the Second World War did anyone any good and then only for purely selfish reasons; the pillbox is still open and provides excellent shelter.

We made our way back through Vellandreath and to the OS for a reviving libation. Is it not odd how things look so different in reverse; we very rarely traverse the dunes in that direction.

I have not repaired to the OS after a run on the beach for some while, mainly as it is not the place it was for retiring to, mid afternoon. Nevertheless the warmth was welcome and with the landlord in attendance it was a convivial interlude. The bleddy hound was not that keen, though, so we did not stay long and returned home for some well earned rest.

I was rather concerned, as I sat here and penned away my exciting adventures, that the electric company I had congratulated on their smart response, had failed to fix the electric pole across the road. There were blue flashes lighting up the window and it certainly was not our Christmas lights. It took me a minute or so to realise that it was in fact lightning causing the flashing, the big clue being the rumbling thunder that followed each flash.

Little did I know that electrical disturbance would be the theme of the night; High Voltage was playing at the F&L. Did you see the subtle literary trick I used there? Well, they were playing for a long while until the electricity failed them. Plunged into darkness and silence they were, time after time, until at last they succumbed and gave up.

I trust all is restored for tomorrow night, as Devil's Creek are playing. I think I may have mentioned them before.

And then a wonderful thing happened. A temporarily redundant barman offered me a lift home. Life does not get much better than that.

December 18ᵗʰ - Sunday

The busiest it has been for some while down in The Cove today. Our next door café opened up for the Christmas rush, which was very nice as it sorted out breakfast for us. Even the beach was crowded when I took the bleddy hound down for a run. Well, when I say crowded it is, of course, a comparative term when you are used to being down there on your own.

It is not surprising that there were a few more around today as it is the first day in a week or more that the wind has dropped out. The sea too has settled, although it must have had a bit of a swansong last night. There are rocks where yesterday there was three feet depth of virgin sand. It certainly has not moved to the other end of the beach, as the rock I sit on was still the same height as yesterday.

As you can see, with all this literary clowning around it was another day devoid of anything very much. And clowning around as we know it certainly would not have been possible without Joseph Grimaldi who was born today in 1779. He invented the white faced clown that makes us either laugh, or gives us the screaming ad dabs if you are coulrophobic. He also came up with the idea of the pantomime dame, oh, yes he did, which is not half as scary until you consider the licence it gave grown men to dress up as women as a form of entertainment.

Talking of scary things the Missus has been running around cleaning, scrubbing and washing in preparation for the grand visitation of the in-laws over the Christmas period. Clearly I have been helping as best I can by making myself as scarce as possible, a habit I have become so accustomed to I might find it hard to break over the next couple of weeks.

Fortunately we did not encounter any clowns or pantomine dames in the F&L when we went up there for the third night running, although there were a few dodgy characters watching the football. We dined with our neighbours, as neither of us had thought about getting any tea in again. We will have to do better from tomorrow night; I would hate the in-laws to feel that they are not welcome.

December 19ᵗʰ – Monday

As the shop is opening on Wednesday it seemed sensible to get a little stock in to spread around the bare shelves. So it was off to Hayle and as you know there is one thing that must be done when you go off to Hayle. We had a little conversation with the neighbours last night about whether Hampsens or Philps were the premier cru of pasties in this neck of the woods. To be honest there is not much between them, but I still prefer a Philps and you can park in their free car park over-looking South Quay, which is better than sitting in the Foundry Square car park looking at the White Hart and paying for a space.

By the time I got back to The Cove it was looking very bleak and the in-laws had parked in front of the shop where I wanted to unload. Very kindly the brother-in-law offered to help unload the van when he came down to move his car. Now all we have to do is get it out on the shelves and he did not offer to do that. I will try the sister-in-law tomorrow; it must be her turn.

Our trusty young dog walker made a timely appearance just as we were finishing off the unloading. She must have been gone an hour with the bleddy hound, which got me off the hook for running her out in the heavy mizzle. She was dripping and bedraggled when she got back and behaved herself for the rest of the afternoon – lest she was dragged out again, I suppose.

I must prepare myself, zen like, for early morning rises, newspapers that I have to beg to be delivered and the delight of meeting your good selves full of Christmas cheer. I still have a little over twenty four hours to save the world. Best I use it wisely.

December 20th – Tuesday

I had a bit of a restless night, banished as I was to the spare room amongst the wellie boots, old bags and unwanted Christmas decorations. I and the Christmas Fairy had one crazy night together, I can tell you. It was no surprise I was up early this morning; she is none too careful with that starry wand.

There was a flurry of activity this morning as I remembered all the things I forgot to organise yesterday. We will now have bread, milk, cream, bacon and the Missus stole a march on me and remembered to order the eggs yesterday. We will all have to cross our fingers that the Laurel and Hardy Newspaper Company has remembered to schedule my newspaper delivery. Actually I was quite impressed this year, after my initial prompt they telephoned *me* to say they had set everything up. I nearly fell off my seat.

Down in the shop there was the detritus from the window dressing and the defrosting of the freezers to deal with. In a room that has been largely undisturbed for a month and a half, it is amazing just how much dust accumulates. It is also quite amazing just how adept we have become at making a purse out of a sow's ear after eight years of practise; you will have to look very hard to see the join. We are as ready as we will ever be for a short shop opening tomorrow – maybe.

With all that in hand it was time for some serious relaxation. With a full house and guests chatting away that was entirely off the menu, so I settled for completing an order for the things I forgot from the cash and carry yesterday. The young dog walker whisked off the bleddy hound so I could not even run her around.

It was then I remembered that I had been offered the use of the neighbour's fields to do a bit of rabbitting. As the guests seem to be quite good at it already, I thought I would do some of my own. I generally knew the location of the fields, but was not entirely sure that they would be appropriate. I parked up on the rough lane and leaving the gun behind took a walk up to have a look-see first. I am glad I did, as when I arrived at the gate there was someone walking their dog over one of the fields and not a rabbit to be seen. I am going to have to think again, as I do not believe that I want a trophy collie's head hanging off my wall.

I will not trouble you with the results of the infamous cards night at the OS. Needless to say my lucky streak is holding firm. Week by week I am running out of shirts. Thankfully they have called a hiatus for next week, which will give me time to buy another one, if I do not get one for Christmas.

December 21ˢᵗ – Wednesday

Happy Montol if you happen to be in the glittering city of Penzance. For the last five years various groups have come together and created a growing celebration of the dark season. The Cornish word Montol can be roughly equated with 'balance', and the word was chosen as the event has been created to balance the Golowan festival at the other end of the year. They even have a little march up to the hill fort, the highest point in PZ, no doubt gaily dressed and making a lot of noise. Well, good luck to them, I say. We need a bit of colour and cheer at this gloomy time of the year.

Here is a nice little story. South West highways have agreed to suspend roadworks on the M5 at the junction with the A30. You will think, 'that's rather congenial of them, helping to let traffic down to the Westcountry flow more smoothly over the festive period'. Well, not really. All the traffic restrictions will stay in place. So let us have another look at that seasonal act of goodwill. South West Highways is stopping work for 11 days thus extending the misery of those that use that junction on a regular basis by nearly two weeks, while the boys have a bit of a knees up. Yes, that just about sums it up.

Well, as I told you, we were due to open the shop for the Christmas period today and we duly did. We were not exactly inundated by customers, but there were a few and a reasonable indicator that we have not entirely wasted our time. Anyway, it was very nice to get back into the saddle, as it were. Yee-hah!

The meagre supplies we drafted in are spread about the shelves, giving an appearance that we have made some effort to anticipate demand. We have even pushed the boundaries of optimism and bought in some fresh fruit and vegetables; the apples are very nice, thank you for asking. I thought I better try some before we have to throw them all away.

December 22nd – Thursday

Happy Winter Solstice and for those of you, including the Montol Festival organisers, who thought it was yesterday, ya-boo sucks. As all good schoolboys will know, (all right, I am sure there are a couple of schoolgirls too), the Solstice is when the Earth's axial tilt reaches its maximum of 23 degrees and 26 minutes. So if you too thought that yesterday was rather short and the night rather long, you are going to have an even shorter and longer one today.

Did I really commit myself to print, heaping praise on the Laurel and Hardy Newspaper Company a couple of days ago for registering our opening? It must have been a temporary aberration, a small moment of weakness. Yesterday we only received four copies of our most popular newspaper, which I have to admit was partly my own fault for not specifying the volume I required. However, having spotted the error of my ways, I had to go to some lengths to amend the omission. I probably should not have been surprised that this morning I was sent the desired quantity of newspapers, but of the wrong title. Further investigation revealed that they had cancelled my most popular title altogether for the next few days.

It is partly for this reason that we normally open a good couple of weeks ahead of any busy period. It can easily take that long to beat the L&HN Co. into providing a sensible and stable supply.

Adding insult to injury we did not get any of *The Cornishman* today. These are distributed by another newspaper company, which now apparently does not have any spares to correct the problem. Given I had arranged the supply over a couple of weeks ago, I am somewhat aggrieved. What really sticks in the craw is that the company that produces *The Cornishman* and *West Briton* whinges and gripes that circulation is decreasing and they are finding it hard to make ends meet. Well, here is a hint: try supplying papers when they are asked for!

The day was grey and uninspiring enough without these shenanigans. There appeared to be a few more people around, however, noticing that the shop was open. Of course, many came in asking for *The Cornishman,* which was aggravating in the extreme.

It was also aggravating for the young lady that came into the shop asking if I knew of anyone who had a small boat for sale, that was not the small boat that I have for sale in the shop window. I would have suggested she look in *The Cornishman,* had I one to offer, but apparently she had already looked in that. She needed a boat as soon as possible to take her around the coast on some mission or other. It struck me that she would have brooked no challenge to the sanity of her crusade, so a challenge I did not brook. If she does find a boat, I trust that it is not anywhere from Pendeen Watch to Porthcurno. The Lifeboat crew has a bit of a Christmas beano tonight and it would not be cricket to interrupt it for a loose nut in a Christmas stocking.

The Missus disappeared off to town this morning for a hair cut, although it is probably called something else for girlies. The hairdresser she goes to must have been very busy of late. I cannot think of any other reason she would have waited six weeks for the shop to be open, before booking an appointment. At least I did not have the bleddy hound to worry about, as our youthful walker took her away for most of the morning and into the afternoon; the beast was fair drooping when she was delivered back. I doubt she will cause much trouble this afternoon.

And now to the F&L for that little Lifeboat bash I spoke of earlier. I do apologise, I remember very little or at least that is what I have been told. What I do remember is, er … Anyway I am sure it was a very agreeable evening.

December 23rd – Friday

The Missus took the parents-in-law up to Travaskis Farm in the late morning to arrive there in time for a spot of dinner. I am destined never to dine at the renowned eatery, so I can only report the hearsay that it offers attractive and tasty fare. I am sure, if you wish, you can get sprouts there, though there is roughly half of you that would spurn the little brassica oleraceas and now I can tell you why. Scientists at the Eden Project, using DNA technology, have discovered that there is a gene, which, if you are unlucky enough to be in possession of, will allow you to identify some bitterness in the sprout. It is believed that the potential sprout eating population of the world is split, with roughly half enjoying sprouts and the other half holding their noses.

While on the subject of completely useless nuggets of fact another group of scientists have discovered that elephants have six toes. Absolutely blinding, I am sure you will agree. Apparently the additional piggy is for balance and stops your umbrella stand from falling over. The really stunning facts in this, are that there are scientists earning a living off the back of counting elephant toes and that it is thought that elephants have had six toes for sixty million years. Why did no one notice before?

I was surprised by the arrival of the bleddy hound's other visiting dog walkers this afternoon. These are not so youthful as the other, but the walks are considerably more hardcore and she is often gone for hours at a time. They took her down to the beach for a run around this afternoon, as a sort of warm up I suspect. They are coming back tomorrow too, so by the end of next week her little paws will be smoking.

And talking of hardcore, which will no doubt have me censored from educational networks in the North East, it is time now for a quiet evening in, I think. In all likelihood tomorrow will get rather ugly, particularly towards the end of it. I intend to be fully prepared.

December 24ᵗʰ - Saturday

Nadelik Lowen, since you will be reading this on Christmas Day, which is, of course, Happy Christmas in the Cornish tongue. This is for everyone, with the exception of the blethering eejits at the Laurel and Hardy Newspaper Company who upset me greatly again this morning by not fulfilling their promise to send me adequate numbers of our best selling newspaper.

The Missus usually concocts some potent brew in our electric wok for passing visitors today and Boxing Day. It is a heady blend of cheap wine, spirit and rotting fruit and handed out freely. It is our little way of getting our own back on rascally customers we have endured during the year. We also throw in some mince pies, if we can find any sufficiently out of date. Unfortunately, even having waltzed off shopping yesterday, the Missus forgot to collect the ingredients from the dustbins of parish.

It was down to me this morning to foray out to remedy the issue of the missing mulled wine parts. I had originally planned to send out to the local cash and carry and have them deliver, but there was no guarantee that they would have what we wanted. I was loath to trip into PZ on a Christmas Eve as I imagine that there would be carnage involved, so it was off to St Just for me. If the town was anything like a mini reflection of what it was like in PZ I am really glad I did not go there. There were people everywhere, many in seasonally fun hats or just with tinsel in their hair. I would have joined in had I only known, but am somewhat at a natural disadvantage – no tinsel, you see. They even had the Pendeen Silver Band playing outside the Co-op. They looked very confident, playing their light Christmas airs, with the gleaming instruments security chained to their wrists.

Perhaps I should be a little more circumspect. In a moment of weakness on Thursday night I was cajoled into joining the Christmas Eve bus that tours the parishes of St Just, St Levan and St Buryan, returning to St Sennen, just past the church on the left, later in the evening. I already have a fatima (like a fatwa but more determined) against me in St Ives after being quoted out of context in the newspaper. It would not do to be barred from St Just as well.

[Space reserved for footnote if still capable enough to form cogent thought and/or write when I get home.]

The decision on cogent thought is marginal so I can try and tell you that all went reasonably well for tow bus loads of peripatetic drinkers. It was an interesting exclusion with uos and dows. Noe all they need to fo is invebt a key boatrd for drunks and we are away.

Now just enough time to leave you the traditional heart-warming image of a small child standing in the snow in dirty tattered clothes and a limp, for added effect, waving and calling out 'Happy Christmas everybody'. Tugs at the heart-strings, don't it?

December 25ᵗʰ – Sunday

I had already agreed with our dog walking neighbours that I would accompany them down to the beach this morning for the traditional Christmas Day dip. Sorry, let me re-phrase that last bit ... to watch the traditional Christmas Day dip. As it happened I was a little late and they went ahead with the dog, but without me. They said they would be quite easy to spot and even then I would see the bleddy hound. Well, when I got to the top of the slip there was already a large crowd of people down on the beach, and to make matters worse it appears that most of them had dogs; you have never seen so many hounds on the beach. Our neighbours had very distinctive Santa hats, yep, you guessed it, so did many others. Fortunately they spotted me and with some frantic waving I managed to meet up with them.

It was in 1864 that the slightly deranged chaps in Hyde Park decided to jump into the Serpentine, and from that day it seems the lunacy had spread and infected us down here. Every year a growing bunch of half naked people throw themselves into the sea on Christmas morning. I, of course, maintain my sense of dignity, such as it is, and keep my clothes on. The bleddy hound, however, is utterly delighted that so many humans find the pull of the waves irresistible, as does she, and happily jumped in beside them.

So, with drowned hound, I returned to the fold for the formal ceremony of present opening, revealing jumpers, smelly stuff and, of course socks. Now, socks are one thing, socks made from bamboo are a completely different kettle of yoghurt. For a start it is difficult to imagine how they made the bamboo go around corners, and for another I do not particularly want to be chased down the street by hungry pandas. It also brings a tingling to the buttocks, reminiscent of those school days bent over the headmaster's desk. Ah, halcyon days.

In previous years it has been de rigueur to attend the OS for a couple of beers ahead of the Christmas dinner. The Missus, keen to stop me interfering in the kitchen, is happy that I maintain the tradition and return only when it is time to carve the Christmas pasty. While I am normally happy to comply with these demands, this year I was hard pressed to stay more than an hour. I do not think I have seen a thinner or more unfestive bunch of festive revellers. Even with the F&L closed at lunchtime for the first time in many years, the OS was barely stretched.

After all that it was almost uplifting to be bombarded in the evening by a plethora of Christmas soap operas, with their usual outpourings of death and disaster. The bunch of monks that gathered around in 440 and decided that today was *the* day, really had not a clue what they were letting future generations in for. Actually, with the calendar they were using at the time we would be celebrating on 7th January by now. I am quite happy not to trade back as this one's almost over now. I should be grateful, however, that there was no airing of *The Last of the Summer Wine Christmas Special*.

December 26th - Monday

There was always going to be a conflict of interest, with a Lifeboat exercise called on the same day as the Boxing Day shoot. Given I had already agreed to assist on the shoot before the exercise was announced, it was only fair to stand by and launch the boat and leave others to recover, while I went up the top.

How typical was it, that that the shoot was called forward by an hour? I might have made both had it not been; but such as it was, everyone turned up late to the shoot anyway. Not even the trailer turned up, so the Old Boathouse van was put to some good use.

The shoot was very well attended, even Charlie Claws was there, (Santa's elder brother), whose aim is such that the safest place to be, is in front of his gun. I believe everyone had a jolly good time and we all retired to the F&L for some hot curry and a pint or five.

December 27th - Tuesday

It is one of those, 'how about that' moments, discovering that it was Carl Zuckmayer's birthday today in 1896. Not the most outstanding name that springs to mind, given that he shared his birthdate with Louis Pasteur, Sydney Greenstreet and Janet Street-Porter, a couple of minor roads and a dual carriage way in Ghent. However the German playwright penned the script for the film Der Blaue Engel that starred Marlene Dietrich, who very coincidentally was born today in 1901. How you, dear reader, lived your life thus far without that nugget of essential fact lodged between your ears is a source of amazement to me.

While you collect yourself from stunned contemplation let me tell you that our day was grey and overcast and, again, warm as toast. Not the most inspiring of days and not many people were inspired to walk out into it either, at least not in the morning.

Not the weather or a late start would stop our intrepid bleddy hound walkers taking her on an extended excursion today. She was gone for three hours or so and covered about five miles apparently. She was a little muddy on her return, but had thankfully avoided any of her aromatic favourites. So that was she subdued for the rest of the afternoon.

If she thinks she will get away with it when our neighbours leave during the week, she has another thought coming. I just happened to be browsing the Internet today looking for a couple of items shotgun related, (sorry, North West education, censored again), when I came across the ultimate dog accessory. It is quite pricey, but I am sorely tempted as we will no longer have a bleddy hound that runs after a ball for hours then comes home and wants to play chase the chicken. Ladies and gentlemen, may I introduce you to the *4 Ball Hyper Dog Tennis Ball Launcher Catapult*. Oh, yes, this is a meaty, beaty, big and bouncy bad boy of a full-blown catapult for launching tennis balls. It will fire them 220 feet and presumably further with a bit of breeze behind you and it will make it much easier to fire them off against the wind, which was a bit of a problem a week ago. It will also be suitable to fire small rocks at her rear end when she decides to misbehave, or ignore you when you want her to come. Oh, boy, I can hardly wait.

December 28th - Wednesday

For the last couple of years we have had a regular visitor to the environs of the shop. I have no idea whether it is male or female, but I am pretty sure it is a song thrush. All right, I am no expert but I am certain that it is not an eagle or a crow and it is bigger than a sparrow and has a pointy beak, which probably means it is not a large sparrow. It has not sung to me yet, but on the balance of probability it is less likely to be a mistle thrush, I have decided.

The little bird has been getting braver through our association. It started last year hopping around in front of the shop and ended by coming up to the doorstep. This year, however, and today in particular, it has excelled itself and is quiet happy to hop into the shop and stand looking at me from in front of the counter. A few days ago it came right into the shop, around by the ice cream freezer and under the nose of the bleddy hound, who was looking elsewhere.

It seems to be exceedingly well mannered and I only have to ask and it will leave. Other birds we have had in the shop get confused and fly into the windows in a blind panic. Our song thrush, even from the complex route at the other side of the ice cream freezer, navigated on the wing round two corners, avoiding the postcard stands and out through the open door effortlessly. The bleddy hound caught the merest flutter out of the corner of her eye and looked completely bewildered as to what had just happened; we are clearly dealing with a stealth song thrush here – and a rather dim dog.

I am not surprised it wanted to come in this morning; our north-westerly blast is back. It was swirling around the shop this morning and, aided and abetted by some glowering clouds and a few showers, made the whole place feel very chilly.

The bleddy hound got run out twice today, (or three times if you include tea up the F&L), once up on the cliff and the other down on the beach. The walkers were disappointed that my *4 Ball Hyper Dog Tennis Ball Launcher Catapult* had not arrived yet, but I said that they would need public liability insurance and a training course before they were allowed to use it in a public place. With this wind especially they could quite easily have someone's eye out, including their own, if they tried firing up wind.

Have you ever had one of those moments of disappointment where delivery has been so off the mark from expectation? The childhood moment where the prettiest girl in class has promised you a kiss, you purse your lips and close your eyes only to find that at the last moment the fat boy in the class has stuck his bottom in your face; Christopher Columbus arriving at the beach at San Salvador and finding a bunch of deckchairs with German towels on them; John Mills slogging over the desert in *Ice Cold in Alex* and finding the bar closed; Jesse Owens coming last in his races at the 1936 Olympics and unable to cock a snook at the host. I am sure you have your own moment of mental devastation to recollect.

Here is mine: I sit down in the F&L for a cottage pie and peas, as advertised on the menu board. When it arrives, instead of peas I get brussel sprouts, squeaky beans and parsnips. Parnsips! I can't stand bleddy parsnips and squeaky beans set my teeth on edge. The brussels and the pie, however, were 'ansum, but I really had set my heart on peas.

What a fat boy's bum in the face that was.

December 29th - Thursday

The bleddy hound's Doom Blaster arrived in the post this morning. I doubt that there is any need to elaborate, but for the avoidance of doubt and for the hard of thinking, this is the *4 Ball Hyper Dog Tennis Ball Launcher Catapult* I have spent the last couple of days eulogising about, except it is a *2 Ball Hyper Dog Tennis Ball Launcher Catapult* which was somewhat cheaper that the 4 ball version. The full name was a bit of a mouthful, or fingerful, as I am typing it, so I have settled on the nickname, Doom Blaster. I had thought that I might call it the dogapult, but I feared that it might be construed that I was instead launching the dog with it, an interesting thought but sadly incorrect.

It was a stroke of misfortune, for them that our dog walking neighbours have gone home and were thus unable to try out the Doom Blaster. The enviable task therefore fell to me, as chief dog walker in their absence. So togged up against the winter blast I headed down the beach, with the weapon concealed in the dog sack I always take down there with me.

I would not put myself up as the Brian Trubshaw of dog ball equipment testing, but I have some experience in this area having both a dog and a previous launcher of dog balls. I will not beat about the bush, nor shall I procrastinate, in revealing my conclusions on this matter. There is nothing worse than having to read a lengthy review in its entirety to see whether the reviewer likes or dislikes the product being tested, when all you really want to know is does it do what it says it will and does it do it effectively. With this in mind let me come directly to the point and tell you without any elaboration exactly what I thought about this new device. I am sure you will appreciate me being candid, without the unnecessary embellishment.

It is a somewhat cumbersome tool that requires a little practice before it can be operated effectively. Even then I found that I could launch a ball only marginally further than with our conventional ball thrower. Cumbersome, certainly; it requires two hands to operate and I had to bend down to pick up the returned ball each time. With a bleddy hound as impatient as ours, it also takes considerably longer to reload on each occasion, resulting in a pestering barking sound about one's ankles.

After some practice I was able to launch the ball a little further than with our existing ball thrower. It does, however, require the user to be standing up to operate effectively and takes rather more effort too. At the end of half an hour of continuous play I felt like an archer at Agincourt, bowed and aching.

We had to fight our way back across the beach. The bleddy hound was way out in front keen to get out of the sand flying over the beach at about her eye level. I was completely worn out by the time we got home.

Not so worn out that I could not find my way down to the OS after a spot of Lifeboat training. The place became packed full by the time the quiz started, but the squeeze was made particularly bearable by AR's sizeable donation to the crew's survival fund that kept us in vital refreshment for a good proportion of the evening.

The quiz was based upon events occurring throughout the year. I had coincidently read and memorised the key events of the year set out in *The Times* newspaper earlier in the day, which you would have thought would have put me in good stead. Unfortunately *The Times* and the compiler of the OS quiz had very different ideas about the events that should stand out as milestones in 2011. I shall spend my time reading *Hello* magazine next year.

At least, on this occasion, we did not come last. I think we were mid field and we did not win the 'chase the ace' either. I just used my newly acquired Agincourt archers' fingers in a parting gesture and turned away to home.

December 30th - Friday

How the Shopkeeper got his Grump

In the land of the fish and the tin and pirates, O my Best Beloved, when the world of keeping shop was young and new, there lived a fine and happy shopkeeper. He was indeed the very model of a modern fine and happy shopkeeper; and the fine and happy shopkeeper wanted for nothing but his shop; and his tinkling and trilling till and his happy demeanour were his most treasured things. And his tinkling and trilling till tinkled loud and it tinkled long; and not more so than when the days were sunny and bright and the customers that came to the shop were happy and smiling because it was sunny and bright.

The customers came from all over the world to see the happy demeanour on the happy shopkeeper's face. They came from South Pacific and Oklahoma, as well as many other wonderful places; and they arrived when June was busting out all over; and they arrived in surreys with little fringes on the top but they all came with their happy smiles and happy, happy talk.

Now, Best Beloved, unbeknown to many of the happy and smiling customers, the fine and happy shopkeeper had been brought up by a band of pirates, which accounted for his love of his tinkling and trilling till and gave him his happy demeanour. It was his mother's mistake that he had been apprenticed to be a pirate, as she had just wanted him to be irate. The shopkeeper's confusion was such that he decided that he did not want to be a pirate any more and wanted nothing more than to be a fine and happy shopkeeper, with his tinkling and trilling till.

As you can imagine, it made the pirates very unhappy that their precocious prodigy did not want to be a pirate. The king of all the pirates called upon his friend who he called Eye, on account of his having just one optical orb, who was the most terrible and most powerful magician in all the land of the fish and the tin and pirates. Together the King and Eye decided upon a puzzlement, a rumbling, tumbling puzzlement that would punish the fine and happy shopkeeper for wanting to leave the pirates. They dearly wanted to take away his tinkling and trilling till, because they knew that that would make the fine and happy shopkeeper very sad, but they also knew that the fine and happy shopkeeper always had the tinkling and trilling till with him, even when he slept. The King and Eye saw that the fine and happy shopkeeper was never happier than when it was sunny and bright and that gave Eye an Eydea, and he started to think Geet Magic, (he was a most powerful magician and could think Geet Magic, for he was proper Cornish too). He was thinking Geet Magic for a very long time, for Geet Magic can take a very long time to think about, and after a very long time he jumped up and clapped his hands and made a sound that sounded like the trundling thump of threatening thunder, and the skies became grey and misty and the rain came down in lumps.

It was a wet and grizzly day, O my Best Beloved, in the land of the fish and the tin and pirates. The grey old sea was bubbling and grubbling, and frothing and troughing, and spuming and looming, and crashing over the mighty and ancient harbour wall. The happy and smiling customers were not happy and not smiling any more. Not only were they not happy and not smiling, but they did not come from South Pacific and Oklahoma and many other wonderful places to visit the fine and happy shopkeeper; and the fine and happy shopkeeper slowly stopped being fine and happy and started being very grisly.

So goes the way of the shop keeping world in the land of the fish and the tin and pirates, even to this very day. If the day is sunny and bright, the shopkeeper is fine and happy, but he is still a pirate with his pirate ways, so beware. When the skies grey over and the sea comes wild and angry from the west, our shopkeeper has forgotten his pernicious pirate precepts but my, oh my, our shopkeeper is a miserable soul.

And this, Best Beloved, is, How the Shopkeeper got his Grump.

The Shopkeeper's Grump is a grievous Grump
Which comes on when the weather is grey.
The cats of the village are nervous and scared,
Lest a boot comes directed their way.
Small children need to be warned as well

That a Shopkeeper with Grump is to fear,
As bringing him ha'pennies for sweets at a penny
Will fetch you a clip 'round the ear.
Don't moan either that your pasty is cold
Or has spent far too long in the oven;
You'll be likely to find it lodged up your behind
With another thrown after your noggin.
Perhaps you may think if you're willing to chance
That his bark is much worse than his bite;
Just take a look up at the walls of the shop
At the heads of those men that weren't right.
So let us all pray for a glorious day
And the sea that shows hardly a lump,
As there is nothing worse or clearly adverse
Than a Shopkeeper's terrible Grump.

The fine and happy shopkeeper would like to doff his cap in the direction Mr Rudyard Kipling, born today in 1865, for lending the use of his Just So stories in such a dangerous and disrespectful manner; and give a nod of thanks to Mr Gilbert and Mr Sullivan whose Pirates of Penzance was first aired today in Paignton (Devon!) in 1879 and whose plot-line was so disgracefully plundered, (as pirates will), for the writer's own ends. He would also give his profound apologies to Mr Richard Rogers, who popped off today exactly one hundred years later.

It was this tripartite coincidence, along with Jupiter being in Mars and the moon rising off the starboard bow, that inexplicably turned a fine and happy shopkeeper's brain to pink blancmange, hopefully just for the day.

December 31ˢᵗ - Saturday

On Christmas Day, I caught the Missus using my ultra sharp fish filleting knife to carve up a joint of beef destined for the dinner table. I did not need to say anything, for she immediately knew the severity of her crime. She spent ten minutes prostrate in front of me, begging my forgiveness for her negligence and the gratuitous vandalism of my best fish knife.

Well, it was something like that, but perhaps more like, "For heaven's sake it's only a knife. Don't be such a child. If you're going to make a big fuss I shall buy you a new one. Now get out of my kitchen." It was that sort of apology.

The 'buying me a new knife' involved me going into town today to buy another one, with my money naturally. In fact it meant buying three new knives. So impressed was she with the effective blade on my knife, that she told her mates and they wanted one too. I should not hold out too much hope that I shall see any of the money back, of course.

The other thing I went in for is a case that will house a computer disk and enable it to be used as desktop storage. I have one that I salvaged from a piece of equipment that has been displaced with the new Bramley Computer TV box.

I went to the computer shop at the bottom of Market Jew Street and told the young chap behind the counter, in very specific terms, what I needed. He rooted about among the boxes on the shelves and handed me a box. "The very thing," quoth he. I asked if it had the very specific cable required to attach it to a computer and he assured me that it was inside the box. All very good, I thought, until I got it home and removed the outer shrink-wrap and looked inside the box. Yes, exactly the *wrong* thing.

In a small specialist shop I certainly did not expect to get the sort of service generally reserved for shoppers in the larger computer stores. I am sure you know the ones I mean, the sort where if you ask for any information about a product, that is not written on the label, they run around in panic like headless chickens.

Much like I shall be doing come midnight tonight when I try and escape the free-for-all back-slapping and random kissing of strangers. It may indeed be the last time we celebrate this event based on a very British midnight. I have read that the Chinese are pushing for a midnight, based on a bunch of atomic clocks, as time based on GMT upsets their satellites. I think we will continue to run on Cornish time. That generally runs a couple of scats behind everyone else anyway.

Just time to tell you that the F&L was definitely the place to be this evening; I even had it in my heart to forgive them for the peasgate affair. The band, Wheal Rock, played a rather jolly set and had the dance floor jumping until just past the back-slapping and random kissing of strangers bit. Good on them.

With the morning tide fast approaching perhaps I should wish you all a Happy New Year. There I have done it. From a grumpy old shopkeeper that is about the best you will get, so get down and darned well enjoy it.

January 1ˢᵗ – Sunday 2012

I cannot say it was a bad start to the year. We were apparently the only shop open in the village and were deluged because of it. It was busy enough yesterday and after a slow start this morning we had a steady flow of happy, and sometimes jaded, shoppers. Even the heavy burst of rain in the mid afternoon did not seem to dampen spirits too much.

I left the Missus holding the fort and took the bleddy hound down to the big beach. She did not get out at all yesterday, so she was ripe for a good run. If we thought the shop was busy, the beach was even busier. There cannot have been a square inch of virgin sand down there; the rest was ploughed up by the prints of a million wellie boots. Well, perhaps not a million, but you get the general idea. There were dogs aplenty and even a couple of ponies trotting around.

It took me ages to get back too; I kept bumping into people we know. I think between us we have completely worn out the phrase 'Happy New Year'.

Well, perhaps not completely worn it out. I have had a few emails from readers wishing us well here. It is unusual that both of you have multiple addresses, but it did give me a power of good knowing you care so much.

So for readers everywhere I wish you all a very Happy New Year and a prosperous one too. At least prosperous enough to buy the next book, perhaps.

January 3ʳᵈ – Tuesday

At seven o'clock the morning Mr JC recorded a 74 miles per hour gust on his rather excellent equipment in a field just south of us.

As I was going into PZ I offered to do the food shopping while I was there and made particular comment that I would use the shops in the town centre. Now the Missus does not hold with my principled stand against the big supermarkets. Because the Missus gave me a sceptical look when I mentioned prices, I decided to take note of what I was paying in the town centre shops. As I also had to go to the supermarket for items that I cannot get in town, I had the perfect opportunity to make a comparison.

I will not beat about the bush, or extend the torture of yet another anti-supermarket moan, so I will tell you that in all cases of my random selection the local shops were between 30 and 50 percent cheaper. This more than covered the additional parking charge that I had to pay. Why would you want to go somewhere to pay too much for food?

Now, before I go, here is another of those little life lessons that are given out free with The Sennen Cove Diary, (or £8.99 if you happened to have to buy a copy), a complementary bonus if you will: never take a plastic shopping basket with you to a supermarket, unless you want the self service attendant to want to punch you on the nose.

By the time I had completed my in town shopping spree for lower than supermarket priced fresh produce, which is predominantly more local and better quality if for no other reason than it has travelled significantly less far, I had filled the two reusable bags I had taken with me for the purpose. When I arrived at the supermarket I discovered that the Missus had left one of The Old Boathouse Stores' plastic shopping baskets in the van, so I decided to use that, rather than collect yet another disposable plastic bag. How socially and environmentally conscientious I am, you are thinking, dear reader. Or possibly, how daft. Anyway, I proceeded to place my shopping in the basket and, once finished, headed for the checkouts.

When I arrived, the queues for the manned checkouts were stretched down the store, so I decided to opt for the self-service machines. I have explained previously the fraught and complex nature of these devices and how sensitive they are if you do not follow their strict rules of use.

When the boffins put the machines together they included a little ruse that means you must place any item once scanned into a receptacle, the increasing weight of which indicates to the machine that you have done so. What the boffins clearly did not allow for was the possibility that some fool may wish to use a plastic shopping basket as their 'own bag' option. I promise you that this seriously stuffs the machine's capability to calculate when an item has been added to the outgoing 'bag' and requires the clever little box to be reset by the attendant after every second item.

I have to hand it to the attendant, as his fixed smile never altered and the only perceptible sign that he was thinking, 'I'm going to punch you on the nose in a minute for using a plastic shopping basket, you goon", was that there were gradually more teeth on display each time he had to come and reset the machine.

Do not do as I did, dear reader. Be a good sheep and follow the rules. Alternatively you could buck the trend, save the economy, and your own pocket, and shop local. You can use a plastic shopping basket to your heart's content and no one will ever complain. It is up to you.

January 4ᵗʰ - Wednesday

The water board truck was in the Harbour car park all night and, this morning, there came another and another. There is nothing quite like a leak, particularly one to the press, to get you top rate service. The tankers have been coming and going all day and a nice little note poked through our door suggests that they might be here for a few days yet.

According to the note they suspect that there has been a collapse in the outfall pipe. They have had to drain the pumping station so that they can get in to fix it. We even made the BBC lunchtime news, apparently, and they managed to find a local chap (in this weather!) for a quote or two. They even had a comment from the SAS, those chaps who do not like lumps in their surfing water not the army ones, who probably would not care.

While the local's report seemed fairly balanced, reading the SAS quote you would think that the world is coming to an end. We are all going to die a horrible death from the nasties that leaked into the sea over the last day or so. According to the quote the sewage was coming out at the bottom of the slip where people were playing, probably small, angelic children, mainly. Well, I am not sure that in 50 miles per hour winds there were too many people playing at the bottom of the slip. The man from

SAS went on that he was retching standing next to it. Um, may I suggest you don't, then? Anyway, it is not important any more. They are all going to die from horrible illnesses, too horrible even to contemplate.

Empty Beach

I should not be too flippant, as he may well have been quoted out of context or misquoted altogether. It was a particularly serious spill so he had a right to be a little upset, but you can see how such things can get blown out of proportion on the back of such reports.

Talking of being blown out, we are still being buffeted by winds gusting up to 60 miles per hour today. It was sufficiently severe not to venture out too far, and when I did head off around the block it was difficult to make headway at times. At last knockings the bleddy hound and I were very nearly blown off our feet at the top of the slip. How she managed to stay grounded I do not know, but she was none too pleased about it that is for sure.

It looks like it may be dropping out a little tomorrow so I might just take her on a yomp up to Land's End. I might even convince the Missus to meet us up the F&L for a spot of lunch. We have not done that for a while. It is best we get out of The

Cove anyway; we would not want the terrible green miasma to get us.

January 5th - Thursday

True to my word I took the bleddy hound on a little trip out up to Land's End. Also true to the forecast the wind had diminished to a mere 50 miles per hour gusts and had veered around to the northwest. Up on the coast path there was absolutely no hiding from the begger and the seas were whipped into a frenzy. Streams of silky white water were clinging to the Irish Lady's skirts, and waves lashed up the cliffs all around, and lumps of foam were flashing past my ears. Actually the last few lumps of foam were poo bags snatched from my pocket, I realised too late. I hope the dog walkers in Normandy appreciate them.

On our way up from Land's End to fulfil the other part of my promise, that I would treat the Missus to lunch, (or did I say meet the Missus for lunch?), at the F&L, we passed the stable field. The place was awash with big black birds. They might have been jackdaws but they were certainly raven mad to be out in a wind like this. (Yes, I know, but it had to be done.)

The good Doc was at Lifeboat training tonight and we learnt more about keeping our victims, ahem saved casualties, alive for a little longer. You will understand that after such intensive coaching we are as keen as mustard to try out our skills. Be very careful as you pass the Lifeboat station if you are down here on holiday. The merest trip and we will have you in a neck brace and oxygen mask before you hit the ground.

Armed with our newly found skills we repaired to the OS and discovered that all this education rewarded us a first place tie in the quiz. Had we been a little more adventurous with some of our answers we would have won outright. As it was we lost the tie-break, but having brought up the rear for so many weeks we left heartened and brimming with good cheer, amongst other things.

Even the wind has dropped off. Things are just getting better and better.

January 6ᵗʰ - Friday

At last our big wind has abated and it has warmed up considerably too. Not that it has been that cold, but the wind made an awful lot of difference.

The damping down of the wind was the opportunity I was looking for to get up to Shrew House to count things. If I had done it over the last few days there would not have been much left to count, probably including the doors, as everything would have been half way across to St Levan. But at least our wind was not as bad as the 'big wind' that took out as many as 25 percent of the houses in north Dublin today in 1839. That was the poorer area incidentally, where the houses were not so well built, but the natural phenomenon also wiped out a few church spires and country house roofs, so that was all right then.

And also today in 1928 the Thames flooded enough to fill the moat at the Tower of London and damage paintings in the basement of the Tate Gallery. Surely they would have been better in the attic where everyone else keeps the stuff they do not have room for.

All in all it is clearly a bad few days for weather and we should count ourselves lucky. I wish I had not said that now, as it has reminded me that was all we did today – count. The blitz on the stock take did the trick though and we have nearly finished.

I like a challenge now and again and it was certainly that trying to put a Diary entry together on a day when I did not see very much of The Cove, and even the bleddy hound did not get much of a walk. I am sure you will all look forward to tomorrow when I shall spend the whole day finishing off the count and keying it all into the computer. If I were you I would skip to January 8ᵗʰ and don't look back.

January 7ᵗʰ - Saturday

Look, it's entirely your fault if you chose to read toady's entry. I have already told you to jump to the next day, on the grounds that I would have nothing to say because I was counting things and not concentrating on items and events that might keep you amused.

Well, now you are here I suppose I could tell you that I did, indeed, step out with the bleddy hound down the big beach since she did not get out yesterday. There are still a few people around, given the number of footprints down there. Much of the sand is back as well. In fact I was able to sit on the high point of my favourite rock. (Gosh, I am really struggling now.) How about the eleven month old dachshund that we met on the way back across the beach? That, at least, will let you go aaah! Or aaaargh if, like me, you are that way inclined. It was wearing a striped jumper with the rings going around the tummy.

All right, I have just had the most bizarre conversation with the Missus. I mean was it best that the rings went around the tummy or should it have worn something with the rings going length ways? Its skin was too big for it anyway, with rolls ramping up on its little legs, so fashion may as well go out the window.

After all that it was time to do some counting. You see, you really should have jumped to the next day. You should not have to rely on me for your daily entertainment, for heaven's sake! There are televisions, radios, music players, games consoles, hand held games gizmos, packs of cards, (remember them?), and watching paint dry before you have to resort to me.

I knew that the Missus was up to something when she did not join me for the stock count and favoured the confines of the kitchen.

Do you remember last year, when I was cornered into walking into the church, somewhat squiffy, with a gingerbread house? Believe me, I do and probably the congregation do as well. Well she has excelled herself this time. She has made a scale model of the church for the children's service tomorrow morning. Given that, as I pen these words, it is half past one o'clock you will have some idea of the grief, blood, sweat and tears that has been poured into this project.

We can only hope that the young Christian children of the village like bodily fluids in their confection. No, do not even think about it.

See, you should have skipped to tomorrow.

January 8ᵗʰ - Sunday

A grey and murky day and much, much worse up the top. Staying under the cloud in The Cove would have been nice but we were compelled to go to church this morning, well, the Missus was to deliver her icon of gingerbread architecture. I managed to stay well clear and take the bleddy hound out to the back field for a run around, where she found some mates to play with.

There is a piece of rope across a make-shift gate at the entrance of the field, high enough for any of the three dogs to go under by crouching down, but not so high that it could not be jumped. Having run around the field all three decided to run, full pelt, out of the gate. The first dog flew clean over, while the bleddy hound hunkered down and went under. The third dog went to jump over but at the last minute had a change of mind and decided to go under. Unfortunately, the change of mind at the rate she was travelling did not reach the legs until it was too late, and she thumped into the rope and came to a very abrupt stop on her back. Getting up and dusting herself off, the look of disgust she gave the rope was extremely comical, not that she appreciated the laughter, I am guessing.

We went at something less than full pelt in the direction of our first trade show of the year, at Fraddon. The mist was varying degrees of thick all the way, (feel free to insert long and repetitive rant about cars travelling on parking lights or no lights at all), so we felt it best to take a well earned break at Hayle. As you all know by now you cannot get past Hayle without a Philps pasty inside you. It also seems you cannot get onto the A30, at least with the Missus on board, without availing yourself of a Costalot Coffee.

You might discern that we were not in the greatest of hurries to get to the trade show. It is the same with all of them, and mainly the reason that we did not bother going to the NEC at Birmingham last year, and will not bother again this year. When we got there we wished we had not bothered coming to this one either; there were no more than ten suppliers there and only four of them were of any interest to us, and all of them were going to be at the Exeter show next week. A desperate sign of the times, or a sign of the desperate times, maybe.

What better an end to the day could you have? To come home after an extended and worthless jaunt and to put your feet up in front of the fire, if we had one, and listen to the urgent tones of one's Lifeboat pager going off.

Yes, at around half past six we had our first shout of the new year. A ten metre fishing vessel that had apparently already been attended to by St Ives Lifeboat earlier in the day, decided to break down just the other side of Longships reef. It was a well attended launch by both Boat and very excellent Shore Crews. Even as the boat launched we were told to get tooled up for a ten o'clock recovery on the long slip, which we duly did.

It was a balmy and moonlit night for TS and my good self, standing down at the end of the long slip at half past nine. The water was as calm as you like and the recovery was textbook. Would you expect anything less from a professional and highly trained shore team? Even the shore team that were there seemed to manage without a hitch.

There, all back to normal after those shenanigans of the last few weeks. Don't take long, do it?

January 9ᵗʰ - Monday

I had not exactly forgotten I was going to take the van in for a service and its MoT test this morning, I just forgot to set my alarm. By a stroke of good fortune a friendly tongue in my ear woke me exactly half an hour before I was due to be at the garage. Well, there are three of us in this marriage, so it is a bit crowded.

I made the garage at precisely eight thirty and the chap said he would have the van back to me before the end of the day. It is the end of the day and I still have the loan car. I can almost hear his meter chalking up the pounds. I am going to take a defibrillator with me when I pick the van up, just in case.

With still some bits to count in the shop and an awful lot of data entry to do, I took the bleddy hound down to the beach for a short run this morning. There were more people in the sea than there was on the beach, with some good surf and little in the way of wind. It was also quite clement down there and ideal for throwing a ball in any direction. I decided to take the Doom Blaster, as it has lain idle for the best part of a week. I am getting quite good at it now; twang and the ball goes for miles, but she keeps coming back for more. Twang and she's off again in another direction. Thwack - Ouch! The flaming rubber band snapped on me. It nearly broke my hand, not to mention nigh on taking my eye out. I cannot imagine I have had more than twenty twangs out of the thing before I got the thwack. So that is my *2 Ball Hyper Dog Tennis Ball Launcher Catapult* consigned to the bin and a lesson learned, as I am beggered if I shall be sending off for replacement rubber bands. An expensive way to buy tennis balls, that is for sure.

It was good to see the Inshore Lifeboat on exercise today while I was down on the beach nursing my wounds. It has not been out in a while due to the sea state. I thought for a minute they had heard my yelp of anguish, (more a tirade of really rude words strung together very loudly), when the rubber band snapped back in my face and had mounted a rescue, caring sorts that they are. Yes, right! They would have been laughing their socks off if they had seen it.

So on top of a broken hand, a slapped face and a rescue mission that ignored me, I have the beginnings of a head cold. Deep down I think that 2012 could be *my* year.

January 11ᵗʰ - Wednesday

The Missus is going away with the girls from next door shortly. She is going to far off places that require a visitor visa waiver, the acquisition of which demands that a big long form to be filled out. It asks all sorts of impertinent questions such as, 'is the applicant a British Citizen, British National or British Subject?' Well, I kind of thought we were all three, having been born here, but apparently we are Citizens as it says so on our passports. I tried to look it up but you would not believe how complex the subject is, even down to the point that if you born before or after 1982 with the same origins you could be two different categories of citizen/national/subject.

The next enquiry on the form questioned the Missus's moral turpitude. I assumed they were asking whether she had ever parted with her favours for profit. The matter could be open to conjecture, since I had to buy her two rings before she would marry me. Does that count? I decided to look it up and found, with some relief, that it is an American legal term meaning had she ever been naughty. Well, had she ever been *caught* being naughty, really? Since Santa has never missed one of her Christmases I can assure them that she has indeed not been naughty, or at least as far as Santa is concerned.

Last of all was the clincher. It made me wonder why we have a secret service burrowing around in the dark corners, being underhand to catch seriously naughty people, when all they really have to do is send out forms with this question. 'Are you now or have you ever been a terrorist?'

I will leave you to ponder that.

January 12th – Thursday

The Missus had taken our newly serviced and MoT tested van into town yesterday for a spot of shopping and had reported some problems. The van had started to sound more like one of Mr Trevithick's excellent machines, which would have been fine had it been a steam engine, which it is not. It has also developed a delay between pressing the throttle and it taking any notice of the demand. I telephoned the garage and they said, in rather worrying tones, that it was probably best not to use the van other than for bringing it to the garage at the very next opportunity, tomorrow morning. The engineer also advised I do my seat belt up very tightly, invest in a fire retardant suit and make sure my last will and testament was up to date. He did not actually say the last bit but his tone was such that I knew that was what he meant.

This very much spelt doom for a little adventure I had planned with the bleddy hound that required the use of some transport to get us to the starting point; a disappointment almost too heartbreaking to bear. The venture also relies on there being a low tide, spring tide preferably, at the appropriate time, and the next opportunity will be in a couple of week's time when it will probably be raining/snowing/blowing a hooley, or all three judging from my luck so far. I do not think the Aeronautical Society of Great Britain would have held truck with such pessimism; they were founded today in 1866, thirty years before the first powered flight.

So I am very sorry but we found ourselves, the bleddy hound and me, walking the well trodden path again. We did the extended version, up onto Mayon Cliff, Carn Olva and Vellandreath Valley before hitting the beach for some repetitive ball throwing.

We did, however, discover that the water board were back in The Cove trying to mend the fault with the drains. It would appear that the blockage in the outfall pipe may well be down below the high water mark. As we mounted Mayon Cliff we gazed down upon a little cluster of yellow jackets among the rocks, standing around scratching their heads. I would have a guess that they must have been officials and managers, as there did not appear to be much work going on. I am not an engineer, so I can only guess at the difficulties of digging up concrete beyond the reach of a compressor and at a place that is covered with water for at least 16 hours a day, and four of those would be in darkness.

Undeterred by such complex mysteries we enjoyed our little tramp around The Cove. And so we should, there are not that many little tramps left. We even came upon some doggie friends that the bleddy hound has romped with since a pup. I must have done something right as she was completely done in for the rest of the afternoon.

Just for something different we had a little Head Launcher's tea party before Lifeboat training tonight. A lump of local lamb made all the difference to the supermarket vegetables that the Missus had bought, but other than that a rather acceptable roast.

I have had a request to include more detail of the Lifeboat training sessions that we have, as you know, every Thursday night. Clearly there are some things that must remain within the hallowed inner sanctum, lest I be subject to the wrath of the elders, strapped to a stake to the slipway at low water, or used as a makeshift span at the next recovery; I need to be circumspect. So this is what I can tell you: we went in and said hello to everyone; we spoke about a possible launch next Thursday, subject to weather and service conditions; we said goodbye to everyone. I hope that shed just a little light on the important work that is discussed at our meetings.

Is it any wonder that after such serious considerations that we feel it necessary to retire to the OS to relax and de-stress.

With the concentration on weighty matters still looming large in our minds it was no surprise that our performance in the quiz was exemplary. Naturally we won by a worthy margin and yes, there were other teams playing, five in fact.

Being such notable Lifeboat personages we decided to dedicate our winnings to the sponsored walk that three of the crew will be undertaking on SOS Day on January 29th, the details of which we had discussed earlier. Oh darn it! There, I shall be keel hauled for such wanton revelation of Lifeboat secrets. I may as well spill all the beans now, that the special three will be walking from Gurnard's Head to Sennen Cove via the coast road, (for maximum exposure), in Lifeboat kit and collecting money on the way. Our Head Launcher will also be attempting this feat, which will give us the opportunity of practicing our recent first aid training in a live environment.

If you wish to be part of this mammoth misadventure please send sticking plasters, preferably those new blister reducing ones, to Sennen Cove Lifeboat Station ahead of the planned event. You could also send money to The Old Boathouse Stores, which will be gratefully received. Just £150 per month will help us save a destitute shopkeeper from almost certain extinction, just text DESPERATE SHOPKEEPER to a number that will cost you lots of money.

[Insert heart-rending images of a down-on-his-luck shopkeeper holding stuffed polar bear and snow leopard toys.]

Open your wallets and say after me, "help yourself". I thank you very much.

January 13th - Friday

It was the sort of day to pack up some marmalade sandwiches and head off on an adventure. Unfortunately with the van back in the hands of the mechanics there was no major adventuring to be done, just a big wide beach at low tide today.

The difference between under the hill in the shade, and the far end of the beach in brilliant sunshine, might well have been the difference between deepest, darkest Peru and the African desert. As the bleddy hound and I sat amongst the rock pools over by North Rocks we basked in near summertime temperatures. The sun waited until I had peeled off two or three layers, including my duffle coat and felt hat, a present from my Uncle Pastuzo, before it went behind a cloud and turned off the heat. I tried giving it one of my hardest stares, but it was to no avail.

Having run out of Paddington Bear references I resorted to collecting the van from the garage, now working properly, and headed off to St Just. First, it was a fitting test to see if the van was, indeed, working properly and secondly we need to have something for tea.

It was shortly after tea that it all started going a bit wrong. I leashed up the bleddy hound for a convenience break, hers, not mine, and headed down the steps. She saves this particular screaming like a banshee for her arch enemy and when she got to the foot of the steps she started using it. Although we raced up the steps and back inside there was a bit of a dust up at the top of the steps. It was not until later in the evening we found that she had been got in her rear quarters and was limping quite badly.

This has rather upset the apple cart, as we need to attend a trade show tomorrow. It will be via the vets first thing I rather suspect.

You will have to wait, as indeed shall we, to see the outcome of this Friday 13th fiasco.

Oh yes, Mr Michael Bond was born today in 1926, that will account for the pathetic attempt to include some Paddington Bear in today's entry. I did not even contemplate the inclusion of his other creations, such as The Herbs. Perhaps I am just not a seasoned enough writer.

January 14th - Saturday

As I suggested yesterday we kicked off with an early start to take the injured bleddy hound to the vets this morning. She was still limping and her and the Missus stayed up all night, as she would not settle. The vet is not one of her favourite places, indicated by her desire to walk in any direction other than the door of the practice.

On the grounds that it would be unfair to burden our neighbour with a less than healthy dog for a couple of nights, it was decided that just one of us would make the journey east for the trade show. I am not comfortable with ill humans, let alone sick dogs, so it was a simple decision as to who should make the journey alone. I telephoned the hotel that we had booked to explain that only one of us would be turning up. They told me that this would not be a problem as they had only booked a room for one person anyway, which was either a stunning example of prescience or incompetence. I will give them leave to claim the former.

January 15th – Sunday

What an action packed day I had, all to do with buying new things for the shop for the up coming season. You will be impressed, I am sure. Well, probably not.

It is the least liked part of the annual process of stocking the shop. We meet lots of keen and enthusiastic sales people, all with a product that will sell by the dozen and we will never regret buying lorry loads of. If just one of them came up and said that they were not sure; it might be a bit of a pup; would not bet on it, I would buy it by the shed full.

Is it not odd how many of us cling to pounds and ounces? Odd then that we have almost universally accepted centigrade, or Celsius, into our language and everyday life without a flicker, or perhaps I am just speaking for myself. It was today in 1962 that the forecast started using it. I can confirm that today in South Devon it is bleddy cold degrees centigrade and that roughly corresponds to brass monkey degrees Farenheit; I cannot imagine that I would find a pawnbroker with intact signage for love nor money.

I shall go and prove it is cold again very shortly, as in this world of equality, non-discrimination and enlightenment I cannot poison myself with nicotine inside in the warm. Fortunately I am permitted to poison myself with alcohol in reasonable comfort, so I shall do that instead.

And if you thought that today's Diary entry was dull and tedious, have some heart; why should I suffer alone?

January 16ᵗʰ - Monday

This is the SCD Home Service for mothers and children at home.

Hello children. Are you sitting comfortably? Then I'll begin.

It was a glorious but very cold start to the day here in the south of Devon and one requiring the use of some sunglasses, as the sun is low in the sky and seems to be in my eyes whichever way I am driving. Do you remember yesterday, children, when I said that I would not have to turn right this morning? Well I told a naughty fib and I turned right, as although I am not going to the trade show, I am going to another supplier in the same direction. I think I might be smacked and sent to my room without any supper when I get home. Did you know, children, that some grown-ups actually like being smacked and sent to bed? We'll save that story for another time.

When I had finished seeing the man with all the toys that I had to turn right to see, even though I said I would not turn right, I went home. Vinnie the van did all the boring hard work driving a long, long way home, although there was very little traffic, which meant we got home in a little over two hours. Vinnie the van and I could never get tired of that view that is there to greet you as you come over the hill. It is none better than at low water, with a clear blue sky and the sun lighting up the far end of the beach as it starts to dip away behind Mayon Cliff.

It was good to be back in the bosom of the loved one; I was able to telephone the Missus from there.

Do you remember we had to take Bo, the bleddy hound to the vet on Saturday morning because she had a fight with a big scary dog that made you all cry? Well we could be forgiven for thinking that there was a big tractor party going on between Sennen and Penzance. We counted twelve tractors in one field alone, (can you count to twelve, children?), and more on the roads, some of which looked like fields with all of the mud about. On the way back today the green and brown fields look more like large lakes as they are covered in polythene to keep them warm. I think, though I could be wrong, (the Missus says I usually am), that this is the early crop of potatoes going in. We all know what potatoes are, don't we children? Yes, that's right, they are those long crisp things that come with your meals from MacBurger Chicken.

A letter of sympathy continues to pour in for the bleddy hound, by the way, for which I must thank H and F on her behalf. She is much better physically, but the signs of mental frailty are still evident. She now waits for me to go down the stairs first, before following me down and is constantly looking up and down the street for signs of her nemesis. I shall consider sensory deprivation, or perhaps electric shock treatment if this goes on, and if that does not work I will try it on the dog.

Well, that is all we have time for today children. Try not to have nightmares over those three mice with impaired vision that had their tails viciously cut off without anaesthetic; the farmer's wife is doing fours years for possession of a knife with a blade longer than seven inches, and wounding with intent.

Jack is recovering in Treliske Hospital, after having his head caved in falling down the hill. Jill, of course, got away with a few minor abrasions. Accusations that she tripped him up were never proven.

And do not worry about the Duke of York's ten thousand men, as they all received top psychiatric help for the trauma they suffered after pointlessly marching up and down the hill. The Duke of York, of course, received his just deserts at the hands of the Health and Safety Executive, and is doing three years in Pentonville for not completing a risk assessment.

Lastly, Little Bo Beep, who was sacked last year for losing her employer's sheep, has won a six figure payout in the High Court. She claimed unfair dismissal, citing mental distress for having to wear unsuitable clothing that the male shepherds did not have to wear, to wit, a big flouncy frock, knickerbockers, ballet shoes and a bonnet that obscured her vision of the sheep. A salient lesson for naughty, fascist farmers everywhere, children.

Be good children and goodbye.

Listen with Mother ran from today in 1950 until 1982. Will children ever be the same again?

January 17ᵗʰ - Tuesday

I was feeling quite chipper this morning so I set about doing something about it. I paid my road fund tax and my income tax, which took a few breaths of wind out of my sails. Given that I was not completely demoralised I thought it best to call up the electric company. As a fall back option it is usually quite effective.

The first number I called was set up as an automatic facility to let customers leave their meter readings. Even my best tinkering could not get it to break through to an operator. The second number, from their website, had no response at all, not even a ringing tone so I elected to use their sales number; if they were going to answer any call quickly I assumed it would be that one and it was. Unfortunately the chap could not help at all and gave me another number.

The last time I called, at least six months ago, the recorded message they play told me that they were hiring at least 700 new staff and implementing new systems to shorten waiting times on the telephone. They are still playing the same message, so I assume that they must be struggling to find suitable candidates out of the 11,000 unemployed available in their call centre catchment areas. As one of their call centres is in Exeter, I do not know if it would be helpful to suggest that there are one or two who appear to be at a loose end camped in protest against something or other around Exeter Cathedral at the moment.

Sorry, I naughtily digress. Where was I? Oh yes, I was given another number to call our electric company on. When I eventually got through, having keyed in my account number on the way, a very nice chap asked if I could tell him my account number. I cheerily told him that I had already keyed it in and that if he told me that part of the system was not working, (again), I would be grievously disappointed that it was still asking me to key it in even though it was not working. The chap was most sympathetic and, rather than see me disappointed, he hung the telephone up on me.

The next lady I spoke to after I telephoned back, this time omitting to key in my account number, actually did not mind having a conversation. In fact she was most helpful to the extent that I almost hung up on her. I am still waiting for my login account confirmation email that she promised me. Phew, for a moment there I thought something might have gone right.

There, you see, that is much better. I had thought I might have to spend the entire day being upbeat and happy. It is so nice to know that there are some things you can rely on, through thick and thin, to bring you down to earth with a bump.

It set me up nicely for another losing streak at the OS cards night too. Some days you just cannot beat when you are happy being a grumpy old goat.

January 18ᵗʰ - Wednesday

In support of the Wiki website going dark today, as a lesson to all of us that we cannot do without freedom of the Internet, there will be no Diary entry today.

Oh, go on then; just a little one, mind.

I was somewhat stranded today as the Missus had gone off early to visit her parents up in North Devon. With the beach out of bounds that only left the walk up to Land's End and back along the cycle path. We could have been anywhere today. Visibility was down to less than 100 yards in all directions and somewhat eerie with it and not a soul in sight. It was also quite damp, resulting in an arrival home with a rather mucky bleddy hound occasioning a re-enactment of Agincourt in the bathroom, without the archers, of course; I do not think they are on until seven.

I am sure Mr Beeton, (yes, Mrs Beeton's well-fed hubby), would have had a Boy's Own book of cleaning bleddy hounds secreted somewhere about his bookcase. I am sure it would have had lots of useful tips like wearing waterproof clothing. I was indeed wearing waterproof trousers, but that was more to do with not being able to take them off while holding on to a dog that would rather be somewhere else, than protection during the procedure. Of course, we would not have had Boy's Own anything had he not been born today in 1879 as he was its publisher.

We would have been even more lost without Mark Peter Roget, born today in 1779, whose fine thesaurus is an essential reference for writers today. Not only providing useful synonyms, but also expansion of words and phrases which is presumably why he originally called it '*Thesaurus of English Words and Phrases Classified and Arranged so as to Facilitate the Expression of Ideas and Assist in Literary Composition.*' It must have been a mighty tome to fit that on the cover.

So as the lexicographer of Eternity etches out the last word in the book of Time, and the grammatician of Fate points out he missed a comma in the introduction, it's time to say goodnight.

January 19th - Thursday

On the basis that the Missus had again absconded with the van, and with the tide not being at all helpful, I took the bleddy hound on the extended round robin. Had it not been for some minor changes I would simply have referred you to last Thursday's entry. This would have saved me the trouble of writing anything and saved you the trouble of reading anything if, of course, you can remember last Thursday's entry or indeed read.

So it is the minor changes I shall concentrate on to avoid the pitfall of repetition. As I descended into Vellandreath there is a short grassy path that had become wet from yesterday's drizzle. It was a complete surprise when my left foot started descending the path rather quicker than the right and very suddenly was at an angle that made supporting my weight impossible. The upshot of this undesirable arrangement of my legs was that I fell over.

On the positive side, being raised by a band of travelling circus performers, I had learnt various methods of falling down without hurting myself. On the negative side, that was a long time ago, even if it were true, which it is not, incidentally. Fortunate, then, that my keen interest in the effects of intoxication, purely on the grounds of scientific research you will understand, also have imbued in me similar skills to which I eluded earlier and I hit the ground with little more than muddied trousers.

Clearly my first instinct was to look around for a witness to my tumble of which there were none, other than the bleddy hound. My second was to establish whether the owners of the path had, anticipating such an event, set up a sign to warn hapless walkers of the danger and again there was none. Such is the power of advertising that my next thought was the phrase, *'where there's blame, there's a claim'* and I found myself reaching for my mobile telephone. Obviously this incident is worthy of many thousands of pounds in compensation for the injury and distress inflicted upon me. Then there is the bleddy hound who, despite showing utter disinterest in my plight, (was that a Mutleyesque snigger I heard when I fell?), was clearly traumatised by seeing her beloved companion laid low by such sheer neglect and will require hours of counselling by trained, and no doubt very expensive, canine psychologists.

Yes, all very unlikely, I am sure. At least it is unlikely that I would get my multi-thousand pound payout before the Missus gets home from her foreign tour, which starts tomorrow.

Much of Lifeboat training was taken up by a theoretical examination of what we would do if a big cruise liner ripped her bottom out on Shark's Fin. With the good Doc present we considered the effects and treatment of hypothermia. Today, in stormy waters, we concluded that it would not look good for many on board, despite the best efforts of all the emergency services available within the vicinity during the 'golden hour'. Though the loss of life on the *Costa Concordia* was tragic the survival rate was nothing less than miraculous.

Have a thoughtful night.

January 20ᵗʰ - Friday

Well, that is it then. I packed them off on the train this morning, the Missus and her two mates, and they are on their way to sunny Florida. I should point out that the train is not taking them to Florida but to the London airport, where an aeroplane will be waiting. I hope that it is a very big aeroplane as the bags they have taken with them had the van's suspension creaking all the way into town.

In celebration I drove to Perranuthnoe, by which I mean a celebration of the girls enjoying themselves, and not at all that I have a fortnight on my own, not one bit. Naturally I shall be heart broken and struggle to get by. Let me start that again. In consolation I drove on from PZ to Perranuthnoe where there is a fine beach. With the tides allowing a small window of opportunity in the mornings it was the right thing to do. It also provided the bleddy hound and I with an opportunity to explore a different environment to the one that we are so used to. I am not entirely sure she gave a stuff, as long as she is out chasing a ball it could be a multi-storey car park in Milton Keynes, (do they have multi-storey car parks in Milton Keynes?).

It was a perfect day for such a jaunt. The sun was doing its best to break through the cloud and was quite successful at times. The wind, being roughly in the west, and the beach being roughly south facing, gave us some respite from the breeze that seemed to be getting quite insistent. We traversed the length of the beach a couple of times, then I found a suitable rock at the west end upon which to perch and she chased the ball from there. We were largely left to our own devices down on the sand apart from a couple of other dog walkers and the encroaching waves.

We hung on until the sea was lapping at our feet, (or paws in her case), then retreated up the slipway. There is a small canteen at the top of the slip called The Cabin. I imagine it is called The Cabin because it is a wooden cabin or chalet, perhaps. It also does a fine brew and a cracking bacon roll at a very reasonable price. It is also open throughout the year and is dog friendly. I recommend it highly. Although I was welcome inside I elected to sit in the garden. For a day in mid January it was perfectly mild under the sun and away from the breeze.

When I returned I thought it best to nip next door and take their dog around before retiring to the flat, but someone had got there first and she was not at home. It is the neighbour with which the Missus has fled the country, leaving me with some intermittent dog sitting duties of which I am sure you will hear more during the days ahead.

In the meanwhile we had some serious relaxation to undertake. Given that I have free reign in the kitchen I also set about doing a little cooking. You may be surprised to hear that a chap on his own is keen to prepare his own meals, rather than resort to an easy life of take-away food. First the choice of take-away meals in the vicinity is somewhat slim and secondly I rather enjoy experimenting. Time will tell if my tinkering provides the required sustenance for my active lifestyle, (def.: walking to the pub/beer fridge and back), or finishes me off all together.

I am sure you can hardly wait for the further grim tales of a lonely shopkeeper. If they should suddenly cease you may assume that my culinary excess has had the better of me, either that or the dancing girls have my full attention.

January 21ˢᵗ – Saturday

I slept fitfully and woke up late, and fortunately so did the bleddy hound else I would have woken up early. I also woke up with a cunning plan, which, once you factor in the bleddy hound, probably is not so cunning any more.

Nevertheless, the morning commenced with the second and final part of my exercise in the culinary arts, the one that I started yesterday. For yesterday I made some dough, well, it is essentially pastry and, once rolled out into very thin rounds, becomes flour tortillas, I had hoped. I resisted the temptation to expound how simple they were to make yesterday, just in case they were not. As it happens they were, though a tad time consuming, and just as good as shop bought ones. I know this as I had some for breakfast, stuffed with salad and ham, and I had some more for tea, stuffed with spiced mince and other goodies. That is probably the last you will hear of my culinary skills. If word gets back to the Missus I will never be out of that kitchen.

Time, then, for part one of my cunning plan, which involved heading out on the diminishing beach to run the bleddy hound around until she collapsed with exhaustion. She did not, but this was of little consequence in my grand design.

When I returned, I went around and collected the neighbour's dog and took her and the bleddy hound round the block for a comfort break, then brought both dogs back to the flat. With her playmate here she cannot rest. She is either playing, or protecting whichever of her many toys her visitor has her eye, or teeth, on. This is part two of the cunning plan - prevent the bleddy hound from having any rest.

Part three came in the afternoon, having returned the neighbour to her own home. I piled the bleddy hound into the van and whisked her off to St Just or, to be more accurate, Cot Valley. Now, I do not know if you have ever been to Cot Valley, dear reader, but it is now a verdant vale more reminiscent of the valleys of the south coast with trees, yes trees, and an abundance of flora. Once though, it was a steaming wasteland beset with industrial goings on, the remnants of which can still be seen today.

It also offers a starting point for walks to Cape Cornwall or, if you are in possession of a small dog that you wish to exhaust, a steep climb and a long descent back where you started. It was the latter I chose for cunning plan part three. I must admit that the climb was rather steeper than I remembered and much faster, on account of having a sprightly bleddy hound, for whom the word 'wait' is some sort of sound that spurs her on, attached to my hand by a lead and dragging me behind her. In fact she pulled for the entire journey, just to let me know that cunning plan parts five to ten would be required to finish her completely.

Still, it was a pleasant enough excursion. It would have been better still if I had been able to let her off the lead. However Carn Gloose is peppered with mine workings and the cunning plan did not involve pulling the bleddy hound out of a big hole in the ground.

On the moors we were exposed to the stiff westerly breeze, but down in the valley it was still and very mild. On the way down we met up with a very boisterous young border terrier, so I let the two play while I watched and enjoyed the additional energy consumption. There were young lambs in one of the fields and, blow me, llamas in another. I hear tell there are ostriches too. Odd place St Just.

It was back home after that, and again I went and fetched the neighbouring dog to reduce the risk of the bleddy hound building up her energy levels. Cunning plan part four complete.

Now you may be wondering why I should want the bleddy hound so completely worn out. Others of you, knowing which day of the week it is, are probably streaks ahead of me. Of course, it is band night up the F&L and I fully intended to go, bleddy hound sitting or not. You see she really is not keen to be left on her own for any length of time, and I reasoned if she was worn out she was more likely to sleep that be upset.

Of course, what I had not taken into account was the toll that all this exercise would take on my well used and knackered old frame. I had time to contemplate this as I dragged myself up Stonechair Lane on all fours. It did not help that I was confronted by the large and grotesque figure of FT looming out of the darkness. It spooked me sufficiently to keep an eye over my shoulder for the rest of the journey.

What cruel irony, then, that after all this extreme effort and cunning plannery, I arrived at the F&L only to find that the band had cancelled their performance. While it did force us to engage in unusual conversation, both in the fact that we had one and the nature of its varied subject matter, it left me with an eerie sense of foreboding. Has the bleddy hound some supernatural power to begger up my night out, because I had planned so thoroughly to leave her home alone?

She plagued me viciously when I got home and I was playing chicken until the early hours. She can survive on her wits next weekend as I am darned if I am going through all that again!

January 23ʳᵈ - Monday

I have already explained that Portheras beach is on our bucket list but that I was waiting until the tides were right before exploring out that way. We are a couple of days off the biggest tides and they are not that big anyway, so with the weather beckoning we headed forth. It was a tough call between wellies and walking boots and whichever I chose was bound to be wrong, so I chose wellies and was right, I was wrong.

There are some long climbs going down to the beach. I ask you, how can you have long climbs when you are going down? I can only assume that the combined short drops and deep slopes are longer and deeper than the long climbs. As with our walk on Saturday, I was disinclined to let the bleddy hound off the lead and again, as with our walk on Saturday, she pulled the arms off me all the way.

The first place I wanted to have a look at was the little fishing station on the west end of the beach. In fact, it uses a steep two-part slipway down into a small inlet known as Boat Cove that is cut off from the main beach by a rocky promontory. This is where I had hoped that the tide would recede sufficiently to allow a walk around it to the main beach. Looking at it at near low water today it seems unlikely that even another couple of metres would have made much difference. I felt very disappointed that I could not pass that way on such a lovely day. I suppose that is where the phrase comes from, sick transit glorious Monday, but there again they did not teach Latin in the Greta Garbo home for wayward boys and girls.

We backed up and followed the coast path further along until we dropped onto the rocky and perilous steps down onto the beach. Given that the bleddy hound is clearly part mountain goat I let her off the lead, which was exactly the right thing to do as she would have had me down on the beach head first.

On the way down we passed a large pile of steel plates and other detritus. Not so long ago the cove was made off limits, as this wreckage had surfaced on the beach. It is the remains of the *Alacrity*, a coaster that ran aground nearby in 1963 and was dynamited to break up the wreck. It is a bit of a mystery how they managed to get the wreckage up that far, as unless they landed diggers from the sea you would not get much more than a handcart down the cliff.

For all the effort of getting down there it is a beautiful and interesting beach. At the west end there is a jumble of rocks, leading onto ledges with deep rock pools. At the other end a fast flowing stream runs down onto the beach, with some more rocks which are just perfect for sitting on and throwing a ball for a daft hound. It was here that the only sunlight poured down and it was warm enough to strip down to a shirt.

We spent some while down there watching the waves, crash up the sand. It is exceedingly quiet, (apart from the waves crashing up the sand), and has an air of tranquillity about it. It also has a steep climb out of it that I was trying to put off as long as possible.

Obtusely, the long climbs we had on the way in seemed to translate into long climbs coming out. With banks of fern either side of the track, I concluded that it was safe enough to let the bleddy hound run free, which I wish I had concluded on the way down. When we arrived back at the van, which we had left at Pendeen Watch, she was fair covered in mud, the bleddy hound, not the van, and other unspeakable things and I was too pooped to care. It, of course, precipitated a regulation shower when we got home, and talking of precipitation we reached the van just as a shower headed in from the west. As a run out it was certainly different from our normal dash to the beach in The Cove, and despite aching legs was rather enjoyable in retrospect.

Time then, for a recuperating afternoon doing not very much at all. Well, almost. I have, in the fridge, some rather 'ansum skirt just waiting to be inserted into a pasty made by an award winning pasty maker. Some of this afternoon was spent making some award winning short pastry, which is when I noticed that I have no baking parchment in the flat to place the award winning pasties on. A trip into town will be required in the morning.

I contemplated the Missus missing all these goodies while I ate my cordon bleu tea, but she is in the middle of the Caribbean just now. I bet they do not do award winning pasties on cruise liners.

January 24ᵗʰ - Tuesday

It was a grey, uninviting and uninspiring day, so much so that I felt grey, uninvited and uninspired to do very much at all. It took me all my reserves to pull myself together and drag, (ha! Drag), the bleddy hound down to the big wide open beach.

I had intended to find an exciting wander somewhere further afield and different from the usual amble. Instead, we ended up exploring the west end of the beach at first, then doubling back towards Gwenver. After some while tossing a ball around we made our way back and, for a change, crossed the rocks onto the Harbour beach before coming home.

Next door's hound was home alone when we returned, so I took both dogs around, then back to the flat. I do not believe that I have ever been so closely scrutinised while putting together an award winning pasty; it quite put me off my stroke, with four hungry eyes looking up at me and eight legs getting under my feet. The end result, an hour or so later, was not bad but I had made the pastry a little wet and the carrot was a little hard – only kidding! As if I would sully my pasties in such a way.

And so to cards at the OS; I could not bring myself to leave the bleddy hound at home, but I had to carry her shaking and quivering down the street. This is, after all, Injun country at this time of the evening and in darkness her arch-enemy could jump from the shadows at any moment. She settled soon enough, with a frothing pint of ale in her paw and propping up one end of the bar. I have to say it did nothing for my game and in all the confusion I left my glasses behind when we left.

January 25ᵗʰ - Wednesday

I have had a hankering for some time to strike out and visit Gwithian beach, or probably more accurately Godrevy beach.

It was on the road up to Gwithian that a change of heart came upon me, and an irresistible urge pulled me into the car park on Gwithian Towans. Little has changed there over the years and the car park is as pot-holed and muddy as it ever was. Across the rough road that leads on to Upton Towans are the tufted dunes of Gwithian Towans themselves.

It has been many years since I walked through these little hills, and as a boy I was sternly warned to stay this side of the rusty remnants of fence that marked the old boundary of the dynamite works. Now as a mature adult, able to judge the danger for myself, I climbed the hills to the left and looked down upon the old bunkers, the outlines of which can still be seen. I felt the need to cast caution to the winds, shirk off those old bonds of authority and stick my nose into one of the old bunkers. Naturally, I sent the bleddy hound first, just in case.

Having laid my ghosts to rest, we continued winding through the hills and valleys of the dunes, eager to land upon the beach. Though my memory of walking through these sand hills is vivid, in my mind the route down to the beach was less so, to the extent of not knowing if one existed at all at this point. Whether it did then or not, it does now, underneath a rather smart RNLI Lifeguard hut. It was a steeper descent than I remembered too, but where once the way was carved by the natural passage of feet, today it is a properly constructed set of steps. The cliffs here are the highest along the whole beach, which does not say much, maybe 60 feet, but the bleddy hound was down there in a flash.

I had chosen this 'Three Miles of Golden Sand', Hayle's tag line, today as the wind was in the south west and the cliffs, at least, would provide some shelter. Did they heck! The wind was fair whistling up the Hayle Estuary and powering across the massive expanse of sand. The loose grains were being blown along a few inches off the ground and looked very much like I was shin deep in a swirling sea of sand.

We headed down, with the wind at our backs, searching for a more sheltered spot, where the bleddy hound could run back with the ball without getting a face full of blasted sand. There really was not one, but we stopped by at a clump of rocks hiding a deep rock pool, where the bleddy hound could swim in safety. This triggered in my mind a hazy childhood memory, of sitting with my grandparents among the rocks at a place named locally as Sheep Pool. I had looked for it before, but concluded that the passage of time had changed the beach sufficiently for it to have disappeared. It seems I was looking in the wrong place before, because as we progressed to the next set of rocks there it was. It is an expansive pool, set between two towering lumps of mudstone and has provided safe bathing water to youngsters for generations.

If I have misled you, I am sure that the Aged Parent will put me right in short order. The place that I refer to is part of Strap Rocks, I think, and lies roughly half way between the dynamite works and the Red River.

Having played, swum, chased the ball, walked at least two of the Three Miles of Golden Sand and reminisced, it was time to head back. We chose the cliff top dunes, as I reckon the bleddy hound would have gone blind with the amount of sand shifting about at her head height. It was not the easier of the routes, and far too much up-hilling for my liking. I suspect my tumble at the end of last week did a little more damage to my left knee than I thought at the time.

It was a shame to leave so soon and we spent a little time just watching the dunes from the shelter of the van. I had the radio on just for a little noise other than the wind blowing in my ear 'ole, and I was mindful that we were lucky enough to have a radio, and a radio station broadcast.

The first radio sets made by the Marconi company, Wireless Telegraph & Signal Company, were manufactured from today in Chelmsford in 1899. The first regular radio broadcasts were made in 1910; a marketing coup if ever there was one. This brought about the first ever joke based on technology –

Toff with first radio set: 'I say, I say, I say, what is on the radio tonight?'

Wife of toff with first radio set: 'I don't know, dear, what is on the radio tonight?'

Toff with first radio set: 'A vase'

January 26ᵗʰ - Thursday

Two chaps can be seen standing in the middle of a desolate northern moor. One is wearing workmanlike dress and is fairly short in stature, though broad and swarthy. The other is more finely dressed, a government man, perhaps. They seem to be discussing some sort of business.

Government man: "So you are the builder of walls, are you?"

Builder: "'edges, my 'ansum. We call 'em 'edges where I come from. Cornish 'edges, best you'll ever see."

Gov man: "I see. You have been recommended, apparently." [Looks at slate clipboard with some sort of parchment pinned to it]. "Can you give me some idea of the work you have carried out in the past?"

Builder: "Sure. There was Mrs George's 'edge just last week there. She wanted to have something to mark the end of her garden. She were some pleased with that, I can tell ee."

Gov man: "Mmm. Anything bigger?"

Builder: "Bigger? Let's see, there was farmer Thomas' field 'ad to be 'edged seeing as his sheep was always 'scaping. That field was at least 'alf an acre."

Gov man: "Bigger?"

Builder: "Look I've been building 'edges since I was thirteen with my old Dad. I'm 46 now. I must have built miles and miles of bleddy 'edges. What zackly are you after?"

Gov man: "Well, the chief wants a wall built, a very big wall, to keep the horrible hordes off his land. They have been causing some problems over the years and things are about to change. He wants them kept out on a permanent basis, so we were thinking of a wall than runs from the east coast to the west, at least ten feet high with checkpoints every mile."

Builder: [Goes a bit glassy eyed and takes a bit of a gulp] "Yes, that's certainly big. I might have to get a bit of help with that one."

Gov man: "Yes it could be a bit of a challenge, but my sources said that you were the best wall, ahem, hedge builder in all the land. Money, of course, would not be an issue; the chief will just collect a few more taxes, especially from the daft hordes across the other side, who we've been bleeding for years. We've been taking money off them hand over fist so a few more denarii won't make much difference. But if you don't think you can manage it ..."

Builder: "Hold on there, me 'ansum. I never said I couldn't do it, just that I might need a bit of an 'and."

Gov man: "I don't think labour will be an issue. We could probably get a few locals to help lifting stones and digging holes, some of the less skilled tasks. Some of them worship a bit too often at the temple of Bacchus ... "

Builder: "They do what?"

Gov man: " They drink a bit, especially the lot round the east end, but the chief reckons that he can make a law to stop the horrible degenerate hordes sending their cheap booze across the border, so that should see to that."

Builder: "And you said something about the money. You said denarry. Woss all that about then?"

Gov man: "Ah yes, I should have said. You will be paid in the currency of the new empire, we call it denarii at present, just a working title you understand. After the wall is built, the empire will be safe and we can do just about whatever we please, including currency. Your denarii will be legal tender in any part of the realm."

Builder: "Oall right then. We'll make a start on un soon as we 'ad a cuppa tay and 'ave un finished dreckly.

Gov man: "Yes, I was just going to come to that. There is a deadline. The chief wants this finished in two years."

Builder: [Laughs sarcastically.] "Two years! A bit of a boy, this chief of yours, I suppose 'ee wants bleddy flags on it too and built of bleddy marble."

Gov man: [Delivers a stony stare.] "Finished in two years – no flags. Building materials ..." [looks around at the rocky heath]" local materials would do just nicely."

Builder: "Right then, best I go get my shovel an' club 'ammer. Incidentally an 'edge this size ought to have some sort of name, something that represents the skilled craftsmanship that went into it. My name's Trembath, by the way.

Gov man: "Don't worry about that, Mr Trembath. The name has been taken care of. It will be called after our great chief, the man who brought us to freedom, who kept the horrible uncultured hordes from raiding our land of its valuable resources and its fine civilisation."

Builder: "Oh?"

Gov man: "Yes, Mr Trembath. It will be called Salmond's wall."

Just in case you were wondering, it was Hadrian's birthday this week and a certain Mr Burns has a bit of a do yesterday.

January 27ᵗʰ - Friday

What a beautiful morning and what a, mainly, beautiful day; just the sort of day for sitting on a rock on Perranuthoe beach and tossing a ball for a faithful dog. Well, actually, it was supposed to be Praa Sands today, just for a change, but we beggered about for so long this morning that time conspired against us. Anyway, I could not find a faithful mutt so I had to take the bleddy hound instead.

I have had a bit of paperwork building up on the desk over the past week and it kept staring at me, throwing down a bit of a challenge to do something about it. So this morning I did something and carved a bit of a notch in it. Not all of it, obviously. You do not want to do something as inspiring as paperwork all at once, especially when you live your life by the maxim, 'never do today what you can put off until tomorrow'.

So by the time I had done some of that, taken the bleddy hound and her mate around the block and had them both back for a bit of a romp, it had just about turned low water. Given it would take me the best part of three quarters of an hour to get ready and drive out to Praa Sands, and add to that the fact the Perranuthnoe has a cracking little beach and a cracking little café in The Cabin, I elected to drop off there.

It was spectacularly sunny, so much so that I had to dig out the sunglasses, (it also goes with the territory down there; it's a bit chic, don't you know). The tide was starting to roll in but there was still plenty of room, even with at least another half a dozen dog walkers there. But by the time we decided to roll off the beach and repair to The Cabin for a cup of tea and cake, (homemade, you know), there were some ominous big black clouds arriving. As we left it had started to shower a little, so our timing could not have been more precise.

Precise, indeed. On the journey home we hit some heavier showers, and as we arrived on the outskirts of Sennen there was evidence of an even heavier hail storm and big black anvil shaped clouds off Land's End. With the sun beginning to set, the colours all about the sky were quite spectacular.

See, even come the Apocalypse we will have something pretty to look at.

January 28ᵗʰ – Saturday

For a while now the van has been making an annoying little rattling sound from the rear end, especially when the engine is in idle or being turned off. The likelihood was that the exhaust pipe was just about to fall off, but having just been through a MoT Test I thought that I might be safe for a little bit. That was until the exhaust fell off on the road down to the Cape Cornwall car park. Well, when I say fell off, it almost fell off, with something still connecting it to the van, letting it drag noisily along the tarmac. Stopping on the single track road to have a look was not really going to be a sensible option, so I decided to see if I could make it to the car park.

With the van making sufficient noise to alarm the sheep in the fields as I passed, it was extremely unlikely that I had not noticed that I was driving a van with something big and metal hanging off underneath. It was with some amusement, then, that I came across a group of golfers waving at me frantically and pointing to the underside of the vehicle. Had it not been for the fact that I was keen to make it to the car park before the item fell off completely, I would have stopped and asked them what the problem was. "My exhaust? Fallen off? What are you talking about, man? There is absolutely nothing wrong with this vehicle. You must have just heard the wind whistling between your lug 'oles."

I did make it to the car park, and having made sure it was not going to roll down the hill and run me over, I got underneath to have a look. Sure enough the golfer was right, there was a bit of my exhaust hanging off. As luck would have it, the middle silencer had rusted through very neatly either end of the box and was dangling off its rubber mount. Some nifty handiwork with a craft knife, that I had secreted about the van for carving up cardboard boxes, soon had the offending article removed. The rest of the pipe work was suitably secure. Surprisingly the van did not sound any different from normal when we eventually drove away either. Nevertheless I think we will be confined to The Cove until I can get it fixed properly.

Having only planned a minor excursion for the morning, I had already decided to take the bleddy hound out again in the afternoon, along the regular route starting up Mayon Cliff. It is only a few miles, with the only climb at the outset of the route and normally, although it does get the heart pumping, it is a walk of only minor exertion. Today, however, I felt utterly drained for some reason, and by the time I reached the top of Vellandreath I was very grateful for my little rest stop at the bench there. It was from here I noticed Head Launcher, who works in the valley, (the term being loosely applied, 'work', that is, 'valley' is quite accurate), and hailed him a friendly haloo. Back came the call, almost as an echo, "Cup of tea?"

For those of you unfamiliar with my habits in this regard, I very rarely drink tea, other than a cup first thing, or coffee for that matter. However, at this moment, a cup of tea seemed to be at the very pinnacle of my list of desires, the elixir that my heart yearned, the pivot on which life itself is balanced. Well, all right, I rather fancied a cuppa. So rather than eschew his kindly gesture, that would otherwise have been my normal response, I fair scampered down the hill and was ensconced in his little hut in short order.

Something very odd happened in that hut. A bond was formed, a reaching out of hearts, a warm ethereal glow enveloping us, perhaps. No, not Head Launcher for heaven's sake, I do not think even Dorothy would have him as a friend. It was the bleddy hound, she jumped into my lap. She never, ever, jumps in my lap and rarely anyone else's. If she sits between the Missus and me on the sofa and we dare reach out and stroke her, that is it, she's off to the far side of the room like a shot. The least affectionate dog you would ever wish to meet; a lap dog she definitely ain't. I tolerated this public display of affection as she was quite insistent, but it was an embarrassing and awkward moment. Well, you try to drink a cup of tea and roll a fag with a panting and unpleasantly aromatic, (yes, she found some badger pooh on the way), bleddy hound on your lap.

Thus refreshed with tea, and shaken out of my erstwhile chronic malaise by the bleddy hound's uncharacteristic behaviour, we continued our journey to the beach. She chased the ball for the best part of an hour and, thankful to say, she was back to her normal indifferent self. We made our way home to a well-earned rest and some tea before, well, before the normal Saturday night shenanigans.

It was *The Dolphins Fly* playing up at the F&L tonight and they had the first advantage over the previous band, in that they turned up. They have been there a couple of times before and I would say that they are the most professional band to play there, with no apologies to *Devil's Creek* who, while utterly brilliant, are amateur by comparison. *The Dolphins Fly* play mostly their own tunes, which are excellent. For some reason they felt it necessary to play some covers for the F&L crowd and, gosh, did they play them well. We had a bit of Beatles, Police, Ocean Colour Scene and believe it or not some Grateful Dead. Even they admitted that they look a little like Simon and Garfunkel and played Mrs Robinson to prove they sound like them too. Their vocal harmonies seem effortless and the tunes were sublime so much so I bought their disc after the set. So did *The Dolphins Fly*? No, they soared.

And so home to a fractious bleddy hound, left alone for three hours. She did not seem in bad shape, particularly having seen her nemesis through the window just before I left. She barked for a full three quarters of an hour. Having run her around, barking and making a fuss she settled.

I left the computer's camera running through my absence. It will be interesting to see what she got up to, but I have a suspicion that perhaps I would be better off not knowing.

January 29ᵗʰ – Sunday

It was never going to be a comfortable day with the Lifeboat Station open to the public and a bleddy hound to cater for. I very rarely get involved with the open days, as most of them are held when the shop is open. To ready myself for this challenge TS and I indulged in a full breakfast next door, which had opened in support of the Lifeboat open day. It was certainly more supportive than the weather that very quickly went from grey to bleak and wet.

Despite the odds stacking up against us there were quite a few people around willing to get wet and to donate a few pounds, while getting a tour of the boat. Unsure of what exactly was required, I manned the reception desk for a while and signed a few certificates for the visiting children. Sitting myself down is the only way to get the bleddy hound settled, and without a proper bed she very quickly improvised with a cardboard box that she crept into and went to sleep.

I managed to get a short while to take her down to the beach for a little ball chasing. I feared she would be overcome with cabin fever had I not. I did cut quite a conspicuous figure down on the beach in full crew gear though. Later I took her for a ride in the ILB launch tractor, which unfortunately toppled her quite suddenly off its seat as we tipped down onto the slipway. She would not get back onto the seat after that for some reason.

While there were quite a few pleasant and very generous people about, far more than you would have imagined on a wet Sunday in January, it was not author inspiring territory. This is why I have left a blank space at the bottom of today's entry for you to fill in your own excitement.

January 30th – Monday

At half past three this afternoon we were the only figures on a desolate and wet beach. Even the two surfers who were there when we had arrived had either beggered off or drowned themselves, as a desperate symbolic gesture against the grey weather.

The pinnacle of excitement this morning was polishing my walking boots and ironing my shirts. There, you see, I bet you were not expecting that today. You must understand that I spent some time as a single man in the 90's. This was when pretending to be a 'new man' by leaving toilet seats down, cooking the odd decent meal and ironing your own shirts was the only way of getting what the 70's man used to get with a bunch of flowers and a dinner out.

I did have a break-through with a major insurance company today. I have been trying to get them to behave properly since the start of December, when they sent me two proposals with two different payments that I had apparently accepted without response. I rather insisted that they send me another correct proposal and since then they have sent me everything but. The final hurdle was negotiating a start date that did not involve me paying twice in the same month, which is what happens if your regular payment date does not coincide with the date that is ten days after the start date. Yup, all that really made me feel like a valued customer.

Luckily, I have the garage that looks after the van to renew my faith in service ethics. I telephoned the chap there this morning to relate my tale of woe regarding the falling off of my exhaust. With a bit of effort he could get the replacement parts in the afternoon, lend me a car in the meantime and have the fixed van back to me by close of play. At five o'clock I picked up the repaired van, along with the bill that was less than I had expected for a job done in a bit of a hurry. Ah, service that makes you smile.

Unfortunately all that left me very little time to prepare the gourmet tea I had rather hoped that I would have. It left me rooting around in the freezer for a surprise box of something we had frozen earlier. We do not bother to identify the meals that we freeze, so it is always a bit of a lucky dip, particularly as everything frozen looks the same. I cannot tell you the times I have had a bolognaise sauce with rice or a curry with spaghetti.

January 31st - Tuesday

How on Earth did we get here so quickly? It does not seem that long ago I was manfully trying to raise a glass at the F&L to welcome in the New Year. It surprised me so much, that yesterday, when the lady from the insurance company said she would start the term on 31st January, I actually asked her why the delay. She had to remind me that it was, indeed, tomorrow that she referred.

So, with only a couple of days left before the Missus gets home from her travels, I decided to go overboard on our day out. The place that had been teasing me for around a week now is Tehidy Country Park that lies between Portreath and Camborne. It is a fair way out for just a walk around, but I was determined to investigate.

There are two locations within the park to start from, the southern entrance off the A30 and the North Cliffs entrance off, well, North Cliffs actually. I selected the latter, on the basis that if the park did not yield up enough excitement we could decamp to Portreath beach for a run around. As it turned out we had more than enough excitement and almost ended up with more than I bargained for in the shape of another bleddy hound.

When we arrived at the small car park there was another dog walker just about to depart. She had a small border terrier with her, but as she drove out the dog came running up to me. The lady stopped and explained that the border had been there when she arrived and was still there now, as she left. She thought that it might have been abandoned. I assured her that I was going for a walk around and that if the dog was still there on my return I would take care of it. Quite what I had in mind I have no idea, but it sounded like the right thing to say at the time.

The dog said her name was Olive, but that was all I could get out of her. She was young and friendly and was very content to chase the bleddy hound around. She followed us all the way round, on our walk through the muddy wooded paths. It certainly made a difference to see trees for a change, as they are rather at a premium further west, but I suspect that the walk is less muddy and more colourful in Spring. Nevertheless it was a pleasant enough tramp around.

By the time we returned to the van both dogs were lagged, and my thoughts turned to how I might accommodate both, to take them wherever it was appropriate to take stray or lost dogs. My mind also turned over the fact that I could suggest that I had found both dogs wandering and be free forever, or at least until the Missus got home when carnage would ensue. It was at this moment that a chap came walking through the car park and the small border ran up to him. I asked if the border was his dog, but he said no. However, he added that he worked for The much maligned council, which maintains the park, and a colleague had mentioned a report of a lost dog.

Now that the council was involved I had the dreaded notion that I would have to fill out lost dog forms in triplicate, while adhering to the dog's diversity policy, for which I would probably have to undergo a training course. He promised that he would circumvent the administration so long as I kept his name out of the Diary. It was while he was telephoning various people to try and get the owner's name and number, that the owner turned up and I breathed a sigh of relief.

Having started out the day with a beige and tan dog, I now had one that resembled a black and tan dog. It was in a flash of inspiration that I recalled our trip out this way a few days ago and the rediscovery of some old childhood haunts; it was time to put Sheep's Pool to some good use.

I drove all the way down to Upton Towans this time, rather than having to labour over the dunes. From here it was but a short walk down to Strap Rocks. It only took a couple of tosses of the ball into the limpid pool for her to emerge clean as a new pin, though seconds later covered in wet sand. Note to self: if the water rates go up much more, it could be cheaper than using the shower at home.

Despite having run a marathon around Tehidy Country Park with a small border terrier attached to her ears, the bleddy hound was keen to chase a ball around. It was considerably less windy than our previous visit and much more comfortable sitting on a ledge with springy mussels at my back and throwing the ball for her. We spent a good hour down there before making our way back.

I once again had to carry the bleddy hound down to the OS so that I could attend the cards night, and once again felt distracted enough to loose badly at the game. If I am sitting, she will settle and behave, but heaven forefend that I should get up to maybe attend the bar, because it is clear I am preparing to go and leave her forever; I do so detest having to sit down in a pub, it just is not natural.

We noted more than a little chill in the air on the way home. Frost tomorrow, I would not wonder.

February 1ˢᵗ - Wednesday

Supristi monkeys! I had to chisel the ice off the duvet this morning. If it gets any colder I may have to relent and turn the new heaters on. There was even some ice in The Cove as I walked herself around this morning. I suppose it cannot get much colder than that.

I procrastinated a little this morning, waiting on the tide to recede, but I had not really planned anything, at least on the scale of yesterday's adventure. I relented eventually and we took ourselves off on a local walk past Trinity Cottages at the end of Maria's Lane and across the fields. I had not travelled this way in quite some time and forgot just how boggy it gets towards the road. Once again I had a muddy little dog on my hands.

I consoled myself with a single pint at the F&L before retracing our steps and on to Land's End. We had sun in a clear blue sky and with the wind in the east we were relatively sheltered on the cliff path. A healthy pace was the only combat against the cold, although I cannot have been moving my fingertips fast enough because they were still freezing off by the time we got back to The Cove.

By the time we reached home she was not any cleaner, so I decided to hose her down on the doorstep. I clearly had not thought this through, as although it got rid of the worst of the mud she was still quite mucky. When I opened the door to let her in the first thing she did was leap onto the furniture to dry herself off; if she had two fingers I am sure she would have raised them in my direction. So much for having the place spick and span for the arrival of the Missus tomorrow, not that I have yet made any attempt to do so. I have also just remembered how muddy the back seat of the van is, that will be used tomorrow when I pick up the girls from the station. It seems I will have a litany of tasks ahead of me before I collect them.

While I sat and considered the litany of tasks I had ahead of me, I became increasingly distracted by the sun soaked beach widening out in front of the window. By four o'clock it had become too much to bear and I togged up and headed down there. I had only intended to be there a short while, but we ended up throwing the ball around for an hour and repaired to the OS for a bit of a warm before heading home. It was then that I remembered that once again I had not prepared my gourmet evening meal, the last lonely repast for a while.

With no real plan for the disparate ingredients I had at my disposal I set about creating on the fly, with some frying onions, floured beef skirt, potatoes, turnip, some peppers and tomatoes and finally a bit of green chilli to spice it up a little. Modesty prevents me from saying just how good the final result was but just let me say this, if shopkeepers made stews it would probably be the best stew in the world. Late though it was, it was exceedingly welcome. I have even put some aside for breakfast tomorrow, really on the basis that I forgot to buy in anything for tomorrow either.

As regular readers you will all be used to the ground-breaking elements in these pages so, hold onto your hats for the first ever Cove Diary recipe.

Ingredients:
500g beef skirt, cubed and rolled in flour (I used wholemeal)
½ litre of beef stock (I forgot to measure but it was about that)
2 cloves garlic (I forgot this, but wouldn't do any harm to add)
1 onion diced
2 good size potatoes, cubed (I used Estima)
½ turnip, cubed (that's swede to most of you)
½ green pepper finely chopped
½ red pepper finely chopped
3 tomatoes finely chopped (I didn't bother but skin if preferred)
1 green chilli finely chopped (optional)
salt and pepper to taste

Method:
Fry and brown the onions in a deep pan and add the garlic. Meanwhile brown off the skirt and add to the fried onions in batches.

Add the stock, potatoes and turnip and cover. Simmer for ten to fifteen minutes or until the potato has begun to soften.

Add the peppers and chilli and simmer for a further five minutes then add the tomatoes and simmer for fifteen minutes more.

Beef skirt does not take much cooking. If you are not lucky enough to be able to get beef skirt and have to use an alternative you may have to simmer the beef for a while longer before you add the potatoes and turnip.

If the resulting stew is not the best you have ever tasted you must have done it wrong.

Bon appetite!

February 2ⁿᵈ - Thursday

Hmm, I think it was the layer of ice on my bald pate that roused me early this morning. I had entreated the bleddy hound to come under the covers with me, on the grounds of some unusually empathic whim of mine that thought she must be cold too; I must have been half asleep still. She eschewed my offer some minutes later, but was as restless as a caged tiger, (sorry, that was the best simile I could come up with at short notice), for the ensuing hour or so. She came back later and laid herself across my head, and I noted how hot her belly was. It was quite comforting until she started licking my ear and I knew, regardless of the hour, that it was time to get up.

Last night the Missus made contact and told me how she longed for one of my famous culinary delights when she returned home. I in return thanked her for the amount of notice that she had provided and vouchsafed that I would do all in my power to provide such a feast. Having already been prepared to drive into town to pick her up from the station, I now had to make an earlier trip to collect the necessary ingredients for the homecoming meal. With the bleddy hound making it perfectly clear she required an adventure of the sort she had been getting everyday since the departure of the Missus, it was plain that today was going to be a challenge.

As much as I would like to believe that the shops in St Just could service all my food needs, even their broad range of products does not stretch to chorizo. I bought as much as I could from there, but had to trek into PZ for the sausage. The look on the bleddy hound's face was priceless when she realised that our jaunt in the van did not have a beach at the end of it and we were on our way home. A softer touch than I would have had a pang of guilt at such a pathetic facial gesture. Oh, come on, she has had a run out every day for a fortnight of at least two to three miles, so don't you start feeling sorry for her.

I left her to her misery as I prepared the fatted calf. She did not do too badly out of it as she had a bit of beef and a bit of chorizo, and I had not planned to leave her completely devoid of exercise. As the train was due into PZ at ten past five, I concluded that it would be an excellent plan to take her down to

Perranuthnoe, fast becoming a favourite location, and for a run on its smooth sands while we waited for the train.

With the sun setting in a perfect sky, the beach at Perranuthnoe was absolutely stunning. It was also less cold than I had anticipated, especially at the eastern end of the beach that was sheltered from the easterly breeze. It was unfortunate that The Cabin shuts at four o'clock, otherwise it would have perfectly rounded off our pre-Missus-collection time. I settled for a cup or tea and some cake at the station that was twice the price and half as good.

The Missus and her mates arrived on time, complete with twice as many bags as they left with. Even so, by the time we got home there was insufficient time to finish off the gourmet feast and consume it ahead of Lifeboat training. I had to make an emergency dash to the excellent fish and chip shop up the top, which is what I had planned to do in the first place, before I was entreated to push the boat out with some home cooking. The meal will wait until tomorrow without being spoiled, especially in the kitchen that is currently colder than the inside of the refrigerator.

Lifeboat training was a frightfully short affair. An exercise is planned for Saturday, thankfully finishing shortly before the rugby starts. With little more to do before then, we repaired to the OS and the regular quiz where, almost embarrassingly, we won for the third week running. We let it go to a tie break, just to give the other team a bit of a chance.

Unfortunately, the tie break question involved the originating date of the Curly Wurly bar. In my first year at secondary school I got into a small altercation over the very same chocolate and toffee confection. During the fracas, another boy, not involved in the original argument, saw his chance and made off with my bar. Who would have thought that this unpleasant incident would result, forty years later, in securing a reward of thirty quid?

I learnt a valuable lesson that day at school – in a fight, always keep your hand on your Curly Wurly.

February 3ʳᵈ - Friday

I feel it in my fingers; I feel it in my toes. Well, yes, I certainly did, but I rather think that the chap that wrote that was not exactly talking about frostbite. Man, was it ever cold this morning.

The ice on the slope up to Coastguard Row was as thick and solid as ever; it was fortunate I discovered this during daylight, as this is part of the late night dash route. There is even ice on the big beach at the current high water mark; there is a geet, thick plate of it where the stream that emerges from under The Beach car park flows out across the sand. Despite its proximity to the warm sea, (ten degrees), it was there late in the afternoon.

There was also a fair bit across the path up to Mayon Cliff, all areas where the sun, at this time of the year, does not yet reach. This will give you a fair indication that it was the round The Cove walk that me and the bleddy hound undertook today. It is the lazy alternative to actually thinking about an exciting adventure, and she was quite lucky she had that.

The Missus slept in until gone lunchtime today. You could, if you were to be sympathetic, put this down to a long period of travel and jet lag, and nothing to do with the fact that this is not long after the usual time of rousing. Nevertheless, it appeared to be infectious this morning. The bleddy hound was not that bothered about going out, although while we were on our own she would have ragged me rotten by midday. And despite the fact I was up, about and doing things from quite early, I was not ever so incited to be overly active either.

It is odd, because you know once you get togged up and out on the path, with the blood pumping around the narrowing arteries, that things will be much better, and they were. By the time we hit the top of the Valley I was as warm as toast and full of joie de vivre. Vellandreath Valley itself was bathed in late winter sun and so warm in the shelter from the light, chill breeze, that you could easily mistake it for a warm spring day. We revelled in it. We revelled even more when we got to the slim sliver of beach, as the tides are really not in our favour, and chucked a ball around and dug holes.

The beef and chorizo chilli, prepared the previous day, was a very fitting repast at the end of such a day, warming to the very pit of the soul. It dovetailed nicely into a lazy and soporific evening, where the Missus caught up on ten days of East Emmernation Street and I played some mindlessly violent and frustrating, (because I am useless at it), game on the games machine.

Nice that everything gets back to normal so quickly.

February 5ᵗʰ - Sunday

Golly, is that what a lie in feels like? I think, by and large, I would prefer to be up early if I were to be entirely honest. After all the sun was out through the few patches of blue sky, the café next door was open with a few hardly souls enjoying the al fresco dining area and it was dry.

It was also a rerun of the cancelled Christmas family dinner organised by our neighbour, which was first arranged for Christmas week. Fortunately, we bumped into our good neighbour, (not suggesting that the other one is bad, just absent), in the morning who asked if we were ready for the event, which we were not. It did not occur to us that it was dinner that he had arranged rather than tea. Nevertheless, we were ready in short order.

The Trewellard Hotel is an old, solid pile, conveniently enough situated in Trewellard. I imagine that had it been in Carnyorth they might have called it something different. Anyway, we have variously dined and lunched there on numerous occasions over the years and it is a comfortable and well run establishment. It was no different today.

The assembled throng of our neighbour's family pretty much filled all the dining space the hotel has to offer. We ended up, with our neighbour, in a downstairs snug that was probably once the cellar. It was a lengthy affair, the dinner, not the cellar, which was roughly square, but we were all served promptly with a Sunday lunch that was very acceptable and had no less than nine types of vegetable accompanying it. Even the fussiest eater would have found something out of that lot.

It was late into the afternoon when we emerged into a rather cloudier day than we had stepped out of. Because the bleddy hound had been cooped up in the van while we enjoyed our meals we decided it was only fair to give her a run out. About the only place between Trewellard and home that does not have too many deep holes for her to fall into was Cape Cornwall, so we repaired there. At least this time the exhaust system on the van did not fall off.

Just before we came away she decided to take a dip in a muddy puddle. Rather than let her back in the van in such condition, I took her down to the beach so that I could throw her into a rock pool to wash her off. Though it worked a treat I had not considered that it was an awfully long and muddy way back to the van from there. I was lucky in that she reached the van largely unscathed, but then disgraced herself by paddling through the same muddy puddle she had rolled in earlier. At least it was paws only this time.

After a large lunch, running the bleddy hound and catching up on a rather exciting, but ultimately disappointing rugby match, you can imagine that the evening was somewhat sluggish. I would hate to disappoint you as well, so carry on and imagine my dozy old frame reposing fitfully, with even the bleddy hound snoring away at my feet. That is what proper Sundays are all about anyway, is it not?

February 6th – Monday

Many of you will agree that The Diary contains nothing but rubbish. It is nice, then, that I can add to this pile by talking about more rubbish.

I think I may have said that The much maligned council has selected another provider to take on domestic rubbish collection across the county from April 1st. This prompted me to look at the alternatives on offer for our commercial waste collection, especially as the current provider has irked me somewhat by starting to charge a 'rental' fee during our closed period. I started the process by issuing them notice to terminate my contract from the end of March. Oddly they were very keen to talk to me about this, but only after I had called to ask if they had received my letter in the first place.

It transpires that they are happy to drop the collection costs and waive the 'rental' fee, to which I responded that they must have knowingly been overcharging me for some while. As to the termination, they insisted that the contract meant that any termination notice would take effect on the anniversary of the contract, which is March 8th, and run for a period of three months. Naturally, during this three months, I would be charged 'rental' and have to retain the bin, unless I wanted to pay nearly £100 to have it collected. As you can imagine all this did not exactly endear them to me to.

One of the alternative suppliers, and the one that will take up the domestic service from April, is considerably cheaper. They are also able to bandy around TLAs, (Three Letter Acronyms), like they are going out of style, so they must be real professionals. I like them already. In the news today they are advocating the use of ATT, (Advanced Thermal Treatment), plants. The council are right behind them on this too. The CMP, (Cabinet Member for Planning), noted that these smaller EFW, (Energy From Waste), stations are more environmentally friendly and crucially more acceptable to the communities in which they are situated than one large plant, like the currently on-hold plant at St Dennis. Well, when I say more acceptable to the communities, the first one planned only has 88 groups objecting to it. I do not know how they can be so censorious, after all we are talking about RDF, (Refuse Derived Fuel), which can only be a good thing, surely? I can see how people can get confused; when I first heard about the anaerobic digester I though it was a keep fit and diet plan.

Talking of keep fit, I managed to fit very nicely into our sofa for the rest of the afternoon and into the evening. With the Missus on holiday I managed to get out on an adventure nearly every day. Now she is back I have done next to nothing. I really must conclude that having a Missus around is bad for my health; I am seriously considering finding her another holiday.

February 7ᵗʰ - Tuesday

Sennen Cove. A few days before the start of the half term week, when school children will descend upon us like snow drops from a grey and sullen sky. They will come from afar and from near, accompanied by pensive guardians pulling with them expansive luggage, like lumbering workhorses pulling a plough. Up into their diverse lodgings they will go, with heads full of concerns and arms full of big winter coats, pondering whether they needed them or no and whether they should have brought extra bedclothes instead.

Sun was everywhere today; sun was amongst the wispy high clouds and carving its arc just above the hilltops as it will in early February. Sun reached into the long flowing grasses of the dunes, that sit and sway like the arms of a hungry Roman crowd baying at the gladiatorial battle between the sea and the sand. Sun fell out along the wide and golden beach, its broad span picking out the tops of waves before they fell upon the sand, like sprawling skaters on some icy pond. Sun picked out the lonely shopkeeper and his bleddy hound as they marched across the expanse, like a solitary Bedouin and his camel seen from some far up air balloon floating over an endless desert.

Shopkeeper sat on a rock in a corner of the beach, and bleddy hound sat in a warm little hole she had carefully crafted with use of paw and snout, as if her constitution were analogous to that of a mole and it was essential for her to burrow deeply to avoid the light.

Shopkeeper was about two-and-fifty years old. Bleddy hound was about three and far too many times faster than shopkeeper could keep up with. Shopkeeper was rather bald, rather red, and though an 'ansum and well-made man, too stern and grumpy in appearance to be prepossessing. Bleddy hound was very small, very hairy, and though (of course) an undeniably nuisance of a bleddy hound, was rather too small and too hairy to be of any use to man or beast alike. On the brow of shopkeeper, Time and his brother Stress had carved indelible marks, like a child with a sharp knife had played noughts and crosses for some length of time on a block of wood – while the countenance of bleddy hound was set about with, well, hair, really.

'Don't you think you are afraid of the sea, now?', I seemed to ask myself. Well I think that I would be if a moderately large wave came in. As it was, the waves were more than moderately large towards the end of the beach, and even larger beyond and out towards the place that is known as Gwenver beach. Even farther out, by Brisons rock, the waves appeared as large as the rocks themselves. It seemed impossible to shopkeeper that men, armed only with a plank of wood, might contrive to ride these veritable monsters, occasioned from the deep, through expert balance, like so many buzzards gliding on a single breeze.

Much later shopkeeper would repair to the ale emporium to play at cards. He would enter the low, dark and gloomy den with tables set about, and two or three old high back church pews set into smoky corners. It was a place where you would half expect to find a man strongly impregnated with the smell of liquor and a white-coated, red-eyed dog, except on this occasion shopkeeper had left bleddy hound behind. It was just as well, since the disturbance of his master's play, as often the case in recent weeks, might well have brought about the relief derivable from a kick and a curse.

Oh. But shopkeeper was a tight-fisted hand at the cards and one that paid him out in neither gold nor favour. Shopkeeper! A squeezing, wrenching, grasping, scraping, clutching, covetous, old sinner! He carried his own low temperature always about with him; he iced his office in the dog-days; and did not thaw it one degree at Christmas. This helped not one jot in the playing of cards, although tonight he did rather better than he had of late.

It should not be of great surprise to you, dear reader that, as shopkeeper returned home in the cold and dark that he, who knew every stone, was fain to grope with both his hands at the stairs to his front door.

Now, it is a fact, that there is nothing at all particular about the post flap on the door except that it is big and shiny. Let it also be said, that shopkeeper had not bestowed one thought on bleddy hound since he had left for cards earlier that night. And then let any of you, dear readers, explain to me why it was that shopkeeper, having his key in the lock of the door, saw in the post flap, without it going under any intermediate process of change, not a postal flap, but bleddy hound's face?

As you may imagine, today's entry was the very Dicken's of a job. If the 200-year-old writer is not, at this very minute rotating madly in his tomb, it is only by virtue of the fact that he is yet to read this seminal work of tosh.

Happy Birthday, Charlie.

February 8ᵗʰ - Wednesday

Our little end of The Cove was alive with activity today. First this morning we happed upon the Picassos slapping some tarry goo on the Roundhouse. Sorry, that should have read, expertly applying a coat of protective paint to the Roundhouse. Then there was a school of fishermen mending nets in the car park. They have been there rain and shine for the best part of a week now; that is an awful lot of nets or not many nets mended very slowly. Some of The Cove's fleet have been out for the last few days, hand lining for pollack in the main and some of the ones I have seen of late have been monsters, that is the pollack, not the fishermen, although ...

The Missus took herself off quite early this morning up to the big city for a spot of shopping. Needless to say I was quite happy stopping where I was; although it did mean that I did not have any transport to go off adventuring. Instead I did another round The Cove trip, as it was far too pleasant not to. The whole bay looked resplendent in the crystal air, the big wide beach set out below us from atop Mayon Cliff, oh heck, I am starting to sound like Dickens again.

I strung out our little jaunt as long as I could, as it was quite temperate in the valley and on the beach. There was hardly a soul about, which will be short lived with half-term next week, so it is best we selfishly enjoy it while we can.

When the Missus returned laden with full shopping bags, (were we expecting guests?), it was gone tea time. I had already anticipated this and had organised the frying of a bit of whiting, which was excellent by the way, as there was no point in sharing it; the Missus hates fish. She also returned with the bad news that the windscreen had developed something of a major crack on the passenger side. I suspect that it was the weight of the shopping affecting the stresses on the bodywork. Let us hope it can be fixed with a bit of potato starch and egg white, as I do not fancy the boys from Autoscreen having much luck with their little machine.

The weather is not going to help much tonight, either. At last knockings, as I took herself out for her last run, frost was already forming on the top of the cars. I might have to dig out my old fighter pilot goggles and flying jacket if I need to drive anywhere tomorrow. Algie, switch the magneto to on, old boy!

February 9th – Thursday

We started out again with a crystal clear day but frosty with it. It took me a while to scrape the ice off the van windscreen so that I could inspect the crack that the Missus reported yesterday. When I took a first look, before the ice had been cleared, there was a long line down the middle of the glass and I was rather alarmed. It turned out that this was just a pattern in the ice, which was a relief. After clearing the ice away I was darned if I could see a crack anywhere. I had to rouse the Missus to ask exactly where it was and it turned out it was hidden by the windscreen wiper, which I already kind of knew about but had fortunately forgotten; as the crack is not obvious the best thing to do, for now at least, is to pretend that it is not there – again.

It was time to seek adventure in foreign parts with a hardy and experienced traveller, so I took the bleddy hound to Porthcurno for a bit of a change. With the sun shining down, and a peak of low spring tides, what could possibly go wrong? I have to say that I was expecting much more sand on show. When you look at the pictures taken from the Minack Theatre, Porthcurno looks a long and expansive beach; when you are on the beach it seems much smaller.

Walking back from the eastern side I saw an object in the water on the west side of the bay. It could have been a buoy, or a man swimming. It disappeared before I could get a closer look so I concluded, at the rate it moved, that it was a seal, although the sighting nagged at me for the rest of the time we were there.

The van was like a greenhouse when we got back to it, and the bleddy hound was rather disinclined to get back in. I opened the door to cool it off before we returned home. Despite my best efforts to look elsewhere, like the road, my eyes were inextricably drawn to the crack under the windscreen wiper; it had taken me ages to forget it the first time.

Later in the afternoon I had to go up to St Just for a visit to the doc. I need to state at this point that the Aged Parents read this column and any mention of the doctor needs some in depth explanation else they will have apoplexy and expire on the carpet. So without further ado and for the sake of the carpet, which, let me be frank, could be an integral part of my inheritance and would be greatly devalued by people expiring on it, let me say that the visit was purely routine and that I am as fit as a butcher's fiddle. I only this mention this journey, as on the way back I scarcely saw the road, as my eyes were pinned to the bleddy crack at the bottom of the windscreen again.

Thankfully the Missus drove me up to the F&L tonight. They had put on a quiz, the proceeds of which were donated to the RNLI lifejacket appeal and it was only right and proper to put in an appearance.

Can I just leave you with this? The first recorded racehorse meeting was in Roodeye Field near Chester today in 1540. I have no idea what they talked about but it must have been popular, as they have been meeting ever since. I understand that canapes were handed around before they ate a meal and hence we have the term hors d'oeuvre – sorry.

February 10ᵗʰ - Friday

I am grateful to the Cotswold Courier for bringing to my attention a 'sailors wanted' advertisement he received in his electronic mail. I must hasten to point out that this was not some unsolicited trawl from a seedy men only publication, but a genuine request on behalf of the Cornish Maritime Trust.

In case you have not heard of this worthy group, in which case, shame on you, they are dedicated to the restoration and sailing of historic working craft and are based in Mousehole and on the River Fal. They are seeking a gritty band of seasoned sailors to man the Barnabas. Oh, do I have to explain everything? It is a double ended mackerel driver, built by Henry Trevorrow in 1881 at Porthgwidden Beach in St Ives. She is 40 feet long and has a dipping lug, (oh, for heavens sake, look it up!), and weighs in at 11.7 tons. She has also been selected to be part of the Queen's Diamond Jubilee Pageant on the Thames on June 3ʳᵈ this year, a veritable honour. Her height and lack of power would make it unsuitable for her to join the pageant at Hammersmith, so it is likely that she will form part of the 'avenue of sail' below London Bridge, near the end of the route.

It is planned that a relay of crews, made up from the Cornish sailing community, will sail her up from Mousehole from May 20ᵗʰ, stopping at various ports along the Channel coast and moor up at Faversham Creek, before the final leg of the journey up to London. All weather permitting, of course. I would say that would be a jolly wheeze if ever there was one, for the lucky crew members selected for the journeys.

Joining her in London will be possibly the oldest boat afloat anywhere. The St Michael's Mount State Barge was built in 1745 or thereabouts and, although rigged for sail, will be rowed down the Thames on 3rd June by a crew of six oars including four from Mounts Bay Pilot Gig Club.

Talking of the ancient and the glorious maritime traditions reminds me that our esteemed coxswain signalled a Lifeboat launch for this afternoon. It has been some time since we were able to go afloat on a training mission, so long indeed that we had almost forgotten what to do. Everything still appeared to work after we had knocked the rust off some important parts, even our very excellent Shore Crew and particularly the Head Launcher.

While the weather had warmed a little, there were some blue hands at the end of recovery; it should be noted that the wearing of gloves is only for girlies. All in all a successful exercise and not a sign of a dipping lug anywhere.

And rounding off our nautically themed entry we should note the birth of Mr Samuel Plimsoll today in 1824 whom, I am sure you are aware, came up with the visible Plimsoll line on a ship to indicate if it was being overloaded, and school children everywhere would wear Plimsolls on their feet during games. Are we grateful that he was not born Samuel Knicker?

February 11th - Saturday

After a single murky day of rain we are back to a bright sparkling day again. It remains to be seen how I might enjoy this spectacle, as our junior dog walker is back on the scene, relieving me of my duties in that respect. Even the Missus took her out for her early morning constitutional - that is the bleddy hound, not the junior dog walker who, presumably, is capable of exercising herself.

I could have done with a lazy day too, as we sat up until the early hours watching the television, as we were unable to contain our anticipation of the final several episodes of a popular Danish thriller. I have certainly improved my knowledge of the tongue, kære læser, but not to the extent that I could turn off the subtitles. The bledig hund was also seriously put out at having to stay up well beyond her normal bedtime.

I tried to revive us both with a little whizz down to the beach at around midday. It was sporting very much a whole leg of sand at the low point of a very low spring tide, as opposed to barely a hint of ankle at high water; I think we may even have had a flash of knicker elastic. Despite that whole expanse of sand you could hardly say that the bleddy hound showed a great deal of enthusiasm, so we did not stay long.

I resisted a trip to the OS to watch the rugby and watched at home instead, and although the result was a happy one, the play was disappointing. Later, despite the absence of a band, I dragged myself kicking and screaming to the F&L. Either the throng that appeared had not heard that there was no band tonight, or they all sought the higher plane of intelligent conversation. Whatever their inspiration they would have been sorely disappointed on either score.

After so much disappointment, in so short a time, it was heartening to behold a wholesome sky on our way home. As you would expect with such a clear night it was rather frosty, so much so that even a thick beer overcoat struggled to protect us. Yes, 'us'. I had the rather pleasant company of a rare Saturday night appearance of Head Launcher. He tagged with PR at the gate to the footpath who very kindly saw me clear across Esther's Field unscathed. Then on the rest of the journey a big red bulbous moon, barely risen and clipped off at the top, clinging to the southern sky, saw me safely home.

I can tell you, it does not get much better than that.

February 12ᵗʰ – Sunday

I managed to wrest myself from my bed at an appropriate hour this morning, despite the demands I placed upon my fragile being the previous evening. It was just as well, because this morning the second Lifeboat training launch of the weekend was organised.

It was a very gentlemanly affair for the Head Launcher's party. Having launched both boats with some aplomb and set up for recovery, we retired to the Breakers Café for breakfast. Even the Missus came and joined us for a frothing cappuccino. What a civilised way to enjoy a Lifeboat exercise, except we almost missed recovery of the inshore boat. The Missus stayed behind while we sauntered off to wait for the boat, no doubt to discuss philosophy with the other intellectuals of the café set. I am pretty sure I spotted Simone de Beauvoir and Jean Paul Sartre in the corner, so she was probably chatting with them.

Much as we would have loved to have stayed to have a light conversation on existentialism we did not want to miss the big boat arriving, which we did not. Recovery was, of course, textbook considering we had the very cream of the very excellent Shore Crew making it look all too easy. One day we shall have to make a mistake, just to show that we are human after all, though we would have to try very, very hard.

Quite by chance our good neighbour dropped by and, with a beef rib the size of a whale bone to get through we invited her and her sister to stay for some Sunday roast. It is not often that we get to enjoy our main meals of the day with some convivial company, but today just seemed to slot together as if it had been neatly planned.

With our good neighbour taking some enjoyment in reminding us that the shop is open in three weeks, tomorrow is going to be a little less genteel.

February 13ᵗʰ – Monday

Well, there is not going to be a great deal I can tell you today. As I said yesterday we needed to do some work to kick start the beginning of the season and that is exactly what we did.

I am sure you would be delighted to hear about our discussions with a new supplier of postcard fudge boxes, or perhaps how many pairs of men's board shorts we might require this year. You would, no doubt, be tantalised by the news that I have signalled to the wonderful Laurel and Hardy Newspaper Company how many copies of the *Daily Express* we think we will need. (I am sure also that it would not surprise you in the least that I am yet to receive a reply.) Despite the immense joy all that would bring you, I know you are teetering on the brink of one of those 'oops moments', that the television would have us believe all women of a certain age are prone to, in anticipation of hearing all about the weather. So to avoid a rather unpleasant scene, unless you are properly equipped, I shall continue without delay.

They said it was going to warm up and according to the thermometer, it has. Why then does it feel twice as cold as it did during the coldest days we had here? It might have something to do with the fact the wind is in the northwest and is piling in our front door. Crikey, it is flaming freezing. It is also not as windy as we have known it in the past but it is certainly making a big fuss of rattling the boards on the shop front.

It was fortunate then that we spent most of the day discussing postcard fudge boxes, ordering men's board shorts and fixing newspaper volumes, else I would have been out in it. Well, I did make one little foray up to the stores at the top. With all that beef left over from yesterday, it would have been a criminal act not to have a sandwich of it with lashings of cholesterol inducing butter and artery hardening salt and on white bread, to boot. Well, for heaven's sake, it's not like it happens every day and if we lived our life according to the daily, and often conflicting advice, heaped upon us by the health fiends, we would die of boredom. It is not surprising an increasing number of us end our days in demented confusion.

Still, the Missus fancies a bit of an expedition tomorrow. We may have to have a serious conversation expounding the definition of the word 'expedition'. I am of the opinion that it should be crossing over some sandy dune and exploiting a boundless piece of beach with the bleddy hound. I rather suspect that she has in mind urban yomping between furniture shops. I cannot help thinking I will end up in a sofa shop in waterproof over-trousers and a pair of wellies, with a bleddy hound gagging for a bit of chase-the-ball up the aisles.

February 14ᵗʰ - Tuesday

So there I was in the middle of a furniture shop, wearing waterproof over-trousers and wellies, wondering where I was going to perch to have my picnic. I looked out of the window at a disconsolate bleddy hound sitting in the van; she had not been allowed into the shop to chase a ball up and down the aisles. My sense of prescience scares the trousers off me sometimes.

It all started with the wind still howling through our keyhole and through the cracks in the front of the shop's woodwork. The Missus was out of the bed this morning like a shot out of a gun; a sure sign that shopping is on the cards. We had to entertain a representative first, an agent representing a number of companies we did not really want anything from. So, after ordering a lot of stuff we really did not want, the Missus set about making a bit of a picnic to take with us; a long shopping trip, then.

If I ever doubted the Missus's sense of geography or logical reasoning I could not fault her on this occasion, and certainly not in the brass neck department. Gwithian beach, our supposed destination, is just north of Hayle so, obviously Travaskis Farm and Redruth, both to the east, are clearly en route.

The Missus has been trawling through her cookery books and has selected some, as yet unknown to me, culinary delights for the week. Part of the requirement is mussels and if possible clams, so even before we got to Penzance we arrived at our first detour and visited every fishmonger in Newlyn. It is not a good time of the year to be seeking out exotic species of shellfish, as during the winter the locals do not drive up a huge demand for that kind of thing. So it was that we left Newlyn empty handed. I could sense trouble in the air.

Sailing past the turning to Gwithian, we headed up to Connor Downs to the rather excellent Travaskis Farm. I cannot complain too much, as the Missus was initially going to do her shopping at Tesmorrisburys. She succumbed to my plaintive request that we shop at somewhere a little more local, and as Connor Downs is local when you are passing through it to go to Redruth, then it was certainly local at the time we passed, if you see what I mean.

Had I not tried to ignore the fact that we would end up at a furniture shop in the industrial heartland of Redruth, I would have made some enquiry regarding its location and the best route by which to arrive there. The Missus certainly had not, and while ignoring the fact that I was ignoring the fact that we would turn up there, ignored the fact that she would have to determine the route and know the location. Following so far?

By ignoring the half-baked directions I was being given and letting my natural sense of direction guide me, we still ended up at the sofa shop. So, there I was in the middle of a furniture shop wearing waterproof over-trousers and wellies, wondering where I was going to perch to have my picnic. The Missus found the object of her desire, which was when I was forced to point out again, that in order to acquire such objects of desire it is sometimes useful to have the funds by which to acquire them, a salient fact that I had tried in vain to convey before we got there and thus rendering the extended journey unnecessary.

Having told the Missus that 'I want, doesn't get' and that she would not have an ice cream if she did not stop crying, I managed to point the van eventually in the direction of Portreath that is, by my reckoning, in the correct direction for Gwithian and its fine beaches and which, more importantly, is devoid of any shopping opportunities.

The inadvertent advantage derived from such a circuitous and stuttering journey was that the tide had retreated a long way down the beach when we arrived. The disadvantage of such a winding and interrupted path is that the bleddy hound was sick on her seat five miles from our destination, which incurred yet another delay while the Missus cleaned up the mess.

Above all, Strap Rocks have something over all the fishmongers in Newlyn; they are awash with Mytilis Edulis, that is blue mussels to you. While I pandered to the hastily recovered bleddy hound and her ball chasing needs, the Missus garnered a bag full of the small molluscs.

When I returned from another poor game of cards at the OS, the Missus had cooked some of our foraged shells. Though a little gritty, they were sweet and juicy and, as I am finishing off this Diary entry the following morning, were consumed without ill effect.

I am not sure the money we saved will buy the Missus a sofa, but it is a small step in the right direction.

February 15ᵗʰ - Wednesday

A form arrived from the Laurel and Hardy Newspaper Company this morning requesting nearly all the information that I had already emailed to them on Monday. I think they expected me to complete the form and send it back but as they had included an email address on the paperwork I forwarded my original email to the new address with the few additional details they had asked for.

I am sure you will forgive me, dear reader, for becoming frustrated and weary from actually having to do some work.

After all I did some at Christmas time and surely deserve a modicum of respite from the grind. By early afternoon, therefore, I donned my walking gear and took to the beach with the bleddy hound. I have to say that she was not overly enthused, so I took her to the OS as a treat. There is nothing she loves more than lying against the bar while I down a pint or two. Ask her next time you see her if you do not believe me.

When I returned home, the Missus, who clearly sympathised with my condition and deeply appreciated the supreme sacrifice I had made in the morning, had spent the afternoon in the kitchen preparing a seafood chowder. I have to say it was absolutely first class and so much better in the knowledge that some of the contents had been garnered for free from Gwithian's bountiful shore.

Golly! Life's good at the sharp end sometimes.

February 16ᵗʰ - Thursday

We are being spoilt by our junior dog walker. Yet another day has passed where we have not had to lift a finger in the ongoing exercise regime of one bleddy hound. Thankfully she is only here for the week else I would lose the use of my legs completely.

I stirred myself sufficiently to attend Lifeboat training in the evening. You will be pleased to learn that the use of hard hats by the very excellent Shore Crew has come to a head, so to speak. We have struggled for some while to combine the use of the hard hat with the chunky headphones necessary for communication between the crew at the bottom of the slipway, the winchman and the boat. Apparently the cowboy hat adopted by the Head Launcher as a workable alternative has sparked some criticism, not least that he looked like a cast member from the film Brokeback Mountain.

I am pleased to report that we have found an acceptable solution that will see the very excellent Shore Crew sporting some state of the art crash helmets similar to those worn by the Inshore Lifeboat crew, except ours will be made from old cornflakes packets and sticky tape.

With such sterling work under our belt we repaired for some well-earned celebrations at the OS and, of course, a return to the battle that is the OS Thursday night quiz. It seems that our absence last week has broken our run of good fortune in winning the quiz three weeks in a row - that and the fact that there were more than two other teams competing this week. We came a pitiful second, second from last, that is.

The ignominy, the shame; it is fortunate indeed that our drooping heads will be obscured by crash helmets next time we are at the bottom of the slip.

February 17ᵗʰ - Friday

From ghoulies and ghosties
And short-legged beasties
And things that go bump in the kitchen
Good Lord, deliver us!

A traditional Cornish shopkeeper's prayer and so very apt for today, at least.

The brother-in-law's wife telephoned this morning ostensibly to talk to the Missus. I would have thought of all people she would have known better than to telephone before mid afternoon. She was a bit reticent to talk to me at first, but when I pressed her she explained that they had been having a few odd things happen in the house. This had apparently been going on for years but the latest development was that she and her daughter had some photographs.

To cut a long, and to some probably a fairly yawnsome, tale short I had her send the photographs to me. I messed about with them using some photograph editing software to enhance the rather grainy images. After about an hour the best I could determine was that it was some sort of large cat with three legs and two tails, or possibly a butterfly with one wing. It was not until later in the afternoon, after the Missus had spoken with her that I discovered that I had the photograph the wrong way up. Even from a sceptic's point of view it did rather look like two characters standing in a doorway.

I have no reason to doubt that the photograph was genuine and, along with the reports of other unexplained activity over a considerable period of time, would suggest some very spooky goings on. I would certainly not propose that the evidence is conclusive and you must draw your own conclusions. I am just glad they are a few hundred miles away.

I managed to wrest our short-legged beastie away from our junior dog walker for a few hours this afternoon, more for my benefit than the bleddy hound's; I was getting a touch of cabin fever. I took her around our usual route.

Mother Nature must have thought it milder of late generally, not that I have noticed, as there was a showing of daffodils down in the valley with hints of other colour here and there. No wonder I miss my little forays out.

Of course, all this walking about does build up a bit of an appetite in a young healthy chap. It does the same for me too. I think I have already explained that the Missus has spent rather a long time in the kitchen this week. We had the chowder the other day, lemon biscuits, and last night a bit of turkey potato pie/bake thing. Today revealed some Yorkshire brack, although Yorkshire brick might have been more appropriate. Not only did it resemble a brick in shape and size, it also made a satisfying thump when it was dropped on the worktop. Nevertheless, having found a suitable chisel with which to prise a sizable lump off of it and lathered it with butter it was actually rather toothsome. Yorkshire brack, madam? One lump or two?

Inexplicably I found myself at the OS for a third night this week. I must be getting to enjoy the place again. I really should come clean having given them such a hard time over the last couple of years. The current management has done an excellent job of installing some character and atmosphere back in the place.

Coming third at cards will account for the happy little chap you might have seen chasing a short-legged beastie around the bottom end of The Cove, no doubt causing consternation among the ghosties and ghoulies community and making them go bump in the night.

February 18ᵗʰ – Saturday

As I walked out along towards the Harbour early this afternoon there looked to be a suspicious group of blackhearts hanging around the wharf. When I drew closer it was certain that it was a group of suspicious looking blackhearts - The Cove seine net syndicate.

The syndicate, a gruesome bunch of fearless fishermen, is very much akin to the Cosa Nostra except they are called the Cosy Nostra on account of the amount of tea they drink. They have their own secret signs and phrases such as, 'fancy a cup, do 'ee?', a revelation that, no doubt, will cause me to wake up with a fish head on the pillow next to me.

Seine netting is an age-old method whereby a long net is driven out in a wide arc on a falling tide around the prey. As the tide falls away and the net is drawn in, vast quantities of oar weed are harvested. The process is less than efficient and on occasion large numbers of fish, namely grey mullet, are hauled in with the weed, leading to much frustration amongst the netters. This time they seem to have been most unlucky, with many boxes of fish lined up outside the Lifeboat station; so many in fact that a large articulated lorry had to be called to take them away.

They were there when I took the bleddy hound out along the slender ankle of sand for a short run once the rain had given way to chilly blue skies. Usually her single minded dash to the beach is such that if someone had built a high wall across the road she would have found a way around it. Today, I had to drag her away from the boxes of fish being piled up outside, in the opposite direction from the beach; unlike the Missus, the bleddy hound loves fish.

They were there when we got back too, with a small army of helpers washing and loading the catch onto the lorry. Such was the bounty, they eventually finished shortly before I decamped to the F&L. And what did the Missus fancy for tea, yup, fish and chips from the rather good chippie at the top. I find it quite bizarre that she likes the occasional fish and chip meal; the Missus hates fish.

February 19ᵗʰ - Sunday

What glorious sunshine we were blessed with today, weighing down on The Cove. We could tell it weighed heavily as there were so many scales on the street outside our door. Sorry, I just could not resist.

The Missus made some cupcakes to celebrate her mate next door's birthday. I love the idea of several little cupcakes instead of one traditional cake. It means that samples can be left behind for my own delectation rather than having to beg a slice off the birthday girl. Selfish? Moi?

It was not long after we got home that we were piling out the door again in the direction of the F&L to join the birthday girl for a birthday meal. We know how to make these days special, I can tell you. We went up to the F&L to join the birthday girl for a birthday meal early, so that we could let the bleddy hound out to chase rabbits in the back field. Well, when I say 'chase rabbits' there are indeed rabbits in the back field at the same time as the bleddy hound gets there. We know this as her ball dropping to the ground disturbed one, sending it bolting for the nearest hedge. I can tell you without fear of repudiation that if I wanted to hunt for rabbit I would have to buy a ferret, as the bleddy hound would rather chase a ball.

It was not until bedtime that we realised in all our excitement that we had forgotten to feed the dog. I think it unlikely that she will fade away in the night, especially as she had most of one of the Missus's lamb chops at the F&L. I think if I were to expire and return as a dog I could do a lot worse than to come back as this one.

February 20ᵗʰ – Monday

Out of my bed this morning like a West Somerset badger from its sett. Well, not exactly, I was not coughing as much for a start.

The game plan was to get out on the road early, get through my chores list and be back in time to take the bleddy hound out before we completely lost the beach. That was the game plan. The fact that I never got through the door until at least half past eleven demonstrates the detailed level to which my plan had been, er, planned. Of course it did not help that I could not find the Missus' passport.

I should explain. It was not my intention to prevent the Missus from ever leaving the country again, although the financial gain might be attractive. No, this was all to do with my accountant or, more accurately, the Government. Apparently it is a ploy to reduce the amount of fraud and to prevent people that are not me from submitting my meagre accounts, though why they would want to I have no idea. New rules mean that although I have been with my accountant for eight years they must now have a copy of my passport to ensure I am me.

So, having found the passport and wiped the accumulated dust from mine, gathering together the other essential items for my journey and walked the bleddy hound round the block I eventually managed to extricate myself.

One of the other purposes of my sojourn was to track down a suitable bookcase. I noted last year that the bookcase in the shop is a little over-crowded and we have such a collection of local interest books now (including one very excellent volume by a local author!), it would be worthwhile separating them. I had considered, after the ripping success of the dog basket plinth and the artful ball stand, that I should make my own. Unfortunately I considered this aloud and, after she had finished laughing, the Missus suggested that it would be more expedient, not to mention more likely that we would end up with something that resembled a bookcase, to purchase one.

Finding a bookcase that met the required measurement criteria, as well as the budgetary constraints took a considerable amount of time. In fact despite thoroughly searching both the furniture shops in Penzance I was unable to find a suitable bookcase. It was a little disheartening to find that when I returned the Missus had found one in the pages of a well-known high street catalogue company, while sitting in the comfort of our home. In fact she had found it ten minutes after I left and never called to let me know. Anyone might think she was glad to have me out of the house.

I was so late in returning that the bleddy hound never got her run down to the beach. Heston Missus had also been hard at work in the kitchen again mixing up some experimental gourmet cuisine. I am beginning to suspect she might be a feeder and is keen to see my lithe and athletic frame ballooning out of control. Fortunately we are open again in a few weeks and it will be back to something out of a tin, if we can be bothered to find the opener.

February 21ˢᵗ - Tuesday

A far more exciting day today. Having read it, you may well disagree but I tell you it does not get much more interesting than this in February.

We started the day with a little Lifeboat exercise. It was actually to test some modifications to the radar system and the boat was out for just over an hour. It would have been a shorter time, but it had to wait a few minutes in the bay for the very excellent Shore Crew to finish their rather good breakfast at the café next door. Come on, you cannot hurry a breakfast like that. As it was I had to leave a slice of toast behind.

It was while we were standing outside the Lifeboat station congratulating ourselves on another textbook recovery, (let us face it, no one else was going to congratulate us), we noticed some goings on down on the beach. There were two chaps in yellow safety jackets surveying down by the tide line. One was traversing the beach laterally on a quad bike, while the other intersected his lines walking up and down the beach. As you might imagine we postulated several outlandish suggestions as reasons for their presence.

With the tide not long on the turn I took the opportunity to take the bleddy hound down. This was not just for her benefit, you understand, but also an attempt to divine the true purpose of the surveying intrusion on our hallowed sand. It took some guile to track the surveyors down. The chap on the quad bike was clearly not going to stop for a chat, as I suspect that the lines he was running required a constant speed and approximate equidistance between each traverse. When I set out, the other surveyor was close by my sitting rock at the far end of the beach, which was convenient, but by the time I arrived there he had moved up into the dunes.

I sat and threw the ball about for the bleddy hound, lulling the walking surveyor into a false sense of security. It worked a treat because after a short while he came down from the dunes and plied his craft close by. On his return up the slope I pounced.

At first he was quite reticent to reveal his purpose, stopping only to say that he was profiling the beach for its shape. He must have seen the gritty look of determination in my eyes and the bleddy hound eying up his pole for her own purposes for he returned with further information. He said that his company had been commissioned by the council and the Environment Agency, as well as other interested parties. I surmised that these bodies would not have commissioned this expensive work in these cash strapped times unless some financial return was envisaged, so I pressed him further. He tapped the side of his nose conspiratorially and urged me not to spread the information further. So I must warn you, dear reader, keep this under your hat.

The council is very aware that this could be a busy year for Cornwall. We have the Olympic Flame starting down here in May, the Queen's Diamond Jubilee and The Old Boathouse Stores will be open. Now that the beach has been properly surveyed, every part of it can be mapped onto a grid of one metre square boxes. Come the season when the beach is full of happy visitors enjoying whatever visitors do on the beach, a council warden will be deployed, clutching to his breast a GPS enabled device that will calculate the amount of beach used by each party. Each square metre of sand occupied, or part thereof, will be charged out at an hourly rate. The machine will happily accept credit or debit cards and issue tickets.

Naturally, the state of the tide and thus the available amount of beach at any given moment and the numbers of people wishing to use the beach will affect the forces of supply and demand. Happily the system will be clever enough to take these factors into account and apply variable charges accordingly. At the head of the slipway and on The Beach car park, automatic signs will be deployed indicating "Beach Full" at busy times.

It goes without saying that The Old Boathouse Stores will step up to the mark on behalf of all potential beach users this year. As you would expect we cannot let such an outrage be inflicted upon our valued visitors and we fully intend to do our bit to help. I have made some initial enquiries and it looks entirely possible that we will be able to provide a clip together one metre square grid so that visitors can assess the area of the beach that they are using; it will be a must have accessory and just £9.99. For those beach users wishing to be forewarned of the cost of their beach usage, a deluxe model will be available that has a calculator strapped to one of the poles for an additional fiver.

Never let it be said that The Old Boathouse Stores does not have the best interests of its customers at heart.

I am so glad we were able to lay any nasty rumours to rest there. So let me start another. The Royal Mail have been in touch over the last few weeks, first to ask me how I would like my information delivered to me - by email, post or carrier pigeon. I elected to have it sent via email as I get far too much post through the door these days.

Today I got an information letter through my door from the Royal Mail. They sent the same information by email too, for good measure. It seems we are due a price hike for stamps at the beginning of April. Unfortunately, due to the consultation process, they cannot reveal what the price will be until the end of March. It must be one of those special consultations as no one I know has been consulted and none of them know anyone who has been consulted. If you know anyone who has been consulted, dear reader, or know if any of them know anyone who has been consulted please consult me, as it would be rather nice to know someone who has been consulted, even by proxy.

Sorry, I digress, where was I? Ah, yes. The rumour to which I refer, although I think it was rather more than a rumour, is that the Royal Mail will be allowed to charge what they like for First Class postage. The proviso is that the price of Second Class mail will only rise a few pennies, so that poor people (i.e. anyone who is not a banker, Royal Mail executive or council chief) can still send letters, so long as they do not expect them to arrive in any timely manner or perhaps arrive at all. Of course we will not know until a few days before the price goes up, so we will have precisely no time to do anything about it but never mind, all those consultees will have been able to sway the Royal Mail away from any unacceptable rise in price, won't they?

Sounds like it will be an excellent summer, what?

February 22ⁿᵈ - Wednesday

First, I ought to come clean regarding the surveyor chaps on the beach lest rabid locals and the disgruntled visitor, (it is quiet this week), beat them to a pulp. The part about being charged to use a square metre of beach is, of course, a product of my over-active cynicism and is complete nonsense. You will get at least a metre and a half.

The bit about the stamps is, as far as I know, true.

A questionnaire was dropped through the letter box from a group called Transition Penwith. Their stated aims are to work towards an 'energy secure future by reducing consumption and decreasing reliance on fossil fuels'. Their concern is that Penwith is stuck out on a bit of a limb and come the energy revolution we will be cut off without a watt between us. Their aims are lofty and I wish them the best of luck, but it did strike me as rather co-incidental it came at the same time that men were surveying the beach. I can see the headlines now; "Penwith goes independent with first Cornish nuclear power station on Sennen beach."

February 23ʳᵈ – Thursday

More mist today than you could shake a stick at, even if you could find one. It is rather thick. It was even thicker up the top as we drove into town and it is at this point you would rather expect me to go into a rant about cars driving with nothing but parking lights, or no lights at all. But the Missus told me I was being boring, as I spotted only two vehicles out of about a dozen I saw coming the other way with any lights on at all. With this in mind I shall not say a word about the complete eejits. Well, you have the Missus to thank for me not going on about people driving in thick mist without dipped headlights on again.

Ah, yes, the reason we were heading into town was to drive past it, which a lot of people do. It is not surprising as it is about as aesthetically welcoming as a bedsore on a warthog's bottom. If the various interest groups spent as much time trying to find common ground as they do trying to be diametrically opposed, then there might be some semblance of a cohesive strategic plan for Penzance by now. I noticed in the paper last week there seems to be some movement in that direction. I just cannot help feeling it might be too little, too late.

Anyway, I digress. Where was I, oh yes, by-passing PZ. We were on our way to Perranuthnoe, for me, again and for the Missus for the first time. To my knowledge she is the third person I have persuaded to visit. If this carries on I shall be looking forward to a vote of thanks and a gold watch from the parish council for services to the village.

I would normally have gone directly to the beach, as the bleddy hound is fair champing at the bit by the time we get there. On this occasion, as we were already running late, I was persuaded to stop into The Cabin first for a top hole bacon bap and cup of tea, while the bleddy hound champed at her bit and eyed up my tasty bun.

I have waxed on before about how fine the beach is so I shall not do so again and besides, I have not had my gold watch yet. Suffice it to say it was a pleasant interlude and the bleddy hound was sufficiently worn out to sleep the entire journey home. While at home it was thick with mist, at Perranuthnoe the mist hung away offshore. Looking west it was clinging like a silk scarf to the hills above Newlyn, lit up by the only puddle of brightness on the coast; a thing of beauty is a joy forever.

Talking of which, a bit of Keats, anyone, since he died today in 1821 and also happens to be one of my favourite poets? I would give you a bit of Elgar as something of a variation, who also died today in 1934, but it has left me with something of an enigma as to how I might convey his talents on the page.

I would normally have given you a briefing on the Lifeboat training tonight and, of course, the results of the OS quiz. Since nothing of note happened at either, here is your Keats.

Bright star, would I were stedfast as thou art--
Not in lone splendour hung aloft the night
And watching, with eternal lids apart,
Like nature's patient, sleepless Eremite,
The moving waters at their priestlike task
Of pure ablution round earth's human shores,
Or gazing on the new soft-fallen mask
Of snow upon the mountains and the moors--
No--yet still stedfast, still unchangeable,
Pillow'd upon my fair love's ripening breast,
To feel for ever its soft fall and swell,
Awake for ever in a sweet unrest,
Still, still to hear her tender-taken breath,
And so live ever--or else swoon to death.

February 24ᵗʰ - Friday

Today, adventure. Despite a very early start for the Missus, and a very late one for me, we managed to get our collective act together and get out of the door before midday.

We have shared our recent early mornings over the last few days. During the cold snap we closed our bedroom window. Now we have it open again the bleddy hound's finely tuned hearing alerts her to her arch-enemy's pawsteps – at six thirty in the morning. She rockets out of bed, barking the place down until she sees the other hound return in the direction of her home some ten to fifteen minutes later, whereupon she stops her row. This is all very well but most of the time the Nemesis returns home by another route, thus confusing the tail off the bleddy hound and leaving her unable to determine when she should stop barking. I am torn between the application of ear defenders so that she cannot hear the approaching enemy, or a strong elastic band to prevent her barking.

While these weighty matters hung in the balance we decided to lunch at Trevaskis Farm. The Missus has dined there several times, mainly while I have been holding the fort behind the shop counter. Consequently I have never eaten there. I have been told it is fare to wonder at, thus my expectations were high.

The place is clean and the tables sensibly spaced. The service is sharp and efficient (even on a February Friday the place was half full), the menu surprisingly broad, with a standard menu and a further list of specials. It is not what you would call cheap, but when the food arrived the prices are commensurate with the quality and size of portion; you certainly get value for money. They pride themselves on good quality ingredients, many from their own resources, and even with the most basic sandwich it is unlikely that the most voracious eater would be left wanting. I thoroughly recommend it.

After a spot of shopping in the farm shop we headed off for Gwithian beach to give the very patient bleddy hound a run. Despite arriving at the Godrevy end of the beach only an hour and a half after low water there was precious little beach to do any running on, which was a bit of a surprise. We back-tracked a little down to the Godrevy Café car park and popped out on the beach at the Red River. Even here, after crossing the beach below the old sand works, we were unable to get around Strap Rocks without being cut off. Never mind, there was plenty of beach for her to run around and chase a ball and we even managed a quick cuppa in the Godrevy Café before we left.

We had the opportunity to have a close look at the Red River on the way back. It still has a bit of a reddish hue and there appears to be red deposits on the pebbles on the river bed, which surprised me greatly. It could have been algae, or any manner of organic material, but I rather suspect there is still a substantial amount of mineral content in the stream. I shall bring some panning tools next time; there's gold in them thar hills, you know.

We returned quite late to our abode, nearly time for tea. It seems that the Travaskis Farm lunch was better value than I, at first, thought, as neither of us were ready for another meal. We will have to think of another adventure for tomorrow, one that does not involve quite so much eating, perhaps.

February 25th – Saturday

I could regale you with tales of high adventure, derring do and vigorous romps on the beaches of West Cornwall. I could have you envisage the bleddy hound and I, with pith helmets at a rakish angle and elephant guns over our shoulders, hacking through treacherous moorland gorse to discover the North West passage to Land's End. I might say, "Let's go hunting, dear" to which she might respond that she preferred fowl.

Perhaps you would enjoy us recounting our perilous climb to the heights of Chapel Carn Brae, traversing glaciers and bridging chasmic fissures with little else but a rusty ladder. I am sure you would be entertained and enthralled and you would *believe*, and why not, it is in The Diary; it must be true.

Alas not, dear reader; would that it were. If it were true I could wax on for a page or more and have you gripping the edge of whatever seat you sit upon while consuming your daily dose of nonsense. As it is you will probably groan with disappointment and switch back to the picture of a scantily clad Rachael McAdams or Keith Flint or whoever is currently in vogue for you.

You see the problem is that I did nothing at all today. I had intended to slip out for a small adventure with the bleddy hound but that was before I realised that the Six Nations was playing again today. Sorry, and all that but there really is nothing to be done but to consume with avid greed every second of the gripping tournament. And consume I did. Ireland and France was wolfed down at the OS and England playing Wales at home, which was just as well; no one likes to see a grown man cry.

After such a howling disappointment there was only one thing to do. I had considered picking up my elephant gun and heading for darkest Africa. I have heard that the ban on ivory hunting has been so successful that there are now more African elephants than they know what to do with, so they could do with a bit of thinning out and I could do with something to put my umbrella in. I dismissed this consideration quite quickly as, although one elephant's foot umbrella stand would be rather twee, another three would be ostentatious.

The trip across the ice fields of Chapel Carn Brae was out as well. It has been somewhat mild of late and I rather suspect that the glaciers will have melted away by now. Not only that, but my rusty ladder has a rung missing. Adventurous I may be, but I am not foolhardy.

No, I settled for a visit to the F&L where the carrying of an elephant gun, while useful on occasion, is frowned upon. They are also not that keen on visitors wearing crampons, as it does make such an awful mess of the floor. I resolved to make the best of things with a beer or two and lent an ear to the jolly musicians that the good landlady had employed to provide some entertainment.

It was a bit quiet for a Saturday night. I ruminated on the way home that even if I had brought my elephant gun the game was so sparse I probably would not have hit a thing.

February 27ᵗʰ - Monday

At this time of year it often feels like we are just marking time before the shop opens. While it might seem idyllic to have such a long period of time with the shop closed, I find myself getting a bit edgy towards the end. I sometimes wonder why anyone would want to live a permanent life of leisure. Granted most people would probably fill the time with ventures to the corners of the globe perhaps, or putting model ships in bottles, but even then I would have thought that endless travelling and stuffing would eventually become a tad boring.

In short I am beginning to look forward to the wherewithal of shop opening once more: meeting and chatting with people again; the merry tinkling of the cash register; the unwrapping of new and exciting stock; the reading of newspapers and looking out at the sun – and the rain; the weeks of fighting with the Laurel and Hardy Newspaper Company; the hours of standing behind the counter with no customers appearing; the clearing up of the floods that occasionally blight us; the getting out of bed on a cold, rainy morning; getting soaked pulling in the milk and the papers.

I do not know, perhaps another few weeks of lolling about would not be all that bad.

February 28ᵗʰ - Tuesday

I have made note previously that we are an official part of the tourist information network for the county. Not that we have received any special training, or have we been supplied with much in the way of resources to support us in this important role. I sometimes wonder if we are doing more harm than good responding to some of the enquiries we receive. In fact, what I am trying to say is that if you want some proper tourist information we are probably the last people you will want to call. There, I have said it.

Nevertheless we do get a lot of emails from the proper Tourist Information Centres, mainly to do with manager meetings. I am not sure that we are actually invited; I think we just happen to be on the mailing list. I have assumed the latter as I have an aversion to meetings, which has emanated from attending far too many that appeared to just be a corporately endorsed excuse for avoiding doing any work.

Not all of the emails we have received have been about meetings, however. The one that dropped into my inbox the other day invited us to attend a familiarisation tour of the Geevor, Levant and Botallack network of mining facilities that make up the World Heritage Site in this area. I selectively assumed that this email was directed at me, as first it was free, secondly, it included a free lunch and lastly, because it was better than spending another day at home sitting on my thumbs.

I duly arrived at Geevor this morning for some free tea and biscuits. There I found myself in the company of around thirty interested, (spelt f-r-e-e-l-o-a-d-i-n-g), parties from a cross section of the visitor industry. Some were proper people from Tourist Information Centres and others, like me, from the service industry. I sat at a table with a very nice lady who runs a bed and breakfast farmhouse near St Buryan and a couple running a larger establishment in St Ives.

We had barely finished our tea when we were shuffled into a nearby meeting room, where a young girl of about twelve gave us a presentation about the World Heritage Site (WHS). It seems she had lied about her age and had secured a position with The much maligned council.

Now, without giving you the whole presentation, the position is this. UNESCO awarded Cornwall the WHS in 2006 after a six year project to prepare the proposal, which was very nice. The much maligned council then had to work out what to do with the award and, as UNESCO do not provide any cash along with the status, how to afford what they decided. The upshot is they raided the coffers of the Rural Development Programme for England of £2.5 million and created a website and are now doing some marketing.

I know that sounds like an expensive website, but the cash has lasted five years so far and the website will be maintained for a further five after the project team is disbanded next year. Six years also seems like a long time to build one, but it has given the various owners and contributors of the WHS locations time to develop their offerings into something worth seeing.

If you want to see the product of their efforts have a look in the new Local Attractions section on the Old-Boathouse.com website. Yes, I know it goes against the grain to click on anything other than the Diary link, but I promise you I am not trying to sell anything in that section.

Anyway, I digress. Now, where was I? Oh yes, in a meeting room in Geevor.

Having been told what it was all about we were given a private tour of the site including a whiz around Wheal Mexico, the underground element. It has been about five years since I last did the tour and I have to tell you they have not been idle. There is a new museum and Wheal Mexico has been extended. It is all rather impressive. We ran around in about two hours and missed a fair bit. I would say a family could easily be entertained for half a day there.

After our free lunch of a large homemade pasty, which would have been very nice had it not been overcooked and microwaved, we piled into a coach for transport to Levant. It would have been very easy to walk there but we were under some time constraint.

Although there is much to see at Levant the main feature is the working beam engine. I may have mentioned that the National Trust that owns and runs the site had to invest in a new boiler recently. I suggest that this is money well spent as seeing the original engine in operation is a wonder to behold. Twenty tons of iron in motion you might imagine sets up quite a stir. Not a bit of it; it hardly makes a sound and there is absolutely no vibration, which surprised me greatly.

I have never visited Levant before and with the top National Trust man guiding us around I really wonder why I have not. Possibly because this is the first year it has been open before Easter.

We finished off the day at Botallack for a nose around the arsenic calciners and a look down at Crown Mines. We were blessed with a perfect day, warm and bright. Although a trip around Geevor would be acceptable in the rain I would certainly suggest a day at the three sites would be better enjoyed in the dry.

Here endeth The Cove Diary Cornish Mining World Heritage Site promotional brochure. I must thank you all very much for paying for my visit. Your hearts must be warmed to know that your hard earned taxes are going towards such genuinely good causes.

I enjoyed myself so much I hardly felt the merest twang of guilt that I had missed a Lifeboat exercise. The very excellent Shore Crew, few though they were and led by the more than capable expertise of TS as Head Launcher, apparently struggled through without me.

I will go now and beat myself with birch twigs and endeavour to repay my debt to society for such a blatant and gratuitous display of selfishness.

February 29ᵗʰ - Wednesday

It is not often you get something for nothing, unless of course you are a shopkeeper involved with the tourist business and get invited to a free viewing and lunch at a local tourist attraction. Sorry, I did not mean to rub it in. But today is your turn, you lucky things. Today you get a whole free day and a whole free Diary entry for nothing, gratis, and without having to shell out a bean. What a bonus!

I am sure you are all sitting there wondering what to do with your extra 24 hours. The ladies, of course, will be otherwise engaged and many of them will be by the end of the day, engaged, that is. Today, of course, the ladies get a free shot, an opportunity to turn the tables on the male of the species and propose marriage, if so they choose. The male of the species, if he has any wits about him, will have spent the day locked in the lavatory or one of the few other remaining male only preserves that the champions of equality have not yet been able to breach.

I could not honestly tell you that I am enlightened but I can admit that I have seen the light, several lights in fact. Last night, while taking the bleddy hound out for her last run, I hesitated at the top of our stairs as I was concerned that a vehicle was coming up the street. There was a puddle of light opposite that I took for a set of headlights shining down the road. It did not take me long to determine that it was in fact the street light opposite, but something was entirely different. You see normally the puddle of light is yellow in colour and this was a bright white.

This morning when I took her around again I saw a council 'cherry picker' up by Myrtle Cottage replacing the bulb in the street light. On closer inspection it appears that they were changing the entire lighting unit, (we do not have lamp posts here, the lights hang off existing electricity poles). They also appear to be radio controlled as there is an aerial atop each unit, in eye catching bright blue, no less. The purpose of the change is unclear, but I would like to suppose that they are being replaced with more energy efficient lights. I hope so anyway, as when I went out later they were all switched on. No wonder it seemed like a very bright day.

I took advantage of all this loveliness in the weather and strolled out with the bleddy hound in the afternoon. The Missus had taken the van into town, so we went for the extended round The Cove walk. It was the first time this year that I had been able to venture out without a coat on.

I managed the entire trip, and an hour on the beach, without a single proposal of marriage. I do not know whether to be relieved or disappointed.

So, as the illicit lovers of Eternity seek a quick clandestine fumble in the shadows of Time, just as the council worker of Fate turns on the street lamp above them it's time to say goodnight.

March 1st – Thursday

"2012 Cornwall Beach Games – Inspired by London 2012. The Cornwall Beach Games are back for a second year ..."

"London 2012 has announced plans for school children across the UK to take part in ... World Sports Day"

"Business opportunities nationally and regionally. Opportunities include: conversion of the main stadium, Aquatics Centre and other venues on the park to post-Games use."

Any common theme that might have caught your eye in those little outtakes? Perhaps I am being a little over-sensitive but it does seem that much of this is London-centric. Frankly I have little problem with that. It was London that won the bid to hold the 'lympics and good luck to them. It is probably why they called it "London 2012" and not "UK 2012". No, what irks me is this insistence that the Games are for the whole of the UK and then not so much the insistence, but the grappling at straws to try and prove it.

The Cornwall Beach Games, for example, being inspired by London 2012. The clue is in the words "back for a second year". What inspired them last year and did the organisers only see it as a one off? "Hey, I've got a terrific idea. You know how the 'lympics are on in 2012, why don't we have a Cornwall Beach Games?" "What, like the Cornwall Beach Games we had last year inspired by it being a good healthy idea but this year we'll do it because the 'lympics are on? Right on"

World Sports Day has simply been hi-jacked. It has been going for years, not that anyone has ever heard of it. It would have happened anyway except on April 27th instead of June 25th. I am sure that Johan Gruijff is immensely pleased with the free publicity, seeing as he was the chap who first developed it.

As for regional business opportunities, I will not even try and book a ticket on the first train up to London after the Games has finished. It will no doubt already be packed with Cornish businessmen just dying to get their hands on a bit of 'lympic stadium, or the Aquatic's Centre swimming pool.

I do not wish to decry the efforts of the enthusiastic few who think we can make a fast buck on the back of the Games, two hundred and fifty miles, (it's two hundred and thirty two point five but fifty sounds better), from its epicentre, but I think they are banging on the door of the wrong bus. I cannot help thinking that there is a certain futility in this attempt to connect Cornwall to the Olympic Games. I just have to ask why? The closest the Games will get to us is the start point of the 'lympic Torch at Land's End and its biggest impact is that it will prevent money spending holiday makers from being able to book accommodation within ten miles of us on May 18th. The Torch itself will have been driven, (driven!), out of Sennen before I have got out of bed, taking with it our best hope of a fast buck from London 2012. Most of the 20 communities through which it will pass will probably miss it anyway. "Betty, has that flamin' 'lympic Torch been through yet?" "No, Ethel, it was s'posed to be here half hour ago." "All right, I'll just make a cup of tea then. … there you go Betty." "Er, Ethel, think you might have missed it. There was this flash of light past the window and a bit of shouting while you was making the tea, then this big fast car drove away." "Begger!"

Sorry, I shouldn't be such a grumpy shopkeeper on such a wonderful day. The Games are a brilliant opportunity to showcase the UK but I won't be dashing out to stock the shop full of Union Flag painted mugs with 'lympic Rings on them. All right, let me make this clear. The first one of you lot that rolls up to the shop after we open on March 10th and asks for a Union

Flag painted mug with 'lympic Rings on it will be shown some very short shrift.

I did promise not to be grumpy about those 'lympic Games so here goes. Later, as is traditional on a Thursday night I attended the London 2012 Lifeboat training session. This passed without incident and concentrated on our upcoming London 2012 Lifeboat Dinner in May. There are a few showstoppers, such as a shortage of London 2012 bunting, but hopefully everything will be sorted out before next week. We think we may have identified a sensible London 2012 after dinner speaker, but we are also keen to have a London 2012 band for the later part of the evening.

Naturally, after such complex discussions, it was necessary for a whistle whetting down the road and to take part in the London 2012 OS quiz night. After being such a grumpy puss about the 'lympics it was probably only fitting that the London 2012 cash prize went to more deserving folk. We came a very close second. Had they only had a few more questions about the London 2012 Cornwall Beach Games, or the London 2012 World Sports Day and the spelling of Johan Gruijff, or possibly even a connections round linked to business opportunities after the London 2012 Games we might have done a lot better.

I have to dash now as I have a 'lympic Rings sew on patch to attach to my London 2012 pyjamas before bedtime.

March 2nd - Friday

I was beginning to feel a little more relaxed, until yesterday that is. After all it is at least six months since that article in the *Western Morning News* (did I tell you I had a review in the *Western Morning News?*) where I took St Ives apart stone by stone and suggested that if I looked back when I was leaving I might have been turned to a pillar of salted pilchards; hake might have been more appropriate.

That was a long time ago now and time is a great healer. Things were beginning to look up and I have been able to step out into the light without a minder these last few months. That was until yesterday. Yesterday I opened *The Cornishman* and there I was, staring back at me; I have never thought myself as page three material before. But that was not the half of it, oh no, that was only a teaser to the real story on page seventeen, where there was the same photograph but bigger, together with *that* review.

In the *Western Morning News* (did I tell you I had a review in the *WMN?*) at least they had the decency to crop out the bleddy hound. Not so in *The Cornishman*, the poor girl has been dragged down with me and will no doubt be a pariah on the streets of St Ives for years to come; she is a marked dog.

But wait, it is just a picture of a dog, right? I am sure there are hundreds of dogs around here that look just like her.

I had a knock on the door this morning. A little old lady standing there asking if I was the writer of the book she read about in the paper. No mystery there, the newspaper said the book was available from here. She said that she was born on Maria's Lane and in fact was the great-granddaughter of the lady after whom the lane is named. "I knew this was the place; I recognised your dog in the window from the picture in *The Cornishman.*"

I spurned a trip down to the beach this afternoon. I shall wait until I have found a suitable pair of sunglasses that will fit the bleddy hound, so that she can venture out incognito. Instead I risked life and limb and drove out to St Just, far too close to St Ives for my liking. It was a necessary journey to collect the essential items with which to arm myself for an important challenge I must face this weekend. I am sure that you are well ahead of me, dear reader, but for the full detail you will have to wait until Monday.

In the meanwhile the bleddy hound and I will be keeping a low profile, making sure the curtains, (if we had any), are shut before we turn the light on, looking over our shoulders when we run around the block and steering a wide berth, from the OS. Did I not mention in all this that the landlady is a proper hake (she is from St Ives in case you were thinking I was just being rude about the esteemed manageress)? I might have got away with it if our Head Launcher had not cut out the article and stuck it to the notice board down there on Thursday night.

I shall still venture down for cards on Tuesday. One of our German visitors from last year left behind her Rosamund Pilcher mask. They will never guess it is me, but I might have to sign a few autographs.

March 3rd - Saturday

Things started out rather well this morning. The weather was rather nice; the bleddy hound did not do her usual six thirty bark the house down; I was feeling just dandy and all looked set for a rather lazy day.

That was before I went down with a virus, a rather nasty one to boot. It laid me up for most of the day trying to recover, and it is definitely not something I am used to. I had taken all the proper precautions and not been anywhere that I should not, so how it got me I will never know, but what I do know is that it was the devil's own job to shift.

Now, do not start to panic. I am sure you will not catch it off these pages on the Internet, or from the pages of the book if that is where you are reading it (poor gullible soul, that you are), although it was from the Internet that I caught mine. It was a clever little virus too, as it shut down my antivirus suite and laid waste to my system files. Because it had slowed down my computer to such an extent, it took five hours for my cleaner to track down all the files that were infected.

I am very sorry if you had envisaged me lying in a cold sweat wrapped in blankets up to my eyeballs. I am sure you were full of sympathy for a moment or two as well. Well, it is most appreciated, especially as after all that hard effort to get rid of the darned thing it resurfaced again just before I was getting ready to go out in the evening. It rather made a mess of me trying to do a Diary entry for today too, and I find myself on a laptop with some recovered files typing away the following morning.

Bleddy computers!

March 4th - Sunday

You have probably guessed that we are making the most of our late mornings, as we only have a week of them left, well, I do anyway. Such is the stuff of paradox, that the bleddy hound will not want to bark the place down either when I am up before her, but anyway I am managing to catch her before she flies off the bed in my sleep now.

Today, though, was not the day for lazing around in bed for too long. It was a day of mighty challenge, of defending the honour of the family, of a fight to the death, (well, maybe slightly over-strained hands), in the arena of cookery. It was the nationally famous F&L Pasty Competition. Yes, nationally famous. Apparently it was mentioned on the BBC One Show on Friday. The press were so excited the photographer arrived half an hour early. (He also left half an hour early as he could not be bothered to wait that long.)

I had already prepared my pastry the day before. It only remained to ready the innards and carefully time the cooking to be ready shortly before we left for the battle ground. The tension was palpable as I entered the bar, the judges were already preparing their palates with copious quantities of Doom Bar and the cups were gleaming on the trophy table.

All right, I will cut to the chase and not leave you dangling in anticipation, waiting on me rambling on about how the panel deliberated with the solemnity of a hanging judge, how we all stood, silently lost in our own contemplation. I will not tell you that our jangling nerves might have had parishioners turning up at the church next door they were so loud they could have been mistaken for church bells. No, I shall save you from the misery of long bated breath and tell you instantly that the winner of the competition was the landlady's daughter, who took away the trophy for the novelty pasty with a filling of chicken and pancetta, I think.

It was after that the judges turned to the traditional pasties. I clearly would not want to frustrate you further by delaying the report that the winner was a paragon of comestible production. It would be cruel of me to string out telling you who that was, although, I am sure you might have guessed by now. Yes, the winner of the traditional pasty section of the competition was ... now I think there are guidelines about how long the pause has to be before the name is announced. I tried to get hold of the BBC and the independent television companies to ask them just how long that pause was supposed to be, but there was no one available for comment. I did look at the television schedules as well, to see if there were any competition shows on whose pauses I could copy, but alas there was none. I am just going to have to guess.

The winner of the nationally famous F&L Pasty Competition (Traditional Category) 2012 is ... fifteen, fourteen, thirteen ...

five, four ... [camera pans from face to face of the competitors] ... three, two, one. Right, let me just open this envelope a minute. Letter opener, anyone?

The darkness of disappointment fell around me. I only made second in a three horse race. The landlady took the prize, snatched from my deserving mitt by a few measly points. That is it; I shall never make another pasty again.

In truth, though, dear readers, I had the opportunity to taste all three traditional pasties before the judgement was made and it was the pasty that I would have selected as well, that won. With other fare the cook has the opportunity to taste and fine tune the product as it is developed. With a pasty, you put it together as best you can and hope for the best. While I thought that I had seasoned sufficiently, it was clear from the taste that I had stayed my hand a little too much in the salt and pepper department.

While I can no longer claim to be champion pasty maker, at least not for this year, we had a jolly little afternoon. The walk home was spectacular too, though chilly, with the sun setting in a bright blue sky bringing out the colour in the crystal clear air. You see, everyone is a winner on days like these.

March 5th – Monday

Oh woe is me or more accurately woe is my computer. My virus issues have escalated and have taken all of my time today. It is a situation as irksome as any I have ever encountered and I suspect I am not out of the woods yet.

I had considered availing myself of the services of a local chap whose skills in this area will be somewhat more up to date than mine. However I am of the opinion, especially after seeing the results that a rescue disc produced, that this is not an ill for mending, and my computer will have to be rebuilt from the ground up. I have saved all of my data, I think, but the whole process of rebuilding from a recovery disc that is four years old will, I know, be both time consuming and soul destroying.

It is not that we do not have other things to consider. The Missus actually ventured down to the shop unbid, to prepare our opening order from the cash and carry. She was going to go down this morning to wash the shelves and put out some stock, but as ever this will be far better done tomorrow. This will continue until Friday when there will be no more tomorrows to put it off until. In fact no different from last year and the year before that, etcetera.

I see that the results are out for that other pasty competition held at the Eden Project. Theirs was boldly called a World Pasty Competition, though the news report I saw only focused on those from Cornwall, but there were entrants from Australia and the USA and I would trust some from Mexico too. Mr Cornish, from the much-maligned Ginsters baking company came away with not just the professional bakers Cornish pasty trophy, but the open category too. One has to assume that the pasties he entered were not anything to do with the products that are generally available from his company. It rather begs the question that if Ginsters can produce pasties of that quality, and let us face it they must have been good to beat the other 120 into submission, why don't they?

Sorry, but I must return to my ailing computer where I have just reached the stage where I can rebuild my operating system. As if things were not hard enough, I have discovered that the recovery disc will not work with my keyboard. If you happen to drop into the shop when we open on Saturday and see a sallow, quivering blob of jelly where you expect a shopkeeper to be, do not be alarmed, that will be me.

March 6th – Tuesday

Well, I reached the end of my tether with this bleddy computer, well not this one, as this one is currently working all right, touch wood. It is the broken computer that I have run out of patience and, particularly time, with. Had this happened a month ago, say, I might have enjoyed the challenge, well, not exactly enjoyed, but I certainly would have had more time to tinker.

No, today was a day to focus on the shop, after all it is our bread and butter and just now we are down to the stale, crusty end of the loaf and the butter's gone a bit funny. Today was a day for going out to the sparkly new cash and carry in Hayle that they have refurbished over the winter. No more dodging drips of rain water from the roof and various buckets strewn around the floor to catch them.

On our way, we stopped off at the shop at the top to deliver a sample of one of the Missus's culinary masterpieces to her mate who works there. I do not know how long it should take to drop off a culinary delight, but I am sure that I could do it in less than the half an hour that it took the Missus. Nevertheless, she came out with worrying information that the Hayle cash and carry was still under construction - most probably. Since we were going to have to go past Hayle anyway to get to the other cash and carry in Pool, if the Hayle one was closed, we decided to drop into the Hayle cash and carry to have a look just in case because, as you know, you cannot go past Hayle without having a Philps pasty, despite having been past Hayle twice in the last few weeks without doing so. Following so far?

When we arrived at Hayle, sure enough the Hayle cash and carry was still in the grips of burly working type people and enclosed in an armour of scaffolding. It certainly did not look like it would be ready any time soon and the lady that we met who works there said that although it was supposed to be ready, it would not be ready any time soon. We repaired to Philps car park to consider our position, because although we knew we had planned to go to Pool if the Hayle cash and carry was closed, we had also planned that while the Missus was filling trolleys in the Hayle cash and carry that I would go off and take the bleddy hound for a run around, possibly in the direction of Upton Towans. While we considered and consumed our pasties we decided that we would still go to the Towans and from there drive on up to Pool and the other cash and carry.

That was all very well until we got to the Towans and discovered that the Missus had not brought her beach boots. Well, we did not actually discover it, as she had not brought them on purpose, since she thought that she would be filling trolleys at the Hayle cash and carry while I alone took the bleddy hound across the Towans. So, unwilling to besmirch her Jimmy Choos, (no, not really, I just thought it sounded rather good), it was left to me to take herself for a run across the fast disappearing sands alone as in the original plan.

I was in the middle of tossing the ball for her when it struck me that it would be a jolly wheeze to take a hike across to Gwithian and have the Missus meet us there. I called the Missus and suggested it would be a jolly wheeze if I took the bleddy hound on a hike across to Gwithian and for the Missus to drive up and meet us there. The Missus agreed that it would indeed be a jolly wheeze, all but for the fact that she had bought a magazine to ward against boredom while I took the dog out. Nevertheless she agreed and that is exactly what we did.

So, running a tad later than we imagined, we made our way to the Barncoose Industrial Estate. The cash and carry is the one we used when we first started running the shop and is much larger than the one in Hayle. We switched to the Hayle cash and carry because it is closer and the staff, at that time, a little more focused on the smaller number of customers that they had. Because the Missus treats the cash and carry like a big supermarket and will insist on traipsing up and down each aisle whether we need to or not, and because the Pool cash and carry is much larger than the one at Hayle it took significantly longer than we originally planned.

You will, no doubt, be able to imagine that after the loading and the unloading of the van the Missus did not feel like cooking another of her culinary delights when we had finished. Now, please keep this under your hat, as I would not like to hurt her feelings when I say that it was actually quite nice to have something very simple tugged from the clutches of the freezer for a change. Please, I am not saying there is anything wrong with her culinary delights, honest, just that it was nice to have a simple meal for a change. I shall now stop digging.

Gosh, after all that running around doing actual work things and writing a paragraph that will, I am sure, come back and bite me severely on the bottom, it was such a relief to repair to the OS for a game of cards. It was even more of a relief to find that I was holding the upper hand for most of the night for a change.

March 7ᵗʰ - Wednesday

Well, that was not so bad. I managed to drag myself from my pit without too much collateral damage this morning, almost before the cock crowed. I am not sure how I would know that it had, since I have not heard a cock crow down here in eight years.

Never mind all that, it was raining when I ventured outside and I am sure it will not be the last time this year. It will however, hopefully, be the last time I have to transport my computer to the expert who is going to rebuild the box, albeit to a very basic level. He is about twelve and lives in the back end of nowhere, and for those of you that are unfamiliar with this neck of the woods, that is a couple of miles south east of St Buryan.

The farm where he lives is rather impressive, or at least the farm where he lives impressed me. The farmhouse itself is an imposing granite built mansion complete with central chapel window. Opposite, set out in a square around a central courtyard, are what were once the barns. These have been tastefully converted into rather exclusive looking holiday lets. It is also on the back road to the Wink in Lamorna a mile away. If I was in the market to rent a quiet little place for my holiday I would say I could definitely do worse.

I would imagine that the somewhat unconditional free advertising would equate rather nicely to the price of a repaired computer, wouldn't you?

As if several hours in a cash and carry were not enough of a shopping placebo, the Missus took the van off deep to do some more shopping in the big city. She returned with all sorts of luxury goods for the bleddy hound, which the bleddy hound pointedly ignored. This was not a surprise since the Missus had also bought a grooming brush, the effectiveness of which she demonstrated on the decidedly unimpressed beast. After that I too would have spurned such lavish frippery, merely out of spite.

I spent much of the day engaged, (it is the modern term for locked in a battle to the death), with the Laurel and Hardy Newspaper Company to promote our sustainable, (another modern term meaning the battle to the death could go on for some time), relationship (the benefit of which is mostly theirs). I am trying to head off at the pass the delivery of an opening stock of magazines of their choice. For some reason they believe that titles such as 'Banana Farming Today' and 'Coal Miners Monthly' will fly off the shelves down here. Having been through most of the contact points they gave me, including a WH Smith store in Swindon, I ran out of time. I now only have tomorrow to make the breakthrough before they arrive on my doorstep on Friday or Saturday.

After all that distraction, and waiting on the arrival of a supplier, there was precious little beach left to run the bleddy hound out on. By the time we headed back the waves were lapping around our toes and we had to head up the slipway below The Beach restaurant.

After such excitement I could have quite happily curled up on the sofa with a copy of 'South Atlantic Oil Rig Worker', but I have no idea where I might find a copy – until the weekend.

March 8ᵗʰ – Thursday

The shopkeeper had been working all morning spring-cleaning his list of magazines that the awful Laurel and Hardy Newspaper Company had thought that they might send him. First with computer keys, then with telephone calls to the high and mighty in the Company, and then with telephone calls to the lower, less mighty and more pliable lower powers in the Company. In the short time he had, he made a rather good fist of it and the lower, less mighty employees of the awful Laurel and Hardy Newspaper Company promised faithfully to not send the bulky list of inappropriate magazines to the shopkeeper's shop.

It was small wonder that the shopkeeper threw down his brush that he had been spring-cleaning with and sent up a cautious 'whoop!' knowing that the awful Laurel and Hardy Newspaper Company could still make a dreadful mess of things.

Talking of dreadful messes, the shopkeeper heard that the toads on the Strategic Planning Committee of the revered council of the county at County Hall had approved the plans for a large park and ride facility at St Erth. He thought that with a name like 'earth' a mole might have found some comfort in it, but it also seems that the people in that area did not seem too upset by the idea - yet.

While today shopkeeper could have spent some time in the shop preparing for his grand opening, instead decided to go up beyond the Wild Wood to Wadebridge, The Royal Cornwall Showground to be precise, to have a look at the food and catering show that they put on every year at this time. It is good to see that the food sector in Cornwall is still growing even in these difficult times, although shopkeeper wished that the salespeople were not so awfully keen to badger you. There were several new producers there and one of these will be supplying an exciting new product that will be in our pasty warmer this year. I can say no more than that, else the whole street will be jumping on the bandwagon – the rats.

It was a perfect day for it, in fact it could not have been 'otter for the time of year. Shopkeeper and Missus stopped about as far from the riverbank as you can get, at the little hostelry known as Smokey Joe's. As the very nice people there brought out each mysterious comestible one by one and arranged them in due order, shopkeeper gasped, "O my! O my!", at each fresh revelation. When all had been delivered to the table Missus said, "Now, pitch in, old shopkeeper." and shopkeeper was very glad to obey, as he had started his spring cleaning with the Laurel and Hardy Newspaper Company at a very early hour that morning, and had not had a bite or sup since that distant time which now seemed so many days ago.

Had he not been stopped, shopkeeper might have been inclined to rabbit on for such a long time that folk might form the impression that he was unlikely to come to an end at all. There was just enough story left in him to explain that in the evening he and Head Launcher and friend strolled out beside the Wild Sea to the Wild OS, in time to imbibe a bit and take part in the great OS quiz night. It was pleasing to see how respectfully they were treated, (to their face, at least), by the inhabitants of that venerable institution. Mothers though would bring their infants, who were fractious and quite beyond control, to the fore and point out that if they did not hush them or not fret them, then the terrible grey shopkeeper would up and get them. While a base libel on shopkeeper, who, while he cared little for his miserable reputation, was rather fond of children when they were somewhere else; but it never failed to shut the little beggers up.

I am sure that Mr Kenneth Grahame, who was born today in 1895, would be greatly distressed if he were to read this Diary entry and it might certainly have put the wind up his willows had he still been alive. Shopkeeper can only tip his hat and apologise for such grave disregard of the work of this proper scribe.

March 9ᵗʰ – Friday

The witching hour approaches. The milk, butter, cheese and eggs arrived this morning. Eggs! Where are the bleddy eggs? I forgot to order them, that is where they are. How many years have we been doing this? Now, if I had been doing my previous job the quality assurance manual would have insisted that I have a checklist for shop opening. Gosh, I think I may have to fire myself.

I am still missing my main computer; I am sure that would have helped. I drove out to the back of beyond (just southeast of St Buryan if you recall) to collect it this morning, and after a brief discussion with the expert we agreed that I should let him upgrade it and hence it would take another few days. It was the right thing to do, but rather stuck a spanner in the works when I went to fax the grocery order through to the local cash and carry, included on which was an emergency supply of eggs. I knew that I would not be able to electronically fax the order, as the software to do that is on the broken PC. What I had not thought through is that the printer is also attached to that PC and I cannot now print the order so that I can fax it manually. That quality assurance manual would have insisted I had a plan B, and while I hated that manual with a vengeance when I was ruled by it in my previous job, I am actually beginning to rather miss it.

The Missus eventually stoked up enough energy to make an appearance in the shop by early afternoon. It only took a couple of hours to do the absolute minimum to allow us to open the shop without putting our customers in danger of injury from tripping over boxes left strewn on the floor and the like. The more complex and somewhat necessary tasks of putting stock out onto the shelves will wait until tomorrow, when we are open. If you are planning to be our first customer I do hope your requirements are slight.

Knowing from experience that the Missus works much better on her own, (no, honest), I ran off to St Just to pick up our bacon and sausages from our very good butcher. You see, you will, at least, be able to have a breakfast if you are the first customer in, provided, of course, that you do not want eggs. I also took the unexercised bleddy hound down to the beach for an hour or so. It is not exactly the last proper exercise she will get until we close at the end of October, but the trips hither and thither to new and exciting locations will definitely be off the cards. When the beach dog ban kicks in at the beginning of May, she will have to make do with half an hour of chasing a ball on the Harbour beach after curfew in the evening, provided that the tides permit.

So after doing approximately three hours work, probably between us, we collapsed exhausted on the sofa for the rest of the evening. Well, you have to build up to these things.

The last thing to do was to set, with shaking hands, my alarm. I was disappointed to note the ease with which the device accepted the low valued digits I keyed in. Anything I have forgotten now will have to join the long list of problems to be resolved tomorrow. Here we go.

March 10ᵗʰ - Saturday

I shall eschew my usual analogy of the amount of beach that was on show at low water today. Suffice it to say that it was a very low tide, possibly the lowest of the year. There was a substantial amount of the mast of the wreck visible and with a little imagination I would not wonder if you could walk to Cape in a pair of wellies.

You might have guessed at just how busy we were today since I had so much time to gaze out upon the unusual tide. Had the weather also not been unusual, in that we have had worse summer days, it would have been deathly. However it did give us a chance to get the shop in order, the shelves washed and the stock laid out.

Talking of Cornish weather, the Bloodhound Project is coming to Cornwall. In case you have never heard of it, this project will see a man, who has clearly taken leave of his senses, strap himself to a Eurofighter jet engine and propel himself beyond 1,000 miles per hour across a bit of sand somewhere in South Africa. A life sized model of the supersonic car, known as Bloodhound SSC, will be on show at the college tomorrow for a while.

So what has Bloodhound SSC and Falmouth College got to do with the weather, you may well ask? Well, Falmouth College has been lent a state of the art piece of weather measuring kit by the Met Office. It will be used to measure the weather conditions trackside while the Bloodhound SSC makes its record attempt sometime in 2013. The college will have until then to tinker and understand the operation of the highly sensitive piece of equipment. It was decided to send it to Cornwall for tests as clearly the weather here and in South Africa is very similar. Using the equipment will enable the college to determine slight changes in pressure and humidity that will be crucial to the success of the project. Once it has been properly calibrated to Met Office specifications, the Falmouth team will be able to predict the perfect dry conditions needed for the speed record attempt shortly before the track is flooded out with unexpected rain.

It is timely news indeed. Today in 1956 Peter Twiss, a former Brooke Bond tea taster, was the first pilot to exceed 1,000 miles per hour, piloting a Fairey Delta 2 research aeroplane; a safer proposition, where you are unlikely to run out of road.

There was a bit of a rumour that the real Bloodhound SSC would be tested in Cornwall, but the exact location is being kept a secret for now.

There was certainly no speeding on Sennen Beach this afternoon when I took pity on the bleddy hound being nailed to her throne all morning. It was not cold in the shop, but chilly enough for a fleece to be required. It was therefore reasonable enough to assume that a fleece jacket would suffice for a run across the sand. The fleece jacket came off after the first hundred yards, followed by the fleece jumper a short while after that; it was steaming down there. I stayed long enough to subsume my entire annual vitamin D requirement and dragged my gasping frame back home.

It is usual for the hordes here assembled to enquire about our winter, our aspirations for the summer and how many Lifeboat shouts we have had over the quiet period. Although we may not show it, there is an inner wince at the last of those questions. I was asked three times today. Did you know that if you dance around a railed grave three times the devil will appear? If you ask a Lifeboat man or, in this case a lowly launcher, when the last launch was, three times ...

At approximately ten to five the pagers went off, suggesting that a launch of the Lifeboat was necessary. This time the Inshore boat was required, or rather not.

On a good day, with plenty of sea, the youngsters of The Cove take themselves out along the breakwater and wait to be tossed off into the boiling harbour. It is a game that must have been a favourite for generations, and in fact a somewhat revered old boy admitted to it later in the evening. It is, to some casual observers, a dangerous activity and possibly it does involve some risk. One such observer was so alarmed that they called out the cavalry.

All in all not a bad start to the season.

March 11ᵗʰ - Sunday

Very peaceful in The Cove today, which is not exactly what a desperate shopkeeper was hoping for. All that summer warmth from yesterday has disappeared too, making for a rather chill sort of day. I should, though, appreciate this period of quietness and make the most of it as we have a visitor arriving in the afternoon for whom the word 'silence' is yet to be defined.

I managed to sidle off in the afternoon with a cast iron excuse that I had to watch the rugby. This was largely wasted, apart from the result, as visitor never turned up until shortly before I got back from the OS.

After swallowing my disappointment, I distracted myself with a count of the lights in the bathroom ceiling. On the face of it this might have looked like a somewhat pointless exercise, but if you like me had read the article in the trade press you will understand that this was a measurement in cost exposure. All those little lights, by order of the European Commission, are going to have to go.

Yes, the suits in Brussels, or wherever they may hide, have decided that those little halogen twelve volt bulbs must no longer be manufactured, I think from September this year. There was no mention of the larger mains halogen bulbs, but what is different about those I have no idea. This is a crushing blow for the retail trade in particular, as many shops use these to illuminate their shelves. Whereas with previous directives the bulbs have been readily replaceable with lower wattage or energy saving alternatives, there is no such option with the MR16s. Furthermore the lighting units, driven by a transformer, are unlikely to accept LED replacements without changing the transformer as well. The directive may cost the retail sector millions.

Of course, this news is likely to send the market into a panic now that I have made it public. You had all best scurry down to your bulb shop and buy up as many MR16 halogen bulbs as you can, before the price goes up or they disappear completely. Naturally, I made sure that I have all I need for the next thirty years at the good old low price before I published this little nugget. Since selling them is not to be made illegal I think my future is assured, especially when they reach their peak price. Some might suggest, quite unkindly I feel, that this is profiteering. I just like to call it my pension.

It is a shame that this investment will take some time to mature; I could do with a new set of earplugs right now.

March 12ᵗʰ – Monday

We were confronted by a thick curtain of fog this morning, instead of the stunning view out across the bay. The fog persisted in various degrees throughout the day. It was as thick as a bag up on the airport straight as I made a quick visit up to St Just in the morning, a disappointing trip if ever there was one. I can usually count on several cars coming along without any lights on, which gives me the perfect opportunity to get at least a paragraph of ranting into The Diary. Today, though, they all had lights on – outrageous!

The fog lifted enough during the day to be able to see a very peaceful bay and a sea as flat as a dish. The light easterly breeze kept the temperature down, but the conditions were good enough for our neighbour, affectionately known as Ben Ten, to try out his kayak with his new stabilisers attached. He had fashioned the addition from bits of scrap that he has collected for the purpose. At one point he was looking for some gash plumbing, but was a bit put off when some wag at the OS offered him some lead pipes.

Visitor came to the rescue of the bleddy hound, who was looking like she may not have got out much at all today. She had already taken her own two dogs some way down the coast path, then returned and took the bleddy hound out along the beach with the ball thrower. It is acts of charity such as this that she will rely upon as summer draws on. I just hope that running up and down our stairs will keep me sufficiently exercised, as I think it rather unlikely anyone is going to offer to take me out for a run.

Well, there is nothing quite like a little Lifeboat exercise to round off the day, so we had one. We were few in numbers shore side, but we are not known as the very excellent Shore Crew for nothing. We even made light work of the oar weed that had collected on the short slip, and had the boat back in and secured without hardly breaking a sweat. What a very excellent Shore Crew we are, to be sure.

The interlude gave the Missus sufficient time to whip up a rather splendid seafood chowder, which we consumed between us last time. I shall have to reign in my disappointment that it must be shared three ways with Visitor, but I suppose she did walk the dog this morning. I had intended to cast aside etiquette and make sure I was first in the queue come serving time and hang the consequences. Instead I found myself jostling in my own kitchen in a rather unseemly manner for the privilege. I succumbed to a somewhat distasteful shoulder barge and a bit of gouging and ended up a poor second then, blow me, she went back for seconds. I can see I am going to have to play dirty for the rest of the week.

March 13ᵗʰ - Tuesday

There is one thing about this persistent fog; it gives me a bit of time to peruse the newspapers. To be fair I only had the morning, as the fog pretty much lifted in the afternoon and gave us a cracking little day after all. And the thing about reading the newspapers is that you find all sorts of interesting little facts secreted about the pages.

Here is a piece that made me think. A lady in St Mawes somehow convinced the makers of the board game Monopoly to produce a St Mawes version. Despite it being the smallest location to have a Monopoly version, I am sure it has much to commend it. There are some top notch restaurants and hotels, so I understand, as well as a castle and a few other historic bits and it draws the rich and famous for holidays in much the same way as Rock does in the north.

I could not help but wonder how Sennen might get on with its own version of the game. For a start we would have to replace the Free Parking square and I guess that the Water Works could go in favour of the Brew sewage works. It would be a struggle to fill the board with streets though. Even if you were lucky enough to buy one, you would be hard pressed to build any houses, especially if you bought a street in the conservation area. Of course, if you had sufficient funds you could easily get over that issue by avoiding the parish and county councils and going straight to the Bristol authority, that will let you build anything anywhere. Then there is the Electric Company; you would not need to worry about passing Go, ever, and you would have to keep stopping play every so often – turning the lights out for added effect.

I had to drop some paperwork into our accountants and from there go and collect my renewed, mended and upgraded computer. It will be a blessing when I have put it back together again and reloaded my applications; I spent the best part of an hour trying to get the cursed web version of email working so that I could send my electronic files to the accountant this morning.

I could not possibly claim that my trip into town was simply an excuse to put myself out of earshot of Visitor, as this is now completely unnecessary. One reader, who I shall simply refer to as AR for his own safety, very kindly sent me a pair of ear plugs. Visitor was not exactly impressed when I told her and promptly issued a fatwa; it is all right, AR, SO19 are on their way as I write.

March 14th – Wednesday

At least we can see the bay this morning and rather weirdly the sea appears to be moving westward very rapidly. I will not pull my punches either; it is a tad cool. So much so we have had the shop door closed for most of the day.

With that in mind we were lucky to get any customers at all today. We did have a German gentleman come in to collect the fish he had ordered on Monday. There were three good sized plaice, carefully caught and packed in ice for his delectation. When we told him the price he became somewhat agitated and declared that he could get three fish and chip meals for what he was paying. We did try and explain that it was a bit like comparing an entry level Volkswagen Beetle with a BMW 5 Series, but he would not be convinced. And so it starts.

On the subject of upsetting the out of towners, it seems the new television series *Fisherman's Apprentice* has stirred up some muddy waters. The series has been filmed in Cadgwith, down on The Lizard and follows a chap trying to learn how to earn a living fishing off a punt. In the opening programme one of the local lads explained that their fishing methods contrast with the big trawlers that are out all year and scoop up fish indiscriminately, or words to that effect. The good old BBC cut to some library footage of a big trawler splashing through some impressive sea. Now the skipper of the big trawler shown splashing through some impressive sea has taken a bit of umbrage at what was said, and the fact that it was his trawler they showed. He complained that his boat is allowed out only 150 days of the year and the scooping is a bit less indiscriminate than suggested. Perhaps I could put him in touch with our German visitor, as the trawler fish are less likely to attract the premium that the day boat fish have.

It will not be long now before the crabber from our own little fishing community will be dropping its pots. There have already been some preparatory rustlings going on. Please note the use of the singular crabber there. Big J has retired and with no youngsters coming up through it is looking a bit bleak for Cove crab and lobster in the future. Also BG has been out most of the winter off and on, handlining for whatever he can get.

March 15th – Thursday

Did I say last week that the residents of St Erth had not made a fuss about the new park and ride plans for their village yet? What I had not realised is that the planners have made no provision for improving the thoroughfare under the railway bridge. It is currently a narrow bit of road on a hairpin bend and if you meet one of the many waste lorries or sludge tankers that service the tip, sorry Household Waste Recycling Centre, you have to wait until they pass.

I have not seen the detailed plans so it may be that the council know what they are doing, though I would not put any money on it. I can also see that these criticisms may have some substance, especially when the council are being ever so shy in supporting some of their claims by not revealing costs or research data. We shall watch and see.

Back in The Cove things could not be more different. I could not find anyone complaining about anything. In fact I could not find anyone. Although that easterly draft has dropped away we did not exactly see a flood of happy holiday makers heading this way. Not even the first dolphins of the year, playing in the surf, drew a crowd.

No, I must retract that last bit, about the complaining, not the bit about the dolphins. It is something I had not yet looked very hard at until a local businessman came thundering into the shop and pointed out his business rates had shot up by twenty percent. This rather upsetting news sent me scurrying to look at mine and sure enough mine too had leapt up by sixteen percent. I had intended to call the council to ask why the national average was 5.6 percent and ours was more than double that, but I was overtaken by events.

The events happened to be the Missus wanting to take Visitor up to Travaskis Farm for lunch and, just to extend their afternoon a bit, Visitor wanted to stop off at Perranuthnoe on the way back. That was my fault. I should not have blown it up to be the destination of choice in several Diary entries and Visitor is an avid reader. Occasionally she reads The Diary too.

I was looking forward to the promised session on resuscitation at Lifeboat training in the evening, as I needed some reviving. We were to have a proper doctor to teach us as well, but unfortunately he never turned up; we will have to go private next time. Instead, we launched the Inshore Lifeboat, twice in fact, and pushed the big boat out on the slip so the crew could play with their equipment.

We have also instigated a little bonus ball gambling to try and raise funds for a band for our Lifeboat dinner at the end of the season. The Missus has agreed to run the programme for us and, bless her, she stood outside the station for about an hour tonight to capture the boys as they tried to get home. We have a few more gaps than names at the moment, increasing the likelihood of a roll-over, but hopefully that will just make next week's a more attractive proposition.

March 16th - Friday

The Government has announced today that they will not be interfering in the development of South Quay over at Hayle; they will leave it to The much maligned council to do all the interfering. That may or may not be a good thing, but it is about time that something happened. I have mentioned before that I went to one of the first Hayle development proposal meetings, when ING first bought most of Foundry some ten to fifteen years ago, and next to begger all has happened since. One of the chaps involved in the latest process has recently dug up some paperwork relating to development proposals that were interrupted by the war - that is the First World War by the way, nearly 100 years ago.

That is nothing. Henry VIII gave Penzance Harbour to the people of Penzance 500 years ago today and they are still arguing about where to put the Isles of Scilly ferry.

There is a quote of questionable origin, 'lies, damned lies and statistics', so here are some statistics to brighten your day and to show that there is some light at the end of the tunnel that is probably a train full of visitors coming the other way.

First, of the seven billion people on the planet, one in fourteen works in the tourist industry. In the UK it became the sixth largest export industry last year and is still growing. While the UK economy grew by 0.9 percent last year, tourism grew by 14 percent. Expectations are that it will grow another twenty percent by the year 2020, most of which will be from Brazil, India, Russia and, particularly, China. Probably not the best time, then, for Devon to fold its tourism body, Visit Devon.

Chinese tourism was responsible for £10 million in 2000 and is expected to be £100 million by 2020. Every Boeing 747 full of Chinese tourists brings around £1 million to the UK. Their average spend is three times that of other visitors to Britain.

You should also know that Yorkshire, which is on a par with Cornwall, gets more visitors each year than the Eiffel Tower has ever; while Spain has 139 Michelin Star restaurants, we have 150, of which thirteen are in pubs, oh yes; New Zealand has 12,000 miles of walking tracks and is capped by Britain with 150,000 miles – boots, start walking.

After assimilating all that riveting information I felt duty bound to drag the bleddy hound down to the beach for a run. She ran, I walked. I think after just a week of the shop being open my feet have lost weight. I put on my usual woolly socks and pushed my feet into my wellies, but they were definitely looser than the last time I wore them, the wellies that is, not my feet; they are perfectly secure on the ends of my legs, I can assure you. Mind you they were every bit as hard to get off when I got home, er, the wellies, not my feet.

I hope you enjoy your evening, no doubt discussing tourism statistics over the dinner table with the other intellectual members of your family (what high regard I hold you all in, dear reader). In the midst of your revelry do spare a thought for the hard pressed Cornish shopkeeper who, after a full day's graft, is busy brushing up on his Mandarin while strumming on a balalaika and watching the back catalogue of *The Water Margin*.

March 17ᵗʰ - Saturday

I suppose I could have danced a little jig in celebration because it is St Patrick's Day, of course, absolutely nothing to do with Visitor making her exit this morning. She went away in her little car laden with local daffodils bought, so she said, from a little place over at Treen. I shall drive out that way later to check the hedgerows to ensure our green lobby are kept happy.

Mind you there seems to be no pleasing some environmentalists; whatever you do you just cannot please them all. Some of the major fish producers have been moved to fish for tuna more sustainably in recent years. This includes some big names like Princes and John West, even Sainsbury's own label tinned tuna is caught this way.

Enter Dalhousie University in Canada, who have conducted a study comparing line and pole fishing for tuna against the purse seine netting method, (that's the one that produces bycatch and is to be frowned upon). I must stop trying to add some suspense into these long wibbles because I know, dear reader, that you are, as ever, miles ahead of me here. Yes, you have already guessed that the purse seine method of fishing came out on top as having a much smaller carbon footprint, in fact 75 percent less. So

385

although the method is less fish friendly, it is more environment friendly.

On the bright side you can now go back to eating cheaper tuna and smugly tell your tree-hugging, dolphin friendly pals to stick it when they criticise, as you are saving the planet, although there will not be any fish in it.

March 18ᵗʰ - Sunday

Well it certainly looked pretty today which is more than what can be said for how it felt. There was a nasty north-westerly, bloomer-tugging breeze that kept me shivering all day. By the end of it I was cold through to the bone.

The Missus drove off early for a surprise rendezvous with her Mum and Dad for Mother's Day, which meant that she would be gone all day. Me and the bleddy hound hunkered down in the chilly shop and battened down our respective hatches against the blow. We were not too bored, or at least I was not, as we had a steady trickle of customers and I have to say that she behaved herself remarkably well, stuck up on her bed with nothing to do all day.

In between customers I had the chance to admire the bright white re-painted road markings across the road. Some chaps from the council dropped by on Friday and freshened them up for the coming season. They did some more at the top of the hill and, I noticed, they had done many in St Just when I went there. They must have worked their little fingers to the bone. I suppose after all that hard effort they could not wait to get their best togs on and go and paint the town red.

I treated the bleddy hound to a run down on the Harbour beach with a ball after we closed, and the Missus treated me by bringing home a rather fine curry from the rather fine curry house in town. It was especially nice of her, given that I have told her that I shall be going out with a girl from Newlyn all day tomorrow.

Oh, now *that* has your whistle whet, I bet.

March 19ᵗʰ – Monday

I met her in the early hours down on the Newlyn dockside, which is where and when you meet ladies of her stamp (so I have been told). I do not know quite what I had expected; I had only seen a faded photograph of her, which was hardly flattering. She looked a little grubby if I were to be honest, in need of a bit of making-up here and there. Worse still she smelled of fish. And why should she not, after all she is a fishing boat.

We shall call her the Girl P, as I am a gentleman, (oh, all right, I am not but she does not know that), and a gentleman would never tell. I have been negotiating for some time to spend a day with her, and last Saturday night I apparently agreed with the skipper that I would be ready for picking up at four in the morning. It was a good Saturday night.

So at half past four on a dark, chilly morning I found myself climbing over the gunwales of Girl P, pulling on a pair of waterproof dungarees and a pair of borrowed, black wellie boots, as mine are green.

It is here I should explain that many members of the fishing community are a tad superstitious: you will hear the term underground greyhound for those little furry things with white fluffy tails and long ears; never take a pasty on board, unless the ends are cut off; always coil line in the direction of the sun; green should not be seen.

Despite being apparently the right size, my borrowed boots were a little on the tight side, even though my feet have lost weight. After an hour or so the boots had become more than just a little uncomfortable and I started to rue not having brought my own. I looked with envy at the boots worn by the crew, all perfectly fitting and, yes, green.

It took a couple of hours or so to steam out to the fishing grounds, south west of Lizard. Today we were to haul three sets of nets, hopefully bagging some valuable monkfish. It was explained to me that these nets were outside the six mile local fishing limit and therefore prone to being run over and cut off by big ships, trawlers and the like, moving through the International waters. It is a risk, but the dividends can be much higher than remaining inside the six mile limit. Even here it is not risk free, as some of the bigger trawlers have been known to turn off their tracking devices and sneak in for a quick trawl – allegedly.

The nets are passive devices and cause very little damage to the sea-bed, where the trawlers will scour through the beds, taking everything in their way. There is great skill in shooting the nets, taking note of the undersea terrain and the strength and direction of the tide at any given moment of the day, in any given week, month and time of year. The mesh was surprisingly large, I suppose two to three inch squares, letting smaller fish through but, naturally, fish of a size other than monk are also snagged, despite a sign every few yards saying "MONKFISH ONLY" – only kidding.

On the way out the crew were joking about the dreaded spider crabs that get tangled up in the nets. Not so much a wasted by-catch, as spider crabs will fetch a useful price on the European market, but just think netting and long spindly legs and you might have an inkling of what was to come. I could imagine the issue, but not the time consumed in untangling the spiny critters, or the sheer volume of them. As a novice, I was taking more than five to ten minutes on each one, the more experienced crew were able to extract them much faster, but even then sometimes were overwhelmed. We must have spent a couple of hours or more on each set of nets.

The process would not have been easy on a stable platform and, although we only had a light swell to deal with, the boat was still dancing about as it rested side on to the waves. It can take weeks of regular sea-going to find your sea legs and I was being thrown about a fair bit and the too tight wellies did not help much either. Fortunately, I have never been susceptible to sea-sickness, which would have been an added impediment to the constant hard physical work that I could already feel taking its toll on my leg muscles, back and arms.

Also taking a toll, was a fair sized brown cock crab of maybe one and a half kilos. I really did not need the warning to keep my fingers away from the claws, as several of the spider crabs had already been nipping at my gloves. I was very carefully pulling away the netting and almost had him free when I concentrated a little too hard on freeing up one of the back legs. I felt some pressure around the base of my left thumb that very rapidly turned to excruciating pain. The begger had latched on with its right claw and was applying increasing pressure. I have to thank the speed of one of the crew who dived in and snapped off the claw, still clinging on to my thumb.

I left further brown crab to the experts. It was less the fear of being caught again, (I suspect you only do that once), than the embarrassment of mucking up around ten quid's worth of prime crab. The greatest disappointment though was, having removed my glove later, there was no deliciously hideous scar to show the grandchildren (if I had any) and no bruising to show the Missus, who therefore dismissed it as a mere nip. In fact the only battle scar of the whole trip was a sunburnt head.

Of all the creatures pulled from the deep that day the monkfish were the most intriguing. They were also ugly as sin. Remember the children's programme *Rainbow*? Think Zippy with teeth. They are roughly triangular in shape, tapering down to the meaty, and expensive, tail. At the wide end there is a cavernous mouth, full of sharp teeth. Anything within range of that gaping maw is snapped at, even as the fish lies gasping its last breath. I unnetted a few and came close once as it lunged forward and snapped its mouth shut – very impressive. Later, when the fish were being filleted, one of the crew sliced open the bulging stomach of a particularly large monkfish. Inside was a young dogfish and another, less recognisable fish, both swallowed whole. Yikes!

We were out for sixteen hours, made more palatable by a really rip-sizzling day with little swell. Six hours of that was travel to and from the grounds, but the boys were busy preparing fish on the homeward leg. I decided to stand back and watch, as having already beggered up ten pounds of their turnover I was not about to deprive them of anymore by getting it wrong. After we made it back to the harbour the fish had to be winched off the boat and put on ice and the crab packed into store pots for market the next morning. I think it was half past nine when I returned.

If you want work, I imagine there are less arduous and more financially rewarding ways of earning a living, but I suspect few are so satisfying in a gritty, down to earth sort of way. You would also enjoy a life full of risk; it is one of the most dangerous jobs in the UK, certainly, but moreover you may not catch anything, a steamer might cut your lines, a seal may take a bite out of each of your catch, or the weather may be against you for long periods at a time. For the first three of those you would have already spent money on diesel before finding out you had not earned anything. Add to this government that makes life increasingly more difficult with a litany of red tape; the skipper had to estimate the weight of his catch before arriving at dock and be within ten percent of actual, or face a fine among many rules, not to mention diminishing quotas.

The Missus did not believe I had been out with the lads all day; she said she could smell Girl P's overpowering perfume on me. I was duly prevented from coming in until I had scrubbed the offending, keen aroma from my oilers. I managed to worm my way back into her affections with some soothing words, telling her it didn't mean anything and it would never happen again, probably. I think what really did it was slipping her a bag of crab claws.

On the other hand the bleddy hound would not leave me alone.

March 21ˢᵗ - Wednesday

I woke up yesterday morning as bright as a button and keen as mustard. Must have something to do with it being the first day of spring, I suppose. Wind forward to this morning and I could do no more than crawl out of bed; I was as stiff as a board. All my wicked seafaring had clearly caught up with me.

I cannot have been all that wicked because the sun shone down on us today, albeit with a chilly easterly blowing in the shop door. There was plenty of swell towards high water to keep the surfers happy and not enough earlier to hold the fishing fleet in harbour; a cracking day all round, as long as we do not mention the budget or toilet closures.

Perhaps we would all be better off if politicians followed the example of the Duke of Wellington in settling their differences. Today in 1829, while Prime Minister, he challenged the tenth Earl of Winchilsea to a duel for saying naughty things about him. They missed each other, deliberately it seems, as a gentlemanly act. I suspect we could not entirely rely on our present day MPs to be as gentlemanly. Quod erat demonstrandum I believe.

Yesterday I took the bleddy hound for a quick run down the big beach. It was not ideal as the tide was coming in and we were left with mainly soft sand to try and play on. Today she was not even that lucky, as our new bookcase arrived.

I have been fed up with the state of our existing bookcase, as we have far too many books to put on it. We also have a good range of local authors (some of them quite famous!) and local interest books that it would be good to separate, or at least put them in a better light. Finding a bookcase of the specific dimensions to fit in the gap we had in mind, was a bit of a trial. I had initially suggested that I make one out of my own head, but the Missus looked meaningfully at the ball stand and suggested we buy one if we could. I must say I could not quite understand her reluctance, but we managed to find one eventually that fitted the bill, and the gap, and it arrived today, two weeks late.

Things have moved on a little since those heady, early days of MFI where various parts would be missing, or the instructions supplied were in Spanish. The object that arrived was complete in every respect and the instructions were so clear that a child of nine could have done it. Unfortunately, I could not find a nine year old child, so I was left to do it myself. Of course, real men do not do instructions and I banged it together in no time. It fits perfectly in the allotted space and the slight rocking will soon settle down when it has some heavy books on it, I am sure. I shall find some other use for the small bag of screws I have left over, they were obviously spares.

I shall retire to my bed early tonight, as Monday has very much caught up with me. Last night, of course, I was drawn to the OS for the now obligatory card night and came second. I shall have to make sure I am dog tired next week too, as it obviously helps.

March 22nd – Thursday

A bit of a grey day today with a few mizzly showers passing through and therefore ideal for doing some work outside that I had a perfect opportunity to do yesterday in the sunshine.

The chap who owns the garage where I have been keeping my boat wants to knock it down over the weekend and asked me to move the dinghy. It took a bit of doing, but I managed to get my behind in gear and headed off with some trepidation to view my boat, that had been in storage for the best part of a year. I was right to be trepid, as the boat was a little deflated and was half full of water. In fact, there was so much water in it that it was impossible to lift the trailer on which it is perched.

I set about bailing out the boat with a small bucket, as it was the only size that would fit in the available pool of water, and emptied that into a two gallon bucket. I provide this level of gritty detail as it will explain how I know that, about an hour later, I had emptied nearly 40 gallons of water from the craft. No wonder I could not move it, that is 400 pounds, (181 kilos if you wish), of added weight. It is up for sale, if you are interested, the boat, that is, not the water. Be quick before the darned thing fills up with water again and sinks without trace.

While I was out I made my first trip this year up to Shrew House. I was pleasantly surprised that it seemed quite dry in there, hopefully something to do with the fact that I had the roof at the back repaired, although, of course, it has not rained for a while either. My cleverly crafted and artistically designed ball stand was still in excellent condition and ready to be deployed outside the shop for the new season. Our net bin followed suit, and all it needs now is for the windbreak stand to be brought down and we will be looking like a proper seaside shop again. Oh, and a few customers would be nice.

March 23ʳᵈ – Friday

The fall out from the budget still rumbles on even in this far flung corner of the known universe. Are we worried about pensioners losing out on their tax thresholds? Do we care that the super rich have had a bit of a state handout, or that couples with a salary over £50,000 will have to put their children in the workhouse when their child benefit stops? No, certainly not. So what has stirred the Cornish heart and brought the people close to insurrection? VAT on hot pasties, that's what.

I was somewhat confused to start with as we have always paid VAT on our hot pasties; if they are sold cold then no VAT applies. Slowly more detail has become available and it seems that the plan is to stop the larger supermarkets and chain stores from selling hot food while claiming that the heated element is for presentation only and the foodstuff is not meant to be eaten hot and therefore not subject to VAT. Think rotisserie chicken in those big, town centre threatening, over-priced supermarkets. Sorry did I say that out loud?

Caught in this closing loophole are the pasty bakers who sell their wares straight from the oven and hitherto have been VAT exempt. Here lies the crux of the Cornish uprising; jobs will be lost and the price of pasties will rocket.

Here is a view that is unlikely to be a popular one. Wherever you go in Cornwall pasties are roughly the same price in a like for like sort of way. This is whether you buy one from a shop like ours, where VAT applies, or from a baker, straight from the oven, where VAT does not. Call me an old fusspot if you will but I do wonder what has happened to that 15 to 20 percent profit differential that has been there for years and years.

However the pasty bakeries of Cornwall should not feel too bad about it; it is not like they were deliberately targeted, unlike the producers of black beer. Mather of Yorkshire is apparently the only producer and has been singled out in this budget to have duty applied to its malty beer concentrate for the first time since the beginning of the last century, when they began. Quite what they did to incur the wrath of Mr Osborne perhaps we will never know. Possibly it may have something to do with the 1200 specific gravity of the brew, or its 8.5 percent alcohol by volume. You are supposed to dilute it before consumption to provide a drink that is "both norishing (sic) and rich in Vitamin C". They were probably still reeling from the shock, when two days later the government announces there will be a minimum price per unit of alcohol. That's what you call a double whammy. Ee bah gum!

March 24ᵗʰ - Saturday

We are quite used to the occasional visitor accosting us well before our usual opening time for an 'emergency' newspaper, or desperately needed disposable barbeque. This morning's lark-like shopper took me slightly off-guard with a request for suncream – in March, for heaven's sake! He said that they had not reckoned on the strength of the sun yesterday and the family had been lightly toasted. How could I refuse?

Much the same on the cards again today, I would say. The sun is shining down on us once more but that lively easterly is still hanging in there. How could I be so ordinary about it? It is a day fit to raise the spirits, as if the Chancellor had not raised them enough.

So glorious was it, that when it came time to take the bleddy hound down to the beach I risked a change into shorts and flip flops. It was like meeting an old friend when my bare, milky white feet touched the sand and I revelled in the splendour of it all. Revelling is not 'zackly the adjective I would use to describe the first dip of the toes into the sea this year. If my toes could have recoiled any further they would have made a nice little frill around my knees. The bleddy hound did not seem to mind at all and insisted that I threw the ball several times into the azure flood. It did not look that busy from up at the shop, but my sitting stone was occupied as were several other suitable spots in the lee of the wind. I had to make do with a slightly squat rock that was not the most comfortable while I warmed my legs in the sunshine.

As you might expect we are faced with questions from visitors everyday and even more so now that we are listed as being a Visitor Information Contact Point. Most of the questions are fairly straightforward and easily answered, but every now and again we get a bit of a teaser that takes some digging to come up with the goods.

Today I had an enquiry over the telephone from a gentleman on behalf of a lady friend in Canada. She wants to attend the memorial service for *HMS Penzance* that she heard was happening this year. *HMS Penzance* was lost in 1940 while performing a lone escort to a convoy and was sunk, with much loss of life, by a U-boat southwest of Iceland. Of the 18 men that survived seven were picked up by the convoy vessel, *Blairmore*. That too was sunk by the same U-boat later the same night. The rescued naval seamen survived.

The gentleman who made the enquiry lost his father, a Petty Officer, that night.

I had to confess I knew nothing of it, but agreed to do some research and telephone our man back if I found anything. It took a little grappling with search engine strings to find a lead, but I found a reference to the Penlee House and Park Committee meeting minutes that spoke of a memorial plaque being prepared. It is too large to fit in the Memorial Garden and will have to be sited in the Park. The Town Council will be making the arrangements for the service and are trying to coordinate with the current HMS Penzance being in port. I telephoned Penlee House and a very helpful lady there gave me the number of the Town Council, which I duly passed on to our gentleman enquirer.

Now, I pride myself on picking up on odd snippets of news and gossip to the point that not much passes me by. I have found it a necessary art, particularly since posting The Diary every day – you did not think I made it all up did you? Well, not all of it. No, the thing that slightly knocked me askance was how on earth did a little old lady sitting in Canada pick up on an event in Penzance that has not even been decided upon yet? When she comes over for the service I am going to have to nick her 'goings on' radar; it must be a very good one.

March 26ᵗʰ – Monday

Our bin men made their last appearance today; the council has chosen a new supplier to take over from next week. The rules have changed a bit too. All household rubbish will need to be placed in bags for collection, and although the wheelie bins can still be used, all its contents must be in bags. This gives those of us with bins along the road something of a problem, as they are constantly being used by passers by for general litter. I have tied down the lid on ours until I can find a suitable and more convenient solution. I also tied down the lid of the bin used by the holiday let next door that brought the current residents out to query how they might use the bin during their stay. A very good question so I am going to have to dream up an easily removable lock before they need to use it next.

It will be a major problem, I suspect, for all the holiday lets in Cornwall. While all residents have been issued with instructions it is unlikely that the visitors will be as clued in or as fastidious if they are only here for a week. It may be even more of an issue in years to come when the wheelie bins die a natural death and the wheels fall off; unprotected bin bags do not last long down here under the ever watchful gaze of the gulls and even the occasional fox.

This is not the worst inconvenience we can expect this season. The Harbour toilets are still shut and as far as I can tell may well remain so. Thankfully, we have some very clear white lines on the roads that we can admire to keep our minds off our bladders. In this austere age we should be grateful for small mercies.

Then, in the warm sunshine, we had a little Lifeboat launch in a training sort of way. It was all rather lovely with the setting sun glinting off the shiny bits of the boat as it rattled down the slipway. It was very expertly put back on the short slip in a stiff easterly and a bigish swell with OG at the helm. Of course, the very excellent Shore Crew kept up their end and the boat was back and refuelled for action in no time.

Although it was still light when we recovered the boat the first bright stars were beginning to shine through. Up in the west was a bright crescent moon, framed by Venus and Jupiter. It is probably a very clear astrological message; do not come to Sennen with a full bladder, perhaps.

March 27ᵗʰ - Tuesday

I am grateful to R&B and I am sure Rhianna is too, although for slightly different reasons. The R&B I refer to have advised me, apropos of the bin rules changing down here, not all holiday lets will be affected as I suggested yesterday. Only those available for less than 140 days in a year will have to watch their bins. Those offering accommodation for longer are classed as businesses and, like us, must have a commercial bin for which you shell out your hard earned shekels. The rules with these are much more relaxed and, should you so want, you could put bits of your granny in and the collectors will not complain, though your granddad might have something to say about it.

As you may remember I had to go to the trade show in Exeter by myself this year due the bleddy hound having been in a bit of a ruck and getting hurt. This week all those key buying decisions that I made on my own are coming home to roost. The first major consignment arrived today.

One of my key buying decisions involved bouncing bug-eyed worms, 72 of them to be precise, which the Missus came upon first as she opened the boxes. She threw one on the floor where it landed with a splat.

Missus: "Why did you buy these? They don't bounce."

Me: "They are highly tactile. Kids will love 'em."

Missus: "But they don't bounce."

Me: "They are highly tactile and come in vibrant colours. Kids will love 'em."

Missus: "But they don't bounce."

Me: "They are highly tactile, come in vibrant colours and have gawky big bug eyes. Kids will love 'em."

Missus: "But they don't BOUNCE!"

Me: "I'm taking the bleddy hound down the beach while you price them up, luvver. Kids will love 'em."

I went and got the dog ball thrower and latched up the bleddy hound to her lead. On the way out I eyed up our commercial bin that you can put anything in. I was not thinking bouncy bug-eyed worms either. We have another big delivery tomorrow and I am taking that straight up to Shrew House and nowhere near the shop or the Missus.

Me and herself had a whale of a time down on the beach. It is much easier for her to swim down in the harbour as well, with less chance of her being swept out to sea, (note to self: go down the big beach more often). I obviously did not spend as much time down there as she would have liked as we had the normal stroppy game of her dropping the ball at the top of the slip so it ran down to the beach again when she was supposed to be coming home.

The Missus must have been busy with customers as, thankfully, few of the other boxes from the delivery had been opened when I got back. I heard a sidelong comment about my magnetic monkeys, but at least they were clinging on to something ferrous. I am going to have to shift the non-clacking clacker balls and the finger flyers that do not have a finger hole before she gets up tomorrow else I fear she will be mightily disappointed with me - again.

On the bright side I came second at cards again tonight. Perhaps I should consider a career in gambling instead.

March 29ᵗʰ - Thursday

Hardly a breath of wind first thing, just the sound of panting as I hefted in our newspapers and magazines this morning, courtesy of the wonderful Laurel and Hardy Newspaper

Company. They have promised me faithfully to halt their onslaught of unwanted titles, but still they come. There were three copies of *Missionary Today* which I nearly put on the top shelf until I saw it was to do with religion in Africa.

We still do not open early enough for some hardy folk, obviously. I was nearly bowled over this morning as some chap thrust the door open with me behind it and asked if we were open for newspaper sales. I suggested he come back after eight thirty when the doors would be open, the blinds raised and the sign on the door would be turned to show 'open' in a subtle display of openness.

Still, it is difficult to be irked on an 'ansum day such as today. Although the breeze started up a bit from the north later on it was still warm and delicious all round. I let the Missus go and enjoy it down on the beach in the afternoon while I took care of a little coach party down from Suffolk. They were a cheery bunch and unafraid to part with a few shillings for a memento or two.

The good people of St Dennis are none too cheery today. They clubbed together to force a judicial review of the The much maligned council's plans to build an incinerator on their doorstep and won. Unfortunately, the council took a dim view of a bunch of feisty Cornishmen employing a democratic process to defeat them, and asked the Minister for the Environment to lodge an appeal. Against all expectation, and with the odds clearly stacked against them, the Government had the decision not to build the plant overturned today. Don't you just love living in a democratic country?

The fight is not over yet, as the feisty Cornishmen have found a bit of very rare grizzlewort on the building site. No one mentioned this before, and rumour has it they borrowed it from the Friends of Penzance Harbour after they used it to upturn the "Option A" plans to transform the *Scillonian* dock. I have a few more grizzleworts I am cultivating on rocks in our roof garden if any campaign group is interested. I sure we can come to some mutually agreeable arrangement. That's localism for you, Cornish style.

We got about as local as you can get for this evening's Lifeboat exercise and launched the little boat out from the Harbour beach. When we first got it, our little Tooltrak tractor was very exciting and new and everyone wanted to drive it. It has slipped down a peg or two in the exciting stakes now that the new tractor launch lifeboat beast has been announced. It has been built by Supacat, the West Country based specialist vehicle manufacturer, and is something to be held in awe. It ranks very highly on the, 'I want one of those', lists every boy has in the back of his mind. I will have to transfer to St Ives if I want a go on it but I suspect the queue might be very long.

We consoled ourselves down at the OS by playing a blinder on the quiz tonight. If we win every quiz from now until the end of time we still could not afford to buy one of the new fangled launchers. What a disappointment. Now, perhaps if I went to the Court of Appeal ...

March 30ᵗʰ – Friday

What with our early summer fast disappearing, and our expected visitors a bit nervous about making a journey they may not have the fuel to get back from, I thought I might be stuck for a subject or two today. How wrong I was.

Let us start with a visit from a chap from The much maligned council. We might ordinarily be a mite suspicious of visits by officialdom, but were rather surprised when he asked if this is The Old Boathouse Visitor Contact Point. When we cautiously admitted that we were, he asked if we would like a box of bus route guides. I select my words carefully here because these were indeed bus guides and not timetables. They show every route in the county, including the endangered species where funding is thinner than the paper on which the guide is printed. It is a very pretty map, with the more frequently traversed routes in different colours to the ones where you are more likely to die of old age than be run over by a bus. While pretty, without the necessary timetable the guide is about as useful as a closed toilet in a beach car park at the height of August.

Look, I have reworked this part more than a dozen times and there is no getting around saying that The much maligned council has made a botch of it. Last year they took on producing a combined bus timetable for Cornwall that was so late it never materialised. Apparently, this year, to get the timetable out early they will produce it before one of the bus company's has released their summer schedule. Are they insane? What is worse is they are using my money to prove it.

So, not content with disappointing our visitors with closed toilets, it seems our venerable Council want to scupper bus use as well. If I were a sceptical sort of chap, I might be convinced that our Council were hell bent on nipping our burgeoning tourism industry in the bud before it has time to bloom.

To add to this timetable misery, because the council has offered to produce timetables, the bus operators, quite reasonably, have not bothered to produce their own, or they did not last year.

It is not just the Council frightening off visitors. One of our frequent shoppers came in with a sorry tale late this afternoon. They have been enjoying the recent good weather with their young Dalmatian up in the valley this week. Today, their faithful hound was chasing a ball into the bushes when she was nipped on the nose by an adder. It is a risk in certain areas, but not normally until much later in the year. Happily to say that the dog made a full recovery after a visit to the vet, but a salient warning to all visiting dogs to beware.

So, with all that nastiness out of the way, it was time to shut up shop and to be whisked into town. Yes, it is rare for me to head out on a Friday at all, let alone to the bright lights of PZ town centre. Tonight is special in that a rather good blues-rock guitarist is performing at the Acorn Arts Centre; at least that is what I was told.

Gosh, where do I start? He was an extremely capable guitarist, that's for sure; a man for whom sex, drugs and rock and roll over the long years have taken their toll, though I doubt that the former had much to do with it as he had a face more suitable for listening to than looking at.

We all love a bit of fancy guitar, but to suffer two or three solos per song, with the chap a prime candidate for top place in a gurning contest, was a bit much. As the evening wore on the intros and the outros were becoming longer than the songs themselves and the caterwauling descended into one long horrible noise.

Towards the end he ventured into Hendrix country and I yelled to one of my companions that if he started playing with his teeth I would feel it necessary to leave. My witty friend gave the repost, "especially if he takes them out first", at which point I nearly spilled my beer.

There was, at least, a little brightness from the evening, which was a certain perverse pleasure from supping my ale in an old Methodist chapel.

March 31ˢᵗ - Saturday

The Laurel and Hardy Newspaper Company excelled themselves this morning. I was not expecting any magazines today, but there was a tote box - a plastic box used for the purpose - sitting on my newspaper bin first thing. With excitement, and just a little trepidation, I pulled open the flaps to see what ludicrous title they had deigned to send us this time. Oh joy; they had supplied five copies of the *A – Z Devon Road Map* and five copies of the *A – Z Devon and Cornwall Roadmap*. Chief amongst these goodies, and something I shall treasure forever, — five copies of the *A – Z Torbay Street Map*.

On an even brighter note our new secret weapon arrived yesterday in the form of Grumpies. I hinted that these were coming several weeks ago after we visited the annual food and catering show at *The Royal Cornwall Showground*. Then I told you that I could not reveal the detail as they would be in the shops down the street before you could say pasty tax.

Grumpies is not, as you may wish to believe, a collective name for West Cornwall shopkeepers, but a Cornish company producing a rather delicious set of pies. There are attractive recipes for steak and ale, chicken, gammon and leek and even a vegetarian option of blue cheese, mushroom and walnut in a tangy lemon and béchamel sauce. We are selling these excellent delicacies either hot or, if you prefer, cold in a little box and we expect to be able to retire on the proceeds by the end of the year. At least that is what the salesman told us.

I would not say they were flying out, but we sold a fair few. I think it was more to do with the chill north wind and a lack of potential buyers wandering around than a question over the attractiveness of the pies. We can hold testament to the greatness of these delights as we sampled, for quality purposes you understand, a steak and ale and a blue cheese and walnut for breakfast.

It was certainly a bit chilly standing at the bottom of the short slip this morning. The Lifeboat went out to play with the helicopter from Culdrose and did a stunning little display out in the bay. We were a bit short shore side because one of our number went out on the boat as they were even shorter boat side, and another went to bail out a flooded holiday let – hopefully not yours, dear reader. Recovery was a bit earlier than we had planned, but the very excellent Shore Crew were, as ever, excellent and ready for all eventualities especially the breakfast afterwards, which I copped out on as I had already stuffed myself with pie.

It is the first of our semi-late closing days. Thankfully The Cove livened up in the afternoon as the influx for this week's holiday started to appear. It was a mix of familiar and new faces, as is usual, and the comforting warmth of a new season settled upon us. It is difficult to express that feeling, but is something like a security blanket, I suppose. Naturally, I no longer have a security blanket, but if you see me at the F&L nursing a pint you may get the general idea.

April 1st – Sunday

Oh, I love it. We have a clear blue sky and, in the morning, a chill easterly breeze. As the day progressed it warmed up some in that sunshine and however you looked upon the day it was bleddy 'ansum.

To cap it all the Harbour toilets have been opened. Save your hoorahs though, if there is no serious negotiation on takeover taking place by April 13th they will close for good on April 16th. Out of seven conveniences in the nearest three parishes only two will remain open for the rest of the year. The much maligned Cornwall Councillor responsible for this area is currently working hard to try and find solutions for each parish, but the issues are detailed and complex and may result in different management for each one. Hardly a recipe for success, I feel. The only sensible solution would be for a body to be formed that would take on responsibility for running public facilities in each district. I know, we could call it a District Council.

It is a memory dripping with irony that this council spent millions of our pounds centralising services under a unitary authority for efficiency and to save money. Many of us said at the time it was waste of time and money. So I urge you to forgive my irresistible descent into sarcasm. It is hard to fathom this council's desire to pass many of its services back down to local level and the parishes, most of which do not have the resources or the skills to manage them.

But let us, sorry me, stop all this gloomy talk. It is a bright sunny day out there and the good folk in Sennen Cove are enjoying every minute of it. The buckets and spades have been flying off the shelves and small children can be seen churning out sandcastles like a Chinese worker's co-operative. Even the bleddy hound is happy, now that her young walker is back down here on her hols.

The Missus went off and deserted me late in the afternoon. It is the birthday of a little chap over at Porthleven who is in dire need of his birthday presents. This left me in charge of tea time for me and the bleddy hound. I found some gurnard in the freezer that I will fry up with a bit of homity pie and a small beer to wash it down with; heaven knows what I shall have.

It reminds me that we have some fish orders to satisfy; the first of the new season. It will give me the chance to practice my certified filleting skills that have sat dormant through the winter. I shall over order just in case and hope that I will still have all my fingers at the end of it. At least I know they will not bite me.

April 2nd - Monday

Whatever happened to today? Everything seems to have gone at a breakneck pace and suddenly, there I was looking up at the clock pointing at five o'clock, smelling slightly of fish and wondering where the day went.

The mornings are a bit more involved now that we are baking baguettes and bread, the newspapers are greater in number, (including Glasgow's *Daily Record* this morning!), and there is gallons more milk to stow away. Though our happy holiday makers were slow to appear first thing this morning, they made up for it a bit later, which took care of most of the first half of the day.

Our current relief Lifeboat is going away for a bit of a service at Plymouth today. It is being replaced by a relief, relief Lifeboat that has been doing some relief at Padstow for the past week. Our venerable coxswain took a few hearty crew up there this morning to bring the relief boat back. The plan was to drop our relief Lifeboat down the long slip and tie her off with a strop, recover the new relief Lifeboat into the boathouse then, when the crew had swapped from the new relief Lifeboat to our current relief Lifeboat, launch it on its way to Plymouth. Naturally, the very excellent Shore Crew were on hand to ensure that the new relief Lifeboat was recovered and our existing relief Lifeboat was launched without a hitch, which it was. What a relief.

That put a dent in the afternoon and then the fish arrived. The filleting went amazingly well and I actually remembered the things that I had been taught some four months earlier. This was a good result, especially for the family that had ordered the fish in the first place. What took an inordinate amount of time was scaling the fish before I filleted it. Well, not exactly the scaling process itself, but the cleaning up afterwards.

Let me explain. To scale a fish you first have to hold it still, which is like trying to hold a wet, round bar of soap between your knees while going up a flight of stairs. Once this has been mastered, the act is to drag a sharp knife blade in a sweeping motion from the tail in the direction of the head of the fish at such an angle that it catches the scales without puncturing the skin. Some scaly fish are easier to scale than others but all, without exception, have scales that ping off in multiple directions at something close to the speed of sound.

The very first time I scaled a fish there were scales on the splash back behind the taps, on the walls and windows each side of the sink and apparently one stuck to the ceiling. I know this, not because I found them while I was cleaning up afterwards, but because the Missus found them after I said I had cleaned up afterwards. Apparently there is one thing worse than cleaning up wet scales stuck to the walls and windows, and that is the Missus explaining to me how hard it is to clean up dry scales that I had missed on the walls and windows.

Bearing this episode in mind, I was fastidious about the post-scale clean up operation. While the filleting of the three fish took no more than ten minutes, the whole operation took the best part of an hour. I would wager my skin that she finds a scale that I missed.

I would also wager that I am asleep before my head hits the pillow tonight and at the rate this day has gone that will be in two minutes.

April 3ʳᵈ - Tuesday

One bit of excellent news today is that I seem to have sold my boat. I have put this out of mind for the last twelve months or so, as it was a constant irritation. I have had to crave favours to store both the boat and the engine and now it seems that I am free. Of course, it could have happened in a more convenient week, but the fact that it happened at all is a blessing.

When I went to pull the boat out of its condemned garage last week and re-inflate it a bit I managed to break the valve adaptor on the pump. Naturally, this is not just any adaptor that can be purchased from any old hardware store; it is a special fitting that is available only from a single Nepalese chandler whose shop is situated on the southern slopes of Mount Kangchenjunga and is open on the first Wednesday of each month, (there is not a great call for chandlers in Nepal). I called, at great expense, but his answerphone message said that he is off to visit sick relatives so he will not be opening tomorrow. Good job I did not buy the tickets first.

I also need to get the engine serviced before I hand it over. Fortunately I only have to go to Penzance for that, but it does mean abandoning the shop while I get the engine out of the store and hump it over there. It is a busy time of the year for marine engineers, so I hope that the one I have in mind has a free spot in his schedule.

It may not be quite so bad, as the Missus abandoned me this afternoon to take the bleddy hound to the dog doctor. She has been limping around on three legs on and off over the last few days, the bleddy hound, not the Missus. Apparently it is probably a pulled muscle and will heal by itself. It will heal faster if she stops running around like a mad thing, but she just will not listen.

Our new refuse collection happened today. I got stuck behind them when I delivered the boat to its new owner this morning, as they swept through The Cove. Contrary to the rumours that they would not be emptying from our wheelie bins, their smart new lorry was more than capable of doing so and was demonstrating this as they went. One of our customers spoke to the bin men who said that they had instructions to be lenient in the first few weeks.

It is a sensible policy as not all the holiday let owners, the ones with domestic bins, have been made aware of the new rules. One I spoke to was concerned that it would be difficult to advise their visitors and impossible to rely on their compliance. I would suggest some interesting times are ahead when the kid glove of leniency turns to the iron fist of intransigence.

So that is enough rubbish for now; I have a busy day tomorrow. I have heard on the grapevine that my Nepalese chandler may be thinking of opening a shop in Falmouth tomorrow. I might have to go and investigate.

April 5ᵗʰ – Thursday

Well, that is a bit better, or at least I thought it was until I got outside and froze to death; those impressive big blue skies were nothing but a big front. In fact the big front came through later on and it rained.

Fair to say it was immeasurably better than it was yesterday, despite the easterly icy blast. I ventured to put out the windbreak stand too, which had remained safely indoors during the monsoon. It soon became plain that I had been a little too enthusiastic, as I watched it try and make its way down the road. This was very quickly rectified by restocking it with windbreaks that I had the foresight to put in the back of the van a couple of days ago. I had very little concern that my cunning plan would be scuppered by a line of customers, eager to plant themselves on the beach in the shelter of the entire stock of windbreaks.

Despite our fraught weather there was a fair crowd milling about, no doubt running off the onset of cabin fever from yesterday. I would like to make clear, that of the many purchases over the last few days, bouncing bug-eyed worms have been flying off the shelves. Oh, all right, I sold one. No sign of life on the magnetic monkey front, though.

You are long suffering, dear reader. Just when you thought yourselves lucky that the long repetitive beach walk passages were at an end, along comes the long repetitive passages about the weather and how the shop is performing. I am sorry, once was the time I could rely on a customer to do something funny and I could hold them up to ridicule in this journal to make you all laugh. Perhaps they would bring their errant children in so that I might lambast them to the edge of libel. Sadly those good old days are gone.

You see word seems to have got around that to misbehave or act in some way out of the ordinary in the shop is to court public derision and humiliation at the hands of your Diarist. I have never seen such a lot of well behaved, more ordinary people in my life than those that now frequent the shop.

It was only last week that a lady threatened me, (quite politely, I must add), that litigation of premier league footballer proportions would ensue should I put into print that she could not reach the sun cream due to her diminutive stature and had to crave assistance. Oh, heck, I mentioned it. Do not worry Doris Schlumberger, The Railway Cuttings, East Cheam, no one will know it's you.

It is probably best that I retire to the Lifeboat Station for a bit of training where I cannot possibly get into any trouble. I salted myself away and cleaned the bell then hid in the workshop and repaired a drysuit while the others launched the little boat. The Inshore Crew were clearly practicing navigation, because they were late getting back. I stood back and watched while they put the boat away.

Having managed to survive training without upsetting anyone or doing anything controversial we headed off to the OS for a pretty much packed quiz night. By staying off the beer, I managed to stay out of trouble there as well. The temperance was not exactly deliberate; I spent so long waiting to be served I gave up. The enforced sobriety did nothing for our score line, although we did quite well, mid field I would say, so it is not a strategy I will be following in future.

Nice to see that the wind has dampened down. It could be a good day tomorrow and I shall need my faculties about me.

April 6ᵗʰ – Friday

They must have come in under cover of darkness; coaches, buses and some, I would say, dropped in by parachute. There definitely were not that many people around yesterday, but when we opened the shop doors this morning we were inundated. I half expected a chorus of 'surprise' it was all so sudden.

It was such an influx that we were very much caught unawares. Pasties were all gone by early lunchtime and our Grumpies took a bit of a battering. The Laurel and Hardy Newspaper Company had seen fit to reduce most of our newspapers for this weekend too, bless them, just to add to our wavering stock.

You can tell it is a sunny day at the start of the season when the Lifeboat pagers go off. You could also pretty much tell what it was too when they went off midway through a rising spring tide. Three or four people were cut off on rocks at Green Bay, over by Porthcurno. One had to be airlifted to Treliske, while the others were brought back to The Cove on the Lifeboat.

The boat launched from inside the boathouse, as it will for urgent responses. It is not a pleasant experience if you are standing in the boathouse at the time, as you are very quickly enveloped in a thick cloud of noxious exhaust fumes. I did not see much of the boat as it disappeared down the slipway as my stinging eyes were streaming and my throat clogged to the extent that it was a tad difficult to communicate to the Coxswain that I had made the boat 'live' by pulling out the retaining pin on the sliphook.

Never mind, the very excellent Shore Crew did a very excellent job of changing slipways for recovery, as the tide passed the point where the boat could safely be recovered on the long slip. We like doing this, as it keeps us fit and healthy and is so much more rigorous than the pilates class we all attend, oh and zumba on Wednesdays. However, we dug in our heels when Falmouth Coastguard called to tell us that the boat had requested a long slip recovery.

We closed ten minutes early today, as it seemed requisite that we attend the Parish Council monthly meeting. On the agenda tonight was a discussion on the future of the Harbour toilets. I had the opportunity to have my say at the start of the meeting, which I had not expected and, as a result, was wholly inadequate. The council members debated, at some length, how the toilets might be run, short of funding. It seems that the Beach car park toilets will only be maintained until the end of the year, after which Sennen Cove could be deprived of these essential services altogether.

I am left speechless that we appear to be in full acceptance that nothing can be done to overturn the much maligned Council's decision to close fifty percent of the toilets in the county. There is bountiful evidence that fifty percent saving can be made through efficiency, but no one in the council seems to be bothered to investigate this route. It is sheer laziness to simply ditch the problem on the already hard pressed tax payer and, in our case, on the few people that seem to give a damn about The Cove as a destination worth visiting.

If I sound incensed it is because I am; it is hopefully the last time I will need to swear on these pages too. It is enough to make your teeth itch and to repair to the OS to see the far famed *Bucket Boys* in action. It is a long while since the OS has been packed to the seams with revellers, many of whom were locals not seen in the place for some time. MB would be fair rocking in his grave, I am sure. If the bean counters at St Awful would wake up and smell the coffee, the OS could once again be a force to be reckoned with.

Ten shillings difference in the beer price will still see me drawn to the top of the hill though.

April 7ᵗʰ - Saturday

I woke this morning with my loins already girded against the strong possibilities that we would be run off our feet again today. I was right to do so, as we were.

We had made a detour via Shrew House to collect some more buckets and spades on our way home last night. We had left the stock in the van because it would have been far too easy to clear it last night with no interruptions. Why not, we reasoned, add a little spice to our lives and unpack, price and put the stock out with customers crowded around the doorway and the till demanding our attention? Darn, it feels good to live on that diet of danger with the cool breeze blowing in your hair, well, the Missus's hair, anyway.

The Missus had a bit of a Che Guevara moment last night after the Parish Council meeting and decided to raise a petition against the closure of the toilets here in The Cove. We cannot imagine that the petition will sway anyone's decision, but it will hopefully demonstrate the weight of public opinion. There is an online petition already in place, but apparently it is only open to people living in Cornwall. Since ninety percent of the users of the toilets will be visitors, this petition will give a somewhat stilted view.

You can tell it is a part way decent day at the start of the season when the Lifeboat pagers go off. You could also pretty much tell what it was too when they went off midway through a rising spring tide. Five people were cut off on rocks at Green Bay, over by Porthcurno. The Culdrose helicopter took off three and the Lifeboat the other two alongside members of the Coastguard.

As a small aside, I spoke with my inside man on the Coastguard Rescue team in the evening. He had waded through a robust surf to bring assistance. While clinging to the cliff fifteen feet up, a big set came in and took away a rather expensive pair of prescription sunglasses. If you happen to find them while you are being cut off by the tide down there he would be most appreciative if you could pick them up for him.

Sorry, I digress, where was I? Ah, yes, the boat launched from inside the boathouse as it will for urgent responses. It is not a pleasant experience if you are standing in the boathouse at the time, as you are very quickly enveloped in a thick cloud of noxious exhaust fumes. I did not see much of the boat as it disappeared down the slipway as I had to run up to the Inshore Boathouse to launch that.

Never mind, the very excellent Shore Crew did a very excellent job of changing slipways for recovery, as the tide passed the point where the boat could safely be recovered on the long slip. We like doing this as it keeps us fit and healthy, which is why we do it two days in a row.

Sorry, did that sound ever so familiar, almost like déjà vu? It did to us too, except an hour later than yesterday, as you would expect with the mid tide an hour later today. It was a little more brisk at the bottom of the slip too with several feet of rise and fall. Still, we are a very excellent Shore Crew and it did help a time pressed Diarist to fill an otherwise thin page with a bit of cut and paste.

And what do very excellent Shore Crew do on a Saturday night to wash away trials of the day? Oh, dear reader, you know me so well. Yes, we (some of us, well, just me really) repair to the F&L where the *Three Minute Warning* were playing tonight. It is a band that has had its share of ups and downs over the years, but tonight was definitely an up. Amongst the normal fare we had a surprise rendition of the Adele hit Rolling InThe Deep and, at least, we did not have wall to wall guitar solos. Neither did Guy have a fan strategically placed to blow his hair around. He did not even have to remove his teeth to play any power chords.

Given that we had cloud all day it was, for once, rather galling to walk home under a star lit sky with the best of a full moon sitting on the southern horizon.

April 8th - Sunday

The cavalry charge of visitors continues, it seems, even though the weather was not that inspiring. All pasties are gone, the Grumpies are doing very well and our bread order was spot on. What a hungry lot we have here. Thirsty too, as our drinks fridge is nearly empty and our next order not due until Tuesday.

The toilet petition has reached over two hundred willing signatures and one or two under duress. There is not one person who has not felt that the closing of toilets in the county is completely ludicrous. The thing is, if we all know it is stupid, how come the council do not?

The buses too have been affected by the cuts. With the new timetables that crept in at the beginning of April we noticed that the two late buses that have been running all through our quiet winter have now been discontinued. The last bus leaving Sennen Cove is now at ten minutes to seven or half past six on a Sunday. If you are coming here from Penzance you had better not miss the quarter to six bus, it is the last one. It is a long journey, that last one, taking in the back roads around Lamorna and St Buryan. We recommend you bring a large Thermos flask with you. Not so much that you might have refreshment on the journey, but more that you have a capacious container at the end of it, as there will be no facilities here for your convenience when you arrive.

On the subject of empty vessels, our inside man in the Coastguard Rescue Team said that he was talking to a visitor on Porthcurno beach yesterday. She lamented that no one had thought to put up a sign warning people that the tide was coming in. I think she has a point; we could put the sign up next to the ones that warn that sand can get between your toes and that the water is wet.

As it happens the sign may not be necessary. It would appear that the good visitors to Porthcurno have learnt that the tide comes in and can cut you off in Green Bay; there was no Lifeboat shout today. We did see Rescue 193 disappear off in the direction of Land's End at one point today, but that could well have just been an exercise, as if they needed the practice. It left a big and gaping hole in my afternoon, as it did in my Diary entry allowing me no opportunity to *copy* and paste, rather than *cut* and paste, as I have been corrected by an eagle eyed reader, from yesterday, to fill the acreage of space.

We shall retire to bed early tonight, as I think we will have a tough day tomorrow counting the rain drops hitting the shop window.

April 9th – Monday

Well, that put a damper on things, quite literally in fact. Mind, while I had been led to expect something of quite biblical proportions what we got was some light rain in the morning, a long period of damp and windiness, then some more rain late in the afternoon. It was much worse at the top when I went up to Shew House for a visit. My big rock that I use to keep the door open was as much use as closed public toilet.

Speaking of which the council cleaners clearly took umbrage at the signage we had erected about the petition, as it was missing this morning. I am waiting on the arrival of some official henchman to work me over a bit and issue a summons for criminal damage to their loos. I will probably have to wait until tomorrow now, as I understand they have stopped paying the council heavies on public holidays as part of their cut backs.

Fortunately it was today in 1747 that the last beheading took place, else I would be a little more concerned.

With all this newfound community crusading I have been ignoring my administrative duties on the invoice front. I now have a nice big pile that sits on my desk and fills me with guilt every time I go near it. I took the bit between my teeth this afternoon, as begger all was happening in the shop, and made a valiant effort to record and file them all. It was while doing this I realised the other reason, apart from sheer laziness, I had left them so long. There are quite a few of them that have not yet been paid.

There was a film many years ago, popular at the time, called the *Wages of Fear* with Yves Montand and Peter Van Eyck, I am sure your parents will recall it, dear reader, for you will be far too young; my grandparents reminded me. The Goons did a parody, of sorts, called *Fear of Wages*. I would have my own slant on this classic and call it *Fear of Payments*. You see, that pile of unpaid invoices seems to draw my eye, even when fully immersed in something as, ahem, pleasurable as penning this daily Diary. It is a symbol of terror every bit as significant as the guillotine was to the French aristocracy, or finding you are holding an empty glass when the time bell rings.

You should be very proud of me, dear reader. I faced my fears tonight after the shop shut and tackled that wicked pile of unpaid invoices. It took a blinding force of heroism, but that unseemly pile is now stacked neatly in my pending file, just under the waste bin. I am sure I shall be spurred on to action when the red ones arrive and even more animated if they arrive with a red faced bailiff attached to them. Ah, the tangled web of running a business.

I note that the heavy lumps of rain we were promised this evening never materialised. I hope they are not wrong about the better than expected weather tomorrow. We could do with a few customers; it would be rather nice to have something to pay those naughty invoices with.

April 10ᵗʰ - Tuesday

There is some advantage to not getting out much. As you may remember the Missus took going out to the extreme and enjoyed some time in Florida and in the Caribbean. I know, not only because she told me, but also when I started seeing the credit card bills rolling in. It was when they continued to roll in on last month's statement I started to be a bit concerned. Either the Missus was running out to Florida every now and then, without me knowing or someone else was charging our card.

Assuming the latter, I telephoned the card company to cancel the card and to try and recover the thirty dollars illicitly siphoned from my account. The stolen card service I called was very efficient, answering quickly and stopping the card without issue. I asked the lady about recovering the funds and she told me that I would need to speak with someone in the contested payments department and she duly put me through.

I like a few bars of Beethoven, which is fortunate, as that is all the on hold tune gave me. It gave it to me again, after a very pleasant recorded voice told me that my custom was of paramount importance to them and that they deeply appreciated the evidently superior level of patience I was exhibiting. These platitudes were wearing a bit thin twenty minutes later, and my enjoyment of the few bars of Beethoven was being sorely tested. It struck me that by waiting much longer the cost of the telephone call would soon exceed the money I was trying to recover. I resolved to write instead, and soon, at least before the cost of the stamp gave me the same problem.

I manned the shop counter today while the Missus dealt with the first large cash and carry order. This meant that I had full exposure to the wealth and variety of our Eastertide customers. One variety we have not yet seen many of is our foreign visitors, though it is early in the season. However I was rather pleased to welcome a family from Finland, our very first from that neck of the woods. I knew they were Finnish because we had the discussion whether Finland was, for postage stamp purposes, in Europe. It is, by the way. I expect you were thinking that I was going to make some tasteless joke about Finland or some pun on the word Finnish. Well, sorry to disappoint but I am sure you know I am high above such cheap humour.

We had a lady in late this evening enquiring about what vegetables we might have. As we stood by the fresh produce refrigerator she asked me if there were any leeks in there. I told her that I hoped not, as we had not long had the chiller serviced;

and that, dear reader, is not cheap humour, that joke cost me ten shillings on jokes online dot com.

I think I should leave you with that. It can only go down hill from here.

April 11ᵗʰ - Wednesday

As the storm clouds rolled away this morning and the clear blue skies opened out you could almost feel in your boots it was going to be a good day. But that was until Laurence Reed of Radio Pasty called.

I sent him an email yesterday to try and get some air time on the plight of our sore threatened toilets. He telephoned this morning to ask if I would say a few words on his lunchtime programme, to which I rather nervously agreed. Little did I know that I would be head to head with the head honcho of toilet services in the council. I do not think that the much maligned council is about to roll over any time soon, but at least the issue reached a wider audience.

The Missus did her bit today by camping out by the toilets in the car park and button-holing passers by for their signature. A couple of people coming from that direction complained that there was a chugger in the car park, (it is a street term, dear reader, chugger, that is, not car park; a combination of the words charity and mugger and relates to those people on busy street corners signing innocent people up for regular payments to charities they have never heard of), and how disgusting it was that it should be allowed down here. I have to agree with them, the Missus has been mugging me for years.

The Missus never reads The Diary; she says she has to listen to it all day. So what is the only bit she reads today? I shall sleep on my un-thick ear tonight.

Sorry, I digress. Where was I? Ah, yes. Despite all this excitement and the good weather it was distinctly quieter today. Had the salesman that turned up this afternoon only arrived a couple of weeks earlier we would have been in clover. Quite why being in clover is a good thing I do not know; it bears some investigation, I am sure. Never mind, our wandering seller is the agent for our thimble man, whose thimbles we ran out of some weeks ago, and whose loss we have lamented since. Until he arrived I could not for the life of me remember who had sold them to us. They are a best seller, certainly amongst the visitors of a certain age group, whose coaches tend to arrive early and late season. Had we a stock of them then, I am sure we would have been run off our feet.

My earlier joust with The much maligned council must have turned what little of my brains I have left into jelly. While the Missus plied her signature gaining skills elsewhere I stood my turn behind the counter. It was half way through the afternoon when a customer that I had served earlier returned. He said that he was certain that I had previously under-charged him. It is not the done thing to argue with a customer unless, of course, he accuses us of over-charging him.

I am appalled. My dubious honour is now in tatters and my miserable reputation trodden in the dirt. On the basis that I do not have a sword to fall on I shall don my hair shirt and beat myself with birch twigs until the feeling goes away. I will doubtless feel better after I have kicked a few little puppies and stolen the sweets off some passing children, or possibly the other way around.

April 12ᵗʰ – Thursday

One little unexpected shower was all we had today to mar an otherwise pretty decent day. Business was steady, pasty orders met sales and we tipped over 500 signatures on the toilet petition. In fact, when our councillor came to collect them, we were able to hand over 534. He suggested that we continue to collect signatures, as the battle was not yet over.

April 13ᵗʰ – Friday

I started the day gazing at the pretty pictures of sunshine and cloud on my computer screen courtesy of our friends at the Met Office, while outside the rain hacked down in heavy lumps. I had fortuitously awoken early and managed to take the bleddy hound round the block before the showers got into gear.

What got me out of bed so early was a nagging thought that we had a crab order that I had forgotten to call in. You see last year our crab fisherman preferred to be called first thing, while he was out in the wild blue yonder. He has since retired and our new fisherman prefers to be called in the evenings. This is going to take some getting used to, so if you are ordering crab I would welcome the reminder of when I should be calling it in. It will save me waking in the early hours with the screaming ad-dabs.

We were unsurprisingly quiet in the morning due to the rain and added to that we had the exodus of visitors on their way home. We picked up later in the day as the sun came out, but I would say that Easter is definitely over.

This Diary writing lark certainly has its complications. It is the third April 13th I have written about, so the 'this day in history' fall-back option is no longer a safe bet. My dimming memory must now try and recall previous entries over two years ago, when my normal span of recollection struggles with what happened yesterday, or remembering to call in a crab order placed earlier the same day. Perhaps it will be my salvation all this exercising of the grey matter, or perhaps it will be an indicator that I should cease these inane ramblings.

I am sure, though, that I have not mentioned that Mr John Dryden was today made our first poet laureate in 1668, although I might have done, I did not check. Interestingly another source has him being appointed in 1667, but either way he did not last long in post after falling out of favour at court. He would not have got even that far today and more probably would have found himself at another form of her majesty's pleasure after penning a verse about a fifteen year old girl losing her virginity.

However I have found a somewhat less controversial verse to leave you with.

Happy the man, and happy he alone,
He who can call today his own:
He who, secure within, can say,
Tomorrow do thy worst, for I have lived today.
Be fair or foul or rain or shine
The joys I have possessed, in spite of fate, are mine.
Not Heaven itself upon the past has power,
But what has been, has been, and I have had my hour.

April 14th - Saturday

It is unlikely to have escaped your notice that one hundred years ago tonight, at 23:40 local time, the RMS Titanic hit an iceberg and sank some hours later. Of the 2,223 on board only 710 survived.

What you might not have heard, although it has been widely broadcast on Radio Pasty, is that one of the lookouts on that fateful night was a Cornishman. In his defence he was one of eight lookouts, I believe, and could have been looking the other way at the time. A rather more inescapable fact is that the chap at the helm was also a Cornishman, Robert Hichens from Newlyn. Being in a prime position to know exactly what happened, he also made it to the first lifeboat to get away.

To be fair, he was ordered to take charge of the lifeboat number six. He was subsequently accused of poor behaviour on the boat, and more seriously, causing the collision by turning the helm the wrong way. The latter nugget never came to light during his lifetime, which was probably fortunate for him, although it does seem he had a rather hard time of it. He died in 1940 on board a cargo vessel in Hong Kong.

It is probably not surprising that his behaviour on the lifeboat was somewhat less than exemplary. Let us face it, if you had just sunk the unsinkable ship I think that you too would have been a little distracted.

I do not know about references to the Titanic, as it was more like the Marie Celeste here all day. There were a few people wondering around, wrapped up against a lively westerly and a few that were not; we did a good trade in woolly hats today. We seemed to manage to avoid the rain that was reportedly falling everywhere in Penwith for most of the day. There was even the occasional burst of blue sky amongst the threatening clouds. Towards the end of the afternoon we had people arriving telling of snow in the Padstow area and several cars in accidents on 'Hamburger Hill'. It seems for the best part of the day we were very lucky.

Lucky too, that the Harbour car park toilets seem to have been given a stay of execution, at least for the short term. There are, however, complications that need to be resolved and the Council will continue to service them to allow time for these to be ironed out. Whether the petition was instrumental in this largesse we will never know, but it cannot have done any harm so a big thank you to everyone that signed up or showed their support.

Despite it being a dour day we were blessed with a minor comedy moment, when a young girl became rather attached to one of our hand-held fans she had been demonstrating. Her long flowing locks had wrapped around the propeller and were proving troublesome to unwind. We resorted to scissors to free her in the end, and although most of us thought it a jolly jape I think the young lady would have preferred if it were not at her expense. She will probably harbour dark thoughts about me into adulthood now and, no doubt, I shall be the respondent in a long legal wrangle to prove that I did not harm her psychologically through my negligence to forewarn her of such a possibility. I shall have to ask the manufacturers to place an additional warning on the label next to the one about small parts and choking, that suggests that the item is only suitable for bald people.

April 15ᵗʰ – Sunday

This story is a bit off our beaten path but, hey, it is a slow day. In the *Sunday Independent*, (Cornish version), there is a report that a football match between Gillingham FC and Swindon Town may be played without any fans being allowed in to watch it. There is some disagreement between Gillingham FC and Kent police regarding the number of officers required. I will not bore you with the details. I just thought what a jolly good idea it was. Just imagine; no crowd control issues before and after the game; no pitch invasions; referees able to go about their duties without being accused of undertaking individual acts of stimulation upon their own person; and no drunken hooliganism, unless the underworked stewards decide to have a tipple or two and get a bit feisty.

And why let football have all the advantages. Imagine the umpire's delight at Wimbledon, not having to tell an over-exuberant crowd to keep quiet; the safety at cricket matches where no distracted observer will ever again be hit in the gob by a cricket ball launched into the Gasworks End; and boat races free from interruption by slightly deranged swimmers. Best of all, although it might be a tad late now, the traffic, travel and security problems solved at a stroke by applying the idea to the Olympics.

The cost savings too would be immense. That hastily constructed bypass into Weymouth need not have been built; and neither would that daft observation tower down on the sea front. In fact all that money spent on the various stadia would probably have gone a long way to salve the national debt.

Unfortunately it is one less thing for youngsters to do with their Dads on a Saturday. You might have read in the press that the National Trust has issued a list of fifty things children should do before they are 11 and three quarters. It seems that they are concerned that children do not get out much these days. There are things such as climbing a tree; building a den; swinging on a rope swing; balancing on a fallen tree; starting fires without matches; and hardest of all, writing out risk assessments for each of these dangerous activities. Is it any wonder that the ill-educated youth of today prefer to rob sweets from corner shops and mug little old ladies? Mind you it seems that several are pretty good at the starting fires without matches, given the number of deliberate heath fires we have had here in the last month.

And talking of risky activities, the in-laws are due here tomorrow for a week. What am I talking about? I am sure it will be a pleasure. Now what football matches are on this week up country that I can actually go and see?

April 17ᵗʰ - Tuesday

I am sure that you are missing tales of walks along the beach by now, just as much as the bleddy hound is missing getting her paws sandy. She has not been out for a proper run for a several days, indeed not since our young dog walker went home, so she was due for a bit of a blast. Therefore, not to disappoint either party, you or the bleddy hound, I went down to the big beach this morning.

I had to hurry back as the Missus wanted to go shopping with the in-laws and a man was coming to stick his head in our oven. I mean that in the nicest possible way, of course. The worst outcome from sticking your head in an oven this side of Penzance is a hot pate. Even that is not guaranteed, as the electric goes off here with severe regularity. If the government ever has to impose a three day week, most folk around here would not notice.

Sorry, I digress. Where was I? Ah, yes, the man coming to look at our oven. This is the oven in the shop, by the way, that has been making the most awful noise of late when we have been warming our pasties. It is quite clearly the fan at fault, as it only makes the noise when running and I assume that a drop of oil in the right place would make all the difference.

I thought it was only garage mechanics that sucked air through their teeth when asked how much a repair will cost. Apparently oven engineers do it too, as I discovered when I asked how much the repair would cost. Naturally a drop of oil was far too simple, and a replacement of the fan was almost certainly required. Of course, there are two fans and there is little point in replacing one without doing the other, and before you know it the cost of repair is fractionally less than the cost of a new oven.

We expect a new oven in the next few days. I suppose we cannot be too disappointed as the oven we currently have was there when we arrived and has provided sterling service for well over ten years. I would not bet a hot pasty on the new one lasting that long.

It is not the only thing that has required repair of late. I might have mentioned in passing that our windbreak stand has a wonky leg. It rocks gently in the wind next to my own very 'ansum ball stand, Custer. I call it Custer because it is the last stand that I shall make after the heartless ribbing I received. I should point out to my detractors that it is still standing and does not rock at all in the wind.

The leg on the metal windbreak stand was bent when it first arrived and, thus weakened, has never been the same since. Having been kicked back into true so many times, it eventually gave up the ghost this year when I heaved it into the van to retrieve it from Shrew House. It lasted over Easter with the help of some duct tape. We are fortunate that the Lifeboat mechanic, RB, is a whiz with a welding machine and last night I dragged the item up to his workshop where he worked his magic on it. It is in better shape now than it was when we bought it, as he also sprayed it with some anti-rust paint.

April 18th - Wednesday

A blustery day Pooh would have been proud of. Winds were topping sixty miles per hour during the night and were still not far off that when I got down to the shop in the morning. Not for the first time this year I had to strap down our wheelie bin and the big bins in the car park were scattered around when I took the bleddy hound around first thing.

Radio Pasty reported a tree down at the Newlyn Coombe crossroads on the A30 this morning. I am surprised they have any trees left down there, as every time there is any sort of wind a tree comes down on the road at that point.

The sea is pretty stirred up too, with white water all the way from Cowloe to the beach and thumping up the cliffs even at lowish water. I cannot imagine we will see much in the way of surfing today even for the most optimistic lunatic. The sea stayed lively all day and provided some cracking photo opportunities for the one man and his dog that actually bothered coming down to see it. In case you missed the scene it did look rather spectacular at high water with the sun out and the waves crashing over Cowloe and the Harbour wall.

The Missus missed it too, as she and the in-laws ran off up to Travakis Farm for a late lunch. They must have enjoyed it as they were gone for hours. When it comes to tea time they will all, no doubt, claim to be full up which means Mr stay-behind-and-run-the-shop will have to get his own. That just reminds me, I was supposed to get some fish out of the freezer but it is now a little too late. Still, it was the Missus's birthday so I suppose she can be forgiven.

They were gone so long the Missus almost missed some friends who turned up to wish her well. They entertained me instead, especially the three young children who reminded me that the first bob-a-job week started today in 1949. I suppose they were a bit young, but there would have been no harm in having them, for example, sweep a few chimneys, as the local fire brigade has recommended, after a spate of related fires. Of course, we do not have a chimney so they would have had to have gone elsewhere to do to their important jobs. I am not suggesting that I did not enjoy their company; you can imagine that I was delighted. I am simply, as ever, being practical.

Now for that tea I promised myself. I just need to find a lolly stick for my fish. Eat your heart out Heston.

April 19ᵗʰ - Thursday

We can all rest comfortable in the knowledge that balance has been restored to the world. Gaia is happy with her lot, or Terra is, depending which side of the Adriatic you favour your deities from.

For once we are not talking about the weather, although the strong winds have abated somewhat and, after some naughty little showers that blew through this morning, we have a bright blue sky with fluffy white clouds over it. And it was the weather that brought about this perfect equilibrium of which I speak.

I waited for the rain to rush off to the east before hooking up the bleddy hound and following her head-long dash to the big beach. You know how we cannot resist all that wide open golden gloriousness, and we have such little time left to enjoy it before the Country Hall wallahs close the beach to little doggies. Of course, if the arrogant few who let their dogs foul with abandon just picked up after them it would not have given the wallahs a reason, although using 'reason' and 'County Hall' in the same paragraph could be said by many to be somewhat contradictory.

It was obvious from right across the beach, standing out like a beacon guiding lost souls, or in this case leading our souls. It was sufficient to let my heart soar and the music of delight fill the air about us. I really do not know how I managed so long without it, as it has been absent for months.

I did try and look the other way but, fearful that it might disappear before I got there or another might be drawn there before me, my eyes kept being pulled back to it. It was Pirsig who said something about it being better to travel than arrive. He was wrong, certainly in this instance, as I knew it would be every bit as pleasurable being there as the travelling to get to it, and right now you are probably agreeing with me – get on with it, for heaven's sake! So I carved a circuitous route (haven't I just), letting the bleddy hound run hither and thither after the thrown ball but always with an eye on our destination.

You see after yesterday's lumping sea the beach has changed. Huge amounts of sand have been scoured from the north end of the beach and seemingly spread evenly across the south and the west, where large rocks have disappeared. Yes, all is now well with the world and we can all sleep fitfully in our beds at night; my sitting rock is back.

As if to prove my point I found this little nugget today. It never fails to amaze me the level of intellect shown by the academics and scientists lodged in our universities and research centres. Without them the world would be still struggling out of the Stone Age and my sitting rock would be lost forever, I am convinced. Take for example the latest research from the European Centre for Environment and Human Health, Peninsula College of Medicine and Dentistry and the School of Psychology at the University of Plymouth – what a sizable team that must have been. Their collective genius has uncovered that exercise in the open air is beneficial to your health. Now, wait before you all go off guffawing at the ridiculousness of such an obvious outcome - it is much more complex than that. Listen carefully as this may add years to your life. It is far better to exercise by the coast or in the countryside than it is to do it in urban areas.

I am sure it was well worth giving up the county's toilet provision and lifeguard cover at Porthcurno beach over Easter so that money was available for such a stunningly crucial discovery. I understand that they are following up this success with research into why Cornish shopkeepers pull out their hair in frustration, and whether their screams of anguish make a sound, when there is no one there to hear them.

On a brighter note, at Lifeboat training tonight we had a doctor of some note coach us in the rigours of resuscitation. It is not the first time we have covered this area, in fact we have covered it quite a bit, but certainly it is the first with such a paragon of the medical fraternity. So, when you come to Sennen Cove this summer rest assured if you should need some resuscitation, we are top of our game in this regard. Just do not slip over and break a limb – you'll be absolutely beggered.

And since most of today's rag-a-muffin collection of ramblings was completely potty, perhaps we should end on a bit of Lord Byron, for the simple reason he popped his clogs today in 1824. He certainly had a bit of a life and allegedly put it about a bit including, allegedly, with his half sister and died while meddling in affairs between Greece and Turkey. I mean what would expect from a man whose dad's nickname was 'Mad Jack'?

I managed to find a few lines of his that would not leave you with, 'handkerchiefs as wet as towels', for he was a morbid soul. This one is about acne ridden youths and verdant sods and is about as good as it gets. It may not even be his, as he entitled the poems, 'Lines Written Beneath an Elm', which he probably found while he was sitting there.

Spot of my youth! whose hoary branches sigh,
Swept by the breeze that fans thy cloudless sky;
Where now alone I muse, who oft have trod,
With those I loved, thy soft and verdant sod;

I trust that is a slightly more uplifting excerpt than the last, that drew some criticism from the Aged Parent. It was only last week he recovered and managed to extract himself from his opium den.

April 20ᵗʰ - Friday

The café next door has not tried to tempt me with any hemlock laced bacon baps, and only time will tell if they slipped some polonium-210 into my cappuccino. This can only mean one thing: another exciting page of The Sennen Cove Diary.

I should start us off in the manner to which you are accustomed and note that the first Badminton Horse Trials were held today in 1949. I find it hard to fathom how they managed to get the animals to hold a racquet, but as they are still going they must have achieved some success.

I cannot see the bleddy hound being attracted to the sport; she is much more interested in a tennis ball than a shuttlecock. I managed to prove this once again with a trip down the big beach, and yes, a sit on my sitting rock that is now a couple of inches higher than it was yesterday, or maybe the sand is a couple of inches lower, causing me to sit on its lower portion.

We were told that showers would be heading our way and that by the afternoon they would be heavier and more prolonged. They did not say it, but for once the 'except in the Isles of Scilly and the far west' was in our favour, as it was sparklingly sunny for most of the day. It did look rather like they were copping it quite badly a bit further up.

It must have been a bit of a spoiler for the opening of the Heartlands visitor attraction, built on the site of the old Robinson's Shaft, part of South Crofty mine, on the borders of Pool and Camborne. They seem to have put a lot of thought into it with botanical gardens, markets, shops, an adventure playground and various exhibitions based around the mining world heritage sites. There are all sorts of events planned throughout the year too, covering the cultural spectrum. It all sounds very nice, just a pity it arrived about five years before the road that will serve it has been built.

By the afternoon I was on the edge of boredom, when our new oven arrived. I had imagined that it would turn up with our friendly engineer attached to it, particularly as I have not paid a bean for it yet. As it was, it arrived by courier with a big note on the outside saying 'open and install me'. It did not really, but it was just crying out for a bit of amateur fiddling.

My first mistake was that I used my trusty craft knife to cut away the packaging. How was I supposed to know that the polystyrene and cardboard only covered the top and bottom leaving the sides open to be marked by a sharp blade? It was not until I removed the protective black plastic wrapper that I spotted the sign suggesting that I avoid using a sharp knife when opening the box. I proceeded with a little more caution, until the shiny new machine sat amongst the discarded packaging, revealed in all its splendour.

Next on the list, was to move the old oven from its perch to make room for the new one. It was when I came to unplug it that I realised that we had followed our electrician's advice some years ago and had the thing plugged into the mains. Fortunately, it has its own breaker on the circuit board, so I did not have to plunge the shop into darkness, or turn off the fridges and freezers, or risk frizzy hair, ahem, by tackling it live. I did, however, have to scrabble around for a suitable screwdriver to loosen the terminal blocks, as our electrician must have used the strength of Hercules to tighten them up.

I shall spare you the details of the detritus that had built up under the old oven. Suffice it to say that I have made a mental note that we do, from time to time, lift up the new one so that we avoid a repeat. When I say lift up the new one, the emphasis is on the word 'we'. It required my own Herculean effort to pull it from its packaging and place it on the pedestal, and I shall ensure that the Missus is on hand next time, at the very least, to ensure the laces of my surgical truss are sufficiently tightened for the procedure.

It was after I had plumbed it back into the mains, but before I turned it on, the oven, not my surgical truss, that, against type, I decided to read the instructions. These stated that before turning it on I should remove all the protective covering, but rather unhelpfully did not suggest where I might find it. Fortunately, my earlier knife incident revealed that the metal casing of the oven was covered in a thin, almost invisible, layer of protective sticky plastic that, though protective, was sadly not knife proof. It took a little while to see where the edges were and an even longer little while to peel it off without leaving any bits behind. The instructions also stated that under European law a certified electrician should attach it to the mains – whoops. I shall expect the men in dark suits to slap me in irons any day now.

My, my, I should not be so free with these stories of the inner workings of The Old Boathouse. You will be thinking that we have this much fun every day and hardly do any work at all. It is not true I tell you; mostly we do really boring things like watch jets dash across the bay a few hundred feet above the waves. It was an F-15 but I could not tell you if it was an F-15c or and F-15b, which I am sure will please the Prime Minister immensely.

Finally, the news that Bert Weedon has shuffled off today rather eclipsed the earlier news that we also lost Levon Helm. He was a leading light in *The Band*, in case you were wondering, and I am sure he is playing Down on Cripple Creek by now.

April 21ˢᵗ - Saturday

For sale: one converted engine house conveniently situated near the conurbation of Scorrier, Redruth. Yours for a mere three-quarters of a million pounds.

Wheal Rose engine house was converted in the late 90's into a residence of note by a clever chap for whom it was a labour of love. I also believe I have seen this on the television's *Grand Designs* programme. One of the key elements of the conversion was that he could not quite find the exact location of the shaft collar and dumped a couple of tons of concrete in its rough location instead.

In its day, between 1826 and 1872, it produced 12,820 tons of copper and 18 tons of tin, and the engine house served a 70 fathom adit shaft for the mine. Call me picky if you will, but I just would not be comfortable owning a home on the edge of a four hundred and twenty feet hole, capped or not.

And talking of big holes, this must be the third day running that they have promised rain and there has been a big hole in the cloud above us for most of the day. We did have the odd shower pass through first thing but nothing of note, but the chill wind has returned to plague us.

Ideal, then to put on the shorts and flip flops and head down the beach with the bleddy hound. Yesterday I was a tad warm coming back from our scamper along the sand, so today I hedged my bets with several warm layers on top and next to nothing down below. It worked a treat, and I need not tell you (at least, tell you again) how satisfying it is to hack across the sand barefoot.

And talking of which I caught the gist of a news item yesterday that seemed to be saying that a group has set up sessions where people can walk along a specially designed course barefoot. All sorts of natural surfaces have been prepared for the walker including grass, logs and mud, a bit like a nudist camp for feet. It all seems a bit odd because, unlike nudists, if you really wanted to walk barefoot somewhere you simply take your shoes and socks off. Why have a special place for it?

These petty musings faded into the ether as I made my way up to the F&L this evening. The *Barracoodas* (sic), a band we had not heard before, were playing an absolutely singeing set. Whilst

I was outside and before they started, enjoying the fresh tobacco laced air, the lead guitarist came out and offered the choice of some laid back tunes, a glam rock set or some of the hard core heavy rock. Well, you can just imagine, can't you. Most of the band members were well aged in the wood and it showed, the experience oozing from every chord and they had good humour too. What a brilliant offering and the joint was truly jumping. They are most welcome back.

As I made to walk home in the unexpected showers it struck me that it would be a blinding idea to cast aside my footwear and walk home barefoot, to experience the feeling of the natural substances beneath my feet. There were, however, two thoughts that struck me in a startling moment of prescience. First, I witnessed the frying pan that the Missus would be striking me with after I made my way across the carpet at home, with feet that had traversed the cow pasture at Esther's Field.

My second thought was, as cow dung has been used for centuries in the permanent colouring of a myriad of items, that my feet might suffer a similar irreversible tinting. I did wish to avoid this and, as every good cowboy knows, you should always strive to dye with your boots on.

April 22nd – Sunday

The universities of Britain are clearly not content with just establishing the crucial facts that exercise near the beach is good for you and that in towns it is not. Researchers, this time at St Andrews, have been studying old books with some bit of kit called a densitometer that measures the amount of dirt on the page and hence which pages have been most read. Ignoring the fact that some readers may have had dirtier hands than others this has helped establish that medieval people feared illness, were self-interested and often fell asleep whilst reading. Four hundred years from now scientists studying copies of *The Cove Diary* will find the pages from two onwards remarkably clean, indicating that people did not bother getting past the first page, or most probably fell asleep before they got there. Medical records from the time will also indicate that the book was recommended as a cure of insomnia.

We were chatting last night, a small group of us, and were congratulating the lady with us who has just secured a job as Education Development Officer at Geevor Mine. It is an interesting job, no doubt, and one to which she is entirely suited. It minded me to ask if I had got my terminology correct yesterday in referring to the Wheal Rose shaft and an "adit shaft". She confirmed that it was correct and that it was a shaft for extracting water from the mine. Flushed with her success and keen to demonstrate the level of knowledge that she had recently acquired, she went on to say that in the mid 1800s the average life expectancy of a miner was 27. Although it might have been a little indelicate of me I begged leave to correct her. If the average age was 27 years they cannot possibly have been minors.

I shall let you return now to whatever you were doing before I rudely interrupted you in the vague hope that I cannot come up with a third groaning pun tomorrow.

April 23rd – Monday

It is a far, far better day today than I or the Met Office expected judging from their forecast. The wind has dropped out and it is warm, yes, definitely warm. They tell us that rain is on the way but until then me, the Missus, the dog and our two visitors in The Cove will enjoy it immensely.

Yep, that did not last long. It was shortly after our window cleaner arrived that the first rain appeared. It was a harbinger of something much worse. No, not two window cleaners, more rain. Not only did our recently cleaned windows get wet, but my lightweight balls were sent down the road by the gale force winds that accompanied it. It surprised the Missus no end when a chap came to our door holding one of them by its sack and asking if it belonged to us.

Quite apart from the effect of the rain we are fewer down here today anyway, as the in-laws went home this morning. I shall have to check our inventory as their little car was creaking on its springs as it took off towards the Cove Hill. I declined the sister-in-law's offer of payment for some milk and a fishing net; it was a small price to pay for the impending restoration of my hearing and mental health. Of course I am jesting; they are welcome down here at any time, most especially when I am not.

On the subject of great pleasures another of mine is being able to say "yes we do, third shelf down on the left*" (* replace with correct location as appropriate) to the question, "you don't have …".

I had a maiden aunt who would berate me as a child for asking questions in the negative, as she believed it to be irritating and rude. Although I have tried to heed her advice through my life it has never been more keenly understood than when we started running the shop. This is possibly the conditioning that her regular admonishing brought about, but most likely because she was right.

"You don't have any sandwiches, do you." You see, it was not even a question, despite jolly old Microsoft Word insisting I put a question mark at the end of it. The problem arises when we, as shopkeepers, answer in the affirmative because it automatically puts the customer in the wrong and creates an immediate confrontational relationship. It is worse still when we have to answer in the negative as it makes us feel inadequate.

Mind you there are many times when we *are* inadequate, especially recently when we keep our fresh stock to a minimum because there are so few people about to buy it. It is also a fact that the visitors at this time of year are those most used to having wild and exotic produce on their doorsteps. I live in dread of the customer just popping in for some asparagus; who thought we might just have some goat's milk; can't quite understand why we don't keep, fresh on our shelves, quantities of pressed lark's tongue flown in from South America.

Either we will have to find suppliers for such rare (at least, hereabouts) products or our customers will have to get used to more run of the mill comestibles. Can of Spam, anyone?

Well, we are spoiled for choice today for notable poets who have made themselves available for a bit of an outing by either being born or shuffling off. We have William Wordsworth and Rupert Brooke both of whom popped off today in 1850 and 1915 respectively. So let's have a bit of Shakespeare who topped them both by, very likely, being both born today, 1564, and dying today in 1616.

In appreciation of today's weather shall we have a little Tempest?

"Were I in England now, as I once was, and had but this fish painted, not a holiday-fool there but would give a piece of silver. There would this monster make a man--any strange beast there makes a man. When they will not give a doit to relieve a lame beggar, they will lay out ten to see a dead Cornishman."

April 24ᵗʰ - Tuesday

I mentioned yesterday the difficulties of maintaining exactly the right stock for the many requests we have from customers. I was roundly criticised today for not sufficiently advertising that we sell disposable cameras. The chap said if it was not for the fact that he was delayed in exiting the shop because someone was in the way, he would have left disappointed and without saying anything. He advised that we should have a sign in the window pointing out that disposable cameras were available in store.

Had he not been in such a hurry I would have politely pointed out that our windows are already too busy with advertisements for art shows, holiday lets, taxis, handymen and recommendations for certain literary masterpieces. Should we add to this details of our entire stock holding, not only would we not be able to see out of the windows, but we would also need to buy more windows to support the list. We are always happy to respond to enquiries – on the understanding that they do not start with "you haven't got …".

It seems that we are not the only business in bother with its customers. Hornby, the Scalextric and miniature railway company that has for years been held up as an exemplar of how to run a modern business, yesterday issued a profit warning. The City is concerned that it is no longer a model business.

Come on, you got away light yesterday, so don't complain.

April 25ᵗʰ - Wednesday

Out in the Egyptian desert in 1859 a small group of swarthy and rag-taggle men carrying picks and shovels approach a tall chap in white suit and hat. He is holding what looks like a large set of plans and is surveying the desert. One of the ragged bunch pulls away from the group and goes to speak to the man with a plan.

Cornish Miner: "You Monsewer de Lessops?"

Ferdinand de Lesseps: "Oui, little person, 'ow my I 'elp you."

Miner: "It's more 'ow we can 'elp you luvver. I understand you want a big 'ole dug."

De Lesseps: "We do, sort of, but your country 'as said they will not 'elp. They have been very rude about my plan. If The General was still 'ere he would beat your behinds."

Miner: "Now steady on, Frenchy. Don't you go mixing us up with they lot from wrong side of the Tamar. Me and my little bunch 'ere es Cornish from Cornwall."

De Lesseps: "Pardon moi, my little diminutive man. Nevertheless it does seem you have come a long way to 'elp ze French with their little project. You must 'ave a raison, eh?"

Miner: "Well, you see Monsewer, we es all miners and mining in Cornwall es lookin' a bit tricky see, so we decided to look for a bit o' work elsewhere. They es going to call it the Cornish day-us-poorer one day. Apparently 'tween 1861 and 1901 two hundred and fifty thousand of us es going to begger off, according to Wikipedia."

De Lesseps: "Wiki quelle?"

Miner: "Never mind me 'ansum. Me and my mates 'ere just thought we'd get ahead of the posse a bit.

De Lesseps: "I am sorry, you digress. Now where were you? Ah oui, you were saying something about our 'ole."

Miner: "Zackly luvver. See, we Cornish es pretty 'andy where 'oles es concerned. Granted, all ours es underground and yours es a bit on top of the ground but to us an 'ole is an 'ole."

De Lesseps: "Mais oui, I see. You think you can dig my 'ole for me. It is a very long 'ole, you know and there are not very many of you. And what is that bag of old rags you 'ave with you?"

Miner: "Bag of ... oh yes, that's the Missus, Susan. 'ad to bring 'er along, Monsewer. You see she makes the pasties for the boys and a nice cup 'o tay to go widden."

De Lesseps: "Pasties?"

Miner: "Yes luvver, pasties. Like your crossants but edible."

De Lesseps blusters a bit but the Cornishman seems undeterred.

Miner: "Now the ground 'ere is a little softer than what we es used to but we 'ad a little chat, me and the boys, and we think we can manage between us. We also 'ave the advantage that we spend a lot of time trying to keep water out of our 'oles but we understand that you actually want water in yours."

De Lesseps: "Nom de plume and sacre blue, you seem to have thought of everything, little Cornish person, but we want this 'ole dug very quickly. We need it finished in ten years."

Our Cornish miner looks a little blank, holds his finger up for a second and goes for a quick conflab with his crew. He draws back to the Frenchman beaming.

Miner: "All right Monsewer. I 'ad a little chat with the boys and they was a bit dismayed at the timetable but they reckon if they worked six days a week and took an hour off for dinner then they could probably stretch the work out that long. They wasn't 'appy mind. They was 'oping to be back in time to see the Royal Albert Bridge open, and I was rather 'oping I'd be there to get a first edition copy of Alice's Adventures in Wonderland."

De Lesseps: "Stretch out the work? It is 164 kilometres, you know."

Our miner pauses. He seems to be making some calculations and mumbling numbers under his breath. Eventually he grins.

Miner: "Yes, that's only 102 miles, I think. You have to 'preciate Monsewer that the rock where we come from is a sight harder than this stuff."

Our man kicks a few loose rocks away with his boot.

Miner: "Anyhow, I reckon that's settled. Just one more thing before we get started. What had you intended to call this 'ole of yours? Just need to have something I can put on my CV."

De Lesseps: "Ah yes, the name. It will be, in Eng ..., ahem, Cornish, The Great Egypt Ship Canal Joining the Mediterranean and Red Seas Built by ze French. It is a working title at ze moment."

Miner: "My, my, that's a bit long winded. Perhaps you would like to discuss it over a nice cup 'o tay. She's a great cup 'o tay maker, my Sue es."

De Lessops comes over all glassy eyed for a second then slowly repeats the last words the Cornishman said with a look of revelation on his face.

De Lessops: "A great tea maker your Sue ez ... Su ez Canal. Mon dieu!"

Just in case you were thinking that your Diarist had completely lost his grip in these slow and weather beaten days I should note that the Suez Canal was commenced today in 1859. The history books do not expressly mention the Cornish involvement, but you know what they say about holes in the ground, don't you?

April 26ᵗʰ - Thursday

I must have told you before how the German tour coaches drop off their passengers in The Cove and frog-march them up to Land's End, making sure they do not spend so much as a penny down here. Some locals informed us that another load had just arrived and I thought they meant that they had seen the coach unload. Not a bit of it. This lot had been dropped at Land's End and were approaching from the direction of the coast path.

It frustrated me rather, as they all wanted stamps. We ran out of our price-marked postcard stamps for Europe last week and have been unwilling to buy more since the price will be going up next week; we still have £500 of stamps from previous price increases that we can do nothing with. Never mind, it did not stop them all buying a postcard or three and very welcome they were too.

Good job not many of them wanted pasties. Getting a pasty in the county today was like trying to find hen's teeth in a pile of rocking horse doings. It seems that most of the pasty bakers in the county had decided to traipse off to London town to protest about losing the extra twenty percent profit they having been making by selling pasties at the same price as me, but not paying Value Added Tax. I cannot help feeling that VAT on pasties will be the least of our concerns after The much maligned council has concluded its master plan of frightening off our visitors. So far they have cut off funding on Blue Flag beaches, closed Tourist Information Centres and most latterly public conveniences.

Not that the Head Launcher's team at the OS quiz night will have to worry much as we presided over yet another win. We are only grateful that the government has cancelled the 50p rate of income tax on high earners. Any more wins and we would have to put our accountant on double time looking for avoidance loopholes.

It must have been the double Lifeboats launch tonight that sharpened our wits for the quiz. The big boat launched into a rolling sea alongside the Inshore boat tonight for a bit of training. It wasn't until after they went that we saw the amount of weed on the short, recovery slip. The very excellent Shore Crew are meticulous about clearing this weed off the slip on the basis that slipping on it while the boat is going astern onto it could lead to a serious shortening of one's height and there are one or two of us who can't afford to lose much more. Still, as you can imagine from a very excellent Shore Crew, we must have done a very excellent job as we are all still the same height as we were when we started.

April 27th - Friday

What a wonderful morning for a bit of an Inshore Lifeboat launch. I clearly was not alone in this appreciation and shortly after the shop opened this morning the pagers went off to emergency launch the boat. One of our last fishing boats, in fact our sole crabber, experienced an engine failure out by Pedn-men-du as he tried to bring some order to his pots after the poor sea conditions of the last week or so. After I launched the boat I mentioned that I had a crab order in for this morning which now looked at risk. It is testament to the values that these fishermen hold dear that as the Lifeboat towed him back to The Cove he got them to drop off at the store, pots to collect my crab order before he was safely brought back into the Harbour.

I was tempted to displace the bleddy hound with the toe of my boot, had I been wearing any, this afternoon.

Very often we avoid the harbour beach because of the amount of oar weed. This provides a host of interesting smells and various semi-edible items that the bleddy hound finds hard to ignore. Unfortunately oar weed in abundance had invaded the big beach this afternoon and as we approached, her little button nose starting a-twitching. It was not long before her ball was forgotten and she was off exploring and nibbling. I managed to drag her away and headed back the way we came, but clearly the rebel in her had surfaced and was, as yet, unsated. The absence of things badgery or foxy did not in the least deter her and why should it when there were dead gulls and cormorants to roll around in.

There were certainly signs of burgeoning life in The Cove when I returned from the beach. It would be nice to think that this was the start of the roll in of visitors for the season; it is nearly May after all. I hope they brought some serious water-proofing with them as Sunday's weather is penned in for being something Noah would be proud of.

I had best attend to my drain tomorrow, or dry out my mop in anticipation.

April 29ᵗʰ - Sunday

I cannot fault the Met Office's forecast for today; it was spot on. I would judge that most of the month's average rainfall dropped on us before lunchtime, and quite a bit of that was blown under our shop door by a rather vicious northerly. Unsurprisingly we had few customers. The rest were proving the old adage that it was a grand day for the high stool, no doubt.

It was into the afternoon when the water started coming in through the back of the shop as well. Of course, had I bothered to clean out the drain at the back while it was still dry I may not have had this problem, but if I had, and the water still came in, I would be worrying that something else was at fault, so perhaps it is just as well that I did not. So grim was it that at one point I considered that it might be prudent to build an ark.

If Noah had been around today I suspect he would not have had such a straight run at it, if you can call taking around 120 years to build a big boat a straight run. The biggest deluge he would have had to face would have come before the Flood.

We find ourselves in a council office looking at an officious little man with a telephone pinned to one ear and some plans set out before him. On the other end of the line is one Mr Noah, who has found himself on the wrong end of a planning enforcement notice.

"Yes, Mr Noah, I have your planning application in front of me now. It seems you want to build a boat in your back garden. A very big boat …"

"... I see, big enough to accommodate seven pairs of every clean beast in the world including the birds of the air and two pair of every dirty beast. These are wild animals, yes? And you have the appropriate licences under the Dangerous Wild Animals Act I presume? ..."

"You didn't think that was necessary since you are saving these animals for, for what was that, Mr Noah ...?"

"... for when the Great Flood comes? Okay, Mr Noah but I really think you need to have a chat with DEFRA about that, just to be sure."

"Now, my colleagues also tell me that there is no plan to seek wayleave to move the boat on completion. You do intend to launch it at some point ...

"... you don't. It will float away by itself on the Great Flood. It is an interesting notion, Mr Noah, but had you considered we are in the middle of a drought currently? [*Covers telephone mouth piece while he snickers at his own little joke*]"

"All right, Mr Noah, let us assume, just for the sake of argument that wayleave will not be required. Consider this; I understand from various complaints that the structure has already been started. The complainants have seen ladders being used on site ..."

"... Yes, I understand that you need to get to the top of the structure to build it. May I ask if you are familiar with the term, Working at Heights Directive? The use of ladders is no longer seen as desirable and you should be using scaffolding. However, the issue raised by the complainants is more to do with the height of the structure and the overlooking of neighbouring properties ..."

" ... No, Mr Noah, I haven't got a clue how many species of animals there are but, yes, I can see your point that you will need a large vessel for them all ..."

"... I don't believe so, Mr Noah. I think I would have noticed an exclusion clause in the Directive for divine intervention and I know for a fact that there isn't one in our planning process. What I can tell you is that if it still there at the end of the month my officers will be arriving to remove it ..."

"... yes, Mr Noah, even if they have to arrive by boat."

I think we might be all right. The rain had gone and the stars were shining bright as I took the bleddy hound round for her last run tonight. Even that fiercesome northerly wind had calmed down to a whisper.

April 30th – Monday

It seems the spirit of smuggling and piracy, fostered for so long in the West Country, is still alive and kicking. The top story here is the frightening proliferation of cannabis farms. The local constabulary has estimated they have increased from eleven to near two hundred. The story sat nicely with another report that the Court of Appeal has reduced the sentences of a drugs gang supplying into the region.

We have a weed problem of a different sort this morning, though. The Harbour has piles of oar weed near six feet high, and several tons of it sat at the end of the launch slip, quite effectively preventing the boat from being launched. You might ask the question, how many people does it take to clear several tons of oar weed from the slipway and it would be a very reasonable question to ask. I can assure you that it takes ten people around and hour and a half, using pitchforks and rakes to drop it off the sides. That would be three Boat Crew and one member of the very excellent Shore Crew with the aforementioned tools and six divisional inspectors, engineers and launch authorities, hands in pockets, looking on.

We did not exactly get an olive branch today to signal the signs of the flood waters receding, but the swallows have moved in again in the apex of the roof next door. We should note that is more than just one swallow. We should also note that the rain forecast for tonight is to be everywhere except the Isles of Scilly and the far west. I shall take it as a sign, and not just that we shall see AG scrubbing the pavement below the nest each morning before the café opens.

May 1st – Tuesday

I managed to fill my day with all sorts of exciting things today. Well, they may not be very exciting to you but given the last two weeks here, getting a mail shot from the World Wildlife Fund would seem exciting to us.

First, I had a little trip into town to see my bone cruncher. I would have gone there sooner, but the girl I usually see has left and the other lady is running the place by herself, so I had to wait for an available appointment. It is not that there is anything particularly wrong, but I have found that by going along for a pull about twice a year keeps me supple and I tend to creak less; an interim service, if you like.

Given that I had never seen this woman before I felt it was a little forward of her to suggest turning me into a pin cushion. She is an advocate of acupuncture in case you had not guessed and, as I found out, she is actually rather good at it. I imagined that I would feel quite silly and uncomfortable with all those pins in me but, so good was she, I did not feel a prick at all.

Ordinarily it is recommended that the patient does nothing too strenuous after such a session, to allow the stretched muscles and sinews to recover from their battering. Unfortunately, I had met up with the chap who is buying my boat in the morning and he was keen to run out for a trial. With the sea state perfectly set for such an exercise, I could hardly refuse. The fact the Harbour beach is still neck deep in weed was merely an inconvenience.

It was I that landed on my behind on the way across the beach, of course. The transom wheels that I had laboured to attach made a terrific difference to all the other times that I had tried to launch the boat. It should be noted that all the previous attempts had been made on my own, which did not help. But it was not all plain sailing (especially given that it is a powered boat), even before we had taken the boat off the trailer. I noticed that one of the brand new transom wheels was flat and having not long ago pumped it up I assumed the worse.

Since neither the buyer nor I had a suitable pump it rather left me no choice but throw myself on the mercy of possibly the most obliging chap that ever lived: RB, our Lifeboat mechanic. If he was thinking, "You mindless idiot, can't you see I'm in the middle of cooking my lunch" it actually came out as, "No problem, I'll just turn the cooker off." It did not take him long to establish that the brand new transom wheel had a puncture and did not take him much longer to fix it, with alarming good grace and humour.

With the wheel reattached to its bracket we manhandled the boat down to the beach, where we managed to haul it over the weed and through a gap in the weed into the water. The engine started first time, also thanks to RB who lovingly serviced it, and we sped out across the bay.

It had been over two years since I took the boat out myself and I had quite forgotten what a good performer it is. Granted that sponsons could have been pumped up a little harder, which led to a bit of a wallowing, bumping ride but overall it was a gratifying experience. More importantly the buyer thought so too.

It was with some relief that I handed over the last of the ancillary equipment, log book and holdall that the boat arrived in. The old adage proved to be true, that there are only two days that you enjoy having your own boat, the day you buy it and the day you sell it.

It also proved the point that after a session of chiropractic manipulation, humping a 75 kilo boat up and down a 45 degree cobbled slope is less than desirable. It was no more gratifying to note that it was the buyer who landed on his behind as we pulled the boat back up the beach and over the slippery weed.

I strongly suspect that as I wind myself out of bed in the morning there will be some creaking and moaning that is unlikely to be the bed springs.

May 2nd - Wednesday

After the excitement of yesterday, today always had the potential to disappoint, and in that regard it excelled. I was thinking about writing to the Oxford English Dictionary, as I believe we have been able to redefine the word 'quiet'.

It could not have been a day with better weather, though. The sun was shining bright from early on until late and turned into a warm and pleasant evening. The afternoon became much busier as the sleepy holiday population suddenly remembered what to do on sunny days, nothing of which resembled shopping.

I consoled myself by filleting a few plaice and preparing some new items for posting on the web shop, in the vague hope that someone might stumble across it one day and buy something. I suspect that we shall see some subtle changes in Internet purchases, as the cost of postage has increased substantially. I am quite surprised that we are still selling postcards for the same reason, with a first class stamp being three times the cost of our cheapest cards.

It is slightly comforting to know that we are not suffering alone. We had three salesmen come by today and all of them reported quietness in the resorts that they visit.

I suggested to the last that it seemed more than coincidental that they all had arrived on the same day, and within an hour of each other. He agreed and confided in me that to save money on travel all the salesmen had got together and hired a coach. It seemed like a smart idea. Perhaps the business to get into will be the hiring out locally of electric cars so that holiday makers, and salesmen, that arrive by train or coach can get around while they are here.

Gosh, I think I might have cracked the next best thing. Do not go telling anyone, now.

May 3ʳᵈ – Thursday

At least I got my jollies today by trekking out to the cash and carry at Hayle. It is a new and shiny store with no holes in the roof. Well, there might be but it was difficult to tell as it was not raining. Of course, the arrangement of goods throughout the store has been reordered, presumably to cause the greatest disorientation amongst their customers. Nevertheless it did not take long to wander around and get orientated again.

The greatest change, other than fabulous automatic doors that open on presentation of new swipe cards they have issued customers with, is the cigarette and tobacco bond. This was always locked up behind a roller door in the past and a member of staff would come along and unlock it for you. Since then the new cigarette display ban has come into force with the aim of preventing young people seeing the attractive, glittering packets of evil weed and being immediately compelled take up smoking. Now, as well as having a heavy metal door, the bond room has a curtain of black rubber strips, the kind you get at the entrances to chiller rooms, to prevent any unauthorised peek at the goodies within. Once inside, the buyer's selection is scanned and added to their account and hastily slipped into an opaque black bag.

These measures are absolutely essential, as we all know what a hotbed of impressionable youth cash and carry warehouses are.

Even at the main checkout the tight restrictions are closely adhered to. Having first checked the vicinity for eagle-eyed youngsters bent on an illicit view of the booty, the cashier reopens the black bag and proceeds, with his head tucked inside the bag, to double check the contents against the manifest.

I would hate you to think, dear reader, that my trip to the outlands was completely without merit, nor would I wish to bring down about my head the wrath of the Hayle Town Chamber of Commerce, fearsome that they are. To this end I must relate that I had a spot of good fortune while I was out in that direction.

You may recall that we have recently replaced the oven in which we warm our pasties and in doing so bestow upon them VAT that allows us to sell them for the same price as a baker who does not charge VAT. (If I say it often enough perhaps the message will permeate). The purveyor of the new oven, who has yet to arrive and pick up his bounty, was to take away the old oven. Given that he has not, we have been driving around with the old beast in the back of the van for a fortnight.

It so happens that just outside Hayle, at Wheal Alfred, is our nearest scrap metal dealer and it was here that I ventured first to rid ourselves of the old lumpy oven. They are an unfussy lot; I do not even need a permit to drive my van into their premises to off-load my metal waste. While it was something of a relief to rid myself of the old oven it is not the good fortune to which I alluded some two paragraphs earlier.

Our van is getting a little long in the tooth. In fact some of its teeth are falling out and to extend the metaphor a little further other of its teeth are going rotten - bits are going rusty. It is what anything of ferrous base will do down here in our salt infused air. One rusty bit has been a particular irritation, since it is the only bit of the exterior that I really lay hands upon and that is the flap that covers the fuel filler cap. Each time I scrape my hand on it when filling up I am compelled to return home to casually browse the pages of a well-known online auction website and then to discover that I spent the money that I could have spent on a new flap on diesel instead.

So, as I was leaving the scrap yard, fortune shone upon me. Well, actually I caught a glimpse of it out of the corner of my eye. There in a corner of the yard was a long wheel-base van of the same make as ours and, even more fortunately, of roughly the same age. I pulled up outside the office, (far enough away from the car crusher to avoid any embarrassing mistakes with our own van), and went to investigate and, sure enough, the dismembered hulk had indeed a flap of the same type as the one I sought. It took me moments to borrow a screwdriver and remove the object of my desire. How chuffed was I; how utterly overwhelmed with elation? And it only cost a quid.

When I returned home it was the most I could do to contain myself, such was my brim-fullness of joy. I kept from the Missus the reason for my happy state, wishing to present her with the finished article – the replacement flap fully attached. I grabbed a screwdriver and it only took a few minutes to complete my task. Dragging the Missus from the shop I pointed out the shiny (well, a bit grubby but not at all rusty) fuel filler cap flap. Had I a troupe of trumpeters to hand I would have entreated them to provide a fanfare to underline the greatness of this moment.

Her response to this crowning achievement of my day? "It's the wrong colour."

Unfortunately the Missus will be further disappointed. No, strike that. The Missus will be extremely disappointed … nay, devastated. Heavens, I do not think I can find an adjective that will adequately describe her upsettedness. You see, I had a telephone call today delivering some bad news from a company that is supposed to be delivering our new sofa.

You may recall the lengths to which I went to try and dissuade the Missus from buying this, *her* object of desire, but I was pushing back against an irresistible force even the most immovable of objects would yield to. When I ordered the sofa we were told the lead time for delivery would be ten weeks, which is roughly a week hence. The sofa company called today to say that due to containers being in short supply; boats from China being very slow; Somalian pirates had intercepted the boat; any or all of the above, that the sofa would be delayed another two months.

Now you, dear reader, may be made of sterner stuff, but I for one am not going to be the one to tell the Missus, or be anywhere near the fall out zone when she finds out that a bunch of gritty Africans are using her sofa to watch back to back reruns of Pirates of the Caribbean.

I throw myself upon your mercy to, perhaps, be so good as to telephone on the pretext of asking if we have such-and-such in stock and right at the very end add that you are sorry to hear that her sofa will not be delivered on time. It would also be most appreciated if you would tip me a wink before you make that call, so that I can put myself at some distance and thus avoid harm or injury. I think they call it collateral damage.

Talking of injury, it was only a few days ago that the Coxswain shared the cheery news with me that the engineering luminaries of the RNLI had come up with a cracking solution to the weed problem on the slipway – remove some of the gratings. We now have four two feet square holes at the bottom end of the slip. The very excellent Shore Crew are cock-a-hoop that our 'tween launch and recovery games of hopscotch now have a little added spice.

The weed on the slip is not the only place it is causing problems. As you may have gathered from previous tales there is some competition as to who will drive the wonderful Tooltrak launching vehicle. Having already seen the amount of weed on the beach, and surmised that a certain amount of difficulty would be forthcoming, I very graciously ceded the privilege to my colleague, TS.

As the tide was receding, our little tracked launching vehicle made reasonably light work of putting afloat the Inshore Lifeboat this evening. By the time the boat arrived back at around low water the weed at the water line was around two feet deep. We watched from the slipway as the machine sank into the weed and stayed there. It took the Harbour tractor to tow it out and for TS to concede defeat and drive to the big beach to recover the ILB.

You will understand that the very excellent Shore Crew are a cohesive team, very much like an inseparable brotherhood, and will stand by each other through thick and thin; so while TS recovered the ILB and took it back to the boathouse for a wash down, the rest of us beggered off to the OS for the quiz night.

Such overt examples of camaraderie rarely go unrewarded and we came in mid-field.

Nevertheless, what a jolly wheeze today was.

May 4ᵗʰ - Friday

Our all-powerful council has decided that it is high time the date of Easter is pinned to a particular couple of weeks on our Gregorian calendar, well, the Easter school holiday, at least.

The council has suggested that it be fixed to the first two weeks of April, which in business terms is not ideal. We would prefer it to be the last two weeks in April. Being a business, and obviously centrally affected by such a decision, we were contacted by the council as they sought to garner opinion on the matter. Well, when I say contacted by the council, I mean that I heard it coincidentally on the radio.

With my interest piqued, I looked on the council website and found a consultation survey on the matter. The opening page asked if I was a teacher, parent or an affected business, except they spelt 'affected business' as 'other'. It is official then, the wonder boys in their ivory towers up in Truro have not the blindest notion that the decisions they make affect businesses.

When will these people realise they are running a council in a part of the country that relies almost entirely on tourism?

At least we still have some people prepared to come and visit us, although these latest ones seem to be coming by boat. I suppose it saves on fuel costs. There has been a proliferation of kayaks dropping into The Cove and camping down, or decamping to, the OS before they push off again. One pair had travelled from London, starting last month, and were making their way around the coast of Great Britain. They had camped on the Harbour beach, which must have been interesting at the moment, and were clearly having trouble locating any bathing facilities.

Another couple, who arrived yesterday, were not as prepared to spend the night on top of some decomposing weed and who could blame them. They dropped off the beers they were carrying with the Lifeboat crew and headed up to the OS for a night of comfort.

I almost headed up there myself tonight and would have done had I been allowed some warning. A friendly soul alerted the Missus to the fact that her sofa will not be turning up when she expected it, just as I rolled in from the Parish Council meeting tonight. Gosh, the air was blue. I did not even have time to fetch my smart new tin hat from the Lifeboat station.

Did I just mention the Parish Council meeting? I went up there to hear the latest about the public toilets in The Cove. It seems some help may be at hand for the Beach car park toilets, at least – yes we all know that a councillor came on the radio and said that there was no plan to close them, but that was last week, so some plans have obviously been made since then. Odd how the council can make some decisions really quickly. The Harbour car park toilets still hang in the balance and rely on some dialogue between the council and the Harbour Commissioners.

It is a world gone mad. I had really thought that in these tough times the council would be doing all it could to keep the county at the forefront of visitor attractions to sustain the influx of holiday-makers and the money rolling in.

Well, the upset is not confined to this little part of the world. It reaches into the very fabric of the nation, to the most treasured of our possessions and traditions, the very stuff that drives us on and makes us the proud people that we are. Then the final blow, the bitterest pill, the deepest cut of all – Weetabix has been bought by the Chinese.

May 5ᵗʰ – Saturday

Well, that is rather nice. After a stuttering start The Cove started to fill up and we have people, real people, running around and doing holiday like things. And that is despite a rather tart little easterly that is cooling us down just a bit. Can anyone explain why, in a tart easterly, my flags of St Piran on the front of the shop are blowing to the east?

Although the holiday feeling seemed to be pervasive we know from long experience that you cannot keep everyone happy. We had an American visitor come through, walking the coast path. I had seen him earlier and he seemed like a nice, cheery chap but after a visit to the OS he was a little put out.

I must immediately assure you that the staff at the OS had done nothing particularly wrong, but the cash machine in the bar there does not dispense cash to foreign credit cards. In fact none of the charging card machines do in this area. The very helpful chaps at the OS suggested that we might assist with our cash back option, but unfortunately our machine will only provide that option for UK debit cards, and we do not do cash advances. As our American friend was staying at a guest house in Lamorna, or possibly Porthcurno, (he told me he was staying at Lamthcurno), that did not take credit cards he was becoming increasingly desperate.

The closest machine available that he could use is in St Just, but given that he was walking in the other direction that was not of much help. He asked if we could take his credit card and provide cash instead of goods, but I suspect that is called money laundering and just a bit illegal. It is not often we have to disappoint; I hope the bed and breakfast at Porthmorna is understanding.

In our advantageous position of Sennen Cove Visitor Contact Point we are privy to key pieces of information long after they have been available to the general public. The latest is a bulky document detailing the facts surrounding the Olympic Torch Relay.

I can tell you that there will be four torch bearers at the Land's End complex, though for the life of me I cannot see where they will be running from and to; it is not that big there. Perhaps they intend to do circuits of the signpost. A further two runners will take the Torch up through Sennen, where it will catch a bus to Newlyn. Two regular bus services will be held up at the Trevescan junction until the relay has gone through, that is the first two buses out of Sennen Cove which will subsequently be delayed further as they follow the Torch cavalcade and several hundred cars in the direction of town.

For each location the writer of the document has set out some interesting facts. For example, '*Penzance is a well known film location in Germany due to the large numbers of Rosamund Pilcher films, beloved by the Germans shot in and near Penzance*'. I did not think I had seen so many Germans about this year and it might take the buses a tad longer to get to Penzance than they expected, too.

Sorry, I was about to call an end to the frivolity when I noticed, '*The first demonstration of dynamite by Alfred Nobel took place in The Poly in Falmouth*'. Of course, this no longer exists.

No, no, I can't take any more. It is time to shuffle up to the F&L for the usual, or in fact something far better than the usual. Tonight we have *The Dolphins Fly*, oozing handwritten tunes of wonderfulness on guitar, both acoustic and electric and polymoog too, uplifting us beyond the plane of joy to the plateau of ecstasy.

I should tell you, before I take you home, that the moon tonight is a 'Super Moon'. It appears sixteen percent bigger tonight than any time in the last year and much brighter. It occurs because of its proximity to Earth, its perigee, at the time of a full moon. Tides are high, or low as you choose. And when you have been dragged onto the dance floor by two young ladies that you told the day before that the F&L was the place to be on a Saturday night, you rather wonder if life can get much better than this. And how I got there from a big full moon I shall never know.

May 6th – Sunday

With so much sunshine, little breeze and attractive white fluffy clouds floating about I would have expected it to be a bit busier. There seemed to be plenty of people wandering to and fro but they seemed to have forgotten the art of shopping to excess. I shall have to write to my MP, although I am still waiting for a response to the last letter I sent him before Easter. Ah well, perhaps he is too busy texting the editor of *The Cornishman,* or whatever MPs do these days.

Still, we are doing our best to keep our visitors down here. Someone sussed our little car park scheme whereby we leave the manhole covers on the sewage system open, trapping the unwary. Naturally I had to feign shock and horror and immediately call in South West Water to come and fix the problem.

I am awfully glad that it was not a very serious problem like a dam about to burst or water gushing from a fractured main, as the chap manning the emergency line was the most relaxed individual I have come across. He took five minutes just recording my personal details, with no sense of urgency at all. He still did not attach any import to the matter when we eventually got to the problem to be reported. He simply asked if it was a round, square or oblong manhole cover. I did sense a little increase in tempo when I said that I did not know what size or shape the cover was, but that it used to cover a thirty feet deep hole. Good to his word, though, some men in a big van turned up a couple of hours later to fix it.

Another boat turned up in the bay in the afternoon and another doing an around Great Britain route. This chap is doing the challenge in a sixteen feet dinghy, apparently a first. It must be challenging too, as his website says he is taking in some of the busiest inland waterways. I am sure he meant inshore and they are unsurprisingly busy with the number of kayaks doing the same. The boat is pulled up on the slipway and presumably will be heading off tomorrow for St Ives, which is a little off-plan looking at his expected route.

I hope he has got a bucket on board; it looks like a typical bank holiday rainy day tomorrow.

May 7ᵗʰ – Monday

The small dinghy that berthed here overnight took its time getting going again and left mid-afternoon. I am not sure about this sailing around Great Britain, as there did not seem to be much sail involved as he chugged out across the bay. Still, he only has to get to St Ives today, although if he had started earlier he would not have got wet.

So, what do we do when things are looking a little blue and our customers have all piled off up the motorway? We put bunting up, that's what we do.

The Parish has been handed several miles of black and gold bunting by the Olympic committee, suggesting some sensitivity on their part. Let us face it they could have provided several miles of Union Flag bunting that would not have seen light of day until November 5ᵗʰ, and even then only fleetingly before it caught light. While the selection showed some particularly clever pandering to the local market, the committee had clearly not considered that between Land's End and Sennen there is very little to pin bunting to.

Rather than see it wasted, an animated member of the Parish Council has been going around attaching it to any object that has stayed still long enough. Both we and the Ice Cream Parlour have some pretty decoration now, and if you come down tomorrow I suggest that you may find some on the wheelie bins, gate posts and telephone box. Whether it will still be there come a week Saturday when the Torch flies through Sennen is neither here nor there; not one of them will see it down in The Cove anyhow.

And since the day was quiet and the evening dour we shall evoke the sentiments of Spring, at least, by a few words from Mr Robert Browning who came to life this day in 1812.

And after April, when May follows,
And the whitethroat builds, and all the swallows!
Hark, where my blossomed pear-tree in the hedge
Leans to the field and scatters on the clover
Blossoms and dewdrops—at the bent spray's edge—
That's the wise thrush; he sings each song twice over,
Lest you should think he never could recapture
The first fine careless rapture!
And though the fields look rough with hoary dew,
All will be gay when noontide wakes anew
The buttercups, the little children's dower
—Far brighter than this gaudy melon-flower!

May 8ᵗʰ – Tuesday

We had a proliferation of coach tours down through the early part of the day, churning out their aging content all over the road. I feared whether I might have sufficient twenty pence postcards for them all, but I need not have worried. I rather think than the recent hike in the price of postage stamps might be starting to put people off, especially those with not much to spare.

It also did not help that the Lifeboat pagers went off at quarter-to-one, just as another coach load turned up and I had to push one or two avid postcard hunters from the shop. The Missus had taken herself off to PZ on a shopping trip and so I had to close the shop to attend the shout. Although I had to eject a couple, at least I did not lock anyone in this time.

Now, usually what happens in these circumstances, when I have to dash off, is that the Missus will turn on the radio scanner and record the details of the emergency call. The very excellent Shore Crew find this extremely useful in understanding how long the boat is likely to be away, as when we are in the boathouse we get no information at all. Because the Missus was off enjoying herself in town we were left a little in the dark.

I say 'we' somewhat guardedly. When the shout went up I found myself with two other very excellent Shore Crew, who had to dash back to work as soon as the boat was launched. Both indicated that they were very busy and may not be able to come back to recover the boat, and not knowing when the boat was likely to come back exacerbated the problem.

Still, being a very excellent Shore Crew and with minutes to spare we found just enough of us to pull the boat back up the slip. If anyone missed the shop being open while I was about my duties they kept very quiet about it. My guess is that not a soul noticed.

Having congratulated myself that I had not done too much damage to our business by attending the shout, I then went and ruined it all. While I had not locked anyone in the shop when I went to the shout, I very nearly did when I closed in the evening. If it were not for the little girly screams when I turned the lights out I would never have known they were there.

May 9ᵗʰ – Wednesday

It would be nice to see some proper summery sunshine again, much like the day we had yesterday but lasting for a week or two. It evoked those summer images of crowded beaches, splashing around in the azure sea and the chimes of the ice-cream van being choked off after four seconds. I was not aware of this but there is legislation surrounding the use of ice-cream van chimes. To give you an inkling, they cannot be used for longer than four seconds and even then only approaching a 'selling zone'. Once used they cannot be chimed again for another three minutes and woe betide if they are used more than once every two hours in the same street. Oh, and, of course, the chimes can only be used between midday and seven o'clock.

I can just see corridors and corridors of offices overflowing with clerks whose sole job it is to make legislation for small businesses as complex as possible. Were these employees traumatised as children by the sound of ice-cream vans endlessly chiming their way around the estates where they were brought up?

We are well used to our faceless bureacrats moving at a ponderous pace but the cities they represent are different case altogether. Take the City of Truro that managed to propel itself to an incredible 100 miles per hour on this very day in 1904. No doubt this inspired other cities such as Birmingham, Bristol and London to aspire to similar rates of pace. Naturally we should be proud that it was a Cornish city that achieved the first accolade but we should be mindful that the City of Truro was, in fact, built in Swindon to start with, and designed by George Jackson Churchward. They do not build cities like that anymore.

And after such an eclectic, or perhaps more accurately, awkward collection of mumblings we should end with a little John Masefield who was made poet laureate today in 1930.

I must go down to the shop again, the lonely shop on the prom
And all I ask is a customer, the receiver to keep her from,
And the till's ring and the door's creak and the pasty baking,
And the flicker of sun on the sea's face, and the whole Cove waking.
I must go down to the shop again, for the call of the newspaper queues
Is a terrible line, with anxious folk keen on the Western Morning
News;
And all I ask is a clear day, with the children baying,
With the flung pound notes and the silver change, and the credit cards
playing.
I must go down to the shop again, with the tattered brown housecoat,
To the grocery aisle and the wetsuit aisle, where the happy customers
float;
And all I ask is a loaded wallet from a rich and 'ansum rover,
And a pint of beer and small tax return when the long trick's over.
With grovelling apologies, Mr Masefield.

May 10ᵗʰ - Thursday

I suppose we are getting a second day of mizzle because we evaded the hacking rain we were promised yesterday but everyone else got instead. But lo, there was surf. One customer expressed her surprise that there were around twenty people who could vaguely be seen through the mist, bobbing around in the water over at North Rocks. After two weeks of flat calm I am surprised the lifeguards were not flattened in the rush.

The lifting mist in the afternoon brought a steady flow of customers. Both of them said how much they enjoyed being here. With such optimism flowing into The Cove perhaps I shall leave walking into the sea with rocks in my pockets until after the weekend. I have also been told it is incredibly difficult to swim thus encumbered, so perhaps I should choose something lighter.

So much for the humdrum of shop life - time to launch a Lifeboat. A textbook exercise from the perspective of the very excellent Shore Crew and we even managed to extract the Tooltrak, the Inshore Lifeboat launch vehicle, from the beach without the aid of the Harbour tractor. It still took twice as long to wash it down afterwards with the amount of weed, now much deteriorated, stuck amongst the tracks. Recovery for the big boat up the short slip was much safer too, with the addition of a high-tech device to stop the hook snagging at the keelway constraint; a rubber tyre at the top end of the hook.

We were so efficient in our efforts that we made it to the OS quiz with moments to spare. It was a hard fought contest and we were only a point behind our arch-enemies, which I might add is extremely unusual, aided by the fact one of their team made a schoolboy error in the last round. Nevertheless neither of us won and the prize went to a bunch of young whipper-snappers who were so close they could have looked over our shoulders. We just wish we had looked over theirs.

Having disgraced myself yesterday and having found no other dead poets to insult I shall leave it at that.

May 11ᵗʰ - Friday

By mid afternoon if you looked out across the big, empty beach it could have been high summer. You will note the use of the adjective 'empty', that is somewhat at odds with the term 'high summer'. It has been busier here on a wet day in February when, at least, you would have seen a bent old shopkeeper and his dog running out across the sand – the dog that is, not the bent old shopkeeper.

With the till stalwartly quiet, it was obvious that the oven man would turn up for his pound of flesh. In fact that is almost all I had about me after a week of throwing away pasties and bread that had been over-ordered. Unhelpfully, he rather insisted on coin of the realm that I just about managed to scrape together. The last few pence I garnered from under the kick plate of the sweet stand. It was fortunate for small children that there were none passing else I would have had their tuck money off them too.

It is a heartening sign, though not that heartening, that we are not alone in the doldrums by the marked increase in sales calls and emails. More often, now, from companies we have not done business with in years or never heard of. I am sure many companies are now ruing their decisions to deplete their teams of travelling sales people; it is not possible to hang up on the salesman in front of you or delete them even, though with some that might have been a welcome proposition.

This year we have certainly seen an increase in individuals arriving at our counter with personally produced greetings cards. In the past we have willingly bought from some of these people who have demonstrated artistic flair or individuality, and we still do. More and more, though, it seems any eejit with a digital box brownie thinks they can take a few snaps and glue them to the front of a piece of card and make a living out of it. We have a few examples in the shop now where the seller has been able to demonstrate some uniqueness, but these are rarities. If this carries on we will have to fashion a 'no hawkers' sign for the front door.

So, with a few shekels left in our pockets, we sought some relief with our neighbours up at the F&L for tea. We headed up early so that the bleddy hound could chase some rabbits in the back field; she does not get out much these days. It was quite busy up there, with one crowd taking over the entire corner of the bar. We were told they were secret policemen on reconnaissance for the flaming Torch relay. I did not believe it myself as there was not a trenchcoat, trilby or a pair of dark glasses between them. Anyway I hope they have been satisfied that the F&L is a perfectly safe place to be; I intend to be there on the evening before.

As I looked up at the star speckled sky and a bright-eyed Venus as I took the bleddy hound out for her last benefit walk I considered how much better it would look if we had an 80 metre tower of tangled scaffolding hanging off the end of Pedn-men-du similar to the monstrosity they have allowed in London town in The Olympic Park I shall write to the Parish Council with my suggestion first thing tomorrow.

May 12ᵗʰ – Saturday

I had fully intended to slip into town this morning to our local cash and carry. The wines that we have been buying for more than a year, and that have served us well by way of sales and presumably suited our customers' palates, have now reached an eye-watering price. They have crept up bit by bit since we started stocking them, but now we need cheaper replacements. Sorry, did I say cheaper? What I actually meant to say was a range of better value, quality wines. At least, that was the plan.

Unfortunately, a life raft floating through the Traffic Separation System had other ideas for my morning. The pagers went off while I was collecting the van keys calling us to a 'slow' launch; fortunate indeed that it was a slow launch, as I was the only one of the very excellent Shore Crew that turned up. While it is perfectly feasible to launch with just one of us, recovery is a slightly different kettle of anchovies. Luckily TS was working close by in St Ives, and our glorious Head Launcher also ambled down from his eerie in The Valley.

It was while we waited on the imminent return of the boat that our crab fisherman hove into view. When I first came down to the shop this morning I remembered that I had forgotten to place a crab order with him the previous evening. Mobile telephone calls to him, and a call over the VHF from another fisherman that I did manage to contact, had both failed to raise him while he was out working. When all else fails, and it looks certain that The Old Boathouse is likely to let down one of its customers, it is time to evoke the emergency services. As the Lifeboat powered into the bay I radioed the coxswain, who very kindly pulled alongside our crabber and placed our order.

After that the three of us made light work of bringing the boat back up the short slip. We are, after all, a very excellent Shore Crew.

They say that good things happen to good people so quite why this happened to us, or to me at least, I have no idea. As I am sure you know, we are frequented by regular visitors throughout the year and this particular couple arrive maybe twice annually. They are a very unassuming pair and, over the years, have taken quite a shine to the bleddy hound. This is not surprising. I think if I saw her just twice a year I might be quite struck by her, especially comfortable in the knowledge that at the end of a week I would be leaving her behind.

Anyway it transpires that the chap is quite an artist, the kind that makes attractive images on paper rather that the kind that makes pointless and grotesque piles of scrap metal – sorry just my own worthless opinion. Today they rocked up carrying a large flat box, which they presented to the Missus whilst I was having a first class breakfast next door with the other members of the very excellent Shore Crew. Inside was a large mounted and framed drawing, in pencil, of the bleddy hound's head. I have to say it was very good indeed and had captured not only her looks, but her spirit as well. It did a pretty good job on the Missus's spirit too and mine, well I can now forever be reminded of the bleddy hound's existence, even when she is not here.

The weather had us busier than of late, despite its shortcomings. So with a few more people around I thought I had better capitalise and try out the second rule of shop keeping: upselling. For the uninitiated, this is a marketing ploy aimed at adding to a single sale by suggesting complementary items. So, when a couple came to the counter with a pot of Sisley's rather good premium strawberry jam, I jovially entreated the buyers to the notion that it would be even better to lather the product onto a scone with some Rodda's clotted cream. The somewhat blank look I received in response suggested that the tried and tested selling technique had not been quite as effective as I planned. Indeed, the look included the subtext, 'what the bleddy heck are you going on about, my 'ansum', which I roughly translated from the German in which it was originally given. This, of course, reminded me of the first rule of shop keeping: know your customer.

Bolstered by our sudden change in fortune, sorry, let me put that a little more realistically. Bolstered by the fact we had more than two customers today, we and our neighbours repaired once more to the F&L for tea. I can tell you we did not have mince or any quince to go with it, and we certainly did not eat with a runcible spoon, however there are some dangers to going to the F&L for tea on a Saturday. Chief among these is that I arrive some five hours before I leave, which is an awfully long time for a chap to be cast adrift in the proximity of a bar. Although I doubt that I shall be standing hand in hand with anyone, there is an outside possibility that I might find myself at the edge of the sand.

But never mind and despite it all, *The Ammunition* was the bees knees and the dogs do-dads. With lead acoustic guitar, accompanied by bass and drums, they electrified us. Songs from Paul Simon, Neil Young and others that we would not have expected lifted us up to heights beyond our guard. Oh, what a beautiful, beautiful night.

While some may call it dancing by the light of the moon, the moon, the moon, most people would call it staggering and falling over. You have to wonder whether they ever saw the clear bright night sky like I did tonight.

Thanks to Mr Lear for allowing me to augment the closing phase with a bit of Owl and Pussycatness. He was born today in 1812, don't you know. Mr Masefield died today in 1967 but we are not going there again.

May 13th – Sunday

Although we had something of a flurry in the morning I cannot say we were any busier; much of the afternoon was spent scratching our bottoms. If this carries on we shall have to start letting the staff go, and since there is only me and the Missus we will have to fight over who goes first.

Also scratching their behinds were the lifeguards down on the beach; the sea was as flat as a dish. I am sure our crab fisherman was not complaining about it, though. He has been out several days in a row now, keeping his pots in order. So bright was his mood he obviously felt inclined to share it with us and dropped by a couple of lobsters and a pile of crab claws. I rather assumed that the lobsters were dead, which is why he was giving them away, and in making that assumption they would need to be in the pot quickly before they deteriorated. I have to confess to making a small gesture of surprise when I put my hand in the bag to fish out the lobsters and discovered that they were very much alive.

It really was quite spectacular looking out across the bay and the big open stretch of beach. It was hard not to imagine getting down there with the bleddy hound for a run around, and I had plenty of time to think about it. Because her arch-enemy lives in that direction we cannot risk heading in that direction in the evening, else I would have taken her.

As it happened I wish I had. She spent the evening pacing up and down and being quite irritating. Had she fingers she would have been drumming them on the table. If she is in the same condition tomorrow I shall take her down there, but we will have to go in the van. Who'd have a bleddy hound?

May 14ᵗʰ – Monday

True to form it was another bloomers day. That is like a pants day but bigger and worse. I managed to run the bleddy hound around before the rain came in, which was the only good thing about the morning. We were lucky enough to see a little sunshine by mid afternoon but with a brisk north-westerly bursting in through the shop doorway.

At least I managed to get away to the Penzance cash and carry in a re-run of the attempt that was scuppered by the Lifeboat call on Saturday. On Saturday I just had the one thing to do, now, two days later, of course, the list was a little longer.

We have a heated towel rail in the bathroom, which I am sure you are delighted to know about. It is an essential piece of equipment, especially during the winter if you do not want to be rubbing down after a shower with a cold and wet towel. Given we are still in the grip of winter, it is still an essential piece of equipment now. On the basis that we have not yet won the national lottery, the towel rail is turned on for the minimum period of time, namely as much time as it takes to dry a towel, by means of a mechanical electric timer, or rather was.

The analogue device has been in place for more than ten years and has outlasted the towel rail. Just recently it has been making a grinding noise, that is very apparent in the dead of night, but worse than that, apart from making a noise, it does not actually work. This has led to trying to remember to turn the heated towel rail on manually but most importantly, remembering to turn the darned thing off again after it has dried the towels. As you can imagine the former action is fairly easy to remember given the alternative of drying with a cold wet towel. Unfortunately, and despite the incentive of not having an unaffordable electricity bill, the latter action is often forgotten. Time, then, to very rapidly replace the broken timer.

There is no such thing as an electric timer shop in Penzance. The shops that might have stocked one did not and the one place I did not want to go, Been and Queued, had one that was seriously poor quality and very expensive, which was not a huge surprise. I also went to the supermarket – yes, I know. Had the other items I wanted been available somewhere else, that is where I would have gone, but they were not, so I didn't. It also did not strike me at the time, but the supermarket is in the proximity of an electrical wholesaler, which would almost certainly have had the timer, but as I only remembered when I got home, we are still without a timer.

I did however manage to get a new bulb for the up-lighter in the living room, that had seemed to give up without a fight a couple of days ago. We have another up-lighter for the other side of the room, but the bulb in that exploded a couple of years ago taking with it the fitting and I have been unable to find a replacement, even if I had a blind clue how to fit it.

How easy it is to forget these mundanities when a glorious tea is placed in front of you containing free crab and lobster. It was only right and fitting therefore to run it off down on the big beach with the bleddy hound, who once again looked like she was about to climb the walls from abject boredom.

I had to take her down there in the van, first to avoid any danger of running into the arch-enemy and secondly as she will not go in that direction in the evening and I would have had to carry her, which does nothing for my hard man image. We were able to park hard by the slope down to the beach, which meant I did not have to bother with her lead, and she happily chased the ball for the best part of an hour.

Before we left for the beach I mentally tossed a coin to decide whether to wear wellies or go barefoot. I chose barefoot, mainly because it was easier, but I ended up wishing I had chosen wellies. I really cannot remember my feet being so cold. They were like blocks of ice when we eventually came up the slope again. It was almost pleasant washing them off with cold water from the hose (sorry if you live in an area that has banned the use of hoses - that was most insensitive of me).

When it got dark I remembered that I had bought another bulb for the up-lighter. It does not take long to replace but can be fiddly, especially trying not to get a greasy fingerprint on the glass. Greasy fingerprints or not the new bulb failed to set the world alight for us, so there must be another problem. This is frustrating, as the next stop will be the fuse which is buried behind the sofa somewhere and requires a replacement fuse which is in the shop.

I had better get some rest now. After a catalogue of failures and a pair of cold feet I shudder to think what tomorrow has in store for me.

May 15th - Tuesday

Blow that, I am off to Hayle for yet another visit to a cash and carry, and this time I might actually buy something to put on the shelves. After all there must be an outside chance that someone might show up to buy something. On the way I also managed to track down the towel rail timer from a salesman who could think laterally.

I mentioned yesterday that I have been, on and off, looking for the little ceramic fittings for the other broken up-lighter so I thought I may as well ask, since an electrical wholesaler was about the only place that might be able to help. Not only did the chap know exactly what I was after he also knew he did not have any. Not only did he know he did not have any he also knew that they would be nigh on impossible to track down, and even if I could they would be imports that would cost and arm and a leg to acquire. Not only did he know all the things he did not have, and could not be had, but he also had the brilliant idea that if I bought a lamp unit I could salvage the bits I required from it, without it costing the earth either. Well, bless my soul, it is not often you get customer service that good, not outside the far end of Sennen Cove anyway.

The Hayle cash and carry store has recently been refurbished, I am sure I have told you. It rather seems that they have refurbished the staff too and sent them on over-the-top customer care courses. I was unable to go down an aisle without being asked if I could find everything that my heart desired. They clearly have also been told to practise their upselling skills by the feel of it. Remember upselling? Two managers chased me around the store informing me of special deals, new products and buying clubs I could join. It was a blessed release to see the light of day again and to let the sound of special offers fade from my good ear.

I had better leave you with a few words from a poet whose birthday coincides with today's date.

In front of me the fire
Grows bright.
I look for pictures in the glow.
All words escape me.
Where we walk, flowers grow;
They multitude about us
Like tender drops of coloured rain
And make us laugh,
As they kiss our skipping feet.
In skipping now I turn
To see the smiling face
That led me to this vale.
To see the eyes,
Whose precipice leads
To those arms
Wherein this flame
Stands tenderly embraced;
Whose tears flood
With happiness divine
This willing vessel.
Close my eyes
With feathered touch of cool caress
And let me drown
In this undarking vale
Until,
In front of me the fire
Grows cold.

May 16ᵗʰ – Wednesday

There is definitely a growing number of Chinese visitors, or at least from that neck of the woods. We had some in today asking for stamps to send their cards back to China, so they were in fact from China unless, of course, they just had friends in China and lived somewhere else. Anyway, it was gratifying to note that, despite being armed with the latest technology to send pictures by email or text, they were still keen to send postcards.

The Royal Mail has changed the price of postage stamps for mail going outside the UK. In a welcome simplification there is only one price for anywhere in the world, although they make a distinction of two world 'zones'. I had to check, but the price of a postcard stamp is the same to both zones. The other happy coincidence is that the price closely matches the price of two old European stamps that we had in abundance. Since the price rise we have been flogging two 44 pence stamps for anyone wanting to send their cards to foreign climes, despite the actual required postage being 87 pence.

This has worked reasonably well and our once redundant stamp pile has now dwindled, at least the pile of 44 pence stamps has. This has worked reasonably well until you try and explain to some Chinese visitors, (or people from that neck of the woods), that from us two stamps are required per card. It took a little bit of time and sign language to get the message across, and once they understood it took me a little time understanding whether they wanted ten stamps for five cards, or sufficient stamps for ten cards. Once we all got the hang of it they just kept coming back and back. They must have been here an hour or more writing cards, posting them then coming back for more cards and more stamps. Our Chinese visitors, or visitors from that neck of the woods, are welcome anytime.

May 17ᵗʰ - Thursday

This flaming Olympic Flame has got everyone lit up. *The Cornishman* decided to publish the West Cornwall route and times today and stated that Cove Road would be shut from 10pm on Friday. It will not be. The main road will be shut from Cove Road turning to Land's End. Our fellow shopkeepers at Sennen Post Office telephoned in a bit of a panic wondering what would happen to their newspaper delivery. Apparently, they had agreed with the delivery driver to have them delivered down here. If that is the case let us hope that it is not raining on Saturday morning, as my little newspaper box has just enough room for my own newspapers.

Most of our delivery companies have shied away from coming at all on that day. Fortunately our pasty company is a little bit more robust, though they have warned they might be a little delayed. As I have told most of them, the flaming Flame will be long gone from here when most of them turn up; the newspaper vans will be the only ones affected.

If the weather is anything like today (you did not think you were going to get away without the weather being mentioned, did you?) there will not be much flaming going on. In fact, with the persistent and bloomer-tugging easterly we have, the runner will have to wear a welder's mask, as it will be like carrying a blow torch.

The head of Visit Cornwall, the tourism group, has told businesses in West Cornwall that they should be in for a share of the expected £3.5 million bonanza that the passing Flame will unlock. He very smartly added, only if the weather was fine. Well then, I shall gird the loins of my till for a share in the 3.5 bob that Cornish businesses will have to forcibly wring from the two visitors who are brave enough to hang around after it has all happened.

Along with the brisk weather, (there, mentioned it again), we had some brisk trade, which surprised us. First, in the morning, we had a coach full of oldies to entertain us. They were clearly keen that the Chancellor was not going to benefit too much from them by way of inheritance tax, as they were all quite carefree with their shillings. It gave us our first quick-fire till ringing since Easter, which was very gratifying. It was also the older generation that provided the bulk of the trade for the rest of the day. While they were not all flush with funds, it was certainly a better poor weather day than we have had all year. If it is the pattern that the seniors are spending the money, I cannot wait for the Chinese oldies to come over; we will all be able to retire.

We also had a visitation by some famous people among the trickle of visitors. Well, when I say famous, famous in that they have appeared in an international seller, after I accidentally locked them in the shop while I attended a Lifeboat shout. They seemed unaware of their renown, or at least they did not turn up with their solicitor, so I assume they must have forgiven me.

There was at least one person enjoying the weather (darn, mentioned it again) out there today, a lone windsurfer in the bay. He certainly enjoyed getting wet; I lost count of the number of times he fell off his sail board. Despite this ineptitude he was clearly determined, as he was out there for most of the afternoon. I cannot imagine that he was one of this year's Olympic team, if there is one for windsurfing; maybe next time.

May 18ᵗʰ - Friday

If we wanted to know why we have not been deluged with hundreds of eager Flame watchers we need only to have asked the much maligned council.

I have long suspected that it has an anti-tourist agenda: funding for Blue Flag beaches withdrawn; beach cleaners cancelled; tourist information centres closed; abdication of responsibility for toilets. After all, those naughty visitors make so much trouble by causing wear and tear on the roads, making the council hire traffic wardens so they do not park in the wrong places and buying second homes, on which they do not have to pay full Council Tax.

The council would also save a fortune on road signage, since all the locals know where they are going. In fact they would not have had to put out 'Road Closed' signs to indicate that the A30 between Cove Road and Land's End will be closed from 10pm tonight. So keen are they to extract every last penny of value from their road signage, that they put these signs up a full thirty-six hours in advance, and a couple of miles up the road towards Penzance. In fact the first sign, I learnt later, was up at Catchall inviting drivers to head towards St Buryan. Our law abiding and concerned visitors have been reading the signs, turning around and heading back.

It is fortunate indeed that our German visitors are either less law-abiding or just plain did not understand the signs, as it seems they are the only ones down in The Cove today.

It appears that it is not just the council that businesses here have to contend with. The Olympic Committee, at least I presume it must be they, have permitted all sorts of commercial enterprises in on this big circus. No particular problem there, after all I assume these large companies have paid good money to be on the band wagon. What does grate somewhat, is that with all the local businesses around here prepared to gear up to service the needs of the hundreds, (or possibly a dozen), of spectators and involved parties alike, the entourage has brought all its own catering with them; so much for businesses basking in the afterglow of the Olympic Flame bringing prosperity in its wake.

It was only through the insistence of the manager of the Land's End complex that ordinary local people were allowed to come anywhere near the start of the relay.

There was an awful lot of policemen in The Cove towards evening; maybe a policeman's ball going on somewhere. Someone said they might be anti-tourist police, or at least that is what I thought they said, mind you I have gone a bit deaf in my left ear. I think the council might have asked them to come in case someone might commit an act of tourism aimed at disrupting the flow of the Olympic Torch.

It is clearly time I relaxed a bit. I took myself up to the F&L with the Missus and the neighbours for a rather enjoyable meal. I stayed for the band, the venerable V8, with he of the fantastic vocal range. As I looked around, expecting a few famous faces ready for the celebrations of tomorrow, all I could see were local people enjoying themselves.

By the time I went home the road really was closed, so I decided to walk down the middle of it. I had travelled no more than one hundred yards when I was nearly run down; two cars in one direction and one in the other and not police or official cars either – that is busier than normal!

The last vehicle to come up behind me was the community bus. It had been laid on, very kindly, by the F&L to ferry revellers home. I gratefully accepted a lift, after all we are to be over-run by happy shoppers tomorrow morning, apparently.

May 19th – Saturday

We were braced this morning, except we were really unsure what we were braced for. The Missus got herself out of bed at 5:30am, a notable event in itself, and took off up to the chip shop to watch as the flaming procession went by.

The press rather unkindly said that someone had made a grasp at the torch in some protest or other. It is not true, I can tell you. Our mate Dunkey was just trying to get a light for the half decent dog end he had found, poor lad.

I missed all the excitement and stayed home to mind the fort, and in the absence of newspapers at the usual time this morning took the bleddy hound around early for her morning run. I had come through the Harbour car park late last night and noted very few cars parked there. It was therefore a bit of a clue to see that the car park was near enough full first thing, so I decided to go back and open the shop, even without the newspapers.

It was the right thing to do. No sooner had the big event up top finished, there was a line of happy hikers pouring down from Pedn-men-du into The Cove. Naturally, they all wanted newspapers, but I pointed out that a bunch of goons with a big candle had chosen my newspaper delivery time to run down the middle of the A30, thus impeding their arrival.

Once the penny had dropped, everyone took it in good humour and as if by magic the Saturday press turned up.

Now, as I am sure you are aware, the Saturday newspapers come with all sorts of bulky inserts. The likes of Tesmorburys have these inserts neatly wrapped in a plastic bag, but us mere mortal newsagents must individually collate the inserts and stuff them manually into the correct newspaper. Please, there is no need for sympathy; we are paid handsomely for this task – a penny a newspaper.

So, you might imagine the carnage of several piles of newspapers and several more piles of inserts and magazines strewn across the shop floor. While customers called in their desired read, I went from pile to pile collating the correct inserts. To add to this confusion the newspapers from the other distributor were delivered to the store back up on the A30 next to the chip shop from whence the Missus had just arrived. When we realised this to be the case the Missus was duly despatched back up the hill to collect them.

Between us we managed to satisfy most demand with me selling one set of newspapers from the shop and the Missus selling the others from the back of the van. The Trotters would have been proud.

The Flame convoy this morning is infinitesimally small beer compared to what is coming our way. You may remember way back in February or March I reported in this very gazette that a team of experts were surveying the big beach. I am very pleased that I can now reveal why this was being carried out.

In the *Western Morning News* (did I mention I once had a review ...), in an article so small I almost missed it, was a report from the Institute of Director's conference. It concerned the opinion that the West was a prime site for the new generation of 'space ports', where British rockets will be launched to service satellites and space stations. There can be no other explanation; Sennen Beach is the new site for British rocket launches.

Naturally, there will be some timing issues, rockets will only be launched at low water on spring tides, but clearly it is an ideal location. Local businesses will be set to make a killing from the thousands of spectators, though there may have to be some fine tuning; Vellandreath will be concreted over to make easy access for the rockets to and from the launch pad and the front of the Old Boathouse Stores will have to be replaced with fire retardant materials. On the bright side we will not have to worry about heating up our pasties, thus avoiding the VAT issue. I have to say, despite the initial disruption I am quite looking forward to it.

May 20ᵗʰ - Sunday

I found myself in foreign parts this morning. I had travelled to the home of the Aged Parent who became an octogen ... octyge ... octi ... reached eighty yesterday. I stopped at a local shop in the town on my way and bought him a bottle of whisky half his age. Of course, on reflection I should have bought him two but he will have to wait for the full ton-up for that.

As it turned out it was not that much of a surprise visit despite my best efforts. The maternal part of the Aged Parent enterprise had caught wind of my dropping in and had spent a fortnight cleaning, preparing beds, killing fatted lettuce leaves (they do not eat too much fatty meat any more) and generally acting in a preparing-for-a-surprise-visit sort of way. The paternal Aged Parent would have to be blind and dumb (he's already deaf) not to have been alerted to a forthcoming event of import. As he put it 'I suspected someone was coming and it was either the Queen or you'.

Nevertheless he seemed pleased to see me, or perhaps the smile was reserved for the forty-year-old malt under my arm, which incidentally was salted away and not seen again while I was there. It was an all too brief visit but at least I was able to be there, which is more than I was able to do for the maternal Aged Parent's eightieth last year as it was during August.

May 21ˢᵗ - Monday

Here comes summer – maybe.

A near perfect day in The Cove today with plenty of warm, yes warm, sunshine, clear blue skies and a lapping sea to look out upon. In fact the only group possibly disappointed by today's appearance might have been the surfers, but surely even they could not begrudge the rest of us some pleasantness. All right, perhaps they would.

And what happens in The Cove when the weather is spectacular. Yes, that's right. Geet, big trucks arrive, unloading dumper trucks and diggers and start trundling up and down the slip to the Harbour beach. While you may be concerned that it is the start of the work necessary to launch rockets from the bay, it is only a little bit of adjustment to the Lifeboat slipway, making it wider so that the very excellent Shore Crew are no longer in peril of falling off it.

Much of my morning was spent composing letters to the council and the Cornishman, ticking them off for the disinformation that led to customers thinking that Sennen Cove was closed for three days. I fully expect to be roundly ignored but it will, at least, make me feel better.

It also made me feel better to see, what might be termed as an average number of visitors to The Cove for this time of year. So busy has it been that we were forced to replenish the stock in our fruit and vegetable fridge well before the bananas started to go soft and black and the lemons and oranges grew a light, furry covering. I also found myself having to trek up to Shrew House for more buckets and spades. It is so long since I was there last I had to squirt a quantity of a well-known easing oil into the lock before I could gain entry.

I tell you, it is almost as if Prince Sunshine has come and kissed our Sleeping Beauty awake after she has been forced asleep by the twin witches, Recession and Poor Weather; perhaps less of a fairytale and more of a pantomime.

With good weather and warmth in sight I stirred myself enough to fix the towel rail timer. I can hardly wait until it is cold and damp again so that I can see if it works.

May 22ⁿᵈ - Tuesday

There, it is cold and damp again. Towel rail works a treat.

I did hesitate, briefly, before exposing this latest nugget hewn from the rock of local press, but, hey, you only live once, even if it is for just a short while. It concerns the appointment of the first lady commander of a warship, HMS Portland. There will be a delay before she gets her hands on the wheel while the ship undergoes a refit somewhere up north. You see, you already expected me to add my own embellishments, such as the curtains did not match the carpet. Shame on you! Well, may as well be hung for a sheep as a lamb. The ship will be based at Devonport where modifications are being carried out which will permit the ship to be berthed without it having to go astern. Personally I think that is a disgraceful thing to say but I must report this story faithfully.

In the time I have left I should tell you that the temporary deafness I was suffering on my port side has been resolved. I tripped up to Cape Surgery this afternoon where a very nice nurse hosed out the affected lug 'ole. It was a wonder to behold, since the last time I had anything similar done it involved a syringe of comic book proportions. I shall spare you the rather unsavoury details but suffice it to say among the astounding amount of detritus I was surprised not to see a shopping trolley and a pair of old boots. Little wonder I could hear begger all. The down side, of course, is that I shall now be able to hear all the abuse levelled at me by lady readers unamused by the previous paragraph.

May 23ʳᵈ - Wednesday

Not one of the busiest days we have had of late but fair, dry and balmy. We are not quite into shorts weather yet, but the flip flops came out today and I disposed of the use of my thermal string vest. I did pause for a moment to consider losing the shirt first, but I do not think The Cove is ready for Rab C Shopkeeper yet.

Things picked up in the afternoon, hopefully bucking against the notion that the Chancellor's Plan A is not working. Perhaps it will be similar to the old telephone boxes where pressing Plan B will get our money back. Mind you the people that are down here do not seem overly concerned about the state of the nation; after all they are on holiday. The ones we should be worrying about are the ones not down here.

Things must be picking up elsewhere too; our sandwich man turned up this afternoon to tell us he did not have any sandwiches. I will wait until he turns up tomorrow to tell him I am not going to buy any.

On the subject of suppliers taking a rise out of us we have had a letter from yet another supplier wanting to issue invoices and statements via email. Of course I understand that the price of postage has gone through the roof and using email will save big companies thousands of pounds. What I object to is that they insist it will, 'improve our service to you', and, 'whilst also being kinder to the environment'.

Just how will my service be improved? At the moment I get a letter in the post that I simply pull out of the envelope and drop into my filing tray and ignore for thirty days. When they start arriving by email I have to remember to print the darn thing, on paper that I bought, using toner that I also bought, on a printer that will eventually flake out when it has printed enough pages.

And the environmentally friendly lark? A piece of paper is still being used as the tax man rather insists on hard copy. Until mail is completely eradicated our postman will still need to come and visit me, just with one less letter, so I suspect the carbon savings are marginal in the grand scheme of things.

How about an honest letter from my supplier, then? "Look, the price of postage is enormous and it is a right good excuse to start sending our invoices out electronically. This will save us thousands per year on paper, envelopes, postage, post room staff and the young lad we took on in accounts to keep an eye on the printer and make the tea, though heaven knows who's going to make the tea from now on. Yes, we know that you will have to shoulder the cost of printing the invoices yourself, but frankly that isn't our problem. Of course the savings we make will be reflected in our prices - until next year when we will conveniently forget the fortune we're saving and blame the price increase on the cost of oil, shortage of containers and pirates in the Saudi Gulf." Perfect, I would be quite happy with that.

In fact I might send that as my response and see if they laugh or send me a cheque – by email, of course.

Shall I leave you with an image of beauty? No, kind of you to say but not a picture of me. As I took the bleddy hound down onto the Harbour slip for her last run, out in the dying glow of the set sun, the smallest sliver of a large crescent moon with Venus at her side, hung above the horizon in a darkening sky. Gosh.

May 24th - Thursday

Yee hah, a rip-woggling day if ever there was one, with not a cloud in the sky. There was, however, quite a big one on the horizon that hung around there all day. It shrouded Cape Cornwall in mist and tried to creep in as far as Nanquidno valley at one point, before retreating again. No doubt it will roll in with the tide towards evening.

Good then, that the film crew were here in the morning getting their shots sorted out. I did not actually see the filming bit, but the important people were here when I took the bleddy hound through the car park first thing – the catering van. I am led to believe that they are filming for the movie version of Les Miserables. How appropriate, I thought, as you probably would not find a more miserable bunch in Cornwall, especially shopkeepers who have had to suffer the doldrums of the last three weeks. I have never seen the stage show or read the book, I would find it hard to read a book by a chap who sounded like he had been named from the phonetic alphabet, but I was under the impression that it was to do with the French Revolution. Quite what Sennen Cove has to do with that I am not entirely sure. One customer, who had clearly seen the show or read the book, said that they might be trying to capture the 'Minchins', a bunch of rocks between Le Harve and the Channel Islands, though I would not have a clue whether that is the correct spelling or no.

I have to say I was rather looking forward to cracking open today's *The Cornishman* to see if my letter had been published. This is the letter I sent them, by email, incidentally, castigating them and the council for disinformation regarding road closures ahead of the Olympic Torch relay. The letter had not been published, but I did get a telephone call from a very pleasant young lady who said she was the Chief Reporter.

I had always formed the impression that reporters were gravelly voiced old hacks from smoking too many unfiltered Gauloises, sitting around in bars wearing battered raincoats and drinking far too much Chateau de Grimolaise. I suppose she still could have been, but she did have a very nice voice – perhaps she smokes filtered Gauloises.

Anyway, I digress, but only briefly. From the conversation I inferred that another, more junior reporter, very possibly lodged in a bar somewhere smoking Gauloises cigarettes and drinking far too much cheap red wine, was working on the story for next week's newspaper. Frankly, I think that might be a little too late and the impact will be lost, but never mind at least it will get an airing. The Chief Reporter apologised for the error on *The Cornishman*'s part, but in her defence she said that the information that they had regarding the road closures was from The much maligned council. How could I not believe those soft and dulcet tones or that our less than illustrious administrative body had fouled up yet again?

At least they cannot interfere, yet, with a Lifeboat exercise that we duly took part in this evening. Both the big boat and the inshore were launched to waving crowds. It was such a spectacular evening we repaired to the small amount of beach the tide had left us and enjoyed fish and chips while we watched the sea come in even further. We are well versed in this routine now, knowing that this ardent sun could be the last we shall see for a while and, bless it, the mist held off and even retreated some.

After a more than perfect recovery we toddled off to the OS for quiz night and since the Lifeboat launch was an hour earlier than previous weeks we enjoyed some quality time wondering what we would do before the quiz started.

These quiz nights have become exceedingly popular over the months and we found ourselves squeezed into a corner of the bar on an especially small table. Half way through, with some rather tough questions, we felt rather squeezed on answers too – who would have thought that Emile Heskey's middle name really was Ivanhoe; we had the answer but thought it too preposterous to write down? We shall have to be braver next time, but even so we came second in quite a wide field.

It was absolutely no consolation to have a nice big, red crescent moon winking at me out of a clear black sky on the way home, petty though it was.

May 25ᵗʰ – Friday

It was so nice first thing this morning that the Missus and I sat out on our benches across the road and fought over who was going to serve the occasional customer when they appeared. When it got to the stage that we were too busy serving to fight we gave it up as a bad job and started do some proper work, well shop keeping anyway.

Now, let me say before I launch into this that the chap whose character I am about to utterly deflate appeared to be perfectly normal, so not a local, then. He was polite, seemed well educated and did not seem to be an axe murderer or a beater of defenceless animals. However he was keen to have some cash back and asked if we could oblige. We are very well versed in the response to this question after being asked a dozen or so times a day and duly explained the rules that if he were to buy a modicum of goodies we would be happy to accept his debit card and, for a small consideration, provide the cash back service that he desired.

There are some people that require small amounts of cash and others, maximising their outlay, as much as possible. Our man asked what the minimum amount was that he could withdraw. We have never been asked this before and at first I was a little dumbfounded, my mind working quickly to try and imagine the consequences of giving a penny cash back in the complex systems and processes that is the electronic banking world. It was with some relief that he settled on five pounds, but could he have it in change as he needed to pay for the car park.

This is where the story really starts. I mean you just would not would you, launch yourself off into the unknown, that is, without a few bob in your pocket against the odd unexpected eventuality? It is like going parachuting without a parachute – 'I never expected I'd need a parachute, anyone know where I can get one?', or going camping in the wilds without toilet paper.

My consternation was diverted half way through the afternoon when I was asked to drop the Inshore Lifeboat down to the beach for an impromptu exercise. This is one of those impromptu exercises that coincidentally coincide with someone's fishing boat that, having left the Harbour through a pile of weed, suddenly finds it has a fouled propeller. Dashed lucky the Inshore boat was out there exercising eh, Rosebloom?

So, with the sun beating down on us still, the Missus and I headed for the Harbour beach again after we closed. We were going to have our tea down there but settled for running the bleddy hound around with her ball instead. We imagined or rather hoped that it would be sheltered down there in the lee of the Lifeboat Station, as by late afternoon that easterly had become quite vicious.

Sitting there in all that sunshine reminded me that it has been announced that a National Solar Centre is going to be set up in Cornwall, near St Austell and there was me thinking that is where the sun shone out of. It has been recognised that Cornwall enjoys the highest levels of the sun's radiation and is well placed to take advantage of this form of green energy. I am sure that it will be a delight for campaigners all over Cornwall to know that those parts of the county not dotted with huge wind turbines will be covered instead with geet glass panels.

I suppose the question has to be, with all this electricity being generated down here from free sources such as the wind, sun, waves and tide how come it is still more expensive than anywhere else in the country?

While we sat on the beach and I pondered on these matters of great import I could not help but notice how the skin on the back of my neck and legs was slowly being flailed away in a sandblasting sort of way; it really was most uncomfortable. It was then it struck me that the Harbour beach would be a great little place for a wind turbine, and on a day like today it would be even better if the blades had solar panels stuck to them.

Do not expect to see me tomorrow; I am straight down the patent office to make my fortune.

May 26th - Saturday

Along with the Laurel and Hardy Newspaper Company who decided they would try and send us a three-fold increase in the Saturday and Sunday Mirror, our bakers also decided to join the party. They already told me yesterday that they could not send any brown bread and I would have to make do with granary instead. Come our delivery this morning it also seems that they could not do any white bread either, as we only had one loaf delivered. I spoke with one of the owners later who cited a mental aberration. I suggested he start selling newspapers; he would fit in quite nicely.

While the hotels of the region are enjoying a boost, I am sorry to report the slightly more risqué establishments have taken a bit of a knocking this week. Just yesterday the council turned down the licence application for a topless club in Newquay. The applicant, a Cornish maid, b'gad, wanted to make a clean breast of it and be up front, but the councillors thought it was just the tip of the iceberg. They suggested some errors in the application and were not prepared to accept such boobs. One was very derogatory about her and her counsel, and said they made a right nice pair. The maid said she needed the income and without the venue she might go bust. At the end of the hearing the distraught applicant said she was going to have to swallow a couple of tipples to calm her nerves, at which point one elderly councillor at the back, whose hearing aid had dropped out, fell off his chair.

Well, that is enough of that nonsense when there is the F&L waiting and the more than excellent *Devil's Creek* playing. How could they possibly disappoint?

I had the desperately good tunes of the band ringing in my newly reconditioned ears and a fuller crescent moon leading me home between the horribly black clouds. You should have seen it casting its blanket out across the sea, you really should.

May 27th - Sunday

Looking at this morning with its bright sunny spells it might have been a day with a little potential. As it turned out it had the potential to completely cloud over and turn our customers into slothful misers. Of course, I mean that in the nicest possible way.

Our neighbour was not having his best day either. Late in the morning the council sheriffs came through and stuck a ticket on his car. It seems he did not have his blue get out of paying for parking card in his window. Later in the day a bunch of around a dozen hairy bottomed bikers turned up on their mean machines and parked all over the pavement next to the café. Our neighbour must have still been ticked off about his parking ticket because he didn't half give them some grief for using up the pavement. I have to say I think I might have been a little more circumspect given their stamp, but give him his due he went back and told them again when they ignored him the first time. He probably called them sissies too. I think I will call him Dangerous Dave from now on.

May 28ᵗʰ – Monday

I think the least said the better about my little trip into town first thing this morning. It was to pay my annual visit to my accountant. It is just about my only trip of the year where the phrase, 'pay a visit', is entirely accurate. I suppose I should be grateful he was not wearing a black cap.

If that was not bad enough I had to go and put fuel in the van over at St Buryan, not that there is anything wrong with St Buryan, I should add. It is rather uplifting, even after blowing what used to be a mortgage payment into the van, to take the lane back to Sennen at this time of the year before the hedge trimmers get out there. The hedgerows are awash with colour, I have mentioned before; the hawthorn is in bloom; pinks litter the undergrowth amid alexander; cowslips and the occasional foxglove. When I reached the end of the lane I was aglow with natural loveliness.

By the time I got back into The Cove there were a few more people about. In fact, I had to fight my way through a crowd of German visitors as they made their way past the shop and up to Land's End. Not one of them was tempted to drop in for a souvenir or two, no matter how tempting we try and make them.

Our products are, from time to time, used for purposes other than that which they were intended. I can cite fishing line used to sew the sole back onto an old pair of boots, or the occasional spade sold to scoop up dog's doings. Today, though, one customer pushed the boundaries of innovation and creativity. Would I mind terribly if she pulled apart a fishing net in order to use the nylon gauze as a hair net? While hair nets very much represent a foreign land to me, I have no particular interest in our products when they have been paid for in full, other than that they provide the value and enjoyment that the buyer expects. For the young lady, now wandering around Cornwall in a shocking pink hair net, I trust those precepts have been met.

Speaking of value we had a senior couple from Yorkshire come by in the afternoon. They bought some small toys for their grandchildren and asked in passing what sort of fish it was that the chip shops used instead of cod. When I asked what they meant, they said that they had been served fish in a shop in Portreath that was listed as cod but certainly was not, in their opinion. They reasoned that cod is white and flaky, and the fish they were served was grey and not a bit flaky.

They asked if it might possibly have been pollack to which they were subjected and I thought probably not. Since Huge Ferney-Wherewithall got his teeth into the fish game, pollack is often more expensive than cod. Plus pollack is white and flaky too. I suggested it might be coley, but I have no idea if it is acceptable to pass it off as cod in a trade descriptions sort of way.

While in no way suggesting that the fish shop in Portreath is one, lest I am beset with their legal representatives, I said that some chippies will buy the cheapest frozen fish possible and have it shipped in from heaven knows where, such as Hull. This clearly was not the right example to give, as it suggested the fish from Hull was inferior and while that may have been acceptable if the couple to which I was conversing were from, say, Blackpool, this couple were from the other side of the Pennines and very quickly took umbrage. There followed a certain amount of rapid back peddling while I extricated myself from the hole I had backed into by explaining that we had a perfectly good fish market just down the road, which was the point I was trying to make. Although I do understand that cod is more plentiful from other ports and therefore likely to be cheaper.

I also fell foul of the Yorkshireman's unerring eye for best value when he berated me for giving him a Guernsey penny in his change.

We ended the day with something of a perfect evening. The sun had broken through late in the afternoon, leaving us in balmy sunshine. The Missus took the bleddy hound down to the Harbour beach after curfew for a run around, and at least this time came back with sand only in the right places. I am not sure we can entirely say that about the bleddy hound, who came back caked and sodden.

We shall no doubt wake up in sandy beds, which is odd since we went to bed in Sennen Cove.

May 29th - Tuesday

I thought it was Thursdays for the grey brigade but we seemed to be inundated with our more senior visitors today. We had Italians too, who seemed undaunted by the trend to pass us by and head off for Land's End without so much as a by your leave. It was not exactly raving busy but there were enough about to give us a steady trickle for most of the day.

I see that the Government has backed off imposing a pasty tax; the tax that never was. The media are still plugging away with misinformative statements that VAT will still be imposed, from October, on pasties sold from warmers. Please get it right, it already is. You have got to wonder what the Government is doing with their other hand while everyone is watching the one with this nonsense in it.

Ah, yes, just spotted it; they raised the school leaving age to eighteen. Typical, isn't it, just as they are planning to re-open South Crofty mine. All this unnecessary education really limits the number of small children available to pull those ore wagons. If the schools cannot teach them to read, write and count in eleven years, do they really think an extra two will make any difference?

And staying with mining I am not entirely sure Mr Davy would have expected a mountain climber who nobody has heard of for years to take his lamp up the top of some geet hill in Wales, 183 years to the day after he popped his clogs, just for the heck of it, carrying an Olympic Flame or not; hardly what it was designed for. I mean, is it dark and full of noxious gas on the top of mountains in Wales?

May 30ᵗʰ – Wednesday

A man at The much maligned council has replied to my complaint about the A30 being effectively shut two days before the Olympic Torch event. If the events related to me are true it is unsurprising that they cannot afford to run the toilets.

I am told that the management always intended that the signs remain flat until the last possible moment. It was the naughty contractors, I am told, that got it wrong – twice.

The signs were distributed on the Thursday, but by 8:30am they had their first complaint that they had been erected. Those naughty contractors must have been out during the very early hours putting them up, earning plenty of overtime. The good managers in Truro told them they were silly and to go put the signs down again. They even sent a Manager of Works out to make sure they had done as they were told.

By 17:30 those signs were back up again because the good managers got another complaint and, once more, they sent out the contractors to put them down again; working after 17:30, yep, overtime lads.

Some rogue must have gone through the route and put them all up, because they were erected again by Friday morning. You know, you just cannot keep a good sign down. Still, at least we had an apology in the last paragraph of the letter. I am not holding my breath for any compo, though.

May 31ˢᵗ – Thursday

I took an early trip up to Shrew House and filled the van full of goodies. I even managed to collect some stock that had not seen the light of day for a good long time. I suspect there is a gap in the space-time continuum up there and items slip out of the present day and return at random points in the future, which is when I find them again. Today we had t-shirts with 'Happy Jubilee' on them, which we lost in 1977.

We were not far off the end of putting out the stock that I had garnered when I noticed that it was three in the afternoon. Where did all that time go? Gosh we will be in June in a jiffy if we are not careful.

Best we go launch the Lifeboat before it is too late. We despatched our Head Launcher, along with another likely looking casualty, off to Cape Cornwall where they were to find an awkward place among the rocks to play poorly. We gave them a bit of time to get organised before launching the Lifeboat. Actually we gave them a lot of time to get organised as we had to wait for the good doctor to arrive, without whom the exercise would have been a bit pointless.

The next time we saw our Head Launcher he was bound to a stretcher and being plopped off the back of the Lifeboat. It was ever so slippy at the end of the slipway, there is a clue in the name, and we struggled a bit and we might have got him a bit wet at that point. It must have been the weight of water in his clothes that made him so heavy, so we had to stop every two minutes to give him CPR. By the time we had hauled him the entire length of the long slip he was not the only one needing CPR. All in all a very useful exercise and a valuable lesson learnt. Yes, our Head Launcher needs to lose weight.

You might want to learn too, what happened to the very excellent Head Launcher party at the OS quiz. All I can say is after our exertions, and one of us suffering mild hypothermia, we did not exactly set the world alight.

Look at that. It is nearly June already.

June 1st – Friday

Yes, the end of the world is apparently nigh and as if to prove it my order of sun hats and sunglasses turned up. Unfortunately, the items I was really after, like the wellington boot stand, raincoats and monsoon survival kits, were in another box that was missing from the delivery. They will no doubt show up at the onset of the sub-tropical conditions we are expecting shortly after the schools go back at the start of September.

Despite the impending doom, a constant stream of caravans and campers arrived in The Cove all heading for the elusive Sennen Cove Caravan site. You remember the one, the Sennen Cove Caravan site that is not in Sennen Cove. The owner of a rather big caravan found himself in a little bother as he could not get around the corner at Tinker Taylor. A very sympathetic Lifeboat mechanic allowed him to drive up into the Lifeboat car park. However, with the slipway workers occupying the top end there is not much room to turn there either, even with the caravan detached it seemed to be a challenge. Ah-ha, not so for this German technophile, the caravan has a remote control and can be manoeuvred under its own steam. Vorsprung durch technik as they say in Germany – possibly.

With the sun doing its darnedest to hang on as long as possible we dined al fresco with our neighbour. It was very pleasant sitting there in the sunshine. Afterwards I took the bleddy hound down to the Harbour beach where we were able to enjoy the last of the emptiness and a smooth, retreating sea for her to have a swim in. It is not surprising we were almost alone, as it is quite aromatic down there at low water due to the continuing breakdown of the oar weed. I say almost alone as there were four small boys playing around the bottom of the short slip. One of them coined it reasonably well when he emerged from the water and declared that he smelled of fish. It is a rough approximation of the type of smell we are discussing, and I am sure his mum will be delighted.

I am afraid I must leave you on a sombre note with the news that one of the more charismatic Cove characters shuffled off today. Born in what is now Tinker Taylor cottage, FT was definitely larger than life and notable in recent years for his early morning bellowing of colourful language out across the bay from his lofty residence. He should however more rightly be remembered for regaling patrons of the OS with his singing of Cornish songs in a deep baritone while clutching pint glass that could barely been seen in his huge hands. "I didn't mean it, you know. Only joking, boss."

June 3rd – Sunday

I was a little bewildered ... now, I better make myself clear here, as I do not wish to injury anyone's sensibility. After all, it only took one comment about confused Cornish people on a television comedy programme to have a Cornish MP raise questions in the House. So let me start that again lest some Cornish person be confused, no sorry, mistaken, that I meant all the people of Cornwall are bewildered or confused ...

I alone was a little bewildered that we were so busy on a rather drab day, until I received an electronic mail from TL who explained all. He tells me in all the publicity surrounding the Jubilee pageant on the Thames there was a picture in yesterday's *Daily Telegraph* of a Tamar class lifeboat launching from Sennen Cove. In the background, and this is where the story really starts, and a little off centre is The Old Boathouse Stores. It is plain to see that we have been inundated with *Telegraph* readers keen to see the iconic landmark for themselves.

It is fortunate indeed that most of our suppliers work through the various holidays of the year, as our shelves have emptied rather quicker than we imagined. These *Telegraph* readers certainly do not mess around while shopping. It has not helped that we were so quiet for such a long time, as we have quite forgotten what busy was all about. No doubt we will get into the swing of things by the end of the week, just as everyone goes home.

We just hope that we do not get the rain the forecasters promise, or we will start to lose the campers. Let us just hope they are not all *Telegraph* readers or we will be truly stuffed.

June 4ᵗʰ - Monday

Another busy day and one with a bit of nice weather, which was very welcome, thank you very much. What was not welcome was our baker, who is catching up quickly with the Laurel and Hardy Newspaper Company in the poor service stakes, deciding to not deliver bread until half way through the morning. It is of absolutely no help to our customers who have come down early in order to feed their young broods a breakfast, preferably before dinner time. Selling them a bucket full of excuses is hardly likely to fill hungry tummies either, but it does seem that our baker has more of them than bread.

He also did not bring enough in the way of pasties either, but that was my fault for not ordering enough. We promptly ran out by midday, which was a tad embarrassing as we did not have any Grumpies to fall back on. Having increased my order for tomorrow we shall doubtless have them coming out of our ears by the time we close, such is one of the many paradoxes of running a shop by the seaside - or would that be ironies.

There are still people that come by that do not mind admitting that they read the Diary from time to time, mostly when they are alone in the shop, admitting it that is, not reading it. However there was a lady today who was about to take things to a new extreme and one that could land me in hot water or leave me stranded or maybe stranded in hot water. She said that she was to have a meeting with the management of the First Bus Group and that she was going to quote me to get her point across. Now, I do not actually recall being ever so complimentary about the bus company in question, so my guess is that she is not going into the meeting to heap praise upon them. This can only mean that the quote she intends to release may be a soupçon disparaging about their service, possibly bordering on the libellous, or would that be slanderous if she is going to say it? I should consider myself fortunate that I do not use the service on a regular basis, nor am I due a bus pass anytime soon else I might find myself at the mercy of a disgruntled bus driver in the middle of a moor somewhere. Let us hope there are sufficient funds garnered from this week for me to make a sharp getaway if necessary.

Of rather more concern than my reputation, was the welfare of a small child on the beach this afternoon. Rescue 193 from Culdrose managed to land on a sliver of sand at the bottom of Velandreath and recovered the youngster from the Lifeguard hut where she was being cared for. No more than half an hour later it was back again to airlift a walker with a broken ankle out over by Cot Valley. Not the sort of busy we like to see on a pleasant holiday afternoon.

June 5ᵗʰ - Tuesday

After some initial heavier showers we were treated to varying degrees of mizzleness throughout much of the day. This clearly delighted the crowds to such an extent that most of them stayed at home. Towards the end of the rain it was starting and stopping every few minutes, which provided some entertainment watching a walker while he alternated between wearing and not wearing his waterproof trousers.

I was unwilling, after the great pasty disaster of yesterday, to be in the same position again so I doubled the order today. As the cheese and vegetable pasties were the last to go yesterday, I made sure that the predominant proportion of today's order was of the steak variety. Yes, dear reader, as ever you are well ahead of me, the predominant proportion of our pasty buyers wanted cheese and vegetable pasties today and we ran out before midday. Similarly, our customers have been buying white bread in abundance, when it has been here, but today, after upping the volume, they fickly switched to brown; rough retribution, perhaps, for laughing at indecisive walkers.

And I have saved the best bit until last although I have not the faintest idea of what I am about to talk about. You see the Missus has set up something called a Twitter account for the shop. Through this ultra modern medium we can apparently communicate interesting news from the shop such as whether crab and lobster is available to order, or new products have arrived. We will also be able to tell people that it sunny and warm in The Cove when the Met Office has indicated otherwise, so expect many Tweets on that account.

I will not be at the tiller of this icon of modernity because, despite having spent 25 years at the cutting edge of Information Technology, and occasionally driving technology into the heart of large companies, I have not a blind clue what this is all about. Apparently, the Missus tells me, our Twitter account is named *@TheOldBoathous1*, although you do not have to type it in italics, and I am sure you, dear reader with your finger on the pulse of current culture, know exactly what to do with it.

June 6ᵗʰ – Wednesday

What a rumbustling rip-gozzler of a day. Who would have thought looking at the ever-changing forecast we had yesterday that we would have ended up with this? It must be said, it looked a little uncertain first thing this morning and for a little while there I was regretting maintaining my high level of pasties on order. But come early afternoon everyone else had run out and we were the only show in town – I love it when a plan comes together.

With The Cove about as busy as it gets, it was an ideal opportunity for the contractors working on the Lifeboat slipway to move in the geet pre-cast concrete sections for the slipway sides. Of course, they could not do much about the timing, as they have to coincide with the spring tides. To be fair to them they managed it extremely well, moving the lorries in and out of positions, where they blocked the road for as little time as possible. They also have a foreman who is a big happy chap who I would think it is almost impossible to be upset with. He is only about fifteen as well.

As entertaining as watching the traffic jams might have been if only we had time to watch, I rather fancy watching the huge low loader come down the hill might have been even more so. There were certainly enough people around to observe the mayhem, and it was good to see a constant crowd down our end of The Cove for a change despite the attraction of the beach. It was crowded down on the big beach too; it could almost have been a summer's day.

Perhaps it was the arrival of our Cornish Earlies, that have arrived late. We have been giving our local farmer a bit of grief, as we did expect them at the end of May. We suspect that today's delivery was just to get us to stop annoying him. We had some for tea tonight along with some of the fish that I did not manage to sell in time. Well, I had the fish; the Missus hates fish, but the potatoes were every bit as good as we remember them. We should have these for the rest of the summer now.

The Missus is tweeting away like a caged canary on this Twitter lark. So far we have six followers, some of which we know. As for the others it is a bit of fun trying to guess; it is a bit like having a benign stalker. Time will tell if there is actually any benefit to it and, as my rusty technical mind slowly pieces together how it works, I am warming to it quite nicely.

At seven o'clock precisely it started to rain, just like it said on the forecast. My sincere apologies to the family attending a show at Minack tonight to whom I suggested that the rain was a little behind schedule. It is only light rain, honest.

June 7ᵗʰ - Thursday

You are like a hurricane ... and I'm gettin' blown away. Neil Young clearly had today in mind when he wrote those lyrics.

We spent the morning in a state of suspense, because the atrocious weather heading our way had been well publicised. In fact the front of one newspaper, the one for people who want to be angry all the time, boldly and, I would say, quite gleefully announced, "70 mph gales ...". Despite the dire predictions, by four in the afternoon we had only managed a paltry 62 miles per hour.

We had a few bright spells in the morning and it was comparatively busy for a while, as some of the visitors made plans to leave. By afternoon, however, the weak lily livered lot had deserted the beach and cleared the street. What a bunch of pansies; it was only a little bit of wind, oh, and driving mizzle followed by lashing rain. Call yourselves holidaymakers? You should be ashamed.

Talking of which, but only in a light and frivolous way, we are required from time to time to exchange items that customers have bought in error. We are very happy to do this, providing the returned item is in saleable condition, unlike the chocolate bars we find occasionally on the shelf that a small child has chewed and put back. A case in point was the lady today who dashed into the shop wishing to exchange the, ... no I cannot tell you what it was because she will be mortified upon the realisation that it was she. Suffice to say that the item she wanted was just a few pence dearer than the item she was returning. The differential, or at least in whose favour it lay, clearly had not dawned on her, as she cheerfully assured me not to worry about the odd few pence. It's all right, I will try hard not to.

But there was no time to worry about that as I had to dash over to Lifeboat training as soon as the shop shut. With no chance that the Lifeboat was going to launch, we set about some simple maintenance tasks. Head Launcher went and serviced the Tooltrak Inshore Lifeboat launching machine, while I went below decks and mended some dry suits.

The dry suits have replaceable collars and wrist bands that keep the water out of the most accessible points. These occasionally whither and tear, then need to be removed and new ones glued into place. I prized open the glue pot with the odd tuppence I luckily found in my pocket, which remmminded me I mmight have had a fffew more of them had I not been dddeprived earlier. Tthere are gglooves aavailable to protect thhe haands but the gglue mmelts the gglooves soo itt is easier to ddoo iit without tthem. Unnfortuunately it iss a verry strong gglue which hass myyy fingers sttickiing tto evvryythiing.

Thankfully, I managed to peel most of the dried glue off and repair to the OS for a very crowded quiz night. It was hard finding a table until a pregnant lady, a man with a broken leg and their frail granny offered us their seats, which was jolly decent of them. We were clearly not at our best, I think I was distracted by my financial loss, and we slipped into obscurity in the rankings. The winning team did the most outrageous double by winning both the quiz and the 'chase the ace' netting quite a handsome sum. Who would have thought that they would have turned out to be scholars and gentlemen - and ladies too and donated their quiz winnings to a very worthy cause? There was a bit of commotion as we left when a man with a broken leg toppled over in the doorway and a pregnant woman went into labour.

I walked home into the gums of the gale, (it was getting a bit old by the time I went home), that is normally reserved for months ending in 'er' or 'ry' only to find that the bleddy hound, despite the weather, was still keen to run around the block. Through all this I could not help the feeling that my pockets felt a bit light.

I just ought to say for the lady who exchanged her item today not to worry, I have forgotten all about it.

June 8ᵗʰ - Friday

There was a howling and gnashing of teeth through the night and into the morning. The wind was howling; the teeth were mine.

When it came to setting up the shop I imagined my balls being battered around in the wind so, although the ball stand needed to go outside, I removed the balls to the safety of the storeroom where they stayed all day. Fortunately, the other items that sit outside in all weathers are a little more robust.

This is more than can be said for the contractors working on the Lifeboat slipways. They had been scheduled to work through the night to take advantage of the spring tides before they diminish, but the little bit of weather seems to have put them off. It was either that, or the large grey seal that has taken up station at the foot of the long slip, that stopped progress.

It has been sometime since I have included a report from our International Correspondent, which is a shocking omission and one that I should put right forthwith.

For those of you unfamiliar with our International Correspondent, as it has been so long, I should explain that long ago we sent MM out across the pond to infiltrate the indigenous population there and send back reports of life in the wilderness. The IC's post is situated in a coastal resort similar in many ways to ours, but just a few degrees warmer, oh, and populated mainly with Americans, whereas The Cove is populated mainly with people from Birmingham.

It seems that we are not alone in being deluged with the wet stuff, although the rain in South Carolina is probably a sight warmer. Now, one thing you should know is that MM keeps an allotment, and things being so much larger in the USA, you might imagine that it is the size of a small farm. Where a couple of years ago the main crop was water melon, this year it seems to be carrots and when it comes to carrots our International Correspondent knows her onions. In fact, she has onions too and has a cracking good recipe for onion and rosemary jam handed down from the little known ancient Native American tribe, the Chericksteinees, that I must share with you if I can persuade her to part with it.

While this seems a world away from the hedonistic lifestyle that we enjoy in Sennen Cove, I must point out that MM's life is not always such a bed of, well, carrots. She reports that recently she attended a wedding and hobnobbed with the rich and influential set in Miami, setting sail to the Bahamas in a luxury steamer onto which her hosts had loaded their personal wine cellar. It is a dirty job, MM, for which we all admire your dedication.

So you see, life the other side of the Atlantic is not so different from our own. We too can take a trip along the coast a bit and board a steamer bound for exotic islands. Although our particular steamer has been port-bound for a couple of days due to the extreme weather conditions, it too has an extensive cellar; apparently a bottle of Chateau Neuf de Lidl can be acquired for a little under a fiver, while in international waters, along with a complementary brace of vintage Special Brew cans.

By evening tide the wind had abbed (that is lighter but not quite abated) and it was still pretty drafty when I took the bleddy hound out for her last run. Many of our visitors have already set their navigation boxes to home and beggered off, however there were signs of a few more arriving.

So as the gardener of Eternity pulls from the ground the carrot of Time, only to find the drought of Fate had shrivelled his root, it is time to say goodnight.

June 9ᵗʰ - Saturday

It is a sad day for us purveyors of beachware. Not because our holiday makers have headed for the hills and taken their wallets with them, although I have to confess that a tear or two did well up in the corner of my eye as I waved them adieu. Indeed, the sadness of which I speak was brought on by the demise of the last of his breed, a manufacturer born to the art and craft of constructing that icon of British beach holidays, the windbreak. Yes, our man who has been supplying the trade for the last thirty-seven years has eventually given up the fight against cheap Oriental imports and hung up his, er, whatever you make windbreaks with.

I am given to believe that he was the last manufacturer of windbreaks, not only in Cornwall, but in the UK. He cited the rising cost and unavailability of the wood for the poles, the materials for the canvas and for the little plastic caps that go on the end. Never will we see their like again. I am minded to save one of each size and have them framed and hung outside the shop as a monument to the last piece of beachware ever made on British soil and, by Saint Piran, it was Cornish.

At least the beach was open for swimming today; it was red flagged all day yesterday and not surprising either. The Lifeguards have become much more visitor friendly in this regard since they started here a few years ago. Back then it seemed that they would put up their red flags if there was a danger of getting wet, let alone drowning.

It was difficult to understand why we were still open until seven o'clock, when by half past five we could have had a ploughing match up Cove Road and not upset anyone. Of course, had it been sunny we would have been inundated and I would have been vindicated.

It could have been worse – I could have been on my own. Each year for the last seven, the Missus has gone off to the Royal Cornwall Show with her mates from next door. This year, with the holiday being put back a week, she was unable to go and has been … how shall I put this kindly, ah yes, grumpy as a room full of Spanish bankers. She will not watch the local news broadcast in the evening as most of it is about the show, and so is the *Western Morning News* (did I mention I once had a review …). I am dreading Thursday as *The Cornishman* will probably have a full colour supplement. I can see the attraction of going as they have all sorts of things to do and see there, for example a chap diving thirty feet into a one foot deep pool of milk. What could be butter than that?

Naturally, I have tried to avoid mentioning the show but it is not at all easy with customers bringing up the subject. I must have nearly not mentioned it at least a dozen times today. Still, she cheered herself up a mite by running the bleddy hound down to the Harbour beach for a bit, late in the day. We shall have to get used to taking her out ourselves as our young walker is going home tomorrow. In fact she had an extra run at the back of the F&L after I was transported up there for tonight's soiree. I could not help thinking, and I do not know, but I think I might have mentioned that it looked a bit like the Royal Cornwall showground up there tonight.

I repaired to the bar while leaving the spinning wheels of the van ringing in my ears. Little did I know at the time but *Melodious Funk*, the scheduled band, were about to give us a bit of a treat. They consisted a lady singer with a substantial voice, a drummer, guitarist, a small maid with a dirty bass saxophone and a saxophone that was not bass but very shiny, and a chap with a guitar that had somewhere close to a million strings; I thought it was a portable harp at first. They played and sung songs, very familiar, from the Mo'town type soul stable from Otis Redding, Erma Franklin and Amy Winehouse as well as a bit of funk from the likes of Average White Band. They did a darned good job – the joint was jumping. They are most welcome back, I suspect. They even won over our resident, dyed in the wool rocker and not many can say that.

June 10th - Sunday

Quite how I missed this I do not know, but *The Diary's* inside man in the Land's End Coastguard told me last night that he was called out to a shout in Sennen Cove on Friday evening. This was the day with the big sea and the red flagged beach just to set the scene. A concerned onlooker called out the Coastguard after seeing some boys jumping off the Harbour wall, followed by several tons of breaking wave.

The irresponsible yoofs on this occasion were local lads who have been messing around in Sennen waters since they were big enough to crawl to the shore line off their mother's knee. While not entirely risk free, these boys roughly know their limitations and have a laissez faire attitude when it comes to the nanny state. Nevertheless, the Coastguard has a duty to give them a ticking off, especially as they have been roused from their tea tables to attend the emergency.

The plot thickened slightly when today we see the same lads in mid jump in a nice big picture in *The Sunday Times*. It seems that quite by chance a professional photographer was on hand to capture the moment. I imagine that it was also coincidence that we saw the same boys with shiny new skate boards out and about this weekend. I have already drafted a letter for the Leveson enquiry.

Despite the nationwide publicity, The Cove slipped gracefully from cosmopolitan crowdedness to sleepy hollow overnight as expected and as usual the weather improved. A couple of days ago we were pegged down to have a nice rainy week and now we seem to be scheduled to have a bit of sunshine. We will, of course, have to wait and see and I do not think I shall be dashing out to overfill our shelves on the information.

I will, however, be seeking to find some mackerel. We have a couple of customers slavering over the thought of having some for barbeques and they have been elusive – the mackerel that is, well, the customers too to some degree. On Friday the sea was so rough that none of the day boats went out and on Saturday, while the boats went out, there was no mackerel to be had. I even telephoned our line fisherman whose punt I thought I saw coming across the bay today. He did not answer my call, probably because, as the boat came closer, it was clear it was not he. Even if it had been we can almost guarantee that he would have been fishing for pollack; he always is when I want mackerel. We are pinning our hopes on getting hold of some tomorrow.

June 11ᵗʰ – Monday

There I was perusing the *Western Morning News,* (did I mention ...), only to find a reprise of the photograph in the Sunday Times of our local lads jumping off the breakwater. The *WMN* was a little less forgiving in the caption, calling it a dangerous game that the coastguards put an end to. They also suggested that the mothers intervened, which is strange way of spelling encouraged.

I think I may have mentioned that we have decided to change our commercial waste disposal supplier. The new one is considerably cheaper than the old one, but the crowning factor in the decision to adopt them is that they will collect our waste cardboard weekly for less money than it costs me to drive to St Just. This is a little academic now, as one of the reasons that the council is much maligned is that they removed the cardboard recycling facilities from the car park in St Just at the same time as they removed just about all the other waste recycling points across the county.

Oh dear, I better have my rant about recycling, had I not, or I will never sleep tonight. Yes, the council has removed most of the recycling points across the county. I suppose the thinking is, that now they have a bright new collection service that collects recycling in half a dozen different coloured receptacles every two weeks, they are no longer needed. This thinking probably works very well if you ignore the fact that this county is one of the major tourism hot spots in the country, something that our council is particularly adept at doing.

The problem arises when the hordes of very well trained recycling visitors that come here on holiday cannot help but want to recycle their waste, nay, they demand it. Increasingly we are being asked in the shop where visitors may recycle the newspapers, bottles and cans that they have accumulated and increasingly, unless they are staying in a holiday let, the nearest point is the much reduced facilities at St Just, or a ten mile trip into PZ at one of the big supermarkets. While recycling is important in the drive to reduce carbon emissions, driving twenty miles to do it probably is not.

Sorry, I digress, now where was I? Oh yes, I no longer have to drive to St Just to get rid of my cardboard. Not that I did so anyway, not ever, not even once, as trade waste was not allowed in the giant cardboard recycling bin that was always full of trade waste. I only ever went to recycle cardboard that had been used in a domestic way, domestically in our flat, honest guv; we seem to have so much cardboard waste from our flat.

So as I returned from town I stopped off at Shrew House where the cardboard that I would never take to St Just had accumulated since, coincidentally, the St Just recycling bin had been removed. Our new waste collection company has promised to collect it all tomorrow, so I have packed it all into the van so that it is on hand. I can hardly wait.

June 12th – Tuesday

At seven o'clock this morning there was a clear blue sky and the sun was splitting the hedges as I walked the bleddy hound around the block. By the time The Cove had filled with happy money bearing visitors the clouds had closed in and we had intermittent showers, despite the Met Office's assurance that we would be rain free all day.

There seems to be a proliferation of pregnant women in The Cove this week. I do hope that it is not catching. We also had a fairly pregnant pause waiting for the main event of the day, which was our cardboard collection. It is all right, no need to rush away and find your tin hats, I shall not be launching into a diatribe of Dickensian proportions on recycling, or suppliers not supplying. I shall save that for tomorrow, if they still have not turned up.

What did turn up today, though, was our first basking shark of the season. Well, actually it turned up yesterday because our man in the kayak that looks like a large shoe, that is the kayak, not the man, who has been out at the crack of dawn all week told me he had seen it, and let us face it if you are in a shoe sized canoe and a thirty feet basking shark heads in your direction you are unlikely to forget it in a big hurry. It stayed for much of the afternoon and since we did not have any at all last year I will take it as a portent of a cracking good summer on the way and with the sunshine breaking through again later in the afternoon, you could almost believe it.

So at seven o'clock this evening there was a clear blue sky and the sun was splitting the hedges as I walked down to the OS for a game of cards. Actually, it was seven thirty but that would not have permitted me to do a cunning copy and paste and win myself a free paragraph. It has also restrained me from issuing that diatribe of Dickensian proportions as, would you not know it, our new waste disposal supplier never turned up to collect our waste cardboard.

But none of that really matters. After all why should it; there are more important things in life. It did not even matter that in a clear field of rainless sky over the entire western approaches and across west Cornwall one single shower decided to plummet down on Sennen Cove, just as I was about to depart the OS. No, bolts of lightening could have thrown themselves in my direction and, believe me, they would have missed. And, yes, when I did head home the rain very kindly abated. I can not imagine why.

Oh, did I tell you? I won at cards.

June 13ᵗʰ – Wednesday

It has not been the best of days for me today; I suspect that the gods have it in for me after winning at cards last night. It must be pay back time.

There is one thing I cannot abide. No, strike that, there are several things I cannot abide such as small, rude and unruly children, football matches that dominate most of the normal watching channels without any real alternatives and dogs that pee up against our newspaper bin while still attached by a lead to their owners. Also, and particularly in this case, it is companies that fail to call back when they have said they will and when you call back to find out why the operative says, "It wasn't me you spoke to". Or is that two things?

Anyway, the latter of those normally generates a caustic response from me such as, "Sorry, I didn't realise I had to speak to the same person every time", or, "Sorry, I assumed you worked for Appalling Customer Services Co. since you answered their 'phone", which normally sets up an antipathy with the operative that accelerates me being passed to a supervisor, or sometimes they just put the telephone down.

So at one o'clock, having been promised our new bin and cardboard collection would come to fruition before eleven o'clock, our new bin was delivered and the cardboard was taken away. The end of a frightfully sorry tale, except, not quite. The lock on the 'new' bin, that looks like it was first used in a working tin mine, does not work, roughly meaning that it will be full a couple of days after it has been emptied, mainly with other people's rubbish.

Talking of small unruly children, all right we were not but I am on a roll so do not stop me now, we were subjected to a visitation by one today. He was with his mother and happily pulling postcards out of our racks. His selection was entirely random and any not to his taste he replaced in the rack. Ordinarily, this is the way of things except that the way he was placing them back in the rack was entirely random too. He had managed to decimate two stands before his mother asked him to desist.

He came to the till with his packet of crisps while mother abandoned him to peruse the rest of the shop. It was then I could see that he had a nasty bump on his forehead. It seems he had already been in another shop with a far less tolerant shopkeeper.

After the bin and cardboard issues had been resolved to some degree the Missus waltzed off to Truro on a bit of a shopping trip. A little while ago she started to make bunting, which I am lead to believe is the new cupcakes in fashion terms. She started with a string that we have in the shop, spelling out "I 'heart' Sennen Cove" I am told; the lettering is in green, which having a red/green colour sight deficiency means it just looks like a string of bunting to me. She has subsequently progressed to doing one for everyone she knows who has had a birthday or suitable celebration, whether it requires bunting or not. She has become so proficient at it that she has repaired to Truro to seek new materials. I urge you, dear reader; if you are anywhere near the shop please do not let the Missus know your name, else before you know it you will be festooned with bunting with your name on it.

June 14ᵗʰ – Thursday

I was surprised to note that *The Cornishman* printed a letter I wrote to them regarding the road closures rolling up to the start of the Olympic Torch relay; surprised, not because it was three weeks after the event, though that did provide some consternation, but because I started the letter holding both the much maligned council and *The Cornishman* responsible in differing degrees. Now all it will take is for someone else to write in and rebuff my claims and this thing could run and run, much like the Olympic Torch relay really, which seems, at the moment, to have been completely forgotten about.

Despite the grievous weather and occasional rogue shopper we had moments of brilliance in the shop. After all it is the last day of going home shopping for many. I was quite amazed at the number of people who were fitfully dressed and had clearly foreseen monsoon conditions – bless them all.

You may not be aware, but most Thursdays we have a Head Launcher's tea party at chez nous (that is French for the only place that will have us) prior to Lifeboat training. We were all set for some training this evening and TS, who lives in Redruth, was well on his way when we received the message that training this evening had been cancelled for reasons unknown. Nevertheless, we enjoyed our rib roast and twiddled our thumbs meaningfully until it was time to head off down to the OS for the obligatory quiz night.

We did not do too badly, although we were beyond arm's reach of the big money. Suffice to say it was prize enough to walk home in the dry and with a few bright stars poking through the gloom.

June 16ᵗʰ – Saturday

We were treated again this morning to a sight of the 'cow' on Cowloe. Our crab fisherman said that it was as clear as it has ever been today. For those of you unfamiliar with this phenomenon it is a flat face of rock that attracts, in certain conditions, white foam and looks very much like a large cow; it is how the Cowloes derived their name, we suppose. Our crab fisherman considered it extraordinary that such an ephemeral natural feature must have been visible from time to time for generations, since the rocks were named a very long time ago.

But all that was nothing more than a preamble for the main event of the day. Ah, I wager you were thinking the F&L, but no. With a few patches of blue sky opening out we pottered around to our near neighbours for their wedding reception.

It was a simple affair furnished with McFadden's pasties and a few light libations with which to toast the happy couple. While newly wed they have been together for a fair few years and the family name has been in The Cove for as long as the cow has been on Cowloe. There were a fair few generations there to help them celebrate too. As it turned out the pasties were a little late in arriving so I had already had a pork pie, some cocktail sausages, fresh crab and a roll that I thought had something in it but had not, and followed up with a cup cake that had as much buttercream topping as it had sponge.

Despite the late arrival of the pasties it would have been rude not to indulge. As I stood and munched on my crust and wallowed in the congenial fusion of guests my eye was caught by some bunting flapping in the breeze. I am sure I have seen that bunting somewhere before.

June 17ᵗʰ – Sunday

It was a far more 'ansum day today than yesterday, which is typical as the Missus is heading off to spend the day with her dad for father's day.

Just before I waved her off I told her to drive carefully. She softened and told me how caring and considerate I was. I told her that everyone needs to be considerate these days as fuel economy is so important, with the price of diesel. She hardened and drove off. I have no idea how she manages to get the van to wheel spin like that.

Naturally, being on my own, it busied up nicely. I also had to content myself with watching the Lifeboat go out on exercise without my involvement. The excellent Shore Crew, (they were hardly 'very' without me), no doubt excelled themselves in my absence. In fact they, Head Launcher and company, excelled themselves in having a breakfast next door without me too. To show I held no malice I wished them an excellent repast and trusted to them that no errant lump of bacon should lodge in their gullets and choke them. After they had eaten, they very kindly in turn told me how wonderful their respective breakfasts were and how very sad they were that I could not join them.

The bleddy hound got lucky too today. She was very likely in for a very humdrum time of it with the Missus away. Although our neighbour was happy to take her round the block a couple of times to sort out her basic requirements, sitting watching the world go by for an entire day is a bit of an ask.

As luck would have it, a couple who have visited regularly for a number of years, R and A, appeared this morning. They are from the north east, a place called Jordan, or at least that is what it sounded like. R came in for milk and honey this morning, which I thought strange as I understood they had loads of it from where they come from; perhaps they are on the wrong side of the river.

Sorry, I digress, well, only so far as is necessary to paint the background for you. Now, where was I? Oh, yes, the bleddy hound's cabin fever. It was a little towards midday when R and A popped their heads in the door and asked if they could take her for a run up to Land's End and, presumably back again, although I did not feel it important to ask. She was gone for some two hours and could hardly walk when she got back. I would doubt if R and A will get her to the end of the road next time; she has a memory for these things, you know.

Later on she staged her own Cornish Rebellion that was a sight more successful than the original, which went slightly awry today in 1497. She refused to move anywhere for the rest of the day and who was I to make her.

The rest of the day continued as busy as the first part. We sold a welcome number of our Grumpies too, as we had no pasties. Word on them seems to be getting around with an increasing number of people already knowing what they are before they arrive.

We have noticed too, that we have turned from a *Guardian* preserve over the last two weeks into a *Telegraph* demographic. Unfortunately, over the weekend I can do nothing about the volume we receive and we are faced, for the very first time, of having more orders than we have numbers of the newspaper. I am considering a lottery for the last one tomorrow, and with the volumes we are talking about I could well retire by Tuesday.

June 18th – Monday

A proper rip-croppling knipper of a day with some glorious sunshine from the off.

Princess Bo, the bleddy hound, was a little grumpy this morning. She has been forced to occupy the bottom bunk in her shop bed out of protest. The Missus brought her back a new bed from her travels yesterday and, pretty though it is, even I could tell it was only big enough for a Chihuahua, a small one at that. Honestly, I could not see what was wrong with the old one, but Princess Bo must have the best, it seems, whether she wants it or not and, for once, she has sided with me and spurned the gift, much to the Missus's chagrin.

A lady came in this morning looking for birthday cake candles. Now, let me tell you about birthday cake candles. Allow me to read you an excerpt from *The Diary* penned by one of our predecessors in the shop.

"It was the summer of '89 when we placed our order for finest birthday cake candles with Cratchett and Slomberg Est. 1765, Purveyors of the Finest Birthday Cake Candles and Funeral Plumes to the Trade. They vouched safe that our order of two boxes of finest birthday cake candles would be with their agents in the veritable East India Company the very next day, and would be telegraphed to Shanghai from whence the order would be shipped.

And so it was that later that same month a steamer departed Shanghai loaded with our order of finest birthday cake candles. Fortunately, since the construction of the Suez Canal, we could expect our order to come to dock in East London, barring disasters, in less than a month. [Readers should note that in the first decade of the 21st century the same shipment could take six months.]

Cratchett and Slomberg Est. 1765, Purveyors of the Finest Birthday Cake Candles and Funeral Plumes to the Trade, sent us a telegram to inform us that our order had been despatched from London to Cornwall on the overnight express and would be in Penzance for us to collect on Tuesday.

We duly despatched The Cove's octogenarian dunkey cart driver, Young Ernest, (thus named to avoid confusion with Old Ernest, his father, who drives the trap), to meet the overnight express and pick up the boxes from

Penzance station. You will no doubt appreciate our consternation when Young Ernest arrived late in the afternoon with a crate the size of a pilchard tank and the wheels of his dunkey cart creaking under the strain of the considerable weight. He apologised profusely in his own manner and said he would be beggered if he was going back to collect the second one until morning.

The crate did indeed appear to be ours since it had Cratchett and Slomberg Est. 1765, Purveyors of the Finest Birthday Cake Candles and Funeral Plumes to the Trade stencilled on the side, along with our name and once we had opened it the contents were definitely the finest birthday cake candles. It was just that there was rather a surplus to the delivery than we had expected, and indeed ordered, from Messers Cratchett and Slomberg Est. 1765, Purveyors of the Finest Birthday Cake Candles and Funeral Plumes to the Trade.

The very next day Old Ernest took us in his trap to Penzance to allow us to send a telegram to Cratchett and Slomberg Est. 1765, Purveyors of the Finest Birthday Cake Candles and Funeral Plumes to the Trade to suggest some sort of error on their part. It was a very expensive telegram; the title alone cost us nearly sixpence.

A week later we received a letter from Cratchett and Slomberg Est. 1765, Purveyors of the Finest Birthday Cake Candles and Funeral Plumes to the Trade conveying to us their heart felt apologies. Apparently, the East India Company Agent's telegrapher at Shanghai knocked his tea over the incoming message and rather than ask for it to be resent had retyped it from his opium hazed memory. Since the package had already been despatched and accepted - Young Ernest had signed the despatch note at the station - there was nothing that they could do. They also, very kindly, enclosed a bill of sale for the balance."

When we first took over the shop in 2004 we noticed on the inventory a fairly significant figure next to the entry for birthday cake candles. We had intended to raise the matter with the sellers but in the confusion that surrounds the buying of a shop we forgot all about it. Forgot, that is, until we opened the garage that was then being used as an additional store. Inside was the remnant of an old packing crate with Cratchett and Slomberg Est. 1765, Purveyors of the Finest Birthday Cake Candles and Funeral Plumes to the Trade stencilled on the side. When we lifted the lid of the crate we were rather surprised to find more birthday cake candles than you could shake a lighted match at.

So when a lady came into the shop this morning and asked if we had any birthday cake candles I told her that we did indeed have a one or two. I led her to where a small selection of the candles normally hangs only to find that the peg was empty. As a small aside I did, however, find the emery boards that the same lady had asked for last week and, at the time, could not find for the life of me. While I thought we had some birthday cake candles in our stock room, we did not and a trip up to Shrew House was in order.

I opened the door to Shrew House and gazed into the gloom inside. The lines of shelves holding birthday cake candles are the first thing you see; there are several of them. The old crate with Cratchett and Slomberg Est. 1765, Purveyors of the Finest Birthday Cake Candles and Funeral Plumes to the Trade stencilled on the side is gone now but I still reflect, from time to time, on a smoke filled telegrapher's office in Shanghai, outpost of the East India Company in the late 19th century with the telegraph clicking away.

Especially I envision the figure bent over that machine whose error, in an opium fuelled state, consigned us to a lifetime supply of finest bleddy birthday cake candles.

June 19th – Tuesday

It is not April 1st, is it? I did not think so. The article in the *Western Morning News* (did I mention …) must be true, then.

There has long been an association between the beasts of the field, predominantly cows, and the production of greenhouse gases. Indeed there are religiously 'green' advocates who will eat no beef purely on this basis. It is thought, please note that, in other words somebody has guessed, that agriculture is responsible for some eight percent of the UK's greenhouse gas production.

It seems that someone high up in government, perhaps an over-inflated fat cat, obviously weary of being asked for some real data on how much gas cows produce, has ordered a study and this is where the story really starts: how to measure the output of gas from a cow. I thought at first this must have been a wind-up because it sound like complete guff, but I am assured this is true.

In industrial locations gases are measured by inserting a probe into the chimney and sucking out a sample of the gases produced and measured. For some reason the project team thought a similar procedure for cows might be impractical; cows do not have chimneys, at least not of the traditional variety. They have opted instead for a system of lasers that measure the gases blown across an entire field.

There are indications that the whole thing might be so much hot air. Lord Stern in his 2006 report on climate change suggested that meat production was a "wasteful use of water". However, in Australia, another study trumped that by asserting that fertile cattle pastures develop soil bacteria that absorb more methane than the cattle on it can produce. Personally I could not give a fart - oops!

Not too far away from the nearest methane producing cow we were having another perfect day down in The Cove. The sun was shining once again, the sea a placid, limpid pool, (bit tough on the surfers), and the temperature beginning to climb - a proper summer's day.

This means that, by and large, all our customers were pinned down on the beach all day and came nowhere near the shop. It is a fine line between having a perfect day and a perfect shop day and, unfortunately for us, today we crossed the line. Still, it was very pleasant looking at it through the shop window while the Missus dealt with the grocery order that arrived today.

What did not arrive today was our first contract bin collection. We were rather looking forward to this, because in conversation with the manager that sold us the service he told us that the bin would be emptied by hand. We tried to convince him that this may not be all too easy as it often contains a myriad of smaller items that might be difficult and time consuming to extract manually. For example, it currently contains two boxes of loose polystyrene chips.

We suspect that the manager has never emptied a bin by hand and his protestations that it is a simple task, carried out elsewhere without issue, may not wholly be shared by the chaps actually doing the emptying.

June 20ᵗʰ – Wednesday

Welcome to the summer solstice.

They said on the radio this morning that rain would be spreading into the county from the south, except for the Isles of Scilly and the far west, which should remain dry. Mmm, at around two thirty the heavens opened and the streets emptied – into the shop. Do not get too excited now, we are only talking about a dozen people at the most.

Yes, we were at our busiest when the rain started coming down as people fell over each other to get into the shelter; I shall have to start charging for such a valuable service. Still, it was not all bad; I sold an umbrella. It is quite amazing how long it takes to choose an umbrella from a stock of identical umbrellas.

But before all that we had a half decent morning. In fact the opening few hours were very warm and sunny as I took the bleddy hound around. We got into a bit of trouble as there is an old dog living at Salt House at the moment. As we approached, there were a few tentative moments then the collie started to follow the bleddy hound through the car park. We were joined soon after by the Lifeboat mechanic's Newfoundland that threw a completely new dimension into the mix. We escaped, but the collie was clearly not ready to return and the owner had a bit of a time to get him back home.

We were more successful with our commercial bin emptying, though not as entertaining as I had hoped. You will remember yesterday, surely you remember yesterday, that we had been ignored for the first collection of our shop waste. I telephoned today and less than an hour later the truck that collects from the street bins emptied ours too. I said disappointing, because they used the machinery on the back of the truck to lift and empty the bin as opposed to doing it by hand as we had expected, and rather hoped. I really cannot understand why the contract manager expected a different truck to turn up as the automatic lift ones are here every day. We will now have to wait until next week to see what our normal collection will look like.

Not long after the monsoon began I had a curious sense of prescience about our troublesome drain at the rear of the shop. I took a tentative peek around the corner of the stock room door and found that the Missus had placed the bleddy hound's old bed on the floor at the far end where, if any water was seeping in, the flood would have started from. This meant heading down to the end of the store room and, on lifting the bed, sure enough, there was a river starting to run through it.

Some drastic action was clearly required and although I started with a mop and bucket it was obvious that I could not mop fast enough; action even more drastic was required. This meant going to the source of the problem.

Ten minutes later I was suitably dressed in boiler suit, waterproofs and wellies. As I headed towards the back of the shop the Missus suggested that since I was suitably attired it was an excellent opportunity to take the bleddy hound out for a comfort break. It is at moments like this that any resistance, such as suggesting that clearing a drain to stop the shop from flooding might be a bit of a priority, is completely useless.

After taking a very reluctant bleddy hound up to the car park for a quick run around I once again headed for the back of the shop. It was worse than I had expected, and the water had backed up such that a large pool was threatening to lap over the window sill into the studio flat next door. Fortunate, then, that a couple of elbow deep forays into the drain and extracting rotting and stinking moss quickly resolved the problem. With a gurgle the level of water in the hole collapsed sending a veritable torrent into the newly created void and into my rubber glove. Finding that the drain was now blocked anew by my hand, the water very quickly went in the only direction left available to it — up my sleeve.

Having cleared the drain and drained my sleeve I returned to mop up the water that had already enjoyed free passage into the shop. As I was waterproofed up, so the Missus pointed out, it was sensible that I should bring in the outside gear while she took care of the mop up operation.

I am rather hoping that our combined activities were enough to avert the wholesale ingress of water, else Plymouth is not the only place that will have an Olympic sized water park. However, after all that running around and rear-guard action, it was with somewhat mixed emotions that, soon after closing the shop, we watched the rain stop.

Still, there is a guts of rain due tomorrow to test my handiwork.

June 21st - Thursday

I must start with an apology.

I received an email shortly after posting yesterday's Diary entry from a couple of Australians, Bruce and Sheila, (not their real names obviously, that is just a silly English idea of what Australians should be called but I did promise Wally and Darlene I would respect their anonymity – oh, begger!). They were a bit miffed that I had used the term, 'summer solstice'. While it is the northern hemisphere's summer solstice this is clearly not true of the southern hemisphere where, presumably, it is their winter solstice.

To save any future offence we shall be using the term dermat, derived from the acronym of Day Earth Reaches MAximum Tilt. People who run off to various points on the earth to see the sun rise and set on this day will obviously be known as dermatologists. This will clear up any rash reactions to the previous terminology and prevent any further confusion.

There may well be some confusion for any out of towners visiting today. Just imagine if you happen to be an alien on holiday from, for example, Omega Centauri. You have been to your travel agent who has told you that Sennen Cove on planet Earth is a cracking little place to visit, why not take the kids and soak up the atmosphere, mainly because there is one. They have picked June because, as everyone in Omega Centauri knows, the northern hemisphere is closest to the sun during this month and obviously hotter. So duly arriving here on June 21st, (they failed to factor in the leap year for the summer solstice, whoops, northern hemisphere dermat), to enjoy the soaring temperatures and the sun-drenched beach, they pop their heads out of their spacecraft made from recycled materials, (everyone in Omega Centauri has recycled spacecraft because their council did not remove all the recycling bins), and look around in consternation.

There is some immediate frantic chatter, much like an argument but in Omega Centaurian, where Mrs OC blames Mr OC for getting the map reading wrong and Mr OC kicks the intergalactic sat nav. "This cannot possibly be Sennen Cove in the height of summer as it is cold, wet and bleddy miserable", says Mrs OC (I paraphrase slightly as my Omega Centaurian is a bit rusty). The kids start a bit of a rumpus in the back seats; after all they have been very good for the last couple of light years only asking a few times, "are we there yet?" The OCs have no choice but to get out and have a look around. They did not bring any rain macs and the local shop does not have any that fit, in that they have two arms and only one hood.

Having established that they are in the right place they conclude that they would have been better off with a staycation and promptly return home. Fortunately, word soon gets around Omega Centauri that planet Earth is a cold, inhospitable planet and that even the warmest places, closest to the sun, are too wet and cold for life to exist in any sense of reasonableness, and a full-scale plan to turn Sennen Cove into a Omega Centuarian Magaluf is postponed indefinitely.

Meanwhile, back on Earth, the very excellent Shore Crew, (I was with them today), gathered to push the Lifeboat out of the station. The aim this evening was to launch and recover the boat without getting wet, which was a bit of a tall order. Well, it would have been if it had been still raining, which it was not. We were a man down too, which would have reduced the odds still further and did not help much when it came to the quiz at the OS later on.

Nevertheless, even with the odds stacked against us, we won in a sizeable crowd. It was unfortunate that another team won too and we came face to face with a tie break, which, of course, in traditional fashion we miserably lost, or was it lost miserably – either way we were miserable and we lost. It would be so easy to blame Head Launcher for Will Smith instead of Tommy Lee Jones, but in truth we should have shot him before we started.

So, begger all that, I'm off to Omega Centauri on the next available shuttle. I hear it's sunny there at this time of year.

June 23rd – Saturday

We did not expect it to be ever so busy today what with it being Mazey Day an' all and with the tail end of Golowan beckoning, even the vaguely interested head in the direction of Penzance. We were not disappointed either, although we still had a steady stream of shoppers popping in for groceries and the odd small gift. We have many odd small gifts.

It was busy enough that I did not have that much time to see the girls' only surf competition, let alone slip on a dress and wig and take part. Obviously, I had a quick glance or two to see what was going on, but people kept walking in front of my 60x field telescope that I set up on top of the pasty warmer. It also did not help that the mount for the tripod is broken, and even the smallest tremor can make viewing impossible let alone the way the counter was already shaking. It would be a shame if it were not a success, especially after the work that went into the advertisement which was in the style of an art deco holiday poster; it was quite stunning.

In the shop we have had mixed success on fish sales. We would love to have a selection of fresh fish in for speculative purchases as many people wish to buy on impulse. However the demand is fairly random and the risk of me being left on a fish only diet when we do not sell is high. We have tried keeping a stock of frozen fish but, understandably, most people prefer to have their piscine delights fresh. As the season gets busier we will try having a fixed fresh fish day during the week, with maybe limited numbers of two or three species available. If, at the end of the season, you see me growing gills you will know that it has been an abject failure.

The tin mines have found something of a runaway success turning themselves into visitor attractions, even to the point of attaining World Heritage status. Now it seems that another hard rock industry is set to follow suit, with a granite quarry in Constantine looking to transform into a heritage site. The area is a prime location as it once had thirty quarries employing over 200 people in the 1800s.

It is early days for the very much locally led project and discussions are underway in trying to secure a lease on one of the quarries. Alongside the project a doctorate student is preparing to create historical audio walks by recording stories and details from local people. All together the project team will leave no stone unturned in reaching their target of having the centre opened. They could not have been bolder in their enterprise and we do hope that nothing will rock their resolve, no matter how hard it is. I suppose if it had been a Welsh quarry they could have put the start up costs on the slate. Sorry, all joking aside we wish them well in their endeavours.

June 24th – Sunday

What is a poor shopkeeper to do? It is a grey, damp and miserable Sunday morning, but strangely balmy. I suppose that is an improvement on cold, wet and miserable, he said trying to be as upbeat as possible. Even the forecast has been downgraded from a week of bright overcastness to a week of dull overcastness and rain. If it were a horse they'd shoot it.

Then something strange, or perhaps miraculous happened, it being Sunday after all, with a geet lump of rain the size of a small planet a few miles to the south of us, a similar sized lump of blue opened to the north of us. It stayed all day, which was nice; the old nag has a stay of execution.

We were not exactly overrun with customers who presumably had seen the forecast and stayed away, but it was busy enough in fits and starts. One lady, buying a small heap of goodies, asked in conversation if my book was doing well. I thanked her and said that I was pleased enough with progress. She then asked if I had written the book myself. I have to confess to being rather taken aback at the suggestion that some other party might have been lunatic enough to have penned 304 pages of senseless drivel and then had the temerity to actually publish it with my name on it. Even I was not daft enough to put my name on the front cover.

Noting my obvious distress, she assured me that apparently proper authors have an editor with whom they must negotiate the content. If this is the case I am rather glad I am not a proper author; I cannot imagine there being much left after a self-respecting editor had got hold of it.

A regular summer visitor turned up today, so I guess it must be summer after all. I remember him well as he and the girl he was with, (you see how circumspect this organ is not to make rash judgements about relationships) always asked for two cheese and vegetable pasties that we had invariably just run out of. They have previously spent the whole summer here as surfing instructors but this year, he told me, he was working in London so only able to visit at weekends. I asked him how the surf was up there in a jokey, conversational sort of way. He replied that there was no surf, but he had been out on the Thames a couple of times on his stand up paddle board, in a teach-me-to-try-and-be-clever sort of way. I should note that he did not intend it that way, as he is one of the most pleasant chaps you could wish to meet.

Just as a small aside, while I was looking up what to call a stand up paddle board to save me looking daft twice I came across an article in the New York Times, just where you would expect to find article on stand up paddling. The writer referenced an experienced surfer he had met who had been riding one of these boards and he was quoted as saying that it helped his balance and speed but most of all it was easier to spot sharks. Point taken.

Despite the Met Office's best efforts it was a beautiful evening. Let us just hope they have got it wrong for the rest of the week too. We can dream can't we?

June 25ᵗʰ – Monday

The pagers went off for a motor cruiser stuck out at the bottom end of the TSS, or it might have been the top end. I was not sure as I never looked at which direction the boat was heading in, and the Missus could not get our scanner to work so she missed the Falmouth Coastguard broadcast.

The reason that I was not looking where the boat was going is that I was talking to one of the engineers in the boathouse. They were there to mend the turning cradle that switches the boat from short slip to long slipway and vice versa as necessary, which is why the boat was out on the slipway, secured by a strop when we arrived to launch her. We found that the cradle was not working during Thursday's exercise and had to turn it using the manual method. It took them a while, but they decided in the end that two of the three phase electrical supplies were wired the wrong way and as a consequence the motor that drives the cradle mechanism was rotating in the wrong direction. Questions were being asked who had changed the wiring in the boathouse since the last successful operation of the cradle.

It was at this point that someone remembered that the Harbour winch had a problem a few days ago; the winder was running backwards. "Aha", we thought. "Aha", said the engineer; the problem lies outside we concluded.

You might recall that at the end of May I reported that the lecky company had come to Sennen Cove to carry out some maintenance work. We were fortunate in that the shop was not affected but the boathouse was, so too was the Harbour winch house. As we contemplated our cradle situation some pennies were beginning to drop. What if the venerable electricity company had done something amiss?

The lecky company were duly called, and at the speed they turned up one might imagine that, perhaps, they felt a little guilty. I could, of course, not state that they were but they did admit, allegedly, that the phases had been reversed and claimed that they were wrongly wired when they found them and corrected the problem during their maintenance. It seems it had not crossed their minds to tell anyone what they had done.

After such excitement recovering the boat was almost commonplace but we managed it with aplomb, after all we are a very excellent Shore Crew.

June 26ᵗʰ - Tuesday

I would not be surprised if you do not recall the tale of the new sofa as it harks back to March. I will not go into chapter and verse as you will have read that earlier in the book (all supposing I do not get an editor who takes that bit out). To recap briefly, there was a war of wills between me and the Missus as to whether she would get a new sofa. So I ordered one. They told us it would be ten weeks from the date of order, which brought us into May sometime. They called us near delivery time and said that it would be another eight weeks to which the Missus nearly had apoplexy.

Today we had a call from the furniture shop asking if it would be all right to deliver it this Friday. Sensing some fun I told the young lady that Friday would be terribly inconvenient and wondered if she could put delivery off for another eight weeks. I do not know which was funnier, the impressively long, dumbfounded silence at the end of the telephone line or the look on the Missus's face when she worked out who it was I was talking to.

The sofa will still be coming on Friday by which time I imagine it will be close to being an antique or the wrong colour.

Once again today the very excellent Shore Crew was called out to launch the Lifeboat to attend a yacht snagged on some debris up off Pendeen. It was one of those calls that could have been a couple of hours or six to seven hours if a tow was required, so the very excellent Shore Crew disbanded to wait on further information. When the Lifeboat returned less than an hour later there were just sufficient off us to mount an exemplary recovery on the long slip.

Fortunately, today the Head Launcher was off playing golf, which I understand quite a few people of his age indulge in. Golf is, of course, not a poor man's pastime and we always suspected our Head Launcher's shabby appearance and miserly existence was the façade of an eccentric multi-millionaire.

June 27ᵗʰ - Wednesday

My hairy alarm clock went wrong this morning and got me up an hour early.

It has become fairly consistent that the bleddy hound goes off like a rocket at twenty-five minutes past six each morning when her arch-enemy walks past; she barks the house down until I get up and lock her in the bathroom with me. The peace is short lived as she goes off again when I open the door twenty minutes (it does not take long to make myself beautiful) later. This has been the way of things for some weeks.

This morning, however, I nipped her barkings in the bud, or so I thought. She had started to growl a bit, generally a precursor to full on mental barking. I had woken with a bit of a start anyway, as I suddenly remembered that I had not ordered the milk. I was going to go back to sleep when the growling started, as our milkman, being the good lad he is, would turn up anyway. So, adjudging it to be nearly getting up time in any case, I duly roused myself and headed for the bathroom to find that the bleddy hound had gone in there of her own accord. I had taken with me my mobile telephone that I use for a backup alarm clock in case the hairy one does not go off and by the time I had finished shaving it still had not rung.

Since I was heading for the shower I decided to cancel the alarm and this is when I found that the time showing on the telephone was an hour before my usual getting up time. Little wonder, then, that it had not gone off. I looked at the bleddy hound, who was by now fitfully sleeping at the door to the shower cubicle, and considered giving her a splash with the cold water hose. I reasoned that it was not really her fault that I was up an hour earlier, but it would make life much easier if she had a snooze button.

June 28th – Thursday

Utter mayhem in The Cove this morning, down our end, at least. Another low-loader arrived with more concrete sections for the Lifeboat slipways and set up position opposite the bus turning bay, while a grown-up sized fork lift truck took each one off individually. Meanwhile, the resurfacing of the Harbour Commission's road between the Lifeboat Station and the Harbour car park got underway, with a cutter marking the limit of the work across the road. Then two buses arrived, far enough apart that the low-loader had to move out of the way twice to let them turn around. All we need now is for the boys to arrive to empty our commercial bin, although that is so unlikely I do not know why I mentioned it.

A visitor told me that there were dolphins in the bay this morning, playing in the surf. He was filming them on his mobile telephone when a lady dressed only in a swimsuit dashed by. This by itself may not have been so unusual other than it was around seven o'clock. Later in the day a lady told me how she had been swimming with the dolphins in the morning, so I presume it was she that had been spotted. She was quite excited until I related how those same sweet dolphins can behave so viciously when they corner a porpoise. I think she may reconsider her position next time, although I did assure her she looked nothing like a porpoise.

Moving on from intelligent sea life our much maligned council has been asked to take part in a national conference on town centre survival today. My heart was momentarily lifted at the thought that our much maligned council had seen the light and had admitted they need some assistance in regenerating our ailing high streets. No, I did not think so. Imagine my consternation, nay, disbelief, perhaps when on reading further it explained that it has been asked to speak at the event. If they were to wax on about the rip roaring success that they have led in Penzance I suspect it would be a very short speech indeed; a lessons learnt summary is far more likely, although I would not bet on it.

But amidst the wasteland of public sector hopelessness perhaps a glimmer of light: the Classic Aircraft Trust has been persuaded to move from the Midlands to the newly set up Cornwall and Isles of Scilly Enterprise Zone (essentially Newquay Airport). It is a charity that preserves, restores and flies classic aeroplanes, as its name might suggest, and, more importantly will bring vacancies for more than thirty full and part time staff to the county. Its focus is on post war aircraft and has flying examples of a Meteor, Vampire, Venom and a Canberra among others. Word is they want to create a new visitor attraction, not that Newquay needs another, but at least this one might to a bit more cultural than some of their others.

We managed to launch the Inshore Lifeboat in the last of the good weather we had this afternoon. I polished my bell and fixed the sleeve of another drysuit for my bit of action. The big boat stayed put this evening since we had already launched twice this week and the slip widening team were in full flight on the long slip.

June 29ᵗʰ - Friday

Did I say it was mayhem yesterday? Nay, it was picture of serenity compared to today's standard.

Allow me to explain. Yesterday the foreman of a group of navvies knocked on the Lifeboat Station door and, with a wink, told the clerk of the Harbour Commissioners that he had a good brea bit of tarmac that he had left over from another job and how he had noticed that the driveway to the car park was looking a little shabby. The clerk of the Harbour Commissioners, being the sort who can spot a bargain when it lands on his doorstep, commissioned the navvies there and then to complete the work.

Lo and behold, this morning our surly, burly workmen arrived at the appointed time to strip off the old surface and lay down shiny new tarmac. Unfortunately, though they were there on time, the machinery required for the job had broken down and a replacement would take a few hours to arrive. Instead of being open again just after midday the road would be closed until well into the afternoon.

Then came the stream of visitors, and queues as they all took turns to turn around. Then came the holiday let owners and cleaners who only turn up weekly and were not around when the notices went up. Given our proximity and availability we usually bear the brunt of any dissatisfaction which arises from issues at this end of The Cove, but on this occasion gripes were few. I think it was apparent that no amount of gribbling would open the road.

When the tarmac did arrive, the workmen set about their task with frightening efficiency and the whole job was complete inside about four hours. I spent the whole day in a state of euphoria as the heady waft of tarmac fumes filled the shop. It is one of those smells that divide the nation with some people unable to abide it; I, on the other hand, would spend my life sniffing freshly creosoted fences had I the opportunity, which, I would contend, is a higher art than licking windows.

Another group who might be accused of sniffing something heady are some teachers in a Devon school. They have employed the use of a 'reading therapy dog'. Yes, that is exactly what I thought. Apparently, the process of having children read to the dog is very good for them, the children that is, it does not say if the dog enjoys it. It relies on the fact that the dog is not judgemental, though presumably if he does not like what is being read to him he will begger off and cock his leg up the nearest desk. The bit that really held my interest, though, is that the dog is not going to correct the child when they make a mistake, which helps boost the child's self esteem. Yes, I am sure it does but I cannot see how that helps the child's reading ability if no one is going to correct them for getting the words wrong. I suggest it would be far more effective if the dog were trained to take a chunk out of the child's backside every time they made a mistake. I bet they would learn to read properly in very short order.

The research on reading to dogs comes from the University of California, where the process has significantly improved children's reading skills, though no one can really be certain as the dogs are not letting on. I thought it best not to dismiss this research out of hand and have conducted my own experiments with the bleddy hound. After many hours with different authors I have established that she is quite keen on Dogstoyevski, with Tom Woof a close second and she is in raptures with Ruff Rendell; she loves a good thriller. Conversely, she left the room howling when I started on some Dr. Suess.

Thrown into today's chaotic mix was the arrival of our new sofa. We had taken care to explain to the chap in the salesroom that the entrance to the flat is a tad awkward for larger items and to let us know should we need to plan to take out one of the windows. He calmed our nerves with the certainty of a salesman who was not actually going to be doing the delivering or the taking away himself, and told us that there would be no problems.

The delivery team looked up at our stairway and the ninety degree turn at the top and shook their heads and sucked air between their teeth in a, it-will-never-go-up-there-my-'ansum, sort of way. The sofa we had ordered was the largest in the range, they assured us, probably why it is called the Big Monster Sofa That Doesn't Fit in Tight Doorways; a clue in the name perhaps. Naturally, I countered with the reassurance that the salesman had given us to which they merely laughed that, you-didn't-fall-for-that-one, sort of laugh.

After some negotiation they came up with the brilliant idea of seeing if the new sofa would come apart. Sensing that this was only half the story, I offered to dismantle the old sofa, which they had agreed to take away for a price, fearing that they would take one look at it, then the doorway and I would get a repeat of the shaking of heads and sucking of air through teeth routine.

It took me a moment to remove the lining from the bottom of the sofa, then another moment admiring the craftsmanship that put this piece of furniture together. Verily it was built akin to a substantial outhouse constructed for the purpose of sanitation and further, there was no obvious way in which it would come apart. It only took another moment to establish that a saw was required and then, after using the saw, another moment to see that a bigger saw was necessary. Much sawing and rending of material later the sofa was every bit as solid as it was when I started. It took much more sawing and rending of material before the entire bottom section would come away, and even then the springs still held the two pieces together. It was enough, however, to get them out of the doorway and into the van. That 25 quid removal service was worth every penny, even if I had to do most of the sawing and rending myself.

Still, I had our evening meal to look forward to.

We have had some casual conversations with our venerable and revered crab fisherman regarding Asian cooking. Not that he is an expert in the art, but his wife is, as she is Asian. He came and had a chat with me this morning and asked what time we closed. After I told him, he said not to worry about cooking tonight as his wife was preparing a Thai meal for us and he would deliver it after we had closed.

True to his word, they both turned up this evening bearing gifts of Asian starters, aromatic sticky rice and a chicken and cashew dish. Along with the homemade sweet chilli sauce it was sublime.

What better than to relax afterwards on our new reclining sofa? Well, it would have been had I not discovered that the delivery men, while clearly adept at taking the sofa apart so that it would fit through the door, were less than expert at putting it back together again. The backrest on my side is loose and does not meet the seat, and when reclining in it the foot rest crashes into the foot rest on the other side.

I do hope we do not have to wait sixteen weeks for someone to come and fix it, but who cares when the world is full of fences to sniff while I read a passage or two to of Little Doggit to the bleddy hound.

June 30ᵗʰ – Saturday

We started the day with a rather swift Lifeboat launch. A boat, on its way to the Isle of Scilly was talking on water after the crew decided that the weather perhaps was not as nice as they thought and turned it around. It was towed to The Cove where a very excellent Shore Crew brought it ashore for recovery by its owners later.

After all that excitement we had quite a busy day in the shop. We sold the last of the pollack in the refrigerator and were cleared out of clotted cream. The cream has been slow moving during the last week so I reined back on the order for the weekend; I should have known better. We also found that despite doing our best to increase our range of Cornish produce there is always something we overlook. A case in point is the couple who started their drive into making us feel inadequate by asking for avocados and after being told that they do not grow in Cornwall made a point of asking for stuffed olives. Another lady who I did not immediately associate with the couple then asked for Australian butter to which I, of course, responded that she would find that the Cornish butter we stock to be far superior (all right, in my humble opinion).

It was when the couple came to the till that I had my first awakening in that the credit card they proffered revealed them to be no other than the Cotswold Courier in persons, long time readers and contributors to *The Diary* and whom I have never met. Even then no pennies were dropping and no rodents were being smelt. It was not until the lady came to the till, dressed in a garish robe with ostentatious costume jewellery that the game was up.

It took me twice for the name on the credit card to sink in, as it did not match the vision in front me. But at the same rate as the scales fell from my eyes the enormity of my gullibility increased. For standing before me in the most outrageous disguise was our very famous International Correspondent, MM. It was a coup of some magnitude and one that I shall suffer for, no doubt, into my dotage and quite the most blatant attempt at being *Diarised* that I almost excluded it through petulance.

July 4ᵗʰ - Wednesday

At least, for once, we did not have to worry about what we were going to have for our tea. Our International Correspondent, Cotswold Courier and party - the Minchhead Set, invited us to join them for a jolly barbeque round at their temporary residence. Of course, I was rather looking forward to some smoked nose of Tao Tome shrew, a little northern hairy-nosed wombat ear or even a Yangtze River dolphin steak nicely griddled over the hot coals. It seems, though, that even the most particular shoppers we have had here for some time were more than happy to concoct a dashed good tea using some Vivian Olds minced steak for the burgers, their rather fine pork sausages along with some beans with bacon and corn mixed with peppers. It was, after all

Independence Day for our colonially adopted friend and, although not something we would ordinarily celebrate, rounded off a rather splendid day.

We had a top hole evening thanks to the convivial company and lively conversation. It was I who felt the soft embalmer creeping up on me first and had to leave before I fell asleep at the table, which might have looked a tad unseemly. It could not detract from the fact that it was a very pleasant evening. We might try celebrating Thanksgiving next time.

July 5th - Thursday

I believe that we have all become somewhat inured to the bad news that pervades our lives from the news channels around us. I think that I can just about put up with the fact that it is costing me £2,000 more to live in a rural idyll than a city crush, or that St Ives is facing the same toilet ultimatum from our much maligned The much maligned council as Sennen Cove did, but with a much bigger bill. There comes a point, though, where the corn in the wind will only bend so far. Today we learn that the powers that watch over our lighthouses from the port of Harwich, wherever that is, have decided to foist upon us a blot so outrageous that it will shake us to the very core.

In 1995 Trinity House converted Godrevy lighthouse to solar power; a sensible option in this day and age and one, you might have thought, that would be the ultimate upgrade. So far the lighthouse had remained an iconic structure, unspoilt since its completion in 1859 and the subject of countless paintings and photographs and, probably, the inspiration for Virginia Woolf's book *To the Lighthouse*. It is not only the squat (if you can call 85 feet, squat) octagonal tower but also its context on the sloping grassy island that sets it apart from any other lighthouse in the country.

So what are the doyens of Trinity House doing that has so incensed my sensibilities? They are installing a LED light, for heavens sake, one that not only will be viewed four miles less distant than the current light but more importantly will involve the construction of another edifice on which to mount the bulb. Two towers on Godrevy rock – what should we expect next? An electricity pylon in Trafalgar Square, perhaps, or a wind turbine on St Michael's Mount I should not wonder.

It was just as well that I did my bit at the Lifeboat station tonight in preparing it for inspection next week. Our esteemed coxswain has long since stopped issuing three line whips for attendance on nights such as this, as everyone stopped turning up. Nevertheless, those that arrived tonight, in the main, threw their all into polishing and scrubbing even if it did mean using the water supply from a neighbour's property as the station's hose would not reach the front of the boathouse.

July 6ᵗʰ – Friday

Let's talk dirty for a bit. You know you want me to; time to get down real mucky and filthy and dish the dirt with no inhibitions. I can almost feel you quivering with anticipation. Yes, those little tubers are covered in filth again, just the way we like them.

I think I explained that the farm had taken to washing them in a process that cleaned off the dirt and left them freezing cold. Apparently they were also supposed to go through a quick drying process that ours clearly did not enjoy. Rather than extending their life in the bag, ours degenerated within a day or two and started to go mushy. We were alerted to the problem by a local who had a bag off us the day they came in, which was just as well as we had not noticed.

We did try and save them but when we opened the bags we found a high proportion were going off. The smell was insufferable and even after washing and drying the remaining good ones, the pong remained to such an extent they were unsaleable. I understand that there is a certain beverage that can be made from potatoes in this condition, but the process is frowned upon in certain quarters and besides I do not have any boot legs, which is essential, so I am told.

Admitting defeat we called our farmer to ask for more potatoes and explained that we had a minor disaster that I would describe when he brought them down. As it was, a young lady turned up hefting a tray of deliciously mucky Cornish Earlies, smelling of the earth from which they were ripped not hours before hand. She explained that the washing rigmarole had not been quite up to their expectations and that we should have had potatoes that had been through the drying process. Having tried the process in full they discovered that it took far too much time, especially when they have had so few dry days to get them out of the ground in the first place.

There, was that not a breath of fresh air and I am so glad I got that out of my system.

Away from the excitement of the potatoes we enjoyed a fairly decent day between the odd showers that were not forecast. There was a fairly sizeable basking shark mooching about the bay for quite some time that provided some distraction. You might have guessed that if I required distraction then it was a pretty sedate day. It was; it was as slow as treacle, which I endured almost exclusively as the Missus was upstairs preparing for the Great Entertainment tonight.

Now I know you will think me an awful bounder for generalising so, so I shall anyway, but if it were us chaps preparing for a dinner party, knowing we also had a business to run, we would have lightly toasted some bread, thumbed open a tin of baked beans and, to demonstrate that we not completely devoid of flair, maybe have cracked an egg over the top (having fried it first, obviously). I would hazard that there are not many of us that would have found the most complex and time-consuming recipes to dazzle our guests with, guessing, probably quite rightly, that their guests' expectations from a business running host would be suitably restrained.

And having written that I fully expect to look on while our guests enjoy their cordon bleu meal and tuck in with the bleddy hound, should I be allowed back into the flat at all.

I was, of course, allowed at the table mainly because the Missus had not had the opportunity to read this draft. It was another perfectly pleasant evening in the company of the Minchhead Set. As they are leaving tomorrow I trust they had a memorable evening if only for the extended four course tea the Missus had laid on and the indigestion that will, no doubt, ensue. We never actually got to the fourth as I think the white chocolate cheesecake and raspberry custard tart accompanied by clotted cream stopped us in our tracks.

We ended with the Missus providing a demonstration on how to pick every last flake of crab meat from a brown crab carcass – all three of them. The proceeds will be packed for a little going away present for each and a sandwich for the International Correspondent who will be travelling away by train.

I trust she has a first class ticket. You cannot possibly consider eating a crab sandwich in standard class.

July 7th – Saturday

Now is the winter of our discontent. Well it certainly does not feel like summer and this shopkeeper is showing signs of discontentment. We had remnants of a small flood through the shop again this morning, though strangely, there was little sign in the store room where it normally hails from. I do sincerely hope we do not have another source.

I cannot, however, blame the flood for the problem I have had with the new paper bags that I put the Cornish early potatoes in. I had a blindingly good idea that by putting them in strong paper bags they would be able to breath and not accumulate sufficient moisture to go rotten when we were still getting the washed variety. They were, indeed, in perfectly good shape as they cascaded out of the damp bottomed bag as I lifted it. I should consider a plan C, I believe.

The Minchhead Set left this morning with fond farewells and a bag of crab meat each along with lashings of clotted cream. Perhaps I can now be spared the ignominy of failing to meet my customer expectations and hope that this week's arrivals are a sight less demanding and show up undisguised.

If we had any customers to be demanding I think I would not have minded but as it was we were quiet in the extreme. It is of no surprise in weather that was more akin to that expected in a normal October and to one of those few customers I managed to sell an out of date packet of muffins. We have not been in this territory before where movement of stock is so slow we have to check such a wide range of perishables on so regular a basis. I suspect we shall have to be a bit more vigilant if we are not to attract a reputation that we would rather not have, after all it only take a few minutes with a very fine pen to add an extra month on the label.

Still, there were signs of improvement in the weather towards the end of the day, which would have been better appreciated earlier on. Nevertheless the youngsters' surf competition went ahead despite the somewhat robust sea state and less than perfect surf. I suppose with that many of them you could afford to lose a few and probably not notice. It just goes to show, maybe, that you can make a silk purse out of a sow's ear. We shall just have to find a few good looking sows for the shop.

July 8ᵗʰ – Sunday

Everyone was in a so much brighter mood; they always are on days like this. The grumpy old shopkeeper managed to lift his spirits a bit and not even a maid trying to get served with a mobile telephone stuck to her ear and in deep conversation with her mum spoilt the mood. I did make her wait a bit, mind, and she did have to ask for her cigarettes three or four times because I did not know if she was speaking to me or her mum. I imagine she had a very good excuse for being so rude; her mum, perhaps, only had seconds to go before she lifted off in a rocket to Mars and she had to buy the cigarettes immediately as her poodle, that was hanging off Pedn-men-du by its paws, needed a last ciggy before it dropped off. I am not entirely without heart, you know.

I would have said a word about the anniversary of Vivien Leigh's demise today in 1967 but frankly, my dear ... no, no, that just would not be right.

Instead we shall have a little Shelley, dear chap he was, who shuffled off today in 1822 and captured this summer down to a tee.

> *When soft winds and sunny skies*
> *With the green earth harmonize,*
> *And the young and dewy dawn,*
> *Bold as an unhunted fawn,*
> *Up the windless heaven is gone,--*
> *Laugh—for ambushed in the day,--*
> *Clouds and whirlwinds watch their prey.*

July 9ᵗʰ – Monday

Another day that just seemed to whip by hardly noticed. I know there was a fair amount of running around this morning for no apparent reason and then I went up to the post office via Shrew House to bank the three shillings and sixpence we took last week. When I returned and unpacked the van, it was gone lunchtime.

We were not particularly busy during the morning. Not, that is until a shower of fine rain whipped through the bay mid morning and suddenly we were full of wet people and a small drowned dog. The rain lasted no more than an hour and the afternoon turned out to be rather pretty. Perhaps it was a meteorological apology for dowsing us when the forecast suggested no rain, regardless it was very welcome.

I was still knee deep in filleted fish when the Missus took the bleddy hound off to the vets. She has a sore paw, the bleddy hound that is, not the Missus, that required some attention and thereafter went off for a hair cut. She has been suffering somewhat in the warmer temperatures with her thick woolly coat. Hopefully she will be a little more comfortable as well as looking half the size.

And finally I have managed to crack the technically challenging options for bunting and put them up on our online store, yes, the one that no one knows is there. If things go well we shall be setting up a sweat shop in The Cove and will be looking for small errant children that we can chain to the benches and work for twelve hours a day on wages of bread and water.

So, small errant children beware. The next time you enter the shop and misbehave could be your last. [FX: Sounds of manic laughter fading into the distance.]

July 10ᵗʰ – Tuesday

It was reported on the radio this morning that there was a rise in the number of cases of SAD of late. That is the Seasonal 'appiness Deficiency, or some such, brought on by dull weather. It is related to a person's low level of joie de vie, normally during the winter months, but due to the noticeable lack of bright weather recently it is affecting sufferers during the summer as well. I do not think I have SAD but it has certainly ticked me off.

Nevertheless despite the grey appearance of the morning and particularly compared to yesterday's unexpected sunniness we seemed to be markedly busier today. When the sun burst through in the afternoon business seemed to tail off. I am beginning to get the impression that people are only coming into the shop to cheer themselves up. Well, we will soon see about that.

One group we did see an abundance of was the Germans and we also seem to have a swelling in the numbers of Scots also. I imagine the latter are here to recover from the shame of their national sporting hero's demise at the tennis at the weekend; it must have been like *Braveheart* all over again but with an authentic accent. But it was the Germans who reminded me that we have once again been let down by one of our suppliers.

We ran out of the 87 pence stamps, which permit postcards and letters, under ten grams, to be sent to any destination on the planet and also Germany. We realised we were about to run out but forgot to order them before the weekend so placed our order first thing on Monday morning. The Missus told me that she had some difficulty in placing the order and that the maid on the other end of the telephone at first wanted to charge us £2,000 for a few stamps. After politely explaining that this was a little steep and significantly higher than our normal orders it was whittled down to just short of £500.

This morning our stamps arrived, (they are sent by special delivery), and we discovered the reason for the inflated price. The stamps that we had in our hands were those required for sending letters up to twenty grams in weight to the far flung corners of the globe such as New Zealand and Australia. We had also ordered some air mail stickers, which apparently are mandatory when sending postage abroad by air mail, and the maid had decided that one sheet of 24 would be sufficient for 400 stamps. If I were suffering from SAD it would have fair near finished me off.

We can, of course, re-order the correct stamps, we were told, but a refund for the wrong ones would have to wait until they had receipt of them. This requires us to wait several days while they send us a special bag in which to put them then we must make arrangements for it to be collected. In all likelihood we shall be out of pocket because of their gaff as well as disappointing so many of our German visitors. There really is nothing worse than a supplier that does not supply.

To console myself I repaired to the OS for the usual games of cards. There were a fair few new players tonight plus some of the new players from last week, sixteen of us in all. Modesty prevents me from telling you who triumphed over all those sixteen players, using the nuances of strategy and cunning, deception and bluff but even to the casual observer it would have seemed a master was at work.

There may be a hiatus in *The Diary* for a while; I understand that the casinos of southern France are more the haunt for the up and coming playboy.

July 11th - Wednesday

I was so overcome with delight at winning the cards last night ... darn it, I was not going to let on, ah well, too late ... ,anyway I was so overwhelmed that I completely forgot to place our milk order – again. I realised this omission at 4:45am when I woke up white and screaming. Unfortunately, it was not quite as simple as picking up the telephone, as I had also omitted to do a milk count so that I knew how much was required.

I was in the minimum of attire when a very bemused Lifeboat coxswain confronted me in the shop. I, of course, had to come clean regarding my forgetfulness and thus opened the door to a raft of amusing jibes. He dropped back in when we were officially open and, in my absence, asked the Missus if we had enough milk today.

Even by the current standard it was remarkably quiet in the shop this morning for the first hour or so. The showers that blew through a little later drove some of the late risers into the shop, including a couple of young walkers who bought a newspaper. I asked if they wanted a plastic bag to protect their purchase from the elements and the young lady said that they intended to shelter in the next door café until the rain abated. I replied that I did not think that the new owners, as charming and obliging as they are, would be overly happy about customers remaining with them until September.

As I may have told you once or twice I am quite keen on fish, eating them that is. This has been something of an advantage since we are very often left with a bit of fish we have not sold in all the ordering we do. It is not always easy to indulge my preference as the Missus hates fish and it is difficult to cook for one, or one and a half if you include the bleddy hound.

Over time I have developed some one person recipes, although the use of the plural might be a little misleading; I have two fish recipes. One, the most complicated, involves resting the fish on a few wedges of lemon in a tin foil envelope and throwing everything I have to hand in there as well. If I am feeling especially decadent I shall pour the resulting juice into a pan and add some clotted cream. The other recipe, if you can call it that, is no more than exotic than rolling the fish in some wholemeal flour and frying it.

Bearing this in mind, you will appreciate my dilemma when I tell you that a lady customer who had bought a fillet from us on Monday came back in today enthusing about the recipe I had given her, – recipe one with clotted cream decadence. So impressed was she, that she has placed an order for some pollack with the Missus and has left a note asking for another recipe. I feel like I am in one of those personality questionnaires that certain women's magazines do (so I have heard): do you

a) steal a recipe from the Internet and pretend it is one handed down from your great granny and hope that it doesn't taste like sawdust;
b) tell the truth that your recipe number two is about as interesting as a cold shower;
c) tell the customer that the cat ate her fish?

C is looking pretty good at the moment, other than the fact that I do not have a cat.

I shall retire to my bed now and hope that there is nothing that I have forgotten that will have me leaping from the covers in the early hours. Not unless, of course, I suddenly think of a blindingly good recipe for pollack.

July 12ᵗʰ – Thursday

It appears that it is not just the weather and the much maligned council conspiring against us in wanting to bring tourism in the county to its knees. The chaps from the United Nations Educational, Scientific and Cultural Organization,

(UNESCO), met in St Petersburg yesterday and discussed the developments at South Quay in Hayle and South Crofty mine. I believe they also had a little chat about my mate Mike's potting shed and the angle of the slope on the top of The Old Boathouse ball stand, but we will save that for another time.

It seems that the long awaited regeneration of the South Quay has come under their scrutiny, it being inside the Cornwall and West Devon Mining Landscape World Heritage Site, and has been found wanting. They also took a dim view of a company actually wanting to do some mining in the World Heritage Mining Site, which I might understand if it were a new open-cast hole threatening to scar an historic monument, but they are not even using the original top site. UNESCO has threatened to revoke World Heritage status from the whole of the Cornwall and West Devon Site unless all work is halted.

How dare we allow some carefully designed development into South Quay so that funds can be made available to restore the historic quay and set Carnsew Pool back to its original operation of regularly sluicing the estuary? What temerity we must have to aspire to grow a mining industry out of the ashes of the last operational tin mine in Europe.

Clearly they have some rose-tinted view that there is plenty of money around to maintain and restore these sites. Without some compromise some sites would fall into further disrepair and, in the case of South Quay, remain an eyesore in perpetuity not to mention the obvious benefits of employment, wealth generation and sustainability. Are they completely mad? I think they would have a point if someone was proposing to put a Tesmorrburys on top of the Great Wall of China but in the context of South Quay, already amidst a retail setting, they should develop a sense of realism.

Still, it is not all bad news. We have been road testing some of the new foods and meals that will be coming to the café next door, soon to become *Little Bo* by the way. Today I was treated to their new burger meal. If by reading the last two words you have in mind some golden arches you really must think again. Try some homemade burgers betwixt two slices of ciabatta, topped with a cheese of your choice, homemade chutney and salad dressing for the salad of leaves, couscous and lentils along with homemade coleslaw. It was unbelievably good and I do not even like couscous. It will also come at roughly the same price as a frozen burger in a limp frozen bap, chips and a lettuce leaf you could buy in some bland chain pub.

If you are coming to Sennen Cove this year you would be doing yourself a disservice not to try, at least once, a meal next door. I suspect that if you leave it a year you might well be looking at an advance booking in The Ivy league. Perhaps I had also better warn you to expect a slightly larger shopkeeper in The Old Boathouse than the one you saw last.

The rotund old begger made his way to the OS for the quiz in the company of Head Launcher, without the intervening inconvenience of Lifeboat training tonight. Clearly the intellectual stimulus of fixing a few dry suits and polishing a few bells was greatly missed, as we foundered miserably. It did not help that we had nowhere to sit to contemplate our answers, but we took some gratification in the fact that we beat the RNLI inspectors who were billeted there tonight.

Time then to walk home in the peace and quiet, (before the bleddy hound got loose), and consider the authority of a team of cultural experts who cannot even spell organisation correctly – apologies to readers across the water, but it really is spelt with an 's', you know.

July 13th – Friday

So, there was I sitting on the corner of my newspaper bin, enjoying the hazy heat of mid summer* and watching the tumbleweed rolling down the deserted street when all of a sudden, out of nowhere, a mother and her young brood approached. The children seemed keen to come into the shop but mother was ever so reticent, sighing, "It's like a newsagent", in a derogatory, "you won't find anything you like in there", sort of way.

"He he," I thought as the kiddiwinks entered my lair, "like a newsagent but with goodies to tempt small children into parting with their pocket money", and it was not long before little whoops of delight were to be heard as they found the pop guns, dinosaur eggs and bouncy bug-eyed worms that do not bounce.

---

* summer: it wasn't raining or blowing a gale.

"Ah ha", said the mother, wise to my cunning plan, "you've already spent all your holiday money", she tells the little mites.

"Begger!" I thought, as I waved them goodbye and went back to sitting on my newspaper bin.

You know you are in deep do-do when not even the children have any money.

As if to demonstrate how quiet we were again today I managed to read my newspaper from cover to cover. It was while I was reading the *Western Morning News* (did I ever tell you …) that I happed upon a review of one of the Eden Sessions, the annual set of music concerts held at the Eden Project. You may recall that I have visited the Eden Sessions for the last five years or so and have witnessed many absolutely blinding bands in an unbeatable location. This year, however, the brass at Eden has booked a seemingly endless list of musicians that I had either never heard of or, if I had, have no intention of wasting my money to go and see. One such band was Blink 182 and, judging from the review, was very glad I did not go. It also put me in mind of someone I knew who was going to see it and how I laughed mightily until she told me she was escorting her teenage son, at which point I just sympathised.

I had heard that the Eden Project were in a spot of financial trouble earlier this year. In my view they went for a bunch of cheaper bands and decided to charge the same gate for them. That seemed a bit cynical to me, especially when they started offering the tickets at reduced prices later when others had already bought at full price. We shall see what happens next year, but it would be an awful shame to loose such a top venue, so accessible to us.

July 14ᵗʰ – Saturday

Things were going swimmingly until, that is, the post arrived. Amongst the usual collection of bills and advertising was a letter from the much maligned council. They were sure that I was aware, which I was not, that they have been conducting a consultation on a review of discretionary business rate relief schemes. They have written to me as I am a beneficiary of one of them. We get 50 percent relief as we are a small store under 1,500 square feet, which I am sure is in metres now, but I could not tell you how many. Now, I am no expert in the way these reviews are conducted, nor am I blessed with second sight, but I am relatively certain that the outcome of the review will not be a reduction in my business rates; quite the reverse I would imagine. Central government has increased the rate over the last two successive years by many times the rate of inflation and now our local chaps want a slice, sorry, greedy chunk of the action too.

The business rates have always been a tax with no perceived benefit to the businesses paying them, but perhaps it is the price we pay for living in the place we do. We have always known, along with the millions of others who visit each year, that Cornwall is rather special. There is the scenery, the food and other draws far too numerous to mention. This small percentage of the Earth's population is now no longer alone in this knowledge; the secret is out. CNN, the American news channel, has compiled a list of 27 places and things which are a must see before you finally shuffle off. Amongst their list that includes the Taj Mahal, the Northern Lights and Sydney Opera House are the Crown Mines at Botallack. Cool, huh?

Being part of such a prestigious list we can probably expect to see an increase in the number of visitors, especially those of limited life expectancy, eager to tick off the visual treat from their bucket list. They had better hurry as I am sure it will not be long before our much maligned council take the mines apart stone by stone to use for road resurfacing or some such in their blind and headlong dash to save every last penny, no matter what the cost.

If I mention *Devil's Creek* you will know that I just had to, just had to, I tell you, head up to the F&L. I was not there long before I was roundly castigated for not providing a band report in last week's *Diary* entry for Saturday night.

Am I really just the far west version of the NME? The band is an integral part of the Saturday night, perhaps sometimes, like tonight, the focus, but I should not be relied upon to, willy nilly, roll out some vacuous comment week after week? I would rather reserve my comments for those musicians that truly make their mark, for one reason or another, to maybe discern the wheat from the chaff.

Tonight was definitely wheat. I suspect you already knew that had you read *The Diary* any other time *Devil's Creek* were playing. Again tonight they were sublime and an evening made perfect by a walk home that, though starless, was at least dry.

I must go now and gird my loins as the parents-in-law are arriving tomorrow.

July 15ᵗʰ – Sunday

For a day with rather grey beginnings it turned into a proper rip-zizzler. For Penberth Lifeboat Day it could not have been better. The excellent Shore Crew, (I could not attend because the Missus had gone off to get the in-laws), sent the boat off at around 2pm to show itself in Penberth Cove.

The boat was still around there when a report of an incident at Porth Chapel came in. The boat made its way around to the cove to show a bit of support, but Rescue 193 carried out the evacuation. It seems that a bit of the cliff gave way and injured someone on the beach. It looked quite serious and the helicopter was there for some time. The Missus happened to see it arrive at Treliske on her way back from picking up the in-laws.

She arrived back home at the same time as the boat was being recovered but unfortunately too late for me to go over and lend a hand. The excellent Shore Crew were a bit short-handed especially as they had to do a last minute slipway change; the boat arrived back with just enough time to recover on the short slip when the long slip was set up. Well, I suppose that will teach them to have breakfast next door without me.

With the sun sitting pretty in a big blue sky we were busy for most of the day. As is usual on sunny days we have a little hiatus mid afternoon, as everyone is down on the beach sunning themselves. Clearly we have not been used to this for the last three months. It also means we are deluged at the end of the afternoon with people returning from the beach. We were run off our feet right up to closing time and a little beyond, which was a delight for a beleaguered shopkeeper with his back to the wall, his nose to the grindstone and his shoulder against the wheel; I wonder if the circus will have me this winter as the contortionist act.

Time, now, to congratulate ourselves that we made it through St Swithin's day without it raining. I was still thinking that when the familiar sight of a line of showers swept in across the bay. Oh, joy!

July 16ᵗʰ – Monday

Day one of Swithin's curse and it seems to be working just fine. Not only did we get a guts of rain come through overnight, but I got a sprinkling as I took the bleddy hound around this morning. The old boy seems to have upped his game too, with thick grey cloud, the occasional mizzle and a fresh chilly breeze just to throw more of a spanner in the works.

It has had an adverse effect on our visitors today because, in their droves, they resolutely stayed at home. It was reported in the news that the latest Census has discovered another half million people they did not know about; I can promise you, they are not down here. Those that did venture out were dressed for winter including woolly jumpers, gloves and oilskins; a sea of sou'westers would not have looked amiss. High summer, my behind!

The high drama of the day was that Rescue 193 was called out again. This time to a gentleman found to be unwell on the Scillonian on its way back from the Isles of Scilly. The helicopter took the gentleman off in a well practised manoeuvre and whisked him off to Treliske. There has been no further news of the chap injured in yesterday's incident at Porth Chapel.

Other than that it would be difficult to imagine a more sedately tedious day than the one we just had. It was so bad that I took some delight in sending a spiteful note to *The Cornishman* regarding the much maligned council's review of Discretionary Rate Relief which, having investigated the plans, appears to be more worrying than it first appeared.

There are several groups that currently receive the benefit, charities and not-for-profit groups such as village halls, sports and arts groups, charity shops and heritage organisations and then there are businesses in rural settlements and small businesses. As the much maligned council has pledged to protect the charities and not-for-profit organisations, guess where the axe will fall? I may be jumping the gun, but I cannot see the much maligned council undertaking a review and then maintaining the status quo.

After this appalling season, finding that I will be paying more than double my business rates next year will, no doubt, bring an altogether different aspect of joy and light to our lives.

Then to cap it all, after we had closed for the day and enjoyed a simple tea, the sun broke through. Swithin, for a saint, you are a real nasty begger.

July 17ᵗʰ - Tuesday

The wonderful Laurel and Hardy Newspaper Company excelled themselves this morning. We do not have a huge demand for *The Independent* newspaper, but it can be missed if it is not delivered. Naturally my first sale of the day was for the title, but unfortunately they had not sent me any. I did offer our customer the alternative title they provided, but he declined my kind offer of The Irish Post.

We had some girls come by later on. They were carrying those circular canes which you can spin around your waist that are all the rage these days. They bought some snacks and it appeared as if they had travelled some way; it looked like they had gone through hoops to be here.

July 18ᵗʰ - Wednesday

Hard on the heels of the news that Ilfracombe is to get a sixty feet high statue of a naked, pregnant woman brandishing a sword, crafted by Damien Hirst *The Diary* can exclusively reveal that Sennen Cove is about to go one better.

You should all be aware that it is our Head Launcher's birthday today. You will be aware because, for the last couple of months, he has gone around telling everyone. It is therefore most appropriate that we break the news today that an eighty feet high statue of a naked Head Launcher, waving his Brokeback Mountain cowboy hat, will be erected at the end of the Harbour wall. As well as providing a thought-provoking monument, visible from Cape Cornwall (except for most days in the last six weeks), the Lifeboat will be able to use it as a mooring, by throwing a line over the protuberance incidentally included in the structure.

While we may not be able to claim that a world famous artist is responsible for the edifice, our local odd job man, Willie Penhaligon, (not his real name, obviously), has spent night and day bolting together old lobster pots, bits of driftwood, scaffolding poles and a bit of lead he gets a bit teasy about if you ask where he got it. Yes, Willie will have a big part in this statue.

As if to underline this momentous day, more in-laws arrived. They had travelled some distance to be here, starting from somewhere northeast of Launceston is my understanding. They have with them their Border terrier, which is quite the biggest and meanest looking Border terrier you ever did see. Unfortunately he is also probably the softest dog you ever did see too and is consequently terrorised by the bleddy hound who, probably quite rightly, suspects the bigger dog is only there to filch and destroy her toys.

In honour of their presence, the sunshine almost broke through at one point in the afternoon. It is, as we discovered only today, permitted a certain number of hours per month to shine through. This is due to the new health and safety orientated EU Sunshine Directive based on reducing the incidence of sunburn and skin damage from ultra violet rays. Naturally, the UK government has implemented the most stringent interpretation of the Directive and as a result today's showing is the last we shall see for a week, or we shall face stiff fines from Brussels, as well as the tops of our ears peeling off.

RW in the café next door proved her exceptional abilities in the kitchen by not only baking a cake for our glorious Head Launcher, but for the father-in-law whose birthday it is tomorrow. Naturally, Head Launcher, being the generous and caring person that he is, graciously offered to share his cake with us before whisking it home. No, don't be bleddy silly, of course he did not. I had considered taking a wedge from it before we gave it to him against such expectation, but I would probably never hear the end of it.

I shall just have to look forward to the father-in-law's cakes tomorrow, although I have no doubt that the Head Launcher will be in to sample them too, as he drops by on his way to Lifeboat training.

So, as the Michael Angelo of Eternity, after years of toil, carves the last minute detail on the fingertips of his statue of the

Venus de Time, just as the schoolboy of Fate takes aim with his catapult, it is time to say goodnight.

July 19th - Thursday

Given that the day developed into a real snurd-grobbler, the sort of summer days that we remember having as children, even if we did not, we were deserted for the middle part of the day — see, we just cannot win. I imagine it will not be long before we get our first drought warnings and the farmers start complaining of crops withering in the fields for lack of water.

What better day to do a little Lifeboat training, especially as last week was cancelled due to the inspector's exercise and the Sunday launch for Penberth Lifeboat Day. I immersed myself in gluing some more drysuits together while the Inshore Lifeboat went out on exercise, and I would wager you could not guess what happened next.

All right, I will not keep you in suspense. We retired to the OS for a Thursday night quiz. What merriment we had, especially as we had the brother-in-law with us who complemented our team by bringing to the table some sporting knowledge. Well, that was the plan anyway. One of his keen responses was that the footballer's name we were seeking started with an 'L' and had about fifteen letters in his name. As it turned out he was absolutely right, but unfortunately that did not count as an answer. We came third. I do not think he will be dashing back down here to play another quiz any time soon. We shall just have to find another sporting expert, or start reading the back pages of the red tops for ourselves.

As we walked home I saw the stars twinkling above us. Now, we have not seen those for a week or two. They were still there when I ran the bleddy hound round and even more of a miracle there was some of the birthday cake left too, although a sizeable chunk was missing. I will have to get my hands on some tomorrow else, even at 89, I reckon the old codger will have the lot.

July 20th - Friday

It is almost pleasant not to see it nice and sunny from first thing in the morning; it adds, rather, to a sense of anticipation of when that moment arrives that transforms the day into the clym-spangler that you were expecting it to be. And it was as clym a spangler of a day that you have ever seen, and so much more welcome after the grim greyness we have had up to this point.

Since we have been told to expect much more of the beautiful sunniness we sent ourselves into a frenzy of making ready the shop for a deluge of customers. Not only will it be sunshiny busy this weekend but it will be school holiday sunshiny busy and that is a completely different kettle of semolina.

To start, I made a horribly long list of goodies to be collected from Shrew House. It was relatively quiet when I ventured up there but when I got back with the van brimming, the shop had become unfeasibly busy. Normally, I would be able to, piecemeal, remove and price items then whizz them into the shop and onto the shelves. With a shop full of people, blocking the doorway and milling about, it is more a case of taking what opportunities there were and loading the stock, wholesale, into the store room to be dealt with later.

So there was the Missus slowly working her way through our full store room when the paper bag man came with a delivery. Not only was this several more boxes to crow-bar into the store, but most of the order was wrong. Actually, I knew it would be because, when I placed the order, the chap on the other end of the line told me not to worry and that he knew exactly the bags I was after.

If that was not sufficient for us to get our teeth into, the local cash and carry driver turned up. I had ordered a significant top up for our shelves, particularly of white wine and bottled water that I expect will be the first to go under the blazing, unrelenting sun. There will be more coming tomorrow, but this order was enough to have the Missus screaming for a cessation in hostilities.

It was then our order of fine bone china mugs turned up.

By close of play we had, more or less, cleared the backlog and hopefully our loins are truly girded for the weekend to come. Now, if we could just find somewhere to put the mountain of empty cardboard boxes that has filled the store room!

July 21st – Saturday

I missed the in-laws leaving, we were so busy, which was a bit of a surprise. It was not that I missed their leaving that was the surprise but the fact that they were leaving at all. The Missus's brother arrived mid-week, you see, so I rather assumed that they would be leaving a week later, blow me, they had hardly got here and they were off. I do not know if it might have been something to do with introducing him to the OS quiz on Thursday night. It is not everyone that can handle the fast-paced quick-fire questions; at top rate our question master can get up to a frisky two questions every fifteen minutes.

There is always something that happens on the first busy day that you would rather it had not. Today it happened to the café next door when their refrigerator broke down. We have a couple of telephone numbers of engineers who fix broken refrigerators but neither would answer the call and a third wanted the manager's first born child as recompense for his services; it was probably fortunate she does not have one, at least not yet.

When the chips are down and the world is about to disintegrate around you there is only one person you can call. Head Launcher arrived in a flash, fortunately not wearing his underwear on the outside, though heaven knows we are used to that. Between him and me we borrowed a fridge from our other next door neighbour and carried it around. While the girls in the café swooned at his appearance all I could do was bask in his ethereal glow; I must recommend to him a decent deodorant.

You might remember that I have had to tie down our bin lid with a bungee cord to prevent loose litter being deposited in it (our new waste collection cannot accommodate loose litter in our domestic bins). I mention this because as I approached the bin I noticed that some considerate soul had obviously read our sign and considerately not put loose litter in our bin. Instead they had slipped the used sweet wrapper under the bungee cord. Now, please, do not think that I am berating this person, after all they had not thrown the litter on the floor and had not used our bin, which you can no longer use for loose litter, and the public bin across the road, which is at least 25 feet away, means crossing a busy thoroughfare. I can fully appreciate their dilemma.

July 22nd – Sunday

You will be aware, dear reader, through some of my modest hints in the past, *The Diary* is very much an international publication with readers in the United States of America, Canada, Australia and Minchinhampton; all English speaking countries, you will note, with the possible exception of Minchinhampton. Well, ladies and gentlemen, boys and girls or perhaps I should add damen und herren, jungen und mädchen, I can confirm that this organ has broken into Europe, Germany to be precise.

A couple, C&W, I think, outted themselves in the shop this afternoon, or was it this morning, telling us that they follow *The Diary* from their home in Deutschland. The lady said that it helped her prepare for her visit to The Cove by catching up on the non-existent events that I mention and the sometimes peculiar goings on that I invent. I said that it must be difficult sometimes because I occasionally lapse into the common vernacular. This is no barrier, she told me, and is regarded as a learning process.

So there you are, not only is *The Diary* firmly embedded in the hinterland of mainland Europe as well as the aforementioned other international locations, but it is educational as well. I expect soon to become compulsory reading in schools across Europe. It may take a while, but I imagine that within ten years it will pretty much see off the European Union, as a generation of burgeoning politicians raised on tales of quiz nights, F&L music evenings and the bleddy hound reach positions of power in Brussels.

Here in the UK you might expect to see a statue raised in Parliament square of a bent old shopkeeper and his dog as we reach hero status amongst the jubilant Euro sceptic MPs at Westminster.

July 23rd – Monday

Gad, the heat, the flies. I half expected Beau Geste to come galloping over the hill, or was he more of a marcher? Needless to say it was another perfect day down in The Cove with temperatures soaring sufficient to melt tin on the street, well, nearly, should you have had the keen passion to do so.

Some people have the keen passion to share the most intimate details of their particular hobby or pastime, whether you have asked to be thus entertained or not. A treasure hunter who was after cheaper batteries than the ones I had for sale for his electronic gadget felt this very desire. Either he was a very bad treasure hunter, or a very good one who had not yet had the opportunity to prove it. Anyway, I was introduced to the toolkit and, in particular, the gizmo that was in dire need of a very cheap battery. Apparently, once you have dug your hole, this is the instrument that tells you that you dug it in the wrong place. I wished him well in his hunt for a cheap battery, especially as he was not that keen to travel to the top of the hill to find it.

I decided to cheer myself up with a little visit to Shrew House. Our happy customers had fair near stripped our shelves of goodies and they need to be replaced, the goodies, that is, not the customers, although …

At least the surfers were happy today. The small god of surfers must have listened to their prayers as we had near perfect swell, certainly from the point the tide turned. It got bigger towards high water and looked gigantic on Gwenver. It is probably no surprise, but exceedingly poor manners, that the surf clubbers who had booked a table at Little Bo Café were late arriving. As we are the café's bar we were late in closing too, but with the bistro tables buzzing it was more bohemian street party than hard work.

As the sun went down on this rather busy day, the sea was beginning to pick up a heavy swell. The spray that was coming off the waves as they broke over Cowloe was turning to gold in the light. I hope our treasure hunter was still around.

July 24ᵗʰ - Tuesday

They found themselves in The Cove under the sun, the relentless burning sun, drying their throats, their skin, their underwear — you would be surprised what people wear under their wetsuits.

They were the lucky ones. We, however, were pinned down in the sweatbox that is the shop in this sort of weather. Our refrigerators and freezers belt out heat morning, noon and night keeping the store unbearably hot. If it gets any warmer, me and the Missus will strip down to our waists. While we may not have any customers it will, at least, keep the flies off our bananas. Naturally, in the winter, this heating effect is non-existent and the shop is usually a few degrees below that of the outside.

Still, we had our customers to help keep up our morale, at least until we strip off. I do not know about you, dear reader, but I find the merry trilling of our till just the tonic. And trill it certainly did throughout the day as sympathetic souls threw their unwanted shillings in our direction. It rather threw me at one stage when a lady told me that I would have more than £30, three shillings and sixpence to bank this week. It took me a minute to realise that I was having *The Diary* quoted back to me. It is not often I am caught short for words. If folk are going to play that game I might have to start reading it myself.

Then, half way through the afternoon the Lifeboat was called out to tow a large yacht to Newlyn from around the Wolf Rock area. This put a small spanner in the works as I had hoped to make it up to Shrew House at a reasonable hour. Instead I went up at an unreasonable hour - that is when Cove Road was still busy with happy holiday makers causing mayhem by assuming that Cove Hill was single line traffic.

The café next door is attracting an increasing amount of evening trade as word percolates through The Cove. It really is a welcoming sight to see this end being brought back to life in the evening and is doing no harm at all to our late trade.

There were a few gathered as we recovered the Lifeboat at around eight in the evening. The very excellent Shore Crew must have looked like little bronzed Adonis's as we hauled the boat out of the water. Well, it was quite bright down there and if you squinted really hard we probably did.

Finally it would not be right to close today without mentioning that it was GO's last day on the winch, (we did suspect he telephoned in this shout himself), as he retired after some fifty odd years of service. We had to prize his knurled hands from the winch lever and drag him screaming out of the boathouse. Naturally, we will send on his bedding, pyjamas and the glass he keeps his teeth in to the mission or wherever he will be staying from now on; we are not completely without heart, you know.

July 25ᵗʰ – Wednesday

Yes, yes, I am sure we all know by now that it was yet another rapastuous and rip-blostering day down in The Cove. I am almost certain that you care not a jot for our sunshine, or that the beach was packed with happy sunseekers and the shop was besieged with happy pasty eaters and happy beachware buyers. And how, you might think, can I be so certain of your carefree attitude and disinterest towards us down here in happy Cornwall? Well, I must tell you it is because you are probably not quite as happy as us.

All right, you might be if you live in Eilean Siar, for example, in which case you would be 7.2 percent happier than us. You might also be rather cock-a-hoop if you lived in Shropshire, Wiltshire or West Berkshire too. These are not just assumptions I have picked willy-nilly or numbers snatched from the air, oh no, these are *official* statistics.

Yes, the Government's happiness index was published for the first time yesterday and the people of Cornwall come pretty high up the list, sixth in the UK apparently. I am guessing that the statistics excluded shopkeepers in Cornwall during the last three months, as that might have seriously upset the apple cart.

We also score pretty highly on the 'worthwhileness' table and in terms of life satisfaction too, although, oddly we are only mediocre when it comes to measuring anxiety. I think I should be quite worried about that. I think that also I might be quite concerned that my hard earned taxes have gone into discovering that a lawyer or doctor in Devizes is a tad happier than an out of work machine operator in Durham. No merde Maigret!

But I was not anywhere near as concerned as the chap who came into the shop in the evening asking directions to The View restaurant. He pointed up towards Sunny Corner Lane suggesting that he knew the restaurant to be up there and said that it looked over Whitsand Bay.

"Aha", said I, "I think you are a little off course, my 'ansum, for this is Whitesand Bay"

"Nay", said he, a little vexed, "I merely dropped an 'e'. This is the very place I seek."

He was quite certain that he was in the right place and, although he did not know it at the time, I could understand how you would not want to be wrong; Millbrook, where the restaurant actually lies, is nigh on ninety miles away. In the end I had to resort to pulling up the restaurant on the Internet then showing him a map of the location.

He did not burst into tears in front of me, though I would not have blamed him, but it did rather look like he went around to the other side of his car to heartily kick his tyres; he clearly did not have a cat with him.

While this drama played out I watched as a bank of sea fog rolled in from the north. It hung around Cape Cornwall for a while but as the sun went down it crept a little further into the bay, Whitesand Bay, that is and played with the light from the setting sun. I am sure it was supposed to be in Whitsand Bay tonight.

July 26ᵗʰ - Thursday

I mooched across the road to launch the boat for Land's End Lifeboat Day. There was just two of the very excellent Shore Crew, Head Launcher and myself, to carry out the deed and with our winchman retired and the Inshore boat requiring a tractor driver down to the beach we were a little pressed, even though we were joined by a third member for a short while. We were in much the same state for recovery, but with Head Launcher on the winch and tractor, (that was some feat, I can tell you), and my good self on the slip and a third member in the middle the operation was smoothly executed. What did you expect from a very excellent (and small) Shore Crew?

Now, ordinarily you would be expecting a trip to the OS for the quiz night. Just never tell me I do not come up with surprises now and again – I did not go. Head Launcher was entertaining his beloved tonight, it being her birthday - just don't tell his missus. I would have cut a pretty sad sight in my team of one had I gone, so I bailed out too.

July 27ᵗʰ - Friday

Our much maligned council made £8.2 million profit, yes, profit on parking charges last year according to one source. This year they are on target to make £11 million. This level of profit is second only to London.

I am not saying anything; it is their business. What I will say is that today started with a bit of a fizzle and stayed that way for much of the day. It is, of course, change-over day and many people have already headed for the hills nursing their sensitive bits after being exposed to the best sunshine we have had in a quite some time.

In Praa Sands our much maligned council reduced the number of waste bins available for the public to use. They had to go in this week and clear up the mess and provide the extra bins to prevent a reoccurrence.

No, not a word. We did have the usual glum faces buying their going home presents. They were not all glum; some were staying for another week. When they see the weather we seem to have been promised they may well change their minds.

The much maligned council has changed the rules on applications for public events making it so burdensome for the organisers of the Penlee Lifeboat promenade fund raiser that they have decided not to run it for the first time in over thirty years.

Completely, schtum. Some customers you know are going to be a little less straightforward than most, just by looking at them. We had a case in point today, in fact it was I who had the case in point - on several occasions. Having already identified the warning signs my worst fears started to be confirmed when she walked away from the till while I was pricing her goods. When the shop is empty this is not an issue but when there is a queue behind the offender it becomes irritating.

I had her goods in order for a quick pricing when she returned, including the stamps she ordered, lest she try and escape again. It was very clear that she was, shall we say, a little less focused than our average customer and it was little surprise that she fetched up less than an hour later asking if she had left the stamps on the counter. I inferred from her demeanour and reaction that I was clearly to blame for this loss.

She returned later to do even more shopping. Once again I had a comment about the stamps and how she was now being forced to buy them again; I must be making a fortune, apparently. It is at this point the words of my once best chum tickled my ear, just as if he was standing at my shoulder, whispering, "smile and take the money". So I did.

The jury is still out on whether the much maligned council will chase small businesses into paying double their business rates by reducing the Discretionary Rate Relief. My letter to *The Cornishman* on the subject might possibly bear some fruit as a chap from the paper called me today to discuss the issue. They will be running a feature on it next week so I will be able to see how much they drop me in it. With my head this far above the parapet I must make a jolly good target. I think I better start saving now.

I shall say no more but you can be assured come the revolution, brother, I shall take great delight in having a pee in the top man's swimming pool and seeing how he likes it.

You might also be assured that since I have had time to pontificate about the much maligned council, things have become a little slack around here. Either that or we are becoming better at shopkeeping. Business did pick up in the afternoon as the new wave of visitors arrived and I can confirm they are all a bunch of heavy drinkers; my wine fridge was completely emptied. Naturally I do not say this in a disparaging or judgemental way; they are welcome to buy as much wine as they like. I shall simply increase my order.

The Missus took the bleddy hound down to the beach for a swim just before we closed. She gets very warm in her woolly fur and loves her swimming, the bleddy hound, that is, not the Missus. It was also very much a perfect evening now that the stiff northerly gusts have abated.

We shall treat these next few days as very precious, I think. Weather is on the change.

July 28th – Saturday

A few rogue showers, they said. Very unlucky to get wet, they said. I always knew I was unlucky. The rain came down in stair rods at around half ten this morning and lasted, in varying degrees of heaviness, for about an hour and a half. So much for a rogue shower.

It was also very much quieter than it has been. Someone suggested that the Olympics might have had something to do with it. They certainly had something to do with the fact that some of our newspapers were well over two hours late this morning. I also do not know what effect our supplier thought the Olympics were going to have on our customer base, but they sent us 81 copies of *The Times* when our normal volume at this time of the year would be around 25. These boys are rapidly catching up on the Laurel and Hardy Newspaper Company and I do not like it.

The weather cheered up in the afternoon, which is more than can be said for the two shopkeepers who were metaphorically scratching their behinds for most of it. It is surprising how difficult it is, when faced with a bit of quiet, to knuckle down and do a spot of shelf filling or tidying up the store room. The Missus got down and did a bit of sweeping up, which was nice to watch. I then watched her clean the pasty warmer and fill up the small bottles of water.

What? Of course I was not idle. I telephoned in the milk order and called our crab fisherman, as we have a party requiring some lobster tomorrow. My finger pads are still tingling I will have you know.

July 29th – Sunday

It is not true what they say about the Germans. They have been living under a shadow for far too long and I mean to expose the true culprits and lay bare the facts for all to see.

The whole sorry circumstance came to light because it was raining first thing this morning. Well, not quite first thing, as I managed to run the bleddy hound around the block without getting soaked. It was a close run thing, as heavy drops were starting to fall as I made the door on the way back. It was dark as a dog's guts (sorry, it is a local phrase) out to the west. Not even the most dedicated were going to venture out before that passed over.

There is a large family that visits a couple of times a year. They are keen beach dwellers whenever the sun is even vaguely making an appearance and go well equipped for a whole day on the sand. The men folk of the family, and this is where the story really starts, were out as soon as the rain started to abate. One enquired about the viability of a day on the beach, as he was buying some supplies, and I remarked that it looked very good.

It was not more than half an hour later I saw him returning from the direction of the beach, a direction that I had seen him go earlier armed with towels and much beach paraphernalia. On his return he was empty handed. The game is up, I told him and the wry, embarrassed smile said it all. He and his buddy had been down to the beach to mark out his spot ahead of all the other unsuspecting visitors who would now have to make do with inferior locations on the sand. Had he not been delayed because of the rain we may still have been none the wiser.

Later, when I had a few minutes, I took out my binoculars and, sure enough, there in the prime spot on the beach were a set of towels and chairs set out. I half expected to see big sign spelling out 'My Plot. Keep Off'. So shame on all of you who have blamed the Germans in the past, it is a large family from up country swagging all the best spots.

Never mind all that nonsense, here's a funny thing. Here is a funny thing. The Cape to Brisons swim was not cancelled this year. Now, that is a funny thing. Actually, to be accurate it is the Cape to Brisons and back swim otherwise there would be an awful lot of people stuck on Brisons.

Given that it was also Lifeboat Flag Day here in The Cove the boat launch combined the statutory show for the Flag Day people and a trip out to Cape to escort the swimmers in case any got into trouble. Despite it being a little choppy and the receding tide carrying a few off around the other side of Cape there were none that needed rescuing. It is just as well since many cover themselves in goose grease against the cold, which makes it a tad difficult to haul them into the boat; I have been told they are slippery characters over that way.

There was about six to eight feet of rise and fall at the end of the long slip for the recovery of the Lifeboat. This makes the operation a little more tricky than usual and requires that the winch wire be at just the right length to avoid too much delay in hauling up. Once again the very excellent Shore Crew carried out a textbook recovery on which we all gave ourselves a jolly good pat on the back.

We were quite busy today in the shop, all told, and none busier than at eight o'clock when we were due to close. There seemed to be a lot of Germans buying beach towels. I did try and tell them they were wasting their time; they are up against professionals, you know.

July 31ˢᵗ - Tuesday

The Missus has caught herself a dose of lurgy and on cash and carry delivery day too. She had also cunningly ordered a big frozen order to arrive today just to really rub salt into the wounds and, blow me, were we not we busy as well.

With the Missus in dry dock I did not have time to get back to our cash and carry supplier who has failed to supply. I know that it was hot last week and they must have had some demand for bottled water but it does not take a genius to put the two together and up their stock. We were delivered less than half of what we ordered which will have us run out in a few days.

Not only that but they also delivered some little cans of flammable liquid, the type used to refill cigarette lighters. These seemed to weigh much less than the last cans we had; it must be lighter fluid. Come on, I have not given you a good groan for a long while.

August 1ˢᵗ - Wednesday

There were a lot of jolly excited people about late in the afternoon. One party were even starting a bonfire on the beach, if only they could find some dry wood. It was all in aid of some bloke on a bike and some bird in a boat apparently winning some sort of ironmongery in the sports day they are holding in London. I heard that the television people were also rather enthused, so much so that they were showing repeats of the event into the night and have unpicked the respective sports people's lives to such a degree we all now know the manufacturer of the nappies they used as babies. The best news, of course, is that the bird in a boat happens to be Cornish. The worst news, of course, is that the bird in a boat happens to be Cornish which means delivery of *The Cornishman* will be delayed by an hour or so while they crowbar in the news of the win and a full page advertisement by the manufacturer of the nappies she used to wear as a baby.

So, with Olympic fever in the air I ran up to the chip shop at the top – in the van, of course. The Missus wanted a portion of chips and, after all, she has been poorly. I reprised my fish stew recipe, mainly because having gone to some lengths to acquire some tasty fresh fish for the masses, my efforts have been spurned.

You really do not know what you are missing; it was some 'ansum.

August 2nd – Thursday

A pretty much black day and nothing at all to do with the weather. Once again we were tricked into believing that showers would plague us, but instead we had just about the best day of the week so far. The beach was rammed for most of it until the spring tide forced many to either abandon their plots or climb into the dunes.

We had moments of calm and moments of complete raving brilliance, especially when people started coming off the beach. We also had a moment of ceremony when top man at the RNLI arrived to present the retirement present, from the crew, and the certificate, from the RNLI, to our departing Winchman. It was a nice touch for a man who had been at the station since before his fifteenth birthday. Of course, back then it was a bit different winching up a dug out canoe by hand.

There was no shirking my responsibilities this week and Head Launcher too realised he could not stay away a second week. We heard on the grapevine that it was very quiet at the OS quiz night without us last time, (in that there were not many people, before you all start). Word had obviously filtered through that members of the very excellent Shore Crew would be in attendance, as the place was jammed to the edges with happy revellers. It was not, but it sounded good didn't it?

It was obviously this crush, had it been there, the weight of expectation and the fact that the much diminished Bar Flies who asked if they could join us that put us off our stroke; our performance was dismal, in that we did not win. It was almost as dismal as the news that brought about this black day.

British International Helicopters has announced that it will cease its 48 years of operations at the end of the season. It cites rising costs and falling passenger numbers, but what really put the mockers on it was that Tesco was successful in forcing a judicial review of the sale of the heliport to Sainsburys. Even if this were to be over-turned, and let's face it Penzance is bound to end up with a third supermarket, it will be too late for BIH.

So with apologies to Mr Auden and apologies to you, dear reader, for not having sufficient time to complete the poem here is Day Fail.

This is the Helicopter crossing the sea,
Bringing the pasty to the Isles of Scilly,
Letters for the rich, social for the poor,
The shop on the quay and maid next door.
Pulling out of Penzance, a steady climb:
The breeze is against her, but she's on time.
Past Tater Du and a farm called Raftra
Turbojet engines making a clatter,
Chopping the air with fast spinning blades
Turning the heads of the pretty young maids.
No longer will birds flock too many to count,
As she crosses the bay and over the Mount
High winds will not stir her course
Nor thick fog close the hanger doors.
No more on Tresco will she be alighting
Or the dogs on the lawn will she be frightening.

August 3ʳᵈ – Friday

The helicopter story continues with our valiant MP stepping into the breach. He has already swashbuckled his way up to the Transport secretary to ask for similar assistance to that provided to the Scottish islands' transport. How brave. I do wonder why all this flurry of activity has only happened at the eleventh hour as BIH signalled their intentions just short of twelve months ago. I know that the Tesco action must have been more recent but I am reasonably convinced it was not started yesterday. Why has there been no plan B on the table before? I do look forward to seeing our man in his shining armour, shortly before toppling gracefully off his rocking horse.

And I shall leave you, on this starlit and clear night, with a bit of Rupert Brooke who was born today in 1887 and this time I shall leave the words unsullied. You will recall that he was a war poet and clearly not prone to a happy turn of phrase. This will be one of the less grim, this one called *Seaside*.

Swiftly out from the friendly lilt of the band,
The crowd's good laughter, the loved eyes of men,
I am drawn nightward; I must turn again
Where, down beyond the low untrodden strand,
There curves and glimmers outward to the unknown
The old unquiet ocean. All the shade
Is rife with magic and movement. I stray alone
Here on the edge of silence, half afraid,

Waiting a sign. In the deep heart of me
The sullen waters swell towards the moon,
And all my tides set seaward.
From inland
Leaps a gay fragment of some mocking tune,
That tinkles and laughs and fades along the sand,
And dies between the seawall and the sea.

August 4ᵗʰ - Saturday

By the time you read this, unless you are particularly early readers, my quiet, remote and content life will have changed immeasurably and my little bubble of constancy and placidity, burst forever – well, maybe a fortnight.

It was certainly busy enough today but it is quite amazing how quickly The Cove can empty when a shower of rain hits us. I do not know where people go but one minute there were lots of people milling about and the next it was like a ghost town. As soon as the rain had passed through, there they were again – a trick worthy of Derren Brown.

Now, since I was diverted from my purpose last week, albeit a very pleasant diversion, I was not to be so swayed this week, especially with my Waterloo (from the perspective of the French side) almost upon me. It also occurred to me that imbibing large quantities of beer might help me forget and, as WG Grace once said, "My advice to you is to drink heavily." Hang on, that might have been WC Fields. I always get those two mixed up as they are very close to each other in the dictionary, cricket and fields.

After leaving you with some Rupert Brooke yesterday it seemed a little over the top lavishing you with some Percy Bysshe Shelly, as it was his birthday today in 1792, but let us face it he is a rather good poet, so there you have it, or rather, here you have it.

Good-night? ah! no; the hour is ill
Which severs those it should unite;
Let us remain together still,
Then it will be good night.

How can I call the lone night good,
Though thy sweet wishes wing its flight?
Be it not said, thought, understood --
Then it will be -- good night.

To hearts which near each other move
From evening close to morning light,
The night is good; because, my love,
They never say good-night.

Goodness, WC Fields was absolutely right. I almost forgot to enlighten you as to the Nemesis I am facing tomorrow. It is the Teenager arriving for a fortnight and this time she is coming armed and dangerous with a pal, we shall call her Red, as that is nearly her name.

I am doomed, I tell you, doomed but right now, I hardly care.

August 5ᵗʰ - Sunday

It was shortly after the Missus, looking at the rain radar, said that the showers were going to miss us completely that it started to rain. It was not busy this morning to start with but that just about finished business off for a while. And, yes, you guessed it, as soon as the rain stopped the street filled up again.

You might have guessed from my chipper demeanour that I have been given a stay of execution as Teenager and Red will not arrive until early this evening. They are coming down by train, on their own for the first time. I hope they manage all right; it would be horrible to think they ended up in Fort William.

Despite the weather The Cove seemed very quiet, unusually so for a Sunday. It was not until late in the evening when a lady came up with a possible reason. Although we were blissfully unaware, it seems the rest of the county and further up the line suffered rain of the biblical sort all day. We were lucky but I doubt that anyone under the deluge gave us lucky beggers a second thought.

Our good weather persisted into the evening. My good fortune, however, was a little more limited as a message came through from the girls that they had passed Truro, and were close to arriving. The Missus set off to collect them from Penzance and returned via St Just, where she collected a Chinese meal to go with them. I have no idea why such a journey should take the best part of two hours, but perhaps the traffic was bad over Leswidden.

It was as I unloaded Teenager's baggage that the reason for the delay became apparent. The aging van is certainly not designed to carry that sort of weight. It must have fair crawled up the hill onto the moors. I must have missed something because she is clearly staying longer than a week.

They went for a walk after tea. It is likely to be the last ten minutes of watching a television programme that is not a soap opera or some sort of Americanised reality show. Oh deep joy.

August 6th - Monday

It was so nice, that Teenager and Red headed for the beach at the first opportunity. They have a little tent so are well guarded against the occasional shower and we did have a little sprinkling earlier on. They also have their bat and ball and a prime spot right under the Lifeguard hut. I cannot for the life of me think why they might have chosen such a location. Perhaps they feel a little safer there.

For our part, we were quite busy after a sluggish start. I even had to make a little dash up to Shrew House for some more buckets and spades. It has become something of a trial getting into Shrew House over the last few days. We have accumulated so much cardboard since the last collection it is now bunging up my store. The joy is that I shall have to squeeze it all into the van this evening as it will be collected first thing tomorrow. I must say that the boys who do the collecting every fortnight are very user friendly. They are very happy to wait while I go and bring the van down from the car park and back it up to their lorry and no longer concerned that after my collection they cannot fit anyone else's cardboard in.

Shrew House was on my list of chores yesterday too. A lady had asked if we had another colour of body board other than the pink and yellow that we had on display as she was not keen on either. I told her that if she came back later I would bring some more boards down from our store. Eager to please, I tore myself away from the busy shop and went up to Shrew House for more boards, as promised. True to her word she returned some hours later and yes, she bought the yellow one that was there earlier. It is all right, do not fret so, I would have had to go anyway.

The Missus took Teenager and Red into town tonight for a little light shopping and a visit to the culinary centre of the known world, McKentuckyBurger. They left shortly after 7:30 and as I finish off this entry at nigh on half eleven they have still not returned. That must be some McMeal. Since she has the van, she must also stuff it full of all the cardboard that currently resides in Shrew House ... in the dark. Into every light shopping and McKentucyBurger life a little cardboard collecting must fall.

And the reason I am not at this moment tucked up in bed, smugly enjoying not stuffing the van with cardboard in the dark, is that I decided that I would take the quiet opportunity to tackle the growing pile of invoices on my desk. This I duly did and it took me a good hour and a half to do so.

I shall spare you all the technical detail but having completed the input I then create a copy using the 'move or copy sheet' facility which requires the ticking of a box to ensure that a 'copy' is undertaken rather than a 'move'. I then delete all the paid entries so that I can see which invoices are outstanding and when they require payment.

Yes, that's right you clever technophiles, I forgot to tick the 'copy' box and ended up deleting all the paid invoice entries for the year and very neatly executed a 'save', consigning my error to permanence. Fortunately, I back up my files every night and was able to recover the file. However I still had to rekey all the invoices that I had very neatly filed away.

I think I would rather stuff the van full of cardboard in the dark.

August 7ᵗʰ - Tuesday

There you go, another forecast telling us to expect a gut's full of rain all day, overcast and nasty. I bet you can not guess what weather we got? Yes, we had a gut's full of rain, it was overcast and nasty all day. Well, it was a day full of mizzle to be fair but it was still pretty miserable.

The inclement weather prompted me to ask a young lady if she was indeed super dry as the name on her windcheater suggested; she looked pretty damp. Perhaps it is the translation from the Japanese writing that is a bit suspect. I know my Japanese is a little rusty, but I could have sworn that the characters read something like, 'over-priced fashion wear' but, if that is true, at least it is British over-priced fashion wear.

Talking of fashion, Teenager and Red set off for Land's End after they got up this afternoon. For a couple of teenagers I thought that was rather brave, the walking to Land's End not the getting up bit, especially given the weather and the fact they are teenagers. Naturally, it took them a while to do their hair and make-up before they went. Well, you can never be too sure who you might meet on the path to Land's End.

Teenager and Red arrived back from Land's End and stayed long enough to change their clothes before they were out again for a stroll down to the beach. It is rather pleasant, not to mention against type, that they enjoy being out and about. Perhaps I should clarify that, as it sounds like it is enjoyable that they are not here most of the time, ahem, when what I really meant was that it was nice to see them enjoying their surroundings rather than being pinned to the new sofa and the television.

August 8ᵗʰ - Wednesday

What a pretty little day. It may have started off and ended a little on the misty side, but down through the middle it had The Cove written all the way through it. The abundant sunshine must have lasted a good few hours, from mid morning to late afternoon.

Teenager and Red launched themselves at the beach from the first opportunity, which was about lunchtime. They joined an enormous throng of colourful dots on the beach and in the water, although there was not much in the way of surf. The girls obviously did not mind too much as they did not come back until early evening.

There was something for everyone today, apart from rain lovers. For the naturalists out there we organised a visit by some fourteen basking sharks, including a mother and youngster. It was not long before you could not see the basking sharks for the number of kayaks that had gathered around them.

Clearly, the Olympics can not be further from these beach dwellers' minds. The same cannot be said for the people of Penzance who plan to honour Helen Glover with an open top bus trip around the town. This should be interesting if they are to commission one of the local tour buses. There will be an initial wait of an hour and then the discovery that it is going the wrong way around. Never mind, there will be another along in a further hour if it has not been held up by holiday traffic. I hope she does not have to take the Western Greyhound back, as her ticket will not be transferable.

And what could make the day more perfect than to dine at The Little Bo Café in the evening. We were concerned that we might have to eat in shifts as they normally close at eight. However, they already had a booking for the Sennen Surf Club who were coming back late so it worked out nicely.

All I shall say to you is Lobster Maryland, Fish Stew (a bit like the Boathouse quick recipe but obviously she had a lot more time to work on hers - the show off) and Chocolate Cheesecake – all homemade. If you have not tried the evening fare yet, why on earth not? You must be completely mad.

It all made for a bit of a late night and I still had not called in all my orders. Still, no matter, it was a rather splendid evening.

And just when we thought it was all over and the café next door had gone quiet I heard a plaintive call from the street below. A dozen weary travellers, just arrived by kayak from the Islands, had thrown themselves on the mercy of The Little Bo Café for succour. It was not the only succour they were after and we were pressed into duty to provide some much needed alcoholic beverage. They were a pleasant enough bunch and it was a pleasure to take their money, ahem, I mean to serve them with invigorating refreshment. It is what we do here for a worthy cause and when asked nicely.

Nice 'ere ain't it?

August 10ᵗʰ – Friday

Cooking in the heat of the shop is not what our tomatoes are doing as, since a couple of years ago, we keep them in a fridge. Now, on the face of it this seems rather a bizarre topic to broach out of the blue, but it is a subject that a lady customer brought to my attention. She told me that by keeping our tomatoes in the refrigerator we are inhibiting the development of an enzyme that makes them sweet. She sounded very knowledgeable on the subject and I have no reason to disbelieve her, unfortunately if we kept them out of the fridge, as we used to, our tomatoes may be sweet but they would also be a soggy mess.

I certainly was not the soggy mess that I was yesterday, as all in all we were not quite as pressed as we were the day before. Come early evening we were coasting and the Missus got it into her mind that she would take the girls out for a pizza. We have a perfectly good pizzeria in Penzance, though we have not used it for a while, but this is not what passes for a pizza to teenage girls. What they were after is a plastic pizza, the ones churned out with little care from national chains and one specific national chain whose most south westerly outlet is in Truro. To be fair to them it was not they who drove this particular insistence, it was the Missus who likes the salad that this chain turns out. I think she also likes the fact that it is in close proximity to large supermarkets that have on their shelves items of desire seldom seen out here in the desperate West.

To make this happen in an acceptable timescale someone would need to run the shop for the last couple of hours while the assembled female company made tracks eastward; a person well acquainted with life and loneliness of a long distance shopkeeper; a steel nerved merchant, a true paragon among tradesfolk. Unfortunately such icons are in short supply in this neck of the woods so they settled for some unsuspecting sop. Yup, that would be me, then.

They were still not home by the time I had finished watching the very informative and mentally stimulating television programme, American Super Idol: Makeover Plastic Surgery at Home, Redruth Edition and although I was tempted with a repeat of the entertaining, The Only Way is Camborne, I demurred and went to bed.

August 11ᵗʰ – Saturday

The Missus had left a shirt draped over my shorts, presumably, for me to find this morning. It was only half light when I got up so I could not be sure, so I left it there and went and put on my of my more sedate shirts, a rather intense blue patchwork shirt of which I am rather fond.

I have other shirts in various hues and even a South Pacific type shirt I reserve for sunny days, as it goes with the mood of the day. Some are a little less obvious but by and large the colours are, or at least started out, alive and happy colours.

When she came down to the shop this morning the Missus was wearing a loud royal blue blouse with a big Paisley print all over it. It was bright and alluring. She asked if I had seen that she had bought me some shirts too. It was the, 'I-spent-an-awful-lot-of-money-last-night-while-out-shopping-so-I-bought-you-something-in-which-you-could-share-my-guilt-and-not-be-too-miffed-with-me', sort of purchase. I told her that I had seen something on the bedroom floor next to my shorts this morning but that I had taken it to be some sort of soiled dish flannel. This remark evoked the sort of response that probably would have resulted in, at the very least, grievous bodily harm had we not been in the shop in front of customers, which is why I said it there.

To prevent an escalation of hostilities I promised to investigate the other offerings that had been bought for me. Having done so and established that the other shirts were about as interesting as a dinner party in a Carthusian monastery I cast caution to the winds with a fresh volley. I pointed out that the blouse the Missus was wearing was bright and alluring and did she not see that the items she had bought me were as dull as a slurry pit; I have seen more gay garments at an Amish funeral.

I see it now, of course. The whole shirt buying enterprise was nothing but an elaborate ruse. Naturally, the Missus will now have to go back to this remote supermarket to return the unwanted shirts and thus have a second opportunity to run riot with our meagre funds. However, even if I had uncovered her cunning plan, my only recourse would have been to say that I actually liked these grey and morbid specimens. I would have been consigned to wear the bleddy things and stalked The Cove like some grey ghost forever.

On a happier note I heard from the International Correspondent today. She had returned home after her extensive travels and unexpected detour to the Dark Continent. She tells me that she stayed with a sheep farming family in the far south who have owned the business for generations and can chart their ancestors back to the Huguenots. I was very interested by this as I always thought that they were the product of mythology; I wondered if their sheep still have golden fleece.

And staying with myths it was mythty on the way home from the F&L too, though a warmer and more pleasant night you could not have wished for, as I walked across the fields. When I arrived at the bottom of the hill the stars were visible – how does that work, then. It was just as well, if they were visible from the top I would still be up there looking.

August 12ᵗʰ – Sunday

We had jokingly suggested that Teenager and Red cook for us this evening but immediately regretted it when they said that they would. It was not a bad salad and the Missus threw in some chicken burgers as she did not want it to get too technical for the poor loves. The washing up is another matter but every journey starts with a cucumber and a bit of lettuce or so goes the old Chinese proverb – roughly translated.

I caught a little of the Olympic Games closing ceremony on the television before I retired to bed with stomach cramps. It seemed to be something of a bizarre spectacle with some quite alarming images (did you see the Pet Shop Boys with big pointy hats being towed by chaps on bicycles wearing pin stripe lycra and scary helmets?); I hope I don't have nightmares.

The most important impact of this event is that after sixteen days we might actually start getting our newspapers at a reasonably hour.

August 13ᵗʰ - Monday

You may be aware, particularly if you have been paying attention, that we are, apart from being a shop, also the Sennen Cove Visitor Contact Point and as if to demonstrate the fact I received a letter this morning with our title on the front. Actually it said Visitor Centre but I shall not split porpoises with you.

If any further proof were required I can tell you that we were asked a question today and we provided an answer. A lady asked where she could go rock pooling and I said that she would have to go down at low water. The next question was, of course, how far away was it and could they walk to Lowater from here. We tourist information types treat these misunderstandings with professionalism and integrity, so after I stopped laughing I took pains to explain the workings of the local tide before selling her a tide timetable.

When we first arrived in the shop we inherited one compressor, inflating balls for the use of and indeed I used it once in the presence of the Missus who has an aversion to balloons and things inflatable that have the propensity to go bang if punctured or, in this case, over-inflated. Being new to the art and a little over-zealous in my inflating this is exactly what happened, the result being that I was banned from using the compressor and the machine was banished to the loft.

Nine years later I have become weary of inflating my balls in the manual method, by using a ball pump. So weary indeed that I have cast aside all resistance and threats of doom and resurrected the compressor. Fret not on behalf of the Missus and her sensibilities; I am not a completely insensitive ogre, no, really, and only inflate my balls in the Missus's absence. It is a joy and I have become adept to the point that there is little danger of over-inflation and the consequent bang. The bleddy hound is not so sure and I have taken to ensuring she is absent also. I have noticed, however, that with every compressor assisted inflation my biceps have deflated in an equal and opposite measure. Maybe I should hand pump a few balls now and again so that I can still lift my pint on a Saturday night; a greater tragedy I could not imagine.

I was provided some assistance in the shop as well during the last hour of opening. Teenager and Red joined with me to serve a customer or two, which was very nice. Our combined charm and stunning good looks must have put many off as we were a little quiet or perhaps it was my withering muscles. Anyway it was a fitting end to a jolly little day that has seemed to fly by.

August 14ᵗʰ – Tuesday

And for today's entertainment we have the swapping over of Inshore Lifeboats. The boys were here for quite a while as they aimed to take the middle boat of a pile of three and replace it with our current boat. Interestingly, or maybe not depending on your point of view, at the bottom of the pile was D-641, Blue Peter IV. The original Blue Peter IV was stationed at St Agnes in 1968 and has seen several replacements since; if I am not very much mistaken that would be Purves, Singleton and Noakes feeling very proud.

Although we do not have a completely full range of sizes of wetsuits we manage to fit most people comfortably. Notable exceptions are young teenagers who have either sprouted upwards without applying the necessary bulk or have not sprouted and have applied unnecessary bulk. We were very pleased, therefore, to be able to fit out a lad who was taller than me by a good head and I would have taken for much older than his fourteen years; he fitted his forty and a half inch wetsuit almost perfectly.

What was not as pleasing was the arrival of a large family and the first errant youth we have had for several weeks. Having the need to touch everything delicate in the shop and being rude and mouthy, the child was clearly desirous of a clip around the ear 'ole, or perhaps some work experience down a very deep hole. Sadly, successive meddling governments have rendered these options for making me feel better inappropriate, not to mention somewhat illegal. I shall have to recourse to drinking heavily later, I suppose, before they make that illegal too.

561

August 15ᵗʰ – Wednesday

Hallelujah! We are saved. Well, if we lived anywhere else I would feel a little more confident.

In the news today Mr Hunt MP, Secretary of State for Culture, Olympics, Media and Sport, (when does the Olympics bit get dropped and does he get a commensurate drop in pay?), has told us to expect a tourism boost of £10 million from the Government, riding high on the back of the Olympic Games. Some of the money is to be used to encourage people to stay at home for their holidays, though simply asking the Met Office not to say it is going to rain when it is sunny in The Cove would be a good start and relatively cheap. By far the largest proportion of the funds will be used to promote the Britain that is outside London; it is believed that only fifty percent of foreign visitors stray outside the capital.

I am minded to write a letter to Mr Hunt MP to ask him not to throw any money in the direction of our much maligned council. In its present frame of mind I can imagine that they might look to employ someone specifically to find additional tourism related areas they can devastate. Maybe they could ban the use of buckets and spades on the beach or perhaps make surfing illegal, that should certainly help.

But never mind that nonsense, the gods have sent me a portent, although I am a bit stuck on working out exactly what it is a portent of.

We have had one of our large beach buckets outside the shop since the beginning of the school holidays, left by some forgetful child, (you did not imagine for a moment that I took one out of stock for the relief of thirsty pets, did you?). Since then it has served many purposes, but mostly that of collecting sand and detritus, oh, and the bleddy hound likes to stick her head in it from time to time but to what end I cannot imagine as her water bowl sits next to it.

It was raining heavily when I got downstairs this morning. While I paid no attention to it, the bucket was rapidly filling with murky water. It was the Missus who noticed first that the bucket not only contained water, but also a very large frog. The bleddy hound was most put out as the frog butted her nose when she attempted to stick her head in the bucket. Since the nearest freshwater pond is out along Coastguard Row I cannot imagine how the frog got into the bucket; I can only conclude that at some point during the night it rained frogs, or at least one frog. Given its size it might have been brought along on a small trailer and may not have been a frog at all, in which case it was towed.

Whatever it was I took it up to Coastguard Row and released it on my way to pick up the van. As I mentioned yesterday a trip to Shrew House was required today for more stock. Down in The Cove, after the rain stopped, it was showing signs of brightening up. Although there was a little breeze the anemometer atop the Lifeboat Station was barely moving. Imagine my surprise when I alighted from the van outside Shrew House to find that I was nearly blown off my feet; the wind was literally howling up there.

Back down in The Cove, as the day progressed, the swell became much larger. Out beyond the shelter of the cliff the sea was being whipped into a frenzy of white-capped waves with large lumps breaking over the Brisons.

This was quite at odds with earlier when our crab fisherman was out in the bay. He came back in to announce that the rope secured to the crab store pot had snapped, rendering it a little difficult to get at. He has a line with a large hook attached, but this can prove a bit hit and miss. What was really required was for someone to dive down and attach a new line. Enter our new hero: the partner of the lady who now owns The Little Bo Café stepped up and before we knew it he was diving off our crabber's boat with a rope in his hand.

It must have been a day of heroes as later on, with waves crashing over the Harbour wall, we had a group of lads in just swimming shorts attempting the long climb along the wall just above the water, (clearly they were not such heroes who would attempt it below the water). It is what we have seen the Royal Marines do during their training and, judging from the stamp of the individuals, we suspected that these were some of those brave lads on holiday. Even with the waves tumbling down on top of them they were clinging on like limpets.

No less brave were Teenager and Red who decided that after being here for more than a week it was the best time to try on wetsuits. They spent most of an hour in our store room trying various sizes of short and full length wetsuits and, here is where the bravery came into it, they let me assess the results. All I will say here is that the neoprene hugged their respective curves and lumps admirably. If I was thinking anything particular I was certainly not going to voice it then, and I would have to be certifiable if I were to leave it here penned in perpetuity. Let it be known, though, that I did not laugh – in front of them, at least.

Talking of scary, we have had a lot of very concerned campers in this evening. The wind is flexing its muscles and we have started to feel the odd gust or two in The Cove. The Coastguard has just issued a storm force 10 warning for Sole and Fastnet, which is close enough, thank you. I would be banging in some extra tent pegs tonight if I were them.

Whatever you do with it ten million quid is not going to stop your tent blowing away.

August 16ᵗʰ – Thursday

Had the seas state been fair I suspect that we may have launched last night to the aid of a yacht sixty miles north with an injured lone sailor on board. Given its position, both Padstow and St Mary's were in the game. He had set off his emergency beacon close to our shop closing time and we listened to the Coastguard direct Rescue 193 out to it instead. Apparently, it was a perilous rescue as the yachtsman jumped into huge seas thinking the high line was his to grab. The winchman, also by this time in the water, had to haul him in along the wire and both were eventually winched back up to the waiting helicopter. This was some heroic action by the winchman, as the conditions were apparently truly appalling.

August 17ᵗʰ – Friday

As we expected it to be a little quieter around here today the Missus volunteered to take Teenager and Red into the sparkling metropolis of Penzance where, I told Red, the streets were paved with gold and every other store was a fashion house. She did not look too disappointed when she returned, although I hope she does not have one of those poker faces and is secretly harbouring a grudge against me.

While they were away the shop was particularly quiet as predicted. This was continued until 42 boxes of ice creams turned up that needed to be stowed away in our freezers as expeditiously as possible. Unfortunately, the delivery coincided with a particularly heavy downpour that drove all those people who were around today into the shop all at once. This presented me with something of a problem as it is very warm in the shop and the ice creams would melt quickly and there was a flurry of activity at the till.

The upshot of these competing of priorities was that the ice cream freezer looks like something has exploded inside it, and at the speed I was going there are a number of customers whose only evidence of being served will be that their pockets are lighter than when they came into the shop. Perhaps they might have felt a slightest breeze across their palms as they proffered their cash.

I think I was still panting from my exertions when the girls came back. Surprisingly, they were largely bereft of carrier bags full of goodies. Maybe they have spent all their pocket money, or perhaps the designer stores that litter PZ high street did not have their size in Jimmy Gabbana's.

Never mind, tonight is the night they get taken out to tea. It has become something of a tradition that visiting parties are whisked off to the Meadery at Trewellard at least once during a stay. They serve plain, wholesome fare, which, though very palatable to the right discerning taste, is not quite my cup of tea. You know the sort of thing, soup in a basket and lumps of roasted chicken on a rustic plank that you eat with your fingers, the chicken, that is, not the rustic plank.

I was very happy to let the Missus take the girls up for the early sitting and stay behind to mind the shop. It was not exactly taxing; my greatest challenge was fending off the abject boredom. The biggest advantage of all was to sit down after I shut up the shop with a beer in hand, a vaguely identifiable ready meal on a tray and something other than Big Brother meets the Kardashian's Next Model Idol in the Emergency Room on the television – utter bliss.

August 18th - Saturday

It was back to normal in very short order and what would a day like today be without a little Lifeboat shout to make it complete. I had just whisked myself off upstairs for a little well-earned zizz when the pagers went off. A yacht had got itself stranded without any wind for its sails the other side of Longships and a tow was required back to Newlyn.

The Lifeboat was very nearly back in The Cove when the Lifeguards told Falmouth Coastguard that two surfers had been seen, possibly stranded, out towards Nanquidno (I have to hand it to the Lifeguard who ran nearly all the way to Aire Point to investigate). The Lifeboat did a sweep of the coast line in that area and concluded that the surfers had found their way safely back.

The very excellent Shore Crew mustered in numbers at five o'clock for a short slip recovery, which was nice since only one other turned up for the launch. It was around six o'clock that the boat finally returned. Fortunately, all that heavy swell from the last few days had abated but there was still a fair amount of movement down at the bottom of the slip at near enough high water. I signalled to the Coxswain that the water was above the rollers on the slip on average and he, very wittily, suggested that I look out for my toes when he came in. Naturally it was a textbook recovery by the very excellent Shore Crew and I can reassure you, dear reader, that my toes are intact as I did indeed look out for them very closely.

August 19th - Sunday

One person more reliant on the weather forecast than most, I expect, is a certain podiatrist from Helston. For the last couple of years he has spurned the use of footwear and has carried out his daily routines barefoot. This nugget of vital news came to light because he was banned from entering his local Tesco store on the grounds that it was dangerous. I can see their point; all it takes is an errant box of cornflakes and he could give his toe a nasty stub, then the years of litigation and recrimination.

In light of this revelation The Old Boathouse will be reviewing its naked feet policy, as we clearly need to address this hitherto unmanaged risk. We have gone to the great lengths of securing a job lot of hobnail boots with steel toe caps in various sizes. These will be issued to all persons sporting bare feet or inappropriate footwear that may pose an unnecessary risk inside our store. We understand that many of you will be in a rush to get back to the beach or wherever you are going, so we have dispensed with boot laces as they may pose an additional hazard if left undone.

Naturally, in this health obsessed society we are conscious that there will be the concern regarding cross infection such as athlete's foot, verrucas and the like. To negate this risk we have installed a three inch deep trough filled with disinfectant, (actually it was an out of date batch of sheep dip at a knock down price but it does the job), that customers will need to walk through before wearing the boots. We apologise for the inconvenience that this might cause, but it is far better than any of you stubbing your toes on a bag of marshmallows that might have fallen onto the floor, and our insurance is so expensive these days.

Anyway, enough of that nonsense, it is time to prepare the Lifeboat for the St Buryan, or was it Cape, Male Voice Choir night. This is the one night each year that the choir comes to The Cove and performs on the wharf. It is usually raining for this event but although the clouds rolled in the wet stuff held off. The Lifeboat moors in the Harbour while the singing goes on and the timing is clearly dependent on the state of the tide.

The Missus had booked into The Little Bo Café for her evening meal with Teenager and Red tonight and the timing was clearly dependent on when the singing stopped and the boat had to be recovered. In perfect style the singing stopped just about the same time as her main course arrived. She was not best pleased as she had to return to the shop while I joined the very excellent Shore Crew to complete the recovery, which was textbook incidentally.

By the time I returned she had inexplicably gone right off her meal. It seemed such a shame to waste it so I finished it off. I am sure, dear reader, you can imagine how delighted she was that it did not go to waste.

Time I sloped off to bed, I reckon.

August 20ᵗʰ - Monday

Today was a different day and not just because it was a Monday and a different date from yesterday, it was because it started sunny and stayed that way. As a consequence we were mobbed pretty much from the moment we opened the doors, which was rather nice.

So busy was it that I had to do an emergency run up to Shrew House. It is a task much akin to deciding to drain the swamp when you are knee deep in alligators – one that should have been done much earlier. Unfortunately, it is not always possible to predict how busy we will be or which products are going to be targeted by our fickle customers. It is a sure bet, however, that once a particular product line has been bolstered it will not be touched again for a week.

One particular stroke of good fortune is that our diminutive dog walker is back on the scene again. This means that the bleddy hound gets run around during the day when Teenager and Red are on the beach strutting peacock like in front of the Lifeguard hut for the last time.

Yes, time has once again run away with us and the girls are going back to their respective homes tomorrow. Never has a period of time gone so fast and seemed to have lasted an eternity. I jest, of course. They have been directed to consider what they would like to do for tea on their last night here; something traditional in a Cornish vein perhaps, encapsulating the high points of their holiday and exploiting the cornucopia of excellent Cornish produce to its fullest extent – McKentucky, no doubt. They surely cannot both be from Philistinia.

Not that we have had the time, but it would have been nice to think that we had introduced them to some real Cornish goodies while they were here and I am not talking about the Lifeguards, either. They have, of course, twice or three times eaten at The Little Bo Café that uses predominantly local produce in its offerings, which was a good start. I did offer them some of the pollack goujons that I prepared near the start of their visit, but both declined. They both had said that they liked, or were prepared to try, some fish but only if it did not taste too much like fish.

So it was to the F&L we repaired for our last supper. It was pleasant and fitting that we should have enjoyed a meal all together and it was pleasant and fitting that it was the most convivial of evenings. I had the chance to talk with both at some length, which is something I have been unable to do for most of the fortnight; it has seemed such a mad rush.

Despite the fact that they have been absent for most of each day, the flat will seem a much bigger place without them. This will be largely because it will be devoid of the female teenager detritus, items that I would be hard pressed to put a name to. I will also be allowed into the bathroom again.

What a strange place it will be.

August 21st – Tuesday

I had a busy morning even before we opened. Because the Missus was driving Teenager and Red to catch the train this morning I had to empty the van of the cardboard that we had picked up from Shrew House last night on our way back from our meal at the F&L. It was fortunate that it was not raining and neither was it windy as I had to pile the cardboard up on our benches across the street.

As well as the cardboard I had to do the normal Tuesday morning newspaper and magazines, the biggest delivery of the week, bake the bread, take in the milk and restock the drinks' fridges. It was then that the cash and carry delivery driver pulled up. The driver and I were only half way through bringing in the large consignment of groceries when our fish delivery arrived just behind the cardboard recycling lorry. That was shortly before the bread man joined the queue. I was seriously considering sweeping the floor in an unusual manner at the same time, but the Missus came back at that moment.

You might have noticed the fish delivery in there. For the last week or so we have been very quiet on the fish front and I have not bothered to push it by getting any in for the impulse buyers either. Someone had placed an order for today, so I added to it to see if we could spark some interest.

The person that ordered the fish had asked for a whole hake for four people to feast upon. I thought this might have been a little ambitious as they are not generally small fish. My suspicions were confirmed when I spoke with the buyer on the telephone and told him the price; the expression on his face was audible. When he came into collect the fish I told him that the fish could be filleted or steaked as he wished and that he did not have to take all of it for which he was grateful.

However, the Missus had only just gone upstairs for a bit of a break and I had to call her back down with my filleting knives and a chopping board so that I could fillet the fish on the fly, in the shop. It had not occurred to me that the small matter of filleting the fish would spark any interest amongst the buyer and his German friends, but I found myself performing the service with a small audience and the occasional flash as they took photographs.

I have filleted a few fish by now and I have a certificate to show that I have some idea what I am doing, but I would not in the least call myself an expert. To suddenly find myself performing a public filleting was, to say the least, disturbing if not slightly surreal. It was probably just as well that they had not the faintest idea whether I was doing it right or not but, note, they were taking photographs. Someone, somewhere, is probably looking at one now on a Facepage wall, (see, I know the right word too), and thinking, 'what's that idiot doing to that fish?'

Maybe it was the helter-skelter of a day or the weather, or both but the Missus and I found today something of a struggle. The cash and carry still sits in the store room and my pile of invoices to process lie untouched on my desk. Time for a bit of loin girding and an early night, I reckon.

August 22ⁿᵈ - Wednesday

Phwoar! What a stonk-gribbler of a day.

We were pinned down behind the counter by a major customer offensive again. The bombardment went on for most of the day until, in late afternoon, we were each able to slip away under the wire and take a quick break.

I do not think I could tell you much about the comings and goings today other that the Missus managed to clear most of the cash and carry order and I stood rooted behind the till. It is a place that I feel most at home, especially during the summer when the trilling of the till is at its loudest. My fingers, though, are but mere stubs at the ends of my hands. Marvellous!

Welcome, then, was an invitation from our neighbour, she that has the café next door, to an evening barbeque in honour of one of the girls who is to spend a year in China. We asked if they were equipped sufficiently in the barbeque department and she said that they did not have one, which was an interesting response from someone holding a barbeque for a maid who is going on a slow boat to China, (I rather suspect that it is a fast aeroplane but it did not sound quite so poetic). It is fortunate therefore that first, we asked, and secondly that we *do* have a barbeque and that she could borrow it for the evening. Fortunate indeed, else we may have ended up with barbequed salad to satisfy our hunger.

As it turned out it was a pretty fine show. Everyone brought a little something and while I thought we might have fulfilled our obligations in that manner by bringing along the barbeque itself, the Missus did some cheesy garlic bread and some sausages. I brought some beer.

Though the clouds threatened rain, it stayed dry and as more people turned up, a little impromptu street party developed. It was a little hard cooking in the darkness, but thankfully someone else took responsibility for that, nevertheless it tasted pretty good even if we did not know what it was. We stayed to help with some of the clearing up, but some of the youngsters and the China bound girl stayed well into the night. Good luck to her in Chongqing, the largest and fastest growing city in the world, apparently. Now I did not know that until last night so it was an education as well as a jolly knees up.

(Chongqing: opened as a treaty port in 1891 and by 1994 had an estimated population of 2.4 million and today has an estimated population of 34 million – next week 34 million and one.)

I have to say it is rather nice living next door to neighbours such as this. I might revise that when I have to get up in the morning but for now that will do very nicely, thank you.

August 23rd - Thursday

Here is a scary bit of news, our much maligned council could soon get more devolved powers and are in talks with Mr Clegg about it. Crikey, they seem dangerous enough with the powers they already have, without giving them some more. It is like having our own personal sorcerer's apprentice up there in Truro but with no wizard to clean up the mess.

Perhaps they are responsible for the cloud thickening up today, although it stayed dry and bright for most of the day and did not seem to bother the army of people camped out on the beach. As upbeat as I wish to sound it was definitely not as busy as yesterday but busy enough nevertheless.

Our ever cheerful coxswain passed by in his van during the afternoon with the happy greeting that by this time next week our visitors will all have gone home. As weary as I might be, it would be nice to think we could have another couple of weeks to swell the coffers before winter. Sadly, though, he is right and we will be looking out on a comparative ghost town in just a few days.

I should come clean and tell you that our much maligned council actually came up with a sound idea, though I suppose someone else might have suggested it to them. They plan to run a pilot in St Just and Treen whereby the street lights are turned off after midnight to save a few bob. The trial will run for a limited period during September. St Just Town Council is very supportive and believe that it will aid in reducing anti-social behaviour on the grounds that the little terrors will not want to hang around in the dark for too long. In Treen the landlord of the Logan Rock is absolutely delighted. He has been moaning like a drain ever since they put the ultra bright new streetlamps in that he cannot sleep at night as it is like daylight in his bedroom.

I shall have to watch the outcome of this trial closely. If it really does reduce the incidence of anti-social behaviour I shall try it in the shop between the end of July and September. The little beggers will find it very hard to displace our fridge magnets, or rip the wrappers off every single pop gun if they cannot see them.

There were no such illumination problems when we launched the Lifeboat tonight in a spot of Thursday night training. Being the most south westerly point in our land we are the last to see the sun dipping away. We launched to an audience in awe and recovered to some bloke who was still fishing at the end of the Harbour wall, as the rest of them had beggered off down the pub. Still the very excellent Shore Crew put on a fine performance just in case, then we beggered off down the pub.

Once again it was difficult finding a table and I can only conclude that this really put us off our stroke. That and many of the questions relating to the Olympics and sport in general along with other questions we did not know the answer to left us dragging behind the field somewhat. If this carries on we will need to find a venue that has easier questions or less intelligent people.

Still, at least it was not raining when I wended my way home. What happy days.

August 24ᵗʰ - Friday

Now, look, I only popped into The Little Bo Café to return the plate on which my last night's tea was delivered, honest. Having a slice of freshly baked coffee cake was furthest from my mind, but there it was on the counter and I could barely see over it to return my plate it was that thick. It was as I was handing over my plate that the coffee cake winked at me, I promise you it actually winked at me. Fortunately, I am made of sterner stuff and manfully resisted the temptation.

It was after I returned to the shop that I started to feel a little tired and distracted. I could not concentrate in the least on the task at hand and customers were starting to look at me oddly, at least more oddly than normal. Sometimes a person must capitulate to the inevitable and accept his fate; the calling of the cake was just too much.

Such was the power of the cake I had left the shop unattended to go and get a slice and when I returned there was a group waiting for pasties. I apologised for the delay but explained that some things just have to be. When they saw the prodigious wedge of cake on the plate I was carrying they all nodded sagely and agreed that it was temptation beyond endurance that I had succumbed to.

It certainly was not justice or my just dessert as I had very nearly messed up a fish order this morning. The Missus had reminded me last night that a customer had ordered some mackerel and I was supposed to leave a message on our supplier's order line. Naturally, I forgot and by the time I had got downstairs this morning I had missed the boat, as it were, or at least the van delivering the fish. I tried a couple of alternatives, neither of whom could help and it was while telephoning one of The Cove fishermen that I noticed a punt heading into the Harbour.

Despite it hacking down with rain I headed on down to meet the returning boat in the hope that they had some mackerel on board. Just as I reached the quay I met with our crab fisherman who, quite fortuitously, was unloading a fish box full of mackerel into his truck. He pointed out how pleasant the weather was here in The Cove, as the rain coursed off my waterproof hood. He said that it was really bad further out and the sea state not conducive to much fishing. Good enough for a few mackerel I thought to myself and quickly struck a deal for a dozen.

I did have to pay the price of having to gut the mackerel but at least I was not left to look silly by having to admit that I forgot to place the order. The customer benefited too by having some really fresh, Sennen Cove fish on his plate.

August 25ᵗʰ - Saturday

Yesterday we had been followed the progress of a towing operation that St Ives Lifeboat had been called out to some forty miles north. They had been called out in the early hours to a large trawler with engine failure and were making slow passage into strong headwinds and a lively sea; at best they were making two knots.

At half past one Sennen Cove Lifeboat launched to take over the tow, still some thirty miles north west of the station. The initial plan was to take over the tow with our more powerful boat and take the casualty back to Newlyn for repairs. As it happened the Lifeboat was relieved by another fishing boat more suitably equipped to tow the large vessel in the heavy seas.

We recovered the boat at around eleven thirty in a tricky but textbook operation.

Then, just when we thought life could get no better, the boat launched again at around half past midnight to escort another crippled beam trawler, taking over from St Mary's boat that had escorted her from the western approaches.

Your mission, should you wish to accept it, is to put together an expert team and recover the Sennen Cove Lifeboat on the long slip. This message timed at 04:50 hours will self-destruct in five seconds – oh, and by the way you only have 45 minutes to complete your mission.

These words echoed around my numb and sleepy brain as I stood on my own in the dark at the bottom of a very slippery long slip waiting for the boat to arrive. There were two others I had managed to wrest from their fitful slumber including Head Launcher, up in the nice and cosy eerie of the winch room. The only two redeeming features I could think of were that it was relatively temperate and it was not raining – yet.

As you would expect it was a textbook recovery, despite having to use the hauling cable to pull myself up to a safe spot on the slipway. With the boat safely housed I was back, washed and preparing the weekend newspapers, the Head Launcher down in the valley supervising change over day and PP off taking wedding photographs all without missing a beat.

Some people might say we achieved the impossible, but to us it was just another day on the job. After all, we are the very excellent Shore Crew.

August 26th – Sunday

Well, you know that it is Lifeboat Day when the enthusiasts arrive before the shop is open to set up their stalls along the road. Every year the Lifeboat Enthusiasts Society sets up its stand of model lifeboats and this year our pal with the clay pipe model of the Round House was back. We have not seen him for a while, but I reckon the old boy was head down in his shed all that time, for he trucked up with around about a dozen different buildings today. I cannot imagine there is a clay pipe left in Cornwall.

One of the models is of the Knill Monument, a granite pyramid near St Ives (more Lelant, really, but I have not upset them yet so we will leave it that way for now). John Knill built it as a mausoleum for himself, but died and was buried in London in 1811. One time customs man and mayor of St Ives he left instructions that every fifth year the monument should be danced around by ten young virgins and two older women singing the 100th psalm. The tradition has survived to the present day and although there is no shortage of older women they have had to loosen the definition for the other participants, else it would have died out years ago.

Head Launcher had some work to do this morning so I stood in to partake of a very pretty little breakfast with TS at The Little Bo Café, as is tradition for Sunday launches. We considered re-enacting the Knill Monument ceremony, but at least one of us did not fall into either of the required categories.

With all the bunting and activity our end of The Cove was a busy little place to be today. The weather held good for us too, even though the cloud increased in the afternoon. We ran out of pasties in the early afternoon which, although disappointing for some, was something of a relief to us as we started the day with so many I thought we might be throwing them away.

Standard for a Lifeboat Day we had a little Lifeboat launch in the afternoon. Some of the fundraisers got on board for a jolly, as did the chap who makes all the model lifeboats. It was once around the Longships and back for a quick recovery where only three of the very excellent Shore Crew were waiting to execute a very nearly textbook recovery. It was me today in the cosiness of the winch room, if you are interested, while Head Launcher and TS did all the hard work.

Our busyness evaporated after that, something we are going to have to get used to, I think.

August 27th – Monday

Despite the rain, which we took in two lumps with some respite for an hour or two in the middle, we had a fairly determined trickle of customers throughout the day. The second wave of wet turned to mizzle at about four o'clock and ceased completely by five, just like the radio forecast said that it would. By six the sun broke through so I trekked up to Shrew House to celebrate.

I had left it a little late, to be honest, and we had to rush rather to get all the new stock out on the shelves before we closed. After nine years, one of the constants in running the shop is that at five minutes to closing, at whatever time that is, we will always get a rush of people. I have no idea why, but the later we close the more pronounced the phenomenon is. If we leave our closing duties too late we have to abandon them to serve customers, thus extending our closing even further. With the door even slightly ajar more people, who probably had no intention of shopping at all, are tempted in.

We are considering not opening at all next year. We will just have a closing time of eighty thirty in the morning and leave the door slightly open. I reckon we will have a bumper year with the hordes of people wanting to buy something just before we close.

August 28ᵗʰ - Tuesday

Someone who wished he had gone home a day earlier was the surfer who cracked a rib or two and had to be whisked off the beach by Land's End Coastguard team. They had a bit of a time of it trying to get down to the beach, given the state of the tide, but eventually managed to get the Land Rover down to Carn Keys, the little black huts out by North Rocks, and stretcher him up to that.

It could have been much worse as the Shark Trust has reported seeing some killer whales in the area. Let's face it, all it takes is one short-sighted killer whale and a surfer in a wet suit does not look a whole lot different to a grey seal. "Hey, bud, look, a geet bunch of grey seals." "Yeah, and they've learnt to surf."

They were first spotted out near the Isles of Scilly but have migrated to near The Cove. The news might deter those pesky snorkelers from getting too up close and personal with the basking sharks. I am sure they would be a little alarmed if instead of some gaping maw they were confronted by a couple of rows of sharp, shiny teeth.

It does look like it may not be too much of a problem if we lose one or two of our visitors to the killer whales as it looks like there will be plenty more. The European Route of Industrial Heritage (ERIH) has just added the Cornish Mine sites to its portfolio. We now join the Spillum saw mills in Norway, the Carbonia coal mines in Italy and Zyviec Brewery Museum of Poland; the Cornish Mines sites complement their offering to the west. The ERIH does little more than promote the sites on its list, but it is a nice accolade and will be a consolation when the UNESCO lot strip us of World Heritage status for building a Sainsbury's on South Quay in Hayle.

Still, even by this evening there were still a fair few people about. We closed an hour earlier tonight but it fooled no one; we still had a rush shortly before we closed.

August 29ᵗʰ - Friday

At low water this morning I was looked on rather suspiciously when I said that the fishing boats may struggle to get out in the next day or so and that complaining about mediocre surf would be the last thing on people's lips this afternoon. My prophecy, well less prophecy more looking at a well known surfing website, was borne out when a sizeable swell came in with the rising tide. It looked pretty vicious and I assume that the lifeguards red flagged the beach as the sea was full of surfers.

I doubt that the Royal Marines, who have been down here all week training, barely noticed the swell or the breeze. They were throwing themselves off Pedn-men-du all day and running around with heavy packs and causing a bit of a stir with the ladies.

We had one of the Royal Marines come in to the shop today for cigarettes. He had a thick French accent and was clearly not a raw recruit. I imagined that he was some gritty and battle hardened, veteran Foreign Legionnaire here to drum some mettle into our soft trainees. He asked for Marlboro, the strongest Red brand, of course, and he probably bit the filters off them before he smoked them. Then he asked for a lighter and I considered offering him a pink one and told him so. In the softest tones imaginable he said he would not have minded at all. I could see immediately how ridiculous that was; you would have to consider your future very deeply before taking a rise out of him for having a pink lighter. He was a very pleasant chap and did not kill me with his bare hands once. I have made it a personal rule never to offer Foreign Legionnaire looking chaps a pink lighter ever again.

Between the Missus and me we managed to shut up the shop with only a small over-run. I had some twine about my neck ready to tie up the bundles of newspapers when a lady asked if it was to anchor me to the counter to stop me running away. I assured her that I needed no such restraint to keep me at my post; I was simply highly strung.

September 1ˢᵗ – Saturday

My word, September already and Christmas just around the corner.

The sparkling weather held back a good number of visitors who were due to leave today; we were serving going home presents and saying goodbyes quite late into the afternoon. We too find it difficult making the transition from the helter-skelter lifestyle of the last several weeks to the more sedate and easy pace that we can expect from now on. While it is quite pleasant to find ourselves closing earlier and being under less pressure, there is an almost perverse regret that it is nearly all over for another year.

We were not the only ones anticipating the end of the season, it seems. Tinker Taylor, the iconic thatch at the top of the Harbour has had scaffolders there all day. Word is that the thatch is too expensive to maintain so it is being replaced with tiles and a nice array of solar panels. Whatever the case, it is going to make it difficult for larger vehicles to negotiate the corner with all that iron work around it in the meantime.

By early evening we were a much quieter Cove than we were this morning; transition complete, I fear. As is traditional, we and our neighbours from the ice cream kiosk have an evening out to mark the event. This year, because it has been so dire, perhaps, we plan to have two. Tonight will be an end of term feast at the F&L, which is the usual venue, and dove-tails nicely with my regular trip in that direction on a Saturday night. It also means, because it is our last later evening of closing, that we can still service the bring-your-own trade for the Little Bo Café, should there be any.

So there I was with a welcome mixed grill on its way when the pager went off. And that, dear reader, was the end to my part in the end of season party. Some silly soul had got himself cut off by the tide at Liberty Zawn, just to the west of Boat Cove near Pendeen Lighthouse. It was already a couple of hours after high water so, logically, he could probably have extricated himself but it was getting dark.

For the first time ever I had to drive to a shout. Of course, according to guidelines, I observed the speed limits all the way down to The Cove where most of the crew were already gearing up. The big boat launched from inside the boathouse and I then took the Inshore Lifeboat down to the Harbour. It was the Inshore Boat that took the casualty off the rocks later and transferred him to the big boat. If you look hard there is some footage of the rescue somewhere on the Internet.

It was no more than an hour later that the very excellent Shore Crew recovered both boats in a textbook fashion up the short slip. In the interim I settled for a rather first class fish pie from the Little Bo Café since, I concluded, my mixed grill was probably in the bleddy hound by this time. As it happened, the Missus turned up just before the recovery and demonstrated that most of the dinner was still intact. I considered keeping my own counsel regarding the fish pie, but then there were so many of the very excellent Shore Crew about that I had absolutely no chance of getting away with it. We are a tight-knit, discreet and loyal group and fully supportive of each other which, in practice, means at the slightest opportunity of dropping a fellow in it, we will.

Head Launcher took me up to the F&L in his new rocket propelled conveyance to continue my night of fun and frolic. This is when I discovered that the originally billed band had cancelled on the basis that the lead guitarist and singer had injured his foot. I may not be an expert in these matters, but I always thought that the guitar was an instrument played with the hands. Never mind, the management had an amazing stroke of luck and had contracted a lone singer with his guitar to fill the gap. He did play some blinding tunes, though possibly not at the production quality that you might expect from some of our Saturday night bands.

Then, just as I was contemplating my walk home under the stars and wholesome waning moon, I met with a certain taxi driver at a loose end. This is a man who could talk with celebrities, such as Johnny Depp, perhaps, and the common man and treat them both the same, mainly because he would not recognise Mr Depp if he fell over him, which is apparently close to what he actually did. And yet he was more than willing to take this weary soul back to The Cove for no more than a thank you. What a gentleman.

Lest you become so alarmed and distressed at the news that Tinker Taylor is replacing its traditional thatch that you start up a campaign group, write to your MP and ride a horse naked through your town centre, I should explain that I was jesting with you. The more knowledgeable among you will have recognised, of course, that it is a Grade II listed building and protected against such vandalism. The inclusion of solar panels is also not permitted under the rules, so they are building a forty feet windmill in the back garden that will barely be visible above the corrugated tin of the new roof.

September 2ⁿᵈ - Sunday

We could not have had a more pronounced introduction to our quiet period; The Cove was as a veritable ghost town this morning. The light, but persistent rain may have had something to do with it. We had some brighter spells later but it was definitely a different place today.

Amongst the greyness of the morning there was a little presentation in front of the Inshore Lifeboat. The local Round Table has had a quick whip around and collected sufficient pennies to buy three dry suits for the station. A Round Table luminary carried out the presentation, presumably wishing that she was in one of the suits at the time.

Unfortunately, I could not attend the ceremony for we were far too busy. Well, busy in the kind of way that the Missus had decided to go off shopping and I was in the shop by myself. There were a few periods of busyness, which were uplifting, and several long resounding silences. It was during one of these that one of our neighbours from the back of us scurried in with her arm held above her head. She looked a little white, which she informed me was the result of slashing her wrist. I was about to suggest a telephone number that she could call, when she assured me that it was accidental.

Fortunately, we have a first aid kit and I have a nice shiny certificate from the RNLI to say that I know how to use it, both of which have accumulated a significant amount of dust. However, the level of confidence that can be instilled by the slipping on of a pair of vinyl gloves should not be underestimated. Had I the time, I would have looked out my nurses' uniform, that I managed to acquire in a nice white polished rubber finish. I concluded that it was made of rubber so that any blood spills would wipe off. I cannot imagine another reason.

Sorry, I digress. Now where was I? Oh, yes, the patient with the slashed wrist clearly was impressed with my level of skill and confidence, brought on by the wearing of vinyl gloves. After I had assessed that there was no glass still in the wound I applied a dressing to hold pressure against it. I advised a trip to the hospital just in case I had dressed the gash too tightly and gangrene set in and the hand dropped off. I will have to check, but I do not think my insurance covers such eventualities. I realise now that I forgot the cardinal rule of first aid: get the patient to sign a disclaimer before doing anything.

I did not even realise that the mist had rolled in, sometime late in the afternoon. Apparently we had it good, as it was as thick as a bag at the top I was told. It must have dropped during the evening because when I took the bleddy hound around for her last walk it was like a scene from an old Jack the Ripper film. I half expected a chap with a tall hat and a cape to come out of the gloom, in black and white, of course.

I tell you, in the stillness there was a faint and distant sound; the Hooper, perhaps.

September 3ʳᵈ - Monday

It was quite fascinating watching the mist roll away this morning; little fingers of white clinging to the rocky outcrops and cascading down the valleys. The Brisons could have been a mighty mountain with its peak shrouded in cloud and was the last place the mist clung onto as it backed out of the Cove. Our baker's man said that we were the only place in Cornwall to still have cloud cover, but the sun broke through eventually.

With such a spectacular day in store, I felt it only right and proper to take a trip out to St Just on the pretext of buying parsley and chives. Over the weekend our crabber dropped in some claws and a spider for us to feast upon. I cooked them yesterday and the Missus picked them. What a team. She intends to put them to good use tonight and make crab cakes that I shall sample with some sweet chilli sauce, thank you. The upshot of all this culinary activity is that we needed chives and parsley.

It is with heavy heart and some dismay that I must report that the little greengrocer in St Just has closed. They never said anything, else I might have been minded to write to my MP, start a campaign group and stamp my foot a lot in frustration. In truth, I am hardly surprised or, perhaps, more surprised that they did not close sooner. They were situated opposite the Co-Operative supermarket and although not the worst of offenders, competition with them must have been tough.

Despite their claim to be gud with fud, (if that is how a Scottish accent looks like written down), they are not very good with chives and parsley or, as far as I could see anything like the breadth of local fruit and vegetable that the old green grocery was. It also means that come pasty baking time I shall have to find another source of local turnips, and for my fish another supplier of top wholemeal flour. It is as close to the end of the world as you can get, I promise.

Then, as I was leaving St Just, a small reminder that the town still has something to hang its idiosyncratic reputation on. Rory Te'Tigo, a man of many parts, was there in the car park. He was the man responsible for the outlandish carved totems along the field leading to Land's End, before they were dragged down with red tape. He also has revived the Well Walks around St Just, looking down very old holes in the ground and jolly interesting it is too; it has given the Missus endless enjoyment ridiculing me for doing it.

There he was in the car park demonstrating, almost literally, that he has yet another string to his bow. He was clutching a stringed instrument very similar to a lyre, but with a larger proportion of wood and with shorter strings, possibly. Look, I am not an expert on musical instruments. I can tell the difference between, say, a piano and a trombone. Me and a group of chums had to move one once and it was very heavy; I have never moved a trombone since. So, anyway the musical instrument that Rory had could have been a North Swaziland kurchamagongle for all I knew and he was playing it to anyone who would listen. Every village should have one – a Rory, that is, not an odd musical instrument.

The crab cakes were bleddy 'ansum, by the way, and I hear a rumour that the St Just greengrocer has moved up the street a bit. The end of the world can wait a little longer.

September 4th – Tuesday

What a day it was today and even more so across the ages. Did you know, for example, that in 1884 the British Government decided not to send its villains to New South Wales any more, discovering it was much cheaper to send them to old South Wales instead. On this very day in 1815 our own Mr Humphry Davy invented the miner's safety lamp; it was not until 197 years later that the British Olympic Torch Committee found a use for it.

I cannot imagine what they will say about today in the years to come other than you could not see very much of it. Our fog has come back and this time decided to hang around all day. Nevertheless it was dry(ish) and warm and you could see enough of it in the morning to keep happy the coach load of pensioners who came in for a visit. We did not sell one thimble or fridge magnet but they near enough cleared me out of newspapers.

Despite the fog we still had a steady supply of customers throughout the day most of them from the German contingent, I have to say. One of these days I shall have to go to Germany to see if it really is so bad over there that it makes Sennen in the fog looks attractive. I have only seen Germany in a couple of films that I have watched and they did not concentrate too much on the landscape.

So, with bierkellers and frothy steins of beer brought to mind, I thought that it was about time I donned my lederhosen, well a pair of grown-up trousers, at the least, and headed off to the OS. It has been at least six weeks since I have partaken in the Tuesday poker night and I have a reputation to uphold, albeit a miserable one. I managed pretty fairly in the first half, upholding my miserable reputation, that is, as I was out inside half an hour.

During the second session things were going pretty well until a rogue ace turned up on the river and took me out of the game completely.

The fog had lifted by the time I wended my way home and I could gaze up at the eight stars of the plough. Um, eight? I had to look long and hard to recognise that the eighth was flashing and moving at some pace. Time I gave up the hard liquor, I reckon.

September 5ᵗʰ - Wednesday

Well, that is just lovely. We have a clear blue sky and lots and lots of brilliant sunshine. It is one of those careful what you wish for days, as although we have wished for this the summer long what we forgot to mention was that it would be rather nice if it did not come with a howling, chilly north easterly.

We also did not ask for a Lifeboat shout when I had let the Missus have a lie in, (yes, I am obviously the most wonderful husband, kind hearted as well as dashed good-looking (in certain lights)) and I was on my own in the shop. I had to run upstairs and rouse her from her tender slumber and leave the Rodda's man guarding the shop while I went across and pushed the boat out with a surprisingly healthy number, (expressly 'healthy number' rather than number of healthy), of other very excellent Shore Crew.

This was the Cornish lugger, Ibis, in a spot of bother up by Pendeen Watch probably the same as was seen messing around in the bay the day before yesterday. With engine failure and the sails blown out she had apparently spent the night up there firing off a flare that no one had seen. Someone that they had sent a text message to finally got it first thing this morning. The Lifeboat was next seen crossing the bay at a rate of knots, (eight to be precise), presumably to stop the lugger catching up with her under a twenty knot tail wind and helped along by a favourable tide. It was probably a slightly different story tugging more than fifteen tons of boat into the same wind once they had gone around the corner.

Following a few hours in its wake was the Stavros S Niarchos seen through the gap between Brisons and Cape. It is a 194 feet long, tall sailing ship in the form of a clipper, think Cutty

Sark, and was resplendent in quite a bit of white sail. As we watched it sail off into the west we wondered if the crew were aware, according to their filed schedule, they were supposed to be heading for St Ives. She was a little later seen rounding the corner with much less sail and a new passage to Mounts Bay.

If that was not a full enough day I have just found out that our Head Launcher has learned to tweet. There will be celebrities the world over tonight wondering what a Head Launcher is.

September 6ᵗʰ - Thursday

Now is the time of the more discerning customer, or perhaps the customer who has more time to be discerning rather than coping with the demands of various exuberant offspring. We are, or course, talking about pasties. There is plenty of choice; six of the eight retailers in The Cove sell them. They come from two or maybe three suppliers, two of which are local. While we cannot claim to sell them under perfect conditions, baked from scratch straight from the oven, at least they are not heated in a microwave. Having changed supplier last year, we have been very satisfied with their quality and very often will eat one ourselves. Yes, they are that not bad.

Lately we have noticed that the baker has a renegade crimper. While all the pasties start with exactly the same sized round and identical weight of filling, some are looking decidedly smaller than the others. Perception being everything, it is driving the Missus up the wall, although I have told her that most customers are unlikely to notice since they are only eating one and have nothing to compare it to, and more importantly no one is being disadvantaged.

What would upset a customer more is getting a cheese and vegetable pasty instead of a Cornish pasty, or more markedly the other way around if you are a vegetarian. One customer asked if I could mark up the bag so that he could tell the difference, something that we do anyway as a matter of course. I did tell him that despite that, it was easy to tell the difference as it would taste of cheese and not have meat in it.

September 7th - Friday

Well, here is a really useful bit of information from the page that normally drops a dollop of hardcore nonsense on your lap in the morning. However by the time you read it, I suppose, it will be as useless as the rest of the witterings. Never mind, I shall tell you anyway.

Some ladies dropping by the shop yesterday asked if I knew why there was a field-sized marquee set up in a field adjacent to Land's End, though I would say that a field is a remarkable good choice of location for a field-sized marquee. Events overtook me yesterday and I never did quite find out. However, the ladies were back in again today brimming with knowledge.

The big tent is for the paraphernalia of a big cycle, as in many cyclists rather than a large bicycle, from Land's End to John O'Groats, commencing tomorrow morning. They said that there were 1,500 people joining in, which seems like an awful lot of bicycles. The Ride Across Britain is sponsored by a big accountancy firm and is supporting the Paralympic Games, the next one presumably, as this one is nearly over, and just to prove it we had one of their official cars parked outside the shop for a while this morning.

We concluded that any attempt to go into Penzance tomorrow morning would be a little fraught, but between us we had no idea when the start would be. As luck would have it two of the organising team came into the shop later on, so I asked them. They assured me that there would only be 600 riders taking part and that they would be leaving at seven o'clock tomorrow morning. Very helpfully the start will be staggered with fifteen minute intervals, so instead of blocking the A30 for an hour, they will be partially blocking it for three or four hours.

But never mind all that nonsense, it was a rip-spongler of a day if ever there was one. It was the sort of day to jump into the van and head for the bright city lights of Penzance. Well, no it was not. It was completely the opposite sort of day to that, but needs must when the VAT man needs his several kilos of flesh and so I had to drop into see our accountant.

I had some company for the trip. Our German friends have arrived from Berlin for their annual visit. They are charming maids, the pair, and were talking of catching the bus in the direction of Penzance, expressly to explore the delights of a certain supermarket chain that sits on the city limits. Since I was heading in the same direction at approximately the same time, I offered them a lift.

This gave me ample opportunity to explain the error of their ways and to point out the rather excellent small shops in the town that would not only provide them with markedly better quality produce, but very likely at a fairer price. By the time we had reached my accountants on the western edge of town my companions were clearly keen to heed my advice and disembarked the jalopy. It was either this or they were just keen to give their ears a rest, assuming that they had understood any of what I had ranted on about.

It was rather busier on the roads than I had imagined for the time in the season. When I returned around an hour or so later it was rather busier in The Cove than I had imagined for the time in the season. Although you could not say that the beach was as packed as it was during August, there was a noticeable increase in the numbers of visitors milling about, and the water in our refrigerator has diminished substantially.

With the sun out and our opening hours foreshortened, it must be time to have a barbeque with our neighbours; the first of the year and probably the last. We would normally have teased one of these out in June had the weather been at all clement, but as we all know it was pants. It was a very small, personal affair but the fare part was excellent, sourced from local shops, well, one local shop.

We did not detain ourselves long after the comestibles were consumed as it was getting dark and, as yesterday, the heat of the day diminished very quickly. In short it got bleddy cold.

There was just time for one last heroic act. A lady pushing her husband in a wheelchair close to the top of the slip eased the chair a little too far towards the slope to avoid some traffic. It very quickly became apparent that she was losing a battle with gravity and the chair, now pointing down the slope, was slipping from her grip. Fortunately for her, there was a very excellent Shore Crew member, ably assisted by the sudden appearance of a member of the Boat Crew. With no time to place our underwear on the outside of our trousers, we acted in mufti to extricate her and her wheelchair bound husband from disaster.

No need for thanks; all in a day's work, ma'am.

September 9th - Sunday

We have not had many crab orders, or fish orders in recent times for that matter. It seems to be a similar story each week where we get a great deal of interest from the new arrivals when they see we sell fish, which does not then translate into orders. Generally, it is the foreign visitors who are more positive about our local fish, which seems to substantiate the belief that the British are not big fish eaters unless it comes in batter. Certainly I have not been so in the past, and it is only since we have been selling it in the shop that I have upped my fishy intake. I would probably eat more if the Missus was interested; the Missus hates fish. However, all is not lost for she does like seafood and we have a cracking little Spaghetti Vongole tonight that she is preparing as I type this.

The last couple of hours in the shop got a bit desperate as the mizzle settled in around us. Since the Sunday papers did not seem too appealing I took up a magazine that the venerable Laurel and Hardy Newspaper Company decided to send me, even though I had not ordered it. It was packed with pictures of desirable objects of the technological sort, none of which I can afford, but it is quite nice looking anyway. I have my eye on an Aston Martin bicycle. It has hydraulic brakes, an on board computer and electric gear changing. The latter will be a boon. I can vaguely remember regularly having to get off my old Dawes racer half way up a hill when I had moved the gear lever a little too far causing the chain to spring off.

After an evening knee deep in paperwork I am just about ready to head off to dream land where awaits my Aston Martin bike, in racing green, of course. In my dreams I would have £25,000 to spare.

September 10th - Monday

All right, I accept full responsibility; it was my fault. Yesterday I evoked the name of the Laurel and Hardy Newspaper Company in a derogatory manner. Revenge was swift and merciless; my newspapers were about three hours late this morning.

They told me that the van broke down. This I can understand, as they use independent contractors to deliver their newspapers and the vehicles that sometimes deliver here are very often on the edge of mechanical reason. It never fails to amaze me, however, the utter fury that failure to secure a morning newspaper at the appropriate time invokes in some customers.

Despite some rather sharp showers that showed up during the morning things were rather upbeat today. There was a smaller coach party through in the afternoon that seemed bent on emptying our postcard stand. My caution in suppressing the postcard orders at the beginning of the year due to the hike in postage prices has clearly been unfounded. If our little sample is anything to go by I would say that the Post Office is quids in.

So it ought to be. You may remember that it sent the wrong stamps to us a while ago, which we duly returned. It was not until my credit card bill arrived that I discovered that it had not provided us with a credit and that I shall now have to cough up for the additional stamps before a credit can be raised. My only recourse was to send an email of complaint as they apparently do not have any telephones. To give them their due the person at the other end responded very quickly and explained that because the Post Office has outsourced its call centre it experienced some initial 'training issues'. It also explains why they do not take telephone calls as the call centre, sorry, email centre has been shifted to Sunderland where the local accent is somewhat pronounced. Why aye, bonnie lad, yau can have yous stamps when the boot cooms in.

As if that were not excitement enough for one day the Land's End Coastguard Team were tasked to an unfortunate chap who had taken a tumble off Pedn-men-du. He was on a difficult to access ledge near the bottom of the cliff and Rescue 193 had to come and winch him off.

The helicopter caused its own little ripple for one of our visitors. Quite the largest greyhound I think I have ever seen came into the shop with his owner seeking some nibbles, the owner, that is, the dog was otherwise distracted. The dog was clearly not entirely happy with the presence of our naval rescue service as he was shaking from head to paw. Such was the frequency of the oscillation that the dog resembled a blur. They hurried on in the opposite direction in short order.

In the midst of all this drama the Missus took off to collect the parents-in-law and bring them to Sennen Cove for a little while. They have been having some problems with their neighbour, who has been making life exceedingly uncomfortable for them. Setting fire to her fence was the final straw and the Missus has gone to evacuate them. It seems a little odd that you can be arrested for, say, being critical about a regional accent but cause misery for your neighbours for months on end and no one can do a thing about it.

September 12th - Wednesday

This should make the basking shark botherers think twice before diving in. A team of divers found some blue sharks about five miles off Land's End a week or two ago. These boys are proper sharks with teeth and have been known to eat people. There was some excitement among the naturalist bodies that the numbers may be increasing, as they have not been seen for a while. Apparently, they do a bit of an Atlantic round trip taking in Norway, South Africa and on to the Caribbean following ocean currents.

You could not blame the blue sharks for being here today, for example; it was quite temperate, though not exactly the Bahamas. We did have a little rain, including one heavy, five minute shower this morning. I know this because I was in it.

The newspapers were late this morning, though not as late as the last late delivery. This, along with a small problem with our credit card terminal put my carefully honed pre-opening schedule into disarray. As I consequence I had only ten minutes before opening to run the bleddy hound around the block. It was while doing so the band of rain sweeping in from the west was clearly evident on the horizon, and approaching fast. There could have been a blue shark snapping at the bleddy hound's tail when the shower hit us, she was so keen to get back home; the second part of her morning routine could obviously wait.

At least she just had her normal collar and lead on. The Missus has taken to making her wear a harness of late, as she does tend to pull. In fits of utter excitement she can quite happily choke herself. Despite the obvious health advantages, the bleddy hound hates the thing. This afternoon I thought I would have a go at putting it on her. When I called her to the door she bounded toward me in quite a state of chipperness at the thought of going for a walk. As soon as the harness was produced she skulked, yes that is definitely the word for it, skulked over to the other side of the room. If she knew any rude words I am very certain that she would have uttered several in my general direction.

Short of an ungainly chase around the living room there was no way that she was going to let me put the harness on her. I had to drop the harness in favour of her usual lead before she would come anywhere close to me. I did get my own back though. When I got her downstairs I made her sit on her chair while attached to the peg on the shop windowsill and produced the harness from my pocket. If looks could kill.

So, you see the bleddy hound is alive and well and causing mayhem. I can not wait until the shop closes and I will be able to exact my revenge with myriad walks of lengthy and difficult progress.

Well, after such unprecedented excitement I shall have to lay down for a bit.

September 13ᵗʰ - Thursday

Ah, that's better; nothing quite like a lying down for a bit and then being rewarded by a stunning little sunrise. This turned into a lovely bright morning, in fact I might go as far as to say that it was a bit of a rip-spongler, even though it starting clouding over in parts from the west in the early afternoon.

The Missus bunked off into town for a spot of shopping in the middle of the day. The father-in-law must have been feeling a tad more chipper today because he went too. It is the first time she has done any domestic shopping since the girls were here during August, which just goes to prove that life does go on without weekly trips to Tesmorbury's. Not that you would guess it from the number of times we see the supermarket delivery van down in The Cove. So if you are thinking of calling up for an order just bear in mind that one of the jolly lot is selling milk at

£1.18 per litre; Old Boathouse price, 93p per litre, our normal price. I rest my case.

The papers here have been dominated by news of the impending badger cull expected to be piloted in Somerset and Gloucestershire. This put me in mind of our own ethnic cleansing that must be very much underway by now. It must be over two years ago that I reported in this very organ that the grey squirrels of The Lizard were to be, ahem, rehomed to make way for a bus load of red squirrels who were to be shipped in. What I did not know at the time is that the same crew were going to do the same in West Penwith. Since then, I have not heard a great deal about it and I cannot say that the silence has been disturbed by the distant sound of shotguns being discharged as the greys are 'discouraged' from their current residence.

But I am not so sure these chaps from Natural England and the like have really done their homework and looked at all the alternatives. I have a plan that will have me written down in history as the Kissinger of Cornwall and the darling of all the conservationists up and down the country. It seems pretty straight forward, that Somerset and Gloucester do not want any badgers and we do not want any grey squirrels. All we need to do is have a list of all the badger habitats up country and all the grey squirrel homes down here and organise a mass home swap. Naturally, we would have to exercise a little caution as we probably would not want to be exporting any grey squirrels with a bad case of mange. It would be bad form, certainly. Likewise we would not wish to be taking on a badger with any health issues like, say, a bad cough for instance.

All right, we might not get it exactly right. There may be the odd complaint akin to the accommodation being worse than an individual squirrel or badger had before, especially from the squirrels that might be missing a pasty or two. I think once we have explained the alternative, a lead breakfast, most of these issues will go away. I just cannot understand why no one has thought of this before.

Anyway, enough of all that nonsense, it is time for a little Lifeboat training and a short training video on how to use the new lifejackets that arrived, as if by magic, during the week. These are the jackets that we all threw our time into in January to raise a few bob for. They are state of the art. Once the unfortunate lifeboatman pulls the release cord, or is even more unfortunate to have fallen into the water wearing one, it will inflate into a full size lifeboat. All right, I might have exaggerated slightly but it is very big, with a hood and visor to protect against the inhalation of water, which apparently is not recommended. It has numerous other bells and whistles, well, a whistle, at least, and a cup holder on the other side. The Boat Crew will certainly be very well protected should push come to shove. The very excellent Shore Crew were also not forgotten and were issued with a rubber ring with pictures of buckets and spades on.

September 14ᵗʰ - Friday

Much effort has gone into creating a dark sky area on Dartmoor. The first such designated area in Europe is on Exmoor and their southern counterparts are trying to catch up. It will enable the viewing of the cosmos in greater detail thanks to the absence of light pollution.

Highly commendable, you might think and an achievement demanding of some respect, unless you are Natural England or the Woodland Trust, who have been inciting school children to go out at night armed with lanterns to make pretty patterns in the gloom. It will not matter how good your telescope is, you will be lucky to see a full moon on a clear night with those hundreds of little darlings waving a torch in your face.

Here in Cornwall we hold no truck with making places very dark or messing around with pretty fairy lights to ruin it. Here in Cornwall we do big manly things; things of great import and grittiness. Take, for example, testing the potentially fastest car in the world. Yes, Newquay Enterprise Zone, (that's the grand name for a few buildings up on the airport site), has been selected to test the Bloodhound Supersonic Car. I did have my doubts at first as, although the runway is built for large military jets, they do tend to take to the air as they start to run out of tarmac and they are not travelling at 1,000 miles per hour. It seems, though, that Bloodhound SSC will not be expected to move at all as it is just the engines they will be testing, including the Typhoon fighter jet engine strapped to the rear end. I do hope that the car has good brakes.

And what is more, here in Cornwall we put the jam and cream on scones the right way around.

Just to show that we can do humility in Cornwall too, though the opportunities are sparse, I should tell you about the woe of the Laurel and Hardy Newspaper Company this morning. Though the company itself should be publicly vilified at every instance of its appalling service, its contracted drivers work long and anti-social hours. Nevertheless, the job at each customer site is hardly rocket science requiring the driver to remember two things: one, drop off today's newspapers and magazines; two, collect the previous day's returns. A certain Internet comparison site company could probably sum this up in one word.

Imagine my surprise, therefore, when I notice that our new driver has remembered to leave us with newspapers but had utterly failed to collect yesterday's. Try though I might to imagine a circumstance that would have allowed one, but prevented the other, I was left dumbfounded.

I telephoned the company to let them know that my newspapers had not been collected. I was informed that they had a 'driver issue' this morning and that other customers had been left with only some of their daily papers and some had none at all. Another driver was on his way to clear up the mess. We are not expecting to see the new driver again, apparently, which is of no great surprise.

Though this particular episode was the result of one wayward individual the litany of service failures from the Laurel and Hardy Newspaper Company can only be the result of abject corporate incompetence and complete disregard for any sort of customer focus. While there is ample room for improvement and the repetitive delusion on my part that things could not get any worse, I have once again been disappointed. I am told that from the beginning of next year it will be our sole supplier of newspapers and magazines. Oh sweet joy!

There is nothing quite like running the bleddy hound on the beach to ease the strains and stresses of the day and to build a whole new set for the evening. It also got me out of the house during the onset of a big dose of Emmerationenders. It was very peaceful down in the Harbour, with just the crashing of a boisterous sea in the background and the thud of small paws on the hard sand. The bleddy hound is relentless with a ball in play and was definitely not ready to head home as bad light stopped play. I should have paid attention to her; Emmerationenders was still in full flight when I got back.

Pass the brandy, Ethel.

September 15th – Saturday

There was so much dew this morning it looked like it had been raining overnight. Everything was really fresh in the bright, sparkling little morning we were handed down. It was busy too with lots of new arrivals who must have materialised during the night; a sling-groggler of a morning if ever there was one.

With a morning this good I just had to venture up to the post office on the grounds that we had an order for a book that the lady was in rather a dash for. I was rather bluntly informed that there has not been a Saturday morning post office service at the post office since May and if I wanted to post my package I would have to go to St Just or St Buryan.

Well, with such a burgeoning sparkler of a morning a little trip out to St Buryan was more a pleasure than a chore, although it did rather negate any profit I might have made from the package I was sending. So with the sun shining and the birds singing, (I can only assume the latter as I would not have heard over the din that the van was making), I made my way to St Buryan Post Office.

The Post Office itself is small and low ceilinged and packed to the gunwales with all sorts of things. If you took the Old Boathouse and squished it to half the size it would probably look much the same on the inside. It is a centre-point for the village and all life is there during the day. This moves wholesale to the pub next door during the evening. Along with the church that sits in the middle and dominates not only the village but the surrounding area it is as typical as you can get of what you might imagine a true Cornish community might be.

I know people who live there who were probably once friends before I wrote this and indeed I have attended a few of the monthly gatherings at the Community House. It is probably one of the last true Cornish bastions in West Cornwall. You can well imagine scenes reminiscent of the original film Straw Dogs, where the locals are not well predisposed to incomers. Ahem, I am sure that this is not true and they are a more than friendly and welcoming bunch – provided you go home again. It was not long ago I spoke with the previous postmaster of Sennen Post Office, a Londoner, who announced that he was moving to St Buyan, largely because of its sense of community. I wished him well and asked him if he had ever seen the film The Wickerman. (In case you have not seen the film, Edward Woodward meets a particularly sticky end after poking his nose into a close-knit community on a Scottish island.) Strangely, I have not heard from him or his family since he moved.

Clearly I need to be a little circumspect in my elaboration on life in St Buryan. After all I am already persona non grata in one West Cornwall town and they were far less likely to set light to a hay rick with me in it.

We were not so lucky with the weather or the customers in the afternoon. As promised the cloud moved in from the west and thickened considerably through the afternoon. It did give us the opportunity to freshen our shelves for the all the visitors we did not have. But that is the way of things for the practitioners of cutting edge shopkeeping. I knew, however, that it was time to stop pushing the envelope, as we keen, top of our game shopkeepers say, when I telephoned the milkman and gave him my bread order.

We availed ourselves of a very excellent fish and chip tea from the very excellent fish and chip diner on the main road, which clearly revived my joie de vie. I have been very taken with their cod cakes, especially with a dollop of sweet chilli sauce, so I had them again tonight. They were every bit as good as the first time too.

I was rather looking forward to sitting in front of the television, sampling the comestible delights and being entertained by some mindless sub-culture programme that abounds on the box these days. I was not disappointed as I had not appreciated that the wall to wall media flood that is Strictly Come Humiliate a Celebrity started this week. It heartened me no end to realise that I shall be subject to this inescapable circus of grimness from now until Christmas.

Such was my utter delight that I pressed the Missus to take me hither to the good old F&L where I could attempt to drown my sorrows, should they have sufficient beer to enable me to do so. This, of course, had to wait until the television coverage of my personal hell had finished.

A walk home under the stars would have complemented the evening perfectly, but at least it was dry. It was when I was coming back through the car park that I noticed the arrows stuck in the back panel of our van. I do not remember them being there before I went to St Buryan this morning.

September 16ᵗʰ – Sunday

It was a bit of a slow start this morning. I mean generally, not just me. It might have been that the whole of The Cove was down on the beach having a surf lesson; there was a veritable army of all ages down there having a go. It must have thrilled the lifeguards to have so much company on a Sunday morning.

It certainly was not ever so thrilling in the shop at first as we had no one to play with. We did not have to wait long, however, before the till started filling up with soggy banknotes and freezing cold coins and the floor criss-crossed with salty wet footprints. That aside it was not our finest day.

This may sound like an exercise in optimism and it certainly drew a few wry smiles from those passing by, but I assure you there is some clever logic behind it. You see I was fed up with looking at a sunglasses stand that was more empty than full and since we were operating at a snails pace today I decided to do something about it.

Now, I should not really be telling you this as I could have my membership of the Worshipful Guild of Sneaky Shopkeepers terminated with extreme prejudice, so I must ask that you keep it under your hat. If you do not have a hat I can sell you one at a very reasonable price, honest guv. You see, the thing is, that during the summer most people will expect it to be bright and sunny. All right, perhaps not this summer but generally speaking. Because people expect it to be bright and sunny they will, in most cases, pack their sunglasses and therefore not need to buy a pair of our reasonably priced, good quality eye shades. Although we do sell a fair number during the summer it is because people have lost, broken, left them in the car and cannot be bothered to go back and get them.

If you are still listening, this is where the story really starts and one of the reasons that we have been admitted to the Worshipful Guild of Sneaky Shopkeepers in the first place. Most ordinary shopkeepers will by now have given up on the sales of sunglasses and will have given over the space to umbrellas, raincoats and galoshes. Not the Sneaky Shopkeeper, oh no. The Sneaky Shopkeeper will know that most of the competition is selling umbrellas, raincoats and galoshes and understand that this is an opportunity. The Sneaky Shopkeeper will know that people, in the main, will not expect it to be sunny and bright at this time of the year and will leave home without a thought of carrying a pair of sunglasses. I am sure, dear reader, you can see where this is heading.

Take today, for example. The forecast for this area was overcast and dull. As I look out of the doorway I can see miles of blue sky and sunshine, yes, bright sunshine that requires the use of a nice pair of UV 400 protected sunglasses. And just how many people can I see who have remembered to bring a pair of shades with them? And just how many pairs of sunglasses did the Sneaky Shopkeeper sell? Unfortunately, quite a few and none respectively, but I stand by my theory and it is early yet in the season. By Christmas I will have cleaned up and attracted the envy and, in some cases, jealousy of my fellow vendors. Either that or I will have sufficient sunglasses to see me through most of next year.

I am glad to see that my comments on St Buryan yesterday have not resulted in any serious backlash. As I always knew, the people there are mature and reasonable individuals and have clearly understood that my words were not in the least inflammatory.

Now if you will excuse me I must go and remove the cat that someone has carelessly nailed to my front door.

September 17ᵗʰ – Monday

I have to report that it was quite the liveliest of mornings, especially if you had to compare it to yesterday. Not only did we have a proliferation of early morning customers, but the fishing fleet were out in force; I spotted their mast lights in the Harbour first thing. Given the tides I suspect that they were on the mackerel which have been in short supply this year and fetch a good price at market.

Also fetching a good price is any company in the payment card industry, who seem to have provided themselves with a licence to make even more money from those using their services. Together, they have spawned the Payment Card Industry Security Standards Council (PCI SSC) whose main job, it seems, is to see how many acronyms they can produce in a given timescale. Here are just some:

QSA – Qualified Security Assessor; PA DSS – Payment Applications Data Security Standard; AOC SAQ (d – Merchants) Attestation of Compliance Self Assessment Questionnaire section d for Merchants. I could go on.

Any company that stores, transmits or processes card payment information must attain compliance with the Payment Card Industry Data Security Standard (PCI DSS) by 1st October this year or face the possibility of heavy fines. To prove that they are compliant, each company or organisation must either have a QSA come to their premises and charge them plenty for the privilege of producing an AOC, or if the company meets a certain set of criteria it may complete a SAQ to produce its own AOC. Are you with me so far? Good.

Now, this is where the story really starts. It is not to the PCI SSC that a company must prove its compliance, it is to the Aquirer, (the company that lets you process payments), or the card company with which you are operating. Each of these, it appears, is permitted to make up its own rules as to how you prove compliance to it. For example, the company that processes my card payments has decided that it will not permit me to carry out a self assessment to produce my AOC, which is perfectly acceptable under the PCI SSC rules, but I must use their facility for which they will charge me thirty quid – per year.

Furthermore, I was preparing to switch to a company that processes card payments on the Internet that is considerably cheaper than the one I use just now. Having checked, I note that they are not on the PCI SSC's list of "Validated Providers" and as such will lose me my PCI DSS compliance status.

I thought that I might write a letter of complaint to the PCI SSC and rail against the injustice of it all. Then again, perhaps I will not bother, they were formed by an alliance of the four major credit card companies. There, not a hint of independence. That is not compliance, that is being complicit.

It took me the best part of an hour to wade through the various documents that explained the degree to which we had been stitched up, at the end of which my frustration was probably palpable.

But the small gods of respite and revenge work in mysterious ways. You may remember the wrong stamps saga to which Royal Mail eventually responded to provide me with a credit, but too late to prevent me having to pay the original amount off my credit card bill. You might also recall the trouble I went to in trying to contact them, as they do not take telephone calls.

Well, I received a telephone call from the Royal Mail this afternoon explaining that they think they have processed the credit twice. I listened with some amusement before I told the chap that I did not take telephone calls on such matters and that he would have to email me the details. I have to say I felt much better after that; a little balance has been restored to my personal universe.

It was not until it was almost time for me to make my tea that I realised that it was recycling collection day tomorrow. This required a quick dash up to Shrew House as we have been storing our flattened cardboard there between collections. It was a pleasant enough evening for the trip with the lowering sun breaking through clouds.

It was on the way back down the hill, looking down on The Cove glittering in the setting sun, that it came to me that corporate blackmail and crass examples of customer service could not do much to ruin all this.

September 18th – Tuesday

Just a bit fresh today with that blustery wind up in the north west, although it did not feel too bad as I took the bleddy hound around this morning. I managed to avoid having her squished under the refuse lorry as it flew around The Cove first thing. After all the complaints of the first month or so of their contract they definitely have got the hang of it now.

We also managed to avoid the early showers but you could not miss the magnificent rainbows that blossomed huge in the west. Quite the most defined that we have seen here in a long while. With that, and a white capped sea floshing over the breakwater, it was some sight for those that were up early enough.

Once again the sunshine brought out the happy people. It is heartening to see that the Little Bo Café is still attracting a good crowd. I do not believe that we have ever seen it quite so consistently busy and it is bringing a real buzz to this end of The Cove. They must be doing something right and it is doing us no harm at all.

We shall be proving their credentials later today as they are providing some coffee cake, my favourite, in celebration of the parents-in-law's sixty fourth wedding anniversary. I do not think that I could contemplate being married for such a length of time; if I wish to be scared witless I just look at our profit and loss account. It is highly likely that the old buffers will eat no more than a slice each of the cake, so I am rather looking forward to cleaning up. Happy Anniversary!

It must be because we have a lot more time on our hands that we can afford to be a little more critical, perhaps. They are only small things and of more interest than irritation so if you are one of these, please do not be alarmed, you are not being victimised. Well, yes you are but not in a bad way.

Take the person that collects various items from a whizz around the shop. When she gets to the till, and I am sorry it is invariably a lady, shock and horror, there is no money in the purse. If I do not have any money, I *know* I do not have any money. How can you not know your purse is empty?

It is like creating a pasty flavoured crisp and forgetting you do not need the carrot flavouring. A Cornish crisp company, well, actually the Cornish Crisp Company was asked to create the pasty flavoured nibble in support of the Mining World Heritage Sites and has inexplicably put a carrot flavour in. We sell their crisps in the shop and a penny from each bag goes to some worthy cause or other. We shall stick with their cheddar and vinegar flavours, I think.

And in our last outing of unfortunate customers a lady asked if I was the gentleman who penned The Sennen Cove Diary. She was clearly not from around these parts, as although I have to put my hand up to be the scribe, as everyone knows, being a gentleman might be a bit of a stretch. I know that you asked not to be included here but do not worry, nameless lady, your anonymity is safe with me. No one in Porthcurno will recognise you or your black BMW X3 from the description here.

Despite being world famous in Sennen and now in PK does not mean that I cannot find it in me to join the hoi polloi down at the OS for a game of cards on a Tuesday night. To prove my new gentrified credentials I wore trousers, which I found did not help at all, in fact quite the opposite. How did I forget to put money in my pockets?

No, of course I didn't, I just thought I would make you forgetful ladies feel a bit better.

September 19ᵗʰ – Wednesday

As if the balance of power were not already sufficiently in their favour, especially as far as the television remote control is concerned, the parents-in-law clearly thought it necessary to call in reinforcements; the Missus's sister and brother-in-law arrived today. I am now seriously outnumbered. I have not been informed as to the length of their stay, the information must be privileged and on a need to know basis, just that I am sleeping in the box room.

Adding to the ripples in my equilibrium our new bank manager paid us a visit. I wore my oldest and threadbare shirt and moved anything of value into another room. After I offered him a cup of tea, I made a point of discussing the high cost of water rates in this county, the number of kilowatts of expensive electricity it takes to boil a kettle and the soaring price of teabags. Since he clearly was not taking the hint I changed the subject and asked him which school he went to; he was obviously no more than twelve years old.

He suggested, after studying our balance at the bank, that we should earn more and spend less, except at the bank where the charges would be increasing. I said I had no more money to pay with, to which he offered to lend us some so that we could, at a very premium rate. I suggested that he meant preferential rate and he replied that he did not.

I was about to thank him for his time as he left, but realised that I had probably already paid for it twice over.

For all that it was a spanking good day with all-over sunshine and a noticeable lack of wind. Again we had a preponderance of good people in The Cove and, by golly, we had a sizeable fish order to get our teeth into. The Hake, a fish I am beginning to like more and more, was in particularly good shape; it was long and thin with teeth at one end. Unfortunately, our customers thought so too so I have very little left, which I know is the point but I was starting to miss my fish stew.

With the world and his wife staying in our small flat I was unlikely to get away with a fish stew for one. My disappointment was obviously starting to show, so the Missus offered me a lifeline and suggested we go blackberrying.

Now, clearly I cannot reveal the exact location of our foraging, but I will tell you that it is somewhere in the Land's End area. Although we left as soon as we had finished our tea and despite being in the last place the sun leaves the south west, the light was fading fast. I would guess that we had the best part of half an hour before the blackberries and the bushes were indistinguishable and grasping a thorn instead of a blackberry was an unacceptable risk. Even in that half hour the pickings were particularly slim. Many of the brambles were still in flower and much of the berries that were there were, as yet, scarcely red let alone black.

I am sure that you can imagine the derision and scorn that was poured upon us when we returned with hardly a tub between us. I did not care a hoot; I do not consume blackberries in great number and I missed Emmerationenders.

September 20th - Thursday

What a gloomy day. The weather was not much better either. The sea was as flat as a dish so the surfers were gloomy too and all the others seemed to be staying away in droves.

I was gloomy as well and not just from the sudden downturn in trade. The jolly old Royal Mail had clearly taken umbrage at my suggestion that I could not deal with their query over the telephone and had sent me a stuffy letter.

The communication consisted of only two paragraphs. In the first they apologised for the inconvenience that their double credit may have caused and now could they have their money back. I was going to add please to the end of that sentence but since they did not, neither shall I. The second paragraph consisted of a grave threat, that if I did not cough up the bunts inside seven days then I would be visited by demons who would pull out my finger nails and do other unspeakable nasty horrors to my delicate personage, or was that delicate parts of my personage. I do not recall, as I was too busy quivering with fear.

If I had the choice I would make them wait at least eight days just to see what happened and to cause them the maximum level of grief. Unfortunately, we are in need of further stamps and there is only one place we can purchase them. With the lack of a cat to kick and the chances of persecuting a small child being rather remote since they all went back to school, I shall have to find another vent for my spleen.

If that were not enough to make your teeth itch, I received the busiest quarter's electricity bill and my VAT settlement in the same post. I really am going to have to buy a cat; I suspect buying a small child might be frowned upon.

Good then that we had a little Lifeboat exercise to take my mind off things for a while. For the first time in a long while I took command of the Inshore Lifeboat launch tractor while the others messed about with the big boat. While the boats were out the Missus laid on a sumptuous meal of sausages that were about to go out of date in the shop, bless her. It was not long before we had scraped off the green bits and consumed the lot.

It probably goes without saying that the very excellent Shore Crew carried out a textbook recovery of the big boat while the Inshore Lifeboat was recovered with expert precision. Naturally we congratulated ourselves with hearty pats on the back before we retired to the OS for a good quizzing.

September 21st – Friday

Ooh, a bit of excitement up at County Hall today. There is the possibility of some blood being spilt on the much maligned council's shag pile, no doubt acquired at great taxpayer's expense to line the Chamber floor. Not quite the ides of March, but the leader of said much maligned council should be looking over his shoulder on the way to the forum.

And what weighty matter has precipitated such drastic action, you may well ask? I may well tell you that in recent weeks the inner sanctum of councillor's voted to outsource, sorry, form a partnership with private companies, to manage a vast swathe of council operations. Nothing wrong with that you might think, whether you happen to agree with the proposal or not; a vote among elected members – democracy in action.

Well, almost. You see the main body of those elected councillors, all 123 of them, had a little vote of their own and came up with 46 to 29 against the motion and despite this overwhelming disapproval the eleven cabinet members pressed ahead anyway. Slightly less democratic, perhaps, but hey, 90 percent of us said we did not want a unitary council and they did not listen to us either.

Such was the ordinary councillors' ire that they have organised a bit of a Julius Caesar job on the leader. I can hardly wait to hear the outcome, but so loved and admired is he that I am sure he has nothing to fear, that and the fact that he is probably safely wrapped up in a metaphoric Kevlar stab vest after the last attempt. With a stunning sense of British fair play they have actually set a date for this showdown: October 16th. Watch this space.

With such skulduggery afoot in the big city it is just as well that we are salted away down here, out of harm's way. All I have to worry about here is where my next crab is coming from. Well, that is no worry at all at the moment as our favourite crab fisherman has not yet finished pulling all his pots in for the winter.

We had a bit of crab yesterday too, as he just happened to have one about his person when I said that we would be placing an order for the next day. The timing of getting it cooked was a little tight as I had to go to help launch the Lifeboat, so I very carefully allowed sufficient time to boil the pot and cook the crab before I left. I had set the pot on the stove and had gone for a little zizz while it worked itself up to a rolling boil and the crab slipped off into a coma in the freezer. I roused myself with minutes to spare to fetch the crab, cook it and still get to the launch in time. That was until I lifted the pot lid and discovered that some helpful soul had taken it off the heat 'because it was boiling'.

I think that I was sufficiently clear in my calm and lilting tones as I set out my expectations for crab kettle boiling operations. In fact my delivery was so soft and measured that I am reasonably certain that I will have the kitchen to myself for the cooking of the crab and lobster that arrived today.

Maintaining the fruits of the sea theme we had to satisfy an order for some wild sea bass today. I do my best to dissuade customers from choosing sea bass as it is phenomenally expensive. Our experience is that no matter how much you pre-warn a customer, when they see the meagre morsel put before them, especially if the fish has been filleted, and hear the price the result is usually shock and disbelief.

Nevertheless the customers in this case have regularly had wild sea bass while here and are inured to the expense. However, for the money they are paying, they have every right to expect a top product and fresh as a daisy.

One of the key ways to tell the freshness of a fish is to examine the gills, so when our fish arrived minus this important organ my suspicions were immediately aroused. I have asked our supplier to desist from this practice on more than one occasion and on more than one occasion have sent the fish back, as I did today. Despite the missing gills it is still possible to tell if the fish is fresh or not, and this one was definitely on its knees. I find this exceedingly irritating, but this supplier is about the only one locally that can supply us.

They redeemed themselves by sending out a replacement that was indeed a fine specimen. The customer was also happy, although they asked if I could vacuum pack the second fillet as it was a rather large fish.

If I thought that my fishy day was over I could not have been more wrong; I was cooking crab and dissecting lobster deep into the evening. Perhaps we should open as a fishmonger next year; I seem to have had plenty of practice. I cannot wait until tomorrow as we have another consignment arriving.

Tomorrow I shall give you chapter and verse on how to fillet a hake. If I have to be knee deep in crustaceans and fish tails you, dear reader, are going to have to be knee deep in crustaceans and fish tales.

September 22ⁿᵈ - Saturday

Saturday 22nd came as a bit of a surprise to me as I had gone through the whole of yesterday believing it to be the 20th despite having penned a Diary entry for the correct date. Such was the fraught and frantic nature of yesterday's progression my mental calendar was undone. Things can only get better.

The sister and brother-in-law went home this morning. I am looking forward to crawling out of the box room and into my own bed again. There is nothing like your own comfy bed to restore your equilibrium. It will also save me walking into the wall as I struggle to find the door in the dark.

It was a deceptively alluring sight as the sun rose into a clear blue sky this morning. It gave the impression of a day that you would just love to run out into. It would be then that the knicker crippling easterly would have whistled up your trouser leg and reminded you that all that glisters might possibly be cold. All the same, not yet cold enough to capitulate and resort to big boy's trousers; not quite yet.

Talking of alluring sights, last week the newspapers carried a report of a chap seen drawing a large pattern in the sand on a beach at Newquay. Today he is here, on Sennen beach creating an enormous work with the aid of one of those rakes used for raking up leaves. I can not be sure that he is the same chap, of course, but the probability is quite high. His name is Tony Plant and he creates time lapse photographs and videos of his work and can be seen on his website, tonyplant.co.uk. I would think that the satisfaction and pride in the work is in its completion as it must be the epitome of a temporary art installation; by half past eight tonight it will have gone.

He may be quite relaxed about losing his work of art as the tide washes it away, but I was quite interested to see how he would react when the seine netters working away below his patterns needed to drag their boat back up the beach. I never did find out, but there did not seem to be any dead bodies down there when I went past later, or the blood splatter consistent with the stabbing of someone with a garden rake.

I would have taken a little hike up Stonechair Lane and taken a picture of it for you all but the Missus had installed herself upstairs to strip six crab of their meat. She was still up there when the tide started to encroach upon it so I am afraid you will just have to take my word that it was a clever bit of geometrical design. If you think crop circles or the Inca Nazca lines on a smaller scale you will get the idea.

Then, all of a sudden, it was time to make my way to the F&L for a seriously good banding. Tonight, a band that needs no introduction except that if I did not, you would not know who they were. It was, of course, the utterly fabulous *Devil's Creek* with their twin set of hardcore blues rock and, later, so more familiar rock tunes. What a glorious night.

It has to be said that the little triangular flags hanging from the ceiling of the F&L are a little irritating. They dangle at just the wrong height and brush against your face and tickle your head if you are standing in the wrong place. I suppose for us hedonistic party goers and avid drinkers they must be some sort of penance. Come on, work with me here.

I had spent some time earlier in the evening studying the rain radar to determine if I needed to be waterproofed before I descended the hill. Both the Met Office and the BBC had promised that the rain would not commence until the early hours of Sunday morning, so I took a raincoat with me. Typically, for once, they were right and I was over-dressed.

As I came down Stonechair Lane I half expected to see that aliens had landed on the beach, using the cleverly crafted and disguised runway drawn out earlier. I know that they had little time to recognise it, but in all the movies I have seen they are much brighter than us.

It did occur to me, though, that if a bunch of weird, unworldly creatures that looked nothing like ordinary folk and spoke in a tongue we could not understand landed in Sennen, how would we ever know?

September 23rd – Sunday

Yes, today was everything it promised to be; rain, of the very wet sort, and wind that pushed the rain of the very wet sort in through the door and all over the counter. Customers, of the very hardy sort, were few and far between. In short it was a poor day of the very pants sort.

It was a poor day for visiting, surfing and just about anything else that required even a modicum of being outside. Bucking that particular trend was a lone kiter down on the empty beach. It may well have been the lifeguards with the kite, trying to pass a little time, as there was begger all else for them to do down there other than move their flags in and out with the tide.

Then, just to prove that the art of lunacy is not yet dead, there was a stream of long distance runners charging through The Cove. These are the people that, each year, find some element of pleasure in torturing their bodies by committing to three back to back marathons over three consecutive days, starting somewhere up by St Agnes and finishing up at Land's End.

I am sure that they all look perfectly ordinary and sensible people when they gather at the starting line. When they pass us by they all look close to expiring, faces grimly set against the pain of screaming muscles and open blisters. I am assuming not one of them is doing this against their will and therefore must deduce that it is done for pleasure. I suppose I can hardly criticise, after all I am running a shop in Sennen Cove in the rain.

But the last word in torture must surely go to the father-in-law. On the first of my breaks upstairs he had the grand prix blazing away on the television. On the second it had developed into football and on the last, a choice that had me running screaming for the stairs, he had found a television channel dedicated to showing repeats of *Last of the Summer Wine*.

Then again, had I not come down at that moment I would never have met the senior couple from across the water, here on holiday to their favourite part of this side of the ocean. They reminded me that they had sent a fan letter to me concerning the book; how could I forget? It was the only such letter. In recognition of the minutes of pleasure my book had given them, (they must have read it twice), they proffered some candied nuts from the Carolinas and some American dog treats for the bleddy hound, whom they surmised must be ill-treated and half starved from what they had read.

They are staying at the OS, which is either exceedingly brave after what I wrote about the place, or they assumed I was writing in jest. Either way it should provide sufficient evidence that the comments were harmless should it ever come to litigation.

At least now I have the tools of retribution; I can crunch my nuts all through *Downton Abbey*.

September 24th - Monday

It is one of nature's strange and unexplained phenomena. Despite our shop door facing almost due north it is a wind in the east or the north east quarter that gives us the most problems, especially, as yesterday, it comes carrying a bit of the wet stuff. Oddly with the wind due north or north, north west as it started out today, we hardly feel it at all.

As you know, the wind was in the east when we settled to bed last night and it made an ungodly fuss about moving to its new direction during the night. It was a strong blow, to be sure, but the noise of it made it sound much worse than it was.

I can also tell you that the rethatching of the Tinker Taylor cottage moves on apace with most of the frontage complete. I do not even need to step outside my door to know that this is happening; we have a good proportion of the thatch inside the shop. We have resisted the urge to sweep it up as, first it is unlikely that we could keep pace with the influx and second it will make an excellent flooring for our Nativity scene come Christmas. Of course, should the thatchers find themselves short at any point I am sure we can come to some arrangement to sell it back to them – times are not easy, you know.

So much so that our survival today was by virtue of the grey pound, bless them all for being here. The little darlings kept coming and kept spending throughout the day. I would say that we had very few people through our doors today under the age of sixty years old.

If our Deputy Prime Minister has his way we will be absolutely beggered as all these old greys with a few pounds salted away will have to give them up to pay the deposits on their grandchildren's houses. Well, blow that for a game of strip ludo. Now listen here, grandparents everywhere, that DPM is a very naughty man. You will have far more enjoyment from spending it all in the shops up and down the country, particularly down the country and specifically this end of Sennen Cove. Not only will you gain so much enjoyment from your thimbles and fridge magnets but you will have the pleasure of seeing a shopkeeper who is oh, oh so grateful.

We were also oh so grateful that the rain held off today and that it was a bright, if breezy, day. A young couple, resembling a pair who had been swimming with their clothes on, came in late in the afternoon and announced that they had been caught in a hailstorm on the footpath up to Land's End. We were lucky indeed, then. We still have their soaking wet fiver on top of the pasty warmer that is not turned on because we ran out of pasties; I had ordered according to the weather forecast for a rainy day.

And just before we closed we had a chap come to the door who reckoned he could hear a sandwich tern close by. It was unlikely to be us as we had run out of sandwiches too. However, I did not like to argue, as he seemed a chap who knew what he was talking about, but our beer fridge has developed a squeak; sounds just like a sandwich tern.

September 25th - Tuesday

I am sure it would not be your immediate thought to compare Hayle in Cornwall to Paris in France. I mean it has not got a replica Eiffel Tower or, as far as I know, a Pigalle district, although the Aged Parent, who grew up there, may correct me on that – or not if he wishes to maintain some semblance of dignity. No, the analogy is a little more by reputation and, possibly, more in my imagination and harps back around seventy years. As I passed the town borders I half expected to see a beret clad resistance fighter on each street corner, steeled against the jack booted foe as the allied forces neared, bringing liberation and chocolate.

I realise that this might be a bit of a stretch but you see Hayle Town Council, as far as I can tell, has been the only group to publicly resist the bully-boy tactics of our much maligned council. Yes, I am quite happy with the words 'bully-boy tactics'. What else would you call telling town and parish councils to take on the burden of running public toilets or else they would be closed down, the toilets, that is, not the councils, although that could well be the next step.

Anyway, our heroes on Hayle Town Council have condemned our much maligned council for putting finances before the taxpayer and spirit of localism. The much maligned council sent them a document that strongly suggested that it could transfer assets such as recreation grounds and toilets to them, yes, here we go again, if "the financial and other benefits to The much maligned council and the wider community are sufficient to justify" it. The town council, probably quite rightly, suggested that the only test against the precept that the much maligned council were interested in was the bit about financially benefitting the council and to hang with everything else. The Town Council went further and said that it believed that it was not just the asset that should be devolved but the funding associated with it. And here they really hit the nail on the head; they also suggested that the devolution without the funding would amount to no more than a tax increase to the taxpayer through the local precept. At last, someone has said it, if anyone is out there listening.

The mayor of Hayle stated, "Where The much maligned council has control over income and expenditure it is reasonable that it controls assets. If the council wishes us to control that asset we should have the same access to income as well as expenditure. It is not reasonable to expect us to take it on with unsupported costs. It is a double taxation to the local taxpayer." I could give her a big hug.

So while they may have their resistance fighters on every street corner and in years to come, little plaques will mark the spot, it does not look like there is any sign of allies at the gates ready to liberate them.

Still, I thought that I had better have a Philps pasty before the whole town was razed to the ground for their daring insurrection. After my comments earlier in the year I am pleased to report that Philps are back on form. It was piping hot and gravy dripped all over the front of my shirt; now that is a pasty. It was probably just as well if it was to be the last.

Signs of Armageddon did verily abound today. I took the bleddy hound around for her usual morning constitutional under warm sunshine and white fluffy clouds dotted about the blue sky. I had just opened the doors and stepped inside when I was very nearly bowled over by a number of customers eager to get into the shop. When I turned to see what the excitement was all about the street was awash under a curtain of rain. These surprise heavy showers persisted for most of the morning.

Later, in the afternoon, we had the rare appearance of a couple of weather dogs, like squashed rainbows, clinging to the cliffs. These are serious portents of doom and, indeed, the Met Office has issued some serious doom warnings for torrential buckets of rain to fall on our heads sometime after midnight and slightly smaller buckets before then.

It must have been my decision to take along waterproof trousers to the OS when I left for tonight's cards that warded off any heavy showers. It was raining when I returned but not sufficiently to make waterproof trousers even slightly essential. I wore them anyway, just for effect; I might start a trend. The bleddy hound loved them as I ran her around last thing and she did not ask once how I did at cards. She can be quite sensitive sometimes.

September 26th – Wednesday

It is a curious bit of weather we are having at the moment. We certainly have not had the appalling conditions that we have heard about on the news, thankfully but it has not been all that pleasant. This particular system has had two bites of the cherry, as well. A couple of days ago it came up from the south and gave us a bit of a slap around the face. Since it has moved up country it has had the temerity to slip back from the north and give us a clout around the back of the head.

The blustery conditions and frequent showers have not deterred everyone. In fact we must have had the most resilient of visitors down this week as we have had a constant dibble of folk through our door all day long. If you were one of them, thank you.

The Missus had clearly had enough of it and beggered off on a shopping trip up to Camborne with the parents-in-law. Quite why she, or rather they, find it necessary to select a supermarket in Camborne when we have two closer to home that are equally capable of providing inferior quality foodstuffs for an overly inflated price, (sorry, just could not help myself), I do not know, and know better than to ask.

She came back loaded with shopping bags containing the ingredients of a meal for me to cook in the evening. It was a less than subtle hint, but I admit that it was my turn. I have to say it tested my culinary skills and I was a little distracted as I had been given some instructions on how I might mend my broken big computer storage box.

I will spare you any further detail as I must attend to the dinner. It would be quite awful if I burnt the toast or the beans stuck to the bottom of the pan.

September 27ᵗʰ - Thursday

It is such a wonderful day, it is, honest. All right, it might be a bit chilly and overcast but it is bright and it is dry. After all that which has been thrown at us over the last few days, that is a wonderful day.

It is also a wonderful day because I had an email back from my electricity company. In fact I have had cause to contact them a few times over the last couple of weeks and I do not mind telling you that they are quite responsive electronically. At least I do not have to do battle with their impenetrable automated telephone system, just impenetrable emails.

My letter to them concerned my latest bill that I had to wrest from them by force. You see they do rather want to bill me annually, which to my mind is a bit lazy and also has the potential of dropping a very scary bill on my door mat once a year.

The problem arose that the bill they sent covered a period starting on 13ᵗʰ September last year. I rather took exception to this as the previous bill I had from them included usage up to 20ᵗʰ November. They also used estimated figures when I had sent them actual figures and they had used these on the first bill. They had helpfully included a credit for the double charging but this was insufficient to cover all the charges.

I was therefore delighted to receive an email from them clearly setting out the reasons for the billing, the over-charge and amendments to the previous bill. I have taken the liberty of including their reply as it should be held up as an example of clarity and simplicity.

"Your latest bill shows payments that you have already made as the latest bill is an amended bill to cover the period from 13 September 2011

until 17 September 2012. The latest bill is not immediately following on from the previous bill because the previous bill is what we term an interim bill, which is a bill that has been produced outside of the billing cycle of when the computer system would expect a bill to have been produced.

As the reads for 20ᵗʰ November was changed from actual readings to an estimated reads which was higher, the charges up until this date was £15.77 more. However the charges after this period would be an equivalent amount less because of this, as the higher estimated reads for 20ᵗʰ November would then be used to calculate the charges from 20ᵗʰ November until the actual reads for 17ᵗʰ September 2012.

The standing charges between 10ᵗʰ & 20ᵗʰ November should be for 10 days, therefore, if anything you are 18p better off now as it had been 11 days beforehand when you had been charged for this period.

Regarding the credit, I will arrange for authorisation to have this refunded to you.

I hope that these explanations clear things up."

Yes, absolutely. Never let anyone tell you that standards in education are slipping.

If that were not sufficient to fry my struggling post-season brain they sent me another email on the subject. This was from another of the company's employees and was equally confusing, but strangely suggested some different reasons for the hiccup. Perhaps they will send me twice the refund too.

Not wishing to dwell too long on such matters of gravity, I can tell you that our wonderful day became even more wonderful in the afternoon as the chilly wind abated and backed around to the west. With the improved weather came an improved number of millers about.

It should be noted, however, that millers about should not necessarily be confused with shoppers about; the latter tend to buy things. I was pleasantly surprised, though, when one of the millers about made an enquiry regarding our fridge magnets, indicating a potential sale.

She asked how much one magnet was then, pointing at two alluring examples, asked how much they were combined. With lightning quick arithmetic, (I was wearing flip flops, which helped), I managed to tell her the sum of the two prices. She looked surprised, nay almost offended, and said that she thought that she might have been offered some sort of discount for buying in bulk. I suggested that two items did not necessarily constitute a definition of the term 'bulk buying', and that if she were to purchase three of the glossy items there was indeed a generous reduction, (I am willing to concede that there may be a small dichotomy of opinion between my definition of 'generous reduction' and a buyer's).

I am sad to report that on this occasion there was no meeting of minds and she shuffled off to get the bus. Perhaps the driver will offer her a discount if she does not come back again.

Here is just a short aside from the normal run of play. I note with interest that schoolchildren can go to the cinema free of charge next week. It is part of National Schools Film Week that aims to instil a greater enthusiasm for the film by watching it together and thus being able to write and talk more about it. Sounds just the ticket, does it not? And what will the little darlings have to watch at the cinema next week? 'Killing them Softly' (18), lots of people killing each other in inventive ways; 'Savages' (15), drug growing and killing people in less inventive ways; 'Lawless' (18), illegal alcohol and violence; 'Sweeney' (15), more guns and violence. That should give the young tots plenty to talk about.

Anyway, enough of this nonsense. I am sure you are all dying to hear what derring do us Lifeboat chaps got up to at our weekly training session. Well, with the sea in no fit particular state for playing around in a boat, we polished the Inshore Lifeboat tractor. It is really shiny now.

And finally I should mention that the Aged Parent's legal team has been in touch regarding my suggestion that Hayle had, at some point in time, some unsavoury character to its community. I have been asked to make it clear that there were no such dens of iniquity and the suggestion that there were, was deeply offensive and insensitive and that the surviving doyens of propriety, Saucy Sally, Naughty Nina and Dirty Gerty will all attest that no such aspect ever existed.

September 28ᵗʰ – Friday

Gosh! Another Friday signalling the inexorable slide towards the end of the month and the closing of the shop for another season. Sounds pretty final, doesn't it? I hope not.

I know it also sounds like we are wishing our time away but it is our holiday that we have saved up all year for. All those weekends that we have worked through; all those public holidays, they all add up, you know.

At least we have only saved them up throughout one year unlike certain chief executives of certain island councils who, through working many weekends and bank holidays over umpteen years, has decided he will take them all at once - all 100 days of them. It may not have been so bad but the ordinary folk in the council, (you did not expect me to pander to the sort of language used in the red top press; I am not a plebeian, you know), can only carry five days holiday over to the next year or lose it. Senior politicians out of touch with the common man? Whatever gave you that idea?

No, it is the common man that we turn to if we need any real help because you are much more likely to get some. A case in point was the slightly new age couple in a slightly old age van that pulled up outside the shop. They were only there a minute before they moved on. The next thing I saw was the van coming back again being towed by our newly clean and shiny ILB tractor. It was the common men of the Lifeboat Crew that sprang into action to help the couple out of trouble. It was expedient to use the ILB tractor as the broken down van was blocking the ILB launch route, before anyone starts asking any awkward questions about misuse of RNLI equipment.

Another of our common man heroes is the delivery driver who turned up today. He is one of our regulars and works for the TNT Company. He is only a small chap, but we have seen him lift huge weights; he is absolute dynamite.

I had to go and visit our doctor in the afternoon up at St Just – now, Aged Parents, there is absolutely no need to leap to the phone and fret and worry. It was only a small amputation and nothing whatsoever to be concerned about; the blood has almost stopped seeping through the dressing and into my sock now and I am sure the patches will come out of the carpet eventually.

The only reason I mentioned my visit at all was that I was browsing a Diary entry from twelve months ago and noted that I mentioned the expansion works at the surgery. So there was I, over a year later, and the work is still going on or rather is unfinished. The work was quite extensive but did not strike me as overly complicated. Either there was more to it than meets the eye, or they contracted the slowest builders in history. Or, of course, they may just be builders who know a cash cow when they see one; not daft is our common man.

Well, with a special curry night penned in at the F&L and a stonking good band as well it would have been very rude not to take advantage of one or the other. I took advantage of both, or I would have done. We dragged the parents-in-law up as well, although they did not avail themselves of the curry and neither did I. What was not apparent from the chalk board was that the curry needed to be booked in advance, which I had not.

My utter disappointment was tempered somewhat by the chance meeting of a bunch of raggedly thieves whom I inadvertently fell among. They entreated me, nay, were most insistent, in a press gang sort of way, that I join them on a jaunt to the pretty village of Goldsithney, whereupon we would embark on a celebration of another acquaintance's birthday. Naturally, I declined their good offer on the grounds that I was there to dine with my nearest and dearest. It was the Missus that insisted that I go, so go I verily did.

What a joyous evening we did have and in the most convivial of company and what is more we were made most welcome in the said far flung establishment. I must make a mental note not to, out of hand, spurn such invitations in future. I was even dropped at my door by the transport that was laid on. So if you saw a discarded bundle of rags outside the shop during the night, do not be concerned; that was me.

September 30ᵗʰ – Sunday

"Dashed quiet out there this morning, Smythe."

"Yes, too quiet if you ask me, Carruthers."

"It is the sort of morning that coxswain fellow might creep up and organise a Lifeboat exercise for. You know, Smythe, to keep us chaps on our toes and all that."

"Dashed if you are not right, Carruthers. It is the sort of dirty, underhand sort of trick you would expect from those Lifeboat coxswain types."

"I very much agree with you, old chap. Looks like a dashed tricky corner to me. The pair of us have been in some tight spots over the years, Smythe, but I think this one might see us done for. Let me say, old bean, that it has been an honour, being at your side through thick and thin."

"Do not be rash, Carruthers, we are not finished yet. I have a plan. It is so simple I can only wonder why I did not think of it sooner."

"Really, Smythe, you are a top man. What cunning plan can you possibly have thought of to get us out of the scrape? We would need a veritable army of crack troops."

"Not really, Carruthers, they are only a small band of hardy volunteers but they are worth ten of any ordinary man."

"You don't mean ..."

"I do, old man; the very excellent Shore Crew, of course."

So there we were, primed and ready and we executed a Lifeboat launch with frightening speed and efficiency.

If it is a Sunday morning then it must mean that the Head Launcher's party slip in to the Little Bo Café for a sumptuous breakfast, worthy that we were after such a breathtaking launch. Sumptuous the breakfast was indeed, and quite the finest breakfast I have had for a long while. If I enthuse much more about the place I shall have to start asking for advertising revenue.

The timing of the event was spot on and we had sufficient time to settle our breakfast before embarking on recovery. Head Launcher and his man at the bottom end of the slipway looked resplendent in their brand new lifejackets. These are a vast improvement on the old ones, as they allow the wearer to work unencumbered. This made absolutely no difference for our Head Launcher.

It would have been obvious to even the casual watcher that, on this occasion, they were treated to a display of the finest precision winching. It was a major contribution to yet another textbook recovery by, what is clearly, a very excellent Shore Crew.

Despite the warning of some grim weather on its way, most of the day was set fair with some breaks of sunshine from time to time. For all that it was remarkably quiet, especially after the busyness of yesterday.

Nevertheless we did have some very pleasant customers come by. One crew of ladies told us that they much preferred to shop in small local shops and were happy to spurn the big supermarkets. They cited the higher quality produce and the more than fair prices, but above all it was the excellent and polite service. I told them how pleased we were to meet such enlightened customers and thanked them for buying locally just ahead of telling them that now I had their money they could begger off. Fortunately they laughed.

We have had our first order for squid today. The Cove boats have been out in numbers all last week hunting the delectable cephalopods and, I understand, have been highly successful. We could have had any number on our slab last week, so when do we get an order? A few hours before some of the biggest seas we have seen all summer, that is when.

Still, we will be able to console ourselves with a Christmas turkey of whose provenance we will have no doubt. Bosavern Community Farm is advertising the availability of a Norfolk Black of your very own on the security of a mere twenty quid deposit. It comes complete with instructions on how to make a temporary pen so that you can keep it safe and well before the big day and, of course, how to dispatch it in the most humane way. For those of a squeamish disposition they will send a chap along to do the dirty deed for you for a few quid more but you will have to clean up the mess on your kitchen floor.

Seriously though, the farm is making the offer of an oven ready bird reared at the farm, which is a blinding bit of marketing for the concern that is still struggling for independence.

There, that is it. Time to fall off my own perch, I believe.

October 1ˢᵗ – Monday

The general public must undergo a great physiological change on 1ˢᵗ October because they stop needing to use the toilet. Our much maligned council understand this particularly well as they have closed the Harbour toilets for the season. The council must also understand that people need to see where they are going in the dark and like the sound of running water as I can almost guarantee that it has left the lights and the water on.

It must save thousands during the winter as the double yellow lines have been suspended so there is no need for Traffic Enforcement Officers. Mind you the last time I saw any down here was before the beach dog ban came into force. I can understand the expense; it took three of them to put a ticket on a van at the top of the beach slipway.

And talking of the beach dog ban, that has been relaxed so that dogs can romp unhindered on the golden sands, just like they have been doing all year without restraint, or retribution anyway. So the dog wardens, (it is nice that they are not Beach Dog Ban Enforcement Operatives), can relax too and save the much maligned council even more money. I am almost certain that we can expect to see half our council tax back come April next year.

As if things could not get any better, the Frenchman dropped by a squid this morning in recompense for a favour that I had done him earlier in the season. Because I am not a tax dodger, I have retained twenty percent of my squid for the Revenue man; I shall post it with my cheque come January; then, a little while later, our crab fisherman dropped by some more, although we did have to pay for those. One is for a bona fide customer and the others are for us, as the Missus has come across a stuffed squid recipe that she wanted to try.

When I was taking the order for the customer's squid it started by them wanting a whole squid as is. It then moved to having it cleaned, which I am happy to do especially since I have some of my own to process. The coup de grâce, though, was that they wanted the ink preserved so that it could be used in the risotto they had planned.

Naturally, I assured them in a confident sort of way that there would be no problem in setting aside the ink. I waited until they had left before I reached for my favourite Internet search engine to see if there was a corresponding page to my query, 'how to extract ink dead squid'.

Whichever method you employ, I heartily recommend a pair of vinyl gloves and a head to toe apron, preferably of the disposable kind, although if you use a cotton apron I can assure you it will be disposable by the end of the process. Just do not use the Catherine I-can-make-very-ordinary-items-very-expensive Kidston apron that is the Missus's pride and joy — oops. Also use a knife, sharp enough to pierce the sack cleanly, so that the highly concentrated ink does not emerge under pressure and if you have used the Missus's Cath Kidston apron make sure you hide the knife afterwards. Lastly, and this is most important, have access to a kitchen that is not shared with a house proud partner who has the sight faculty of a bird of prey with binoculars. Said partner will, no matter how diligent you have been in clearing up after you, notice that spot of diluted ink you missed on the floor, wall or ceiling and even if you managed, by some miracle, to wipe clean all the spots there will be a smudge on the fridge door or a grey tinge to the work surface that will be invisible to ordinary humans. So, good luck with that, then.

We were going to have the squid tonight, stuffed with chorizo, rice, coriander and other goodies. Unfortunately, the bleddy hound had to be taken to the vet, (I can say that now as she no longer reads these pages since she found herself appearing less). She has been complaining of a sore front paw for a short while; the problem comes and goes. I threw her chicken for her last night and she limped back without it and sat in front of me dangling her paw; it was truly pathetic. I told her they shot horses for less and she beggered off to seek some sympathy from the Missus.

Anyway, her poorly paw put paid to my grand plan of taking her down to the big beach in the late morning to take advantage of the new freedom and the rather pleasant weather. It is highly unlikely that it will be so pleasant tomorrow, and we shall have to wait for the outcome of the veterinary report.

On the positive side, as the Missus headed for town at a late hour to catch the open sessions at the vets, she will come home sporting a curry from the take away in town. I have been hankering for a bit of Indian grub since my disappointment on Friday. I can tell you it was 'ansum, but exceedingly hot.

I look forward to tomorrow with trepidation.

October 2nd – Tuesday

I know, this is it. It is what you have been waiting months for; the moment of all moments that you have fretted over and pined for throughout the long summer months. You have absolutely no need to tell me how your lives have been incomplete, as if a big bottomless cavern has opened in your hearts.

Look, I understand. Do you think that it has been easy for me all this time? It feels like I have been marking time this last six months, making up some jolly tale or other to entertain you, knowing all the while that it is not what you have been wanting to hear.

I mean, that I would write something like ... it started out in a 'ansum sort of way, warm but overcast with brighter spells and a bit of a strong breeze starting to rise in the south west. Then you would say something like, "Albert, ee's on about the blessed weather again. Is that all the wretched man can write about?" When all I was trying to do was set the scene a bit so you knew what it was like here. You see, a thankless task.

Anyway you were really lucky; it might not have happened today at all. In the afternoon the promised rain materialised and, as they said it would, it came on persistent and it did not stop either. The tide was just about right for it as well and receding, which meant that there was plenty of time. There is, after all, no need to hurry something you have been waiting such a long time for.

Can you see what it is yet?

All right, I admit that I am just playing with you now. It is time to come up with the goods, cut to the chase and come clean.

I took the bleddy hound down to the big beach this morning; a whole six months and a day for a moment that we have all waited for. In celebration, I took a bully beef roll down with me and a small off-cut for her as well. Not that I should have bothered, as she was too busy chasing her ball and digging a geet pit in the sand.

It was a little bit blustery at the far end, so I was thankful that I brought a jacket, but I assure you that it was still very much bare feet and shorts weather despite everyone else wearing full waterproof gear.

The recent big sea had torn up the near end of the beach somewhat; the bleddy hound ran after the first couple of balls like a thoroughbred steeple chaser. All right it was a lot less gainly than that, as all I could see was her little woolly bottom up in the air as she leapt over the holes. The sand at the other end is ramped up against the rocks and all that I could see of my sitting rock was about six inches of granite. I managed to find a suitable resting place for my hastily arranged picnic though, and we had one whale of a time.

There, I bet you are all giggling like little schoolgirls now you have had your fill of bleddy hound on the beach again. Oh, you are so easily pleased but I have no doubt that in a couple of months it will be, "Albert, ee's on about that bleddy hound on the beach again. Is that all that wretched man has to write about?" You fickle bunch.

Well, no actually, I can write about cards at the OS on a Tuesday night if you like. Not a great deal, I grant you, as I did not win – again. But I certainly did better than the last few weeks and that is something to be celebrated. Perhaps I will take the bleddy hound down the beach again tomorrow.

October 3rd – Wednesday

We had a rather pleasant surprise in the post this morning. A postcard from the Minchhead Set who are living it up on the South Carolina island of Hilton Head, at the International Correspondent's mansion there. The postcard had a map of Hilton Head Island on it. I had not realised how similar in shape the island was to the county of Cornwall, mainly as I have never had a postcard with a map of the island on it before, I suppose.

The Minchhead Set, if you recall, caused me a great deal of consternation by disguising themselves as ordinary shoppers and asking for outlandish products such as Australian butter, lark's tongue and fried pigeon feet. It pleased me greatly to hear their report that Hilton Head Island shares more in common with Cornwall than its shape; they do not have such items either.

Unfortunately, we cannot say the same about the weather as we struggled to make the Island's 82 degrees (Fahrenheit) in the peak of our summer, let alone autumn. Nevertheless, once our showery and grey morning shuffled out of the way the afternoon blossomed into splendour. It would have been worthy of another stank down the big beach with the bleddy hound had the Missus not slipped off with the mother-in-law on a bit of a sly shopping trip.

And sticking with the meteorological theme, it seems I am not the only person frustrated by the Met Office's tendency to downplay the forecast. A chap who owns a theme park in Devon has threatened to sue the agency if they get the forecast for next Easter wrong. He says that it is the 'needlessly pessimistic' forecasts that are driving visitors away, particularly with the increase of late bookings. No poo Poirot! The number of times we have had a forecast for a day's worth of rain and it turned out to be a couple of ten minutes showers is irritating in the extreme.

Our hero has been collating data in support of his plan and has given the Met Office until Easter to pull its socks up. Perhaps, I should send him a copy of The Cove Diary. There is enough data on dodgy forecasts in there to give him a cast iron guaranteed win in the courts.

October 4ᵗʰ – Thursday

This must be bizarre request day. From early on I have been inundated with strange or unreasonable demands. I know we are the Sennen Cove Visitor Contact Point but, as Dirty Harry says, a visitor contact point must know its limitations. All right, perhaps he did not but he would have had he tried to run one.

First up was a foreign couple with a small child. They were taking a little stroll up to Land's End and wanted to know where the nearest toilets were, as the most convenient ones appeared to be locked. I mean, how demanding can you be. It can only be another 400 extra yards carrying a small child for heaven's sake!

Then came the lady who had scoured West Penwith for a pebble lamp for an elderly relative. Obviously, word has got around that we are the world centre for rare objects of retro kitsch. If you are interested, we also stock flared trousers, cheesecloth shirts, ashtrays in the shape of a green hand and alloy CND medallions the size of a dustbin lid.

A short while later another couple stopped by to ask why, with so many people still about, were the Harbour car park toilets locked shut. I felt that I should stand by our much maligned council against such a slur on their good name. I told the couple that clearly the much maligned council will have carefully studied the impact of such an early closure of essential facilities and will, no doubt, have established that no visitors, (other than a foreign couple with a baby), come to the county after the end of September. Clearly, all the other people were residents and had access to their own toilets and, by the way, what did they think they were doing here so far outside the visitor season?

Tiresome that it might have been, I also managed to keep up a happy front when our next odd enquiry was levelled at me. Daffodil bulbs! In the name of heavens, I know we have a bit of a reputation for stocking most things that a visitor might require during a couple of weeks stay down here but Daffodil bulbs, I ask you! The only bulbs we have had are light bulbs, and we even gave up selling them after the silly rules from the EU meant you could only sell the ones that take forever to come to full power and when they do you may as well have stuck a glow worm on your ceiling for all the light they give out.

Then at last, after a stream of complaints and enquiries, a young man who was a little more vociferous than most of the others who had asked, wanted to know why on Earth the toilets were closed. I said to him that I would tell him what I told the other countless people who had asked today, that there was simply no demand for them to be open at this time of year.

I had to field these questions alone, as the Missus had gone into town ahead of the Lifeboat Dinner on Saturday night (sure she only went last week too). There must have been some queue as she was gone nearly five hours. When she returned I thought I would let her have a go in the hot seat and I took the bleddy hound down to the beach again.

It was such a lovely afternoon, too, with plenty of sunshine and even the breeze was warm. On days like these she does get a brae bit thirsty, especially with a mouth full of sand she gets from digging her pits, so I filled a small bottle of water to take with us. It was when we were settled down amongst North Rocks I unwrapped her travelling water bowl (yes, of course she has a travelling water bowl. Did you expect her to slum it with an old plastic dish or something equally cheap?), and offered her a drink. It was only then, rooting around in the back pack, that I realised I forgot to pack it. Have you ever seen a bleddy hound look disappointed and disgusted at the same time?

I have to say I could have stayed down there all afternoon it was so pleasant, but needs must when you have a shop full of customers wanting to know why the toilets are closed so early in the year.

October 5th - Friday

I had every intention of venturing into town today to do a bit of shopping. It would mark the start of my end of season assimilation back into what could be termed normal society after months of almost monastic life down in The Cove. It was not to be.

I had wanted to replace my fish filleting knife that had inexplicably failed half way through a largish plaice; the blade snapped clean off. I think the Missus believes that I have been affected by this, as she insisted she went to town instead – again. I do not know if she thinks the big city is a little beyond my sensitivities and that I should cut my socialising teeth on, say, St Just a few times first, or perhaps she is just waiting until I decide to put on my grown-up's trousers.

Whatever the case, the restriction prevented me from carrying out some remedial work on my ball stand. You remember the ball stand? The work of art that I created from proper wood and made out of my own head. What do you mean, is it still standing? One of the wheels, after many months of continuous use in all weathers, has seized. This makes dragging it in and out of the shop something of a trial.

Mindful of the Missus's kind suggestion that it should have been fitted with bigger wheels from the outset, I bought some bigger wheels to replace the small nylon casters I used originally. Never let it be said I do not listen to the Missus; it may be true, but never let it be said. Unfortunately, and my argument for using smaller wheels in the first place, is that the new bigger wheels are too big for the legs of the stand. There will need to be some clever jiggery pokery and an element of blunt instrumentism employed to meld the two into a cohesive operational unit.

Being completely out of jiggery pokery, my blunt instrument in need of a new flange and my movements into town restricted by the Missus, it looks like the wheels will have to wait.

She surprised me later; she came home. Rather, I meant she came home with a present. It was a chopping board to go with my new filleting knife. The board was yellow. I told her that, given its size, I shall use it religiously from now on every time I have to fillet a minnow or a stickleback.

Narrowly avoiding a demonstration of how sharp my new knife was, I decided to use the last few seconds of our opening today to count our takings. It did not take that long. It was our first day of continuous rain for some while. I do hope that it is not starting a trend.

October 6th – Saturday

You have to have a chuckle now and then. Today's came courtesy of the aged gentleman of The Cove, he who makes Methuselah look like a teenager. I am sure you remember him. He was the chap who sliced his thumb off with a circular saw, because he was distracted slightly by a bus turning up.

He came in earlier on for some groceries and a little later I delivered a freshly baked loaf up to his house. He was back down later on for his regular Saturday dinner time pasties for him and his missus. It was only when he left, I realised he was using a thumb stick. Well it made me chuckle anyway.

I had to have something to laugh about with a wicked little north easterly whipping up my trouser leg and rattling my bloomers. It was, however, dry and sunny, which was very welcome. It was also deeply appreciated by the hordes that turned up to wander about and sit and look out on the sun lit vista.

Just the sort of attraction to bring in the Far Eastern contingent that we hear will be our salvation in the years to come. And just to prove that this is not just some smart suit talking nonsense, a couple of young students from that neck of the woods collared me as I worked outside the shop and asked where the bus stop was, which I was glad to point out to them.

They returned a couple of minutes later to enquire which bus they should take to get them to St Ives, as they had heard that it was a good place to find a fish restaurant or two. It was ten minutes to five in the afternoon and I must have given over a look akin to the sharp intake of breath a garage owner gives when you ask how much it will be to repair your vehicle, because they started to look a little worried.

I resorted to my bus timetable that I keep under the counter for such moments, as I still have not updated the summary versions on the shop window since the schedules changed. It was as well I did, as I had the slight suspicion that they would have to travel to Penzance first, then change buses for an onward journey to St Ives and I had no idea which bus they would need to change to.

To be perfectly frank the bus timetable was not in the least helpful as to which bus they should change to; I had to thumb through all the buses until I found one going on that route. Even with my doctorate in bus timetables, and vast experience unpicking their complexities, I did not find it easy establishing the routes and the times for this young couple to complete the journey. How they were supposed to manage is beyond me.

Here it is: first they must wait for two hours for the 18:52 bus that will take them to Penzance. This should arrive at 19:37 which is two minutes after the bus leaves for St Ives. They must now wait for a further hour for the 20:35 bus to St Ives that will get them there at 21:11, probably not the best time to be looking for a fish meal even if they still fancied it, after taking over four hours to travel 15 miles.

Fortunately, it takes only five minutes to get to the Land's End Hotel, which is where the RNLI dinner was taking place tonight. I do not know what the Missus was doing in the bathroom, only that whatever it was took a very long time.

The last such venture up there was an unequivocal disaster as the food was grim, largely inedible and fortunately in short supply. This left those even remotely associated with the organisation of tonight's party a little nervous. Despite it being a little pricey the hotel put on a very good show this time around.

The speeches were mercifully brief and the after dinner speaker, the PR lady from the RNLI, was entertaining and with a slide show to augment the performance. Having been asked to arrange musical entertainment that transcended the wide age groups present, our man with guitar and keyboard did a pretty decent job. Some of you may have heard of the Bingo Twins of which he was one half.

However, the highlight, for some of us, was to be awarded the Queen's Jubilee medal. It is a proper medal too, with a ribbon and pin an' all. I know it is quite unlike me to come over all serious at the end of a page, and especially on a Saturday night, but I am really quite proud of that.

October 7ᵗʰ - Sunday

It is the first time in a long while that I have seen first thing on a Sunday morning, but I did promise the RNLI PR lady a copy of The Cove Diary before she left. I must tell you it looks no different - the day, not the book - than on any other day, so I do not think I will bother again.

I probably deserved a lie in this morning after yesterday, helping visitors on and off buses, attending prestigious dinners and fixing wheels on ball stands. In fact I probably deserved a medal – oh yes, I got one.

Sorry, did I not mention fixing wheels on ball stands yesterday? How remiss of me. I had thought I might have to wait until Monday because, as I said, it required some items that I did not have. But never let it be said that I am not resourceful; I am not but never let it be said. I managed to find a little jiggery pokery in a cupboard under the stairs, and the flange on my blunt instrument responded to some TLC and duct tape. Thus armed, I set about sawing, screwing and applying cable ties when the wood I was screwing into split on the last turn of the screw. What an achievement just using my ingenuity, the sweat on my brow and a bit of old bench; I doubt the council will even notice it is missing. The movement of the ball stand is now so smooth you could waltz with it – sev-en!

You know, on Friday I could have sworn there was a whiff of something in the air. It was the sort of smell that gets the dander up, livens up the senses and sets the spirit soaring. I could not quite put my finger, or rather my olfactory neuron's cilia on it and it lingered into the evening.

Up at the Parish Council meeting, or so rumour has it, they discussed the matter of the toilets in the Beach car park. Previously this Parish Council had voted to accept our much maligned council's offer of 30 pieces of silver to run and maintain those facilities under its own aegis. I was a little disappointed, nay, miffed that our boys (turn of phrase; there are girls on it too) had rolled over so readily and so cheaply, after all it does not take an accountant to realise that 30 pieces of silver would not last long in the running and maintaining of a busy toilet block.

Last week I reported, or rather exalted Hayle Town Council for voting to tell our much maligned council to take a hike on the transfer of assets and now I understand that Penzance Town Council have followed suit. At Friday's Parish Council meeting, or so rumour has it, our revered councillors woke up and smelt the coffee and voted to do much the same, apparently, or so rumour has it, on the basis that the lease agreement was too onerous.

That smell I was talking about? Maybe, just maybe, it was the smell of a glorious revolution rising into the air; an Oktober revolution, perhaps. The wind of change is blowing through this county. Whether they like it or not this growth of Cornish consciousness is a political fact – we hope.

The wind of change was blowing across the beach too when I took the bleddy hound for a run early this afternoon. The rain was just beginning to gather itself for a dowsing so my timing was immaculate, for a change. It was blowing too when I crossed the moors for our Chinese meal tonight. Tomorrow could be windy too.

October 10ᵗʰ – Wednesday

It was while I was standing there minding my own business and wondering where all our customers might be that the Missus's mobile telephone rang. She had a mystery caller yesterday, and since I had little better to do, I answered the call.

The very pleasant gentleman on the other end said that he was from Vodafone and that the telephone call was being recorded for my own safety. I cannot tell you how relieved and safe I felt in the knowledge that Vodafone was taping my conversation. He then told me that he needed to ask some questions to make sure that I was who I said I was. I told him that I had not said who *I* was and I only had his word that he was who he said *he* was.

Undeterred, he said that he would ask me some security questions and started with asking me my post code. I said that I would be delighted to provide him with the requested information just as soon as he had demonstrated to me that he was indeed a caller from Vodafone. He said he could not do this due to the Data Protection Act which I found a little odd. There must be some way of proving who they are without divulging personal information.

Just as I was about to suggest that he write to me setting out the details of his purpose he put the telephone down on me. Even though I understand that these telephone chaps need to get through a target number of customers each day, I felt that this was abrupt and not just a little rude. Things are slow; I feel a little letter writing coming on.

So slow in fact that I resolved to take the bleddy hound around on her first land based walk of this part of the season. You know the one, up to the look-out on Pedn Men Du, across Mayon cliff, down Maria's Lane across Carn Olva, down Vellandreath valley and back along the beach. I was quite surprised how remarkably fit I was after a long summer pinned down in the shop. I only had to stop for oxygen a couple of times along the way, that and a fag at the top of the valley.

After a morning of mizzle and greyness, the afternoon was blissfully summer like; I really wish I had not taken a jacket. On the beach it was balmy and the lapping waves were crystal clear. There were also a fair number of people down there, many walking their dogs. The near-high water also helped to make it look busier than it actually was. We found some space at the western end of the beach and, her longish walk clearly having not diminished her energy levels, threw the ball about for a bit.

I was a little peckish when we returned home. Some rather deep coffee cake beckoned from the Little Bo Café so I popped in for some. Now, the last thing I wanted to do was to pass any criticism on the place that has been as a shining beacon in the culinary darkness of The Cove but needs must, I am afraid.

Their coffee cake has hitherto been of the highest quality, deep, thickly layered with butter cream and altogether completely devoid of walnuts; not a one; totally absent; lacking walnuts in every sense; a walnut free zone; walnutless; not a walnut in sight.

I cannot fault them for their honesty; they did tell me it was a coffee and walnut cake. It also had little walnuts sitting on top of it where the coffee beans usually are. I bought some anyway thinking that this must be some sort of mistake. Perhaps it only had walnuts on the top of it because you just do not do that to a perfectly good coffee cake, do you? So it was to my utter disappointment, shock, disgust, disbelief, horror, chagrin and dumbfoundedness to discover that they had actually put walnuts in the coffee and walnut cake. I hate walnuts.

There is some poor, unsuspecting begger at Vodafone who is about to receive a scathing letter on customer service completely unaware that, but for some walnuts, he might have got away with it.

October 11ᵗʰ - Thursday

It is definitely getting worse. The wind had veered around to the north west and turned into a real knicker-twister, we had heavy rain in the morning and showers in the afternoon and those customers we did have seem to have run away. We did have one couple in this afternoon, dressed in the manner of Nanook of the North and who could blame them; it was just horrid.

I resumed reading a book that I had started before the summer busy period. I had used the book mark for some other purpose, so I have spent a couple of hours trying to find my place, although I have been told on a number of occasions that I should know it already. It is a little disheartening to read most of a chapter only to find a bit at the end that you readily remember. It is also frustrating to read a chapter and come across a revealing bit of plot that you had not read the build up to. A bit like reading The Diary, I suppose, not that you will find any unexpected plot endings, though you might find some bits you remember, but it is disheartening and frustrating. I gave up in the end and started another.

All this finger drumming and toe tapping did give me some time to look at the dog fight that was going on over the bay. A couple of large great black-backed gulls (possibly) were harrying a couple of smaller gull-like birds (maybe a tern) ... let me start that again. There was a big bird and a small bird having a dog fight, presumably because the smaller birds were getting food by working for it and the gulls were not because they do not work for it. The smaller birds were also having to work hard to evade the attack, but the big birds, despite their size, were quite adept in aerial manoeuvres. The gulls (they were, I am sure) are quite vicious in a very mean sort of way. I have heard that they have been seen holding the heads of smaller gulls under water until they drown so that there is less competition for food, or perhaps they are born sizist.

Tomorrow we shall have a dissertation on the lesser spotted sand gribbler and its ability to whizzle gurnets while on one leg in high winds. I am sure we can hardly contain ourselves.

Just as well that we had Lifeboat training to distract me from my nature gazing before I went stark staring bonkers. We learnt that City of London III will be returning to the fold, hopefully, early next week. I fear a bit of bottom scrubbing may be in the offing, as she has been afloat for the last few weeks on trials.

Talking of trials we ended up at the OS for the regular Thursday night quiz, minus a Head Launcher. I can hardly say we bowled out the opposition tonight, but I was fair near bowled over by a hefty head wind on the way home. The night sky was a mass of stars, not that I did much looking up with my head bowed into the gale, but I found it strange that from an apparently clear sky I was getting a face full of rain. Just one of those days, I suppose.

October 12ᵗʰ – *Friday*

Bond looked out over The Cove then back at the sorry state of his brand new DB7. He could not believe that the sump was still sitting on the speed humps outside Sennen School along with the contents of his oil tank and the mechanism that made blades poke out of the wheel hubs. This was a serious inconvenience to his mission to preserve democracy in Cornwall.

He remembered that he had passed an Inn just before the light on the Aston's dash had lit up, warning of impending doom. There would be plenty of time for a quick tipple before the 00-AA turned up with a replacement vehicle.

Bond scanned the bar. He was highly trained to examine a scene such as this and build an instant assessment of threats and opportunities. There were five ordinary looking visitors, two appeared to be couples and a man on his own. There were two bartenders, one, whose name badge said he was Smith, was casually cleaning glasses with the end of his vest that he had lazily pulled from his trousers. The other was talking to the man at the bar; Bond knew he may have to wait a while to be served.

Eventually the talking barman noticed him and came over to ask what he wanted. "Vodka Martini, shaken not stirred," growled Bond, a little miffed at having to wait.

The barman looked at him blankly, so Bond repeated his request which at last elicited a response. "Sorry sir but we don't have any bottles of Vodka Martini. We don't do those bottles of alchopops any more. Half a Rattler do you?"

Bond raised his eyes to the ceiling along with an enigmatic eyebrow. "Look I have had this drink in all the best bars all over the world; it is a classic. You must know how to make a Vodka Martini." Then with uncharacteristic patience added, "Look, I am a fair man, I will give you a further five more chances between you to get it right," said Bond fingering the handle of his Walther PPK under his jacket.

Bond waited and watched as the two barman scurried around behind the bar frantically trying various combinations of drinks. Each time Bond shook his head as another miserable concoction was placed in front of him. At last he turned to the first barman and nodded at the second, "That is a Smith with a vest on and you have had your six," he said coolly, reaching inside his jacket.

Before he left Bond turned to the others in the bar, "Don't worry about any more drinks, these two will sit this one out; they're just dead."

By this time Bond was feeling a little peckish. He had heard about a first class fish and chip shop up on the main road and took a stroll up the hill to try it out. On entering, the owner recognised him immediately. "Ah, Mr Bond, I had heard you were in the village. Please come in and I'll show you around; it is a little quiet at the moment. I am W by the way."

Bond was a little taken aback at being recognised so easily, yet again. He was after all, an international spy reliant on anonymity and inconspicuousness. He accepted W's invitation to look behind the counter and into the back where there were all manner of machines for the preparation of chip shop type food. It was while he was looking that a customer came into the shop. Bond suddenly felt that he should be on his way. "So, W, you expect me to walk," he asked. "No Mr Bond," replied W darkly, "I expect you to fry. There's fish in the fridge there and batter too."

Bond made his excuses and headed for the door.

Making his way back down the hill, Bond, still unsated, found himself in the small Little Bo Café. "Ah, Mr Bond, we had heard you were hereabouts. I'm Plenty O'Cake."

Bond scowled. What was the bleddy use of being a spy when everyone knew who you were and where you were but he put on a brave face. "But of course you are. I am Bond, James Bond but you knew that anyway," he replied with a hint of bitterness.

"So you are Plenty O'Cake. I must be dreaming," mused Bond as he was unusually fond of a bit of coffee cake. "Is that a bit of coffee cake I see on your counter?" asked Bond trying not to sound too desperate."

"It is," replied Plenty, "would you like it with walnuts."

Bond feigned a look of shocked surprise at the prospect of having walnuts in his coffee cake, "My dear girl, some things are just not done, like drinking Dom Perignon '53 above the temperature of 38 degrees Fahrenheit. That's just as bad as listening to 12 Volt without earmuffs."

Plenty laughed and told Bond that 12 Volt were not really as bad as a coffee cake with walnuts in it. She watched Bond devour a slice of unnutted cake and was taken rather aback when he caught her looking at him eating.

"You don't actually think I enjoyed what we just had, do you? What I did was for Queen and country! You don't think it gave me any pleasure, do you?"

"But of course, I forgot your ego, Mr Bond," Plenty snapped back, "James Bond who only has to eat a girl's coffee cake and she starts to hear heavenly choirs singing. She repents and immediately turns to the side of right and virtue, apart from the odd caramel slice, but not this one Mr Bond."

"Eck," thought Bond, "these Cornish maids are a bit tetchy. Good job I didn't ask for a bit of Rodda's with it."

"Anyway, enough of this nonsense, Plenty. I have to take out the highly fictitious leader of this exceedingly imaginary much maligned council before the whole county goes to the dogs."

"What, the highly fictitious leader of this exceedingly imaginary much maligned council? Who could possibly want to take a contract out on him?" asked Plenty, a little incredulous.

"Oh, jealous dictators, outraged voters, humiliated junior councillors. The list is endless," smiled Bond.

Bond raised an eyebrow and stepped outside just as the 00-AA arrived with his replacement car. Plenty looked on as Bond raced off up the hill and on to his mission.

"You'd never believe he's been going at it for fifty years, would you?" she muttered to herself.

October 14ᵗʰ – Sunday

There are only so many ways you can tell someone that we do not have or stock a particular product. It makes no difference how local the producer is, or how much sense it makes that we should stock it, or how dumb it is that we do not, if we do not have it no amount of argument or discussion is going to make it suddenly appear.

We had a gentleman in yesterday after a product that we should have had and did not but the lady that came in today was truly insistent. So convinced was she that we should have had the item that it took me ten minutes to convince her that we did not. Even then she urged that I search the depths of my soul to make sure I did not have one hidden away there and when I said that I had looked and found it empty (yes, there is very little where my soul should be) she had to ask if I was certain.

There are also only so many ways you can tell the bleddy hound that she was not going to get a major run out today. To be honest we should have got it out of the way in the morning when there was a decent amount of beach to be had. When the Missus eventually got around to being ready to take her it was high water and hardly an inch of sand visible on either beach.

She has survived the summer long without exercise, the bleddy hound that is, as well as the Missus, but now we have given her a taste of it she expects it every day. It is a shame we cannot just send her out with a knapsack and a sandwich and see her around tea time.

She created so much fuss, the bleddy hound, that is, not, for a change, the Missus, that the Missus took her up to the fields for a run around. It was good that it had not rained today, as she came back marginally less muddy than she did last night when she got a short run at the back of the F&L when the Missus took me up.

As you can tell it was another slow day in The Cove. Nevertheless, I took myself to bed early. Well, you never know when something might happen, like a Lifeboat shout at half past two in the morning, for instance.

October 15ᵗʰ – Monday

Well, I must have second sight. At ten past two this morning we had a Lifeboat shout. If I really did have second sight I would have sat this one out.

The boat was tasked to carry out a shore line search for a yacht that had left Mousehole on Saturday evening and was overdue in Bideford. Penlee and St Ives also launched to cover their patches.

I shall not dwell on the outcome, which was tragic and puts my own woes somewhat into perspective. The Lifeboat found nothing but, come light, various bits of wreckage began appearing all over The Cove and, as I type, our end of the road is packed with news vans, police and coastguard vehicles.

My own woes commenced when the Lifeboat returned to station at around six o'clock this morning. It would have been yet another textbook recovery by the very excellent Shore Crew had everything gone according to plan. Unfortunately, we had a bit of a problem down at the bottom end of the slip which required some unsnagging right at the water's edge. I should explain at this point that the water's edge was rather fluid, if you will excuse the pun, and was coming in three to four feet lumps. It was while I was doing a bit of unsnagging, with my foot in the keelway, that an especially large wave scat me backwards. This would not have been so bad had my foot followed me, but it decided to stay put and left me with a decidedly odd sensation in my right boot.

I was lying down by this time and, with the retreating sea flooding over me, it seemed a remarkably sound decision to stay put and not try getting up again; I was not entirely sure that my foot was still attached to my leg, at least in the normal fashion.

I managed to drag myself up the slipway in the manner of a classic horror Igor. Having established that my ankle was not broken, I retreated to the comparative safety of the winch room where I switched places with Head Launcher. Being a member of the very excellent Shore Crew it would only have been permissible to retire injured had the entire leg been missing, and even then I would never have lived it down.

I had rather assumed that my injury was simply a muscle strain treatable by some rest, ice, compression and elevation. Given that it was essentially a workplace accident, I felt that a precautionary trip to the doctor may be advisable. To save shutting the shop our very kind neighbour gave me a lift to the surgery at St Just.

It was rather a long wait, being a Monday, and I have to confess to almost dropping off in the waiting room once or twice. When I eventually saw the medic he told me that I should have gone directly to casualty. This was clearly not a man versed in the ways of the very excellent Shore Crew; surely this was just a scratch, a mere flesh wound.

The doc assured me it was not and in fact I should be in rather considerable pain. I was not. He did, however, bring a small tear to my eye when he delivered his verdict that my Achilles tendon had snapped and that I should immediately go thither to the hospital in Truro to have a cast placed around it.

So here you find me, dear reader, cast up (in a very alluring pink) and incapacitated to a degree. Things are going to be very different for the next three months and that is if I am lucky. If I am unlucky I shall require surgery and a much longer period of cast upness. Ouch, that did hurt.

October 16th – Tuesday

First, let me thank you, dear readers, for your heart felt concern and sympathies; both of you were most kind in your sentiments.

Both the Missus and I have been bowled over by the offers of help from the surrounding community too, which were coming in almost before the mishap; news spreads quickly here and, clearly, bad news even faster. I might just surprise one of you as I need another lift up to Treliske on Friday and it would be a bit much to ask our neighbour again.

I had another long and tedious event up at the hospital again today so the chap with an ultrasound pen could poke around to see what was what. Poke around he did and none too gently either. Before he could have a go I had to have the cast removed, which was an interesting experience. The technician used what appeared to be a small circular saw. I had a good look at it and I am darned if I could see any calibration for the depth of cut. I said to him that it was rather disconcerting and, while I was sure he had done thousands of such procedures, I was not necessarily to know that. He reassured me that he had been well trained and thanked me for allowing him to have his first go on a real patient. I will not ask again.

Perhaps I should apprise you of the state of my mobility. As you might imagine, I have been issued with a pair of crutches. My first attempts at trying to move in a forward direction under the supervision of a nurse resulted in her watching me through the fingers of her hands that she had covered her face with. When I told her that we have steep concrete steps to negotiate up to the flat she telephoned for a physiotherapist whom, she said, would be able to provide me with more expert tuition.

The physiotherapist was an 'ansum maid and jolly with it. Clearly the nurse had forewarned her of my lack of dexterity with a pair of ski poles and had brought with her a Zimmer frame. After witnessing another precarious attempt with the crutches she suggested that I may be more comfortable with the walking frame. She also advised that I discard both aids in favour of my bottom when needing to ascend or descend our steps.

I have been practicing with the crutches, though not on our steps, and I think I have made some improvement. At least I have not yet fallen over. However, the amount of effort required to travel even the shortest distances is substantial not to mention painful. You will therefore, no doubt, appreciate my apprehension when I sought directions today from the fracture clinic, where they removed my cast, to the scanning clinic and discovered it was far greater that the shortest distance.

I arrived white and panting and in a state of near collapse at the scanning clinic, which appeared not to raise even the slightest concern on behalf of the receptionist. I manfully resisted the offer of a wheelchair back to the fracture clinic on the grounds that I may have to wait some time for a porter to be found. Fortunately, a nurse with a strong sense of the practical borrowed one, a wheelchair, that is, not a porter, from the reception area and had me back where I started in double quick time and in better fettle.

On a slightly different tack I should tell you that we were once again beset with coastguards, police and newsmen in The Cove under sunny skies. Our local bobby had his hands full, but with others about he was redirected to a cement mixer that had toppled into the hedge just the other side of Crows-an-Wra. We passed it on the way to the hospital. On a straight stretch of road it was not apparent how the disaster had occurred. There were two police cars in attendance directing traffic and, presumably, looking for some concrete evidence.

That will be it for today, then, but fear not there is plenty more mileage in this leg lark yet. You would be amazed at the lengths your Diarist will go do when he starts running out of material. So, for now, down on Cripple Creek, it is goodnight.

October 17ᵗʰ - Wednesday

There I was, so focused on my foot I completely forgot about the high drama up at County Hall yesterday.

You may remember the whiff of revolution being in the air, the seemingly undemocratic behaviour of the inner sanctum of councillors and the prospect of blood being spilled on the carpets of or much maligned council's chamber floor. Well, everything seems to have gone as planned, with much recrimination and alleged backstabbing going on. The deputy leader of the much maligned council who stepped down from his post last week clearly having seen some scribbling on the wall of the executive washroom is now, surprise, surprise the new leader. Et tu, Brute, perhaps.

Thank heavens that we would never see that sort of skulduggery here in The Cove; that slippery manoeuvring is completely foreign to us.

Back in the real world we had a bit of a stunner out in the bay at high water this evening. With winds reaching over 50 knots from the south west, the sea was boiling with large waves crashing up on the cliffs from Cape to Aire Point. The Harbour wall regularly disappeared under a pile of white water and the only sand visible on the beach was up into Vellandreath.

Fortunately, the Missus took the bleddy hound down to the Harbour beach before it was inundated and I am sure she was very grateful, the bleddy hound, that is, not the Missus; she was wrapped up like it was winter. With the sun shining all day I did feel a little jealous.

I was allowed to do a bit of shop keeping while they were gone; the Missus has been quite insistent that I do unlikely things like rest and relax. Unfortunately, for me, those two things are mutually exclusive except when I am sleeping, so it is probably just as well, with the amount of effort it takes to get around, I am doing quite a bit of that.

Gosh, is that the time? Best I head off to bed.

October 18ᵗʰ – Thursday

I made another appearance in the shop today much to the Missus's annoyance; apparently resting means staying upstairs. This, however, does not necessarily meet with my definition of resting as you will, no doubt, recall that the parents-in-law are still staying with us. How can a poor fellow rest with the ever present threat of *Last of the Summer Wine* being screened at any moment.

In the shop I can be helpful to a degree. I can serve customers, provided that there is no requirement to go and fetch something. Serving a pasty requires a little more ingenuity as it necessitates the employment of both hands. Just picture in your mind Gilbert's Eros statue in Piccadilly and you will have some idea. Then I can tick off our magazine delivery and fill out the returns form while the Missus physically puts them out on the shelf, or in the returns box – or not.

We have a range of top shelf magazines that are designed to get the young person's blood boiling. I am sure this is a familiar sight in many newsagents. Of course, the thing around here that excites and titillates the youth beyond measure is surfing, (what *were* you thinking), and we have such titles as *Surfer's Path*, *Wavelength* and *Surfing USA*. At the outset of taking on the shop we were advised to arrange these along the top shelf to discourage penniless grommits from spending hours thumbing through them. This has worked to a degree but it also disadvantages the shorter surfer. I have, once or twice, sailed close to the wind by advising some of these that the magazines are height restricted.

Now the whole purpose of telling you all this, apart from being very effective at using up white space, is that while the Missus is not a surfer she is also not that tall either. This generated a fair amount of humour when I asked her to bring down the copies of Wavelength that were being recalled. Perhaps I should add that the humour may possibly have been a bit one sided.

In a similar vein a lady of The Cove related to me that she had been, like me, incapacitated at one time. Her late husband, noticing that she was unable to carry out simple domestic tasks and being an utter Cornish gentleman came to her aid. He went to Penzance and acquired a stool from Andrewartha's and, also being a master craftsman, cut the legs off to the right height. "I was able to peel the spuds at my worktop then," she said. "He was resourceful, like that." I shall have to take a leaf out of his book and devise some standing stool for the Missus.

Our flags have not been out at the front of the shop since the weekend as the she cannot reach the post holes. We have had offers from tall passers by but have turned these down on the grounds that we would have to rely on the coincidence of another tall passer by, passing by at closing time. I am sorry but I think we shall be flagless until we close in another couple of weeks.

I had to spurn attendance at Lifeboat training tonight on the grounds that the crew room is up a long flight of steps; the seat of my little boy's trousers can stand only so much stair bumping. I understand that they set about training half a dozen excellent Shore Crew on winch operations to account for my absence. Only half a dozen, I thought.

We could have done with around that number to assist us with the quiz at the OS. I thought that losing a faculty accentuates the performance of the remaining organs. Clearly losing a foot does not count, as we were rubbish. I also noted that my performance with the ski poles was much reduced even after a mediocre imbibement. If I am to last out on Saturday night I may need some assistance.

Does anyone have Lance Armstrong's number?

October 19ᵗʰ - Friday

Another episode all about my leg, I fear. I can see all of us getting pretty much bored with this very soon and given that this is my world at present the alternative is going to be a big blank space. I shall press on for now but I suspect that this bleddy foot may well have killed us off.

I have progressed to number two on the list of unsuspecting volunteers pressed into taking me up to the Royal Cornwall Hospital in Truro. It was an early start, as my appointment was at ten and we were uncertain of the amount of traffic that we might encounter. As it turned out we were half an hour early.

It was a meeting with the main man and I was rather expecting a five minute chat, a booking for surgery and to be sent home directly. The main man, as it happened, was having none of that and insisted on removal of the cast so that he could have a good poke around. He said that the ultrasound procedure was all very well but all it showed was that the tendon was ruptured, and that we knew that anyway. What it did not show was how badly it was ruptured and how far apart the ends were, which I thought was the whole point of going through a second eighty mile round trip and a replastering job.

Within a few seconds of placing his thumb on the injured part he was able to tell me that I probably did not require surgery so long as I abided by the rules of engagement. The first part of the rules was to have my foot recast in the equinus position, which I imagined, worryingly, was something to do with horses. Apparently, it is the 'fixed position of the foot in a plantar flexed attitude of the forefoot in relation to the rear foot'. In other words pointed downward as far as it will go, no matter how much it hurts in getting there, which it did – considerably. I was quite taken aback that there were no thick strips of leather made available for putting between the teeth during this procedure. I did ask the technician but he said he did not need one.

Foot thus pointed, the technician swiftly went about setting a cast upon it lest it spring back up to a normal attitude as it was trying hard to do, even without my conscious help. And that was it; I was there less than an hour – how efficient.

My chauffeur of the day pointedly refused any remuneration for his services, so I suggested we stop by Smokey Joe's on the way back where, at least, I could buy him a hearty breakfast. It was busy and we had to wait a while, but at least I could put my foot up on an adjacent chair. When it arrived it was a welcome repast and just as good as the last time I was there, in slightly more comfortable times.

I have been instructed to keep the foot elevated as much as possible, which is difficult as there is no resting place under my computer desk. This is the desk that has me positioned at the back of the television screen, the most comfortable position for reasons described yesterday. However I relented as I do wish this thing the best possible chance of recovery.

Two hours after lumping my foot atop a pile of cushions it occurred to me that I could no longer feel my toes which looked considerably larger than I remembered them being. I was also slightly concerned at the dark blue hue that they had taken on.

I vaguely remembered through the haze of pain being instructed to be observant for this condition and to return immediately to the hospital for attention. Yes, return immediately to the hospital that is forty miles distant and without any transport. I telephoned the fractures department and was answered by a recorded message that they would return my call, which they did not. I tried the main reception desk where the young lady told me, rather alarmingly, that I was on the verge of an instant demise and should seek help immediately, before she passed me on the emergency ward. Here, the nurse was a little more reserved and suggested that I could get help at West Cornwall Hospital in Penzance.

So, shortly after closing the shop, the Missus took me up there to be freed of my boot of torture to be replaced with a slightly more comfortable one. For being a good boy and not crying too much the Missus rewarded me with a rather nice curry. Sweet, ain't she?

October 20ᵗʰ - Saturday

Someone up there is clearly not all that keen on me. Why else would we have had stunning blue skies, warm sunshine and, in the afternoon, a beach fit to walk a herd of bleddy hounds on? And where was I during this rip grubbling day? Yes, on my sofa with my leg stuck on top of a pile of cushions.

I have been nagged into submission. That and a keen desire to give recovery its best chance, well, as far as is reasonable anyway. However I did manage the best part of an hour in the shop, long enough to notice a sharp upturn in trade.

It would appear that some of the private schools are out and some of our regulars are back in The Cove. It also means that I did not order enough bread and pasties, where in the last few weeks we have been buried in both.

See how exciting it can be sitting in a chair and doing nothing? Good then that the Little Bo Café has instigated a Mexican and Central American theme night. For this event they have invited a guest chef who, I am led to believe, has been top dog in some fine dining restaurants across the world and who just so happens to be the friend of a friend of theirs.

If we ever doubted the rumours, there was no doubting the superb squid in lime and coriander, or the potato in coriander cream sauce with chorizo, or the chicken in tomato sauce, or even the hake ceviche. Crikey, we were treated beyond measure and, I suspect, in a cook off with the best restaurants in Cornwall the evening would have given them a good run for their money. All this and next door too.

As a small aside I should tell you that ceviche was the first meal that I prepared for the Missus after I met her. For the uninitiated it is a fish dish made with raw fish 'cooked' in lime juice. The recipe I had followed included the use of scotch bonnet chillies and various white fish. She asked me if the meal was cooked, which I asserted that it had been, though I omitted to say exactly how, and after tasting it she used some words that I had not imagined a lady to have in her vocabulary. It laid the foundations for a long lasting relationship, me knowing that she was not necessarily a lady and her knowing that I occasionally bent the truth in my favour and was not at any time to be trusted.

Time then to celebrate that happy joining by insisting that she take me to the F&L in the full knowledge that I would not be enjoying a walk home under the perfect sky, studded with bright points of light. Oh mercy, what further suffering must I endure?

Bugaloo Dudes play a fine set of slightly unusual, but perfectly acceptable covers. The fact that I was tucked away in the snug paying lip service to having my foot elevated and unable to see them only slightly detracted from the enjoyment. Part of this enjoyment included the many enquiries related to my casting and the friendly abuse I received. This was going quite well until someone found a black marker pen and now my cast is littered with humorous comments that were probably quite amusing half way through a Saturday night pub session.

Ah well, at least I did not fall off my poles. I must be getting better.

October 21ˢᵗ - Sunday

I am immensely grateful, I think, to SH who convinced me to persevere with The Diary for a bit despite having begger all to write about. As time progresses and you have had enough of how many steps it is to the bathroom today and the statistical variation between gulls flying left and right across the window you may wish to throw rotten fruit at him.

I am sure that you will be delighted to know that I am adapting to my new life quite nicely. All it takes is a little ingenuity and innovation. For example today I managed to cook up some goujons of pollack.

Despite knowing that tonight I am to enjoy some fish stew that was left over from yesterday's Mexican theme night at Little Bo Café, the pollack needed to be eaten or thrown away since it had been sitting in the fridge since Friday. Given that I am being a good boy and cannot move from my foot-elevated position on the sofa some clever arrangements needed to be made to allow me to prepare and cook the fish in the living room.

I have a small lap table and one of those cantilever tables normally used to reach over a bed. With a chopping board on one table and a small primus stove on the other I was able, with some assistance from the mother-in-law, to slice the fish, roll it in some seasoned wholemeal flour and then transfer it to the frying pan on the other table. This required no small amount of dexterity and some care that the hot oil did not splash into my lap or other sensitive part, or even not to knock over the primus stove and set light to the carpet.

All right, of course I did not cook the fish in the living room; I have hurt my foot not had my brains removed. Yes, yes, I realise that some might say it was a close run thing. Trouble is if the Missus thought for a moment that I had been banging about in the kitchen, shuffling pans of hot oil and a spatula and playing with sharp knives while balancing on one foot she would probably hide my crutches and kick my good shin to make sure I did not do it again. So, dear reader, you are sworn to secrecy (and that especially includes you, DG).

Just to rub a little salt into my wound, my pager went off at around half past twelve. I was in the act of struggling to my foot when I realised that I do not attend shouts for the time being. I did make it to the window to watch everyone turn up. I did not imagine that I would be so affected, but I cannot remember when I have felt so frustrated and impotent. All right, there was that one time, but she said it could happen to anyone.

Anyway, I digress. I may well have to turn the pager off else I will only end up annoying myself every time it goes off. The shout was cancelled in the end, but not before the Inshore Boat had gone afloat in the harbour. It was likely to have been a surfer in a spot of bother, as there was a significant swell in the bay today and the surf was full of little black heads bobbing about.

In fact the bay was a spectacular scene with large rolling waves blown back at their crest by an easterly breeze. Even at low water, with the bay looking calm and innocuous, great plumes were thumping up on the Cowloes, the Brisons and the reef running up to Cot Valley. The whole canvas was lit by the warming light from the dipping sun.

Gosh, you really should have been here.

October 22nd – Monday

The RNLI has very kindly offered to provide any sort of support that they can, without prejudice naturally, during the period of my recovery. I was asked to fill out a form and if I had any questions whatsoever to telephone a rather pleasant lady at the Poole Head Office.

Well I did have one or two questions regarding the use of a Lifeboat to take me up to Truro for any future appointments that I may have there, so I telephoned the lady I refer to. On not receiving an answer I left a message that some hours later had not been returned. I had noticed that when I left a message that the telephone system allowed the caller to press a zero to be returned to the operator, so I telephoned again with this in mind.

On pressing the zero key on my telephone a rather sweet voice told me that I was being returned to the operator.

"This is the Microsoft Exchange automated telephone system. Please state the name of the person you are trying to contact."

"Well, I was rather hoping that I could speak with the operator, like I was promised."

"I'm sorry. I didn't hear that. Please repeat the name of the person you are trying to contact."

"The operator. Can I speak with the operator?"

"I'm sorry. I didn't hear that. Please repeat the name of the person you are trying to contact."

"Reception. Operator. A bleddy human being!"

"I'm sorry. I didn't hear that. Please repeat the name of the person you are trying to contact."

Time to get serious, then, "Hello, I am a DONOR and I want to leave you a million pounds."

"I'm sorry. I didn't hear that. I will connect you to reception."

Ah, thank heavens, it has given up and is transferring me to someone who can help, no doubt.

"This is the Microsoft Exchange automated telephone system. Please state the name of the person you are trying to contact."

Good grief, this system is unbreakable, most unlike Microsoft. I had considered asking for the Chairman, whose name is included in the letterhead on the letter that I had been sent, but opted for the name of the inspector who had visited me last week, Nigel.

"Did you mean ... Nggl?"

If it was trying to match on mispronounced sounds what hope did I have? I told it yes and it connected me through to a lady called Jennifer. Unfortunately, Jennifer was not in Poole, she was in Saltash and although the computerised telephone system could connect me to any branch in the country, it seems, Jennifer could not. She did give me the number of the main reception at Poole and I just hoped that it was attended by a human being, which it was.

While I have been a little unkind to the Institution, to hold it up to ridicule in this manner, it should be noted that it was its internal telephone system that was run in this manner. I assume that it saves costs on employing a person to operate the telephones, which, being a charity, is highly commendable.

There, hopefully they will still have me back when I am better.

I was allowed down into the shop again today. I think that the Missus feels sorry enough for me to permit a little respite from my prison cell. I reckon it is also so that she does not come upstairs to find claw marks where I have been climbing the walls.

Of course, it is really the sympathy that I truly crave. It is not likely to last very long, so I am making the most of it. Things like the suggestion that if I sat outside with the bleddy hound and a penny whistle I could probably make a few bob. Most people, though, elect to cheer me up by commenting how painful it must be and how they have heard how long the recovery period is and, best of all, relating how a family member of theirs had the same thing ten years ago and still walks with a limp. Warms the heart, does it not?

There are those, though, with some genuine knowledge to impart, like AR who telephoned to give me tips on handling my ski poles and the lady who had some success with a homeopathic remedy. Today an Australian visitor boldly strode up to squeeze one of my toes. Fortunately, I have some training in the dark arts and realised that this was not a curious antipodean Masonic greeting, but the fact that he was testing my capillary refill reaction. He then went on to scold me for letting my foot rest below the level of my pelvis. He was right, of course, but it was only for a short while.

It was all over far too soon; once around the exercise yard and back to my cell. I did get a glimpse of the sometimes clear sky and other times grey and cloudy. The air was warm, the sea less robust that yesterday. Not bad for my little trip out. Then I awoke and looked around me, at the four grey walls that surround me and realised, yes, I was only dreaming.

Oh, I almost forgot to tell you. It was only after a chance conversation with my editor in chief, (that's big sis to me), that I remembered. It was on the first day I had my shackles slapped on and, perhaps, unused to its bulk and restriction when I swung my leg under my desk ... I broke my bleddy middle toe.

They are starting to call me 'lucky' down here.

October 23rd - Tuesday

Our pleasant sunshine has gone and we have been treated to a misty, damp but mild day; just the sort of day for taking yet another trip up to Truro to see if the boys of the local A&E have reset my plaster correctly.

Head Launcher turned up to give me a lift today. It was, after all, his turn in his smart pocket rocket and especially as he had assured me he was taking a couple of weeks off work. As it transpired, and despite some notice, his bosses had not responded to his request for leave and he was supposed to be at work. He came anyway as that is the sort of chap he is.

It was heartening to know that I am not the only one who has a bee in his bonnet about motorists who fail to turn their lights on in the fog. As Head Launcher said, all you have to do is turn a switch; it is not hard. What a team: a grumpy shop keeper and a grumpy Head Launcher.

I also met a grumpy receptionist who insisted that I should not have just turned up at the fracture clinic, despite my protestations that it must have been one of her colleagues who said that I should. I got a 'tut' when I explained; I did not know that people in front line customer service roles still 'tutted'. I thought millions of pounds worth of training had consigned that to the past in favour of big smiles and 'have a nice day'.

Despite the frosty reception, I got in to the plaster workshop inside five minutes and was back out less than fifteen minutes after I arrived, with a shiny new plaster with no rude witticisms written on it. I was almost as relieved as a Gloucestershire badger.

Now, I did not explain that after years of working together in the very excellent Shore Crew meant that Head Launcher and I are highly trained and efficient in our duties, and this is probably why both of us had mobile telephones that only had one bar of electricity left inside them. On this basis, we had agreed to turn our telephones on one hour after he had dropped me off to see if either had left a message for the other regarding my collection from the clinic. If you are still following, dear reader, and have not dropped off to sleep or found a patch of wet paint to watch dry you will, of course, have calculated that I now had 45 minutes to wait until the nominated contact time.

There are two main observations that struck me as a planted myself in the waiting room. The first is that the NHS is clearly confident that it can meet all its challenging waiting time targets set by government, as they have dispensed with the notion of comfortable seating. The second is that the NHS has conducted an in depth study regarding the social background and gender of fracture patients and concluded that only women's knitting magazines are required in the waiting room.

Not even in the extremity of discomfort could I bring myself to read a copy of *Prima,* and the signage regarding the use of mobile telephones and desisting from smoking only gave momentary relief. I cast about the room looking for a bearded lady or a chap with two foreheads who may have provided some ghoulish entertainment and, yes, I am fully aware that gaining any sort of enjoyment from looking at a chap with two foreheads is to be frowned on.

It was then I happed upon a lady, clearly grandma, with a young chap on her lap. She was reading to him from a book called Topsy and Tim and, as she was facing me in the next row, I could hear her quite clearly.

I have to say that Topsy and Tim do have some adventures. Today they were going on holiday on an aeroplane and had been invited to the cockpit by the pilot, who showed Topsy and Tim his instruments. Back in their seats they pretended to play with the instruments and fly the plane. The book, though, was very clear to point out that Topsy and Tim knew deep down that it was really the pilot flying the plane.

It concerned me more than a little that the book appeared to lack a sense of realism. I mean whoever heard of a maid being named Topsy unless, of course, her parents had singled her out for a life on the stage or, perhaps, as a high class escort. That would have made sense, and I did come in half way through the story.

I was less enamoured with the next book which was a Noddy story. It was like no Noddy book I remember. Some of the main characters were missing for a start, and I am sure that Mr Sparks did not run the garage. It was also littered with unnecessary life tips such as sweets are bad for your teeth. Who wants to hear about that when you are trying to achieve a little escapism? No, it is Topsy and Tim for me, for sure, even if it does have the foundations of a disastrous life for one of its characters. Let's face it, Topsy is either going to be a movie star or a crack addicted call girl when she grows up and I know where my money is; she does not stand a chance with a name like that.

Anyway, when grandma had finished reading the stories I was surprised to look up at the clock and see that time had flown; it was nearly time to turn on my mobile telephone. As I left to wait for my lift outside I thanked grandma heartily for her public reading. I am not sure how that was received and did not wait for a reply, though perhaps I should have.

My big toe has gone numb again in the new plaster and I may well have to repeat today's episode. I wish I had got grandma's number now; the trip would be a breeze.

October 24th - Wednesday

I have been smote down by an unseen hand; a bug, perhaps, picked up from the hospital waiting room yesterday. I do not think there is any cause for alarm, as there is nothing super about this bug, merely inconvenient.

I shall not dwell on this matter, as I am sure you have quite enough of misery. I shall simply say, by way of explanation, that I have been asleep for most of the day, hence a rather thin Diary entry.

During one of my more lucid moments I did manage to read the *Western Morning News*, (did I tell you I once had a review ...). Well, I say lucid but it is extremely likely that I was suffering in delirium; I have always liked Italy. The front page headline announced that the councillors of our much maligned council have voted to award themselves a twenty percent hike in pay, as well as an eleven percent increase in petrol expenses.

The main excuse that they gave was that they wanted to attract a younger set of people to become councillors. I think they may have missed the point; our current councillors have been behaving like five year olds in a school playground over the last week or so. What we desperately need is more mature councillors, oh, and ones that turn up. Over ten percent of councillors did not vote in the most important decision since the Unitary was formed. I know, I know, that seems very harsh – but fair, I felt.

I fleetingly thought that while I languish here I could prepare my own campaign for the elections in May. Crikey, I must be poorly! I have been awake for more than five consecutive minutes. Nursey will not be at all pleased.

October 25th – Thursday

I awoke feeling like a new man but with no idea where to find one. There was not a vestige of the smiting I received yesterday, which, on reflection, may possibly have been a result of the repleccioun of two slightly out of date cream éclairs the evening before. Darn those naughty French.

However, it was not all roses in the yeerd as when I looked out of the window this morning it was clear that this would be one of those days I am growing to diffye. The sky was clear, and the early morning sun lighting up the Harbour wall made this an excellent day to be running around down on a largely empty stronde with the bleddy hound. It was not all doom and gloom, as a rather lively easterly wind had set in bringing with it a bitter chill. Thank hevene.

I did not get to feel the chill wind at all during the day as the Wyf reminded me that I should be a good boy. I have tried to make my being a good boy as comfortable as possible by surrounding myself with the nedes of life such as deyntees, books and papers, telephone, glasses and a network connected laptop. This also minimises the effort committed by others, so that they do not have to constantly run after me.

The greatest danger in all this is the access I have to the Internet. It is such a marvellous resource and, if used sensibly, can conseille, enthral and entertain. Without it The Diary would not be the centre for literary excellence and font of undeniable truth that it is … oh, all right, but if you read that on the Internet I bet you would have believed it.

I extensively use the Internet for research too. In years gone by I have been responsible, (responsible: I get the blame if it all goes wrong), for sourcing chaffare based on a client's specifications and nedes. Since the birth of the Internet this task became immeasurably easier, or at least faster, (not necessarily a good thing when you were paid by the day), and less onerous. More recently I have used these skills to recommend chaffare such as cameras and computers to friends and family with confidence and drad of their disappointment.

I still like to do this to disporte, and this is where the ensample really starts, and with so much spare time on my hands I have been doing it rather a lot. The problem arises when I get down to establishing price as the only place this can be determined is from the sites actually selling the product. Byynge and having these desirable thyngs delivered to my door is just a few clicks away.

The television in the living room has lines down the left side of the screen where the matrix has failed, my headphones, which are currently pumping a bit of Tom Petty into my erys leave bits of black plastic behind where the covering has disintegrated; this laptop is a bit slow. It would be oh so easy to replace them all.

Of all the thyngs I have ful faste, the water, the glasses, the books, the telephone, only one thyng is missing: my credit card.

But joy of joy, the Wyf has relented and has allowed me to wiggle off down to the OS for quiz night and the sheer love of it. She understands that the love wol nat been constreyned by maistrye; when maistrie comth, the god of love anon beteth hise wynges, and farewell, he is gon! Love of beer is a thing as any spirit free. Boys, of kynde desiren libertee, and nat to been constreyned as a thral.

And if you were thinking throughout that I had lost control of my mental faculties, my fingers, my spellchecker or all of the above that last paragraph should have reminded you that today is the anniversary of Mr Geoffrey Chaucer popping off in 1400. You should also note that 'disporte' had a rather purer meaning in the 14th century, you naughty people.

It has also gratified me and very possibly my Eng. Lit. teacher, whose name my sister will remember, that the hours of studying the Franklin's Tale were not entirely wasted, although the rest of the time clearly was as we were rubbish in the quiz.

October 26th – Friday

The drivers of the First Bus Group have decided to hold a strike today as they have rejected the company's pay offer. This means that we have suffered an appalling service today with fewer than one bus every two hours and none at all in the evening. This is outrageous. Oh, wait a minute, sorry. That is the normal timetable I am looking at.

After that opener let us just hope I do not have to take a bus anywhere anytime soon.

I managed to get a little trip downstairs and the Missus needed to do a few things upstairs. This suited me just fine as I was running a little low on sympathy. Unfortunately, we were also running a little short on customers so I was not quite as sympathised with as I would have hoped.

I think I might have explained how the Missus has waited on me hand and foot and catered, nearly, for my every need. I had always assumed that, over time, the willingness would falter as the level of sympathy declined and the irritation factor increased. I did not, however, expect it to evaporate completely just over a week after the accident.

My needs are few, no really, and I do not ask for much. In the mornings she will ensure my clothes are easily within reach and that there is a mug of tea waiting on my desk when I have eventually dragged myself to it. After that I am near enough self sufficient, with my survival pod over by the sofa.

It was yesterday morning that the axe fell. I had just hauled myself to the living room where she was stationed looking at handbags on the Internet and noticed that there were no clothes set out for me. Not a problem, I thought, I can always drag my aching frame all the way back to the bedroom and fetch them myself, which I duly did. When I eventually returned, hot and perspiring from my efforts, I sank, with some relief, into my desk chair gasping and ready for a reviving mug of char. And there it was ... no bleddy tea!

Well, dear reader, it is not like I have shown a lack of gratitude, or have taken for granted the services that have been lavished upon me. I know that I can also make my own tea should push come to shove, but one thing I cannot do is transport it from the kitchen to my desk. I ask you, a simple mug of tea delivered to my desk. Is that too much to ask? Must I beg? If you prick me, do I not bleed?

I do not know what made her realise my disappointment. It might have been the soulful look, the gasping sounds as I sat at my desk or it might possibly have been telling my chums at the

Lifeboat Station who all then made mention of it, one at a time, when they saw her last night.

Anyway, whichever subtle artifice it was, my tea was waiting for me this morning. I do not know if mentioning that it seemed a little cold was a good thing or not. It tasted a bit gritty too, but I thought it best not to say anything, bless her.

She must be getting quite fractious, though. When I visited the kitchen later I noticed that she managed to break one of our wine glasses, quite a job too; there was powdered glass everywhere.

October 27ᵗʰ - Saturday

Today looked very nice through the window and that is just where I saw it from – all day. I do not know if the Missus read yesterday's Diary, she usually does not, but I was not allowed out to play today. There were large portions of bright blue sky, white fluffy clouds and bright, bright sunshine, which looked very alluring.

She might, of course, just have been kind as I understand there was a rather a nasty, knicker-ripping northerly blowing and I am still wearing shorts. Actually, I could hear the wind whistling in my ear 'ole from the safety of the sofa, and it did sound mighty indeed.

The most exciting thing that happened today, and one that I shall be eternally grateful for as it gave me at least one more paragraph, was a young gannet deciding to practice a bit of flying and diving close in to the shore and right outside our window. It dived into the Harbour water and looked rather stunned after it surfaced; I would guess that the water at the point of entry was probably no more than ten feet deep. It did a final pass across the window and what a magnificent sight it looked; shame about the slightly bent bill.

October 29ᵗʰ - Monday

Our weather conditions are certainly unsettled. Even the Met Office could not mess up a forecast for this, whatever they reported. Today we had showers lining up across the bay to dowse us down between smatterings of sunshine. It was definitely better than it was last night, as it seemed to rain continuously then.

This, of course meant that the steps leading up to the flat were wet, a situation that drives ice cold fear into any individual that has to negotiate them on his behind. Naturally, I am not allowed out and was perfectly safe or dry bottomed, at least. The Missus is strenuous in her efforts to ensure that I do not have to make an appearance in the shop. Except today, when she inexplicably had to carry out some task or other upstairs, requiring me to be downstairs and between which lay the [FX: dramatic, deep musical notes] the wet steps.

Actually, at the time of my descent the steps were reasonably dry and I cast aside the waterproof trousers that I had, with some difficulty, shuffled into.

The hour I spent in the shop whistled by; it was rather busier than the last week when I was down there. Consequently there was not a great deal of time when I was sitting with my cursed, encased leg elevated.

All of the cast fitters, and the doctor too, used the term that my leg was now in a tube. It was related as a warning that, at the time, I did not quite appreciate the meaning of. It was only later when I had spent any length of time with the foot not elevated that the true meaning of their words became apparent. It is the rushing of blood to the toes and its apparent ineptitude at getting back up the leg again that seems to cause the problem and produces a feeling akin to having my leg in a vice. It throbs too. This phenomenon is never more acute than after my leg has been elevated for a long period of time – such as a few hours prior to being asked to attend the shop for a while.

So, during my period behind the shop counter in a continual upright position, serving customers, my little toes turned a deep blue and throbbed like an Ayia Napa dance floor. I should point out that I have never been on a dance floor in Ayia Napa, so I am working from my imagination here. I have seen pictures on the television and I once, mistakenly, went to Le Palais, that once was the Hammersmith Palais where big bands used to play, and was alarmed at the volume of the noise that was sufficient in bass notes to make my diaphragm jump.

Sorry, I digress. Where was I? Oh yes, my foot was fair thumping as I served customers. It is a sensation that is easy to get used to, but you never quite shift the feeling in the back of your mind that it cannot be terribly therapeutic. Nevertheless, it was wonderful to be in the company of other members of the human race and to feel the raw slap of fresh air about one's parts – yes, I am still wearing shorts. Ladies, please control yourselves.

I was so enwrapped in the sensations of freedom that I paid no particular attention to the frequent squalls sweeping across the bay. Not, that is, until the Missus returned and gave me my marching orders. It then suddenly occurred to me that the steps that I was about to ascend were now soggy and that in short order so too would be my rear end.

Although she told me that she had considered letting me suffer this ignominy, the Missus had softened and had brought down with her my waterproof trousers, bless her.

October 30th - Tuesday

I was woken in the middle of the night by a desperate feeling that I had forgotten to do something, that and the fact that the Missus had once again nicked the bed sheets off me. The former matter resolved itself into the omission to order some fish for the morning, so I pottered into the living room to leave a message on our supplier's answering service.

Had I not done so, and slept fitfully through the night, I would have missed the sight of the moon drenched bay. If you recall in the old movies, night scenes were filmed during the day with a heavy blue filter on the camera lens. They may well still do it in new movies, who knows? The bay last night was very much reminiscent of this effect, with every part set out in fine detail, down to white capped waves and glimmering beaches and with little cotton wool clouds dotting the sky. Had I slept peacefully I would have missed all that, not to mention disappointing a fish buying customer.

It looked rather pretty in the morning too, first thing, with the rising sun lighting up the white wave crests and Harbour wall. A cloudy, grey aberration followed which then cleared away to something of a fine day. So fine, indeed, that the parents-in-law went and sat across in front of the Lifeboat station for a couple of hours in the afternoon.

I even got to have a little time out as well. The Missus cleared off to the farmer's market behind the school in the morning with the mother-in-law, leaving me behind the counter for the best part of an hour. Two days running, she must be softening.

It was not overly busy while she was gone, but I was able to have a brain stirring conversation with one or two customers. An older lady asked if I had seen her glossy egret, which had me a little concerned until she explained that it was a rare bird. I told her that had it fallen upon my head I probably would still be none the wiser and, after assuring me that it had not, she went off in search of someone who was a little more helpful.

November 1ˢᵗ – Thursday

I slipped off with the Head Launcher's party to the OS for the quiz again tonight. I had the foresight to telephone ahead this time to reserve a table in the area level with the door. It is not that I cannot do stairs, short flights are manageable, but they do still present something of a challenge and this is while I am in full possession of my faculties. Call me unadventurous if you will but even a reputation as miserable and tattered as mine still needs to be maintained.

And talking of adventurous it has come to my attention that amidst my Chaucerian madness of last week I completely failed to mention my method of transport to the OS last week. On the basis that I could not join the fun and games of Lifeboat training, and my urgent need to secure a seat in the aforementioned level area at the OS I decided to form an advance party of one and form a bridgehead before the main forces arrived. The Missus, clearly in a moment of heady enthusiasm, suggested she wheel me there in the father-in-law's wheelchair.

The road between the Boathouse and the OS is, to the general vision, flat and ordinary. When you are being pushed in a wheelchair, or, more accurately, when you are pushing a wheelchair, it is very apparent that there is a long and steep incline, becoming steeper the harder you push. I do not think the Missus will be offering again and I am rather glad she did not tonight as we were lashed with hail storms.

Incidentally, the venerable company of Head Launchers came a respectable second in quite a wide field tonight, floored only by Oscar Wilde.

November 2ⁿᵈ - Friday

Something of a big day for me and my foot; it was the day I would find out whether three weeks of being plastered was actually a good thing for a change.

Head Launcher was on hand again to transport me hence to the big city hospital and the judgement that hung in the balance. Despite having to do a few errands on the way, we arrived a little before time and contrary to popular belief I was on the examination table at exactly the appointed hour having only waited a few minutes.

I was attended by a team of caring professionals. A cheery chap saw off, quite literally, my cast while a couple of buxom nurses fed me grapes and soothed my furrowed brow. Yet another brought some heady elixir in a chalice of gold and all the while cherubs danced and played their pipes and lyres; some parents just cannot control their little ones. There was not a hint of the horror stories, or concerns in staff shortages and extended waiting times prevalent in the press. I am minded to write to the Health Secretary and tell him that Treliske Fracture Clinic is clearly over-staffed and the root cause of the financial uncertainty in the heath service.

All right, maybe I exaggerate, just a little, but I was certainly transported to a heavenly plane when the good doctor announced that all was well in the Achilles department and I could now progress from the restrictive cast to the restrictive 'boot' instead.

A rather humourless, but nevertheless polite and efficient member of the Occupational Therapy department duly arrived with a rather fearsome looking device in a bag. It had the appearance of an item I had last seen in a chamber of horrors, used to torture confessions from unfortunate innocents of the Spanish Inquisition. I had considered asking the dour chap's name, but decided against, just in case he might reveal himself to be a descendant of Tomás de Torquemada himself.

It took ten minutes just to unwrap the multiple elements of the boot of death. An allen key is then employed to adjust the angle of the foot, and afterwards this was pressed into my palm with strict instructions to keep it safe and bring it with the boot and my leg to future visits. I suggested that since it was such an integral part of the equipment and its operation that it would not have been beyond the design team to have constructed some appropriate pocket for it on the device. This was met with the kind of look that I imagine Orville gave Wilbur when he suggested that his flying machine might possibly be better off with wings.

The fitting of the boot of death took a further ten minutes with straps, bars and hooks and more Velcro than is decent. I suspect that any spontaneous acts of passion requiring its immediate removal will have long evaporated after the last fastener is released. Not that any spontaneous acts of passion are remotely likely; we are married after all and I do not get out much.

My deepest disappointment is not its unlikely construction and clumsy appearance but the boot of death is a very boring blue in colour. Apparently there is no joy and delight in the world of boots of death; the colours pink or mauve are, as yet, a distant dream.

I wish I could tell you that the rest of the day came up to scratch with the excitement of the morning but it did not, well, not quite ... until.

You might recall a few weeks ago that our neighbours in the Little Bo Café upped the ante of excellent dining in The Cove by holding a Mexican and South American theme night. So successful was it that they decided to run another and tonight we were treated to an Asian night.

What can I tell you about perfectly made sushi, squid with roasted garlic, marinated and seared beef with noodles and a fish stew with cabbage, squid and mussels that was mouth-wateringly out of this world. I will not berate you further for not attending had you the opportunity to do so, if you did you are beyond help. All I can tell you is that should you miss another you should kick yourselves and for this purpose I will quite happily lend you my boot of death.

November 3ʳᵈ - Saturday

I had a fitful night's sleep last night, despite the boot of death, thank you for asking. I had thought it a tad more cumbersome at first but with the knowledge than my recovery is on track I have been walking, and sleeping, on air.

To celebrate, I managed to do absolutely nothing today, which would have made for rather thin reading had it not been for an item of spectacular news.

As I have made you aware, on countless occasions, we are a small cog in the Cornish tourist information machine, being as we are the Sennen Cove Visitor Contact Point. This, I am sure you will agree, allows us, in some small measure, to take credit for the results of the British Travel Awards which cited Cornwall as best holiday county 2012. I would have been more assured of our single contribution had the county not won it last year as well, before we were the Sennen Cove Visitor Contact Point, but we will not dwell too long on that thought.

It is likely, too, that we had much to do with St Ives winning best coastal town as well after my, ahem, glowing recommendation of the town in the published Cove Diary. They too enjoyed this accolade last year, the year in which the book was published.

I probably cannot claim too much of a hand in the Eden Project's success in winning best UK tourist attraction, against the likes of Legoland and Madam Tussauds, unless it was to do with the fact that I did not go there this year. Neither can I assert any involvement in the Fal River winning a silver award in the best waterways/lakes boat operator, or Minack a bronze in best heritage attraction. In all Cornwall picked up eight of the 24 available awards in the UK category of the awards extravaganza, including four gold medals. Good ain't we?

If there were a better excuse to go and celebrate at the F&L I certainly could not think of one. I dragged along the boot of death, as it seems to be rather attached to me at the moment, and I am very glad that I did.

The band, *Hooked*, were indeed a sumptuous example of the deliciousness that makes evenings on the hill great and good. They, with a blond and raucous female lead, played some rocking tunes that encompassed a whole happy genre such as Wheatus (whatever happened to them), Green Day, Foo Fighters and, what an absolute delight, a rendition of 99 Red Balloons including the red balloons dancing around the bar. How inspired. What fun.

It did not escape my notice that the band members were wearing big heavy boots with straps up the side and silver heels. I think maybe that me and my boot of death have started a trend.

November 4th – Sunday

Another blustery day of sunshine and showers with the bluster reaching over forty miles per hour on occasion. It was piling in from the west, which was better than some other directions it could have been piling in from, but not ideal for a swansong to a fairly bleak year.

Still, on the bright side I do not have to pull myself out of bed before the sun has risen and force myself out in the cold and damp to see what delights the Laurel and Hardy Newspaper Company has left me. No, wait a moment, I have not had to do that anyway for the last three weeks, the Missus has. Perhaps I shall just be happy for her instead; after all she absolutely detests getting up early.

The closing of the shop is, for me, always a day of mixed feelings. The freedom to be lazy in the mornings and come and go as we please is always attractive, or is normally welcome when I have two feet to play with. Ranged against this is the loss of contact with the everyday visitors to the shop, although based on today's performance there will be precious little of that. After all, if there were still plenty of people around we would be staying open.

At least the bleddy hound may benefit by some more exciting exercise than she has been used to recently. This week we had the young maid on her holidays to help us out, else she hardly would have got out at all. Now that she has gone home, one of us will still have to get up at a reasonable hour for the morning constitutional. Sadly, due to my predicament, this duty must fall upon the Missus. I did not snigger, honestly I did not.

November 5th - Monday

Well, the Missus had to get up dead early anyway this morning to meet the newspaper delivery driver. We have to send back all the magazines, and there was an abundance of Sunday newspapers, and not all of it would fit in the newspaper box outside. I managed to get away with this last year by sending back the magazines piecemeal through the week, but there again, it is my area of responsibility.

During the normal running of the shop we split up our roles and responsibilities for fairness. I take care of the ordering of newspapers and magazines, bread, pasties, milk, butter, Rodda's cream etcetera and the Missus is responsible for criticising me when I get the volumes wrong.

She was determined to get her lie in this morning and promptly went back to bed when she had sorted out the papers and the bleddy hound. I got up with her this morning, but find it utterly impossible to return to bed once I have got up. As a consequence I had my breakfast at midday, by which time I was pretty desperate. Although I am quite capable of making a cup of tea or a sandwich, I still have not found a way of transporting it to the living room without leaving a trail of whichever down the corridor; all suggestions on a postcard please to 'Starving of Sennen'.

Perhaps someone could also suggest why, with a rather fierce northerly wind blowing all day, the weather vane on the Lifeboat Station seemed to be pointing to the east. Despite the wind it looked rather pleasant out there, although I never got to find out, with large portions of blue sky dotted with massive lumbering storm clouds. We got away scot free until the early evening when we were lashed with a spectacularly heavy hail shower for ten minutes.

Fortunately, the Missus was early enough to miss this when she voluntarily, and without being prompted, took the bleddy hound for a walk. She went up to Brew Farm and wandered around the fields up there, which I thought was particularly brave and gave the little girl some new places to explore; I think the bleddy hound enjoyed it too. Naturally she found some badger or fox doings just before she came back and dabbed it nicely behind her ears – the bleddy hound, that is, not the Missus. This is precisely why I tend to gravitate to the beaches with her; it is far less trouble unless there is some scabby fish around.

Tonight, being the 5th, I would normally have wormed my way into an evening at the F&L where a firework display and massive bonfire, (most likely unaffected by the heavy hail storm), would have attracted hundreds of small children, running around and screaming with delight. This year I have demurred on the basis that the firework display and massive bonfire would have attracted hundreds of small children, running around and screaming with delight; I would have felt like a skittle in a bowling alley free-for-all.

November 6th - Tuesday

The Missus finally got her lie in this morning. Even I tarried far later than I would do normally. The mother-in-law took the bleddy hound out and the Missus, woken by her alarm to find the dog missing, got up in such a fright that any benefit she might had had from her extended rest was immediately wiped away. Such is the stuff of mighty plans.

She had to be up fairly early anyway, since the father-in-law had an appointment in town. It is most unlike the Missus to miss out on a trip into town, especially when she did not need to be back for any particular purpose, so she did not. They were gone for hours. Had I realised quite how long they were going to be gone for I would have watched a big loud crashy film on the living room television, but as I thought I would probably not have time to, I did not and now rather wished that I had. Watching on a small computer screen while wearing headphones is all right but it does not really replace being able to hear the hunter's gun go off on the left hand side of the room and Bambi's mum thump to the earth on the other, now does it?

Did I just mention headphones in that last paragraph? I think that I did. You may recall that the pair that I was using is rather old and the black pretend leather that used to cover the ear pieces has fallen apart and leaves little black bits of pretend leather all over my ears. They are also not very good at shielding the people around you from whatever you are listening to, and the Missus has complained vociferously in the past that she can hear my music in the bedroom while I am listening to it in the living room. I have also been far too polite to say that, while listening to my music in the living room, I can also hear her complaining vociferously in the bedroom. It was time to find some new ones.

Despite my fairly broad criteria that the headphones I was looking for should produce good sound across the musical range, should not leak the sound out, or let the Missus's vociferous complaints in, and not cost the Earth, I do not think that I have ever found a more difficult research project. I suspect that this is mainly because headphones are such a personal item that it is difficult to provide a truly objective opinion on them.

First it would appear that the vast majority of headphones are produced for bright young things that like their music on the move. Headphones are necessarily lightweight and small for this very purpose. It surprised me greatly that among these, very few manufacturers have the slightest concern that the sounds listened to on their devices, almost by definition in a public place, might be heard by those around the listener; almost none of these devices are leak-proof.

Of the remaining options I was able to whittle down the field to about three likely contenders. When I starting seeking independent reviews of these I could find no two that agreed in their assessments of sound quality, comfort or even whether sound leaked or did not. In the end I had to take an educated guess for the most appropriate, and ended up with a pair that had to be procured from the German manufacturers in Germany; they were German.

They arrived yesterday via two locations in Germany, Barking, Tamworth and Bodmin carried by a company that prides itself on its efficiency! I have to say they are very nice and do not leave little bits of pretend leather on my ears, and I am completely unable to hear any of the Missus's vociferous complaints. I concluded that since I do not hurt anywhere that perhaps she is not complaining vociferously and that I have chosen a pair of headphones that do not leak.

Given that I have been cooped up inside these four walls for far too long I thought that I would make a break for the border and a game of naughty cards at the OS tonight. The boot of death is rather more forgiving at having my foot dangle unsupported than the cast was, although I am told that I should not make a habit of it. The Missus also seemed somewhat keen to see me go; I might have caught the words petulant and grumpy between songs belting through the headphones.

I duly arrived at the OS to discover that they had set up the card table in the bar area below the steps. Had they known that I was attending I might have guessed that this was some psychological ploy, but I had to concede that it was just bad luck. Throughout the first half of the game I thought that this was the run of things for the evening but in the second half I triumphed magnificently. Shame then, that in my glory I made a complete bog of getting up the steps.

Should I ever be awarded the Nobel prize for literature, (please do not scoff; it is so vulgar), I shall be remembered, not for my eloquent prose, but for falling flat on my face in front of the dais on my way to collect my medal.

November 7ᵗʰ - Wednesday

Gosh, if I wrote today up it would look ever so much like yesterday. Is this the way of things to come, I wonder?

The Missus got up late, the mother-in-law took the bleddy hound around and they all went shopping in PZ. The end.

All right, the post lady brought me a new toy to play with. It is not a very exciting toy. It simply allows me to add more exciting toys to my home computer network, as the existing box has run out of plug holes. The whole affair was not very time consuming, as all I had to do was plug it into the electricity, join it to the original box and it just worked. I like it when things just work.

I know that was not ever so exciting, but it did give me an excuse to watch a loud crashy film on the living room television to test my new connections. No, it did not involve Bambi's mother being shot; it was much louder and crashier than that. I also missed the last twenty minutes of it, as the parents-in-law returned just as the bad guy was going to get his just deserts. I suppose it is plausible that the good guy could have been mangled, but the film did not strike me as cerebral as that. I shall probably never know now.

One of the big stories in the newspapers today (the Missus actually had to buy one in town) was the state of the region's bathing waters. Some of the waters, the closest being Wherry Town in Mounts Bay, have been deemed to be unfit against the existing EU standard. In 2015 an even more stringent standard will apply and the much maligned council will be made to put up signs saying, 'do not enter the water or else you will melt', or something along those lines.

The root cause of all this misery, apparently, is that it rained rather a lot recently and dirty things have run off the land and into the sea. The really worrying thing is that our very expensive water company has been charged with making everything all right again. The reason why, we are told, that our water company is very expensive, nay, the most expensive in the land is that they have not long finished a project called Clean Sweep. The objective of Clean Sweep was to ensure that water entering the sea was nice and clean and would meet EU standards.

Let me just summarise for a moment. We are paying the highest water rates in the land to pay for a project that made sure our bathing waters are clean and meet EU standards. Our bathing waters are starting to fail EU standards because it has rained. The company that charges us the highest water rates in the land are being asked to run a project to make sure our bathing waters meet EU standards. Yes, I think I have that now.

So, with that delightful thought in mind I shall take to my bed and probably stay there.

November 8th – Thursday

Up early this morning, by the Missus's clock anyhow, as we have a big adventure before us, well, before me, I suppose. Another trip to the doctor but I tell you this is high adventure for a wounded chap whose normal day is four walls and a book. Actually the book is rather good, a ripping yarn my big sister had sent me, all about this chap with a bell attached to his hat and his friend with huge ears. Sweet, ain't she?

Anyway, I digress slightly. I have negotiated with the NHS to the degree that I no longer have to traipse all the way to the big hospital at Truro, and may now traipse slightly less far to Hayle.

It is a completely different prospect at St Michael's, with a much more personal feel to it. For example, the very nice man at the reception desk offered me a wheelchair to take me to the treatment room, whereas at Treliske I had to plod with my unaccustomed pegs to a much further room without any aid at all. I had barely arrived outside the room, when the doctor stuck his head out and invited me in.

Just in case you are interested, I had the angle of the foot on the boot of death reduced by ten degrees. This may sound fairly straightforward, and for me it was. For the good doctor, however, it was an unimaginable trial, as he was unfamiliar with the operation of the boot of death and it took him more than fifteen minutes to make the adjustment. Even now the foot part does not dip down when I apply pressure to it as it should, meaning I am unable to perform part of my exercise regime. I trust that the physiotherapist who I am seeing on Monday is slightly better informed on boots of death.

We thanked the chap on the reception desk for the use of the very nice chair. It was brand new and had carbon fibre wheels and leather seat with go-faster stripes. He said they were very expensive and, pointedly, that they were collecting for another. I dropped some coins into his box and made a mental note to beware of hospital reception staff bearing wheelchairs; I shall plod next time.

Now, you know full well that you cannot possibly visit Hayle without indulging in a Philps' pasty. When I mentioned this to the Missus I could tell from her expression that she did not hold fully with this tradition. She suggested instead that we voyage to Trevaskis Farm for luncheon for an altogether better class of fare and who was I to argue, she has been there often enough.

For one at such odds with tradition, she was most insistent that we stop at the Costafortune Coffee house tacked onto the end of some big name stores at the Loggan's Moor end of town. Again, I was in no position to argue mainly because she was driving, and my protests would have been no more than wasted hot air. We sat outside as, even in my little boy's trousers that fate has demanded that I still wear, it was reasonably pleasant.

Now, I do not drink very much coffee, or rather I do not drink coffee very often, preferring mostly the life-enhancing properties of Adam's ale or, failing that, any other sort of ale. So, on the odd occasion that I do sample a cup of coffee I feel that it should be done properly and come accompanied with one of those little spiced biscuits that often come with the coffee maker's name upon them. It was therefore something of a disappointment when the Missus emerged from the sliding doors sporting a tray of the steaming beverage with not a hint of biscuit to be seen.

It is most unlike me to voice such disappointment, so I must guess that the Missus read the uncharacteristic look on my visage. All right, there is the slightest possibility that I might have dropped a subtle hint such as, 'where's me bleddy biscuit'. Either way she left me with the coffee while she returned inside to fetch one.

I am sure that you have heard the saying, 'be careful what you wish for', and it is certain that I shall do so in the future. The Missus came back sporting a bag, rather larger than one required for the transport of the small spiced biscuit that I craved. She told me that they had none of the sort I demanded, but had bought a bourbon, a custard cream and a jammy dodger for my delectation. Even then I could not help feeling that there was some disparity between the size of the bag and its apparent contents. Not so, I can assure you. The Bourbon was the size of half a brick and the others in similar proportion. I shall never ask for a biscuit with my coffee again.

Needless to say, I did not eat all of the biscuits or even all of one, as I would never have finished the Trevaskis Farm lunch which was rather special and large. Despite being a little full, it was still very hard to drag myself past the range of cakes they have on offer by the till. What a very naughty place to put them.

After such a lovely morning gallivanting, it was rather a pity that I had to endure twiddling my thumbs while the Lifeboat went out for an exercise in the late afternoon. Given the hour, the excellent Shore Crew suffered something of a shortage of numbers. I am sure no one would have noticed if I had slipped over to run the winch for them with my good foot.

November 9ᵗʰ - Friday

I am very glad that we chose yesterday to explore out in the great wide world. This morning we had bands of light mizzly rain sweeping the bay, and after an interlude of brighter weather the mizzle came back with a vengeance and settled in.

The bleddy hound was unwell during the night and as a consequence I was up with the lark, a very lazy lark I grant you. It was not until later in the day we discovered that the illness was entirely self-inflicted; consumption of tennis balls is not to be recommended. The Missus followed shortly after - getting up, that is, not eating tennis balls - as she had arranged to take the mother-in-law for a hair appointment in St Just. She returned in the interim armed with tasty comestibles, including a McFadden's pasty.

I think I have mentioned before that I have had mixed results from my previous encounters with McFadden's of St Just. On this occasion I must grant them a, 'not bad at all' award, although it was rather dry. The bleddy hound certainly enjoyed the morsel I saved her, and I would not refuse another from them if it were offered.

In all it was a quiet day, which allowed me to poke off some letters that I had been meaning to write for some time. Our International Correspondent must have had a similar moment not so long ago as I received from her a parcel in the post, along with a get well soon card; they have those in her neck of the woods too, it seems. It was not so much the contents of the parcel that was a surprise, although I am looking forward eagerly to reading the history of her private island home, it is more what it was wrapped in. Either our feisty correspondent has fallen on harder times than I imagined and could not stretch to wrapping paper, or she was sending a subliminal call for help, as it was encased in newspaper.

The sheet used was from the island's local newspaper holding a recent date and appeared to be the front page. The main story was from a court report featuring a chap accused of the heinous murder of an islander, robbed at pistol point, shot and his body carelessly hidden under palm fronds at the water's edge. Well, I must tell you, dear reader, my image of a peaceful island paradise and refuge to our International Correspondent evaporated in a flash. A hardened and gritty reporter though she be, I hardly think that this hotbed of vice and depravity is any longer a suitable home for a lady of her sensibilities. I have written to the newly elected President of her land demanding her immediate evacuation and resettlement to a more suitable environment. So hold on MM, help is on its way, just as soon as he has fixed his economic meltdown and mopped up all the water in New York.

Phew, now I am able to rest more easily, I decided to accept a long standing invitation to a curry and cards night somewhere in the locality. The organiser had sensibly offered to send a car to pick me up and, suitably blindfolded so that I cannot reveal the location of the event, I was delivered up.

In a smoke filled room, somewhere close by, the sleazy underbelly of Sennen life gathered. A dreadful crone delivered us drinks and offered around Havana cigars as we pitted our skill and cunning against each other. Over the next five hours I lost my money, shirt, house and the bleddy hound, so it was not all bad. I have yet to tell the Missus she will be living with Big Al from now on, after a tense hand that saw his five aces beat my full house, the swine.

November 10ᵗʰ - Saturday

We had some dark and heavy rain clouds passing through today, and some of them stopped for a bit of a sprinkle. However, a sparkling little day nonetheless and the conditions gave rise to a rather bright display of multiple rainbows.

It was enough to prompt the Missus to take the parents-in-law out shopping, and for lunch up at Trevaskis Farm. I elected to stay put today with the bleddy hound, and we amused ourselves playing variously chess, backgammon and just for kicks a little baccarat for which she wore a black tie for effect. I have given up playing scrabble with her as she makes up the most outrageous words.

And that was the measure of my day, although I managed to watch the most part of *Young Frankenstein*, a film by Mel Brooks that I vividly remember watching with the Aged Parent in the cinema. It is good old fashioned humour and I recall that we were both in stitches watching it. Funny films now seem to be much less subtle.

It was all just marking time for the main event that was, of course, a trip up to the F&L. *Three Minute Warning* was in residence tonight, long standing visitors, and very serious rock players with a good amount of humour. I seem to remember that they were a bit off form the last time they played, so it was good to see that they had introduced a few new tunes and had rediscovered their mojo, whatever one of those is. It also helped that I can now stand up by the bar with the help of a stool to rest my dickie leg upon; I no longer feel an outcast sitting in the corner.

But the deepest cut of all was stepping outside at the end of the evening and looking up at the star studded sky and knowing that I would not be walking home under it. There are some things you just cannot console a poor lad for.

November 11ᵗʰ – Sunday

I wrote to the International Correspondent today to thank her for her present and card, after all it would have been a bit rude just to convey my thanks through this organ.

I chose Sunday to complete this task as I imagined our reporter attending the courtroom day by day to report back the twists and turns of the murder case or, at the very least, to shout encouragement from the side lines such as, 'hang 'em high'. It struck me that I should establish what possible punishment the perpetrator might face, as some States in America still uphold the death penalty.

My research did reveal that the State in which our venerated International Correspondent resides does in fact have a death sentence, one of 33 States that still do. The crime committed unfortunately, or fortunately depending on your point of view, meets the criteria for which a death sentence may be passed down, and the convicted criminal may select from death by electrocution or lethal injection. Since 1976 some 43 people have met their fate in this way, and if the villain of the piece has any hope of clemency he should note that out of a total of 684 death sentences in the State there have been no recorded commutations.

I realise that this is a little gloomy for a pleasant little Sunday in November but I do not get out much. But take heart, if that is your mood, that many States have abandoned their capital punishment policies. Surprisingly, Michigan abolished theirs in 1846 followed by Wisconsin in 1853. Since then a further fifteen States have repealed their Acts including Connecticut which did so this year.

If all that were not bad enough, on this day in 1946 Stevenage was officially designed as Britain's first New Town.

And just to prove I can do happy as well, I had some technical success this morning. Ever since my great computer crash earlier in the year the volume on my computer, at least through headphones, has been held back, restricted and not at all what you want after a Saturday night of heavy rock at the F&L. Last night's poor performance through my new headphones galvanised me to do something about it this morning.

After an hour or so tweaking I had a breakthrough and now the Fleet Foxes, among other venerable musicians, can fry my brains at proper head splitting volume.

Well they would have been able to; the Missus has reasoned that since the old headphones, her headphones, breathed their terminal breath under my usage the new ones are now, by rights, hers and has commandeered them. I am sure there is a lesson to be learned there somewhere. When I work out what it is I shall let you know.

There, you cannot say that reading The Diary is not an education, at least on occasion.

November 12th - Monday

A grey and mizzly start down here in The Cove this morning following on from a thick band of rain that came through over night. Of course, it is not allowed to rain here during the day, although sometimes it forgets, like between April and August this year.

The sea state was good enough for the whole fleet to take to sea during the low water period in the morning. I assume that in the main they are still hunting the squid. There was quite a ground sea running towards high water in the early afternoon and we had one lucky fisherman at the end of the breakwater who narrowly avoided getting wet, or worse, by coming away just before the sea came over the top.

I had some excitement myself today, as I was allowed out to go to my first physiotherapy appointment at West Cornwall Hospital in Penzance. I had fully expected to be pulled and twisted and made to feel extremely uncomfortable, but I was disappointed. All he did was take off the boot of death and tell me about the pulling and twisting and being made to feel uncomfortable in the time ahead, when the boot of death was removed for good. Nevertheless, I still have to attend weekly, so that the angle that my foot sits at in relation to my leg may be upwardly adjusted.

To demonstrate his intentions, he adjusted the boot of death then and there, so that I am another ten degrees nearer a normal attitude. Some might say that I will never attain a normal attitude, but that is another story. The chap did however have knowledge of boots of death, and fixed it so that the foot will dip if I am able to exert sufficient pressure in a downwards direction – I can hardly wait.

The mist was lifting as we made our way home again; my little freedoms are very short lived. Not so for the Missus, who took the bleddy hound up to Land's End when we got back. I am not entirely sure she has exactly the right idea about this dog walking lark, as she drove up there. I shall have to have words with the bleddy hound and perhaps between us we can put her on the right track.

I am rather hoping that the weather is clement tomorrow and I can get the Missus out of bed, for I have plans, I tell you, plans.

November 13th - Tuesday

I know that I made it look rather like it was my idea yesterday, but it was actually the Missus who suggested a trip out to Praa Sands today. Well, she suggested Praa Sands, but I knew she really meant Perranuthnoe and that suited me just fine. I knew that while she was running around a wind blown beach with the bleddy hound I would be up in The Cabin partaking of cups of tea and a bit of cake.

Wind blown it was indeed, and the choice of Perranuthnoe was not an ideal one as the wind was coming in southerly today and under a sullen grey sky. At least it was not raining. My bit of cake, however, was quickly translated to a very nice bacon roll, as the tides dictated that we should be there as early as possible to give the Missus the best chance of having some beach to play on and the bleddy hound some rock pools to splash around in.

Having spent the best part of an hour in an increasingly warm and busy Cabin I decided that I would take a stroll (clank and hop really) down to make sure she had not been swallowed up by the incoming tide. At the top of the slipway there is a very handy concrete platform with a wooden bench, and I plonked myself down for a gaze at the still very much active bleddy hound as she cavorted on the beach. Also at the stop of the slipway was a lady talking to a man from the much maligned council.

I had a scowl from the Missus when I suggested going straight home knowing full well she had neither coffee nor bun, so we retired back to The Cabin. We tried sitting outside as it was still quite busy inside, but that southerly wind really was quite insistent. As luck would have it a table became free and we pottered inside for some shelter and another cup of tea for me.

The lady who had been at the top of the slip with the man from the much maligned council was in there as well, and when he left she turned to me to say that she really wished that I had not sat on the bench. I raised an inquisitive eyebrow that is sometimes more effective that swiping my crutch across the back of her nut. She explained that the land on which the bench has been erected (can you erect a bench?) belonged to her, as did The Cabin I surmised, having looked at the plan she showed me. Still at a loss as to her complaint, she went on to tell me that the parish council had erected the bench and the surrounding railings without recourse to herself, and she was clearly miffed.

She had the platform installed specifically for wheelchair users to sit and observe the beach without having to attempt the steep slipway, which was highly commendable. I did not like to say, particularly as I was sitting in her canteen and had not yet finished my tea, that I thought the wheelchair user might have some difficulty in reaching her platform as the slope to it was hard enough negotiated on poles. Or rather they probably would get down there, if they did not overshoot at some speed, but they would have been very hard pressed to get back up again.

Her jocular complaint that I had sat on the bench indicated to the man from the much maligned council that some elements of society did find having a bench there of some benefit. I made a mental note to ensure that I carried out some research before employing the use of a bench in future or, at least, to have a look around to see who is watching.

Despite all that I very much enjoyed my trip abroad and we were out for quite a considerable period; it was nearly four o'clock by the time we got back. The bleddy hound slept all the way back so it was clear that she enjoyed herself too.

November 14ᵗʰ – Wednesday

What an absolutely splendid day; blue sky with just a hint of haze on the horizon and a big sea to wonder at. There were large rolling waves caught in the light and, as the east wind peeled off the top of their breaking crests, they showered rainbows behind them like great swirling multicoloured capes.

The Missus was fortunate enough to be down amongst it all early in the afternoon as she ran the bleddy hound down across the beach. She must have known that I was envious, as she brought some home with her. She had stopped to take a picture of the crashing waves down at the water line and found herself in the middle of one. She was soaked through when she came home, and so was the bleddy hound.

November 17ᵗʰ – Saturday

It was the sort of day that any Lifeboat Coxswain worth his salt would have called for a Lifeboat exercise. It was no surprise therefore, that at nine o'clock this morning the Lifeboat rattled down the slipway on an exercise. The aim today was to work with Cape National Coastwatch Institute in finding a buoy set adrift from the boat. Two members of Cape NCI were taken along onboard to observe the whole exercise.

Had the timing been better, the excellent Shore Crew would have indulged in a spot of breakfast at The Little Bo Café before recovery. As it was the café did not open early enough on this occasion, and the breakfast was postponed until after recovery. This proved to be a good plan, as a few members of the Boat Crew joined with the Head Launcher's party to enjoy a sumptuous breakfast together for a change. So cordial was the arrangement that you might have though some peace envoy had a hand in it.

It was after breakfast that the trouble started, when the Head Launcher's party repaired to the flat for a post breakfast coffee. I probably have myself to blame as somehow the conversation tripped over a certain vampire movie, and I mentioned that I liked the theme tune from a television based series of the same ilk. Head Launcher wholeheartedly agreed with me and announced that he wanted that very theme tune to be inserted into his mobile telephone to be used as a ringing tone.

Now, it is the Missus who is the expert in this field and as Head Launcher had not the first clue how to operate his telephone (that often extends to answering it when any of us call him) it fell to her to perform this task. Our next problem was where to acquire the theme music from and, as there appears to be many sources, some of them legitimate and some of them rather less so, which one to chose. This itself took a considerable amount of time and effort.

Having acquired the music and downloaded it onto my computer the next step was to transfer it to Head Launcher's mobile telephone. While the Missus could load the tune onto her Bramley smart telephone, it appears that Bramley, while very good at talking to other Bramley products, refuses point blank to talk to any other product outside the Bramley stable. We eventually managed this seemingly Herculean task by using three computer and mobile telephone products and two methods of wired and wireless communication.

We have no doubt that Head Launcher will still not answer his telephone if we call him, as he will be too interested in listening to his new ringing tone.

A fragile peace reigned afterwards. Having plundered the depths of our combined technical knowledge, Head Launcher left for an appointment which our kindly given efforts had apparently made him late for. The peace did not last long. Just as I settled to listen to some music on my headphones that I had managed to wrest from the Missus's clutches (mainly because she had taken the bleddy hound out) our new guest crashed through the door.

Horseracing and football commentators employ a volume and verbal compression to be wondered at. Believe me, they are but mere amateurs, playing with a skill they have little command or knowledge of. If you wish to hear a true exponent, a zen master in the art, then drop around to the flat during the next week. My new, non-leaking, super slick headphones? I may as well have had toilet tissue over my ears.

It was with no small measure of relief that I trekked up (sorry, the Missus took me up) to the F&L to have *Even Nine* fill my tympanic cavities and sooth my cochleae with loud and sympathetic home written sounds.

They started up late but that is forgiven. The first two tracks, their own, sounded like Snow Patrol on speed, if I knew what that meant. Of course, in my youth, I never inhaled, or, erm, swallowed, honest. From there they moved effortlessly into some soft punk of the Buzzcocks and back to some of their own.

They were energetic, electrifying and utterly brilliant songsmiths and cunning musicians. Most of the songs were their own and they mixed them so simply with bits of Killers, The Who and, just before the break, a sparkling rendition of Midnight Oil's Beds are Burning with a guitar solo so sharp and keen. The lead singer and bassist melded seamlessly with lead guitar and their voices so clearly complimented each other. It was no surprise to find out later that they were brothers.

Not only were they good, so good that I spent a whole five pounds on buying their disc, but they were loud too. I do rather hope that the incessant ringing in my ears persists through tomorrow morning at the very least.

November 18ᵗʰ - Sunday

Something of a busy little day down in The Cove. The fishing fleet were out in numbers, although I could not see them at first as there was a fair amount of swell and white capped waves. There looked to be a few happy diners at Little Bo as well.

We did not escape either, although we were busy in a grim sort of way as the father-in-law is a brae bit poorly. We have had teams of medical professionals queued up to provide attentive care and medicines to the old boy for most of the day. All right, a doctor turned up first thing and a couple of nurses rolled up later in the afternoon, but for all that they were busy little demons working away for some while.

I think I must be coming down with something too. The Missus announced that she was heading into town to the big supermarket as we had nothing in for our tea. It might have been the heat or the lack of beer, but I suddenly realised that my mouth was working and my voice was saying that I wanted to go too. There was a stunned silence for a moment or two. I could tell that the Missus was trying to work out if I was speaking in jest or I whether I had turned into more of a gibbering wreck than normal, or that a crack had opened in the space/time continuum. In the end she did the right thing and talked me down gently. I am feeling much better now.

I think what caused it was that I had finished the last book that my sister had sent me. This has left me weak and vulnerable to the continuous rumble that seems to accompany our latest visitor wherever she goes. At one point today she asked if she had dozed off in our easy chair. I said that it was entirely likely as I recalled a period of silence that preceded the question.

She left with the Missus to go shopping, a period during which I hoped my ears would stop bleeding. I gave the Missus strict instructions to return with some reading material or failing that some Blu Tac, which is ideal for sticking in your ear 'oles. Anyway, I wished them well and told the Missus to take as long as she liked upon which instruction she fair near fainted.

She prepared a cracking little tea with the morsels she had collected. She is good like that, the Missus.

November 19ᵗʰ – Monday

Not only did I get a trip out to St Just today but, later in the afternoon, I got to go to Penzance as well. Clearly this was not a pleasure trip, but you cannot have it all. It was my weekly visit to the physiotherapist to have the boot of death adjusted, so that my foot is now another ten degrees up from where it was last week. My man delivered some excellent news: I only have to put up with the boot of death for another three weeks if all goes well. After next week, I should be able to put some weight on the leg I have not used for seven weeks; I anticipate some periods of being inadvertently horizontal.

I am going to have to think up a suitably outlandish story of how I came to be sporting the boot of death. Today, as I waited in the hospital reception area for the Missus to finish her shopping trip, a lady with a small child asked what I had done to my leg and how the accident came about. Having briefly explained the Lifeboat incident, I was somehow elevated to instant super-hero status. The lady proceeded to tell everyone that came to sit in the vicinity with increasing embellishment, until at last I had saved several families and babes in arms from certain death in monstrous seas while fighting off attacks by great white sharks with total disregard for my own life. No wonder they gave me a medal.

I was very pleased when the Missus turned up and I could extricate my heroic form from the clutches of the maddened fanatics. I half expected my clothes to be torn from me by hands eager to gather the merest fragment of memorabilia. When I eventually poddle off, I shall instruct my trustees to ensure that my body is encased in concrete to prevent my grave being defiled by relic hunters.

I can only imagine that the good people of The Cove had been misinformed as to the time of my arrival, as there were no palm fronds covering the road as we drove through. The only throng greeting me was the throng that currently lives in our flat, and they have long since been inured to living with a demi-god. It was all a bit of an anti-climax really.

Part of the reason that the Missus ran into town during my hospital appointment was to see if she could find the books that I have been seeking. Unfortunately, she was unsuccessful and after I had scoured the Internet for them, I note that the only place they are available is on the website of the wholesaler we use.

I think I have spotted an opportunity and shall be acquiring a small stock of these books to sell on our own website. Of course, there is the possibility that they are not generally available because no one wants them, which, if I buy a substantial stock, is bound to be the case.

In the meantime I still have a few pages left of another book I am finishing off, not that I had much opportunity to read it. Another crowd of medical professionals came to visit the father-in-law late in the afternoon as he had languished all day, spurning the best efforts of the mother-in-law and the Missus and giving them great cause for alarm and distress. Within a few minutes of their arrival he responded, Lazarus like, to the nurses' instruction to sit up and take sustenance and is now making leaps and bounds down the road of recovery.

He will, no doubt, be up and about tomorrow and all over the television remote control.

November 20ᵗʰ – Tuesday

There is a chap down on Lizard who has got himself a licence to harvest seaweed. They must have some special and rare seaweed down there, because if he had asked us he could have had as much as he wanted from here for free. In fact the excellent Shore Crew would, I am sure, find a few bob if he were to take it from the slipways after a bit of ground sea.

Apparently, the fellow has been a shipping lawyer and lecturer and fancies a change of air. The plan will be to dry-cure the weed, powder it and sell it on to top restaurateurs who will use it for all sorts of nefarious purposes, probably. His licence means he must demonstrate that his work does not have any adverse ecological effects. Quite how you prove that I would not know, maybe take the seaweed away and hope nothing else dies.

Anyway, if you see a chap down on Lizard shovelling geet loads of seaweed give him a wave and a shout. He goes by the name of Algie – oh, please yourselves.

Meanwhile, down in The Cove, nothing happened. Our rain cleared out quite early but it was still grey and dismal. I was confined to barracks, which left me climbing the walls. It is good exercise for upper body strength – something that I do not need at the moment. After seven weeks on crutches I have biceps that Charles Atlas would have been proud of. You must remember Charles Atlas, the bodybuilder. He died at Long Beach in 1972 when mourners came from miles around to kick sand in his grave.

Well, I am sure you can see where this is going, so I had better pack my poles and head off to the OS for the obligatory game of Tuesday night cards before it is all too late. Thus far I have been fortunate that it has not been raining during my transport to the end of the road. I am not entirely sure that the father-in-law's wheelchair is waterproof or, if it is, whether wet weather tyres should be fitted before the journey.

I wrote that last paragraph shortly before I left and shortly after the weather man said that it was not going to rain in this neck of the woods. So when I popped my head outside the pub door at half time, I was somewhat surprised to find that it got wet, very wet indeed.

I had to telephone the Missus to ask her to bring my waterproof coat with her when she picked me up. On the seat of the wheelchair is a block of foam or sponge, if you will. I am sure you can imagine the effect. The Missus certainly did and rather cleverly she used my coat to cover the seat. We did not need the wet weather tyres, although I was nearly turned out at the bottom of a particularly sharp slope that, in dry weather, I would have bounded over on my poles.

I promise you that this is what passes for excitement in my life. It was certainly more exciting tha the cards, that is for sure.

November 21ˢᵗ – Wednesday

It was the sort of day to run out along the beach or out to foreign parts for a long walk with the bleddy hound; to investigate new and exciting locations, new peoples and civilisations, to ... well, it would have been had there not been a myriad of other priorities and appointed tasks to carry out.

The Missus took our ailing van into the garage for a bit more mending today. The knocking that we had, turned into a different knocking after the CV joint had been fixed and we were told it was probably the inner CV joint this time. Had I known that we had an inner and an outer I might have asked him to replace both at the same time. Naturally, whenever the garage mechanic test drove the van the knocking dutifully kept silent.

Talking of knocking, we still have a line of medical professionals coming to our door. Just so she does not get left out, our visitor took mother-in-law up to St Just surgery for her anti-flu injection. The Missus started cleaning and tidying the flat and I started to wonder that we might have some royal personage attending the father-in-law this afternoon. Apparently, this is the sort of thing you do if the doctor herself is expected; nurses, unfortunately, must cope with the general squalor that we live in.

I think it must be suffering early onset of diaeta claustum morbus, the main indicator of which is the irrational desire to utter diatribes of complete gibberish while standing on one leg. It is also known as Long John Silver's disease after the first identifiable case or more commonly cabin fever.

The Aged Parent has clearly identified the early signs and has sent Red Cross parcels containing books in the hope that they might distract me from my course towards oblivion. Both books are mighty tomes, one of which is a currently popular story book. The other is a factual study that at least will be educational. After reading it I will be a veritable expert on the habitats and behaviours of the dung beetles of the lower Amazon delta; it promises to be a cracking good read.

November 22ⁿᵈ - Thursday

It was a wild and windy day and no mistake. The sea was boiling from first light, yes I was up that early, (all right, it does not get light until around half seven so it was not that early) and the wind, although pretty placid in The Cove was howling over the top of us – 62 miles per hour recorded on the Isles of Scilly. We were dry for most of the morning but the rain in the afternoon more than made up for that.

I did not get much time today to start reading my new remedy for cabin fever. It seems that The Old Boathouse is the place to be seen for any self-respecting medical professional these days. We did not have to summon a doctor today; one turned up unannounced mid morning to check on his patient. I have to say that we cannot have any complaints regarding NHS service in this neck of the woods.

The Missus, conscious that we had not taken our guest out to play since she has been here, decided that we should lunch out at Travaskis Farm, whether our guest wanted to or not. Initially I thought that she had read my mind yesterday and had planned an excursion to relieve my pent up tension. As I was only included as an after-thought, I can dismiss any hope in that regard.

Although it was dry when we left, we could not have chosen a worse day to venture out. Radio Pasty was advising that anyone driving should only sally forth if necessary amidst reports of floodings and tree falls. I am sorry, but I regard me going outside my four walls to be therapeutic and therefore utterly necessary. They were not far wrong, by the way, we were fair near blown off the road on the Hayle by-pass, and whilst we sat and fattened ourselves on over-indulgent fare the heavens opened around us.

On the way back our half of the road down to the Loggan's Moor roundabout was awash with a muddy river running down the hill. There was standing water in a number of places and, although less severe, there did not appear to be any let up in the rain.

We stopped at a well known clothing emporium on the way back, as I need a pair of training shoes for when the boot of death is eventually removed. I also need a pair of shorts, as the ones I am currently wearing are the only ones that I have that will fit over my encumbrance – that is the boot of death in case you were wondering. I was to be disappointed on both counts as first, they do not selling training shoes at all and secondly, asking for shorts in the middle of November attracts the sort of expression reserved expressly for confrontation with escapees from a lunatic asylum. I bought some jogging trousers instead, which I thought must be the ultimate in irony.

The Missus and the guest had already decided that they would eat at the Meadery at Trewellard this evening, or at least bring home a take-away from there. With this in mind, I ate heartily at Trevaskis and elected to have a little homemade soup in the evening. To bolster this diminished repast I had the Missus buy me a cake to take home from the farm which was the size of a small mountain. You will notice the use of the past tense, as I ate the lot and afterwards felt as sick as a dog. I am sure that this will see me through the evening.

Indeed, I feel the size of a small mountain now. I shall not need to eat for a week and, if I had donated the food, I am certain that a village in a poor part of the world would probably have dined fitfully for the same period.

Not that any of this matters a jot, for in the matter of the OS quiz we manfully struggled to a notable second place behind two other teams who had joint first. Not that any of that mattered a jot, for in the matter of the 'chase the ace' draw, I won. Yah boo sucks etcetera. Naturally, I was happy to share my good fortune and especially with Head Launcher with whom I divided the spoils in the same proportion that he did with his win some time ago.

I know he does not take this to heart as, after he had dropped me off at home, he opened his window and kindly said that he hoped I did not fall down our steps and break my neck, which was a nice thought, and waved goodbye. I think he must have been holding something as he was only able to wave with two fingers.

November 23rd - Friday

Another of the laziest of days. I watched as another of the long line of medical help came and went. The father-in-law is well on the road to recovery now and we can probably expect his presence in the living room any day now. He must be getting better, as he managed to find the strength to watch an entire episode of *Last of the Summer Wine*.

It was the sort of day that we should have gone out and about, what with a welcome break in the weather and nothing better to do. This, of course, was not possible after all I went out yesterday and two days in a row would just be gratuitous.

The Missus made her escape into town in the afternoon. She came back with a pair of training shoes for me, unfortunately a size too small despite the fact that they had the appropriate size written inside of them. I am sure it is a conspiracy by the small children working in backstreet sweatshops. One day they will march upon us in the safe knowledge that we will all be crippled by wearing shoes a size too small for us.

As you might imagine, sitting on a sofa all day long reading or watching the occasional television programme does not provide much scope for interesting Diary writing. At least the chattering dogging my left ear has gone; the guest left this morning. It cannot have been the most exciting holiday she has ever had either.

Any more of this nonsense and I might be compelled to start knitting.

November 24th - Saturday

Even if I had intended to fight my way out of the vicious circle of laziness today, I might well have changed my mind. It was a thoroughly miserable day, raining from the outset and the bay thick with grey mist, or was it just the rain we could not see through?

As the Missus had an extended lie in this morning and with breakfast time long gone, I threw myself on the mercy of The Little Bo Café to provide some succour. This did not quite extend to the effort of pulling on my waterproofs, bumping down the steps on my behind and dragging my withered leg through their door to prostrate myself before their altar of fine food. Much as I realise that such a display of heroism might well have induced a few swoonings among the young waitresses, I elected instead to be slightly more humble and use the telephone to place my order.

My doorstep delivered sausage, bacon and onion toasted roll was so much the better for having the bleddy hound shut in the bedroom with the Missus; she usually insists that I share some with her, the bleddy hound, that is, not the Missus. I did leave the empty wrapper on display, simply to demonstrate that treats are not hers by right. Now, I know what you are thinking, dear reader, but she is not a poor little dog at all; she is spoiled beyond measure. Someone in this family has to be cruel to be kind, although I do admit that on this occasion I was purely being cruel.

In any event Julie, our postie, always brings with her some little treats for the bleddy hound, even when we do not have mail. In fact, she is on leave next week and has brought a bag full to cover her absence. I cannot think of a reason why anyone should lodge a complaint against her for bringing her own dog along in her van while she delivers mail. It seemed like such an act of pettiness against someone with such an imbedded sense of kindness.

To add insult to injury to the poor hard done by bleddy hound, the Missus took her out for a run up at Land's End in the afternoon. She was very keen when she realised she was being taken out but that was before she had stepped outside the door. It took her around three milliseconds to realise it was raining and immediately came back in again. The little bedraggled and lagged bleddy hound that returned some hour later was a very sorry sight to behold. How I laughed.

But then it was my turn. It had rained solidly all day long and was certainly not letting up to give me a clear run down the steps and into the van without getting wet. There was some powerful wind swirling which nearly took the van door off its hinges one minute and crashing shut upon my legs the next as I struggled up onto the seat.

The Missus had already warned that there was a torrent of water coming down the hill when she returned earlier in the day. We reckoned that it would be worse by evening time, which it was, but we had not expected, first, the scattering of large stones on the first corner and then, further up, that the bank had collapsed and was heaped up on the road along with a bush or two.

Preceding vehicles had cut a way through the mud, so we had little issue in getting past the obstruction, fortunately. It did not occur to me, of course, that if we had trouble getting to the F&L in the little distance we had to travel that others, from further afield, would have even greater difficulty and, indeed, would have been utterly foolhardy to try. Nevertheless, there was a small group from Newlyn who were, who had come to see the band and the band, who were not, and had quite sensibly cancelled.

Never mind, there were a few hardy souls who had trekked in from the locality and we employed ourselves in, I hesitate to say intelligent conversation, but conversation all the same that was refreshing for a Saturday night.

The disappointed band of revellers from Newlyn stayed the distance, despite become increasingly concerned about their journey home. It did not help their condition that someone from home had sent them a picture of the bridge at Newlyn that was up to the parapet with boiling floodwater and presumably cutting off the Mousehole road completely. There were similar problems reported on the back road through Polggia with a deepening pool cutting off the road at Skewjack Farm.

The rain ceased at some point during the evening, but the wind hung on in there to give me a hard time getting out of the van on my return home. I dare say we will hear more tales from around about. As dark and stormy nights go this one was certainly one of the filthiest in recent times.

November 25ᵗʰ - Sunday

It was quite an innocuous looking morning, so much so I half expected to see a dove with an olive branch in its beak. On reflection that is hardly likely to be of any comfort as I imagine that it would have had to fly quite a distance to find an olive tree.

We did, however, enjoy quite a peaceful morning and listened to the reports of doom and disaster coming in from across the country. The pictures from Newlyn were quite shocking, especially when you consider that at low water there was nothing much stopping the water from flowing out.

The Missus announced that she was going up to what passes for a large shopping centre around here at Hayle. It was purely a practical trip to exchange a shower stool that she bought the last time we were there. Although I have managed to date with a foot stool, this item will make showering for me much more comfortable (please ladies, a little decorum) apparently, and anyway the Missus wants her footstool back that she uses to reach high shelves in the kitchen.

I stowed away in the van, as even a mediocre shopping trip is better than the alternative. I was expecting to see scenes of havoc that last night's wind and rain had wrought on the countryside, but other than a few piles of pebbles, sediment from rivers of runoff from the fields and a few puddles of standing water, there was very little.

The further east we travelled the worse the weather became. It was not long before the radio news announced another bout of apocalyptic rain and high winds moving in from the west. Weather warnings have been issued and places that had already borne the brunt yesterday look like they will be in for it again this evening.

It was raining heavily as we came back into Sennen and the skies in front of us were hung with black menacing clouds. It looked like a scene from an over-enthusiastic disaster movie until the rain got even heavier and you could not see the sky at all. It eased off a little to allow me to bump up the steps, but continued in varying degrees of heaviness through the rest of the day and into the night.

Time, then, to batten down the hatches and consider ourselves lucky that we live in a first floor flat. Come to think, we

691

are a ground floor flat at the back but at least our foundations are solid rock, which is not the same as rock solid but hopefully we shall still be at this spot in the morning.

We will try hard not to consider that today is the anniversary of the Great Storm of 1703 that was the worst ever recorded in southern Britain.

November 26ᵗʰ – Monday

It was evident from the howling of the wind that it was our turn to get a bit of a slap in the face today. Quite often, with the wind coming straight at us, it sounds much worse than it actually is. Today, however, it was just as bad as it sounded reaching nearly sixty miles per hour in gusts. The wind had turned to the north during the night and was clearly dissatisfied at the way residents of The Cove had set their bins out down the street as it decided to move them about a bit.

The sea did not look too bad first thing while at low water but later in the day it was a boiling mass of white peaks and troughs laced through with ribbons of wind blown surf. Just to add a little edge to the proceedings the rain came with it in fits and starts.

It was no time to be faint hearted as I had my weekly appointment with the physiotherapist today. Fortunately, it was not raining much when we headed off to PZ and had abated again when we got back. In the meantime my foot was straightened by another ten degrees and it is now apparently at 90 degrees to my leg, although it feels and looks nothing of the sort. I shall have to get my set square out later and test it.

I now have carte blanche to place my full weight upon this pin and, should it prove possible, to walk about without the aid of sticks, at least inside where the landing will be soft.

I have never before had to consider the inherent mechanics involved in the act of walking. So, having placed my worse foot forward with a modicum of weight placed upon it and swung forward my best foot, I had absolutely no idea what came next. I had to study the minute detail of every flex of muscle and the action of each joint on my good leg to determine what I should do with the bad one. I have come to the conclusion that walking is not quite as simple as it looks.

The other consideration, and one that merely exacerbates the process, is that the sole of the boot of death is around three inches thick. Should I be able to overcome the technical issues related to the normal walking process, unless I can find a platform shoe for the other foot, I can only imagine that any motion at all will be circular and in an anti-clockwise direction.

There may, of course, be advantages: I can traverse slopes where the rise is on my left with ease, for example. A walk along the South West Coast Path from the direction of Bude would be a synch, I am sure.

I had to wait in the main reception area again for the Missus to return. I sat out of the way this time and tried, in my luminous bright yellow waterproof jacket, to make myself as inconspicuous as possible. No, of course it did not work. I was wearing a luminous bright yellow waterproof jacket, for heaven's sake.

A chap sporting his own pair of sticks and platform boots, that at present might be extremely useful, came across and asked if he could pose some questions to me. He said that he was acting on behalf of the Care Quality Commission and wished to garner responses from patients regarding their experiences to match against the more scientific analysis carried out with the hospital management. I was happy to help, since my own experience has been nothing but positive across all the contact I have had.

The only negative experience I had was with the Missus who said she had been waiting for twenty minutes for me; during my interview I had been unable to look out for her.

The Missus went out again not long after we had got back to take the mother-in-law to look at a flat that they had placed a bid for in the much maligned council's home allocation service. It was something of a procedural visit as the supervisor had already warned them that the flat was far too small for a couple and barely suitable for a single person. It seems that the administrative process to have the flat reclassified is too onerous to pursue.

And there was me thinking that it would all be over by Christmas. Looks like I will have to order a bigger turkey.

November 27ᵗʰ - Tuesday

The wind persisted all night until the morning when it started to rain heavily as well, which was nice. Rather than get out today it was obviously the thing to do to have people visit.

First up we had a new lady doctor arrive to have a geek at the father-in-law. She was young, red headed and turned up in a smart sports car. "Well, I say. Hello", (to be read in your best Leslie Philips). I had considered asking the Missus to ring the surgery and ask if I could change doctors, but there again I cannot run very fast at present.

She gave the old boy the once over and declared him fit as a fiddle and that he needed to get up and move about a bit and come and join us again in the living room, if only for an hour or so each day. Father-in-law was very responsive, for some reason, and later got up for a jog around the block. This new doc must have healing hands, or something. The visit must have been infectious, as I was able to slip into the kitchen, make a sandwich and carry it myself back to the living room, tripod-like; I only needed to use the one pole.

The Missus once again tripped off into town today, ostensibly to change my new training shoes into ones that actually fit. All this gallivanting off is rather rubbing salt into the wounds, especially when she arrived back with about a dozen shopping bags. If anything is going to encourage me back to full health it is the thought that I might be able to discourage her from all this impulse spending. All right, I also believe in the tooth faerie and the possibility of porcine aviation.

Our second visitor of the day, if you do not count the parcel delivery man who insisted that he could not deliver our parcel to the flat as it was addressed to the shop, was a very nice lady from the much maligned council's housing team. As you know I am trying to find the parents-in-law a suitable flat in Thurso, which I have told the Missus is a small hamlet near Sancreed. The lady from the much maligned council, who has eventually recognised their plight, is helping us to increase the parents-in-law's chances of being allocated a home a bit larger than the shoe box they saw on Monday.

She arrived shortly after half past three, with two forms that needed to be completed. The questions asked fully examined the ins and outs of the last few inches of a hen's digestive tract, such was the depth of their inquisition. When she left at gone five o'clock, she was fair weighed down by all the paperwork and supporting documentation.

Interestingly these workers employ a safety feature that requires them to telephone the office at an appointed time to reassure their co-workers that they have not succumbed to any harm Clearly, this is an essential procedure if, as I suspect, they have to visit some of the more unsavoury characters in the community. I am sure that it works very well when the people in the office have not all gone home at four o'clock.

My new found two-leg cavorting was not entirely the result of our new doctor's visit earlier in the day, I must confess. A long time reader and veteran medical man, after reading of my issues with the mechanics of walking, was able to provide some very useful coaching. I employed his advice later on my trip to the OS for my usual Tuesday night cards and was able to reach there without assistance.

I will telephone him today to ask if he has any suitable tips for not coming last at poker.

November 28ᵗʰ - Wednesday

What a very pretty day for a change, although I suppose there is a certain charm and visual attractiveness to big dramatic rainstorms too. It was the sort of day to cast caution to the winds and drag the body out to enjoy the spectacle and revel in nature's bountiful gifts. It was that sort of day, but it was also bleddy freezing, so I stayed at home in the relative warmth.

The Missus dutifully went out to run the bleddy hound around the Harbour. Then she went out again to take the neighbour's hound around as she discovered while she was out that our neighbour is unwell. The Missus was wrapped up like an Arctic explorer; I have no idea what she will wear when the chill really sets in.

I am not looking forward to it. If it gets too much colder I will be bullied into turning the heating on. The parents-in-law are already starting to look a little blue. Maybe I will drop a couple of hints about the price of electricity and their old codger's heating allowance.

Mind you I took some hitherto untried dramatic action a couple of days ago. There had been a much heralded initiative by a number of bodies including the Eden Project and the local NHS trusts to form a collective to bid for power from the energy companies at a lower rate than we could individually attain. It seemed like a ripping idea, although it was also supported by the much maligned council and the St Awful beer company, which was a tad disconcerting.

Anyway, I left it until the last moment as I rather thought that I had committed to a two year deal with my current supplier. However when I checked my online account the termination date was marked with "n/a" so I took the plunge and accepted the Cornwall Together offer and switched my electricity supplier – for the flat anyway.

There is still time for it to go horribly wrong, and I suspect that after the year long contract is up the new company will exact its revenge for daring to gang up against it. Nevertheless, the principle was sound and the project is looking for new areas to pit itself against.

As I clearly did not get out at all I shall have to resort to a bit of William Blake to get me out of trouble since he was born today in 1757. This poem is all about a visitor to Cornwall who gets lost and how a friendly soul finds her and helps light the way for her German motor car to guide her back over the Tamar. Quite appropriate, I thought.

Once a dream did weave a shade
O'er my angel-guarded bed,
That an emmet lost its way
Where on grass methought I lay.

Troubled, wildered, and forlorn,
Dark, benighted, travel-worn,
Over many a tangle spray,
All heart-broke, I heard her say:

'Oh my children! do they cry,
Do they hear their father sigh?
Now they look abroad to see,
Now return and weep for me.'

Pitying, I dropped a tear:
But I saw a glow-worm near,
Who replied, 'What wailing wight
Calls the watchman of the night?

'I am set to light the ground,
While the beetle goes his round:
Follow now the beetle's hum;
Little wanderer, hie thee home!'

November 29ᵗʰ - Thursday

Recriminations have started surrounding the floods in Newlyn. The main complaint is that sandbags were not readily available. Now, in retrospect the good old days of Penwith District Council, a supply of over 600 bags were held locally to be distributed quickly to where they were needed. Unfortunately, centralisation has taken its toll. The much maligned council has been quoted in the press as stating that sand bags would be made available in times of emergency on an as needed basis, in fact they actually said the request would be looked at sympathetically, whatever that means. However, sand bags would not be made available on the results of a bad forecast or even an Environment Agency flood warning.

So that is clear then. When the flood water is lapping at your doorstep that is the time to call up the much maligned council. Well, no actually, as this is roughly what happened except no one could get through to the emergency line as it was inundated.

This sort of policy making seems to be all the rage. The EU was happy to provide millions of Euros to build fish processing plants in Spain that could cope with 300 tons of mackerel an hour. At the same time they levied quotas on the fishing fleet that would ensure nowhere near this volume would ever get to the factory; a stunning example of joined up thinking.

However, some of the complaints coming from Newlyn might be a little unfair. While they have been flooded before it has always been from the sea on spring tides and with strong southerlies, of which on this occasion there was no risk; the river has never before given them a problem.

None of this pontificating, of course, helps anyone that was knee deep in muddy flood water on the night. Due credit should be awarded to the Coop, though. No sooner than the flood had abated, they were cleaned up and open for business.

On the other leg I seem to be fully operational on one pole now, in the flat at least. Stairs are still a bit of an issue, even being able to use both feet to balance upon, especially those leading down from the flat. I did give them a bit of a test but the treads are quite narrow and the boot of death quite long.

However, I did manage to get up them in an upright condition when I returned home from the OS quiz in the evening. I am going with the theory that a few beers improves my balance and make the steps deeper and my boot of death shorter. I will be imbibing heavily before I leave the flat tomorrow to see if it works for the descent. I will get the Missus to stand at the bottom in case I fall in a heap to the ground alongside the shattered remnants of my theory.

December 1ˢᵗ - Saturday

At last, a day when lots of things happened; shame I cannot be fagged to write about it.

Oh, go on then. First up, a Lifeboat training exercise scheduled perfectly for half past nine in the morning. Perfectly, because by the time the excellent Shore Crew had prepared for the recovery, the Little Bo Café was open and welcoming of *very* excellent (I was included) Shore Crew members. Head Launcher invited himself up to the flat for a preparatory cup of coffee before we headed off for a spiffing breakfast next door.

Perfectly also, because by the time we had finished breakfast it was time for me to head up to the F&L for the Feast Day shoot. Not that I was taking part in any shooting, more is the pity, but I was in the seat to take entrance monies and set out the shooting order. With a crisp, chill wind blowing across the car park I was sitting pretty in a cattle trailer with my cash box and paperwork.

Despite the fact that the trailer was sparkling clean there was a certain aroma in the air from the Feast Hunt that had gathered earlier in the same spot. Regardless of whether you are pro or anti hunt there is no denying a certain splendour in the pageantry involved, not that I have ever seen it as I have never been early enough.

I repaired back to the F&L ahead of the others to count the money and prepare the accounts, not an onerous task, to find that I was just in time for a rather special rugby match. I have been unable to watch any of the other November test matches as they are aired on premium satellite television so this was something of a treat, and even more so as England won convincingly and against the odds. This wrapped up a rather splendid morning, if you can call four in the afternoon the end of the morning.

This left just enough time to head back home for some tea before turning around and heading back up to the F&L for the evening session. Just as we were preparing to leave the pagers went off requesting the Lifeboat to launch to seek some kayakers who were overdue to wherever they were going. We had seen these adventurous types in and out of the Harbour in the afternoon. The crew had not even the time to get togged up before the pagers went off again to say that the launch had been cancelled.

This was excellent news as, naturally, I would have been riddled with guilt had I left my compatriots pinned to the station while I quaffed frothing ale and enjoyed myself. Well, at least until after the end of the first pint.

December 2nd – Sunday

A dire day of mizzly rain and, perhaps, a day of revelation.

For a little excitement I decided that I would go and collect a bit of breakfast from the Little Bo Café next door.

I can now go down our steps as well as up in an upright condition, even without beer, so I was able to go on my own. For many of you this is a mere small step but for me this is a giant step in the direction of independence for damaged shopkeepers, I will have you know.

I was glad I went today, as I discovered that it is the last time that one of the regular serving girls will be there for a while. She is to go off travelling in the big wide world for three months, and will take in such heady destinations as Vietnam, Cambodia and some of the less familiar South Sea Islands. I am really quite envious as they sound adventuresome and exciting places to visit. I shall have to catch up with her on her return and live the adventure by proxy.

When I turned around to find a seat on which to wait while my breakfast bun was being prepared, I was hailed by a couple I had not noticed when I came in. They asked kindly how the repair of my ankle was progressing and I told them that soon I shall be embarking on my programme of physiotherapy. They are both fit and active types themselves and knew a thing or two about what sort of exercise is best for which part of the body. They said that when the time was right I could borrow a wobble board from them, and they highly recommended its use.

I let them finish their breakfast in peace and contemplated the possible beneficial properties that performing Rolf Harris impressions could have on my Achilles tendon.

I am sorry to report that breakfast was the most exciting part of the day which is why I have made such a meal of it, so to speak. I felt that it would be somewhat gratuitous to visit the F&L for the last of the Feast weekend celebrations and to listen to the Cape Singers perform. As a sop I read another couple of chapters of the book that the Aged Parent sent me. I am pleased to tell you that I now have a detailed knowledge of the lifestyle, reproduction cycle and migratory habits of the small-eared, red-toothed shrew.

The Missus ran off into town to gather the remaining articles for what proved a rather excellent Sunday roast meal. I have been enjoying having my meals placed upon a tray and delivered to my lap over the last weeks. It was as the Missus brought to me the various elements of my roast dinner that she twigged that perhaps the necessity of this operation is waning. As the hot gravy approached, the important facts that I had sat for three hours at a table collecting monies for the Feast Day shoot and had for the last two evenings propped up the bar at the F&L, prised the scales from her eyes.

It is testament to her restraint that the gravy remained in the jug and not in my exposed lap, but I rather suspect that I shall be having my meals at the table with everyone else from now on.

December 3rd – Monday

I am now in possession of a boot of death with a full minus ten degrees of upward movement that will allow me to propel myself forwards in a near normal walking motion. I have tried it out and it feels marvellous. No doubt I will soon be able to climb mountains, ford streams and undertake a myriad of sporting activities - pish, and they said I would never play the violin again. If they ever want to remake *Reach for the Sky*, I would put Kenneth More to shame.

In joyous celebration of this breakthrough, I fair leapt at the chance to wander down Causeway Head demonstrating my adept and light-footed walking skills to the assembled crowd of stay at home mums, personages of pensionable age and the over preponderance of work-shy malingerers lining the streets. Surely, there would be no other sort of person out and about during the working week.

Now, I would not have you think that I was stereotyping the rough looking ne'er-do-wells hanging around outside the pubs and on street corners, so if I am wrong I apologise profusely. Most of these dozens of people are probably actively seeking bar work or practicing to become street researchers, I am sure.

I do, however, need to be careful, as I have been told that the permanent attachment of the boot of death is coming to an end. I am only a short time away from having no visible sign of impairment and yet will still have to walk with a stick or a pole. To the untrained eye I will indeed resemble a work-shy malingerer or rough looking ne'er-do-well, even more so than usual.

I had considered having a t-shirt printed explaining the nature of my injury, and that I was not a drain on society's resources. However, I think it would be much more fun to have a t-shirt printed explaining that I was a work-shy malingerer and how much I appreciated the tax paying reader's financial support. This may, of course, provoke some non-passive reaction from certain tax paying readers and may represent a mortal risk to my person, so perhaps I should reconsider. After all, a genuine work-shy malingerer could take off on his heels, sharpish, in such an event whereas I, being only a pretend work-shy malingerer, could not.

It would be good to be able to tell you that after such an active morning I returned home, thus enlivened, and threw myself heartily into the preparation of my business accounts. They are once again due and there is a plethora of paperwork to prepare for the accountants. While the taxman is a bit of a pushover and will bow to a decent enough sob story, the VAT man is a hard and bitter taskmaster and will not.

It would have been good to tell you that I obediently performed my necessary duties diligently, but I did not. I dallied, procrastinated and made excuses for myself. I learned all about the production of carved toothpicks by the Indians of the Thar Desert in the tome that the Aged Parent gave me, and I scoured the Internet for gadgets that I cannot possibly afford. In fact, I demonstrated complete unproductive inactivity and felt not one iota of remorse.

Oh gosh, I think I have become a work-shy malingerer. Perhaps you will spare some alms if you see me outside the pub with my shabby bleddy hound during the working week.

December 4ᵗʰ - Tuesday

It was a bright sort of day, the kind of bright that lets you see the hail showers as they dash across the bay towards you, driven by the gusting north west wind. Wrapped up in the right sort of weather proof clothing it would not have been so bad as to stop a bent old shopkeeper and a bleddy hound from setting out across a perfectly empty beach almost as big as the cloud scudded sky itself.

While my mobility improves daily, it is still not sufficient to allow me this freedom. I can only look out of the window and imagine the wind driven hail slapping into my face and the bleddy hound's look of utter distain at being dragged out in such disgusting weather.

I have to admit that the terrors of my incarceration are getting the better of me. The tedium that tears at my very soul is more than a poor boy can bear. Had I been higher born or married, I would almost certainly have been taken into hospital for observation; this is clearly a case of acute boredom, or severe tedium and I would have the world's press holding their breath for news of my improving condition.

As I am not high born and neither did I marry into the aristocracy (although the Missus does get treated like one) my boredom is ordinary and I shall have to lump it like everyone else.

I did, however, get off my sorry behind and plough some effort into preparing my accounts this morning. What joyful distraction it gave me for a short time. I am sure that you imagine a gathering of documents, a recording of details and a collation and sorting and filing but I assure you my accounts require the use of imagination and, ahem, creativity. With any luck I shall show that the shop made no profit at all this year. Oddly, our Cayman Islands branch seems to have coined it in.

This is partly the reason why I have to be so careful about winning at cards on a Tuesday night, honest. I once again demonstrated this caution tonight, and would have risked being blown off my sticks on my way home by the buffeting wind were it not for the insistence of a young bar lady that I should travel home in her car.

Had it not been for this intervention, I should have you know that it would have been the first time since the accident that I walked to and from the OS by myself, unaided and without the help of a net.

Bleddy do gooders, I was relishing that milestone.

December 5th - Wednesday

There was still a bitter north westerly blowing into The Cove today for which, later, I was rather grateful.

The parents-in-law have been promoted up the housing list and are now capable of bidding for properties with an inside toilet. This has broadened their choices somewhat, and the Missus took the mother-in-law out to have a geek at a bungalow in St Just; father-in-law is still too poorly to travel and anyway his opinion on any matter, like mine, is included only as a formality.

This left me some rare peace to enjoy before an onslaught of terminal ferocity that was heading rapidly in our direction; the other in-laws were coming to pay their respects to the heads of the family ahead of Christmas. At least this time they have taken up digs in a holiday let next door. I suspect that even they might feel a smidgeon of guilt at evicting a poor cripple from his bed so near to the season of goodwill to all men.

I have had some success in training the parents-in-law to accept that the property in which they are staying is devoid of central heating. It is due to its construction that it is incredibly difficult to heat to central heating levels without firing up the electric heaters until they are melting from the walls and using electricity equal in value to the GNP of Cameroon.

Undeterred by these restrictions, the Missus made every effort to accommodate our new visitors by turning our front room into a fair facsimile of the tropical biome at the Eden Project. I managed to find a moment when her back was turned to switch off one of the heaters and thus avoid a major blackout on the South West grid. It also averted the imminent growth of creepers and palms behind the sofa.

I hope it was nothing to do with us that the far west looks like it will escape the deep frost that will affect most of the country tonight. It certainly was not going to put off our much maligned council from gritting Cove Road which was a first, or at least a rarity. They usually wait until several cars have come down the hill sideways. Perhaps the Missus told them the in-laws were coming.

December 6ᵗʰ – Thursday

A startling early start this morning for the pair of us; I had an appointment with the consultant looking after the dodgy peg at just after nine o'clock in the morning. The Missus tried very hard to complain about the early hour of the appointment but knew full well that she, in a rash moment, booked it herself.

I tried very hard to complain about the fact that the Missus planned a trip to Truro directly after the appointment, but knew full well we were already about a third of the way there. She also promised to sweeten the pill by buying me breakfast at Smokey Joe's Café on the way. I know, I know, you cannot go to Hayle without a visit to the Philps excellent pasty emporium. I have no excuse; it just seemed like a full breakfast sort of morning. Anyway I got my comeuppance, as the Missus decided to powder her nose when the bill came.

I had rather more luck when we got to the outskirts of Truro as there is a large shoe store there. The Missus has been trying to get a pair of running shoes for me – she has great expectations - but none have fitted. At least here I was able to try them on myself. I was given short shrift when I asked for just the left one.

We dropped into the big hospital next to return the walking frame that I was given because my ability on crutches gave the nurses such a fright. Now that I am proficient in their use and that the worst of their use is over, the frame is surplus to requirements and gets in the way rather. Despite having had to sign away my life when I was allotted the item, lest I keep it as a memento or sell it on a popular auction website, the process of returning it was rather perfunctory. I hope that I am never asked to demonstrate that I have dutifully returned the frame, because I will be utterly unable to do so.

I expected to be transported into the centre of town for the Missus to go shop to shop on a Quixotic quest while I acted the Sancho Panza amongst the bustling crowds. Fortunately for me, she decided she could get what she wanted from the big superstore just outside town.

Partly for fun and partly as I needed by now to powder my own nose I went into the store with her. It is a superstore of such superness that it is arranged on two storeys, the toilets, of course, being on the upper level. Thankfully, the store sported a lift to hoist me to the first floor.

On my return I noticed that the store was so super that it also had an escalator, or more accurately an inclined moving walkway, down to the main shopping area. I have contemplated attempting an escalator in my mind's eye on a few occasions but discounted actually doing it on the basis of the moving centre of balance that I would encounter. Given that this was slightly different from an escalator in the areas of steps (lack, thereof) and angle, and therefore depth of potential fall I decided that I could come to little harm by giving it a go.

It was on the final approach that I discovered that it was moving far more rapidly than I had anticipated. With so many people about, and having strode with such purposeful gait, I felt that I could not now pull out. Also, out of the corner of my eye there were a few people on the upward moving walkway looking at me with, 'how is he going to manage that without falling over', looks in their faces. In short, I was trapped.

Rapid choices flashed before my eyes: sticks first, with centre of balance going forwards and risk landing on my face, sticks last, with centre of balance going backwards and risk landing on my bottom. At the last moment a final and enlightened choice presented itself and I swung forward on the moving hand rails landing with sufficient grace to allow myself a look of smugness to the upwardly travelling audience.

Now travelling comfortably on my two feet, I had a finite length of time to consider my exit strategy. I was after all about to land on a fixed platform while travelling forwards at a rate faster than I had travelled at any time for the last six weeks. The choices were somewhat fewer than the approach. After a quick assessment sticks forward was the only option and hope that I could slow my forward movement without air-brakes, drogue chute or tailhook and arresting wire.

I was heartened by the sight of an ambulance sitting outside the main entrance and fixed my eyes on the landing platform. This did not help as the striped panels of the moving escalator conspired to form some sort of optical confusion very nearly upsetting my perfectly timed lunge forward. I think I should avoid escalators in future.

December 7ᵗʰ - Friday

The in-laws dived out quite early on and were gone for hours. Apparently, they had a little nose around Penzance, and went off to look at the bungalow that the parents-in-law have made a play for over at St Just. While they were out, the chap who showed mother-in-law around the shoe box they had bid for a week or so ago, telephoned to let us know that another more suitable flat was going to be available very soon. It was a very nice gesture since he was not under any obligation to do so, and now I have made it public he will probably be in hot water with his bosses.

The way things are going the parents-in-law will have their own little place very soon. Although I think it might be a little too soon to cancel the turkey, I have a bottle of Louis Roederer Cristal '90 in my beer fridge just crying out to be broached in celebration. I think you must have a very low opinion of me, dear reader, I mean, of course, to celebrate their good fortune.

Meanwhile, our much maligned council are debating applications from the major supermarkets to carve up the remains of St Austell, presumably to ensure that the millions that they spent on the in-town regeneration are completely wasted. One development, at Coyte Farm, should just about deliver the *coup de grace* all by itself. The supermarket, together with a shopping park, has the same retail space as all the town centre shops put together. Phase two will see the creation of 250 new homes to ensure there are people to shop in the new shopping centre. The new residents will probably never know that St Austell ever existed.

Closer to home St Buryan looks like it might increase by a third of its current size. Some helpful bunch from West Sussex wants to build 90 new homes close in on the west side of the village. Naturally, there are one or two locals who are none too keen, believing it will ruin the character of the ancient settlement. Since it is unlikely that there will be 90 new jobs created for them all in St Buryan, I would be rather more concerned about traffic jams on the Penzance Road, which is single file in many places. I also cannot see them having the best of welcomes in the St Buryan Inn either, where you can hear a pin drop if a stranger walks in.

If I had a suspicious mind I might form some conspiratorial link between all this new development and the introduction of flights from Newquay to Liverpool. I shall be keeping my eye out for a new generation of Cornishmen with dark curly hair and thick moustaches.

December 9th – Sunday

It was a veritable grey vacuum of a day devoid of one iota of excitement in the small sphere of my acknowledgement. I did, however, manage to finish off the heavy volume sent to me by the Aged Parent. I now know all there is to be knowed about correct use of English grammar, surviving a night in the Brazilian rainforest with its complete list of Brazilian rainforest hotels, and harmonious living with a house full of visiting random family members.

I have now commenced reading a lengthy Swedish thriller, in the original Swedish, of course. Fortunately, the Aged Parent's paperback also has a complete Swedish to English phrase book in the appendix, which has proved invaluable for the first six chapters.

The likelihood of getting six paragraphs, let alone six chapters out of me today are slim. The writing situation is grave indeed.

Talking of which, I notice from the local press that Barnoon Cemetery in the posh bit of St Ives is to receive a bit of a makeover. Well, a make under if we are to be precise. It seems that there is a movement (perhaps it is an underground movement, sorry) to let churchyards become overgrown with wild flowers, rather than neatly clip and mow them. There is even a voluntary body that promotes the idea, Cornwall Living Churchyards.

However, the real drive in this case is not so much to do with letting nature look after itself, but more to do with how much our much maligned council can save in shekels. To underline the fact, Cornwall Living Churchyards, who probably know a thing or two about how to do it properly, know nothing about the plans in St Ives. The Town Council has been informed that this will go ahead in the near future and are quite warm to the idea, although they admit that it would probably happen anyway even if they objected.

The idea has already been trialled at St Uny in Lelant, where the living churchyard has really taken root. A spokesman for the Cornwall Living Churchyards suggested that the plan was to let a few wild flowers grow, not to completely neglect the place. Apparently, the much maligned council contractor has not been seen there since the policy was started and it is now getting difficult to get into it – alive or dead.

Gosh, just about six paragraphs, but there, I am afraid we shall leave today's nonsense. There is no earthly point in flogging a dead dunkey – it was not even so good as flogging a dead hoss.

December 10ᵗʰ – Monday

At least it was not grey today and, being Monday, I get to go out for my weekly foot hold in Penzance.

In fact, it was an entirely pleasant day in terms of the weather and the entire fishing fleet was out in the bay, glittering white in the morning sunshine. Sounds romantic, doesn't it, unless, of course, you are the one out there, covered in squid ink and freezing off your oarlocks for a pittance. Well, it is their career choice.

As alluded to just a moment ago, my choice was to head off in the direction of PZ. Well, it was hardly a choice, but I had been led to believe that there may be some good news on the boot of death front, so I was rather looking forward to it. True to his word, the boot of death is now an optional extra, although I am supposed to only be without it for a few hours each day, slowly increasing to several hours a day.

I had taken the right shoe of the new pair that I bought the other day in Truro, just in case I was allowed to ditch the boot of death. Although the right foot is still rather swollen, I was able to cram it into the shoe with its laces spread out as far as they would go. Moments later, I was hobbling out of the door with the Missus carrying the boot of death at arms reach (it has become rather aromatic during the period I was wearing it and unable to wash – sorry if you were half way through your cheese on toast when I mentioned that, I shall try and provide some warning next time).

I had hoped that we could go and celebrate at the new Brazilian restaurant in town. Yes, the cosmopolitan centre of the universe, aka, Bread Street sports a Brazilian café that has been highly recommended to me. Unfortunately, it does not open on Mondays so, as the Missus wanted to go to Costalot Coffee, we ended up at the only half decent eatery within walking distance, Renaissance Café in the Wharfside Centre.

Renaissance has been there for dunkey's years, during which time I have eaten there once. I could not quite remember why I had only eaten there once in all that time but after I arrived I remembered, it is because it is highly over-priced; a sandwich will set you back the best part of eight quid, but does include a side salad that looks more like a salad dressing. I had a ten inch pizza that was very nice and probably not over-priced at nine quid.

I waited outside the café while the Missus went around the clothes shop opposite. Out of the corner of my eye I noticed that a brown, speckled gull was watching me from the parapet, standing on one leg. At first I thought he must be taking the Mickey, but on closer inspection he had no choice as he only had the one foot. I sympathised, naturally, and wondered at how well adapted he had become, gently swaying in the breeze. Then with one last, especially robust gust of wind, he fell off.

I made it down to the car park, carefully avoiding the escalators, and back to the van still in my normal footwear. So that I do not get over excited I am provided with a wedge that will fit into my shoe. This ensures that I will not be tempted to turn up my foot too far or too violently. Alternatively, I could wear a pair of the Missus's stilettos although after several hours of use they do squeeze my toes rather, ahem, I mean, I imagine that they would.

In fact, I avoided the boot of death for the rest of the day. Its only function is to ensure that my foot does not move in a direction that it should not and with my foot elevated, as I have been told that it should still continue to be, it is unlikely to go anywhere that it should not. It was also the first night in seven weeks that I went to bed without it. I am sure I should pine awfully for it.

Will I 'eck.

December 11ᵗʰ - Tuesday

It was rather a splendid day despite the fact that it was darned chilly outside. I know this because I went out in it.

The Missus was waiting for a telephone call, and the bleddy hound was becoming increasingly unsettled waiting to relieve herself. It was clear that the Missus was to be unmoved by the bleddy hound's desperate indications and so I stepped, falteringly into the breach.

It was not quite so simple. I had to make my way down the steps first, lest the bleddy hound dragged me down in her exuberance, and then pick up the lead thrown from the open door. As it happened, the Missus had to come down the steps anyway to unwrap the dog from her lead that she managed to become tangled up with.

By the time I had got to the top of the Harbour I discovered just how cold it actually was. It is the first time in seven weeks that I had taken her around the basic relief route and, unsurprisingly, little had changed. There was a fair build-up of oar weed on the Harbour beach which we have not seen since spring, but otherwise every stone and weed was in their place.

It was something of a trial getting the bleddy hound to stop trying to pull me over, so I let her off her lead. She stayed with me for the first half of the run, but got bored when I took too much time climbing the slope up to Coastguard Row. After that I was playing catch up. I lost sight of her completely when I had to slow down again crossing the slope at the bottom of Stonechair Lane and made my pathetic, lonely way across the RNLI car park.

I half expected to see her at the top of the neighbour's steps having a chat with her mate through the letter box, but she was not there, nor could I see her on the road. It was as I approached our own stairs that she bounded down to see where I was at last. Well, I do not think it was as a result of any concern, it was probably more that it was cold and no one else was likely to let her into the flat.

I pointedly ignored her for the rest of the day and took sheer delight in shutting the door on her when I went out later to the OS. Not only did I make it to the OS with two shoes on and only one stick, I spent the rest of the evening moving around with no stick at all. Now all I have to do is learn how to not be the first one out at cards and all will be well with my world.

December 12ᵗʰ – Wednesday

We have been having some success with the mail order side of our business through the website of late. That sounds rather grand. It is not, but just about pays for itself and gives me a little thrill every time an order appears in my email inbox. In fact, I had an enquiry that I almost dismissed as a hoax, spam or phishing email as it was clearly from abroad and had a hint of the enigmatic about it. I replied as tentatively as possible without giving too much away, until a second arrived asking how to place an order using a VISA credit card. I was still a little suspicious, but gave a quite detailed set of instructions as to how this might be achieved. I heard nothing more for a week, then an order arrived for a Cornish scenes calendar all the way from San Francisco.

The Missus had been forced to carry out all the wrapping and posting of our website orders while I was unable to easily get downstairs. Her main complaint was that the orders came in piecemeal, meaning individual trips to the shop to pick and wrap the items and individual trips to the post office to despatch them. I made a mental note to place a notice on the website asking customers if they could coordinate their purchasing to keep the Missus happy.

Sorry, I digress. Now, where was I? Ah yes, I digressed before I even got started. The point I was trying to arrive at was that for the first time in a number of weeks I was able to go down to the shop myself to pick and pack the latest two orders. It was rather nice to be down in the shop again and even nicer that while I was down there I bumped into a passing chum and we had quite a little chat. It was because of this that I missed the opening time for the post office. Well, I did not miss the opening time for the post office, the Missus did, as that is still the one part of the process I cannot do alone.

It became greyer in the afternoon for the second run, er, hobble around with the bleddy hound. This one was rather enforced, as the Missus and the mother-in-law had gone into town. Their visit was rather enforced too, as after several weeks of up hill struggle it was agreed that the best course of action was to admit the father-in-law into hospital for some intense getting better treatment.

The Cove is a quiet place, as well as a fairly close community, and especially during the winter there is not a great deal to do or talk about. So when a bright ambulance turns up, there is not a soul whose interest is not piqued. So far I have been asked three times why an ambulance was parked outside our door. I have told the enquirers variously: the Missus in one of her violent rages hit me with a frying pan; the Missus's back went into spasm during some outrageously athletic bout of love making (I have a stunt double for such occasions, obviously); Nelson Mandela wanted to visit the Home of the Sennen Cove Diary before it was too late.

The father-in-law is comfortable, as they say, and is at least doing as Matron tells him, which is more than he was doing for the Missus or mother-in-law and is the root cause of him being there in the first place. I think if I were in his shoes I would be twice as rebellious and cantankerous to boot, with not a nurses bottom left unpinched. You can do that when you are 89 so he tells me.

December 13ᵗʰ – Thursday

I took the bleddy hound out first thing this morning. I think that was a mistake, as expectations will be that I can now do it all the time and the likelihood is that it will be raining tomorrow morning. However, it was quite pleasant out despite the low leaden clouds and the threat of a few light showers in the air. Over towards Cape there was a big bright patch throwing some contrast on the big rolling waves trundling through the Tribbens.

Out across the bay, the waves were having their tops blown away by the east wind as they raced in towards the wide beach. Oddly, the wind did not seem too severe where I was.

The Missus and mother-in-law were off again in the afternoon to visit the invalid. They were gone for hours. They went off again in the evening and were still gone when I made my way down to the OS for the quiz. I would have gone across to Lifeboat training but the bleddy hound does not do too well being left on her own for extended periods. While I did leave her on her lonesome later when I went to the OS she was as sick as, well, a dog by the time the Missus arrived ten minutes later.

December 15ᵗʰ – Saturday

The Missus was out of bed like a greyhound out of the trap this morning. This is most disconcerting; she never, ever gets up early. They had arranged to be with the father-in-law for an unofficial visiting session in the morning and were out of the door before nine o'clock.

The brother-in-law decided that it was a right good idea to trip next door for breakfast, and he was not wrong, I know because I was there too. It was only after we got back that the other brother-in-law arrived looking rather envious, but pretending that he was not. It did not take much to convince any of us that going to the OS for a few hours would be a top hole idea.

From our seats at the bar we were still able to admire the big sea rolling in, the big fluffy clouds and a rainbow. One of the brother-in-laws has a nice shiny Bramley mobile telephone that can do all sorts of things including taking pictures of rainbows. Unfortunately, the brother-in-law has not the faintest idea of how to make it do all sorts of things, including taking pictures of rainbows, so he had to ask the barmaid to do it for him. We then had to ask her again how to find the taken picture on the smart shiny mobile telephone so that I could see what it looked like.

We chatted away on many subjects and one in particular enlightened me no end. It discussed both the joys of Christmas and the chaotic and high pressure life east of Penzance. Apparently, brother-in-law wanted to take his grandson to see Father Christmas, and having discovered that the one closest was fully booked (and did sir want to book in advance for January) found another at a farm nearby. It cost £15.50 per child to see the big chap as well as tour the farm, and grandfather duly had his money ready at the gate when he was surprised to be told that the total price was £38. When he made a polite enquiry as to why this might be, he was told that the three adults in the party attracted a further charge of £7.50 each, oh, and by the way if you wanted a picture with the darling youngster with the jovial bearded one himself that would be an extra tenner. Happy Christmas everyone!

We arrived back in time for tea, which was handy and not at all planned in any way. The Missus has been experimenting with her new mixer, before it is consigned to the corner to collect dust in perpetuity, and managed to put together some rather good chocolate éclairs. I shall have to leave her alone in the kitchen for a few hours again some time.

There then followed a hiatus while the assembled company made a further visit to see father-in-law in hospital. This was, after all the main cause of the gathering. Father-in-law is starting to do quite nicely, thank you for asking, and apparently enjoyed an ice cream today. All the visitors were charged £7.50 to defray the costs.

Not so in the good old F&L in the evening time, where entrance was for free. We had considered spurning the usual Saturday night frolic, as both brother-in-laws were driving in the morning. However, when push came to shove one decided to restrain his consumption and the other decided to make his missus drive.

It was a rather sedate evening by normal standards but the band was lively and played some cracking good tunes. We, no doubt, chatted on many subjects, but for the life of me I cannot remember a single one, but I do not think any of them included Father Christmas.

December 16ᵗʰ – Sunday

Well, I did not get away with it this morning even though I delayed and procrastinated for ages. Showers were passing through, the Missus was in bed, and the bleddy hound needed to be taken around the block.

In the end I capitulated, donned my water proofs and stepped outside just as it stopped raining. I was standing at the top of the steps trying not to be pulled down by an anxious bleddy hound when there was a substantial flash, a thunder clap and a sharp shower of hail. Unsurprisingly, the bleddy hound suddenly stopped pulling and headed for the front door and cover, which was just as bad as her constant tugging, as the unexpected release of pressure upset my balance and had me toppling backwards. It is a good job Sunday mornings are quiet in The Cove as I believe I said a few things that were most unchurch like.

With the Missus dashing to and from Penzance three times a day the bleddy hound does not get a look in for exercise save for a functional walk around the block with me. In the middle of the day the beach looked just ever so enticing and I reckoned, that if the Missus could run me down to the slipway in the van, I could at the very least throw a ball for her down on the sand at the OS end.

There had been showers blowing through all morning so I took some precautions with waterproof gear. Although it took a little effort getting down the slope, we both thoroughly enjoyed ourselves for the best part of an hour. It was just as well that I do not rely too much on the stick any more, as it was completely useless on the soft, wet sand.

I found a rock to sit on eventually and watched the waves out on the Cowloes and across Pedn-men-du crash and explode, white, against the grey skyline. Yes, a grey skyline. While the sky above me was sparsely populated by big, white fluffy clouds, the sky out to the west, where the strong wind was coming from, was harbouring thoughts of dropping some wet stuff upon us. Sure enough about fifteen minutes later we were lashed with rain, not that it mattered a jot to the bleddy hound who just insisted I throw the ball some more.

Despite having some pretty effective waterproof trousers and jacket, I have not yet dared to try on a pair of wellies or my walking boots. It is all very well being dry from head to ankle, but if your feet are soaking wet you may as well not have bothered, I thought as I removed my dripping socks.

December 17ᵗʰ - Monday

We had to be at the hospital at 12:00 for my physiotherapy appointment, but the Missus had arranged to wave at the father-in-law from the back of the hospital a little earlier. Previously, she was able to visit first thing in the morning as he was in a room of his own, but he has since been moved to a general ward so she has to wait until normal visiting hours.

After seeing my physiotherapist (carry on doing what you are doing and I'll see you after the holidays - thanks) we headed into town. First, it was to waste some time before the 2:30 visiting hours begun and secondly to find something to eat.

The Missus had asked where I fancied going for lunch and I told her that I had heard that the Old Coastguard at Mousehole had formed a good reputation since it had reopened. I knew that it might be a tad expensive, but the mother-in-law was with us and I thought it would be nice to treat her. To say that I also thought that she might cough up for it would be a horrible slur on my already deeply blemished character, I shall have you know.

While I thought that I said the Old Coastguard at Mousehole, I must have actually said Blue Snapper in town, because we ended up at Thirty Five, which was Blue Snapper before the team discovered a hole in the roof and got into an argument with the landlord as to who should pay for the repairs. Thirty Five is in town and close to several shops, which is probably why I did not have a chance of going to the Old Coastguard at Mousehole, which is not, even if I had said it, which I apparently did not. Nevertheless, it was a very acceptable meal at a more acceptable price than the one we had last week and especially as the mother-in-law did not cough for it as hoped.

By the time we had finished our dinner and the girls had finished shopping it was time to go to the hospital to visit the father-in-law. He has been moved into a sunny spot in the corner of the general ward and he looks a lot brighter than he did when he went in, which is handy. He says that he may be released later this week, although the nurses and doctors may have a different opinion, so let us just hope he continues his upward spiral.

As there are only two people allowed in to visit at the same time I made my excuses so that the Missus could come in. As I made my exit, it surprised me a bit to see that the spritely, red headed doctor who has been attending the father-in-law has her own room at the hospital. There was no mistaking that it was her room as it was labelled 'Acute GP Clinic'.

I know what you are thinking. You are thinking that I should have stopped writing just shortly before I started that last paragraph. Well, you could be right, but inexplicably my delete key has stopped working.

December 18ᵗʰ - Tuesday

Since the shop is opening on Thursday it seemed right and just that we should do something about it, like buying some stock to sell. I had dropped a couple of hints last week but the Missus was, and still is, very focused on her poorly dad and in no mood to think further than a day ahead.

It was actually the Missus who, this morning, announced that we would be heading up to Hayle to the cash and carry and thence onto the hospital. I did express some misgivings that it would mean that I was once again waiting in the van for two hours outside the hospital and the Missus suggested an earlier start tomorrow instead. Somewhere between me going downstairs to do my list for the cash and carry and having breakfast the Missus decided that there was still enough time to go today, and get back in time to drop me off and go to the hospital.

I was quite surprised at the time as to how well my dodgy ankle held up to the punishment that I gave it walking around the cash and carry and lumping geet heavy boxes of goodies, then doing it all again getting it out of the van and into the shop.

As it was still a reasonable day I took my foot around the block while attached to a bleddy hound on the end of a lead (actually, I let her off the lead as we go around otherwise I would spend most of the circuit on my behind). My foot then got a well earned rest for the remainder of the afternoon before I took it down to the OS for the usual poker night.

Having already discovered on Sunday that my comfy running shoes are not waterproof and knowing that it was scheduled to rain quite heavily, I had to wear my stout walking shoes down to the OS. In normal circumstances these are the most comfortably shoes I have ever owned. Currently, however, that is not quite the case and extended wearing does cause a few inflation issues.

I shall spare you the exact details, but suffice it to say that when, in the late evening, I looked at my dodgy ankle and the attached leg and foot it was rather apparent that it had not held up to the punishment I had given it quite as well as I thought.

This gives me a cast iron excuse to do absolutely begger all tomorrow – again.

December 19ᵗʰ – Wednesday

It was an exceedingly lazy morning and all the more so since one of us will be up at sparrow puff tomorrow morning to open the shop. I do not think that waving my 'fit note' from the doctor under the nose of the Missus will hold any sway whatsoever.

I did however have one rather essential task to perform this morning, and that was to call the esteemed Laurel and Hardy Newspaper Company.

If you are a seasoned reader you will understand the necessity of calling a newspaper delivery company that has already been emailed with our opening and closing dates and a list of newspaper titles and volumes, and which has responded to confirm that it has read and understood our requirements. That was not entirely true. A representative telephoned to say that she understood we were opening on 20ᵗʰ December and could I let her know the newspaper titles and volumes required. I then explained that the newspaper titles and volumes were included in the same email that stated our intended opening and closing times, if only she had realised that sometimes emails go beyond the bottom of the computer screen. It was then that she found her scroll button and said, 'oh yes, I see them now'. Marvellous!

With this, and a whole nine years' worth of lunatic incompetence to fall back on, I telephoned the Laurel and Hardy Newspaper Company this morning to ask them if my newspapers had been set up for delivery tomorrow. It was of no surprise to find that only a handful of newspaper titles had been set up for random days over the open period. It took twenty minutes to talk the operator through the changes. I still have absolutely no confidence I will have anything like the right newspaper titles or volumes delivered tomorrow.

What we will have is pasties, bread, fruit and Rodda's cream because I remembered to talk to all those suppliers and they, for their part, read or listen to my requests and deliver what they have been asked. I am grateful for that because otherwise I would have to assume I must be doing it wrong.

So with a busy day ahead in the shop (all right, we all know that it will be as dead as my ballroom dancing career but we can dream, can we not?) I shall take my leave of you and drink heavily.

December 20ᵗʰ - Thursday

I could be wasting my time with this particular Diary entry as you may never get to read it. Perhaps I should have said goodbye yesterday. You must have heard by now that thanks to the Mayan people not being able to count past 21 in this year that the end of the world is nigh.

I was invited to an end of the world party tonight that promised to be quite wild, as you might expect. I had to turn it down, as I have to get up early tomorrow.

Oh, please yourselves. Anyway I happen to think that it was just a simple Mayan administrative error.

Somewhere in the Mayan capital of Tikal in an anonymous civic building of the administrative district a slightly concerned senior civil servant looks for a lacky.

Boss (Mayan civil service): "Ikan, come 'ere a minute my 'ansum."

Ikan (Junior Clerk): "Yes, boss."

Boss: "The halach uninic has noticed that we seem to be running out of calendar dates."

Ikan: "Yes, boss. That maid Eme was supposed to be doing the next ten years but she's not been in since the high priest sacrificed her favourite goat last month."

Boss: "Oh, right. What you doing at the moment?"

Ikan: "Counting pencil sharpeners."

Boss: "Oh, right. What's a pencil?"

Ikan: "Dunno Boss. I only got as far as counting sharpeners."

Boss: "Okay, stop doing that then. The halach uinic has got a bee in his bonnet about running out of days on the calendar. Seems 'ee thinks if 'ee runs out of days on the calendar that the day won't actually 'appen."

Ikan: "You'd 'ave to be some special to think that, just cus we don't have a calendar for a day that the day int going to 'appen, eh Boss."

Boss. "Well, since we int had a day yet that int had no calendar for it, might be ess true. Anyway, unless you want your inside organs on a priest's slab I suggest you get chiselling."

Ikan: "Right you are, Boss. When shall I do up to?"

Boss: (Irritated) "Just keep going till I tell you to stop."

(Some months later ...)

Ix Chel: (Ikan's Missus): "Hello, are you Ikan's Boss."

Boss: "Who are you?"

Ix Chel: "I am Ix Chel, Ikan's missus."

Boss: "Who's Ikan?"

Ix Chel: "He works for you. He is a clerk in the counting pencil sharpeners department."

Boss: "We don't have a pencil sharpeners department any more. We 'aven't 'ad one for they this past six months on account of no one knowing what a pencil was."

Ix Chel: "Well, that's where 'ee was workin' when I last saw 'un."

Boss: "When did you last see 'ee?"

Ix Chel: "When 'ee left for work six months ago."

Boss: "Oh. Begger."

Ix Chel: "What?"

Boss: "I sent him to work in calendar production."

Ix Chel: "When?"

Boss: "Erm, about six months ago. 'ell, best I take you down there and tell 'un 'ee can stop."

Down in the bowels of the civil building, in a darkened room is a pale and wan little man, working away by the light of a candle.

Ikan: "'ello Boss. 'ello Luvver. What you doin' 'ere?"

Ix Chel: "What do you mean, 'what am I doing here?' You int been 'ome for six months."

Ikan: "Well, someone's got to earn, luvver, especially the way you do spend it."

Boss: (Keen to avoid the crossfire) "So, Ikan. 'ave you finished that little job I set you?"

Ikan: "Dunno, Boss. You said to keep going 'til you come and tell me to stop."

Boss: (With slightly embarrassed glance at Ix Chel) "Well, I didn't zackly mean you not to stop, ever. I thought you would use some initiative. Anyhow, 'ow far you got?"

Ikan: "I was just about to finish the entry for 21st December, Boss."

Boss: "21st December? What have you been doing all this time?"

Ikan: "21st December 2012, Boss."

Boss: "Oh, begger. The halach uinic will go bleddy mad. We're supposed to be making cutbacks and 'ee'll see all this as a geet waste of time and money. We're doomed, Ikan."

Ix Chel: "Look, boys. How about you tell the halach uinic that you found the best mathematician and astronomer in the land to work out the last day ever? That way 'ee will never have to worry again about running out of calendar days and 'ee will be remembered for all time as an intellectual and prophet."

Boss: "Brilliant; a life saver. One thing though."

Ikan & Ix Chel: "Wassat?"

Boss: "What if 21st December 2012 really is the end of all days?"

Ix Chel: "You would 'ave to be some special to believe that. Anyway all of us will be pushing up the poinsettia by then so not our problem. Only the gods know what the people at that time will think. There's a thought though, Ikan."

Ikan: "What's that then luvver?"

Ix Chel: "Just scribble a note in the last day there 'end of all time' or something like that. That will really get them going."

[FX: *Sounds of wicked laughter echoing around empty corridors*]

December 21st - Friday

They do say that as you get older time seems to travel a bit faster. They must be right, whoever they are, as today seemed terribly short to me. I suppose that we should be grateful that it happened at all, at least after eleven minutes past eleven. Perhaps it did not and I am just a ghost writer.

It was also grey and miserable today.

It must be even greyer and more miserable for the islanders on Scilly as Land's End Airport (it's an aerodrome, honest) was water logged and out of action and all flights had been diverted to Newquay. Newquay has its own problems and was fog bound. At least they have a decent enough excuse not to send any Christmas cards this year.

Incidentally, if you are one of the many, many readers (alright, I have had two) who sent me a card this year, thank you very much. Clearly I would reciprocate but you are far too numerous (well, you have to draw the line somewhere) and I do not want to be writing Christmas cards all bleddy year. In fact I do not want to be writing Christmas cards. Please do not think me miserly, miserable, ungracious and ungrateful; I am very grateful.

A very merry winter solstice to one and all!

December 22nd - Saturday

I think the most excitement I had today was collecting my electricity meter reading for the new company. I still have had no response from the Cornwall Together programme regarding my enquiry that I could get a quote for power equivalent, or actually lower than their collective bargaining quote. I have even written to the newspaper and, come to think, I have not had a response from them either. Perhaps everyone is too embarrassed to admit that they have been had.

A pod of dolphins popped up late in the afternoon for a little play. It was obvious that they soon realised that they were up against a meter reading in the entertainment stakes and very quickly beggered off.

December 23rd - Sunday

It was still quite grey today but largely dry. Whether this had anything to do with the fact that we had real customers come into the shop in numbers we can only guess. And just to note that when I say 'numbers' this is purely a comparative term and means that there was more than two.

I suspect, though, that we have started to see a beginning of the Christmas influx. I spoke with a regular visitor who said that they had avoided coming down yesterday due to the awful weather. Perhaps others had thought the same too. Those who have decided to come by train are probably still somewhere east of Taunton.

The Missus thought that today would be a good day to go and buy some vegetables. It was necessary as we would have had no tea else, but as I waved her adieu I had the feeling that it would be a very long time before I saw her again. Additionally, she was just popping in to see a friend who was visiting another friend at a house on Sunny Corner Lane before she went off to see her brother in St Just – oh please, do try and keep up. The Missus promised she would just stick her head around the door and would not be at all long. I saw our neighbour later who had been there; I am surprised that the Missus did not have a cricked neck when she came back, as her head was poked around the door for at least an hour.

When the Missus did eventually return from her shopping expedition she reported tales of carnage in the aisles and queues longer than a Russian bread line, although that is probably quite a dated simile – how about longer than an MP's expenses sheet. Nevertheless, she still managed to come back weighed down by vegetables and items obviously from someone else's shopping list that she must have consulted in error. She nearly did not recognise me as my beard had grown long and grey by the time she returned.

Never mind, we have the delight that is the television Christmas schedules to entertain us tonight; thank heavens I have a book to read, even if it is in Swedish.

December 24ᵗʰ - Monday

I had asked the Missus to pick up some essential items from Shrew House yesterday and since she completely ignored her mobile telephone messages had to make a separate trip up to get them. A chap had been in for a dog ball thrower which, inexplicably, we had run out of. I also asked her to get some footballs as the bottom tier of the cunningly designed and artfully built ball stand had been empty since the end of September and was looking rather silly.

I may have indicated before that the pumping up of these footballs requires some strength and, particularly, stamina if there is more than a few of them. This is why, after some years, I have dusted off the compressor that was buried in the attic as I possessed neither strength nor stamina ... until now, that is.

You may recall that a little while ago I noticed that my upper body strength had improved after a couple of months of operating my crutches; I could crush walnuts in the crook of my arm I am sure, should I have the desire so to do. I set about the task of inflating the footballs with some alacrity and, if I may say so, some flair. My fist flying up and down the pump handle was a mere blur, and my strokes steady and consistent. If young ladies had been present, I am sure that they would have swooned at the metaphoric urgency of it.

So there I was pumping up some footballs when a group of customers came into the shop. The ladies in the group were clearly admiring the metaphor of my flying fist and steady and consistent stroke; I noticed a little colour in their cheeks. The man looked at my work questioningly. "Christmas balls", I said helpfully. "The same to you," he cheerily replied.

I am very pleased that I have that out of my system now. It leaves room to tell you that we had yet another quite busy day with a few more real customers coming through the door. The chap with the dog ball thrower request actually came back and bought one, which was quite a surprise, and we were able to satisfy a fair few last minute Christmas gift requirements too. What utter gems we are.

Each year at the OS we are bullied and cajoled into buying a few numbers on a patchwork board in the vain hope of winning an out of date bottle of beer or a battered box of mince pies; I have, thankfully, not won for many a season. I had quite forgotten that it was drawn on Friday, until the landlord and landlady arrived half way through the evening and announced that I had won a prize. They produced an envelope, which I opened eagerly in the hope of discovering a worn fifty pound note or a voucher for an evening's worth of beer, perhaps.

No, not a chance; I am now the proud recipient of a voucher for a one night stay at the OS. Might be useful if it snows next year while I am playing cards one night and cannot get home or a landslide takes the road away or perhaps some wag nicks my crutch. For certain, in the unlikely event of any of those happening, I will have left my voucher at home.

Oh, Merry Christmas everyone – bah humbug!

December 25ᵗʰ – Tuesday

Singing in the Rain on the television and a sudden sense of déjà vu of me and my sister going at it hammer and tongs over viewing supremacy of the hired Christmas television (only for two weeks, mind) with the Aged Parents, who presumably were not so aged at that time, trying in vane to referee the match. I did not dare look at the schedule just in case The Great Escape was on the other side; that would have been just too scary if it was.

It must be bleddy Christmas and that was certainly the ghost of Christmas past. It could have been a ghost town this morning when I took the bleddy hound around. Despite doing my best to ensure a lay in, I was still the first one up, in our household at least. Probably not so in the whole Cove, as those opposite the Roundhouse were not spared a moment's rest over night, as the wind had blown open the doors and the alarm was going off. The doors were still banging off their hinges when I went past at half past eight.

Although it was windy, there were signs of brightness and the rain held off completely for the Christmas Day swim. There were hundreds of complete eejits down on the beach, barely dressed, and ready for a dunking. I met some of the blue, shivering souls on my way down to the OS for the traditional morning meet up with pals. Despite being completely mad, they did very well and managed to raise £500 for three different charities this year.

Being under strict instructions to be home before dinner time, I behaved myself impeccably, honest I did. It was certainly busier than it was last year, but that might have had a bit to do with the short sharp shower that drove everyone inside. Nevertheless, there were quite a few chums to share some festive cheer with, and noisy small children in their Christmas gear were surprisingly well behaved too.

While the showers persisted through the day there was plenty of sunshine too and we were treated to a Cove Christmas spectacular with stunning rainbows, crashing sea and those grey misty bands of rain sweeping across the bay. Along with a high wind, conditions were perfect for the half dozen kite surfers tempted out for an early play. They came in a bit close to the swimmers at one point, but judging from some of the tricks they were pulling I would say they were very well practiced.

And so to the over-stuffed after dinner collapse and excessive television watching that is the lazy man's Christmas afternoon. I really hope that I do not have to do battle with the parents-in-law over the television remote, as there is no referee this year.

December 26ᵗʰ – Wednesday

Ah, Boxing Day. It must nearly be all over.

Not concerned with making business as good as it might be, the weather decided to stick the boot in. It was a truly horrible morning, with wind blown rain heading along Cove Road, and black as pitch again as I ferreted around getting the shop open.

The Roundhouse has had its door nailed shut. I am assuming that the owners could not get down here to lock it up properly, but at least the alarm has been turned off. It also meant that the bleddy hound did not jump out of her skin every time the door banged open, bless her.

The wind and rain was not an ideal backdrop for a morning of traditional shooting of clay pigeons up at the field behind the F&L. Just as well that the last of the rain blew through shortly before I got up there and lasted for most of the shoot. As you know, I was unable to join in at Feast time, but I was determined this time to have a go as well. There were more people having a pop this time than at Feast, and so much the merrier for it too. I only had a couple of rounds but, surprisingly, did reasonably well and did not fall over even once.

Just as we were about to commence the penultimate round another lump of wind lashed rain came in and we were bogged down in the horsebox shelter for the best part of an hour. The wind was howling even as we resumed, which made interesting sport of trying to hit the clays as they floated and bobbed both down and across the field at random.

I was lucky enough to get a lift back down the hill and just in time to see Rescue 193 hanging off the cliffs at Carn Gloose. It was clearly not an exercise and on investigation it seems a small dog had taken a tumble off the coast path. It was not an ideal day for walking the coast path, and even less than ideal to have a dog running around up there. I am sure the Coastguard would have preferred not to be up there too.

It was just as well that I was not up there as I would have missed my bubble and squeak, which is not only a first class bit of nosh, but also acts as a finishing flag on the Christmas celebrations. Therefore we are back to normal in the shop tomorrow, where I shall steel myself lest any other unschooled punter decides to ask why we do not have a seasonal sale on. The mere thought of it sends a seasonal shiver down my wallet.

December 27ᵗʰ – Thursday

I felt a little uneasy walking the bleddy hound around this morning. We battled, more than walked, into storm force winds hacking across the car park from the west. Even nearing low water big waves were being thrown against the rocks of Pedn-men-du and the wind was howling and whining through the power cables. Strangely, the bleddy hound, she who will run screaming from a rattling plastic bag or flapping door, was completely unaffected, even when the lid of the public bin across the street rattled and banged. She was, however, up the steps to the front door well ahead of me for once.

The sea out across the bay was once again a spectacle to behold, despite there being hardly any visible ground sea, just a white churning mess. Even near low water the waves were still half way up the beach. Later on, Mother Nature really pulled out all the stops, as the sun broke through and the tide rolled in attracting a lively crowd of surf watchers – surf watchers who were not particularly interested in shopping, apparently.

Yes, it was another day of thumb twiddling, although we did manage to sell all of our pasties. We also managed to sell some woolly gloves that we had miraculously managed to get out of the store room and display in the shop. If we sell any more we might actually have to replenish the stock at some point, which is more than I can say for the fresh fruit. This is probably why the Missus thought I was bananas opening at Christmas.

I forced myself down to the OS for the quiz this evening. It was not busy, which was quite gratifying in a perverse sort of way. Team Head Launcher was a bit short handed as Head Launcher never turned up, but not quite as shorthanded as last week when nobody but me turned up. We did not do too badly, given that we were up against a team using their mobile telephones to acquire some answers. I think I would be dreadfully embarrassed having cheated to that extent and still lost.

I was embarrassed anyway, as I had brought my full rainproof gear with me on the premise that the Met Office had promised heavy and continuous rain for the evening. I am sure that you can imagine the derision I received while donning my water proof gear just before leaving knowing that it was as dry as a desert outside.

December 28ᵗʰ - Friday

The weather has done all it can to begger up my year and today was no exception.

It was actually quite temperate first thing this morning. That fierce wind had died away and the rain that was due overnight never really amounted to very much. The bleddy hound and I had a very uneventful walk around the block after I had sorted out the shop, and then nothing really happened until late in the morning.

Late in the morning the Missus went shopping.

I had decided to be useful today if it was quiet again. As you may remember, each year after we close we must record all the stock we have and enter it on a spreadsheet so that we know, first, what we have and, secondly, what we have used through the year. The latter information allows us some guidance when we reorder repeat sellers, such as postcards.

Last year, I deliberately reduced the number of postcards we ordered as I had assumed that the greatly inflated price of a stamp would deter people from sending cards. In fact, I had not ordered so many cards because I was being tight and was trying to reduce our over-stock, but the other excuse sounded better and made it look like I was being clever and strategic. Whatever my excuse, people kept on buying cards regardless of the price of postage, and it meant that we ran out of some lines early and have very little in the way of spares on less popular lines. This is almost the way it is supposed to be.

So, can you guess what the grumpy old shopkeeper counted boys and girls? Yes, that's right more postcards than you can shake a second class stamp at, and that is many several fewer than last year for the reasons stated. Therefore, my counting of postcards was not as onerous or long lasting as it could have been. In short it was the easy option.

That said it was just as well I did not elect to choose a lengthier task. As the day progressed we were blessed with more and more customers – well, people who came into the shop and looked around a bit. Then at around half past two there was a crowd starting to gather opposite. Some broke away and came into the shop and others were looking, clearly tempted. My hopes were raised; business was looking up.

It was then that the dry weather that had persisted all day gave way to a heavy shower. It was a short, heavy shower, but was sufficient to clear the street. It never recovered.

We did not get another spot of rain, not even with a Met Office weather warning in place for this evening. Not a bleddy drop.

December 29th – Saturday

Mmm, was I being rude about the weather yesterday? I did not think that I was that unkind. Certainly not so much that it should wish to teach me a lesson by raining hard and incessantly from the moment I opened the shop doors this morning. I suppose it could have been even more obtuse by raining on me as I took the bleddy hound around the block first thing, but it chose instead to suggest that it was going to stop altogether. It was teasing.

The sea was rather appealing in all this, with white water powering over the bottom of Pedn-men-du and thundering through the Tribbens. It was even more attractive later on with a bit of sunshine lighting it up after the rain decided to let me off a bit and abated. Much later it spent a good hour pummelling the Harbour wall in quite an athletic display.

I note that the Met Office has, for the first time ever, issued a landslide warning, aided and abetted by the British Geological Survey after several landslides had been reported across the West Country. I had thought that it mainly referred to further up where the cliffs are less rock hard and manly than here in the Far West but, oh, how wrong could I be?

Close to home I noticed that there has been another slip from under the Chy Ryn's driveway at the far end of the Harbour car park. It is not really surprising to be honest, since the fall consists entirely of earth; not a rock or stone in sight. I think that there was a biblical reference about not building your driveway on soft earth, as when the rain comes down and the streams rise and the wind beats down, your smart Mercedes Benz will fall down a hole, or something like that.

The rain did certainly come down in the morning but in the afternoon the assembled crowds that magically appeared had to play Russian roulette with the showers, some of them quite heavy. I played this very game with the bleddy hound and won, so perhaps my luck is improving.

I was looking out across the beach thinking that it looked just about perfect to take a small bleddy hound across it for a run with a ball. I looked at the bleddy hound and could see she was looking at the beach thinking that it looked just about perfect for me to take her across it for a run with a ball. So that was settled then; time to take a small bleddy hound across the beach for a run with a ball.

It had not rained for at least two minutes, so the timing was ideal. I donned my wet weather kit, collected the ball thrower and the back pack containing dog paraphernalia and the bleddy hound and set off for the beach. No, sorry, the back pack containing dog paraphernalia did not also contain the bleddy hound, she was separate. It was not entirely easy holding her back from tearing down there at 90 miles per hour, but we made it unscathed. It was fearfully windy down there and about a third of the way across I decided that it was probably best to turn about and stay at the western end.

Having turned around, the bleddy hound got it into her head that we were going home. No amount of wresting the ball from her and throwing it in the opposite direction could dissuade her. I did my best to keep her out for a bit longer, but she was determined. We must have been gone no more than three quarters of an hour.

We had a comparatively busy afternoon after I came back. We noticed from last year that it is busier coming up to New Year. There were some familiar faces amongst the crowd too, and it was rather nice to be serving people more often than reading a book for a change. It was even nicer to see that one particular book by a local, ahem, author is still popular; a lady bought three copies all bound for the other side of the world. I think I just heard someone rather unkindly remark that it was best place for them.

December 30th – Sunday

Gosh, we seem to be very quickly running out of year. I might have to hurry in case I miss it.

It was an exceedingly fine day today. It was overcast and grey and, from the reports of those that were out in it, extremely chilly and the sea was big and somewhat violent all day long. There you go, an exceedingly fine day; it did not rain. It did however lose me a crab line sale. I had to explain to a potential customer that taking a small child to the water's edge in these conditions, however irritating the child, was not exactly best practice.

We were busy too. There were loads of people milling about up and down the road and down on the beach. Also, I cannot remember seeing so many dogs around than there were today. It does make me wonder whether the dog ban on the beach has an impact on the number of visitors during the summer. Mind you our local heroic bobby reported that he had not seen so much dog mess down the street either. I wonder at the complete eejits who do not pick up after their dogs and at the furore when bans are introduced.

When the Missus pointed out that it was pointless doing the stock take of postcards that were in the shop while the shop was open, I scoffed. The number of postcards we shall sell, I told her, would not amount to a hill of beans in this crazy world. She seemed a little put out at my put down, but said that we would always have Camborne.

I was rather pleased that she went upstairs today to do some knitting, or watching a television programme she had recorded. During her absence, we had rather a lot of people come through the shop and every single one of them, it seems, bought a postcard or two. We shall of course, dear reader, keep that little nugget of knowledge between ourselves.

Our customers did buy other things as well, including all of our pasties, which was good, and little children still seemed to want to buy ice creams of which we have very few left. In the main they had all, young and old, disappeared by half past three.

Then, like the rising of the sun in the morning and the turning of the tide, at five minutes to closing, the five minutes to closing rush. It is so nice that there are things you can still rely on.

December 31st - Monday

Ooh! Nearly there!

I seem to have been completely wrong footed by the busyness of yesterday, or that is what I thought. Of course it was raining this morning; coming down in geet healthy bucket loads. That did not inspire me very much, and I do not think that we saw our first customer until half way through the day. It was not until I went and looked at the refrigerator and noticed that we had gone through half of tomorrow's allocation of milk that I realised that it had actually been busier than I had thought.

I reported a while ago now that many of these happy souls are increasingly expected to be from Asia in the coming years, and clearly today was a good day to begin for some. A gentleman and his companion came into the shop looking to buy a map of the area, he said. The girl was wearing a smog mask, and since it is not smoggy down here, in fact as far from it as you can probably get on the mainland of Great Britain, I wondered if they were planning on taking the map without payment. Apparently, this accessory appears to be some sort of fashion statement since she was also wearing it in the motor car as they came past later.

Anyway, I digress. Now, where was I? Ah yes, the chap wanted to buy a map of the area, so I pointed out the one inch map (it is probably something in centimetres now) on the top of the book case, which I informed him was a first class walking map. He told me that he was driving, so I showed him the next map up that covers all the way up to the Lizard Peninsula, but he again told me it was too detailed and that he wanted a road map of the whole of Cornwall.

Having pointed out the correct map to him he asked where he might get a lobster meal in the vicinity and also where there might be a town that was interesting to look at. I considered for a moment, after all if you are interested in vacant looking shops and people sitting in their doorways with ragged looking dogs playing penny whistles (the people sitting in the doorways, not the ragged looking dogs, although ...) Penzance is your place. If, on the other hand, endless streets of pretentious art galleries and shops selling nothing but fudge and sea shells you would not find on a beach within one hundred miles, then I would steer you more in the direction of St Ives.

With the rain abating, and visibility increasing, I suggested he take the coast road out to St Ives where, at least, the drive is very pleasant and he was more likely to find a restaurant selling lobster, even if the shops and ambience were not to their taste. I also suggested that Falmouth might be worth a poke around as well, as the town centre manager there has really pulled the community up by its bootstraps in the last year.

To this he said that it was unlikely that he would have the time as he had to be back in Weymouth by the evening. I do hope the service in the restaurants in St Ives is up to scratch as he could be very late getting back to base, else.

I am not overly excited by the New Year's Eve frivolity, but there was an excellent band playing at the F&L, many of my chums would be there and the they sell beer; consider it an extra Saturday night if you will.

The band was excellent. No, they were exemplary. They were *Even Nine* and played all the right songs in all the right places and had a rather packed F&L jumping, jiving and fully entertained. Everybody who was anybody was up there. It was so busy that even people who were not anybody were there too, and what a jolly shindig it was.

And before we all knew it we had slipped, with unerring certainty, into yet another year.

Happy New Year, everyone!

January 1ˢᵗ - Tuesday

I think I made a bit of a mistake with the opening days for this Christmas period. We have always shut at the end of the first day of the new year as everyone has always beggered off the day after. This year, however, it seems that everyone has booked in for a week's holiday and will be here until at least the weekend. And we shall be shut.

It is too late now, as it would take me a week to get the Laurel and Hardy Newspaper Company to register that I wanted to remain open and supply me with newspapers. We have also run out of other essentials that it would be difficult to resupply. So, in short, we are closing and that is that.

As if to rub in just how wrong I got it, we had the busiest day of all today. It did not start off all that well, but as soon as I had my breakfast roll out on the counter with a nice wedge of pate ready to eat, the crowds descended upon us, or rather me. I did not manage to finish my breakfast until after dinner time. I need not consider myself alone in this phenomenon as the second person in the queue of this deluge said he was also a shopkeeper and he said that it happens to him too. Still, I would do without breakfast, dinner and tea if it meant having a shop full of customers when I needed them.

However, I did managed to finish my Swedish book, which means I can watch the Swedish film of the book – in Swedish - tonight. I have to wait until the in-laws have gone to bed though, else it will clash with Eastemmeration Street or some such I expect. Still, since I made the mistake of not extending our shop hours, the shop will not be opening in the morning I can get something of a lie in.

January 2nd - Wednesday

There is nothing quite like the sound of the theme tune to *Last of the Summer Wine* to get a person out of the house. I had intended to leave anyway, but not necessarily white and screaming or in such a hurry. It was not like I was procrastinating; I was in the middle of rounding up invoices and such like from our week of opening.

My planned lie in was rudely disturbed by the insertion of a canine tongue into my slumbering lug 'ole, so I had plenty of time this morning. I got up and took the bleddy hound around the block. It was not unpleasant out, although a little misty, and the temperature mild and that stiff wind had died away. Ideal, then, for a little trip out.

I was keeping an eye on the beach as it widened before the retreating tide. I explained yesterday how inviting it was but today, at least, with the shop shut, I had the opportunity of exploiting it. So with time getting on, that theme tune was just the thing to spur me into action.

The bleddy hound was apparently delighted to be going on a proper run for a change, and so was I. It was rather liberating to be striding out across the sand without rod, staff or ski pole. All right, striding might be slightly overstating the case but I was certainly without my sticks, although there were one or two sticky moments where the sand became soft under foot or uneven.

One of these incidents was trying to cross the outfall from the stream that runs out from Vellandreath. I have heard from a couple of people who have said that they have never seen the stream so full. One of them reported that the water is lapping over the top of the bridge that runs between the cottages. We probably have the esteemed head gardener to thank that it is not much worse, as he regularly cleans the stream's course, but there is no need to tell him that; he has enough encouragement already.

It is no surprise, therefore, that the delta formed as the stream pours out over the beach is extremely wide. It was also quite deep in places and I had to be a little cautious. I had rather hoped that I could get up to have a look at the top end, but the sand was impossibly soft for me and the stream would need leaping at that point; leaping is not a forte at present or even, I suspect, in the repertoire.

As you might note we forayed out quite some distance from my usual safe area at the western end of the beach. Indeed, we got as far as my sitting rock just the other side of the black huts of Carn Keys. I hesitated to go further despite the fact the Escalls Vean was accessible, as I had to be sure we could get back again. I wager, though, that it will not be long now before I am gambolling over the fields and valleys like a spring lamb. I can hardly contain myself.

I had clearly run all the gambolling out of the bleddy hound; she collapsed in a little woolly heap when we got back and refused to move for the rest of the evening, save for going to get her tea.

It did not escape me that it seemed ever so quiet out. The beach was near deserted compared to yesterday's crowd and there were very few people milling about down the road. I shall have a chat with our neighbours in the café but it would seem that perhaps we were not wrong to close the shop after all. I can stop beating myself with birch twigs now.

January 3ʳᵈ - Thursday

A grey and overcast day. That must mean it is time to bury ourselves in the shop and do the stock take, ahead of the trade shows this month.

We would have got on very well, I am sure, if the telephone had stopped ringing for more than five minutes at a time. Most of the calls were for the Missus, so at least one of us was able to plough on regardless. After that the district nurse turned up for the old man so the Missus went and attended to that, but at least one of us was able to plough on regardless. The Missus had set a sensible time limit for our exertions so we did not carry on and burn ourselves out, and when she came back again this time limit had expired. It is all right, though, because at least one of us was able to plough on regardless. Sorry, did I make a bit of a meal of that?

Talking of interrupted projects, it is nice to see that the Penzance harbour development seems to have sprung into action. The Government has released funds after the various bodies agreed - well, agreed might be a little strong, maybe stopped fighting long enough for something to be actually done.

From what I can see the St Mary's side of the project will go ahead, and in Penzance they will be able to do a bit of dredging. The dredging is presumably on the grounds that the action group, Friends of the Bits of Weed Growing in the Mud in Penzance Harbour, can be dissuaded from kicking off a judicial review and, of course, whether the twenty billion amoebas living in the mud can be successfully re-homed elsewhere without affecting their single cell rights thus averting a spoiling campaign by Friends of the Mud Dwelling Amoebas in Penzance Harbour activists.

Although eight to ten million pounds has been released, the Government are apparently still looking forward to seeing a business case which seems a little cart before horse to me. They are aware that there is still some controversy (which is a nice way of putting it) related to the plans for the south harbour wall and have asked for this element to be separated out in the business case, presumably so that they can whip back that part of the cash should it all go pear shaped.

Lastly, it should be noted that the Government has praised the relationship between our, much maligned council and Penzance Town Council. This can be roughly translated as they are relieved that no representatives of either party has, so far, managed to bludgeon one of the other to death yet.

I am sure you would find it hard to imagine such controversy and confrontation happening in quiet little Sennen Cove, unless, of course you know where the bodies are buried. Here the regular launching of the Lifeboat provides a vent for macho posturing and keeps the levels of testosterone at manageable levels.

As if to prove the point our esteemed Coxswain called up an exercise for this very evening. The crew, so manly that even the women sport moustaches, gathered in great numbers for a launch into the best sea state we have had for several weeks. The excellent Shore Crew conducted themselves with aplomb, which is odd as they usually conduct themselves with a peach (please yourselves), and carried out a perfect launch and near textbook recovery. By the time the boat had returned, so had the rough seas and the recovery was undertaken in what looked like some

January 4ᵗʰ - Friday

Still grey and overcast; it is like living under a duvet. While that probably means that I should have ensconced myself in a little stock taking, I jolly well did not.

The father-in-law was due in to see the quacks at Treliske today. We had arranged for some burly ambulance people to come and carry him down the stairs since we still are not sure if he can manage them by himself and they duly arrived and carted him off. The Missus and the mother-in-law followed on in the van, leaving yours truly and the bleddy hound to look after ourselves.

I sat for a while enjoying the fact that *Last of the Summer Wine* was not playing on the television then did a bit of work type things on the computer. It was not until a little later that I realised that I could be watching the last of the Swedish films of the book now, instead of waiting until everyone had gone to bed. So that is what I did.

It was towards the end of the film that I noticed that the bleddy hound had been eyeing me purposefully. It had been fully two days since she had one of her longish runs out on the big beach and clearly this has now translated to it being her god given right to expect them more regularly. To be honest I am grateful for the excuse and, after a couple of months of sitting on a sofa with my leg up, in dire need of the exercise.

It was close to three o'clock by the time we hit the street. We could not have left a great deal earlier because of the tide, but there was plenty of empty beach to enjoy. Neither did we go as far as we did two days ago, but she was content to chase after the ball and sit in a sandy puddle to cool off. We met a few new friends and a few old ones while we milled about and watched two of the braver fishermen bring home their boats. There is still a fair bit of swell out there, born witness to by the number of surfers heading for the waves, but judging from the gulls the catch was good.

I had thought to dally at the OS briefly on the way home, but this is injun country at this time of the afternoon. The bleddy hound's mortal enemy lives close by and is known to wander with her owner in the afternoons and she was none too pleased to be there. The whining and the pulling at her lead were all too much, so she relented and did let me have one pint.

The father-in-law had returned during my absence. I have no idea what they did to him at the hospital, but apparently he was so chipper that he asked if he could climb our steps rather than be carried up them. I am told the scene resembled Chris Bonington bringing the Olympic Flame to the summit of Snowdon during the summer, except he did not have a torch.

He is a sly old devil. If he is that fit he can take the bleddy hound around the block tomorrow while I have a lie in.

January 7ᵗʰ - Monday

It was an absolutely super day for doing something completely unfathomable. I started almost as soon as I got up. It seemed like the right thing to do.

I had, in fact, started yesterday and had become stumped almost as soon as I had started doing it. Being a Sunday there was no one to call for help, so I had to give up. I hardly slept a wink last night as the anticipation and excitement were just too much.

I must have looked like a small child on Christmas morning as I ran to the computer to start all over again in the safe knowledge that someone would be at the end of the telephone to offer assistance. If you have not already guessed I refer, of course, to me completing my PCI DSS compliance questionnaire. If you have been following closely you will know that this should have been completed by the 1ˢᵗ October and by not doing so I incurred a rather hefty fine, sorry, I meant 'management fee', as my acquiring bank so euphemistically put it. They will continue to charge a further 'management fee' for each month that I remain non-compliant.

Alright, to recap, all businesses that accept credit card payments must spend a few bob becoming compliant with a Payment Card Industry Data Security Standard set up by, oh yes, the credit card companies themselves. If they do not then the businesses become liable to large fines if a fraudulent transaction is detected, and also become liable to huge management and non compliance fees.

So in order to become compliant I must complete a form, but unfortunately my acquiring bank will not accept the completed form unless it has been assessed by a qualified assessor. Oh yes, they have a tame one that they recommend, and they will provide this service if I pay my acquiring bank a management fee. Sorry, I know that sounds confusing but it really is not. This is not the same management fee that I am charged if I do not complete the form, this is a completely different management fee I am charged for completing the form.

Anyway, I am sure you are completely on top of the whole issue now and I can proceed with my story.

So I telephoned the assessor who will assess my completed form for the management fee I pay to my acquiring bank. They very quickly told me what I needed to know and I was on my way typing in answers to complete the questionnaire.

It is difficult to judge just how many pages of the questionnaire there were, but at a rough guess I would say at least twenty. As I proceeded through the pages it became very apparent that by answering certain questions in a certain way then I very quickly sailed forwards through the form. Now, I know some might say that this method of responding to questions is sometimes called 'lying', but I prefer to think of it as how the question is interpreted. For example, when it asked, 'have all authorised staff been properly trained in keeping credit card details secret', I had a very stern word with myself and answered, 'yes'.

By and large the questions were posed as if I were the information director of a fairly large company and as a consequence were completely inappropriate for a one man (and woman) show with one credit card machine and a website that people occasionally trip over and buy something from. To cover my rear end I now have a 'data security policy' and an 'incident response plan', which, in case you were wondering, is a couple of paragraphs written on the back of a fag packet. Having also second thought my way through all the questions I am also the proud possessor of a PCI DSS Compliance Certificate and will no longer be charged the monthly management fee. I can hardly wait until next year when I must go through the entire process all over again.

It was also very apparent that no one was really assessing this form at all and, unless I am very unlucky, no one ever will. As an experiment I introduced some real words in a nonsensical sentence in one of the free form areas. In a testament to the utter futility of this process I still passed with flying colours.

It took me a little while to calm down after all that excitement and it was just as well that I had a plan in mind to bring me back down to earth. We are, after all, in the middle of doing our stock take and there is one particular part of that which still needs to be completed: Shrew House.

Given that we expect it to be lashing down with rain tomorrow, and colder thereafter, it seemed to be the ideal day to do it. As I still have not discovered whether I can drive or not the Missus came with me. Surprisingly, we had the job done in less than a couple of hours; what a team. An hour after that I had also completed the input process and we are now up to date. It does mean that we must press ahead with the rest of the shop tomorrow as our first trade show is at the weekend.

The rest of the day paled into insignificance, really, although it was probably not that insignificant for the bleddy hound. She ended up at the vets in the evening to have something unspeakable, but routine, done at her tail end; the look on her face will stay with me forever.

Since we were in town it did mean that we ended the day with a rather fine curry from our rather fine curry house in Penzance. Now we have not done that for such a long time and I hope we do it again rather sooner than I have to do another PCI DSS form.

January 8th - Tuesday

I am beginning to think that I should have been a fisherman. Particularly a Japanese fisherman, out on the high seas seeking a particular type of fish.

I did not see much of today for several reasons. First the fog and mizzle had descended upon us and stayed all day. I did not go up there but I was told that it was much worse at the top. Later on the Missus and I disappeared down to the shop and between us completed all we needed to do for the stock take – whoopee – but it did take most of the afternoon.

First up, though, I had to settle a small matter with the Laurel and Hardy Newspaper Company. For some reason they had decided to charge me a full thirty three percent more for delivery than I am used to. This tipped the balance on the quiet newspaper sales over the Christmas period and, in short, I made a loss on selling them. I reported this important slip to them last week and they promised to get back to me, which, up until this morning, after I had given them a nudge, they had not.

The Missus took the call and was informed that a credit would be forthcoming for the over-charge. I had to call them back again as, in the meanwhile, I had received another invoice with the same mistake on it. The lady I spoke to apologised that the mistake had been made, but told me that the department that had made the mistake had blamed me. Despite having placed my customer number in the title and the first line of my email requesting newspapers for the period, they insisted that I had not told them that I was an existing customer and they had set me up as a new one. It is a wonder that I had any papers at all over Christmas.

I brought her attention to the fact that the same over-charge had been made again and would require another credit and in all likelihood the same error had been made on the invoice due today that I had not yet received. I also noted that I expected two more invoices and that, no doubt, they too would have the excess delivery charge, perhaps she could make sure that the final invoice reflected a credit for all the incorrect charges; a tall order, I know and I have no expectation that it will be correct.

Yes, that fisherman's job is looking more attractive every minute.

The Missus had to take mother-in-law up to see the doctor this afternoon for a check up. They were to see the rather fancy doctor who had attended the father-in-law recently. I considered offering my services as an escort, just to hold her hand, the mother-in-law that is, not the doctor, although … ; it is the sort of kindly son-in-law that I am. However, I thought that the gesture might have been misconstrued.

Instead I stayed at home and started the mind numbing task of entering all our collected stock data into the spreadsheet that I had prepared. I will not go into detail, as I gave you chapter and verse last year, I recall. Suffice to say I have numbers floating before my eyes; perhaps I shall have to visit the doctor after all.

I would not have had to worry about any of this as a Japanese fisherman and in fact, right now, I could be considering my retirement. A few days ago one lucky fisherman landed a bluefin tuna that cracked the previous record price for bluefin tuna by some margin. The new record is, wait for it, 1.8 million dollars or $8,000 per kilo if you prefer; that is roughly eight times better than the price of silver. That is probably something like £15 a (small) mouthful in a Tokyo sushi bar and they do not even have the overhead of having to cook it.

I am sure that there is a down side to being a Japanese fisherman but just now I really cannot think of one.

January 10th – Thursday

Despite the fact that the big rolling waves did not look that inviting to go out upon today, the sea will be a much safer place to leave your crab pots in future.

The problem arises for those fishermen that dare fish near and beyond the six-mile limit, especially off Lizard Point which I learned when I accompanied a local lad on his boat in that area last year. The mainly foreign fishing vessels quite regularly run over crab pots and fishing gear and carry them away with trawls or anchor cables. South West fisherman have been asking for years that the offending vessels, that can be tracked on AIS, be prosecuted.

Our local MP, bless him, has clearly single-handedly, by the look of the report, managed to sway the chief executive of the Maritime and Coastguard Agency to act. It seems that from now on the charts for the area of concern will be marked, "fish pots", so that all vessels will be aware to take caution when traversing, trawling or dropping anchor there.

I think our local representative and officialdom in general may have missed the point somewhat. When I spoke with the local fisherman who told me about the problem I do not think he was suggesting that the foreign vessels mashed up the pots and lines accidentally. Showing where the pots are on a chart is not going to help a great deal.

However, these seafaring matters were far from my mind as the Missus drove me up in the direction of Hayle this morning. It was the latest visit to see the specialist foot doctor who, unsurprisingly, wanted to look at my foot. He told me that all appeared to be well and recovery was progressing normally, but alas I would not be participating in this year's London or New York marathons and it was highly unlikely that I would ever play the piano or violin ever again, at least not with my foot. He said that it had been a pleasure and he did not want to see me again, a sentiment that I wholly reciprocated.

As we have been invited to a wedding (yes, we still know people young enough to be getting married and for the first time, at that) we can actually attend (it is being held before the shop opens) and as the Missus has made it clear that she will not be seen dead with me dressed in my sand coloured, hand tailored suit, I am looking for one that she will be seen dead with me in – er, I mean, oh never mind. Given that there is a large clothing retailer on the outskirts of Hayle we repaired there so I could at least have a geek at their suits. Well, that would have been the case but, although they had plenty of suit type trousers, there was not a single suit jacket in the place.

This is not a major problem as I had already looked in on the suits available from the small clothes retailer in town and, frankly, I would rather they had my shillings than Mr Marks and Mr Spencer who probably already have quite a few shillings from other people. The suit I had already seen was a nice shade of black. I had decided that a black suit would probably be a good idea as, while we still know people young enough to get married, we probably know quite a few more who are old enough to be planted reasonably soon and a black suit would do for both occasions with a cunning deployment of a different tie.

There is yet another option in nailing down this suit and one that I had not altogether fully appreciated. As we are heading east at the weekend we shall be near the big city lights of Exeter – it is a cacophonous and busy place near Devon, the last I saw it, and I was not much taken with it then. As I said I did not fully appreciate the reference the Missus made at first, as last year I went to the trade show by myself and avoided Exeter like the plague. It is, of course, a place that has shops and as the Missus likes shops I will, no doubt be dragged kicking and screaming about the crowded streets at some point during our visit. I am told that they will have suit emporiums aplenty. I can hardly wait.

Never mind, I shall put all thoughts of such torture aside for now as I am to attend a Lifeboat training night for the first time in several months. It was everything that I remembered it being and I even shamed some of the excellent Shore Crew into cleaning the brass bell that had been left unattended since my demise three months since.

January 11ᵗʰ – Friday

The heavy swell has taken its toll over the last few days and much of the reef at the bottom of the slipway has been uncovered. There are also a number of deep rock pools there that the bleddy hound delighted herself in, especially on the way back, hot and panting. The number of pot holes out across the sand made the going a little tough for me and it was something of a relief to reach the sitting rock for a rest. With hardly anyone about and the weather perfect I would not have missed it for the world.

January 12ᵗʰ – Saturday

It was never going to be easy getting out of the house this morning. We have in-laws staying, no, other in-laws staying for the duration of our absence and the Missus wanted the flat to be spick and span for their arrival. This meant ironing the silver and polishing the bed linen or something like that; it is technical and I do not pretend to understand.

We left for the other end of the world at around eleven thirty and got as far as the Costalot coffee house at Hayle. Now, ordinarily, you cannot go past Hayle without having a Philps pasty but since we already did that once this week we decided to burn our principles and have a sandwich instead. As we also needed some isotonic chocolate biscuits to munch on in the hotel room we dived into Mr Marks and Mr Spencer's excellent emporium and picked up an unhealthy snack or two to serve as breakfast.

We did not leave Hayle until near two o'clock, but some of that had to do with the petrol station nearby that was having some technical problems. We had to queue for some while, which is a novelty for us as we normally fill up at the local petrol station that never has a queue or, if in town, during the week when it is quieter. The filling up of the van is an experience that has the palms sweaty at the best of times, as the numbers on the petrol pump leap forward at an alarming rate and seemingly endlessly. When the whole process came to a halt without warning I was not sure if I had broken it or it had somehow determined the balance in my bank account and decided that giving me more fuel was far too risky.

When I went into the shop to enquire it was clear that the problem was not mine alone. It certainly had more to do with the technology, and quite a lot to do with the chap behind the counter who was doing a first class impression of a headless chicken. Offering to return at some unspecified point in the future to pay for my diesel did not seem to elicit the jovial response that I had expected. Perhaps I should have been a little more circumspect, since he had just chewed the ears off the customer who had preceded me.

We arrived late at the hotel, which is at least half an hour outside the shopping streets of Exeter. After I had registered and we had unpacked our bags I pointed out to the Missus that it would be impractical to go shopping now as it would take at least half an hour to get into town, even longer to find a car park that did not have a height restriction and by which time the shops would be getting close to closing.

I know that the Missus does enjoy the shopping bit, especially as we live so far from a proper shopping centre. I gave her my heart-felt commiserations and comforted her for as much as thirty seconds before I headed off in the direction of the bar.

Oh, come on. It is not like I did not suffer as well. The bar is not in Cornwall and did not have a band playing.

And one more thing. I was assured that the hotel had free access to the Internet, hence I held no concerns regarding filing the daily Diary. The hotel does have free Internet access but not in our room that is right at the end of the block and therefore out of range of the signal.

January 13th - Sunday

It was a bit of a trial getting the Diary published this morning. I had to tiptoe down the corridor in my pyjamas to try and get a signal, and on about the fifth attempt to connect I realised that I had not keyed in the password that the receptionist told me about yesterday. It was a good job that no one saw me; I do not wear pyjamas.

We were up and gone before breakfast was served, for our first meeting with a supplier in Bovey Tracey, which was a bit galling as our hotel rate included breakfast. Bovey Tracey is not far away and easy to get to from the hotel we are staying at, but the journey was accompanied by a slight whimpering from the driver's seat. The Missus had run out of hotel coffee the previous evening and none of the garages we passed provided a Costalot coffee franchise, which is apparently the essential brand, and rather set her on edge. It was not until just after our meeting that we managed to find a petrol station, fortunately nearby, that had the appropriate supplier in its forecourt shop.

We ate at this garage too, and for a roadside convenience eatery it was not at all bad. It also satisfied the cravings of the Missus who had clearly entered into a state of withdrawal. I shall consider booking her into a Betty Aston Martin Clinic when we get back. It is like the Betty Ford Clinic in America but is quintessentially British.

Our entire afternoon was eaten up by a traipse around the trade show at the Exeter Westpoint showground. The Missus had suggested we spend a couple of hours in Exeter shopping, but I said that it was doubtful we had sufficient time. I was given the warning, that if we for some reason got back to the hotel with time to spare, I was not allowed anywhere near the bar as a lesson for not letting her go shopping. As I suspected, the time at the showground raced by and we did not get back to the hotel until nearly six o'clock. I do not think I will get away with diverting her from her shopping trip tomorrow, unless by a stroke of good fortune Exeter has a half day closing on Mondays.

Last night we ate in the hotel bar area and selected from the 'light bite' menu as we were not overly hungry and the dining area was very busy. Tonight, however, we decided to push out the boat and book into the restaurant. I was not overly convinced that our booking had been taken, as the barman wrote my request down on the equivalent of the back of a fag packet. It also did not inspire confidence that last night the Missus's dinner was delivered but they had completely forgotten to register my choice at all. We ate separately, just like at home.

Just before we retired for the night the Missus reported that little flakes of white stuff were falling from the sky. I sincerely hope that they begger off before morning or that will severely disrupt our day and the likelihood of getting back to Cornwall at a reasonable hour.

January 14ᵗʰ - Monday

We did not have to get going as early as yesterday morning. In fact it was a distinct advantage to me as the later we were the less time we would have to procrastinate in Exeter doing the horrible shopping thing. It also meant that I could go and get breakfast for which, later in the middle of Exeter, I was very grateful.

First off we had a little trip up to Cullumpton, for yet another supplier which does not attend the trade shows. I can understand its stance, as it does have rather a wide range of stock. It would have been a mammoth effort to move that lot up to Exeter for just a few days and it really was not that far to travel.

Unfortunately, it did not take that long to go through their range and list down the various items that we will take on for next year's stock. This meant that there was plenty of time to run back down to Exeter for the dreaded shopping spree.

I have mentioned before that we have had issues in Exeter with its car parks. Being in possession of a van whose overall height I can never remember, and certainly not in both feet and inches and metres, rather means that multi-storey car parks are out of bounds. None of the signs pointing to the city's car parks indicate whether they are multi-storey or not, which makes it a bit of a game of Russian roulette as to whether we will arrive at a car park we can use.

We breathed a sigh of relief when we arrived at the car park we had chosen at random to find that it did not have a roof, or at least not at first look. It was not until we had taken our ticket and entered the enclosure that we saw that there was space for about fifty cars in the open, which was full, and thereafter vehicles were expected to enter the multi-storey section. We were just about to make our exit when a van very similar to ours, but sporting a roof rack, headed for the multi-storey entrance with no hint of hesitation. Thus encouraged I suggested to the Missus that if they could make it so could we.

It still gave the Missus the jitters as she drove under the height restriction. It made absolutely no difference that a van higher than ours had entered before us; the approaching roof looked very menacing and it fell to me to leap out of the van to observe and reassure the Missus as she moved forward.

We then spent several hours discovering the streets and shops of Exeter. You should have seen her little face light up as all those big stores came into view. They even have a brand spanking new John Lewis store, which, unfortunately, was a good mile from where we had parked. I am sure that you can imagine that I could barely conceal my delight as well, as I was dragged from one boutique to another. I did, however, manage to find a replacement set of waterproof trousers that I have been after for a while. You can be sure that 2013 will now be the driest year on record.

After wandering the alleys and the avenues of the Westpoint showground (someone should write a song about that, the alleys and the avenues, not Westpoint showground) for most of the day yesterday, and trudging between the stores today, my poorly stump of a foot was throbbing a bit. I was grateful when we got back to the van and on our way homeward.

The Missus bought me a copy of the *Western Morning News* earlier (did I ever tell you I once had a review ...). Now, it is said that many newspaper reports may be taken with a pinch of salt, but I can confirm without doubt this newspaper's front page story was bang on the money. It reported that Exeter City Council made £3.1m from car parking charges last year, an increase of 38 percent. When the figures are released for 2013 showing an even bigger increase I can tell you that £6.50 of it will be mine. The report headline was that Westcountry councils are making £189 per minute from parking and I can tell you, it certainly felt like it.

It was sheer delight dropping over the brow of the hill into The Cove in the evening, especially as we had to make two further shopping stops on the way back. Mind you if we had not we would not have eaten later. Then it was into the waiting arms of the in-laws and a bleddy hound that pointedly ignored us all evening. Yes, within an hour we might as well have never been away.

January 15ᵗʰ – Tuesday

Last night's rain had melted away leaving us dry and pretty in the morning if a little chilly. All right it was downright cold in the draft we had first thing.

It was a little better later in the morning when we drove into Penzance for my latest visit to the physiotherapist. I had not seen him for three weeks as Christmas had intervened, and when I saw him again today he said that he did not want to see me for another three to four weeks. I do not know if I should be getting the impression that he does not like me very much, but I am getting the impression that he does not like me very much. I am glad I am not paying for this else I would want my money back.

He did say that my recovery was going very much according to plan. Well he would say that if he did not want to see me very often, would he not? I am not entirely sure we can call this a plan; it is more a non intervention policy. However he was very clear that I should stay away from marathon shopping excursions and the Missus should not tempt me by going herself. At least that is what I told the Missus he said.

Since we were in town and it was a Tuesday, for a change I suggested we might try the new tapas restaurant in Bread Street. I quite fancied some tapas washed down with a cerveza or two. The Missus simply smiled at me and said that, first she was not that hungry and, secondly had my physiotherapist not just said that I was not to go wandering the busy shopping streets? Darn it, I thought, hoist by my own petard.

Ignoring my childish tantrum, she whisked me home where the big beach was spread out below us as we came down the hill. It was crying out for a small dog and a grumpy shopkeeper to go and trudge across it throwing a ball. It was also a grand time to try out my new waterproof trousers, not that it was raining but they are also windproof.

After my clean bill of health from the physiotherapist, and after walking several miles over the last few days, I was encouraged to step out a little further today. The tide was well out and we had plenty of time to explore, so we made our way over to North Rocks. It was abundantly clear when we arrived where all the sand from the south end of the beach had gone over the last few weeks. Much of the familiar rocky land marks at the north end are completely obscured, and the larger ones are barely above the sand. In many places I would say that the depth of sand has increased by five or so feet.

We also had plenty of space to conduct our survey and throw the ball around; there were only two other people on the beach with me and even then some distance away. The weather was perfectly reasonable so we spent quite some time messing around. The messing around also gives me sufficient time to rest the dickie foot before making my way back. The bleddy hound on the other hand was chasing the ball all the way out, all the time while we were there and, unusually, most of the way back. Mind you even she slowed up a bit towards the end.

Gosh, it is just fine and dandy to be back.

January 16ᵗʰ - Wednesday

We were both out of the traps dead early this morning. The van had to go in for a service and to acquire its MoT test certificate (since there is no MoT any longer, should that not be a DfT test certificate?) and that means it being at the garage in Buryas Bridge as early as possible. There is, of course, a small dichotomy between my first thing and the first thing the Missus uses, but by and large we were there roughly on time.

He is a good man and lets us use one of his spare motor cars while our van is being taken apart. He usually makes sure that there is at least a thimble full of petrol in the car before we take it away, but on this occasion the tank was nearly one quarter full; he must be slipping.

We took advantage of his generosity and slipped into town, which was the reason that we both decided to drop the van off this morning and I did not lanquish in bed and let the Missus do it on her own. I have already told you I have a wedding to be ready for and we needed supplies for tea this evening so there was plenty to do.

We were shopping in town, for me, expressly for a suit for this wedding that we have been invited to. Our local clothing store had just the thing but not before the salesman had rather pointedly raised the issue that they were rather short of 'long, portly' jackets.

Nevertheless, the good chap did find the perfect jacket and trouser combination and suggested that a waistcoat may also suit – presumably to cover up the portly element of sir's deportment.

Thus outfitted for the wedding of the year and hopefully one or two more formal events, such that I receive some value from my purchase, I went about collecting ingredients for our tea.

Ordinarily I would make the pastry for pasties the day before to allow it to rest but since I had promised the pasties for today I could hardly renege on my offer. I knew as soon as I had done it that the pastry was too wet and later when I started to fill them I noted the pastry was also too thin. Nevertheless the final offering was none too shabby, though a tad late to table.

The cause of the delay was a spot of first aid. Fret not, I did not have to dash out with bandages and rubber gloves up to my elbows. No, this is a first aid, or rather casualty care course, as it is rather more than first aid, run by the RNLI. It is an updated version of the course we undertook three years ago and is required for us to maintain our certification. The course will run two days each week for four weeks so it covers quite a bit. I am partaking in the afternoons although another session is run in the evenings for people who work for a living.

January 17ᵗʰ - Thursday

Most the rest of the day I have been glued to the computer screen making up the orders that we pencilled in from the trade show.It was while I was pasted to the screen that I noticed our sometime neighbours from around the back of us waving from across the road. These are the people that take the bleddy hound on extended walks when they come down. The dog was holed up in the bedroom with the Missus at this juncture, so I went down the corridor to see if she wanted to go with them.

I could hear the scratching at the door and whimpering as I approached and was relatively certain that it was not the Missus, but I opened the door to make sure. Now, I would imagine that you have seen movies where the unsuspecting victim opens a door only to be flattened by a torrent of water, or seared by the back draft from a raging fire. Well, I was flattened by a torrent of raging bleddy hound as she headed for the front door. Seemingly, she had heard the neighbour's dulcet tones and was going mad to get out long before I had got there.

She came back some while later with a slightly muddy undercarriage from her running around over two and a half miles of footpath and moor up to Land's End and back. It was just as well that she got her exercise in this manner as I had another casualty care session in the afternoon that prevented me from taking her.

January 18th – Friday

The dog walking neighbours took the bleddy hound for a run mid morning and she came back about two hours later pretty much uninterested in anything that did not involve sleeping. This made me somewhat redundant, short of taking her out in the morning and once more late in the afternoon.

However I did, very quietly, pass over another hurdle on the road to recovery. While the Missus was sleeping and the in-laws occupied, I slipped out for a little play in the van. This was a proper play, in the driver's seat with the engine running. Yes, I drove the van. This is something I have been unable to do since the accident and has left me entirely dependent on the Missus for my mobility to anywhere outside The Cove.

I did have a little proactive go in the empty Harbour car park to make sure that I could stop, especially in an emergency, and I did ensure the van was pointing uphill in case I could not. Thus encouraged, I set off up the hill to the shops, not a huge journey but enough to prove myself capable. I cannot express the joy of being on the open road again with the wind in my hair as I raced along. All right, there was no wind in my hair as the van does not have an open top and I do not have any hair and we were hardly racing, but you know what I mean.

Later on the Missus took the in-laws out for a drive, which rather quickly translated into a shopping trip. Clearly, I was not trusted on a journey that far. They came back from the big city with the van loaded with goodies and empty of fuel. She and I then went out as soon as they came back to get a Chinese meal from St Just. I cannot believe that they can go out shopping for the best part of five hours and not come back with any tea.

Mind you I probably spent rather more than they did with our postcard lady. She arrived promptly at one o'clock, had a cup of coffee and left about fifteen minutes later. Having already prepared the order yesterday, there was not much in the way of selling that she could do, which is the whole point of preparing the order yesterday. Apparently, the same is true of shopping lists!

January 19th – Saturday

A decidedly pleasant day, particularly on the weather front. It was the sort of day you would take an impatient dog down to the beach and let her run riot for a small measure of time.

It was colder down on the beach than I had imagined. My fingers were blue and numb by the time we reached my sitting stone. Before we got there and just as we were starting our quick march out across the strand we bumped into Picasso, you must remember him, I certainly do as I have a wood coloured corner of the shop front that still requires a coat of paint. I did not acknowledge him at first as the last time I saw him he had a small black dog. He now has the largest black dog you ever did see, although it does not walk strangely.

It was good to catch up with him and out of politeness I did not mention the outstanding painting job. I also understand that he is to be married in April and out of politeness I asked him where my invitation was. He thanked me for my congratulations regarding the wedding and we agreed that you probably could not expect to be happy all your life. He added that my invitation was in the post and would probably arrive at the same time the corner post of the shop front is painted.

Soon after the rest of my body started catching up with my fingers I felt that it might be a good plan to retire from the beach. Picasso had told me that he was heading for the OS but had added if he was still there when I arrived back from running the bleddy hound then he probably would not be getting married after all.

It is likely that he is still getting married as he had left the OS by the time I got there. The bleddy hound was not exactly the most delighted dog in the world at having to divert to watch me down a quick beverage or two. It also did not help that just inside the entrance was a big dog that was none too friendly and further along inside was another puppy that was far too friendly. In fact the whole pub was packed with dogs. I am sure that it would have been quite amusing if someone had walked in with a cat.

As it happened there appeared to be hardly any amusement whatsoever. I had only just commenced a second pint when the bleddy hound started tapping me on the knee and looking up at me with a pair of let's-go-home eyes. If she had a watch and a concept of time I would have no doubt that she would have looked at her wrist and tutted; she is definitely the Missus's dog.

The Sitting Stone

Having eventually been dragged home I took the opportunity of taking some documents down to the shop for shredding, duff batteries for the collection box and rubbish for the bin. I fell in with a passing pal while I was down there and we watched as a gritting truck passed by. First, I was quite surprised that a gritting truck passed by given that it is unlikely that we will freeze tonight and secondly that it passed by at all, unless someone has been sensible and seen that it is a route to a lifeboat station – no, do not be silly. I did note that it was only gritting the return side of the road. He was clearly Cornish, making absolutely sure our visitors could get home again.

January 20th – Sunday

It was some pretty day we had but cold, oh so cold. It was not so bad first thing when I took the bleddy hound around the block and when I came back the flat seemed to be all right to me. The mother-in-law told me it seemed a little cold and as she had not been outside I assumed she meant the flat, so I softened and turned on one of the heaters. It was after that I started to get cold myself.

Fortunately, we had been invited out to dinner by our neighbour who has a family dinner at around this time of the year. It at least meant getting up off my behind and moving about a little bit. The venue was new this year too and the name initially did not mean very much. It was not until we got there, up on the moors above Lelant that I realised that I have passed by the place a number of times. The Balnoon Arms very much lent itself to the kind of gathering we were party to with its big open bar with plenty of space for an extended family of more than fifty.

There were so many of them that a coach had been laid on especially for the occasion. Being a Sunday it was, of course, a carvery and very good it was too. It was, however, slightly surreal that we had to choose the size of carvery we were to have from small, two slices of meat, through medium to a large four slices of meat. The choice was even more difficult in that we had no idea how big a slice might be. I opted to go down the middle and ended up with more than enough for a lad trying not to grow.

When we returned home we fully expected to have a worn out bleddy hound on our hands, but as it transpired, the neighbours behind who had taken her shortly before we left had brought her back shortly after we left. They had started out only to find the bitter cold so debilitating that they had to turn back. I could hardly blame them. As I took her around the block after we returned the cold was seeping in through my bloomers and tugging at my fortitude.

Needless to say there was a long evening gathered around the one bar of our electric heater. I know, I am just a big softy, but I do not mind pushing the boat out a bit for the old codgers every now and then.

January 21ˢᵗ – Monday

We had a telephone call this morning from the lady that panders to my feet. Hey, you know you have made it when you have a lady that panders to your feet. Either that or you have some really bad feet. Anyway, she called first thing this morning to ask if we had any snow in The Cove.

It took me rather aback, as when I took the bleddy hound around this morning I reckoned that it was a tad warmer than it was last night. Mind you it could hardly have got very much colder than last night; it was bitter. I had even closed the skylight window in the bedroom just to let the temperature rise slightly above freezing before we went bed, and so that the warmth from the electric bar in the living room did not all float out of the bedroom window. I did open it again before we went to bed so that we had some fresh air during the night and the only part of me that gets cold during the night, my head, I wrapped up in the dog's blanket which turned out to be ideal.

So, when I got the call in the morning asking if we had any snow it came as a bit of a surprise. Then I looked outside and noticed that one or two of the vehicles that had arrived in the morning had around an inch of snow on top. There was a dusting of snow, too, at the top of Vellandreath. All I heard down here was a bit of rain splashing on the window.

Not to be outdone, the father-in-law had a medical visitor in the shape of the head district nurse. She was here for quite some time catching up on the events of the last couple of months. I held on for as long as I could but I am afraid that I could hear breakfast calling from the kitchen and I certainly was not going to ask all the assembled company if they wanted some. I sat in the corner eating my scrambled egg on toast and pretended they were not there.

The Missus announced that she was heading off to St Just shortly after things had settled down. Given that I have spent far too long sitting around at home gathering dust, I told her that I was coming too. Besides, I need to renew the road fund licence and having found all the appropriate documents was properly equipped.

The Missus immediately complained that we would have to go to Penzance for the road fund licence and she wanted to return home quickly with some ribbon she was sure she could get in St Just. I decided to go regardless; a trip out is a trip out, after all. It also allowed us to see how the air traffic control tower is progressing. When we passed by the other evening the control room was all lit up and, my, it did look ever so grand. I am sure it will be a fitting addition to Land's End Airport (it's an aerodrome) if they ever have an aeroplane fly out of there again.

As things turned out I was able to get the road fund licence from St Just Post Office, but the Missus could not get her ribbon from the town. A trip to Penzance was in the offing anyway.

It has been a while since I have been to the bottom end of town and especially to the Wharfside car park. It seems that our much maligned council must have had some spare pennies to spend as they have changed the parking ticket machines. It is now necessary to key in your vehicle registration number before a ticket can be purchased.

This prevents the heinous crime of passing the three hour ticket that you have used ten minutes of onto another council tax payer. I am guessing that the much maligned council spent a fair amount of money in determining that transferring tickets was causing serious loss of revenue, at least as much as the survey and the cost of ticket transfers, times the life of the new machines in operational years. Who knows? Perhaps a dodgy looking character with a van full of cheap parking ticket machines turned up at the council offices one day, "'Ere guv, want a job lot of parking ticket machines. I'll do yer a good deal." (Note: men selling dodgy parking ticket machines are always from London.)

Whatever the case they are a serious pain in the bottom, as I had to go back to the van to collect my glasses as I could not read the layout on the keypad. It also took three times as long to get a ticket and with only a few of us wanting one on a cold

Monday in January we quickly formed a queue. Anyway, with all that money with which to buy new machines you would think that they could have got ones that give change.

Never mind, they will not be needed soon. Our much maligned council are hell bent on closing Penzance town centre and with the opening of the new supermarket on the helicopter site we will all soon be able to park for free. If you do not have a car, do not worry. As part of the new supermarket deal a new bus will be laid on to take people from the town centre to the supermarket at no cost. It is advertised as a bus service to take people into town but we know what they meant.

While I still could, I bought a road fund licence holder from a shop in town to stick to the windscreen. We have a new one, you know – windscreen, that is, as the old one had a big crack in it – and the old holder would not re-stick. I also stopped into the book shop to see if I could find a new book. There were plenty there, but they wanted me to actually buy one whereas I am so used to having them donated for free.

So with nothing left to do we were soon back home where I could watch the calming vision of a big angry sea bring my blood pressure back to normal. 190 over 95 – perfect.

January 22ⁿᵈ – Tuesday

Another interesting bit of sea to have a long look at, especially out towards high water. The breeze blowing back the tops of the waves as they came rolling in and thumping up the cliffs from Aire Point to Cot Valley.

Even now there will be some fishing going on, which is my way of saying that I have a little bit of news concerning fishing coming up. It seems that not everyone is happy with the burgeoning campaign to get rid of fish discards. You may find that strange and how could anyone agree that throwing back fish that exceed quota be a good thing.

Well, the Danes are particularly vociferous on the matter; their main concern is the additional costs that modified practices of reducing discards will involve. Here in the UK a South West fisherman has put his head above the parapet and has some science on his side. Apparently 40 to 100 percent of flat fish survive the discard process. Should discards be banned then this proportion of fish will be killed and serve no beneficial purpose; essentially, worse than discarding them. Heavens! This argument looks set to run and run.

But wait, I also have some good and wholesome news. The excellent Shore Crew have had to make their own entertainment for the last few months as the satellite dish attached to the aerial mast on the side of the boathouse has been somewhat less than attached. It blew off during some robust winds and I cannot remember exactly when. Today a satellite dish repair man arrived, and standing on top of the ILB fuel store replaced the dish. Oh, the sheer joy of it; we will be able to watch the second half of Emmerdale Farm on Thursday nights when the boat is out on exercise.

And you may have noticed from the clutching of literary straws that next to begger all happened today to tell you about. So rather than continue to flagellate this particularly expired dunkey I shall withdraw to fight another day.

January 23ʳᵈ - Wednesday

After yesterday's disaster I thought I better do something today. Then I realised that I have the next instalment of my casualty care course in the afternoon so I would have precious little time to something very exciting.

Mind you, why do something really exciting when we have such a rip-gurgler of a day to look at. It was bright with much blue sky and sunshine and, early in the morning, quite a bit of golden sand to appreciate. I observed it jealously thinking that it would have all disappeared by the afternoon when I usually take the bleddy hound out, but there again I would not be able to take her anyway today.

Hang it, I thought. I shall take her down there this morning and dash the consequences. That is the kind of devil may care attitude I woke up with this morning, and who would blame me. After all, I am sure the ancient codgers can pander to the Missus's every need for an hour or so; I would hardly be missed.

I had these thoughts at around nine o'clock this morning, shortly after low water. By the time I was getting ready to go out the tide seemed to have covered half of the available beach. I know that it is neap tides at the moment but that really is taking the Mickey.

It did not bother the bleddy hound much and we made it down to our sitting stone without getting our feet wet. We met a few other dog walkers on our way out, but by the time I had got comfortable on my rock and looked back we were just about alone on the beach. It was not until we were on our way back that we met another group coming the other way. The lady asked what kind the bleddy hound was and for once I managed to restrain myself from telling an enquirer that she was part nuisance and part pain in the bottom. I did add, though, that to keep her curls we stick her paws in the electric socket every morning. I was expecting a small polite chortle, or perhaps just to be ignored. What I did not expect was to be asked if that was really so.

It was quite a relief to return to the Lifeboat station to practice some of the things we had learnt from the previous sessions of casualty care. We were all given the opportunity to be manhandled and to manhandle our fellow lifeboatmen, including strapping each other in stretchers and pumping air into each other. What jolly fun all this looking after poorly people is, well, at least while they are not really poorly.

It was almost a shame to retire to play a game of cards at the OS. At least I had more success in reviving my fellow man than I did in winning a hand of poker. I did, however, have a wondrous star filled sky to gaze up at on my way home. That just about made it all worthwhile.

January 24ᵗʰ - Thursday

I rather spoilt my quiet little walk around the block with the bleddy hound this morning. It was such a pleasant day too.

For the last week or so the builders working away in Myrtle Cottage have been somewhat thoughtlessly parking their vans in Coastguard Row, leaving the smallest of passage ways to get through. Had I been firing on both pins I may have let this slip, as passing by would not be so troublesome. As it is, squeezing through on one and a half pegs is, and they have been getting more sloppy about leaving some space.

I spoke to one of the drivers a while back about it and he kindly moved his van without a fuss, mainly as he was in it at the time. This morning, however, two vans were parked and between them completely blocked the roadway. As much as I hollered, I could not make myself heard, so had to retrace my steps back around and through the car park.

When I set off I had intended to be quite reasonable in my remonstrations with the workmen and their somewhat inconvenient parking. By the time I had hobbled back through the car park, however, and climbed up the slope to Myrtle Cottage's door I had prepared my verbal shotgun and loaded both barrels.

Teasy Shopkeeper: "Those your vans parked inconsiderately in the road there?"

Workman: "Yes."

Teasy Shopkeeper: "For over a week now I have struggled to get past your vans inconsiderately parked there. Even the fully fit would find it hard today and I am sporting a recovering injury my 'ansum; for me it is impossible or impassable, if you prefer. If your vans are there tomorrow I shall request the local constabulary to adorn your vehicles with nice shiny penalty notices."

Workman: (now affronted) "There's no need to be like that. You could have asked nicely."

Teasy Shopkeeper: (now more teasy) "I did when I spoke with your co-worker last week. Being nice did not seem to work, did it?"

Workman: "Oh. I'll park them down the front, then."

Teasy Shopkeeper: "Very good. Thank you."

On reflection I think that my hard man image might have been enhanced had I not had a bleddy hound hanging off a pink lead in one hand and a full poo bag hanging off the other. I shall bear this in mind next time I am remonstrating with workmen.

It would have been a sight worse if I had been in possession of my latest accessory which arrived this morning in the post. I have been suffering a bit with a cold head, as opposed to a head cold, during the night as our bedroom is unheated and we leave the window open. I said that I nicked the bleddy hound's blanket the other night, which was ideal, but she has since nicked it back again. Subsequently, I have variously used a t-shirt and a towel neither of which really cut the mustard.

With this in mind I trawled the Internet for a hat suitable to be worn at night and that did not resemble at item worn by a certain nursery rhyme character. Well, I have to say that my exhaustive search left me exhausted but turned up two options. One was to procure a sensible hat from a company based in America that looked perfect but expensive, if you include the postage and the exchange rate. The other option, of which the choices were legion, was the acquisition of a hat resembling an item worn by a certain nursery rhyme character. To make matters worse only one of the online shops was a clothes retailer and all the rest were fancy dress shops, which rather added credence to the belief that this was an item of jest, inviting derision and mockery.

What I am trying to say here, is that I am now the possessor of a Wee Willy Winkie hat, without the bobble, I will have you know, which I shall be wearing hence forth during the cold snap to keep my head warm during the frozen nights. I shall have to let you know tomorrow whether it worked or whether the embarrassment was far too much. It does also mean that I will have to go to sleep after the Missus if I do not want a picture of me wearing it on Face Page going viral across the globe.

January 25ᵗʰ - Friday

I know, I know, you have all been watching the news with dismay seeing that mackerel is now off the "eat with a happy heart" and onto the "eat with caution" list. You can blame the Icelandic and Faroe Island chaps scooping them up with gay abandon, or the fish for beggering off outside EU member state waters. Either way, it is unlikely to sooth your furrowed brow after forcing yourself to enjoy mackerel over a nice bit of cod or haddock.

But fear not. I have some excellent news for you mackerel loving gastronomes. Both the Marine Management Organisation and the Marine Conservation Society who decides what gets onto the, "eat with caution list", have both been quick to report that it is still perfectly acceptable to eat south west handline caught mackerel and in abundance too. So, what are you waiting for? Ah yes, you are waiting for the Old Boathouse Stores to open its doors again so you can order your handline caught mackerel from a reputable source (even if the shopkeeper is highly disreputable).

The bleddy hound has been a tad under the weather for the last couple of days with a bit of an upset tum. I told the Missus on her way out to the shops to get a nice bit of cheap white fish and I would make the bleddy hound something mild with rice and fish. She returned a couple of hours later with a geet lump of haddock; I should have guessed that the words, 'cheap' and 'dog', are mutually exclusive in the household.

Anyway, I halved the fish and made up something bland and inoffensive for the bleddy hound's tea. Sorry, did I say inoffensive? "If you think I'm putting that anywhere near my mouth, my 'ansum, you have got another thought coming. You think it's so good then you bleddy eat it." This epithet was written all over her face as she took one sniff, looked at me then beggered off back into the living room. After that she would not touch anything else.

Well, there is absolutely no point in flogging a dead horse. Perfectly aware that I still had half a haddock fillet in the fridge and with plenty of cooked eggy rice still left I knocked together some kedgeree and had it for breakfast the following morning and very nice it was too. I did try some more on the bleddy hound but she was having none of it.

Now, if the bleddy hound is off her food you know that she really is unwell. It also meant no beach walking for either of us and a quiet day all round. The Missus was making noises about taking her to the vets, but we decided to leave it another day and this morning she actually went looking for her food bowl; a good sign. I still decided to let her rest another day, particularly as it was tipping it down outside with a smart puff of wind too.

It was a shame that we could not get out; the household is full of ill people at the moment with only me not suffering. I would suspect that is just a matter of time, though. With a bit of luck we shall have some weather tomorrow and I will be able to escape, all supposing I have not been struck down too by then.

Now, if you will excuse me I shall go and address my haggis.

January 27th - Sunday

I pretty much had my day mapped out for me, for it is SOS (Support Our Station) day at the Lifeboat station. I did have a little time to myself before that kicked off, which left me just enough time to drag the bleddy hound out.

The blasting wind had obviously followed us home last night; I could hear it this morning whistling around The Cove roof tops. When I walked past the boathouse it fair near bowled us over and was in our faces as we cut across the car park. It did not seem that cold but as the day worn on it seeped into the bones.

It seems an odd time of year to run a fund raiser. Many of the Lifeboat stations across the country will be in the same position as ourselves with few people about. We were fortunate that it was sunny, if not warm, and the promised rain held off until the evening. We had a few visitors, many of them local, but also a few from further afield who were shown around the boat and took tea provided by the ladies of the fund raising team. I suspect that much of the tea and cake went to the hypothermic crew staffing the event and very nice it was too.

With the sea boiling all day there was never any danger of getting either of the boats afloat and there would have been few spectators too. As the tide turned to flood the waves got bigger and bigger and in the light from the dropping sun looked something spectacular crashing over the wall and up and over Pedn-men-du.

I thought I had better whip the camera out and slip down to the Harbour car park for a few shots and, blow me down, the car park was packed with storm watchers. Where were they all day when we needed them?

January 28th - Monday

It did not look that wet or stormy. All right, it looked a bit wet and stormy but I decided to take the bleddy hound down to the big beach anyway. After all, I have new waterproof trousers and a big waterproof jacket and, yes, I do know that the bleddy hound does not, but she does have a big thick woolly coat that the Missus back-combed last night; she looked like a furry snowball with a face sticking out of it. It required urgent modification else we would not be going out together again; I have a miserable reputation to uphold.

Fortunately, hardly anyone was around and although it was raining a bit (and certainly enough to damp down the fur ball) we were not deluged. Even as we walked across the bleak beach it was hardly a monsoon. I did stop short just beyond Vellandreath because the sand was dryer and starting to fly at about shin height, or bleddy hound height if you will, and I was feeling sympathetic.

It was when I turned around that I discovered it was rather difficult to stand upright. The wind was hacking across the beach in 50 to 60 miles per hour gusts. I must be streamlined from the rear as I really did not notice it. We did not bother to throw the ball as I am pretty sure it would have gone backwards.

I had been gone so little time that the in-laws, who were being taken out, were still there when I got back. I was dripping and so was the bleddy hound. At least now she had a few curls back and looks more like a country girl and a little less like a Crufts entrant.

And that was pretty much the end of the excitement of my day unless you count looking out of the window at a big, unrelenting sea. These are definitely not days for dashing out and doing things. No, these are days when you let the Missus dash out and collect the doings for a first class bit of mussel and prawn chowder which you then eat too much of and spend the rest of the evening regretting it. Marvellous!

January 29th - Tuesday

Despite the fact it was still damp and stormy it was a marginally more interesting day today, but only because I managed to drag my lazy frame out of the house and go and do something.

The Missus excelled herself in getting out of the house and doing something, as she went off on a shopping trip to Plymouth. Thankfully she went with some pals and took the train, leaving me with the van and strict instructions to take next door's hound out every now and again.

But for that little proviso and the fact that our own bleddy hound would need some out time too I would have taken the van and been gone most of the day. As it was, part one of my big trip out was a little journey over to St Just to see the doc.

Now, before the Aged Parents fall onto the carpet in apoplectic concern this was a little straightforward check-up to make sure that nothing had fallen off since the last little check-up and everything is working as it should. Since part of this examination includes a blood pressure check I felt it sensible to avoid the young, red-headed doctor who has visited the father-in-law on occasion, as I have a suspicion that it might have skewed the result somewhat.

Rather cunningly the surgery has introduced a robo-receptionist. Given that the real live receptionist is still present I must conclude that this is not a step down efficiency boulevard, but a method of determining that the patient's mental faculty is firing on all cylinders. The machine invites the incoming patient to enter the day of their birth onto the screen by selecting from the available choice. It is clearly a complex mind game as the screen only contains numbers up to 31. The patient has to be mentally competent enough to realise that they actually meant the *date* of your birth rather than the day – unless, of course, it is even more cunning than that and there is some complex formula from which the patient should be able to deduce a number that relates to a day of the week, in which case I failed miserably and can expect, at any moment, to be carted away by men in slightly soiled white coats (there is a recession on, after all).

In the time left available to me I should continue swiftly, then, to assure the Aged Parents that I am in fine fettle or as fine a fettle that any slightly overweight, heavy drinking (against the latest Health Department scale), couch potato of a shopkeeper of my age is likely to be. I do however need to return next week to have a blood pressure monitor fitted – again – just to ensure that the practice gets good value out their investment in the tool.

My next trip out was slightly more enjoyable. This time I ventured into town to gather some goodies for tea. With the Missus away deep I must fend for myself, and this means selecting any meal at all including those not on the Missus's favourite list, such as fish; the Missus hates fish. Naturally, I elected to gather the fresh items from the local independent stores in town where, as you will know by now, dear reader, fresh fruit and vegetables may be acquired at better value if not wholly cheaper than the naughty supermarkets on the edge of town and, in case you were wondering, I was able to park for a pound.

Also in town is a shop that sells photographic and optical equipment such as telescopes and binoculars. For a fee they will also source third parties that will fit a tripod bracket to a field telescope (I bet they do not do that at Tesmorburys) which is handy as we have a field telescope that requires the fitting of a tripod bracket, as the original is broken and has been for some time. They promised to telephone me with a quote but I did see a pair of high powered binoculars in the window going for a song.

Off then to collect some fish from the shops opposite the fish market. If I were particularly pedantic about the number of food miles my fish had travelled I would have thought that two hundred yards would have me cock-a-hoop. I picked up a side of smallish hake for a fiver; job done.

The last job I had in town was to talk with the chap in the little television shop along the promenade. The Missus has been complaining that the television in the bedroom does not pick up all the channels that are available off the St Just transmitter (which, incidentally is fewer than the number of channels available off the Redruth transmitter and somehow we are charged the same television licence fee for this inferior service). She has berated me for being unresponsive to her needs, which is poppycock; it has only been two years since she first asked.

I also wished to gain some advice regarding new televisions. Our set in the living room shows an increasing number of dark lines down the left hand side of the screen when it is first turned on and after the set has warmed up dark splodges appear in the middle of the screen causing the actors to appear to have big bruised foreheads. More recently it has also appeared to only display programmes that I am uninterested in, and particularly a preponderance of *Last of the Summer Wine* episodes, that is becoming increasingly irritating.

In my research so far it appears that the better screens all sport this new fangled 3D feature which I do not really want and are stacked with technology that will become redundant within six months of buying the set. I already have this technology available to me through cheaper external boxes that can be replaced or upgraded at a fraction of the cost of replacing the television.

Our man agreed that the manufacturers appear to be pushing their high end boxes but maintained that the next models down were just as good in terms of picture quality. Unfortunately, he also raised the prospect of switching to a plasma screen which is better at displaying motion that the LCD screens. It means that I must go through that whole argument again and decide which technology I really want or, indeed, whether I want a new television at all if it only shows programmes that I do not watch.

After such an exciting interlude, well, it was for me, I returned as I need to be available to take mother-in-law off to St Just for an appointment. Before that the bleddy hound and her neighbour needed to be walked around and the tea needed to be prepared. I tell you, life these days, well, just today really, is one headlong rush from job to job.

Certainly not so for next door's dog. Later in the evening as I waited for our fish to bake in the oven I ran both her and the bleddy hound around for the last time before the long distance shoppers came home. The weather had started to fall apart and as I looked out of the window I could see, admittedly light, rain coming in horizontally between us and the boathouse. As I anticipated, the bleddy hound made short work of her business and made to go home. Unfortunately, next door's dog which clearly did not want to be there in the first place, procrastinated for twenty minutes until I took her back to the first place we visited before concluding her task. It was like going shopping with the Missus, which is why I did not go today, oddly enough.

January 31st - Thursday

In a day that was unlikely to yield much in the way of interesting stories I am exceedingly grateful for this little warm potato dropping into my lap. It follows on from what I was saying a few days ago about the Marine Conservation Society downgrading mackerel on its what to eat list. They were quick to point out that the handline caught mackerel were still a sustainable option and very much on the menu.

Underlining this view the local chaps have come up with an understandable example of what the Cornish fishing impact is against the EU quota for mackerel this year. It suggests if we view the whole quota as one mile of Cornish coastline (no, a proper mile, not a Cornish mile) then the Cornish handliners part of that would equate to the first 3.5 yards. Further, in 2012 out of a Cornish handline quota of 1750 tonnes the fleet only managed to catch 648 tonnes. I can well believe this as it was the devil's own job to get hold of mackerel last year.

February 1ˢᵗ – Friday

Please do try your best to avoid telling the Missus that there are only six weeks left before we throw open the doors of the shop again, will you? Sometimes six weeks can seem interminable, say, for example you are waiting for your new sofa to arrive or the last of the season's *Last of the Summer Wine* to be shown on television. When you are the Missus and quite comfortable with the shop being shut, six weeks is the blink of an eye or the apparent useful life of your latest handbag.

The Missus and the father-in-law drove the events of this particular day of the few we have left. The father-in-law had an appointment up at St Just with the angelic doc and the Missus suggested a bit of dinner up the F&L if the father-in-law was still up for it, which he was. They picked me up on the way back, and we found ourselves near enough the only people there. They all had main meals while I had a baguette (one has to consider one's sylph-like frame, don't you know. The last time I was able to consider it without bending forward was 1983, I believe).

I had already planned the next phase by asking the Missus to bring along the bleddy hound's beach kit that includes the ball thrower. I had her drop me at the far end of the Beach car park which saved me a hundred yards or so. I had made it about a hundred yards across the beach when my mobile telephone rang, which in itself was a surprise as I usually forget to turn it on. It was the Missus telling me she did not have a key to get in, so I had to retrace my hundred yards to give her mine. It is always the little things, is it not?

By the time I had reached my sitting rock I was ready for a rest. The sand has been so eroded from the north end of the beach that it was a struggle even to get up on the low end of my rock. It was also exactly the wrong place to be, as in line with one of my ball throws was the ancient remnants of a seal which the bleddy hound took an immediate interest in. Despite throwing her ball in all the directions away from it, the decaying beast seemed to be a continual draw so I cut my losses and walked back.

Having already wet my whistle at the F&L I was in the mood for some gratuitous over indulgence so I dropped by the OS too. For once the bleddy hound did not seem to mind too much and let me over indulge quite happily. I might have to do that more often now we only have six weeks left.

February 2ⁿᵈ - Saturday

Well, today was something of a race against time. Everything required some precise timing and cunning tactics for it is, of course, the start of the Six Nations Championship and missing any of the key games is unforgivable.

The first game to watch today started at half past one in the afternoon. Before that there was a bleddy hound to exercise as it would have been a bit unfair to let her suffer, the poor hard done by thing.

And where was the Missus who could have performed such a necessary task? Ah, she had bunked off on a big jolly to Wadebridge where the bride of the wedding we have been invited to was having her hen night, or more exactly her hen afternoon. I am sure that someone will enlighten me before long, but I was unaware that Wadebridge had acquired the status of the place to be when having a hen afternoon. Yep, the Missus has just returned and informed me that Wadebridge is not the centre for hen night delight, it is a place called Hustyns, and that was not either.

However I had a whale of a time, to begin with at home, watching the first match as, apparently, there was nothing else on television and then at the OS for the second match when, apparently, there was. I came away directly after the match had finished and when I got back I took the bleddy hound around, bless her. Not long after I got back the Missus arrived home.

Now, the Missus did not inform me as to what sort of time she was getting home. I did ask but apparently no one could tell me. With this in mind and with no intention of missing an evening at the F&L and knowing full well that walking up would probably be beyond my ability I was faced with little choice. Oh, come on, you would have done the same, I am sure. I telephoned our local cab company; he who can count Mr J Depp among his bessie mates (sorry, is that right – Microsoft Word says no but what does it know about street culture).

The first reaction I had was, as expected, incredulity that anyone, other than a complete girlie, would hire a cab for less than a mile's walk. I tried to explain that the dodgy foot was to blame only to be told that, apparently, the Missus had told him that I had achieved a complete miraculous recovery. Having explained that I was not yet quite that fully recovered he was more that happy to come and fetch me despite the ridiculousness of the journey.

To top off something of a blinding day and a first class evening I got it in my head to walk home. As I got to the turning to lead me down across Esther's Field I remembered that I had forgotten my torch. Ordinarily I might have chanced it as I know every part of the path quite intimately, but I know that a couple of stones have fallen across the path since the last time I was down it and the stiles can be treacherous. I swallowed my pride and took the main road back home only to be passed by the excellent Mr P in his taxi cab. I watched as he dropped someone off opposite the Lifeboat station. Had it been raining he might have had a different wave as he passed me on the hill on the way back up again.

February 3ʳᵈ – Sunday

After all that running around yesterday I was a bit weary this morning. It was the Lifeboat engines that roused me from my slumber, the last time they shall do so hopefully. Obviously, I was still excluded from the activity but from tomorrow I am signed back onto the work register and shall no longer be living off immoral earnings. While I am not one hundred percent match fit, I can slowly integrate myself back into society – if society will have me back.

I did put a tentative foot, the good one, back into the station as the boat came back in again. I watched from the sidelines, but instantly felt part of it all again. Head Launcher came back home for a cup of coffee and TS gave our casualty care trainer and her partner a tour around the Lifeboat. It was some tour, unless he was showing them around St Ives as well; he was gone for ages.

The Missus took the old codgers out for a trip, and I took the bleddy hound down to the Harbour beach for a bit of a short run around. We had been watching the mist roll in and out since first thing, sometimes filling the entire bay. There must have been some bright about as the gannets showed up brilliant white against the grey backdrop. It is odd how they like a bit of weather and rolling sea to go with their fishing. Even then, I thought I was being a little over cautious by wearing my waterproofs but clearly not as we caught the only shower of the day.

She ran her little paws off on the beach and even did a bit of swimming before we headed back. It just gave me enough time to start watching my third rugby match of the weekend before the in-laws came back. They did not want to watch anything else, which was fortunate as it was another blinding good match. I reflected on how athletic the players are now compared to when I first started watching; I bet they do not come off at half time for a couple of fags and a swill anymore.

I had the temerity earlier in the day to rail against the proposal of yet another roast dinner for Sunday tea. I do not mind having a roast meal once in a while and, for a change, occasionally during the week. To have to suffer a roast dinner every Sunday week in and week out in metronomic drudgery is, at the very least, dull and unimaginative. To my utter surprise the Missus and in-laws yielded to my reactionary ways and bought the contents of a stir-fry. My penance, though, for my insurrection was to cook it and do the washing up. A small price to pay, I promise you.

For the rest of the evening I basked in my successful revolution in the full knowledge that they will be ready next time and a roast it will be. Roll on the shop opening when the Missus will not have the time or inclination to cook one.

February 4ᵗʰ - Monday

This month is already off to a flying start and nothing much yet to show for it.

I had to take a trip into town to pick up the telescope that cannot be mended. I had a little think about those big binoculars they had in the window and thought better of it. For that money I could have a couple of the rust spots on the van fixed. This was another reason for heading into town, as I had been told of another body works chap in Drift who I could not find the other day when I looked. I found him today, but he was not that keen. He said he was near retirement and the job was too big. That was worrying; how long did he expect the job to take?

He also suggested we have a word with the mechanic who looks after our servicing, as he would also do the job. I thought that he might, but kind of assumed he would be a bit more expensive than the other two suggestions I have had. I dropped by anyway and he wants the van in for a morning so that he can have a proper look and give me a quote. If it is going to take him couple of hours to do the quote I can probably wave goodbye to the van for a month for him to do the work. In fact, I will probably have to leave him the van to pay for it.

I was not much more successful looking for a waistcoat to go with my bow tie I intend to wear at the wedding. To be fair, I am not surprised; you would be hard pressed to find anything to go with the bow tie I have for the wedding. The Missus also drew a blank in the same store looking for a jacket to go with her wedding clothes. Having spent an entire day in the city of Plymouth buying a wedding outfit, then changing your mind, it was highly unlikely that a little independent clothes shop in PZ was going to come up trumps. I have to confess to liking the place very much. They still have sales assistants who call you sir (if you are a man) and have tape measures around their necks that they do not need because they know your size just by looking – even if it is a 46, portly.

I made the mistake of agreeing to meet the Missus at the bottom of town in the van. She was 'just popping in' to a store to get some frozen rice and would be waiting in the Wharfside car park by the time I arrived so we would not have to get another parking ticket. It was on my fifth circuit of the car park when I realised that believing that the Missus was traversing the entire length of the high street and only going into one shop was a little over optimistic. Had I parked as soon as I got there, it would have cost me less in parking charges that it did in diesel driving around waiting for her to turn up.

As we settled into a quiet little afternoon back in The Cove, we were disturbed by an odd buzzing sound coming from above. I raced out to see what it was but it was gone by the time I got outside. I was a little luckier later when I heard it again as I took the bleddy hound around the block. It was a curious iron bird floating above our heads, something that I could vaguely remember from the dim and distant past. Ah yes, it was an aeroplane coming in to land at Land's End Airport (it's an aerodrome). It has been so long since a flight either left or arrived there I had quite forgotten that there was a service at all. It must have given the resident bunnies up there a bit of a shock too.

Still, we will enjoy it while we can; there is a bit of rain coming in the next few days, so it will be back off to Newquay for the rest of the month.

February 5ᵗʰ – Tuesday

Well, if you ever wanted to see a sky glowering and full of menace, this morning was your chance. Just such a pity you were not here.

The wind had been powering through all night long and there had been a bit of rain with it. The wind was still powering through during the morning, the afternoon and into the night as well with varying degrees of wet. You would have thought that it would have run out of puff by then. In short, it was a most unwelcoming day.

With that in mind it was a surprise to see the Missus up with the lark, I have no idea where she got it from. She did have to take the mother-in-law up to St Just for an appointment, so she had no choice really. However, I only had to look at the time and the Missus's state of unreadiness to understand that it was me taking the bleddy hound around and I was not going to take any chances in doing so; it was weather proofing from head to toe.

Out to the northwest the sky was the colour of a big heavy bruise amongst a gathering of big threatening clouds. We were buffeted all the way around, but at least the sky was beginning to clear a little. I had intended to take her along the beach in the afternoon, but with a late low water and the wind pushing the waves up the beach there was no chance of that. I took her around the block again instead and it was no different from earlier, other than the car park was half full of weather watchers.

And if you think that there should be just the slightest bit more substance and interesting stuff included with today's Diary you try being here when it is like this.

February 6ᵗʰ - Wednesday

Do not ask how I get myself into these situations; they just seem to happen.

As I rooted through my emails yesterday, sorting the prime bully beef from the spam, I saw an email that was entitled Turner's House. A company that works on behalf of movie producers is looking for locations suitable to act as the artist Turner's home for a start. When they are looking for movie locations The Old Boathouse is the obvious first step.

They do not need much, just a Georgian house close to a river, another empty one to act as the interior, another to represent Somerset House, which, while it still stands, has been subdivided inside since Turner's time, oh, and they have to be away from cars and roads and empty and free for filming for several weeks. I know that the Diary readership is teeming with folk of superior class so you will be tripping over yourselves, I am sure, to offer your summer or winter residences for the film.

I did a quick recce around Penzance this morning as I went up to stock up my larder for the weekend. You did notice that, didn't you? The use of the singular possessive adjective, 'my' larder. Oh yes, I am to be left to my own devices over the weekend, in fact from tomorrow if all goes well, as the in-laws are going back to their home in North Devon for a few days. I shall not have it all to myself, of course. I shall have to vie for prime viewing schedules and space on the sofa with the bleddy hound. She is being left to my care and I am not, repeat not, to leave her on her own, say for example, on a Saturday night while I begger off up to the F&L for a darn good banding. If that is the case I just hope she like blues rock, as Devil's Creek are playing and I am darned sure I am not missing that.

We came back from town just in the nick of time to carry out the last of my casualty care course across the road. This involved putting ourselves in common casualty roles, such as having our hands and legs broken or hacked off or suffering from sea-sickness, diabetes or being drowned. I saved the Oscar winning moment for the end where I was, 'man with horrific burns on face and hands'. Apparently there has been a picture circulated that I am sure you will see on the front page of *The Stage* in due course.

I also had no idea that I was so far up the poker ladder either. It seems that by simply turning up, I am second best in league. All right that may sound a bit grand. I am second best out of the people that occasionally turn up at the OS for a game of cards on a, now, Wednesday night. After a little confusion it also seemed that if I could win tonight I would be top of the league, head of the pile, top man, best of all the players, king of the hill, top of the tree. Yes, I came third.

The way my luck is running I will probably discover this weekend that the bleddy hound has developed a liking for re-run episodes of *Last of the Summer Wine* and will howl incessantly unless she gets to see it.

February 7th - Thursday

Thank goodness that wind has died down. I think we were all fed up with that howling through our keyholes. It also meant that there was a little bit of beach to play on today and the bleddy hound has been beachless long enough. With high water in the early afternoon, it was a bit of a race against the clock. I did not want to take her down too early, but I did want to be back before the in-laws set off back home.

There was plenty of beach for our purposes when we did get down there, although the bleddy hound did not seem to have her eye on the ball, so to speak. In fact I saw the reason for her distraction before she did, it was that decomposing seal again, but this time down at the bottom of the slipway. I managed to get her away and threw her ball far enough down the beach that she forgot about her smelly seal. It was odd that it had come down to the southern end, as when I arrived at my sitting stone it was clear that all the sand had been dragged up to the north end.

We had been watching a hang glider sail around, having jumped off Carn Olva, the hang gliderist that is, not us. It is unusual as most of the jumpers off this lump of rock tend to be paragliders. As we walked back along the beach after our play, I noticed that the hang glider had passed over our heads a couple of times and appeared to be quite low. On the next pass it was clear he was coming in to land so we stood back to give him some room, whereupon he made a faultless landing (I assume it was faultless; I am not an expert. He landed on his feet and did not look hurt in anyway. I would say that was faultless).

It occurred to me that the machine is an object of lightness and grace in the air. However, on close observation on the ground it looked big, heavy and cumbersome. It also occurred to me that he almost certainly would not get it along the beach by himself, let alone back up the hill. Time to leave, I thought.

Well, I would have left pretty smartly but for the fact that the bleddy hound was sidling towards the seal remnants. It was rather comical watching her circle around pretending that she was interested in something else but all the while edging a little closer to the smelly lump. I am sure she would have nonchalantly whistled a tune and put her paws behind her back if she could. In the end, I had to put her back on her lead and drag her up the slope, the little minx.

Shortly after I got back the Missus departed with the in-laws. You can imagine my distress, I am sure. I took out the hose to wash down the van, put some wax oil on our rust spots and topped up the screen washer, anything to delay them just a little longer, you understand. I waved them away with my hankie hoping that they did not see the little tear in the corner of my eye.

It was time to go to the OS for quiz night by the time I had cleared up the empty bottles, spent party poppers and the last of the revellers had left. There was no Lifeboat crew training tonight, so I went directly there with the bleddy hound in tow. Now, I am sure that I have mentioned that she will not head in that direction after dark in fear that she might bump into her arch enemy en route, so I am compelled to carry her. Did I say that the wind had diminished earlier? Well it had earlier, but by the time I carried the little girl down to the OS it was howling again – the wind, not the bleddy hound -, and piddling rain to boot, and fair near pushing me off my feet, especially with my somewhat delicate balance further disturbed by the heavy hound in my arms.

I knew that one of our team would not be there because he is in Colorado and the other because he is in Redruth, both undeniably fair excuses I would say. I am eager to learn the excuse the last member of my team has, who lives no more than a stone's throw away but the upshot was that I was a man alone, but for a bleddy hound, in my quizzing efforts this evening.

Allow me to point out, especially for the benefit of a particular, erstwhile, member of the Head Launcher's team that there were two teams of five, another of two and me playing by myself. Allow me then to say, ya boo sucks to you; I came second all by my lonesome - and the bleddy hound could not use her smart phone as the Internet was turned off.

February 8ᵗʰ - Friday

Our little bit of breeze seems to be persisting. I could hear it whistling around as I took an extended lie in along with an unenthusiastic bleddy hound. When I eventually roused my ponderous frame I discovered that it was quite a pleasant looking day out there.

Having whisked her around the block first thing, I took stock and realised that for any decent amount of exercise we would need to head out early. I had it in mind to attempt the north face of Mayon Cliff in a daring free-climb and then abseil down Vellandreath. It had hung over me as a constant challenge for the last three months, and today I was set to take it up.

The whole idea was to end up on the beach at the end of the run, so timing was fairly crucial. We set out at around midday so that I could take the coast path up to Pedn-men-du with careful steps to ensure nothing was going awry down below. It was not easy, as I kept forgetting I have a damaged ankle only to be reminded by the rough terrain when I stepped out too far. Having reached the top and checked that all was in perfect working order, I set out along the cliff top and Maria's Lane where the going was much smoother.

I was caught rather unawares as I approached the south side of Vellandreath. The path narrows to a single foot width and with a substantial wind piling into me from my left side I gracefully toppled over. My right leg must need more beefing up than I imagined. It was also a tad worrying heading down the sandy steps onto the beach under Carn Keys with the bleddy hound nagging for the ball around my feet. Overall, the walk was less bothersome than I anticipated and my ankle seems to have benefitted from the experience, although the rest of me was desperate for a pint at the OS.

Before I got there I was accosted by a young lady. I know, I should be used to it by now. This particular lady entreated me to follow her up to her car so that she could show me her etchings. I have a keen appreciation of art of all kinds so I let her lead on. Before you berate me, dear reader, for setting a poor example I must tell you I am familiar with the lady in question as she is a frequent visitor with strong connections to The Cove.

Strong indeed, as amongst her souvenirs, as it were, she had uncovered two old documents. Both are technical drawings, the first dated 1899 is an early drawing of the Harbour wall and the second, dated 1908, is a blueprint of the same. She had no idea how it came about that they were in her possession, but would happily donate them to an appropriate body in The Cove and this is why she collared me.

She felt that they should be on public display, since they are of local interest, but was unsure where they might be hung. The Lifeboat station was suggested given its proximity to the wall, but the Harbour Commission is probably the appropriate body which unfortunately has nowhere to display them.

Furthermore, there was the issue of preservation. The only ancient things I have any knowledge of require excessive heat and a television showing constant reruns of social comedies that have long since ceased to be amusing. I am not entirely convinced that this is appropriate for old documents. No, what I required was a real expert.

I started by telephoning Plymouth University, as I imagined that they would have archaeological experts coming out of their ears, but apparently not. It was suggested I seek assistance from a museum and our closest was the Royal Cornwall Museum in Truro. I spoke with a very helpful lady on reception who gave me the name of another lady, an expert in the field, but not immediately contactable. I have sent an email and will apprise you for your delectation, dear reader, with the results of this in depth enquiry so you too will know what to do with old bits of paper.

Of all the odd things I am asked to deal with from time to time this is one of the most curious. Let us hope it ends well, with them displayed somewhere locally and most importantly without my name being attached to their upkeep.

February 9ᵗʰ – Saturday

It all started far too early this morning as there was a Lifeboat exercise that required the attendance of the very excellent Shore Crew for the first time since mid October. Yes, this was my first taking part since that accident.

Everyone is a little nervous about just how far I can push this activity, so it was decided early on that I should drive the Inshore Lifeboat launching vehicle today. It only requires the use of my hands to drive it, although feet are useful to stop yourself being thrown out of your seat on rough terrain. Rough terrain such as the Harbour at lowish water as it was today at launch time. Even with the optimum route chosen there are several large boulders to negotiate.

The water was even lower at the time the Inshore Lifeboat needed to be recovered, and although I did try and get far enough out it soon became obvious a big beach recovery would be easier. It takes a little while to drive down there in the Tooltrak and I had not quite appreciated how narrow the slipway was, with not a great deal of space either side of the trailer. Fortunately, I had a co-pilot on this occasion and between us we managed to avoid falling off the wall, and selected the best place on the beach from which to drop into the water.

It is surprising just how big those little waves actually are. They were slapping against the forward blade with a nice big bang. We had to readjust and go further down the beach and even those little waves were troublesome. And no less troublesome was the narrowness of the slipway going up, and this time without being able to see where the wheels of the trailer were. I must apologise to the small child at the top of the slip – it did not look that close at the time, honest.

I was down on the beach again within the hour with the bleddy hound who was none too pleased about being left alone for so long. I had left going down to the beach with her rather longer than I intended too, with the beach at the far end rapidly diminishing.

It was somewhat surprising just how quickly the sand had diminished too. Yesterday there was sand all the way up to the path coming down from Carn Keys, today I think I would have struggled to get down on the beach. My sitting rock, too, was so proud of the sand that a ladder would have been useful even for the lower portion. Two days ago I was sitting on the higher part with no trouble at all.

There is a sand bar just to the south of North Rocks, but that does not account for half the missing sand from the beach. There is also such a hole at the bottom of Escalls Vean beach that it is impassable through to Gwenver even at low water on a spring tide.

Luckily, such a passage is not required to get me up the hill to the F&L. Yes, I spurned Mr P's excellent taxi service and took to Shank's pony instead. Mr Shank should really have the animal seen to as it was so much like walking. I do not think that I had fully appreciated the difficulty of the challenge, as I was left weary and panting on the post opposite the supermarket at the top. I was also rather warm in my full water-proof gear and woolly hat, a costume that I was derided for wearing both as I arrived at the F&L and shortly before I left. That is until it became apparent that outside it was raining heavily. I believe the expression is ya boo sucks to the lot of you.

There was a little something that marred the complete enjoyment of the evening. It was when I dropped that bleddy hound off at the neighbours on my way up the hill. She sat at the glass door just looking at me as I walked away. I felt like a complete heel for all of two minutes and by the time I came home she had clearly forgiven me. I even took her around the block when I got back, which is also the first time since that accident. I must be better.

February 10ᵗʰ - Sunday

Honestly, I have no idea where today disappeared to. I know I woke up late but that should have left a substantial part of the day to enjoy and yes, I did enjoy it but it seemed, oh so short.

I was able to drag myself around the block in my waterproof gear. No, no, I did not sleep in it last night, honest. It was necessary as all that rain that eventually hit us last night was still here first(ish) thing this morning. It persisted for much of the morning and the early afternoon too.

My duel objectives of the day were to ensure that the bleddy hound had a bit of exercise and that I made it into the OS before the start of the Ireland versus England Six Nations rugby match. The two were inextricably linked; if she had insufficient exercise then I would be distracted by her fidgeting beyond measure during the game. The timing, too, needed to be spot on as the tide was threatening the beach towards the time the match started.

I could not have timed it better, with the best seat in the house still available at the bar and the bleddy hound suitably exercised. Having divested myself of my heavy protective clothing and setting the hound down the match preamble was just about finishing. What with all that, convivial company and a right result I could not have asked for more.

Shortly after full time the Missus turned up to take away the bleddy hound and signal that my bachelor weekend was over. Looking back at the list of things I have done, it seemed so much shorter than the list of things I had intended to do. Three days gone in a flash.

February 11ᵗʰ - Monday

I had already decided to take it easy today. Oh, all right, I have not exactly pushed physical or mental activity to the limits on any day recently. However, my exertions, particularly up the hill, had taken their toll on the duff peg and that was really apparent yesterday on the beach. I thought it might be a good idea to give it a rest today and I thought that before it started raining, before you say anything.

Yes, it did rather mean that the Missus had to take the bleddy hound for a run in the inclement weather. I am sure running after a sandy and wet ball did her the world of good, and it cannot have hurt the bleddy hound either.

I did intend to have a little crack at the security light that sits at the top of our steps. It died quite a long time ago now and I have procrastinated about replacing it. About six months ago I spent some time looking for exact replacements on the Internet but could not find one. I need an exact replacement because it is screwed to the PVC door post and I really would prefer not to have too many holes in it.

The reason why this has come to the fore again is that the dull and redundant unit has become possessed. Not for the first time it has randomly woken up and refused to go off. It has been on since Thursday, I think, and has remained on all through the night, which is irritating because after I have turned off everything at night I keep thinking I must have left a light on, which I have but not accidentally.

This morning I got as far as turning off the lighting circuit at the fuse box and the security light duly went out. Unfortunately just around dusk the blessed thing came back on again. It will be a couple of days before I am sufficiently irritated again at which point I shall have to try and remember to take out the bulb.

February 12ᵗʰ - Tuesday

I think I must have told you that it has come to the time when the old van must have a bit of bodywork done to it, as the mud is no longer capable of holding together the rust all by itself. It was this that got me out of bed before first thing as I had to take the van to our regular mechanic who also does a bit of bodywork from time to time.

He had suggested that he would need a couple of hours to do a proper job of assessing the work to be done. This is comforting in that the assessment would be detailed, thus, presumably, leading to a more accurate quote. However, if I was a cup half empty sort of chap, I might reason that if the job could absorb two hours of uncharged work then the accurate quote was likely to be substantial. Surprisingly it was not. The van is now booked in for mid-April and there will be a loan vehicle on hand to boot.

I was just considering running the bleddy hound down to the big beach when Head Launcher came knocking. There was some work being carried out on the turntable that he thought I should be involved with, or at least know about. While we were there we helped winch the boat back into the house, which, as it worked out, was very good practice.

It was while I was sitting down to pen this very page that my Lifeboat pager went off for an emergency call. A fishing boat had fouled its propeller just off Porthcurno and required a tow back to Newlyn. I can hardly say that I sprang into action, but it was a reasonably swift launch nevertheless.

A quorum of the very excellent Shore Crew stayed at the station until the boat returned and we were joined by other supporting members. The sea and state of the tide were highly reminiscent of a certain day in October. I vaguely wondered if some demon might have transported me back in time to endure my torment over and over again, but then I thought that even demons would not be that nasty.

It was a tricky recovery. The lifeboat had to withdraw for half an hour to let the sea state calm a little. Even then the search light on the boat was picking out waves coming over the Harbour wall and the frothing white water beyond. Still, in the end it was a textbook recovery, which probably goes without saying, as we are now a very excellent Shore Crew again. And how lovely it was to be able to say that after such a long time.

February 13ᵗʰ - Wednesday

It was still mizzling when we attended the shuffling off ceremony of an old Cover. As shuffling off ceremonies go it was pleasantly performed, with some rather attractive tunes. It was attended by just about everyone that is anyone in The Cove and most repaired to the F&L for a sip and a sandwich. Not a bad send off for a good chap, no, not bad at all.

With the rain dissipating I decided to take the bleddy hound on a bit of a journey. Going to the beach is a bit old hat despite the fact that she loves it, so I we went first in the direction of Pedn-men-du. When we got to the top I had a moment's indecision: Land's End or Maria's Lane. While it seemed a bit of a challenge, I elected to head off to Land's End as there is nothing quite like a bit of a challenge.

We headed back along the cycle path despite expecting it to be largely under water. Certainly for the last couple of years the run-off from the surrounding fields has submerged significant portions of the path, not exactly to the depth of making it impassable but difficult nonetheless. There seems to have been some work carried out, ramping up the path edges and clearing some drainage areas. It certainly appears to have worked as the path is mainly dry.

I have noticed, particularly while crossing rougher terrain, that I see very little of the countryside. With a still somewhat imperfect leg it seems that I walk with my eyes pinned to the path before me, carefully picking safe spots to place my foot. I have no idea what I missed because of this.

By the time we arrived back at Maria's Lane I would normally have turned back via Pedn-men-du to The Cove. Today, however, I threw caution to the wind and continued my walk along Maria's Lane. When I got to the end, again, I contemplated shortening the walk by heading down the hill but again I spurned such a shortcut and made my way over to Vellandreath and down the valley.

Now, by this time we had walked the best part of three miles and I have to admit to a certain amount of tiredness creeping into my legs. However, within a hundred yards of the beach it was utterly clear that the previous three miles meant nought to a bleddy hound that lives and breaths only for the beach. She was highly animated and racing off ahead of me, looking very excited and urging me to go faster.

I had already contemplated the issue that faced us at the bottom of the path down from Carn Keys. As I mentioned a few days ago the sand has been eroded leaving nothing but boulders to negotiate. These, of course, meant nothing to a bleddy hound completely focused on the ball in my hand. I was loathed to throw it and have her dash headlong over the rocks, but she resolved the problem by dashing headlong over the rocks anyway. I threw the ball to stop her coming back whereupon she promptly lost track of it. Despite my best efforts at directing her gaze in the direction of the clearly evident yellow ball she would only search roughly two yards from the end of her nose. I would hate to consider the state of the nation if we had to rely on hounds of her stamp to sniff out illegal substances or explosive threats.

There was no way I was going to venture over the boulders myself and had already decided to follow the dunes down towards Vellandreath and join the beach from there. Before I had a chance to make a move another dog claimed the bleddy hound's ball and it was recovered by a rather helpful owner. This was all very well but in order to join him on the beach I had to walk roughly in the opposite direction. Being out of speaking range and having already waved in recognition that he had the ball it must have looked obtuse, to say the least, that I was now walking away. Worse still, because I was painfully aware of the situation, I hurried best I could so that it now looked like I was making best speed to get away from the helpful chap.

We stayed on the beach for a while tossing the ball and digging holes. I will not bother with the three mile walk in future, at least not for the bleddy hound's sake, as it clearly just gets in the way of chasing the ball.

February 14th – Thursday

Well, I asked the Missus last night how she might like to romantically celebrate the anniversary of the sticky end of one of the possible St Valentines of history. On one notable St Valentine 's Day before we were married, I took her to the cinema to see the film Hannibal, which I thought was suitable given that saints generally have a rather horrid terminal moment. I am not sure she saw it that way. However, since she fell asleep before the end of the opening titles I have never made the same mistake again, and today was not going to be an exception. I suggested instead that we romantically trip off with the bleddy hound to some romantic beach somewhere since it was such a pleasant day, to which she responded that the bunting she is making for the wedding we are attending would not make itself.

So, dear reader, what I am trying to explain is how the bleddy hound and I found ourselves on the road to a romantic beach somewhere for a romantic afternoon out.

During the summer last year I was busy making plans to tour the beaches of the Lizard during our winter break. This admirable objective was seen off when I put my foot in it just before our winter break started. Now that I am a little more mobile I thought that I could, at least, try a Lizard beach or two before we had to go back to work, and this is how we found ourselves heading off to Gunwalloe and Church Cove.

Unsurprisingly, Church Cove is thus named because it is a cove and there is a church there. The church is notable for being the only Cornish church to be built on a beach, and for having a separate tower for a reason that is not altogether obvious. The tower is apparently the oldest bit dating from the 13th century. The beach today was largely covered in shale with patches of grainy sand. What I had not appreciated is that there is a river running through the beach, the other side of which is another shale beach but beyond that a length of bright sand. The majority of people were that side, obviously having been here before and knowing better than to follow the official signs to the beach.

We played around for a while, but I was sore disappointed. As I headed up the beach in search of beaches new I met a lady who was clearly a veteran hereabouts. She said that this beach was usually sandy, but as an alternative Fisherman's Cove might be better.

On my way out I discovered another beach to the north of the church which was far more interesting. It was strewn with lumps of granite that I thought unusual until I saw that the authorities had dumped huge lumps down the cliff side in an effort to reduce the erosion. Although there was far more shale here, making it difficult to move down to the sandier areas below, it was far better for a small hound to run about and douse herself in a plethora of rock pools. It was so different from sandy Sennen beach and very refreshing for it.

We made our way back up the road to where we parked the van. It was rather odd to see cows in a farmyard so close to the beach setting. It was also a bit of a challenge to direct the bleddy hound along a line that did not involve cow output, having only had her hosed down yesterday after her Land's End trip.

I had intended to drop down into Fisherman's Cove and possibly go on to Loe Bar, as I have rather an affinity with bars, but I missed the turning to the former and the sign to the latter did not seem to lead there. A very quick plan B came to mind and I set my controls for the heart of Perranuthnoe. As we all know by now there is a very nice big beach and above all a rather superb café selling tea and cake.

I did try very hard not to rush the bleddy hound around the beach but that cup of tea was calling hard. I was rewarded with some fine comedy moments where the bleddy hound did not see some hidden deep pools on the beach and almost disappeared as she chased the ball. I know, I should not laugh really.

After such an exploration it was very enjoyable to order up a cup of tea and a geet wedge of raspberry and white chocolate cheesecake that only the utmost of restraint stopped me from having a second slice of.

The bleddy hound has never been a great traveller, not since she was a pup. She had endured a twenty mile trip out to the Lizard with no complaint. She had come all the way back via some quite winding roads and eventually dropped back down into a resplendent Sennen Cove. I left her in the seat while I collected our baggage from the back of the van. By the time I opened her door she had been sick.

Little Bo Café opened today for the first time this year. They laid on a special St Valentine meal in the Italian style and the Missus agreed to abandoning her bunting and came with me. You see we can be romantic, after a fashion, if we try really hard. It is indeed unlikely that I shall be romantic with anyone else for a day of two as there was rather a surfeit of garlic in the dishes I chose. Sorry, were you expecting me to wax lyrical about the perfectly cooked tuna steak or sing the praises of spaghetti al dente with pesto, herbs and garlic oil or a stunning little hazelnut cake with chocolate sauce and cream and not a hint of cavallo in any of the dishes. If you wanted that sort of in depth description you would have been far better off being there, and believe me you would have been far better off being there.

February 15ᵗʰ - Friday

I was about to seize the day when I suddenly remembered that the replacement security light arrived yesterday. I had not even unwrapped it but when I did I discovered, to my delight, that it was an identical model to the possessed version hanging on the door frame. This meant identical drill holes in the door frame, identical cable lengths and identical position for the conduit. What more could a DIY dunce require. As expected the new light fitted perfectly and was installed so easily.

Flushed with this unmitigated success I bagged up the bleddy hound's ball thrower and headed beachwards in the blazing sunshine. As it was shortly after low water we were able to go all the way over to North Rocks and gallivant about the deep rock pools there. We had a new friend join us half way back across the beach in the form of a proper hound at least three times bigger than she and only ten months old. Apparently, he had just discovered luuv and was a bit keen on the bleddy hound's womanly charms. Despite being dragged on the lead half way across the beach in the opposite direction he came all the way back, once released, just to be with her. On his behalf I have to say that he was not at all pushy and was a perfect gentleman; he just would not go away.

I spent the evening opening our front door and waving my hand in front of the security light sensor. It was gratifying to watch the light come on and, more importantly, go off again a little while later when I could open the door and test it all over again. It was either that or watch murdering love rats running a pub in East London while their brother's best friend's wife's half brother they did not know they had run off with the offspring of a transgender café owner's mum's boyfriend's ex partner in a suburb of Manchester. I do not know about you, but that light had me riveted.

February 16ᵗʰ - Saturday

I could have let Saturday come and go without lifting a finger and I very nearly did. I spent the entire morning scratching my behind, although I suppose included in that was some book preparation and then the Missus got up and suggested she take the old codgers out for a run around.

It took all my effort after listening to some loud music and numbing my brains on some mindless games to get up off my backside to actually go and give the bleddy hound a run. Even then it was not strictly necessary, as our young dog walker is back for the week.

I had completely forgotten that she was expected and had already taken the bleddy hound around the block for the first thing. She was having her breakfast when our girl turned up and immediately put the bleddy hound in a tail spin – breakfast or walk, breakfast or walk. Breakfast won, but she ate it so quickly it scarcely can have touched the sides.

It was late afternoon by the time I got around to taking her out again. We dropped down to the Harbour beach as I had absolutely no intention of getting geared up for a long walk. It was also the first day in a while when the sea had been dead calm and ideal for a bit of a swim – for her, of course; she does so love her swimming. It was quite easy to loose track of time down there too as the sun was warming up the beach nicely, we were largely on our own and it was exceptionally peaceful.

So that was enough peace for a moment or two, for heaven's sake, must be about time to head off to the F&L and a darned good banding.

The drummer and the lead guitarist had to be competent as they spent most of the evening enveloped in a dense cloud issued from the band's smoke machine. Despite that they played some fearsome old time rock and roll and some new rock and roll, some soul and some blues and many in between. The dance floor was jumping from time to time and more so in the second half. Overall, there were some pleasing and different tunes making up a bit of a fresh front for a Saturday night at the F&L.

All that remains is for me to tell you about the walk home. Oh yes, these days I walk home and how beautifully was I treated tonight? There was a six day old moon peaking out from behind a few errant clouds that looked resplendent, and a myriad of stars to gaze at between wondering where my boots were treading.

Oh, man, it is so good to be back on my foot again.

February 17ᵗʰ – Sunday

Oh, what a naughty boy I was today. I asked the Missus to do the getting up this morning while I snoozed fitfully in my pit until ten o'clock. Unforgivable, I know, but it was the first time in many weeks that I had done so.

It could have been a template for the day but for a telephone call late in the morning reminding me that I had agreed to take the first steps in joining a surf club today. Fortunately, the call came after we had had our breakfast roll from next door, otherwise I might have felt guilty about having one.

Now, I should point out that when I say surf club you should not immediately picture your portly Diarist in skin tight neoprene balancing, hang ten off the end of a Malibu, running a left hand break over at North Rocks. Far from it I am happy to report. No, the whole purpose of joining the surf club is to enable me to use the gymnasium.

Now, I should point out that when I say gymnasium we are talking about the old men's club, that is the men's club which is old rather than a club for old men, which has an exercise bike, a stepping machine, a multi-gym and several rowing machines sitting currently unused. It is also likely that I am the only, or at least hopefully first, member of this exclusive venue solely for this purpose.

I do realise that on the face of it this does seem like rather an extreme action for a comfortably proportioned shopkeeper to undertake. This should not, however, be taken as some sort of indication that I am about to throw myself headlong into a regime of early morning jogs out across the beach, snacks of muesli, natural yoghurt and prunes or, worse still, start wearing tight lyrca bodysuits. Heaven forefend. I still have some self respect, well, no I do not but it sounded like the right thing to say, and no matter how hard I try I could never be Robert Redford as I am far too fond of beer, to quote a Dr Hook song.

No, this whole venture certainly started as a remedy or easing programme for my stiff right ankle. If it so happens that there be ancillary benefits and by and by I emerge from the men's club sporting a Charles Atlas six pack then so be it; I shall go and kick sand in my tailor's eye when I ask him to take my trousers in. Anyway, I shall be trying out some of the facilities starting tomorrow morning. If I can lift my fingers after that then I shall let you know how it went in tomorrow's page.

February 18ᵗʰ – Monday

I have to report that I am grievously disappointed; I feel short changed and hard done by.

I said yesterday that I fully intended to use my new gymnasium membership to the full and would start the using it to the full today. Having taken the bleddy hound around the block and had a cup of tea and gathered together my gymnasium bits I set off the fifty yards or so down the road. The place was empty when I arrived and remained so until I was packing up the equipment, which saves so much embarrassment.

I started off on the exercise bike for which I had brought some batteries so that the on-board computer would work. It certainly sparked up with no trouble at all and the rudimentary buttons were self explanatory, well, seemingly so. I set the number of kilometres for a sensible target and started to pedal. After five minutes or so I had to stop as the seat was clearly in the wrong position; I am certain that it is not intended that the soft tissue is pinched in that manner.

After another ten minutes of cycling it became apparent that I was not getting anywhere. Now, I know that the machine is rooted to the floor and is not supposed to physically travel anywhere. What I refer to is the notional distance set up on the computer which had not diminished one metre. This was a little irritating, as I had hoped to boast later how far I had travelled this morning. Nevertheless, having got into my stride I used my somewhat less complex measuring device, my watch, to determine that I had cycled for at least twenty minutes.

Not wishing to over exert myself in my first ever gymnasium session I stopped and set up the rowing machine. The calculating device on this exerciser not only was easier to set but worked as well. I can tell you that I rowed for just over 2,000 metres and was not sick once, despite a heavy swell and strong easterlies.

It should go without saying that I felt pretty good about myself. I also felt pretty good. My six pack, I am sure, was developing nicely and I am certain I heard some wolf whistles from the Saga coach that was pulling away as I made my way back. Strangely, no one at home said anything but I put that down to jealousy. Naturally, I went straight to the bathroom to examine the results on the bathroom scales; surely I must have lost half a stone at least.

And therein, dear readers, lies my astonished disappointment. The only pounds I seem to have lost were those that were wrested from my purse on the promise of health, fitness and a loss of weight. All right, the purveyors did not expressly state all those benefits but we both knew what they meant. Were it not for the hefty and non-refundable outlay I am in no doubt that I would never set foot in the place again. What a waste of time.

Well, I was certainly not going to waste any more of a lovely day such as it was today. The sun had been shining since early morning and the only blight on the perfectness of the day was a rather stiff and chilling easterly breeze. The tide was still only just on its way out, so when I set off with the bleddy hound I went up the hill and took the long way around to give the beach some time to expand a little.

It was a rip-stoggler of a day to be out and about and in the safe knowledge that at least my two mile hike would have shaved a couple of inches off my waistline even if 2,000 metres on a rowing machine had not, it was clearly time to celebrate. So on the way back I stopped in to the Little Bo Café and availed myself of a slice of isotonic coffee cake. Oh, come on, after the exercise I have done today I am sure it will hardly register and it was a very slim slice.

I have pencilled in a rest day for tomorrow. I would not wish to over do it, now would I?

February 19ᵗʰ – Tuesday

I have more than once explained that we are heading off to a wedding in some foreign part in the next few days, all right, tomorrow to be precise. The location is a rather grand looking country house and since our van is not grand looking in any respect I thought that I had better try and do something about it.

It was never going to be a perfect solution, or even a half decent solution and probably not a solution at all. It might just offer a slight improvement if I threw some water over it and made, at least, a small attempt at brightening it up a touch. What I did not appreciate was that by doing so all that happened was that the rust spots become more evident.

The other thing that I had not thought through, and that came to mind as I travelled to St Buryan's car wash, was that the back road between Sennen and St Buryan was caked in mud (or something similar). I realise that the one hundred and sixty mile

trip to the wedding will do the van no favours, but it would be
quite nice to start the journey with a relatively clean van. The
brisk east wind did a cracking job of drying the van off, so at
least the dried mud thrown up by the tyres would not stick. It
was fortunate that I ran into Picasso while I was there who
recommended that if I returned via Catchall on the main road, I
would be less likely to encounter mud on the road.

Frankly, I think I am on a hiding to nothing but I have, at
least, made an effort.

Ah well, I suppose I should go and pack my humble rags for
the next few days. The Missus is keen that we leave a day early so
that we can have an extra day on the road, suggesting that we
should reward ourselves with a slightly longer break. I rather
suspect it is because the incoming in-laws who will be here
tomorrow to look after the old codgers can use our bed
uninterrupted. Me cynical? How dare you.

February 20ᵗʰ - Wednesday

It is highly unlikely that you will guess where I am just now,
so I should just tell you that I am in Okehampton. Judging from
my school learnt explanations of names of places, that they seem
to not bother with any more, I might suggest that it means
somewhere by a river – ton – and possibly something about an
Oak, spelt wrong.

Who knows, all I can tell you is that I think I must have
passed through Okehampton when I was a small lad, perhaps. I
cannot say that I remember it. You could easily be mistaken for
thinking that you had travelled back in time. The High Street, at
least, looks like it still lives in the 17ᵗʰ century but for the modern
shop fronts, the streetlights, yellow lines on the road, the bollards
… all right, apart from all that it looks really old. There is much
to discover in the few hours we have tomorrow morning.

So, right now, you will understand that I capitulated and
deserted the family home. I did leave it until the last possible
moment imaging that the European Court of Human Rights
might have saved me but in the end, and despite the barricades, I
was evicted.

The Missus had slipped into town first thing to have her hair
done; it is obligatory the day or two before a wedding so I am

told. I took a leaf out of her book and did my own hair this morning too. I have to say that I cannot imagine how it takes three hours to do hair, as it only took three minutes to do mine.

Three hours! And this was despite instructing her hairdresser to do only half a head of highlights, and even then it seemed to me that the hairdresser had ignored her as her whole head had been highlighted. Some things, perhaps, I shall never understand.

So, after an uneventful journey, we are ensconced in the White Hart Hotel that apparently dates from the 17th century itself. Our room is about a mile from the front of the building along some narrow corridors and up several short flights of steps that are so numerous and unexpected there is only one warning notice and that is in reception.

Much as I would adore to reveal more, I am afraid I have run out of time.

February 21st – Thursday

All right, so we missed breakfast because we slept in longer than, at least, I had planned. I am sure that it would have been fine as nearly everything else is about this hotel. Yes, nearly everything, with the small exception of the shower that is one of those attached by a hose to the bath taps, and if they could have found a smaller showerhead even I would have had to run around underneath it to get wet. Not only this but the water temperature varies randomly from ice cold to scolding which may have been entertaining for someone watching me as I hopped in and out of the flow.

No less entertaining was the lady in the car park who reversed into another car park user with some force, moving the victim's car a couple of feet with the impact. The lady climbed out of her vehicle with a face full of concern. She checked, in detail, the rear of her own car, saw that it was unmarked, got back into her car and drove away. If she so much as glanced at the car she had backed into I would have noticed, as she was right in front of me when she did it. I left her registration number and my details with reception for the victim to use if he or she so desired.

We did a bit of exploring in Okehampton as we had some time to kill. There is a Victorian arcade close by the hotel that whether by accident or design had been very well preserved. It is venerated by the Okehampton people website and lauded for its quirky, independent shops, many of which were strangely shut when we walked up mid-morning.

Across the road there was another arcade, much more modern but with apparently thriving stores, cafes and quite the biggest butchers I have ever seen. With a couple of the big name stores in the high street too I can imagine this would be all you would need for normal shopping. I noticed as we left that there is quite a few new housing estates, and a fairly large building project for more on the outskirts. I would say that the town centre shops probably have quite a bright future ahead of them.

We met our neighbours and friends at Exeter motorway services at around lunchtime. They had left this morning to go directly to the wedding venue. After a short break we fell into convoy with them as the place we were heading to is deep in the countryside between Minehead and Bridgewater. The lead car had an ancient satellite navigation system on board, clearly programmed by someone with a sense of humour. It led us a merry dance by suggesting that we exit the motorway one turnoff before Taunton and took us across country.

The sun made an appearance, after being absent for the whole day, just to bathe the wedding venue in golden light as we turned into the drive. It is a country house complete with deer park, duck pond and trout stream, and a pigeon loft no doubt, making me immediately wish I had brought my gun. It sits below the village, complete with its own impressive towered church in green rolling hills of the Quantocks. Our sumptuous room looks over a perfectly manicured rose garden and up the valley to the church. It is a good job we leave on Saturday, as I am sure the poor of the village would be expecting our carriage to turn us all out to the Sunday service.

You will have to excuse me as the time has arrived for the bar to be opened. It would be ever so rude not to mingle with the other guests.

February 22nd - Friday

It would be fair to say that it is likely that most people had an exceptionally enjoyable evening yesterday. The number of grey, listless characters wandering the corridors in the ancient building in the morning might possibly be taken for ghosts.

As the Missus was intent on making herself beautiful for the occasion, and knowing this would take some time and tribulation, I went for a walk. I had plenty of time, as it only takes me a few moments to make myself beautiful.

I am sure that the estate has some very pretty walks to enjoy, but unfortunately I knew none of them so I walked up the drive and onto the main road. This afforded such glorious views back down the valley to the manor house and beyond that to the sea. Short of risking life or limb on the main A39, the only other place to walk was into the village up the hill. This turned out not to be hugely entertaining, other than watching the dustbins being emptied, so I cut my losses and walked back to the big house.

I delayed my journey to note the stream issuing forth from the ground inside the deer enclosure. It was not at all apparent where this flow was sourced, as it was too strong a stream to be a spring, I assumed. I imagine that this enclosure was also used to its full last evening, for the stag night, of course. Oh, come on, I spared you, it could have been worse, I could have suggested that it was an expensive evening and far too dear.

This being a wedding venue specifically, the whole day was cleverly mapped out for us. We were instructed where to be and when, we were fed and watered appropriately and they all came together in a well orchestrated cacophony of splendour. The only fly almost in the ointment, perhaps, was that the bride's father was a tad ill and only the medical experimentation of some family member saved the day.

Into the evening we tumbled, with a million photographs taken, herds of animals slaughtered and consumed, vineyards decimated and chocolate factories emptied. Small children, dressed in fairy outfits beyond their imaginations, peaked and cascaded into their little world of dreams as older ones danced and twirled and tumbled into the deep evening.

February 23rd - Saturday

And then suddenly it was all over. A room full of ordinary people, dressed ordinarily, ate their breakfast and prepared to drift away into the snowy morning.

Oh yes, we had a dusting of snow overnight that decided to come back in a little more force shortly after I had cleared off the windscreens of the van and two or three other cars. Nevertheless, it made for pretty pictures in the grounds of the manor house and the great stag that decided to hold a lonely vigil down at the fence nearest the house.

I was keen to return home as there was a rugby match to watch in the afternoon and what could be more important than that? Ah, yes, a trip to a shopping village some thirty miles distant – in the wrong direction, naturally. I mentally recalculated the latest leaving time from the new location, silently obviously, and hoped that I could arrange our leaving before it arrived.

The gods were clearly kind to me and we travelled home without further interruption and arrived just in time to watch the rugby match.

February 25th – Monday

I found myself against the clock this morning; I am getting less and less of the bed recently. I also had to rush around a bit as the Missus had booked the bleddy hound in for a hair cut early in the afternoon. I suppose it was only fair as everyone else had had a haircut for the wedding, and to be brutally frank she was more llama than small dog.

As the Missus was also going to be absent for the rest of the day, off up to Truro for a show at the Halls for Cornwall, I needed to ensure I had something edible for tea. Since the Missus was not going to be joining us I had my mind set towards some fish; the Missus hates fish. Nevertheless, I was not going to be alone either, as the parents-in-law would be here and the mother-in-law is partial to a bit of fish.

I was heading round to the Strand in Newlyn when I remembered that there is a perfectly good wholesaler in Stable Hobba that will sell fish retail as well if pushed. I straight away spotted a nice small hake that clearly had my name on it, and would serve to supply some goujons for breakfast as well if I fancied it. I told the chap that I also needed some fish for the mother-in-law and asked if he had a bit of fish with plenty of small bones in it. I came away with a medium megrim that would probably do the trick.

I almost missed an appointment with our postcard man that I forgot I had arranged. It was a brief meeting as I had already set out the order. As soon as he was gone I headed down to the gymnasium again. I have to say that I quite enjoyed the last session and was looking forward to this one. I had it in mind to push myself a little harder today and row the 5,000 metres faster than I did last week. I know what athletes mean now, as I hit the wall today; I will look where I am going next time I let myself in through the back door. (Sorry, that was the second awful pun today and, I promise, the last.)

The Missus returned from the dog hairdressers with a dog half the size of the one she left with. I do not know what the dog hairdressers do, other that shear the fur off the beasts, but the bleddy hound was completely shattered when she came back. I decided not to take her out as she looked so tired and anyway I had lost the beach with the tide nearly all the way in.

That was the sum of my efforts today but for the cooking of some fishy goujons for breakfast, despite someone having thrown out my wholemeal flour. We had fish again for tea, which the mother-in-law survived, bones an' all. She is a hardy one, you know.

February 26th - Tuesday

Grey, cold and miserable. Yes, the Missus seems to have caught some sort of bug and her demeanour mirrored the day beautifully. The bleddy hound was not to be left out and has been struck down with some malady of her own. She made this wholly apparent this morning with a very insistent tongue in my ear suggesting that I might rue not letting her out directly.

We had planned to deliver the contents of last year's collection to the beneficiary over in Marazion this morning as they promised to show us around the Sand Rose Project properties there. However, I could not raise anyone on the telephone and, besides, the Missus was in no fit condition to attend even if I had.

Nevertheless, I wanted to head into town anyway to acquire my first ever MP3 player. Now, what, you may be thinking, does a grumpy, born in the age of the gramophone shopkeeper want with a music emitting device more commonly associated with the bright young things of today's hip, happening scene? Well, it is simply this: the lot of a solo exerciser is a cold and lonely experience in the Sennen Cove Men's Club. While I am cycling to oblivion, or rowing beyond it, I like to have some musical accompaniment to transport me and with ear phones blocking my aural canals I cannot hear my body complaining.

Of course, it is never as simple as just driving into town with one objective in mind and I soon had a shopping list, albeit a very short one, to complete. Before I even got beyond the barrier to the car park I had to stop and return for my credit card. I had quite forgotten that the Missus had driven to Truro and back the previous evening and quite naturally the fuel tank was the closest thing to being completely empty. She has an almost childlike assumption that motor vehicles run on thin air or, at least, the fairies ensure there is sufficient diesel in the tank to transport her wherever she might roam. As I drove to St Buryan to fill the van up, I considered she might be right.

Still, having completed my chores and returned home I, at least, was able to spend the entire afternoon priming my new musical box with a cornucopia of musical delights. This was neither quick, simple, nor pretty because Mr Gates's media programme is not without its quirks (often known as bugs or as Mr Gates would have it, features) and the cheap MP3 player I acquired is hardly state of the art. Anyway, I suppose it was entertainment of a sort watching spurious albums split themselves into individual folders per track and others confuse 'artist' and 'album' as they were copied about.

Fortunately, I had to attend to my tea before frustration and irritation got the better of me. The Missus, who had languished in bed all day, was still there come tea time, which was just as well as on top of a bug I am sure she would not have welcomed an MP3 player in the eye as I threw it across the room.

I am afraid I must go now as there is just enough light left for me to see my way as I paint a big black cross on our front door.

February 27th - Wednesday

Overcast and grey, they said. Miserable and cold, they said. Tee hee, not 'ere my 'ansum. We have a lovely, horizon to horizon blue sky and a large warming sun although if you get caught in that easterly breeze, yes, it was a tad knicker rattling.

The Missus was up before me this morning which was no surprise since she had slept most of yesterday. Unfortunately, she was not up for running the bleddy hound around, who was feeling much better thank you for asking, so I had to drag myself from my pit and do the duties. I was not alone as again today we have a group of local fishermen hanging, furtively, around on the corner of the boathouse; surely they cannot all not have homes to go to?

I continued my health drive by jogging, well, all right, sauntering, down to the men's club and taking up on the exercise bicycle and the rowing machine. It was as much to try out my new MP3 player as it was to exercise my creaking limbs. Yesterday I was not sure that it had charged its battery at all during the hours that I had it plugged in. First thing, I was convinced it had not charged itself as whichever button I pressed it would not come to life, every button that is apart from the power up button that is cunningly disguised as a control panel lock. It is also the first device that I have ever seen that displays completely white cells as a battery strength indicator which was the root cause of my confusion.

Regardless that I had just cycled several miles up hill and down dale and had rowed 5,000 metres across treacherous seas, the draw of a wide open spring tide beach under brilliant sunshine was just too much to resist. I did stop to wring the sweat from my brow then saddled up the bleddy hound and headed out to the far end of the beach. It was glorious.

The sand had really piled up on the southern side of North Rocks and a long sand bar runs out from the beach a little further south still, pushing back the normal tide line by 100 to 150 yards. There is another bar to the north and between these is a deep pool harbouring dark secrets, no doubt.

Secrets and mysteries, indeed: I met with my geologist friend shortly after arriving, coming across North Rocks and clutching hold of a couple of sizeable pebbles of flint. He said he had seen examples here before and wondered where they might have come from. He dismissed the theory of a shipwreck which may have spilled its flint ballast, as there was insufficient volume of the rock and it certainly was not indigenous, although there is some to the north end of the Isles of Scilly. He also mused that it was once worked at Mayon Cliff Castle and may have been brought in by sea for that purpose. My pal is certainly steeped in local knowledge and I have a feeling I shall have to distil him 'ere long as it is all interesting stuff – to some of us at least.

When we, the bleddy hound and I, eventually came away, which was some time as it was a rather special day, the bleddy hound lagged behind me looking rather downcast. I thought that it may be that she was a little tired, as she did not want to me to throw her ball for her and she had been poorly not 24 hours previously. She trailed me so slowly that there were occasions I had to stop and wait for her. When at last we made it to the slipway she stopped and mulled around the rocks there, failing completely to follow me up further. She was not tired in the least; she just did not want to come off the beach. It is like going out with a petulant child sometimes. I bet Ranulph Fiennes never has this problem, but then again we were not chased off the beach by a bit of frost bite; we are made of sterner stuff.

However I really did not want to move too far in the afternoon as my pins were aching, just a little. I did get a little rest before I was reminded that we had very little for tea and that a trip up to the village was required. When I returned there was a group of fishermen hanging around the corner of the boathouse, looking rather furtive. I cannot help thinking that I have seen them somewhere before.

They had disappeared by the time I headed down to the OS for my game of cards. I had missed last week's game as I had been spirited away to Okehampton. I find it hard to believe that it was a week ago already. I made my presence felt for my return by being triumphant. I am sure they will not want me back again so soon.

February 28th – Thursday

Again the beach was calling. I am sorry but I really cannot resist a big wide beach like that; it is against nature to do so. It was not so jolly or bright today but perfectly set for a long stretch out across the sand, a few throws of the ball and a saunter back. Once again the bleddy hound made a show of dragging her paws back across the beach. This is new behaviour and I am not entirely sure that it is reluctance to go home. She will have to find another way to tell me, as I do not have the first clue what she is trying to communicate.

And now, at last, I can reveal what our furtive fishermen were all about, if you have not already guessed. It is, of course, the season for a bit of grey mullet to enter Whitesand Bay and for our fishermen to spend days watching and waiting until they appear in just the right spot. The process is as old as The Cove itself: a Hewer spotting where the shoal is and directing the boats to the right place, a seine net shot from a punt to surround the shoal and a bunch of syndicate owners standing by to work in the net and prepare the catch for market.

Two punts were out this morning but missed the main body of fish. Later some part of the shoal entered the Harbour and the seine net was shot and the captured shoal held against the dropping tide until they were clear of the water.

We watched for a while after a brief Lifeboat training session where we prepared the station for a major visit next week. At that time more than a dozen oil cloth clad gentlemen were out holding the net up. The sound of the flapping fish was most apparent, rather like waves running over a pebbled beach. In the reflection of lights from the slipway the hundreds of fish flashed against the night.

As I returned from a victorious quiz night, the boys were just finishing off. I could not possibly tell you how much fish were landed, first because I do not know and secondly, I would probably be strung out on the beach if I did. I can tell you that it was not quite as much as last year that seemed to be a modern day record. I am sure though, despite the late hour, that the boys will be ready tomorrow as well if the mullet make another showing.

March 1st – Friday

What an inspiring day. Well, not really. I was inspired enough to chase the bleddy hound around the block and then take myself down to the gymnasium for a bit of a cycle and a row, which made me feel much better.

When I came back I resolved to actually do what I had intended to do yesterday and go down to the shop to complete the stock take that we had started in January. I let slip to the

Missus that I was also going to defrost the freezers, which should have been done at the end of October. The whole purpose of letting slip this little nugget is that the Missus would have kittens at the thought of me letting the melt water flood onto the shop floor. This thought would be too much to bear and she would doubtless follow me down to do this task herself.

I was down stairs for all of ten minutes when the Missus came down to do the defrosting work herself. I love it when a plan comes together.

It took more than an hour to not only count every grocery item on the shop shelves, but also to note any 'use by' date the product might have. Some items, we knew, would have already slipped beyond a saleable date, where others would need to be watched carefully to ensure they disappeared from our shelves before their due dates arrived.

With the shop shelves complete, and the only remaining area left to count being the store room, I left the Missus with her hairdryer and dripping freezer shelves to take the bleddy hound down to the beach. As I am away deep tomorrow she will not get anything like a decent run, so I thought that I had better treat her today. It was much of a repeat of yesterday, but a little further up the beach as I had left it well after low water to come away. The other thing different from yesterday is that I detoured via the bar of the OS on the way back. Well, there was no need to hurry back now, was there. Those freezers take ages to defrost, even with the aid of a hair dryer.

So, with duly whetted whistle I returned to the fold, kicked off my walking boots and returned to the shop to finish the stock take as if nothing had happened. The data entry of the collected figures will wait until Sunday, I am sure.

What a perfectly well orchestrated day. Apart from the three hours of enforced tosh on the television in the evening it almost could not have worked out better.

March 2ⁿᵈ - Saturday

Leaving behind a Lifeboat exercise, four intrepid adventurers set forth to the environs of heroic Plymouth. After all, Mr Drake supposedly spotted the Spanish Armada from there and calmly finished his bowls before dashing out to finish them off. Then years later we learn that a big storm probably did for the Armada and Mr Drake only had a few stragglers to deal with, those that the Irish had not eaten.

Anyway, while the excellent Shore Crew, no doubt, struggled through their task without me, the four of us headed out to do battle but not quite of Armadian proportions. We were the four most point laden players from the OS poker nights and were to pit our skills against lots of other four players from pubs and clubs across our region. To the victor the spoils of an all expenses paid trip to Las Vegas to take part in another contest, while the remaining seven runners up took home a sliding scale of cash prizes.

I have been eligible to take part in this party on other occasions but have demurred, either on the grounds that the event was held in Bristol – far too far for a game of cards – or that it occurred during shop opening season. I did not particularly hold out any high hopes of victory for myself, but I have for a long time harboured a desire to visit a casino to see what the fuss was all about. Even if I fared poorly at cards, I could always play on the tables for a self imposed ceiling of treasure.

So having finished fifth, er, from last in the cards I set about learning what one does to beat the system and stay solvent in a gaming palace. First I studied the games available, then watched as others tried their luck. Given that we arrived at the venue just before midday I was surprised at the number of people already there. It transpired that many of these were cards players, and while they were still involved with the poker I had pretty much a free reign of the games.

I started with the roulette and wondered at the absence of a revolver on the table. The croupier immediately noted my concern and explained that this was English roulette and the Russian version only came about once I had lost all my money, car, house, wife in the English version. I reasoned that it might take a while to reach that point as the minimum bet on single numbers was 25 pence.

I employed a well used but complex system of choosing the numbers on which I placed my 25 pence tokens, which stuns the onlookers into silence as my hands deftly flicker over the board. In some circles this method is often known as random selection.

It seemed to work reasonably well, and with the odds of winning on an individual number being 35 to 1, and given I had covered quite a few numbers I soon started amassing a small fortune. Being aware of the number of closed circuit television cameras in the venue and having seen numerous casino scenes in movies where the lucky big winner is spirited away by heavies and roughed up, or worse, and left in a dirty back alley, I decided to cut and run with my small fortune before anyone noticed.

I waited until the dust settled and the excited crowds had diminished before settling at a blackjack table. Here the chances of winning are increased but the returns are reduced, so the minimum bet is much higher; three pounds for heaven's sake. Here you merely have to beat the dealer's score but no higher than twenty one to win. If you are fortunate to have an ace and a face card dealt to you the return is increased for the win.

I cannot say that it was a very interesting game other than struggling to quickly sum up the total value of the cards laid before me quicker than the dealer, in order to avoid looking stupid. It was difficult to say how long I was there, or how many hands that I played, but I came away with a profit and over both the blackjack and the roulette I tripled by initial stake, such as it was.

I suspect that I could never become a gambling man to anything of a significant degree as, for one thing I did not register the slightest glimmer of excitement or thrill as the little white ball dashed around the roulette wheel or as the next card was issued from the shoe. Secondly I am far too fearful of losing and the subsequent agony of the, 'if onlys'.

There was no such outcome for one of our valiant players, as against all the odds, he found himself on the last table out of nearly eighty players. He had been down almost to no chips at all on several occasions throughout the hours of play, and now he looked in for a real chance. For what appeared to be an interminable time, with the minimum stake climbing up into the thousands, he whittled away the opposition until at last he came out as winner. Unfortunately, due to some misunderstandings of the past, it was doubtful that he would win a visa to America so he swapped his prize and the glory for the cash awarded to the chap who came second.

My original expectation, one that I had been given by the veterans with me, was that we would be returning home with plenty of time to repair to the F&L for the usual Saturday night banding. However, due to the latter day Drake in our midst we did not leave Plymouth until late in the evening. I did put in a late appearance at the OS to spread the news since it is the OS that sponsor us on this event. It would have been very rude of me not to endure a couple of libations while I was there, would it not?

With the excitement gone I felt quite tired as I limped home. I must remember to remove the Derringer from my sock next time.

March 3ʳᵈ – Sunday

Bump! Back down to Earth after living the jet set life yesterday; dogs to walk around the block, stock sheets to input and grocery orders to place. I did have a blindingly good idea that we should all go up to the F&L for Sunday lunch but then realised that we had all just had breakfast and that I should have said it earlier. Never mind, though, we resolved to go up for tea instead. Job done.

The boys were up early and on the mullet again. I could not see them at first and only the presence of their cars in the car park alerted me. Then I saw them just short of North Rocks, roughly where my sitting stone is, with the net shot and the tide receding. It was not long after that we saw the tractor come past with boxes of the fishes still flapping around.

Finding and landing these fish requires some time and patience, not to mention experience and expertise, oh, and a seine net. All that effort when all they really need is a bleddy hound.

I took her down to the beach early in the afternoon, as the hugeness of it all was spread out under a brightening sky and looking ever so attractive. It was cold, mind, seeming rather colder than the rest of the week or maybe I was just used to being in an insufferably warm casino all day yesterday. After a brief chat with some pals when we first got down on the sand, we struck out towards North Rocks.

Strangely, the stream falling out of Vellandreath had taken a sharp northerly direction when it hit the beach at first today and its delta spread out just beyond Carn Keys. It was in this stream, out of the full expanse of beach, that the bleddy hound dropped her ball. I saw her sniffing in the stream and walked on knowing that she would catch me up in her own time. What I had not expected was to look back at a rather sheepish looking bleddy hound with a whole, if rather tatty, grey mullet in her maw.

As I went back for her ball, in which she had no further interest, she gave me a wide berth and headed on towards North Rocks looking for somewhere to either eat or bury her trophy and definitely out of my reach. I could tell this by the way she kept looking back at me. Only extreme cunning and skulduggery was going to resolve this matter, I could tell.

Fortunately for me, I was helped in this task by a large dog ahead of her that was giving her some cause for concern. She stopped to assess the danger then remember that I was coming up behind her, looked back and moved out of my reach, then remember the other dog and stopped again. It was during one of these stopped moments that I caught her by the collar and luckily the shock made her drop the fish.

Usually, I can draw her attention by throwing the ball while I dispose of the item I do not want her to have. I should realise that she is also getting wiser, smarter and has some skulduggery of her own now. She made a quick feint for the ball when I threw it but was right on my case when I turned and threw the fish over some big rocks near the water's edge. She spent the next ten minutes trying to get around the rock at the fish and nothing could dissuade her. I ended up having to retrieve the decoy ball myself, the little madam.

She did come around eventually, and chased her ball again nicely until I made the mistake of throwing it vaguely in the direction of her lost fish which revived her memory and had her sniffing over the rocks again. She now knows exactly what grey mullet smells like. I shall rent her out the next time the mullet are in the bay so she can stand, pointer-like, on Pedn-men-du and show them where the shoal is to.

After such unmitigated excitement, what better way is there than to finish the day with a pleasant repast up at the F&L. It also marks the end of the in-laws' stay with us as they are set to return home on Wednesday for a trial run. This is a shame as the pay per use electricity meter for the portable heater they have been using arrived yesterday. I do hope they did not see that as unwelcoming, or that I have had someone programme the television to play loud rap music every time *Last of the Summer Wine* is selected from the schedule. I am sure, though, they will miss my friendly little jests.

March 4ᵗʰ - Monday

We are slowing pulling together our first orders of the season for perishable goods. Naturally, we leave these until the last minute. We often leave lots of other goods until the last minute too, but that is another story. Since the last of our rock with Sennen Cove running through it ran out last year we have to order some more. Given that no one else will want this we have to order a fair bit to make it worth the producer's while. We are told that it could take up to a month as we have to wait until the producer is heading our way in his truck from Blackpool!

Still if you think that Cornish rock from Blackpool is daft, spare a thought for the crisp manufacturer that uses an ex-footballer to advertise its products. They are in hot water for having the temerity to actually use real chicken in its roast chicken flavour crisps and real pork in its smoky bacon flavour. I thought we should be grateful, at least, that there is apparently no equine content but surprisingly it is the vegetarians that they have upset. Previously there was no meat content in these flavours at all and the vegetarians could pretend that they were ever so naughty by indulging in a little pretend meat eating; they are now outraged. I can only assume that the carnivores never realised that there was no meat in their meat crisps or they are just far more laid back than their veggie counterparts.

Fortunately, there was some real pig in our Old's gammon steaks we had for tea. It reminds me that we will soon have our famous St Just butcher delivering to us a whole range of local, wholesome meats with absolutely not a hint of hoss. All supposing, of course, I actually remember to place the order.

March 5ᵗʰ - Tuesday

There were a few discouraging spots of rain first thing and I did not think it was supposed to rain until tomorrow. Just lucky,

I suppose. At least we were to spend most of the day under cover as it is the last of the trade shows before we open.

On our way we had a few errands to run, the first being to drop the funds collected in our countertop jar to this year's designated charity. Actually, it was not the designated charity that we took it to, as we had called the designated charity only to find out that they are a little pressed financially and suggested that the money go to another charity that was likely to be able to use the funds more sensibly. They are a little further out in Redruth but since we were heading in that direction, sort of, we said that we would drop it off on our way today.

Having relieved ourselves of such a heavy burden it was only right and proper to go immediately to Scorrier and the Smokey Joe's fine establishment to avail ourselves of a breakfast. We had earlier passed through Hayle, where as you know you cannot pass without partaking in a Philps pasty, but despite it being St Piran's Day the tide was in (it is a matter of tradition) so we could not. Anyway, the Smokey Joe's breakfast was exemplary and very much sorted us out for the entire day.

On reflection it is a bit of a mistake having something to eat to the way to this particular trade show as it is all about catering. Many of the stands have food that is freely available for the visitors to sample and thus you can very much sort out a complete meal for free. This year the show was considerably smaller than in previous years and much less well attended. One thing I can tell you is that if you intend to visit Cornwall this year you will be spoilt for choice when it comes to beer, coffee and ice cream as it appears that these are the only suppliers left to do business with in the county.

Being so small we did not spend too long at the show and were home before tea time. This gave us plenty of time to help in the sad task of packing up the in-laws for their journey home tomorrow. Distraught? It was like hacking off a treasured limb.

March 6th - Wednesday

I made very sure that I had polished behind my ears and washed my shoes this morning as we were due for an audience with the RNLI royalty this morning. Every five years the top brass at the RNLI carry out what is termed a Coastal Review that involves visiting every station in the country. It is a little more than just a meet and greet. It is an opportunity to feed back issues from the factory floor and for the top brass to roundly ignore them.

They were a personable bunch and I am glad that I wore my light coloured trousers and deck shoes, as I fitted in exceedingly well. They shared with us our statistics that the All Weather Lifeboat's average distance to a casualty is seven point three miles and the Inshore Lifeboat's average is just over a mile. The big boat launched on average eighteen times each year. They acknowledged our problems with oar weed clogging up the slipways from time to time and were aware of the efforts to try and solve them. For some reason they never mentioned my foot. I was very disappointed.

I returned home in time to go to the gymnasium before the in-laws left. This put me in good stead for helping to move their accumulated detritus down to the van. There was a substantial amount in various forms of luggage, carrier bags and cooler bags. Yes, they took a tremendous amount of food back with them and they even took the bed that they have been sleeping in. The van was fair bursting at the seams when we squeezed the last item in, which was the mother-in-law. I did a quick check to make sure that I still had my clothes on as I waved them goodbye.

Clearly, I would have loved to give you chapter and verse of how we embraced and promised to write, how we consoled each other and how I had ensured that the Missus knew exactly the direction in which to head but it would be far too upsetting. I consoled myself, after they had gone, with a glass of premier cru Champagne that I had secreted under the floor boards. I know, I know, it is an odd place to keep a bottle of champers but it surely did not escape your attention that the mother-in-law has been living here for nigh on six months.

Even now it is a little difficult to forget they were here. I keep finding small reminders like empty bottles of Cockburns and father-in-law's used boil poultices, and the aroma of horse liniment and carbolic still hangs heavy in the air. They did leave me one last special surprise: when I turned on the television in the evening to watch the news a channel was already tuned in, yes, that's right, *Last of the Summer Wine* was showing. I am almost afraid to go to bed lest I wake up in the morning with a picture of the cast's heads on my pillow.

Since the Missus is away deep with them until tomorrow I had to take the bleddy hound to cards with me in the evening. She has no concept of poker; her face is a dead give away when she has two aces.

I have related before that she will not walk in the direction of the OS after dark on the grounds that she might run into her nemesis, the dog from up the road. This evening, however, she quite happily trotted almost as far as the chip shop before she stopped and looked back. There, under the streetlight outside the Lifeboat station, I could see the shadowy figures of the dreaded dog and her owner coming up behind us. Fortunately, I do not think that the bleddy hound recognised them as she did not start screaming but I rather fancy she thought that it might be them as she kept looking back. I carried her the rest of the way just in case.

I will not dwell too long on the outcome of our cards night only to say that I stayed in longer than the current South West Regional Champion. I can tell you that the bleddy hound behaved impeccably, as indeed I am certain that you would have, had you been tied to a radiator all night.

For the first time in a while I could not see the flat glowing like a hot coal from outside the OS. When I let myself in there was stony silence. I reflected briefly on the loneliness and loss before I turned the volume on the powerful sound system to maximum and played shoot the baddie on my dust covered games machine until way into the night.

March 7ᵗʰ - Thursday

It was raining when I got up this morning and still raining when I was about to take the bleddy hound around for her morning constitutional. Consequently I slipped on my water proof trousers and waterproof jacket and waterproof shoes and as I stepped out of the door the rain stopped. It was also milder today than it has been for a while so the extra layers I was wearing were not only unnecessary but uncomfortably warm as well.

I disappeared down to the shop to wrap items that had been ordered and to ensure that they were properly addressed. With the parcels duly wrapped I noticed that the rain had made a reappearance and was coming down upon us in stair rods. Consequently I slipped on my water proof trousers and waterproof jacket and waterproof shoes and as I stepped out of the door the rain stopped for which, at least, the bleddy hound was grateful. I have already explained that it was mild and, for sure, the midges half way up the hill were certain of it.

The trip up Stonechair Lane is at best an onerous one. It is a hard slog and there is not a great deal to look at. Well, all right, there is the view out across the bay which is delightful but rarely appreciated. All I see is the tarmac path under my feet as I concentrate on my heart thumping nearly out of my chest and my clogged arteries bulging fit to burst. I take a brief few seconds by the Stone Chair to answer the request from my lungs to provide more air than they are capable of holding and at this point I can distractedly take in the view.

It was on the way back and half way across Esther's Field that the mobile telephone rang. Most people by now realise that I rarely take my mobile telephone anywhere with me, and on the odd occasion that I do I mostly forget to turn it on. It is for this reason that I assumed it to be the Missus, first because I missed her this morning when I tried to call her at the parents-in-law's house and secondly because the Missus delights in calling my mobile telephone with the express purpose of berating me for either not having it with me, or having it with me and not switched on.

Shopkeeper. (In over-friendly and loud tones) 'allo!

Caller. Blah, blah, blah, blah, blah, Scotland.

Shopkeeper. I heard Scotland.

Caller. Blah, blah, Royal, blah, Scotland.

Shopkeeper. Look, I am in the middle of a field, the wind is howling in my other ear 'ole. You are going to have to slow down or speak up; preferably both.

Caller. It ... is ... your ... bank ... manager.

Shopkeeper. (Following a bit of a stunned silence) Er, very nice to hear from you. Look, I am in the middle of a field ...

Bank Manager. Yes, you said. Is now a good time to talk about insurance with you?

Shopkeeper.!
It might have been the telephone call, or perhaps the unnecessary dressing for the weather that never happened twice in the same day, but my will to live somewhat evaporated for the rest of the day. I did take the opportunity, however, to play mindless shoot the baddie games on my games machine for far longer than I should have done.

After a rather sedate Lifeboat training session we decamped to the OS for the usual quizzing. Well, that I had assumed was the plan until I arrived and found that my Head Launcher team chums had deserted me ... again. Despite being rather short for team mates the few that stood by me stalwartly did something of a blinding job as we won after a tie break. This would have been entirely unnecessary if the one eejit on the team had not insisted that the first cartoon cat was Corky instead of Felix which wiped us out of the last round instead of having a perfect ten.

Never mind the same hopeless eejit also went on to win the 'chase the ace' raffle and bagged a happy bunch of notes to take home. Life is particularly unfair on occasion I have found.

March 8ᵗʰ - Friday

The last day of freedom for a while and what a rip-spongler of a day it was too. The sun was out, it was mild, and a bright and happy Cove was spread out under a clear blue sky. Just right for spending in the shop sweeping and mopping and dusting.

I headed down to the gymnasium as close to first thing as I was ever likely to get this morning. I had put my glasses on so that I could see the numbers on the combination lock on the box where the key is kept, only to find that the number was already set and the box was open; I was to have some company it seemed. I tentatively opened the door to discover that the floor was strewn with mats, and the mats were strewn with ladies bottoms clad in leotards all pointing in my direction.

The lady who runs the yoga classes told me that she had to book the Men's Club room as her usual place was unavailable. She did suggest I join in, but I told her my leotard was in the wash and ran away very quickly.

So with my exercise regime in tatters I consoled myself first with a run up to the post office and secondly by giving the back of the van a good clear out. We had removed some storage boxes from the van when moving the in-laws out and I had noticed how much rubbish and dirt had accumulated over the years since I last cleaned it out. The storage boxes needed to be returned to the van as they were sitting in the middle of the shop floor, so before I did so I took a broom and mop to the interior. The mopping did not seem to make much difference but at least the rubbish has now gone.

By this time the Missus had come down to help get the shop ready for tomorrow's grand opening, well, opening anyway. This consisted of clearing out the rubbish and sweeping the floor. Heck, we are good at the shop opening lark now. There is no stock on the shelves, but the shop will be open on time.

Given that this was the last day before opening I thought that I had better give the bleddy hound a run down to the beach. Being such a lovely day, although it has started to cloud over a little, I dispensed with the usual waterproof gear and heavy fleeces. We were half way to the beach when I felt the first rain spots on my hatless head. The shop is not open yet and already the weather has it in for me.

There was only an ankle of sand showing on the beach as it was close after high water. It was heavy going in the soft sand close to the high water mark. I think she felt so too, as she was not that keen on chasing her ball. We stopped short of Carn Keys and she made a half-hearted effort at digging while the rain came and went. Out on the horizon a more serious lump appeared to be approaching so I headed back towards The Beach complex, so at least we had an option of some shelter. I found a suitable rock to sit on and wondered why the bleddy hound had wandered quite so far away from me and without her ball at that. It was when I saw her legs up in the air I realised that she had found the last remnants of the dead seal I had been trying to keep her away from some weeks earlier. She will get short shrift if she tries sleeping on my head tonight, that is for sure.

Well, that is it. If everything is not ready now it is too late.

March 9ᵗʰ - Saturday

Here we go again. Up earlier than any self-respecting lark or gastrically challenged sparrow, run the bleddy hound around and straight into the thick of it.

Surprisingly, it was not the Laurel and Hardy Newspaper Company that let the side down this year, although they did initially propose bringing us newspapers only six days a week, it was the other lot. Fortunately, the other lot only supply two newspaper titles and neither was very much missed today.

A month ago it was suggested to me that I should undergo a review of my medical case, so that the RNLI could be assured that I was fit enough to resume duties. Given that I resumed duties over a month ago, the medical was a bit academic but it was the first opportunity that the Lifeboat Medical Advisor could see me. My appointment was at half past ten this morning and just to add a little spice to proceedings a Lifeboat exercise had been arranged for half past eleven.

Of course, the fact that this was our first day open and I had cause to not be in the shop for most of the morning delighted the Missus no end. I did assure her that only the launch and the medical were pencilled in for the morning and the recovery was actually in the afternoon which did not seem to impress her at all.

So it was that I found myself in the St Just clinic at the appointed time only to discover that the good doctor was running half an hour late. It was fortunate that the medical was a cursory affair; I had already demonstrated my fitness by performing back flips down the corridor to the doctor's room. How could he argue with that? I immediately set off to return home to make the Lifeboat launch, especially as I was launching it.

As I approached the junction in St Just I noticed an elderly blind man and his dog waiting to cross the road. I stopped to let him pass, but he stayed resolutely glued to the pavement. I reasoned that, of course, he could not see me and honked my horn to indicate that he might safely cross. When this failed, I got out of the van and went to see if he needed any assistance. I was immediately informed that I was a blethering eejit and that the dog would not cross in front of a vehicle with its engine running and how I had ruined his entire day by making matters so much worse for him. So that will teach me to try and make tea with the milk of human kindness, but I could not help wondering how much worse his life was about to become with the onset of electric cars.

I returned to The Cove in good time for the Lifeboat launch having not stopped for several small children trying to negotiate a zebra crossing, sped closely past some nervous horses and roundly ignored a little old lady with one leg struggling with some heavy bags and trying to thumb a lift. Had the RNLI car park had a space for disabled badge holders, believe me, I would have parked in it.

The boat was due to co-ordinate with Penlee Lifeboat and the Culdrose helicopter and look for a 'Dead Fred' dummy, set adrift south of Penberth an hour earlier. They were to be gone for two hours, and were it not for a burst water tank, Head Launcher and I would have had plenty of time to partake in a Little Bo breakfast. The burst water tank probably saved my marriage. I did not mention the rugby that started about ten minutes after the completion of yet another textbook recovery by the very excellent Shore Crew.

For a first day we were quite busy, but there again the weather was very much on our side. As usual it does not take long to get back into the swing of shopkeeping and by tomorrow it will be as if we have never been closed.

Well, there is only one thing to do after spending your first day serving the general public and that is to be one of the general public and fall upon an ale house in the locality. Tonight, quite by chance, I selected the F&L since they appeared to be sporting some sort of music night that I thought would be nice, just for a change.

Then when it all came down to go home I had to, once again, suffer the derision of my peers as I slipped on my waterproofs with the dryness of the outside calling into question my sanity. And then, as if by magic, half way home, the rain commenced cascading down upon my oil-skinned frame. Hah! I bite my thumb at you, you deriders, you.

March 10th - Sunday

You will not get much out of me today and that is for certain. Much of the essential operational pieces that produce *The Diary*, fingers, elbow joints and the occasional firing of a synapse, are inoperable due to the cold. It is not so much the cold itself, it has been colder this winter, but what I am doing in it that counts. Had I been running out with the bleddy hound or launching a lifeboat, I am sure the cold would not be so much of a problem. The fact that I am standing behind the shop counter with the door letting in an increasingly insistent, and decreasingly temperate, easterly blast is the root cause of my woe.

By early afternoon all semblance of resistance evaporated and I closed the door which was of some benefit. It was of even more benefit that I had negotiated two hours in the afternoon to sit in the warm and watch the rugby on television. It did mean losing my lie in, but there again it was not quite as cold this morning as it was in the afternoon, so that was not so bad a swap.

The weather was supposed to deteriorate in the afternoon but from where I was standing, looking out across the bay, the skies brightened as the wind and cold increased. Waves crashing up the side of the Brisons, Cape and Aire Point looked pure white in the patchy sunlight and lingered with the spray blown backwards into the air. Closer in, the sea was flat but for the strong wind making it look like it was draining away to the west and, increasingly, white tops speckled the bay.

I left it to its own devices after that and settled down in front of the television. By all accounts I will need snow shoes tomorrow and a warmer pair of bloomers. I can hardly wait.

March 11th - Monday

If we thought that yesterday was slow and cold, so very cold, today almost came to a full stop and was even colder it seemed. Even a session at the gymnasium only held off the deep chill for so long.

With the cold holding the customers at bay and little else going on I am afraid it was an even duller day than yesterday. There was snow, of course. I understand that The Lizard had a little dusting, and one of our customers said that he saw a flake in The Cove. We did have some pretty dark and unforgiving sky out to the west in the late afternoon, but that was rather nicely juxtaposed with the widening expanse of blue appearing from the east.

At least I had the first of our deliveries today. It was a nice little introduction of a few boxes from our postcard company. This one does so like to drop our order in piecemeal, so I have learnt to keep an accurate record against our original order so that I can keep track of what they have sent, and what they have not. Still, it was nice to be able to fill some of the gaping holes on our postcard stand which even the few customers we have had, have complained about.

It was a pleasure to sit around in the evening getting warm, until the bleddy hound signalled her intention that I should take her out. All that blue sky had done us no favours at all; man, it was proper cold with wind cutting through my many layers like a knife. I shall be pulling my Wee Willy Winkie hat down tight tonight, I can tell you.

March 12th - Tuesday

The stock orders are coming in thick and fast now, well, we had another two today. Again two rather short orders dealt with in very short order.

I had a call, too, from a supplier just about to send an order. The chap supplies rather nice bookmarks made in leather with Sennen Cove embossed on them. He wanted to know whether we wanted the writing in white this year as apparently it shows up better on some of the darker coloured ones. It took me a second or two to work out what he meant as he has a rather thick Northern accent and I was, of course, listening in Cornish.

Then he embarked on a bit of up-selling and, for some reason, I struggled even harder to understand him. He asked if I wanted any framed fridge magnets, which seemed a little bizarre to me until I found out that he actually said friend fridge magnets, with which I was even more perplexed. There was another item he was trying to push as well, but he gave up with that when I failed to grasp what it was on the third attempt.

People complain bitterly that so many call centres are based in India and that the agents' accents are sometimes hard to fathom. My Internet Service Provider prides itself in having its call centre based in England and nine times out of ten I struggle with understanding their agents. It is based in Yorkshire.

I had intended to take a trip into town today to try and find a replacement newspaper box. That is the one that sits outside the shop and is where the newspaper delivery boys put the papers in the morning, and where I put the returns in the evening. It has suffered over the years, what with people using it as a seat and being blown down The Cove in high winds, and now leaks like a sieve.

As it happened, the Missus complained of a toothache last night during tea, so I reminded her to call the dentist for an appointment. Neither of us had expected that she would get one today, but the receptionist, after berating her for not having a check up since dentists first walked the Earth according to her records, found a cancelled appointment she could have. No, it was not at two thirty.

This rather put a spanner in the works of my venturing in to town, and left me with two small orders to process. It also left me with a poorly bleddy hound. She had an upset tummy over the weekend but had recovered. This seemed to be something of a relapse. One of the main indicators of trouble is her failure to run into the kitchen at 90 miles per hour when I silently peel back the foil lid of one of her dinners, and this morning she was just not interested. This meant a trip to the vets.

In between the dentist and the vet I managed the second journey of the year up to Shrew House and this time to retrieve stock and not just count it. I had kicked myself over the weekend because a customer had asked for goggles which I was sure were in the store room in the shop. Quite a keen search revealed nothing, so I guessed that I must have seen them up at Shrew House. When I got there I did a thorough search and they were not there either. My stock sheet says that there are 26 somewhere, because I counted them. Either 26 pairs of goggles have gone missing, or I counted 26 pairs of imaginary goggles during the stock take. I would have said that either scenario is probable cause for concern.

Piling stock into the van, piling it out again into the shop, cutting off labels and pricing are all clear indicators that we are well and truly open again. It has not felt like it in the last couple of days, as the high wind has prevented us from putting the nets and famous ball stand out at the front of the shop, or even having the front door open. The ball stand is all right, it would withstand much more ferocious weather than this, but the lightweight balls in the top tier tend to float off down the road.

After all that, it was the type of evening to curl up in front of the fire and feel all cosy and warm. Since we do not have a fire I shivered and did the VAT return instead.

March 13ᵗʰ – Wednesday

Happy Anniversary to us, apparently. We tend to forget every year, and every year we are reminded by the arrival of cards from our respective parents. I think I have said before that it is far better us both forgetting than just one of us, and by that I mean me, obviously.

With the excitement of opening the cards over and done with, and a healthy row around the Men's Club completed, I had rather set my heart on going into town. I imagine that there are small gods of anniversaries that abhor people forgetting them and set about making punishments for them. Mine was that whenever it looked like I could get out the door something happened to scupper it.

First the Missus was expecting an urgent email to do with the father-in-law's medical care. This would ordinarily be a straightforward case of going to the computer and opening the email. However, because the Missus reads all her emails on her shiny Bramley iSmallCushion instead they tend to build up on the email server up the line. As this particular email could not be read on her iSmallCushion because of some clever security measure she had to go to her computer, whereupon she discovered that she had 1,560 emails waiting to be downloaded.

Normally, the frustration incurred waiting for the last one to pop out of the telephone line is all hers. I have suggested several times in the past that it might be beneficial to carry out this practice more regularly and as the delay was stopping me going out, the frustration was all mine.

With the email issues eventually sorted, I was once again primed to leap into the van and head towards town. It was then that a smartly dressed sales person dropped by. To make matters worse I had invited this smartly dressed sales person to come to demonstrate his wares. I just wish that he could have done so a little more quickly. As it transpired he took so much time, that our accountants, one of the main reasons for heading into town, had shut for lunch so there was no point in dashing out until after it.

In between running the bleddy hound around the block and placing some regular orders the time ticked by until it had got to the time when I could sensibly head off again. Enter sales person number two. Again it was one that I had invited to come, and again it was one who just loved the sound of his own voice.

I did eventually get to town you will be pleased to hear, I am sure. The first stop was to investigate Been & Queued's selection of newspaper bins. We had seen one that resembled a park bench and were sorely tempted, especially given the number of people that use it as a seat. In the end, though, practicality triumphed and we have one that is less a seat but more voluminous.

Thanks to my sojourn we also have illumination in our vegetable fridge. The tube light has not been working for almost the entirety of last season and was a fleeting moment of irritation every time we went to switch it on, only to be forgotten until the next switch on moment.

So after a thoroughly useful trip into town, I slipped back just in time to be told to slip out again as we had nothing for tea and required a Chinese take-away instead. Even this trip was worthwhile and not just because it gave us something to eat. On the journey home I was treated to a spectacular sun as it sank into clouds on its way to the far horizon. Glimpses of Longships bathed in sparkling light, multi coloured cloud with shafts of sunlight bursting through. It is a wonder that I managed to stay on the road.

Then later, after cards (I came second, by the way), another treat as the clouds drifted away leaving a star studded heaven to gawp at. I am led to believe that a comet was showing out in the western sky, though having never seen a comet before I had no idea what I was looking at. Quite a stunning anniversary present nevertheless.

March 14ᵗʰ - Thursday

Well, that is much better. It even felt slightly warm as I walked the bleddy hound around our end of The Cove this morning. It might have been because I had to do a fair bit of rushing around as the girl had been ill during the night and, although I shall spare you the detail, it needed some attention.

Because of this the Missus carted her off to the vets for the second time this week leaving me to deal with the onslaught of customers, which meant I read quite a bit of my book. Unfortunately, another order arrived and had me wading through piles of postcards again, so I actually did do some work today. I can feel the sympathy oozing down the telephone wires to me.

The Missus also forced me into doing some domestic work too, after delivering an ultimatum. We have two rather fine uplighters which once graced a posh hotel up country somewhere. One gave up the ghost more than ten years ago and the other blew up while we were here a couple of years back – or possibly more if you believe the Missus. If they were not fixed before Easter, she warned, they would be heading to the council tip, sorry, Household Waste Recycling Centre.

As I said, they are rather fine lamps and I would be loathe to part with them. I had already made some effort to find a solution to their not working and had bought a floodlight about six months ago that has the same internal parts as the uplighters. Salvaging the right bits from the floodlight would hopefully give me the right bits to replace the broken ones in the uplighters.

The Missus sent me upstairs when she got back from the vets and set me to work fixing the lamps. The first came apart surprisingly easily and I was able to swap the corresponding working part in the floodlight with the broken one in the uplighter and, blow me, it worked first time. Sorry for the language but I am not used to things working first time or, indeed, at all.

I am more used to the result I had with the second broken uplighter, which failed to work despite my best efforts mainly because I got confused which of the parts were from the new floodlight and which were from the broken uplighter as they were identical and I had put them together on the table. I am not an expert electrician but I am guessing that a fizzing noise coming from the lighting unit when it is plugged into the mains is not necessary a good thing.

In the end I ran out of time and shall have to have another crack at it tomorrow. I may even need to get a new floodlight so that I can be sure which parts are new and which are old.

I absorbed some chill-out therapy over at the Lifeboat station by polishing the Shore Crew bell while the Inshore Lifeboat dashed off into the dark for a little exercise. By the time the boat returned I was ready and keen for the OS quiz which once again the Head Launcher and team mascot eschewed. We did however have an extra team member to last week to assist, but even then we came a poor third - joint at that. I did learn that the comet I was chasing was only visible briefly, and close to the rising crescent moon which seemed a little like too much hard work for me, especially as the moon appears to rise behind the Pedn-men-du headland. If a comet wants to be seen it should be a lot more reasonable than that. I contented myself with watching Jupiter that is much less shy.

The bleddy hound did not give a hoot about the stars as I took her around last thing. She is on nil by mouth for 24 hours which must be complete torture for her not to mention the Missus who is a sucker for her sad eyed look.

March 15ᵗʰ - Friday

The morning was temperate and dry so I elected to go into town in the afternoon when it was tipping it down. I said yesterday that work on the second uplighter had not gone quite according to plan so I had to go and get another floodlight for its salvageable parts. I also had to get a couple of halogen bulbs as I had not realised that the one that came with the floodlight is a 500 watt, whereas the uplighters are rated for 300 watt bulbs. I am glad I noticed before I burnt a hole in the ceiling.

Naturally, I was given a list to go with my own which unfortunately meant parking at the top of the town then parking again at the bottom of town. Yes, I do realise that I could quite easily have walked from the top of the town to the bottom of the town but if God has intended us to walk such distances in the pouring rain he would never has given us the motor car.

In fact it was the Missus who said that I did not need go to the top of the town as I could get her shopping in Tesmorburys which is vaguely next door to where I would be getting my floodlight. Why, I asked her, should I wish to go to Tesmorburys when I could park and walk about the same distance to proper shops where I could purchase better quality goods for probably less money and not be concerned that my shopping may include bits of budgie or whatever else was going cheap this week. To be fair, it is unlikely that even the likes of Tesmorburys could screw up a few tomatoes, chillies, some coriander and a few rashers of bacon, but a principle is a principle.

I also had to visit the new visitor centre near the station. Well, I say new but it is the old Visitor Information Centre that the much maligned council used to pay for until it decided that it did not need tourists any more. It is now run by the National Trust and a very good job they have done with it too, the best part being that it is actually open. The centre appears to do all sorts of extra activities including selling tickets to the Acorn Theatre which was the purpose of my visit. I shall elucidate further when the time comes, but until then you will just have to wait.

So warm was it in the new visitor centre and so long did it take to acquire four tickets that my soggy trousers had almost dried out by the time I left. I took great delight in passing by Tesmorburys on my way to get the floodlight and again as I passed back. I dropped off at our local cash and carry to see what wine brands they were selling this year, then rushed home with my booty.

That rain hung in there until well after I had pulled in the famous ball stand, net bucket and windbreaks which were all dripping wet. The till also reflected the bleakness of the day which rather reflected this shopkeeper's demeanour. However, my mood brightened considerably when I sat down to repair the last uplighter. After a bit of a scare when I put it all together and it did not work I was much relieved when I discovered that it was the bulb at fault. I even remembered to call in the milk order and send off for needed supplies from the local cash and carry. Can life get any better?

March 16th – Saturday

One thing you can say about Cornish rain is that it knows how to rain properly. We even had a sharp hail storm thrown in for good measure half way through the morning.

We had another Internet order come through some time during the night. You would have to fleetingly wonder who would spend the night trawling the Internet for a magnetic monkey. Such thoughts aside, it needed to be posted and I had assumed it would slip into a padded envelope and be easily posted with a large letter stamp attached. When I put it through my postage template it touched the sides, suggesting a little extra was required.

This will explain why I found myself on the back road to St Buryan half way through the morning given that the post office in Sennen does not open on Saturdays. It turned out to be a bit of a waste of time as the man in the post office assured me that the package would easily be sent as a large letter. It was not an entirely wasted trip as I also needed to fuel up the van, but had I been able to post my package locally as I intended, the fuel could have waited and I would not have ended up getting wet for the second day in a row.

By the time I got back the Missus was champing at the bit, keen to head into town to buy a new steam iron. She had wondered about buying one of those steam generating irons and asked what I thought. Having a quick look at the Internet and discovering that the cheapest was over one hundred pounds I suggested that it might prove to be irritatingly cumbersome on the occasion when she came to iron single items in a hurry, say just before going out, and mercifully she agreed with me.

While she was gone I set about constructing the new newspaper bin. It suggested that no tools would be required during the process so I took a big mallet with me as, in my experience, a big hammer is always required during these processes. I was not wrong either, as the flimsy clip together parts needed a hefty thump to get them to connect properly. All right, a big hammer was not exactly necessary but so much more satisfying than a thump with the palm of the hand.

By the time the Missus got back the new box was sitting pretty in its allotted space complete with large rocks in the base to hold it down. The old box was duly hoisted into the back of the van and will have to be taken to the dump, sorry, Household Waste Recycling Centre on Monday as I will need the van's back empty for a delivery on Tuesday. The new box seems slightly less robust than the old one, and only time will tell if I should have persevered with the old one a little longer.

I had already told the Missus that I would be watching the important Six Nations rugby match at five o'clock. If you were a witness, dear reader, to me telling the Missus that, you might have described it as pleading and begging but this is my Diary and I shall describe it as I like, thank you. The semantics are academic anyway as I found myself in a sparsely occupied OS to watch the match. I had considered watching at home on a bigger screen, amongst my home comforts but, being the considerate sort, I did not want to impinge on the Missus's free time after the shop shut by having a sport that she does not like blaring away on the television. It had not crossed my mind that there was probably more beer at the OS, honest.

It was just as well. As most of you will know, England suffered miserably; I can only tell you how much I enjoyed the game, look you, boyo.

And now for my retribution for weeks of snooty 'I have my waterproofs so blow you' that you must have read here now and again. I have no idea why I decided to leave my gear behind, especially as the television forecast assured me that it would be raining despite the Met Office saying that it would not. You would, no doubt revel in the knowledge that my trousers were soaked through before I made a few hundred yards. They were even wetter by the time I got home and met a rather insistent and much recovered bleddy hound that wanted to do a circuit despite the atrocious weather.

I humoured her, naturally, after all I could get no wetter. Well, that is what I thought before I stepped in rather a deep puddle that I should have known was there. She, of course, was keen to play as we stepped inside the house. Still dripping wet, as was I, it was a hard fight to try to get her to understand that I did not want her damp and smelling form tucked up beside me for the rest of the night.

That is another thing you can say about Cornish rain: it is really wet.

March 17ᵗʰ – Sunday

The first lie in of the season and very nice it was too. I had a dreadful dream last night that England had lost miserably against Wales in the rugby. Thank heavens it was just a nightmare.

The morning I woke up to was looking pretty good too. Lots of sunshine, a car park with more cars in it than since the end of last season and, after a slow start, a good smattering of shopping visitors. The group of kayakers leaving the Harbour this morning must have thought so as well. They left in a big bunch and before you knew it were way out in the middle of the bay. They certainly looked like they might know what they were doing and all the kayaks seemed to be sleek, sports jobs but what I know about kayaks can be written in big letters on a small piece of paper.

The rain held off all day apart from the moment I stepped outside the door to take the bleddy hound down to the big beach. Fortunately, I had learnt my lesson from last night and ignored the wall to wall sunshine that the Met Office were advertising on their website and was togged up against a monsoon. She has been feeling much better for the last couple of days so I reckoned she could do with some leg stretching, as indeed could I since I have not been out walking for well over a week.

It was pleasant enough when we got down there although it was more crowded than we have been used to. We are off spring tides now but there was still plenty of sand to be getting on with and I especially timed our foray for low water time. When I say plenty of sand, there was certainly an expanse of it but the topography has changed yet again and my sitting rock is again proud of the sand and not sittable upon. Walking on a little further there was plenty of places amongst North Rocks so we parked ourselves there and tossed the ball around a bit.

Being St Paddy's Day it was quite obligatory to stop by the OS on the way back for my bi-annual pint of the black stuff. I may have mentioned before that I am not really that partial to the Guinness outside of Ireland but it must be mentioned, especially as I have in the past lambasted the OS for many reasons, that their Irish stout is well cared for and just a shame that it is over-priced. Oh, darn it and I was trying ever so hard to be nice too.

It was of little surprise to meet the family that I had met on the beach on my way out still supping when I got back. My understanding is that they are a bit of a rough lot down from Essex, wherever that is, but since there was no one else to talk to I settled down with them and let them buy me a beer. I had to make my apologies when it came to my round as someone has to run the shop while the Missus cooks my tea. I dare say I will buy them a pint too next time we happen to be in the same alehouse together. I shall be checking in through the windows from now on, just in case.

It turned out to be a dashed fine evening with crystal visibility out across the bay. The cliffs were bathed in warm colours as the sun set and lighting up the cloudy sky. Spring's a-coming I should say.

March 18th - Monday

The bleddy hound has done for me it seems. I noticed yesterday while trying to lift my pint of Guinness to my lips that my upper right arm was pinching a bit. It got worse during the evening and at night caused a few wake up moments as I turned on it. What with the effects of walking lopsided for a few months as well, I am not exactly in prime condition.

Fortunately, the injuries did not interrupt my Monday morning cycling and rowing but, with a large order being delivered tomorrow, I thought that I had better try and book in with my bone cruncher to get it sorted.

The last time I went there one of the chiropractioners had just left and I had to wait some considerable time to be fitted in. This time, however, a new chap has been hired and they were able to offer me an appointment almost immediately. Being made of stern stuff I was able to heave my aching frame into the van and make my way to PZ for the appointed time.

This will be my fourth chiropractor since I have been going to this particular practice, and while each has had a distinctive style I have never been disappointed with the service from any of them. We shall call this fellow Biggles because his name firmly reminds me of the First War pilot and his sidekick, particularly. I hope I did not show my astonishment when Biggles opened the door and introduced himself, as that would have been quite rude. However, I am sure you, dear reader, would have been astonished in equal measure as Biggles, although slightly taller than me, is clearly only twelve.

Nevertheless, despite his tender years, the boy is a whizz at the old bone twisting and crunching. Here is a neat little trick you can try at home boys and girls. It probably requires the help of a chum if you have one. Lying flat on your back raise your arms straight over your head and have your chum place your hands together as if in prayer, should any of you recall the practice, with your fingertips exactly aligned. With your palms pressed firmly together, bend your elbows and bring them down to your chest. If your fingertips are still aligned then you have nothing to fear, however, if like mine one set of fingertips lags behind the other then you are a bit skew whiff somewhere.

I was quite amazed by this little demonstration of skill, and even more so after he pressed at obviously strategic places on my ribs and repeated the trick, and noticed that the gap between the fingertips had reduced. Further pressing and poking reduced the gap still further until with a flourish he revealed them to be level again. If that is what they are teaching twelve year olds these days I take my hat off to the Education Secretary.

By the time I came back to The Cove the Missus had been knee deep in deliveries and the Little Bo Café was packed to the gunnels. I know this because the Missus insisted on having a cappuccino with her mate and I fancied a bit of the chocolate cake that had caught my eye earlier. Obviously, with all the exercise I am getting in, geet slices of chocolate cake can be eaten without any adverse effect on my waistline. It is true; I read it somewhere.

Then without warning all the people disappeared. It might have had something to do with the little bits of rain we had appear from time to time. Nevertheless, not a bad day for a mixed weather day in mid March, let us hope that this is not a flash in the pan. And I could not go without mentioning that we also had our first after hours' shopper of the season. Things are almost back to normal.

March 19ᵗʰ - Tuesday

It seemed to be going swimmingly with the Laurel and Hardy Newspaper Company this year. I should have known that it could not last.

I had their invoice this morning and on it they have once again over-charged me for delivery. I suppose I should consider myself lucky that they did not charge me for the one day they delivered last week as there is no such thing as a sliding scale; a weekly delivery charge is implemented if you have papers seven days or one day usually.

Determined to nip this in the bud before it gets out of hand like it did over Christmas I called the helpline number. This is the same number that I called over Christmas when I was over-charged and they were able to sort it out. However, when I called this time I was told that they had nothing to do with accounts and that I should call Blackburn, and helpfully gave me the number. I redialled and spoke to a lady in Blackburn who told me it was nothing to do with them and I needed to speak to Plymouth. When I told her that it was Plymouth that advised me to call Blackburn, she had a hissy fit and told me to hold on the line while she gave Plymouth a piece of her mind. She was back on the line directly saying that Plymouth would have nothing to do with it and that she would pass me off instead to Reading.

The very pleasant lady in Reading told me that it was nothing to do with them and that I should really speak to Plymouth. It was a very good job she was a very pleasant lady. Having explained, she agreed to investigate and call me back with the solution. I am still waiting for the return call.

Now, you must all be watching with some bemusement the antics going on at County Hall, the seat of the much maligned council. It is a bit complicated but I shall try and put it as simply as possible and use the analogy of the infant's school playground, which, as it happens, is an entirely appropriate analogy to employ.

So, imagine if you will that there are two gangs in the playground, Gang C and Gang LD to pick two imaginary names out of thin air. There is also a group of older children who take all the big decisions and there is a small group of monitors who make sure there are enough toys to go around.

With me so far? Good. So it came to pass that the older children were going to force their Mummies and Daddies to cough up some more pocket money as otherwise they could not afford enough toys for everyone. However Gang LD was not happy with this and said that if they stopped buying batteries for the toys they could still afford enough toys without upsetting the Mummies and Daddies. Strangely they managed to get some of Gang C to agree with them, which was very odd as Gang C never, ever agreed with Gang LD even if it was a good idea.

Because so many of the younger children got together to agree no more pocket money was required, the older children had no choice but to do what the majority wanted. Even while this decision was being made the Toy Monitors were leaping up and down saying that the plan would not work since if no more batteries were bought then some of the toys would not work and that meant there would not be enough toys to go around. However, because the Gang LD were so happy that they had made the older children do what they wanted they did not want to listen to the Toy Monitors.

So now that the decision has been made the older children, who come mainly from the Gang C, have found out that they cannot afford any more toys and that some children will need to go without. Because the older children come mainly from Gang C they are making sure that the children who do the going without are nearly all Gang LD children. This vindictive approach has made the Gang LD children very angry and some of them are starting to cry.

There, dear readers, I hope that has sorted that out for you. There is no proper ending to the story as the children, ahem, sorry, I mean the Councillors are still squabbling as I relate this sad tale. You can rest assured, though, that whatever happens it will not be anyone in the playground that really suffers.

As if life were just a bed of roses our largest single order of the year turned up this afternoon. I am sure we must have had bigger orders in the past and some, certainly, like this one turn up secured to wooden pallets. Previously our drivers have kindly waited for us to remove the goods from the pallets as we have nowhere to store these, or indeed do we have any method of disposing of them. Today's driver decided to be not so pleasant and left three pallets sitting, literally, on the main A30 obstructing traffic, because he could not get them over the grass grown up outside Shrew House. I thanked him for his kind consideration and trusted that someone would return the favour to him in due course.

I now have a couple of wooden pallets if anyone is interested. I understand that they make good firewood and fortunately it is still quite chilly. I am hoping that someone will steal them from outside Shrew House where I left them. It is, of course, expected that the honest community in which we live will become even more honest in respect of my pallets and they will still be there this time next year.

I shall find out tomorrow as I have to go back up to Shrew House to sort the delivery out as I only had the time yesterday to shove it randomly inside. It is nice to have something to look forward to.

March 21st - Thursday

Just as we settled back into a bit of a rhythm again a big lorry pulled up outside. The very nice driver said that he had a pallet full of goodies for us. Remembering my less than satisfactory meeting with the other lorry driver on Tuesday I asked, before he unloaded, if he was willing to take the pallet away. This very nice driver said that he would be more than happy to remove the pallet and even helped with the unloading.

Having thanked the driver very much and waved him adieu a van pulled up. The driver of the van also had a delivery for us, though not quite as large as the delivery that was in the big lorry. I helped him unload another set of boxes and place them inside the shop as there was precious little space left in the storeroom.

We carried on with the original delivery and the lorry load that had just turned up, sorting out what needed to stay in the shop and what needed to be transported up to Shrew House. Then, as if by magic, yet another van pulled up outside with yet another delivery. How many is that now? No matter, we had a total of five deliveries in very close order which I would say is very much saturation point and about four more than we could cope with.

Saturation point, indeed. I noticed by about mid afternoon the glisten of a little puddle forming under the grocery shelves. This seems to be the flood of choice now and is connected to the main drain for the flat, rather than the drain I have emptied on previous occasions that takes only run off water. This second drain is in a more awkward position and probably beyond my current capability. By the time the shop closed the puddle had spread across the first aisle and mopping was having little effect, although turning out the lights and locking the door seemed to make it much better.

March 22ⁿᵈ - Friday

The flood in the shop was not as bad as I imagined. There was a bit of a flow across the floor from one side to the other, and quite a bit under the cardboard laid down to absorb it but did not. Half an hour's work with a mop and bucket and most of it was gone. There could, I suppose, be a bit of a lake under the card stand but as I cannot see under there, to all intents and purposes, it does not exist.

It seems West Cornwall copped it quite badly during the day and evening yesterday. I spoke with the Lifeboat mechanic who is the first point of call for anyone who knows him and is in trouble. He had already been out to his missus who got stuck on the road out to St Just earlier, and late in the evening he had another call from another maid whose car was floating around in a puddle the other side of Crows-an-wra. Even by morning the road from Crows-an-wra to St Buryan was a bit dodgy in places, I understand, and what a surprise, flights in and out of Land's End Airport (it's an aerodrome) were suspended.

I had a stroke of luck in that there was a break in the deluge first thing that allowed me to get my newspapers in before they turned to papier mache. It was still dry when I started to take the bleddy hound around, but was starting to revert to heavier rain by the time I got back. Fortunately, I was fully togged up and unaffected by the renewed downpour.

We were not given much of a break from the relentless flow of deliveries today either. Another couple turned up during the morning so we still have a storeroom full, and it looks like we have not made any headway since yesterday despite the shop shelves filling up.

If you are reading this and watching the rain pouring out of the sky at you, fear not. Our rain disappeared quite early during the morning, or at least earlier than was planned, and it has given way to some cracking blue skies and sunshine. I was sorely tempted to take the bleddy hound down to the big beach later on, but the Missus was busy upstairs preparing my tea that I was going to have to cram down if I were to be able to have it at all.

Yes, I have plans tonight that involve trekking into the big city, something that we have not done for some while. The 'we' is the usual suspects from the F&L who enjoy ripping apart, or praising in equal measure, the various bands that turn up there. This evening we are not waiting for the band to come to us and have acquired tickets, paid for with real money, to see a band and, unfortunately, on my recommendation. These events usually involve some good natured ribbing of the organiser regardless of the merit of the band although there have, in the past, been some real howlers.

It did not help that one of our members had read that the evening was to be interspersed with poetry, but despite my cultureless companions' misgivings we were able to avoid the verse by hiding in the bar until it was over. *Dworniak Bone Lapsa,* were surprisingly good for a band recently born out of nothing and reminiscent, perhaps, of old style Genesis or to some Pink Floyd with some Celtic airs thrown in – at least that is what it said on the packet. They suffered more than a little from repetitive lyrics and lacked the inventiveness of the original bands, but still they knocked out some pretty tunes. The band consisted of bass, twelve string and lead guitar with support from a slide guitar bed which looked rather like an Expo x1 electric organ and, for one song, a saxophone. One of the wags here present noticed Quentin Tarantino on slide guitar and James May taking lead locals.

Although we all agreed the band had some potential, I did not escape rib free. Unfortunately, the performance ended once they had played their complete album, just over an hour in length which seemed to leave us a bit short changed.

Given the spare time we had left before the taxi arrived we repaired to a nearby hostelry where the assembled company enjoyed a game of lambasting the organiser. So, not an entirely wasted evening out then.

March 23ʳᵈ - Saturday

We have emerged from the shadow of the rain clouds only to be frozen in our socks by a knicker tugging, ice cold easterly. We appear to be the lucky ones.

Some of our regular visitors have been turning up over the last couple of days hailing from the snowy regions further up the line. One couple from Derbyshire told us that the snow had not retreated since it arrived in January. It might lead to some concerns if all our customer are snowed in for the first busy period of Easter.

There were certainly no concerns for those already here. The sea was dotted with happy surfers from early on this morning and stayed that way all day. The swell was half decent and, in the curious misty light we had today, the surf was showing up pure white all around the bay. I could never get tired of watching the waves coming in with a punchy offshore breeze tearing away at the tops as they break. It makes them look like they are flying in with big smoking capes flowing out behind them.

It seems I had plenty of time to watch them too. Although we had plenty of busy moments (for the time of year) we also had long deep silences. At least we had the opportunity to clear some more incoming stock including some balls that needed to be inflated.

You may not recall the fact that after nine years I resurrected the electric compressor so that I do not have to wear myself out hand pumping the balls that arrive flat packed. Because we have only one delicate ball needle that screws into the business end of the compressor and because the compressor spent the winter in the loft, the delicate ball needle was put away separately for safety. So safe was the delicate ball needle that it eluded discovery and neither myself nor the Missus could remember where I safely put it.

I found it after a two day search by employing the logic that I would have put it somewhere en route to the loft. This rather meant the bedroom and I eventually uncovered it nestled alongside my knickers in my knicker drawer. Where else?

So with balls happily inflated, I set my sails for the F&L for a second banding in sequential days. Although *Jonestown* was in a different league to the band we appreciated last night they did, at least, play for a little longer. I am sure that I have reviewed *Jonestown* before as they are regular contributors to the fun at the F&L, but for completeness sake I should tell you that they are three guitars, including a bass, a lead singer and a drummer who belt out popular modern rock tunes in a wholly acceptable manner.

They were joined later by a, how shall I put this kindly, a slightly more mature maid from their entourage of groupies who had clearly, thus far, enjoyed her evening. She picked up one of the spare guitars, thankfully not plugged in, and mimed along with the band. One of the usual suspects suggested that it was reminiscent of the classic Robert Palmer video for the song Addicted to Love. If you do not know it, do look it up, it is visually stunning. The association was a bit of a stretch and it was late in the evening, but I could see what he meant.

I have to confess to being a little fatigued after the previous night so, although, the usual suspects gathered around I found myself strangely detached. I cannot say that I did not enjoy the evening, because I surely did, it was just that the mind was willing but the body required some encouragement.

I had taken the precaution of wrapping up in many layers for the journey home as it was a mite chilly. Even one's beer overcoat seemed insufficient in such conditions. It was pleasant and surprising given the attendant cloud, however, that the way back was lit by a two thirds full moon; I hardly needed my new torch at all.

The bleddy hound has very quickly got back into her habit of becoming over excited on my return and insisting on barking loudly for the first fifty yards of the last run around the block. Naturally, she was denied this pleasure while I was laid up with my dickie ankle, but clearly has a long memory. If you find yourself staying in the environs of the RNLI car park during your holiday this summer that will be her waking up the offspring it has taken you an hour to put down at around eleven thirty.

March 24th – Sunday

We abhor having to shut the shop door during our opening hours. We lost count of the numbers of people who cannot work out where to push to open it, despite a big metal plaque at about eye level with the word 'PUSH' written on it. In fairness the door is a little stiff to open after the dampness of last week, but if it were not it would not stay shut.

We were not exactly inundated with customers, even those capable of opening the door were in short supply. Those that did make it out mostly wanted fire lighters and kindling. It is a crying shame that we do not have the space to sell firewood; selling it would be easier than falling off a log.

We assumed that today would see some respite from the deluge of orders we had during last week. Not a bit of it. Two local companies that we have bought from asked if they could deliver today as they were in the area. The first was all the St Piran and Cornish memorabilia such as keyrings, flags and piskies in various forms and a St Piran baseball cap with 'Sennen Cove' on the front, thankfully spelt correctly.

The second delivery came from a company that specialises in surfboard wax. For the uninitiated this wax is rubbed onto the surface of a surfboard to keep the water off and enhance grip. We have been trying to find a supplier literally for years with no success. This year our main beachware supplier actually acquired some, and we ordered it in to arrive with the huge delivery that came at the start of the week. Typically, it did not arrive and is not expected until at least May. Even more typically, having waiting nine years for a supplier, two turned up at once.

The second supplier of surfboard wax appears to be the only UK supplier and just happens to be Cornish. They do surfboard wax in a range of colours and shapes, the foremost of their range in the shape of a pasty. This was too good to pass up and we called them for a sample supply which arrived today in the hands of the company owner. These waxy pasties will be on the website in short order if you are interested or even interested in seeing a picture of it.

So as a consequence of all this delivering and putting out of stock I spent a considerable time in front of the computer screen in the evening trying to update the website. I managed to get some of it done but the call of sitting down in front of a picture of a warm fire was just too much. This was soon overtaken by the attraction of a picture of a warm bed.

Good night, oall.

March 25th – Monday

It did not look too bad when we started off today. Most of the little jobs about the place have been finished, it was just that there was rather a lot of cardboard to get rid of and the man with the recycling van does not turn up until next week.

It was at this point that I resolved to take it up to Shrew House and try to remember to bring it back again next Monday evening. I know, I know, it is very likely to remain at Shrew House where it will be in the way right up until the end of the summer when I eventually remember to bring it down. When I went and got the van, however, I remembered that it was still full of the old newspaper bin that I put in there last week. If I cannot remember that, how on Earth am I to remember the cardboard?

Fortunately, the cardboard fitted into the van around the newspaper bin, but I decided that it was high time I went and visited the tip, sorry, Household Waste Recycling Centre. Since it is a little way to go I thought that I would take anything else that needed tipping, er, recycling that I could fit into the van. Mindful that the radio and newspapers here have been alive with reports of fly-tipping, and the fact that the much maligned council has tightened its grip on misuse of the tip, sorry, Household Waste Recycling Centre I knew that I could not take any of the old display stands which are cluttering every corner of Shrew House. This only left an old shopping trolley used to transport the bleddy hound around the Royal Cornwall Show when she was small, yes, bought for that purpose and used just the once, and our old toaster that gave up the ghost shortly before the in-laws departed.

I was just about to leave Shrew House on my way to the tip, sorry, Household Waste Recycling Centre when my eye caught the old double glazing window unit that our installer had left there some three or four years ago promising to remove it when he had finished doing our windows. It has since been comprehensively smashed and several thousand snails of varying sizes have taken up residence in between the shattered layers.

I have a thick pair of gardening gloves on board the van against what contingency I have no idea, possibly lifting old windows into the van. I was rather glad that I did as some of the remaining shards look pretty fierce. I almost discovered how fierce as I carefully lifted the unit into the back of the van. As I did so one of the pointed shards dropped out of the upper portion and brushed my leg as it fell. I know that I have been highly trained in the arts of casualty care and, in particular, the use of a tourniquet, but had not contemplated a self application. I also think it would be difficult writing the time on my own forehead which apparently is essential according to our instructor.

I was a sight more careful taking the window out of the van, but even then one shard fell out just behind the van and another just at the edge of the geet bin set aside for the purpose. I should point out that both fell away from any part of me that bleeds.

What I should also point out is, despite the dire warnings that the much maligned council had employed a team of Dobermans to patrol the site, I was not so much as glanced at regards my vehicle type or cargo. I probably could have shipped in commercial detritus of any size and been wholly ignored. It was not as if the practice of checking was not carried out at all, quite the contrary. A car with a trailer parked right next to my van and another van just the other side of that. Both drivers were placed under scrutiny and made to reveal their home addresses, have their permits stamped and their inside leg measurements taken. I have to confess to feeling somewhat inadequate when I left, or perhaps I have chanced upon a cloak of invisibility.

The latter cannot be true as the Missus spotted me straight away as soon as I got home and promptly told me it was her turn for a break since I had been gone so long. It was pretty much a lonely vigil I held in the shop for the rest of the afternoon; the icy cold blast is keeping the customers at bay quite successfully. The shop door is closed again too which is not helping, but at least there is some entertainment value in watching the few customers we do have attempting to open the wrong side again.

We also had a couple with a small child enter the shop. They were seeking some sponges that they could attach to the corners of the table in their accommodation to save their offspring hurting himself when he ran into them. He was already sporting a bit of a shiner from doing so previously. I would have thought that the natural process of experience would have been enough and anyway we did not have the type of sponges required for the job. The mum sighed and said that she would just have to resort to traditional parenting, which I thought was a little extreme and somewhat old fashioned.

I shall have to find some way of keeping warm downstairs if this weather continues, which it seems might be the case. I had thought about putting on some warm clothes but they always seem to get cold before I have put them on. I must be softening, though, as I let the Missus have both wall heaters on in the flat tonight. I cannot say it was that comfortable; I kept seeing my electric bill flash before my eyes.

March 26th - Tuesday

There was a quantum leap in the number of people mooching about today. Some of them even came in the shop once they had worked out how to. It has either got warmer or people have just become more accustomed to it and, let us face it, we are sheltered on this side of the county.

I am certainly not sheltered from the Laurel and Hardy Newspaper Company which has still not called me back regarding my over-charges. They must have decided to try and not upset me this week so they omitted to send an invoice or, in fact, any paperwork at all with this morning's delivery. It did not work; I was still upset.

I had barely got over this trauma when the grocery order arrived. Actually it was not so bad especially as the Missus had dragged herself out of bed early to help. It is always a bit of an eye opener when I go through the price lists for the first few grocery deliveries that arrive. Our last orders will have been made at the end of September last year so we have five to six month's worth of price rises to accommodate. The biggest leap is for tobacco products and some alcohol naturally, but there are also significant gains in some foodstuffs.

Our prices cannot be too obscene as we were slightly busier today, it seemed. It might have something to do with the sunshine showing itself for much of the morning and early afternoon. It was very pleasant but I am not sure that it warranted the first sale of sun tan lotion we had today, or indeed the first of this season's bikinis over the weekend.

I considered if they were right to be respectful about the sunshine as I took the bleddy hound down to the Harbour beach in the afternoon. She has not been out for a day or two and was showing signs of cabin fever. Actually, it was more signs of abject boredom. She tied herself in knots when she saw I was taking the ball thrower with us, and then proceeded to do nothing but dig a big hole when she got down there. This rather left me to stand around scratching my bottom and getting increasingly cold the more she dug. She seemed surprised when I gave up after half an hour and told her we were going home. She expressed her disgust by bringing her ball to the top of the slip then dropping it so it rolled back down again.

As luck would have it, shortly before we closed, our neighbour dropped in to say that her son was walking their dogs back from Land's End and would the bleddy hound like to go? Darned right, I thought and ushered her into the car. It must have dried up considerably along the path as she returned in quite good nick. If she is really lucky I might take her down to the big beach tomorrow. After all it will probably be the last opportunity before the end of the season.

March 27th - Wednesday

I have never considered myself a pipe smoker, although I did try it for a while and still have a rather nice Meerschaum pipe tucked away in the attic somewhere. It was all the fuss and mess and poking around with pipe cleaners that put me off. However, it seems that others know better than I.

It was a while ago now that I bought a new knife sharpening system. I can say it is a system because there is rather more to it than just a rough steel pole the thing you attach to your work top and pull your knife blade through. I have examples of both of these tools and even have a sharpening stone, but none seem to return a blade to the condition it was in when the knife first came out of the box it was bought in.

It was a chance conversation with a self-confessed knife fetishist who had endured similar problems in the past that put me in the direction of this new knife sharpening system. The fellow in question swore blind that the system was the holy grail as far as knife sharpening was concerned, well sort of, as this one has been found. I thought no more about it and bought one from a well-known online auction site which is apparently the only place it can be bought.

So excited was I when it arrived that I set it to use immediately. It took a little while to work out what to do with it as it has a number of parts that need to be joined together or used in concert. It did come with instructions, but as we all know instructions are for girlies and wimps, not real men. Fortunately, I had seen a demonstration of the tool on MeCylinder, the Internet video website, so I had a fair idea of what it was all about. Briefly, there is a hand held brace for holding the knife and a series of abrasive fingers onto which a long wire is attached. The wire then fits through a hole on the brace thus giving the abrasive finger the perfect angle at which to strike the blade. There is a different hole, and therefore a different angle, for different knife types and blade sharpness's.

My first attempt did not produce the expected results. The blade was a little sharper than it was when I had started, but no more sharp than if I had used a steel and nowhere near the advertised ability of slicing a hair down the middle lengthways.

844

Having scratched my head for a day or two I noticed that the demonstrations always suggested a knife blade of consistent depth; all our knives are wider at the back than they are at the blade. This had me thinking that the angle at which the abrasive edge strikes the blade is probably wrong. If I had one I might have taken to a Churchwarden to contemplate the matter.

It took another couple of attempts to find the right hole in the brace, but today I cracked it. In the absence of any hair to test the blade on (the bleddy hound would not stay still long enough) I used the edge of a piece of paper and the knife sliced through that most satisfactorily. It was one of those moments of self satisfaction, you know the ones, epitomised by Sherlock Holmes settling back in a high backed leather Chesterfield tugging on his Calabash.

Later in the afternoon I put the blade to good use in preparing the vegetables for a pasty tea. I nearly had apoplexy when I found the turnip the Missus had bought from the supermarket; it looked like a fat carrot. Fortunately there was another turnip, bought from a local store that was proper size and interestingly half the price. It would have been enough for me to bite the end off my Tapered Liverpool.

Oh gosh, the pipe smoking; I almost forgot. It seems that the clever people at the online auction place know all about people who buy knife sharpening systems. When I went there to leave my comments about how good the seller was, as you are encouraged to do, I noticed that there was a panel at the bottom of the screen. It told me that people who bought knife sharpening systems also bought pipes, pipe ashtrays, pipe lighters and pipe cleaning tools.

There is no escaping it; the time has come and the writing is on the wall. I shall be up in the attic dreckly, seeking out my briar and Meerschaum. The next time you see me will be through a cloud of tobacco smoke with a Dublin clenched between my teeth.

March 28ᵗʰ - Thursday

If I were to show you a picture of the bay today with no other explanation you would think it was high summer. There was the placid blue sea, crystal clear with the sand, rocks and weed beds visible as if under a sheet of glass. There was a slight, almost imperceptible haze, like a thin gauze curtain between us, Cape and the Brisons. Further in, the wide expanse of beach at low water stretched out in pastel colours towards North Rocks which were almost underlined by a long finger of sand bank pointing out into the lapping sea. But for a few palm trees you would be hard pressed to distinguish it from a Caribbean shore.

Oh, there is one thing that might give it away. There is not a figure in sight that is not wearing a thick coat and woolly hat, all right there might be a few woolly hats in Jamaica. This will be because the temperatures are once again Arctic.

Once again there have been major changes to the topography of the beach. The sand is building up at the northern end; my sitting rock was just about sittable upon yesterday and today it is just about visible. Much of North Rocks has disappeared too. As if to demonstrate just how against nature this was, the bleddy hound proceeded to remove great portions of sand by digging an enormous trench. I noticed this mainly because she had her rear end towards me and every so often showered me in wet sand.

March 29ᵗʰ - Friday

I can definitely say that I have seen better days. The number of visitors hardly had us ruffled, and the juicy looking weather that we had yesterday was nothing but a distant memory. Nevertheless, despite the blossoming of flowers held back and the frozen conditions, I heard my first popgun of spring in the toy aisle today.

Yes, visitors may be in short supply but the charming spring lambs seem to be ever more abundant as they tear through the peace and neatly stacked shelves of the shop. Another visitor that can be seen all year round, but more prolific at Easter, is the brass necked climber, seen throwing itself off the top of cliffs and scrambling back up them again. These hardly creatures were out in force today, but were seen scurrying for cover when the rain started.

The normally cheerful sand striders were completely absent from the beach leaving it open to a couple of rare kite flyers and a few dog walkers who will shortly be leaving our beaches for the summer season. By the end of the day the rain really took hold, and any self-respecting spring visitor either found a high stool to perch upon, or hid themselves away in their warm burrows and nests.

Us shopkeepers, clearly made of sterner stuff and quite apart from the fact that we booked it yesterday, headed out to The Beach for a bit of nosh. It has been some while since we have been there, and an even longer time since we have actually paid for the meal. It has not long ago been a minor wedding anniversary for us; coincidentally we both shared the same one. Also the Aged Parents dropped a couple of bob into the card they sent which took care of the tip, well, some of it, at least.

They must have known we were coming as they put us at the back out of the way of everyone else. From there we were able to look out on the bay and the swell that had increased late in the afternoon and now looked to be about to break over the restaurant. We were treated incredibly well, with mussels to start and, between us, seafood linguine and scallops. To beat it all the management paid the bill, which was very nice. I wish I had known earlier as I would have had a pudding and twice as many beers.

The bleddy hound, who had been waiting in the van for us, had been ill when we got out; she does not do being alone at all well. It was also still raining, but fortunately I was togged up in water proofs to give her a little bit of a run around so that she could get over her trauma.

Other than that it was a most satisfactory end to the most appalling day. Let us hope that is all behind us now.

March 30ᵗʰ - Saturday

What a pretty looking day we had and for once nothing froze and fell off.

It is not very often that I find myself agreeing with the Met Office, but on the front of the *Western Morning News* (did I ever tell you I once had a review …) it says that the Met Office had to admit that its advice was, "not very helpful". All right, I know that it is a cheap shot and they were only referring to one event last year but I really could not help myself.

I had promised myself a trip up to Shrew House today, well, actually I had promised myself a trip up to Shrew House yesterday before it started raining. We had some gaps in our wetsuit range that needed filling, just in case anyone fancied getting into the water with just two and a half millimetres of neoprene wrapped around them. We also had sold one or two footballs and the beach shoes needed topping up.

The bleddy hound was getting a bit fractious and in one of her, I'm-not-going-to-sit-still-on-my-shop-perch sort of moods, so I piled her into the van and took her with me. It was not long before I discovered that she was also in her, I'm-not-sitting-still-in-the-van sort of moods, and she was an utter nuisance in both directions. Never mind I will make her suffer later when I take her out of a slightly warm flat and make her run around the block.

And that is not the only thing that is not rosy in the garden. The Harbour toilets are not open and it seems are unlikely to be. Rumour has it the much maligned council are blaming the Harbour Commissioners for failing to come to the table. I have absolutely no doubt that if I were to ask the Harbour Commissioners they would have a similar tale to tell. With this less than conciliatory mood abounding, I can only see the stream of unspeakable fluid that is seeping from the toilet entranceway becoming a river before the week is out.

The beach car park toilets are to be taken under the wing of the much maligned council. We know this because up until yesterday they were still closed for refurbishment; I have not heard whether they opened today or not. The Parish Council after a bit of a false start woke up to the fact that despite a big bribe, oops sorry, I meant large assistance fund, they were really not experts in running toilets and told the much maligned council to stick their bribe, er, incentive payment.

Our neighbours at the Little Bo Café have already suffered as a result of the lack of conveniences. Last week they were inundated with queues of passers-by wishing to use their toilets. RW said she was loathed to put up a sign stating that her facilities were for customers only, but the state they were in at the end of the day was not remotely amusing and she may be forced to do just that.

I will leave you to cross your legs while I explain the ins and outs of a trip up to the F&L this evening. I did not immediately recognise the name of the band from the advertisements on the board and the Internet. I also did not recognise their faces as the last time they were here I was tucked away in the corner of the bar, unable to join the party. It was their footwear that gave it away, as the lead singer and lead guitarist were wearing boots of death – how could I possibly forget.

I hope that it is not too revealing to say that I have a long time fantasy of long legged, blond, blue eyed guitarists. Unfortunately, our man tonight was just not my type. It may be a little unkind but it was not me that suggested that he was reminiscent of Rocky from the Rocky Horror Picture Show, but I could see what they meant.

All that aside they were loud and brash and keen and joyful. Tunes from Billy Idol, Wheatus – you got to love them, The Buzzcocks – you know the one, various girly singers and a bit of Skunk and Nancy, what a duet they were. It was not necessarily all my kind of music but it was fun, lively and entertaining. What more could you possibly want on a Saturday night?

I was rather hoping for a night sky full of stars on the way home, after all it was a clear, bright sky dotted with them when I left to go up to the F&L. No such luck; it had clouded over completely on the return trip and all I had to light the way was a village elder and a bright torch. Thank heavens for the bright torch; the village elder was next to useless – he will, of course, say he was next to me!

March 31st – Sunday

Where did everyone go? They cannot all have forgotten to put their clocks forward, surely? It is diabolically quiet, even for an ordinary Sunday let alone Easter Sunday, darn it.

Some wag is spreading a rumour that the toilets will not be opening yet on health and safety grounds. The fear is that ladies might become attached to the seat, given the icy conditions.

Actually, I should not harp on so about the cold. I have been getting messages that all you poor souls up country have been suffering in far colder temperatures, you poor lambs. Well, the solution is simple: there is obviously plenty of room down here, so stop whinging and get yourselves on the next bit of transport to Sennen Cove. Don't forget your wallets.

At least we are not the only ones sitting on our thumbs today. The Lifeguards must have found it pretty tedious as well. I counted five surfers in the water at any one time, and only one of those was out the back and at any risk of needing saving. They do have a grown up four by four this year, with a yellow flashing light that they seem to enjoy making good use of. They would have been hard pressed to zip up and down with their quad bike, as the path up to the Lifeguard hut is virtually cut off by the lack of sand at that point, although I noticed that the quad was parked up outside the hut.

We were lucky enough to get a little activity in the early afternoon with a little brightening of the sky, but as the wind increased later the numbers diminished again.

And that, ladies and gentlemen, is as exciting as it got today, well, almost.

I did promise faithfully that I would not comment upon a regular visitor who dropped in at five minutes to closing for a newspaper. You know, one of those newspapers that had been carefully counted, put in piles and tied up neatly with a newsagent's knot. I did promise, so I will not make comment at all, not one, honest. I only mention it to show the utter restraint that I exercised on such a slow day and with such an obviously newsworthy item. Good aren't I?

The Last Word

There, that is all you are getting. If you have reached this far without the aid of painkillers, alcohol or artificial stimulants, well done. Now, go and lie down in a darkened room for a while.

This really is the last Cove Diary Book ever, as the quiet consensus is that one book was unfortunate and the second was sheer carelessness. You may still dip into the intellectual wasteland of the Cove Diary by seeking it out on the Internet at www.old-boathouse.com or you may wish just to use this address to add to your privacy policy so that your offspring do not accidentally come across it.

It only remains for me to thank you for your kind perseverance and trust that your mental health recovers dreckly.

About The Author

The Diarist is the product of a marriage between the houses of Cornwall and Somerset. His parents discovered early on that they would have preferred a child, so he was raised by lamas in the wilderness of West London. Spurning school at the age of eleven, he spent his formative years salting pilchards and baiting crab pots until, at the age of twenty five, he worked out why people were avoiding him.

Adopting a life of heavy drinking and enforced celibacy he discovered that there were worse ways of earning a living and spent 25 years doing one of them. As if that wasn't punishment enough he bought a shop in West Cornwall where he continues to live and occasionally work with a long suffering bleddy hound and a wife he takes for longs walks.